Economics of Education

"This important volume presents the main economic models and latest evidence on some of the key questions in the economics of education, from long-time questions like the effect of smaller class sizes on learning outcomes to frontier questions such the value of social-emotional skills. It also includes a valuable overview of the Spanish education system and an introduction to econometric methods for impact evaluation. I recommend it to both professors and students at the intersection of economics of education and international education seeking to understand the rationale for leading education policies and the extent to which they have had the intended effect. It will become a key resource in my classes."

—Alejandro Ganimian, *Harvard University, USA*

"This volume brings together top scholars to take on some of the most pressing challenges in the economics of education. The chapters draw on solid empirical work and lay out policy-relevant insights across key topics such as school choice, teacher effectiveness, and educational equity. I was particularly drawn to the chapter that digs into gender gaps in educational outcomes. The book does a great job of unpacking the drivers behind persistent inequalities and what can be done to address them. This book is a must-read for researchers, policymakers, and anyone looking to back up education reform with strong evidence."

—Almudena Sevilla, *London School of Economics, UK*

"This book provides an excellent overview of topics in the economics of education. Its chapters go beyond introducing topics—they provide rigorous analytical frameworks for understanding the research on them. I highly recommend it to all interested in how economics and empirical work illuminate educational systems and policy."

—Miguel Urquiola, *Columbia University, USA*

"This edited volume covers an expansive range of essential topics in the economics of education literature. Researchers and policymakers alike stand to benefit from these deeply researched chapters filled with cutting edge research. I recommend this book to anyone interested in better understanding the Spanish education system or the application of applied microeconomics to the issues of education policy and practice."

—Matthew Kraft, *Brown University, USA*

Antonio Cabrales · Ismael Sanz
Editors

Economics of Education

An Introductory Textbook

palgrave
macmillan

Editors
Antonio Cabrales
Department of Economics
Universidad Carlos III
Madrid, Spain

Ismael Sanz
Universidad Rey Juan Carlos
Madrid, Spain

ISBN 978-3-031-90910-8 ISBN 978-3-031-90911-5 (eBook)
https://doi.org/10.1007/978-3-031-90911-5

Translation from the Spanish language edition: "Economía de la Educación" by Antonio Cabrales and Ismael Sanz, © Fundación Ramón Areces (Ramón Areces Foundation) 2024. Published by Fundación Ramón Areces (Ramón Areces Foundation). All Rights Reserved.

English translation of the original Spanish edition published by Ramón Areces Foundation, Madrid, 2024

Cover credit: Image by Inspiration GP

This Palgrave Macmillan imprint is published by the registered company Springer Nature Switzerland AG
The registered company address is: Gewerbestrasse 11, 6330 Cham, Switzerland

Preface

This volume brings together a series of contributions by leading scholars in the economics of education, with the shared objective of providing a comprehensive, rigorous, and accessible introduction to the key issues, methods, and debates that define the discipline today. The book is designed for advanced undergraduate and graduate students, researchers, and practitioners interested in understanding how economic theory and empirical tools can be applied to evaluate and inform education policy. While each chapter can be read independently, the volume has been carefully designed to function as a cohesive whole, introducing essential methodological foundations, applying them to various educational issues, and drawing policy-relevant insights.

The motivation for this book stems from a growing demand—both in academia and policy circles—for robust and evidence-based analysis of education systems. Education is at the core of human capital formation and social mobility, and its role in fostering innovation, productivity, and social cohesion has never been more critical. At the same time, education systems face complex challenges: persistent inequality, changing labor market demands, and questions about the most efficient use of public resources. This volume addresses these challenges head-on by emphasizing causal inference, carefully measuring outcomes, and contextually interpreting results.

Our primary objective is to bridge the gap between theory and practice. This book not only discusses education from a normative or theoretical perspective but also offers robust empirical evidence based on causal inference methods, many of which are at the frontier of applied microeconometrics. Understanding "what works" in education policy requires moving beyond correlations and identifying causal relationships—a challenge that this volume explicitly tackles, both in the dedicated methodological chapter and the empirical analyses presented in each substantive chapter.

The book is organized thematically and methodologically to follow a coherent narrative. The opening chapter presents indicators and trends of education systems across OECD and EU countries, setting the empirical foundation for the following chapters. Chapter Empirical Methods: A Brief Introduction to Causal Inference introduces the primary empirical methods used to estimate causal effects in education research, including difference-in-differences, regression discontinuity designs, and instrumental variables. It serves as the methodological backbone for the empirical chapters that follow. Chapters Evaluating Educational Policies in Practice to Non-cognitive Skills then apply these tools to various substantive topics. Chapter Evaluating Educational Policies in Practice assesses the effects of the Texas Top Ten Percent Rule and school-starting age policies, illustrating the importance of natural experiments in education policy evaluation. Chapters The Impact of Class Size on Academic Performance through Teachers: Much More than a Profession focus on inputs into the educational production function: class size, families, peers, and teachers. Each chapter examines theory and empirical findings, demonstrating how different factors influence student outcomes and how policies might effectively target these factors.

Chapters Foreign Language Knowledge and Early Childhood Education extend the analysis to foreign language acquisition and early childhood education, exploring the returns to specific forms of human capital investment and the importance of early interventions. Chapters Post-compulsory Education and Tertiary Education: Access, Financing, and Cost-Effectiveness shift attention to post-compulsory and tertiary education, addressing the returns to academic and vocational pathways, equity in access, and the design of financing systems. Chapters School Choice through Gender Gaps in Education explore education systems as mechanisms of allocation and stratification. Chapter School Choice reviews theoretical and empirical findings on school choice, while Chapter Educational Inequality focuses on educational inequality and its intergenerational consequences. Chapter Gender Gaps in Education examines gender disparities in academic achievement and aspirations, highlighting the role of biases and structural constraints. Finally, Chapter Non-cognitive Skills addresses the growing literature on non-cognitive skills. It reviews the definitions, measurement strategies, and policy implications of traits such as perseverance, self-control, and social skills. The chapter underscores how such skills, although harder to measure, are crucial for both educational and labor market success.

Each chapter presents rigorous empirical analyses and connects to real policy challenges faced by education systems worldwide. For example, the chapters on class size and peer effects use identification strategies such as instrumental variables and regression discontinuity designs to address endogeneity problems common in education research. The chapter on teachers links labor market dynamics to educational outcomes, reflecting a growing literature that studies teachers as key agents in the education production function. Similarly, early childhood education and non-cognitive skills chapters highlight how skill formation is a cumulative process, where timing and complementarities between inputs matter critically.

A unity matches the diversity of topics in approach: all authors aim to evaluate the effectiveness of policies and interventions using causal methods and high-quality data, including administrative records, standardized test scores, and survey data. This empirical orientation reflects a broader movement within the economics profession, which has increasingly emphasized evidence-based policy and the rigorous evaluation of interventions. The book also benefits from the contributions of economists working at the intersection of education, labor, and public policy, which allows for a rich, interdisciplinary perspective.

This book is a valuable resource for university students, scholars, policymakers, practitioners, and those interested in improving the quality and equity of education systems. It encourages readers to critically examine what policies are effective, for whom, and under what conditions. We hope this volume will contribute to a more informed public debate and foster the development of evidence-based education reforms.

We are especially grateful to the researchers who have contributed to this volume and the institutions and colleagues who have supported its development. This project reflects a collective effort to strengthen the economics of the education research community. By offering rigorous, accessible, and policy-relevant analyses, we hope this book will catalyze further research and informed decision-making.

Madrid, Spain

Antonio Cabrales
Ismael Sanz

Contents

List of Figures

The Impact of Class Size on Academic Performance

The Effects of Classmates (*Peer Effects*)

Teachers: Much More than a Profession

Foreign Language Knowledge

Early Childhood Education

Post-compulsory Education

Tertiary Education: Access, Financing, and Cost-Effectiveness

Educational Inequality

Gender Gaps in Education

Non-cognitive Skills

List of Tables

Educational System Indicators in OECD and EU Countries

Evaluating Educational Policies in Practice

The Impact of Class Size on Academic Performance

The Impact of Families on Education

Post-compulsory Education

School Choice

Gender Gaps in Education

Introduction and Methods

Educational System Indicators in OECD and EU Countries

Ismael Sanz

1 Introduction

This chapter presents key indicators of the educational systems in OECD and EU countries, organized into four sections. The first section analyzes data on students and teachers, focusing on enrollment rates, teacher working conditions, and the learning environment. This section focuses on access to non-compulsory education stages such as early childhood education, vocational training, upper secondary education, and higher education. The second section examines indicators related to education funding within OECD and EU contexts, including total expenditure, spending per student, and grants or scholarships. The third section addresses critical outcome indicators, such as early school leaving, graduation, and grade repetition rates. It also reviews international student performance in primary education through the Progress in International Reading Literacy Study (PIRLS) and the Trends in International Mathematics and Science Study (TIMSS), and in secondary education through the Programme for International Student Assessment (PISA). Additionally, it examines adult literacy, numeracy, and problem-solving competencies in technology-rich environments, as measured by the Programme for the International Assessment of Adult Competencies (PIAAC). The chapter concludes by exploring the relationship between education and employment, highlighting the connection between educational attainment, unemployment rates, and income levels, as well as the transition from education to the labor market.

I. Sanz (✉)
Universidad Rey Juan Carlos (URJC), Madrid, Spain
e-mail: Ismael.Sanz@urjc.es

London School of Economics (LSE), London, UK

A. Cabrales and I. Sanz (eds.), *Economics of Education*,
https://doi.org/10.1007/978-3-031-90911-5_1

2 Indicators of Enrollment and the Learning Environment in OECD and EU Countries

2.1 Early Childhood Education Enrollment Rates

Participation in early childhood education and care (ECEC) varies significantly across OECD and EU countries, reflecting differences in policies, cultural attitudes, and resource allocation. As of 2022, enrollment rates for children one year before the official primary school age were nearly universal, exceeding 90% in most OECD countries and reaching 100% in eight. Notable progress has been observed in countries like Saudi Arabia and Türkiye, where enrollment increased by approximately 30 percentage points over the past decade, attributed to expanded compulsory education and targeted ECEC policies. In contrast, countries with lower maternal employment rates, such as Hungary and Türkiye, tend to have lower enrollment rates for children under 3 years old, influenced by extended parental leave and cultural norms regarding caregiving (OECD 2024).

Differences in the structure and provision of ECEC programs also play a critical role. For example, countries like Finland, which offer tailored one-year preparatory programs, ensure a smooth transition to primary education through curriculum alignment. Meanwhile, integrated systems in nations like Sweden and Lithuania provide continuous services from birth to school age, supported by substantial government funding and capped parental contributions. This contrasts with countries where ECEC for children under 3 is primarily out-of-pocket, creating financial barriers for low-income households. Spain's recent initiative to create over 60,000 places for children under 3 by 2025, funded through the European Recovery and Resilience Facility (RRF), exemplifies efforts to address these disparities.

Table 1 provides a comprehensive view of early childhood education enrollment rates across OECD and EU countries from 2005 to 2022, highlighting notable disparities between age groups. Enrollment for children aged 3–5 reached an average of 83%. Countries like France, Germany, or Spain show consistent high enrollment rates for older children, with universal participation in France since 2005. In contrast, the United States and the United Kingdom lag behind, reflecting variations in policy emphasis and funding mechanisms. Table 1 also highlights the significant disparities in early childhood education enrollment rates for children under 3 years old across OECD and EU countries from 2005 to 2022. On average, only 27% of children under 3 are enrolled in formal early childhood education programs in OECD countries, with the EU average slightly lower at 22%. Germany and Spain show marked progress over the years, with Spain increasing enrollment rates from 15% in 2005 to 42% in 2022, reflecting targeted policy efforts to expand access. However, other nations, such as France and the United Kingdom, continue to report limited participation in this age group. These findings underline the importance of targeted policy interventions to improve accessibility and equity in early childhood education. By addressing affordability, availability, and parental leave structures, countries can better align with global education goals, such as the Sustainable Development Goal 4.2, which

Table 1 Trends in early childhood education enrollment rates by age group (2005, 2015, 2020). *Institutions include public and private providers*

	Starting age for early education	Start of primary education	Age of compulsory education	Early childhood education (0–2 years)			Early childhood education (3–5 years)		
		2022		2005	2015	2022	2005	2015	2022
				2005	2015	2022	2005	2015	2022
France	2–3 years	6	3	9	4	4	100	100	100
Germany	0 years	6	6	17	37	40	87	96	93
Spain	0 years	6	6	15	34	42	98	97	97
United Kingdom	0 years	5	4–5	–	–	19	–	68	67
United States		6	5–7	–	–	–	64	65	61
OECD		6		**–**	**24**	**27**	**74**	**82**	**83**
EU-22				**–**	**22**	**22**	**78**	**87**	**88**

Note Early childhood education = ISCED 0. Early education services must meet the following criteria: (1) Appropriate educational objectives; (2) Be provided in institutions (schools or similar institutions for a group of children); (3) A minimum intensity of 2 hours per day of educational activities and 100 days per year; (4) A regulatory framework or curriculum recognized by national authorities; and (5) Be staffed with personnel holding pedagogical accreditation
Source Education at a Glance 2022 and Education at a Glance 2024

aims for universal access to quality ECEC by 2030. This alignment ensures the developmental benefits of early education and broader socioeconomic gains through increased workforce participation and reduced educational inequalities.

Early childhood education and care are crucial in cognitive and emotional development, learning, and student well-being (Duncan et al. 2022). Children participating in high-quality early learning programs are likelier to achieve better educational outcomes later in life. This impact is particularly significant for children from disadvantaged families, as these programs can help bridge learning gaps in home environments (see Chapter 4 on early childhood education). Moreover, expanding access to early childhood education can reduce educational inequalities and facilitate parental workforce participation, contributing to economic growth and well-being.

In the EU, the expansion of early childhood education has been driven by additional impetus from the objectives set at the European Council in Barcelona in 2002, aiming to provide full-time subsidized childcare places for one-third of children under the age of 3 by 2010 (European Commission 2024). The EU-level goal is that, by 2030, at least 50% of children under the age of 3 should participate in formal childcare, and at least 96% of children aged 3 to the start of compulsory primary education should participate in early childhood education. For this EU-level target, children are considered to be participating in early childhood education only if they are enrolled in programs classified as educational under the International Standard Classification of Education (level 0/early childhood education), intentionally designed to support children's cognitive, physical, and socioemotional development (European Commission 2024). The 2024 proposal by the Commission aims to increase participation in early childhood education, particularly for children in vulnerable situations or from disadvantaged backgrounds. Recent progress has been particularly notable in countries like Portugal and Lithuania due to reforms. However, participation rates vary significantly by age, with older children showing higher enrollment levels due to compulsory attendance requirements in the year before primary school. For younger children, participation gaps are more pronounced, with affordability and legal entitlements playing a critical role. These findings underline the need for comprehensive policy frameworks to ensure equitable access to ECE, particularly for the most vulnerable populations.

The quality of the program is critical to its success. The Perry Preschool Project and the Abecedarian Program in the United States, which will be examined in detail in Chapters 3 and 4 on the impact of class size and early childhood education, for instance, employed highly qualified teachers with university degrees and maintained low child-to-staff ratios. Heckman et al. (2010) highlight that early childhood education programs modeled on initiatives like Perry can deliver an annual return on investment of 7–10%, comparable to the post-World War II return on equity in US stocks.

Despite efforts to increase access to early childhood education, the likelihood of participation remains highly dependent on family context and income, particularly in early educational development services that rely heavily on private funding sources. Data from the European Union Statistics on Income and Living Conditions (EU-SILC) survey reveal statistically significant differences in participation in early childhood education across half of the EU countries for children experiencing socioeconomic disadvantages in terms of household income, maternal education, or risk of poverty or social exclusion (Flisi and Blasko 2019). On average, in OECD European countries, children aged 0–2 from low-income households were approximately one-third less likely to attend early childhood education (including centers, homes, and organized family childcare) compared to those from high-income households (European Commission 2024; OECD 2020a). In nearly all EU countries, the proportion of children at risk of poverty or social exclusion attending formal childcare remains consistently lower than those not at risk (Fig. 1). The participation gap for children under 3 years of age averages 15.8 percentage points across the EU, with countries like France, Malta, and the Netherlands exhibiting disparities exceeding 35 percentage points. This underscores the need for targeted interventions to improve accessibility and equity in early childhood education.

The figures corresponding to Graph 1 are higher than those in Table 1 due to differences in the type of programs measured. OECD data reflects attendance in programs with an educational component, while the EU-SILC survey records participation in formal childcare, irrespective of its educational intent. Additionally, the timing of the EU-SILC 2020 data collection may have been affected by school closures due to COVID-19 in some countries, a circumstance not reflected in the OECD data. These differences highlight the varying approaches and challenges in assessing participation rates across regions.

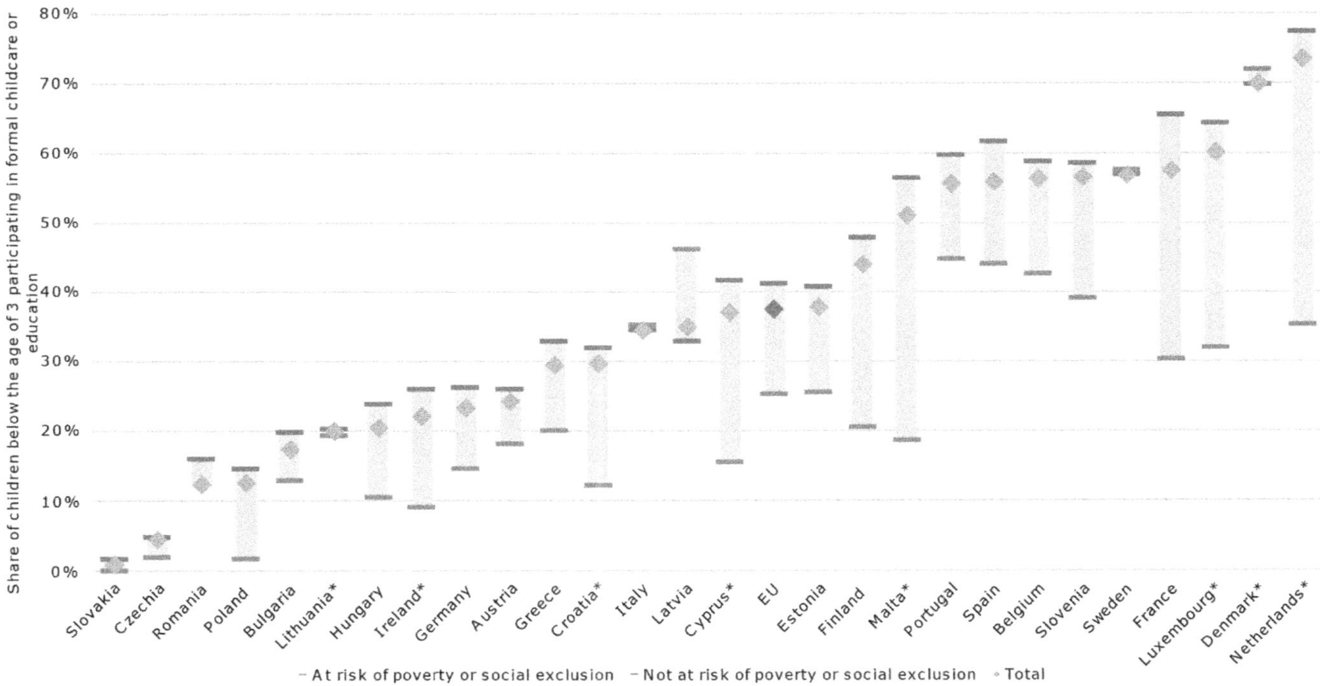

Fig. 1 Share of children below the age of 3 participating in formal childcare or education, by risk of poverty or social exclusion (*Source* Chart extracted from the European Commission (2024). Based on Eurostat database [EU-SILC 2023]) (*Note* Countries are displayed in ascending order according to the total share of children participating in formal childcare. Low data reliability for the category "at risk of poverty or social exclusion" is marked with an asterisk; data for Romania in the category "at risk of poverty or social exclusion" are not available and have low reliability for the category "not at risk of poverty or social exclusion." The upper age range is defined by the compulsory primary education starting age in each country)

2.2 Trends in Primary, Vocational, and General Secondary Education

The trends in student enrollment and graduation across primary, vocational, and general secondary education reveal significant patterns in the global educational landscape. Primary education remains foundational to compulsory education systems worldwide, with near-universal enrollment rates among children aged 6 to 14 years across OECD countries. The average enrollment rate in this age group reached 98% in 2023, reflecting a sustained global commitment to universal primary education as part of the Sustainable Development Goals (SDG 4). In most countries, primary education is publicly funded, with 85% of students attending public institutions. However, in some contexts, such as Belgium, Spain, and Chile, government-dependent private institutions account for a substantial proportion of primary enrollment, often functioning similarly to public schools due to significant state funding and regulation.

The introduction of policies to extend compulsory education has further bolstered enrollment rates, particularly in countries that have integrated pre-primary or upper secondary education into compulsory schooling frameworks. Since 2013, twelve countries have extended compulsory education at these levels, targeting subpopulations such as disadvantaged groups, where enrollment rates remain comparatively low. For example, the inclusion of pre-primary education as a compulsory stage in France and Belgium has significantly improved access among children from socioeconomically disadvantaged backgrounds.

Despite these advancements, disparities persist. While most children progress seamlessly from primary to lower secondary education, the transition to upper secondary education—comprising both vocational and general pathways—reveals stark differences in participation and outcomes. Vocational education and training (VET) programs, particularly at the upper secondary level, play a critical role in equipping students with practical skills and facilitating their integration into the labor market. However, the proportion of students completing VET programs varies significantly across countries.

Table 4 illustrates the distribution of graduates in 2020 between general secondary education (e.g., academic tracks like high school) and vocational education at the upper secondary level (Table 2).

This data highlights considerable variation among countries. For instance, vocational pathways in Germany and Italy are almost as popular as general ones, reflecting robust VET systems and a high degree of alignment in labor market. Conversely, countries like Spain and the United States exhibit lower shares of VET graduates. In Spain, this imbalance can be partly attributed to higher dropout rates among vocational students; data shows that over 30% of students who begin vocational programs fail to complete them. Countries like the United Kingdom stand out for their high proportion of VET graduates, emphasizing the value placed on vocational training as a viable alternative to traditional academic pathways. Notably, the UK's government-supported apprenticeship schemes have contributed

Table 2 Distribution of graduates in 2020 between general programs (upper secondary education) and vocational education (upper secondary vocational training)

Country	% General secondary graduates	% Vocational education graduates	Total (%)
France	55.0	45.0	100.0
Germany	53.0	47.0	100.0
Italy	44.3	55.7	100.0
Spain	64.7	35.3	100.0
United Kingdom	35.0	65.0	100.0
United States	100.0	0.0	100.0
OECD Average	62.7	37.3	100.0
EU-22 Average	56.3	43.7	100.0

Source OECD Education at a Glance (2022)

to this success, providing structured pathways for students to gain work experience alongside theoretical knowledge.

Efforts to address the challenges in vocational education have increasingly focused on dual VET models. These programs, which integrate classroom learning with workplace training, have been particularly successful in countries like Germany and Austria, where they account for most vocational enrollments. Dual VET programs enhance employability and reduce dropout rates by offering students direct exposure to industry environments.

Global trends underscore the importance of expanding and improving vocational education. In the EU-22, vocational education accounts for 43.7% of secondary school graduates, compared to 37.3% in the OECD average. The disparity suggests that further efforts are needed in many countries to elevate the status and accessibility of VET programs. Moreover, addressing gender imbalances remains a priority, as vocational education often reflects traditional occupational stereotypes. While 51% of graduates from general upper secondary programs are female, women only account for 46% of graduates from vocational programs. Addressing these gaps requires targeted interventions, such as promoting STEM fields for girls in vocational tracks and offering mentorship programs to encourage broader participation. Women are underrepresented in technical and engineering tracks, while men are less likely to enroll in healthcare or education-focused programs.

In conclusion, strengthening vocational education systems requires a multifaceted approach. Countries could invest in infrastructure, expand dual training opportunities, and promote inclusive policies that address dropout rates and gender disparities. Aligning VET programs with labor market needs will improve graduates' employment outcomes and contribute to broader economic growth and social equity. Students from families with lower educational attainment or immigrant backgrounds face notable barriers to completion. Completion rates are consistently lower for these groups across all countries with available data. Ensuring equitable access to quality education across all levels remains a shared goal for OECD countries.

2.3 Trends in Tertiary Education Across OECD and EU Countries

The evolution of tertiary education across OECD and EU countries underscores its critical role in fostering innovation, driving economic growth, and enabling social mobility. Over the past few decades, participation rates in tertiary education have surged, reflecting concerted efforts by policymakers to expand access and meet the labor market's growing demand for highly skilled professionals. This trend highlights the increasing value placed on higher education in knowledge-based economies.

2.3.1 Educational Attainment and Expansion

As of 2023, 41% of adults aged 25–64 in OECD countries held a tertiary qualification, aligning with the OECD average and slightly surpassing the EU-22 average of 37%. Educational attainment levels vary significantly across countries, with the United States and the United Kingdom leading with 51% and 53% of adults, respectively, holding tertiary qualifications. Conversely, countries like Germany (33%) and Italy (22%) report lower levels of attainment, emphasizing the disparities within advanced economies.

Short-cycle tertiary education programs play a pivotal role in many countries by equipping students with job-specific skills. In the United States, 10% of adults have completed short-cycle programs, which constitute 40% of first-time tertiary graduates. Similarly, Spain's emphasis on vocational training is evident, with 13% of its adult population holding a short-cycle tertiary qualification, compared to the EU-22 average of 4% (Table 3).

Table 3 Educational attainment of people aged 25 to 64 (2023) *Percentage of adults with tertiary education*

Country	Short-Cycle tertiary education	Bachelor's or equivalent	Master's, licentiate, or equivalent	Doctorate or equivalent	Total
France	14	12	15	1	42
Germany	1	19	12	2	33
Italy	0	6	15	1	22
Spain	13	11	16	1	41
United Kingdom	9	27	15	2	53
United States	10	25	13	2	51
OECD	7	20	14	1	41
EU-22	4	15	18	1	37

Source OECD Education at a Glance (2024)

Table 4 First-time graduation rate and characteristics of tertiary graduates

	% of first-time graduates by educational level (2021)			First-Time graduation rate of under 30 s (2019)		
	Short-cycle tertiary education (2–3 years)	Bachelor's degree	Master's or equivalent	Total excluding international students	Men	Women
France	–	–	–	–	–	–
Germany	1	86	12	37	34	41
Italy	2	83	15	35	29	43
Spain	43	45	12	54	47	60
United Kingdom	23	76	1	43	36	49
United States	40	60	–	–	–	–
OECD Average	16	76	8	38	31	46
EU-22 *	13	78	10	37	30	45

* *Note* The EU-22 data refer to 2019
Source OECD, *Education at a Glance* (2023a), p. 241; OECD, *Education at a Glance*, 2021, p. 208. https://www.oecd.org/education/education-at-a-glance/

Table 4 provides information on graduation rates for individuals under 30 years old in tertiary education. First-time graduation rates exclude those who had previously obtained any higher education qualification, such as individuals completing short-cycle tertiary programs and subsequently earning a university degree or advancing to a master's program. The first-time graduation rate by the age of 30 thus measures the proportion of first-time graduates under 30 compared to the total population under 30.

Although the most recent internationally comparable data are from 2019, the graduation rate reveals notable variations across countries. For example, first-time tertiary graduation rates for individuals under 30, excluding international students, range from 35% in Italy to 54% in Spain, the highest recorded in the OECD. These figures surpass the OECD average of 38% and the EU-22 average of 37% (see column 4 of Table 7). Columns 1–3 highlight the distribution of first-time tertiary graduates across short-cycle tertiary programs, bachelor's degrees, and master's programs. Countries like Germany and the United Kingdom exhibit strong emphasis on bachelor's degrees (86% and 76%, respectively), whereas short-cycle tertiary education plays a more prominent role in the United States (40%) and some European countries like Spain (43%). These patterns reflect the diverse priorities and pathways within the OECD and EU tertiary education systems. On average, 16% of tertiary graduates in OECD countries completed a short-cycle vocational program. These programs provide students with specialized skills tailored to labor market needs, enhancing employability and facilitating smoother transitions into the workforce.

Vocational education and training (VET) programs play a pivotal role in bridging the gap between education and employment.

The strong emphasis on short-cycle tertiary education in Spain, where it accounts for 43% of all tertiary graduates, contrasts with the EU-22 average of 13% and aligns with the United States' significant share of 40%. This highlights the role of vocational education in meeting labor market needs. The data in Table 4 emphasize the diversity in educational pathways and the increasing importance of aligning tertiary education with labor market demands across OECD and EU countries (Tables 5 and 6).

Diverse pathways and institutional types, including public universities, private institutions, and short-cycle vocational programs, have facilitated the expansion of tertiary education. Across OECD countries, 63% of students graduating with a bachelor's degree in 2022 attended public institutions, although private education is gaining prominence. Since 2013, the share of graduates from public institutions has decreased by three percentage points, reflecting the growing role of private providers, particularly in regions such as Latin America and Asia.

Despite this progress, disparities in access remain significant. Socioeconomic background, parental education levels, and immigration status continue to influence students' ability to enroll in and complete tertiary education. Students from less advantaged backgrounds are less likely to participate in tertiary education and face higher dropout rates. For example, first-generation students and those from immigrant families often encounter financial, cultural, and institutional barriers that hinder their academic success.

Tertiary education participation has seen a reversal in gender trends, with women comprising 56% of first-time entrants in 2022 across OECD countries. However, gender disparities persist in specific fields of study. STEM disciplines (science, technology, engineering, and mathematics), which are highly sought after in the labor market, remain male-dominated. Only 15% of female first-time entrants choose STEM fields, compared to 41% of male entrants. In contrast, men are underrepresented in fields such as education and health, with just 4% and 8% of male students enrolling in these disciplines, respectively.

Efforts to address these disparities include programs like Ireland's STEM Passport for Girls and Spain's STEAM Alliance for Female Talent, which aim to encourage female participation in STEM fields through mentorship and collaboration with industry partners. Additionally, countries like Luxembourg and Germany have implemented broader initiatives to promote gender equity in tertiary education, such as training teachers to adopt unbiased teaching practices and creating role model programs for female students in male-dominated fields.

2.3.2 International Mobility in Tertiary Education

The globalization of higher education has led to a steady increase in international student mobility. Between 2013 and 2022, the proportion of mobile students—those studying outside their home countries—rose across nearly all OECD countries. Central and Eastern European countries, such as Estonia and Latvia, experienced

Table 5 Statutory teacher salaries in early childhood and primary education in PPP dollars (2022)

Annual salaries in public institutions								
	Early Childhood				Primary Education			
	Starting salary	Salary after 10 years of experience	Salary after 15 years of experience	Maximum salary	Starting salary	Salary after 10 years of experience	Salary after 15 years of experience	Maximum salary
	(1)	(2)	(3)	(4)	(5)	(6)	(7)	(8)
France (Euros)	34,611	38,651	40,683	58,751	34,611	38,651	40,683	58,751
Germany (Euros)	–	–	–	–	70,419	80,750	85,699	91,713
Italy (Euros)	32,981	36,160	39,584	48,015	32,981	36,160	39,584	48,015
Spain (Euros)	44,650	48,516	51,715	63,910	44,650	48,516	51,715	63,910
England (Pounds)	34,732	–	55,726	55,726	34,732	–	55,726	55,726
Scotland (Pounds)	43,895	55,096	55,096	55,096	43,895	55,096	55,096	55,096
United States ($)	45,931	50,953	68,905	76,985	44,992	61,054	66,251	78,190
OECD ($)	34,563	43,063	45,981	57,118	36,367	46,782	49,968	61,075
EU-25 ($)	32,541	39,061	42,586	53,626	35,175	42,682	46,894	58,742

Source OECD Education at a Glance (2023a)

Table 6 Statutory teacher salaries in secondary education in PPP dollars (2022)

Annual salaries in public institutions								
	Lower secondary education				Upper secondary (general program and vocational training)			
	Starting salary	Salary after 10 years of experience	Salary after 15 years of experience	Maximum salary	Starting salary	Salary after 10 years of experience	Salary after 15 years of experience	Maximum salary
	(1)	(2)	(3)	(4)	(5)	(6)	(7)	(8)
France (Euros)	37,720	41,760	43,792	62 169	37,720	41,760	43,792	62,169
Germany (Euros)	77,905	88,442	93,085	101,510	81,141	91,729	96,742	1,10,694
Italy (Euros)	35,447	39,151	43,038	52,725	35,447	40,084	44,235	55,106
Spain (Euros)	49,905	54,243	57,758	71,235	49,905	54,243	57,758	71,235
England (Pounds)	34,732	–	55,726	55,726	34,732	–	55,726	55,726
Scotland (Pounds)	43,895	55,096	55,096	55,096	43,895	55,096	55,096	55,096
United States ($)	46,018	64,196	69,439	79,031	48,187	63,026	69,641	75,988
OECD ($)	37,628	48,605	51,613	63,332	3,974	50,841	53,456	65,658
EU-25 ($)	36,446	44,444	48,606	61,090	36,985	45,986	50,082	63,474

Source OECD Education at a Glance (2023a)

particularly rapid growth, reflecting efforts to attract international students through targeted policies and English-taught programs.

International students are disproportionately represented in STEM fields, with 30% of mobile students enrolling in these disciplines, compared to 19% of domestic students. This trend highlights the alignment of international education with global labor market needs, as STEM skills are highly transferable and in demand. However, fields such as health and welfare see lower participation rates among mobile students due to regulatory challenges and the costs associated with degree recognition.

Countries have implemented various measures to attract and retain international students, including streamlined visa processes, work permits, and post-graduation employment opportunities. Finland, for example, has introduced centralized English-language application platforms and joint degree programs to facilitate international student enrollment. These initiatives enhance the global appeal of tertiary institutions and contribute to local economies, as international graduates often join the workforce and drive innovation in their host countries.

2.3.3 Policy Implications and Future Directions

Tertiary education systems across OECD and EU countries face a dual challenge: expanding access to meet growing demand while ensuring equity and quality. Policies that address financial barriers, such as scholarships and income-contingent loans, can help level the playing field for students from diverse backgrounds. Initiatives to promote gender equity in education, particularly in STEM fields, are crucial for reducing disparities and tapping into underutilized talent pools.

Vocational education and international mobility represent critical opportunities for innovation and growth. In conclusion, tertiary education remains a cornerstone of social and economic development in OECD and EU countries. By addressing persistent disparities and leveraging the strengths of vocational education and international mobility, countries can ensure that their education systems remain dynamic, inclusive, and responsive to future challenges.

2.4 Teachers and Learning Environment

Teachers' salaries and working conditions play a critical role in attracting, developing, and retaining a skilled and high-quality teaching workforce. Across OECD countries, teacher salaries vary widely depending on the level of education, years of experience, and qualifications. Between 2015 and 2023, nominal teacher salaries increased by 28–29% on average across OECD countries at the primary and secondary levels. However, after accounting for inflation, the real increase was much smaller, ranging from 4–5%. This modest growth underscores the challenges in ensuring that teaching remains an attractive profession, particularly in the context of rising costs and competing career opportunities for tertiary-educated workers.

Teacher salaries in OECD countries are, on average, 81–88% of the earnings of tertiary-educated workers. In comparison, school heads earn 22–38% more than tertiary-educated workers, reflecting their additional responsibilities and leadership roles.

2.4.1 Variation Across Levels and Countries

Teachers' salaries increase with the education level taught in most OECD countries. Upper secondary teachers often earn the highest salaries, followed by lower secondary and primary teachers. For example, statutory salaries for upper secondary teachers are typically 15–20% higher than those for primary teachers. Additionally, the wage progression throughout a teacher's career varies considerably. In some countries, the maximum salary for teachers is nearly double the starting salary, particularly when higher qualifications are involved.

In countries like Germany, teachers experience significant salary growth as they advance in their careers, while in other countries, such as Italy or the United Kingdom, salary progression is more modest. Variations in salaries are also influenced by local factors, such as the cost of living, as well as additional allowances for teaching in remote or socioeconomically disadvantaged areas, which are provided in about one-third of OECD countries.

2.4.2 Working Conditions and Teaching Hours

Table 7 presents data on the number of teaching weeks, days, and hours for educators in public institutions across different education levels. Teaching hours and the number of instructional days vary widely across OECD and EU countries. In early childhood education, teachers in some countries work significantly longer hours annually than their counterparts in others, reflecting different educational priorities and reporting standards. In primary education, instructional time is often concentrated into fewer days per year, with longer daily schedules. For instance, teachers in some countries work fewer than 185 days annually but often have schedules that maximize daily instructional hours.

In secondary education, teaching hours reflect the balance between classroom instruction and other responsibilities, such as preparing lessons, grading, and professional development. Countries with strong vocational education systems, such as Austria and Germany, often report fewer annual teaching hours for secondary teachers due to the integration of on-the-job training within their education models. By contrast, academic-oriented systems in countries like France and the United Kingdom typically require more classroom hours.

Table 7 Number of teaching weeks, teaching days, and net teaching hours for teachers in public institutions during the academic year

	Notes	Número de días de enseñanza al año						Horas al año de enseñanza					
		Early childhood	primary	Lower secondary	Other	Upper secondary (general)	Upper secondary (vocational traijing)	Early childhood	Primary	Lower secondary	Other	Upper secondary (general)	Upper secondary (vocational traijing)
		(1)	(2)	(3)	(4)	(5)	(6)	(7)	(8)	(9)	(10)	(11)	(12)
France	1	162	162	–	–	–	–	900	900	720	–	720	720
Germany	1	225	193	193	–	193	193	1755	691	642	–	620	617
Italy	3	189	174	174	–	174	174	945	766	626	–	626	626
Spain	1	176	176	176	176	176	176	854	854	656	656	656	656
England	–	190	190	190	–	190	–	–	–	–	–	–	–
Scotland	2	190	190	190	–	190	–	855	855	855	–	855	–
United States	4, 5	178	178	179	–	178	–	900	908	893	–	888	–
OECD	–	***194***	***183***	***183***	**–**	***182***	***185***	***1007***	***773***	***706***	**–**	***679***	***695***
EU-22	**–**	***196***	***178***	***179***	**–**	***178***	***183***	***1067***	***703***	***632***	**–**	***618***	***646***

Source OECD Education at a Glance (2024)
1 Typical teaching time (teaching time required for most teachers when no specific circumstances apply). 2 Maximum teaching time. 3 Minimum teaching time. 4 Actual teaching time. 5 Reference year: 2018.

3 Educational Financing Indicators

3.1 Total Educational Expenditure, Public and Private

Educational investment is a key driver of economic growth, productivity, and social mobility. Governments across the OECD allocate significant resources to education to foster human capital development and reduce inequalities. However, the level and distribution of education funding vary considerably across countries, reflecting differences in economic structures, demographic trends, and policy priorities. While education funding tends to follow long-term economic trends, it does not react significantly to short-term GDP fluctuations, as governments often maintain or even increase educational spending during economic downturns to sustain investment in future generations (OECD: Education at a Glance 2024).

Table 8 presents total expenditure on educational institutions as a percentage of GDP in 2021. This expenditure includes public, private, and international funding directed toward institutions such as schools, colleges, and universities that provide teaching services or education-related activities. However, it does not account for private spending outside formal institutions, such as private tutoring, textbooks, or the living expenses of tertiary students.

Across the OECD, education expenditure represented 5.9% of GDP in 2021. The EU-25 reported an education expenditure of 5.4% of GDP, demonstrating a relatively stable investment level despite economic pressures. Notably, some countries such as the United Kingdom (6.7%) and France (6.1%) allocate a higher share of GDP to education, whereas others, including Italy (4.6%) and Germany (5.8%), report lower levels of investment relative to their economic output. The United States remains a unique case, dedicating 2.3% of GDP solely to tertiary education—far above the OECD average of 1.5%—reflecting its reliance on private funding in higher education.

Spending patterns also vary across different educational levels. Early childhood education, which is increasingly recognized as critical for long-term academic success, accounts for an average of 0.9% of GDP across OECD countries. France and Germany allocate above-average shares to this level, whereas Italy and the United Kingdom invest less. Primary and secondary education typically represent the largest portion of national education budgets, with primary education absorbing between 1.2% and 1.9% of GDP in most OECD countries. The OECD average for secondary education stands at 1.9% of GDP, but this figure masks significant differences depending on whether countries emphasize general or vocational programs. In post-secondary, non-tertiary education—an intermediate category between secondary and higher education—spending is generally modest, averaging between 0.1% and 0.2% of GDP.

Tertiary education financing reflects substantial cross-country differences in funding structures. Countries with publicly funded university systems, such as Germany and Italy, allocate around 1.0–1.3% of GDP to higher education, whereas the United Kingdom (2.1%) and the United States (2.3%) invest significantly more,

Table 8 Total expenditure on educational institutions as a percentage of GDP (2021)

	Early childhood	Primary	Secondary					Post-Secondary non-tertiary
			Lower secondary	Upper secondary			All secondary	
				General program	Vocational secondary	Total upper secondary		
	(1)	(2)	(3)	(4)	(5)	(6)	(7)	(8)
France	0.7	1.2	1.3	0.7	0.5	1.2	2.5	0.0
Germany	1.1	0.8	1.3	0.4	0.6	1.0	2.3	0.2
Italy	0.5	1.2	0.6	–	–	1.2	1.8	–
Spain	0.8	1.4	1.0	0.6	0.4	1.1	2.0	–
United Kingdom	0.4	1.9	1.0	0.9	0.4	1.3	2.3	–
United States	–	1.6	0.9	0.9	–	0.9	1.8	0.0
OECD	0.9	1.4	1.0	0.5	0.5	1.0	1.9	–
EU-25	0.9	1.3	1.0	0.4	0.5	1.0	1.9	0.1

	Higher Education			Total Education Spending (including R&D)
	Higher Vocational	University	Total Higher Education (Including R&D)	
	(9)	(10)	(11)	(1 + 2 + 7 + 8 + 11)
France	0.4	1.3	1.6	6.1
Germany	0.0	1.3	1.3	5.8
Italy	0.0	1.0	1.0	4.6
Spain	0.2	1.1	1.4	5.7
United Kingdom	0.1	1.9	2.1	6.7
United States	–	–	2.3	–

(continued)

Table 8 (continued)

	Higher Education			Total Education Spending (including R&D)
	Higher Vocational	University	Total Higher Education (Including R&D)	
	(9)	(10)	(11)	(1 + 2 + 7 + 8 + 11)
OECD	0.1	1.4	1.5	5.9
EU-25	0.1	1.3	1.3	5.4

Source OECD Education at a Glance (2024)

largely due to high tuition fees and private contributions. The extent of public versus private funding in higher education also varies widely. In some countries, such as the United States, private sources—including tuition fees, endowments, and philanthropic contributions—account for a substantial share of funding, whereas in much of Europe, government support plays a larger role (Table 9).

Beyond overall spending as a share of GDP, another key measure of education financing is expenditure per student, which accounts for variations in population size, enrollment rates, and wage structures. Table 9 provides data on total expenditure per full-time equivalent student in purchasing power parity (PPP) USD. Across OECD

Table 9 Total expenditure on educational institutions per full-time equivalent student (2021). In USD equivalents using PPPs for GDP

	Primaria	Secundaria					Primaria y Secundaria
		ESO	Secundaria Superior			Total secundaria	
			Bachillerato	FP Media	Total secundaria superior		
	(1)	(2)	(3)	(4)	(5)	(6)	(8)
France	9,673	12,139	15,279	18,142	16,266	13,874	12,119
Germany	11,587	14,197	15,681	20,394	18,098	15,614	14,343
Italy	12,008	9,760	–	–	11,059	10,569	11,096
Spain	9,077	10,658	10,482	14,188	11,668	11,159	10,173
United Kingdom	12,513	12,716	14,609	14,370	14,539	13,695	13,141
United States	14,321	15,302	16,775	–	16,775	16,018	15,186
OECD	10,658	11,941	11,379	13,216	12,312	11,942	11,352
EU-25	10,337	12,111	10,967	13,072	11,664	11,696	11,123

	Terciaria			Primaria hasta Terciaria (Incluyendo I + D)
	FP Superior	Grado, Master, Doctorado	Total Terciaria (incluyendo I + D)	
	(9)	(10)	(11)	(13)
France	17,468	19,315	18,880	13,545
Germany	7,981	20,788	20,760	15,767
Italy	4,697	12,746	12,663	11,439
Spain	10,770	15,354	14,361	11,123
United Kingdom	29,292	29,552	29,534	16,052
United States	–	–	36,172	19,973
OECD	12,266	19,775	18,105	12,647
EU-25	11,317	18,571	17,578	12,275

Source OECD Education at a Glance (2024)

countries, average per-student spending across all education levels stands at $12,647, though this figure varies significantly by level of education and across countries.

At the primary level, spending per student ranges from approximately $9,000 in Spain to over $12,000 in the United Kingdom and Germany. At the secondary level, per-student expenditure also varies significantly, with Germany and France allocating over $15,000 per student, while Italy and Spain remain below the OECD average. In some cases, spending on upper secondary vocational programs is lower than on general secondary programs, reflecting differences in resource allocation and instructional costs.

Higher education spending is particularly heterogeneous. The highest levels of per-student expenditure are found in the United Kingdom ($29,534) and the United States ($36,172), where high tuition fees and research-intensive institutions drive costs. In contrast, Germany, Italy, and Spain report significantly lower levels of tertiary spending, with per-student investment levels around $12,000–$15,000. These differences reflect not only the cost structures of higher education systems but also varying degrees of public subsidies, tuition policies, and research funding priorities.

Several factors influence education expenditure levels and distribution across countries. First, demographic trends play a crucial role: countries with aging populations may allocate relatively less funding to education due to declining school-age populations, whereas countries experiencing demographic growth may need to expand educational infrastructure. Second, teacher salaries—one of the largest components of education spending—vary widely across countries and can significantly impact total expenditure. In some countries, higher teacher salaries are offset by larger class sizes, maintaining overall cost efficiency. For instance, OECD data show that while teacher salaries in Spain are above the EU average, class sizes are also larger, resulting in lower per-student spending compared to smaller-class-size systems.

Additionally, vocational education and training (VET) funding differs across countries, with some investing heavily in dual education models that combine classroom learning with on-the-job training. Early childhood education funding is another area of variation, with some OECD countries providing near-universal public funding while others rely more on private contributions.

Education financing across OECD and EU countries is shaped by economic, demographic, and policy factors that influence both total investment levels and spending efficiency. While some countries allocate a higher share of GDP to education, others prioritize targeted investments in specific education levels or rely more on private funding.

3.2 Scholarships and Financial Aid in Higher Education

Higher education funding policies vary significantly across OECD and EU-25 countries, with different approaches to tuition waivers, scholarships, and student loan systems. Table 10 presents data on financial aid eligibility across major OECD and

EU-25 countries, showing notable differences in how public and private funding mechanisms support students in accessing higher education.

In several European countries, tuition waivers are widely available at public institutions. In France, 76% of undergraduate students benefit from tuition exemptions, similar to the 78% of students in Spain's Higher Vocational Training programs. In Italy, the proportion of tuition-exempt students at the Master's level reaches 84%, reflecting strong public support for postgraduate education. In contrast, in the United Kingdom, the tuition waiver system is largely absent, as higher education is primarily financed through student loans. Germany, although lacking detailed data on waivers, has a well-established student financial aid system (BAföG), which provides means-tested grants and loans to eligible students.

Scholarships also play a key role in higher education financing, with significant variation in how they are awarded. In Spain, 53% of undergraduate students receive scholarships, a relatively high proportion compared to France (42%) and Italy (39%). However, at the Master's level, only 24% of students in Spain receive scholarships, which is lower than in France and Italy, indicating a policy focus on undergraduate rather than postgraduate funding. This aligns with the principle that the private returns to education increase at higher levels of study, making it more justifiable for governments to concentrate public funding on undergraduate students rather than those pursuing Master's degrees.

Student loan systems are prominent in some countries, particularly in the United Kingdom and the United States. In the UK, 96% of students finance their studies through loans, reflecting a system where tuition fees are high, but repayment is income-contingent. The United States also relies heavily on student loans, with 53% of students receiving either government-backed or private loans. Germany, although it has lower tuition fees, still provides loans to 22% of its students through the BAföG system.

These loan systems operate on the premise that students borrow money before entering higher education and repay it once they start earning income. Countries such as Germany, the UK, and the US have implemented income-contingent repayment systems, where graduates contribute a portion of their earnings to repay their loans, with exemptions for those earning below a certain income threshold. This system is designed to make higher education more accessible while ensuring that graduates with higher lifetime earnings contribute more to the cost of their education.

Research on these financing models highlights their distributional effects. Cabrales et al. (2019) examine the impact of income-contingent loans in different contexts, demonstrating that such systems can be progressive. Their simulations using administrative earnings data suggest that students from the highest income quartile would repay nearly the full tuition amount, while those in the lowest income decile would contribute very little. Furthermore, their findings indicate that shifting to a loan-based system could reduce the proportion of government-funded university financing by 16 to 56 percentage points.

Across OECD countries, there is an ongoing debate about the balance between public and private contributions to higher education funding. While some countries, such as France and Germany, maintain strong public support through tuition waivers

Table 10 Eligibility criteria for public scholarships or grants for higher education students enrolled in public and private institutions (2022–23)

		Students benefiting from tuition fee waivers (public institutions. 2019–20)				Tertiary students receiving (%): (2022–23)			
		Higher vocational training	Undergraduate	Master	PhD	Only government-guaranteed private loans or public loans	Only public scholarships	Public scholarships and government-guaranteed private loans or public loans	Neither public scholarships nor government-guaranteed private loans or public loans
		(1)	(2)	(3)	(4)	(5)	(6)	(7)	(8)
France	1	76	42	31	–	1	33	–	66
Germnay	1, 2	–	–	–	–	–	–	21	79
Italy	–	–	39	38	84	0	45	0	55
Spain	–	78	53	24	–	–	40	0	60
England	1, 3	–	–	–	–	96	0	0	4
United States	1, 4	–	–	–	–	7	35	38	20

		Average annual amount of public scholarships (USD converted using PPPs) types of scholarships/grants	Public or government-guaranteed private loans	Scholarship types/ aid			
				Universal	Need based	Merit based	Targeted at disadvantaged population groups
		(10)	(11)	(12)	(13)	(14)	(15)
France	1	4547	18,771	No	Yes	No	No
Germnay	1, 2	5384	5174	No	Yes	No	No
Italy	–	9715	–	No	No	Yes	Yes
Spain	–	–	–	No	Yes	Yes	No

(continued)

Table 10 (continued)

		Average annual amount of public scholarships (USD converted using PPPs) types of scholarships/grants	Public or government-guaranteed private loans	Scholarship types/ aid			
				Universal	Need based	Merit based	Targeted at disadvantaged population groups
		(10)	(11)	(12)	(13)	(14)	(15)
England	1, 3	–	23,384	No	Yes	no	Yes
United States	1, 4	2202	2879	–	Yes	Yes	Yes

Notes The data do not refer to students receiving public financial support (BAföG) but to those eligible to apply for it
Government-dependent private institutions instead of public institutions
Loan distribution refers only to ISCED levels 5 and 6
Source OECD. Education at a Glance (2024) and Education at a Glance (2022)

and scholarships, others, like the United Kingdom and the United States, have shifted toward private financing through student loans. Italy and Spain, meanwhile, have adopted a mixed approach, with a combination of scholarships, tuition waivers, and relatively modest student loan programs.

A key policy consideration is whether to increase tuition fees for higher-income students to expand financial aid for lower-income households. García-Montalvo (2020) analyzes the effects of a tuition increase in Catalonia's public universities, showing that higher fees for wealthier students allowed for an expansion of need-based grants without negatively affecting low-income student enrollment. Surveys conducted in Catalonia reveal that while many students perceive tuition fees as high, a significant majority (80.9%) support an income-based fee structure, and 81.2% believe that full tuition waivers should not apply to families earning above €30,000 for a household of four.

Overall, the design of higher education financing policies must balance equity and efficiency. Countries that rely heavily on public funding face fiscal constraints, while those that emphasize private contributions must ensure affordability is maintained through targeted financial aid. As student debt continues to rise in some systems, particularly in the US and the UK, policymakers across OECD countries are reassessing the sustainability and fairness of different models. The challenge lies in ensuring that financial aid mechanisms—whether through scholarships, tuition waivers, or student loans—effectively support access to higher education while maintaining long-term financial viability.

4 Educational Outcome Indicators

4.1 Grade Repetition in Primary and Lower Secondary Education

Grade repetition remains a key educational outcome indicator, influencing student progression and overall academic achievement. While some countries continue to use repetition as a means of supporting struggling students, its effectiveness remains contested. Across the OECD, the share of students who repeat a grade varies significantly by country and educational level. On average, across OECD countries, 1.5% of students in primary education and 2.2% of students in lower secondary education repeated their current grade in 2022 (Table 11). While grade repetition is relatively rare in primary education, it becomes more prevalent in lower secondary education. The highest shares of primary school repeaters among the countries analyzed in this chapter were recorded in Spain (2.13%), the United States (1.75%), and France (1.21%), while the lowest were observed in Italy (0.33%) and Germany (0.60%).

In lower secondary education, Spain (7.79%) and Germany (2.64%) exhibited the highest repetition rates, while Italy (1.84%) and France (1.08%) reported lower figures. The OECD and EU-25 averages stood at 2.17% and 2.13%, respectively.

Table 11 Share of repeaters in primary and lower secondary, by level of education (2022)

Country	Primary education	Lower secondary education
France	1.21	1.08
Germany	0.60	2.64
Italy	0.33	1.84
Spain	2.13	7.79
United Kingdom	–	–
United States	1.75	1.77
OECD average	1.47	2.17
EU-25 average	1.19	2.13

Source OECD. Education at a glance (2024)

Research indicates that early grade repetition tends to yield negative long-term outcomes, increasing the likelihood of students dropping out or performing poorly academically. In many countries, the practice is being phased out or restructured to emphasize remedial programs and personalized learning interventions instead of grade retention. Several OECD countries, including the United Kingdom, Norway, Iceland, and Japan, do not use grade repetition at all. Instead, these systems rely on alternative measures such as targeted interventions and differentiated instruction to support students struggling with grade-level content.

Grade repetition remains more prevalent at the upper secondary level, particularly in general education programs (Table 12). In 2015, the OECD average for repeaters in upper secondary education stood at 5%, declining to 3% by 2022 (Table 12). This downward trend is indicative of policy shifts aimed at reducing the financial and social burdens associated with grade repetition. Spain exhibited a significant reduction in upper secondary repeaters, from 11% in 2015 to 6% in 2022. Similarly, Italy saw a decline from 6 to 3%, aligning with broader European efforts to minimize repetition rates. France also witnessed a substantial reduction, from 6 to 2%. In contrast, the United States maintained a relatively stable repetition rate of 3% over the period.

The gender distribution of repeaters shows a clear trend: boys are more likely to repeat a grade than girls. In 2022, boys comprised 57% of repeaters across the OECD, with a similar proportion in Spain (57%) and France (55%). Research suggests that boys face a higher likelihood of grade repetition due to differences in academic engagement, behavioral expectations, and socioemotional factors.

The COVID-19 pandemic temporarily altered grade repetition patterns, as many governments implemented policies aimed at minimizing disruptions to student learning. Countries such as Germany and Spain introduced policies to discourage grade repetition, leading to a short-term decline in repetition rates in 2021. However, post-pandemic, some countries have experienced a rebound in repetition rates as students who struggled with remote learning faced challenges in catching up with academic expectations.

Table 12 Share of repeaters at upper secondary and post-secondary level (2015 and 2022)

	Upper secondary general programs		
	Share of repeaters		Share of boys
	2015	2022	2022
	(1)	(2)	(3)
France	6	2	55
Germany	–	–	–
Italy	6	3	46
Spain	11	6	57
United Kingdom	–	–	–
United States	3	3	52
OECD average	5	3	57
EU-25 average	4	2	55

Source OECD. Education at a glance (2024)

France has recently revised its grade repetition policy. From 2013 to 2024, repetition was permitted only under exceptional circumstances. However, new reforms have granted more authority to school councils, allowing for greater flexibility in deciding whether a student should repeat a grade. Similar policy shifts have been observed in Belgium, where first-grade students in the Flemish community are now required to either repeat a year or switch to a different study track if they fail their final exams (OECD, Education at a Glance 2024).

Countries have increasingly sought alternatives to grade repetition, including early interventions, tutoring, and competency-based assessments. These measures aim to provide students with targeted support to improve learning outcomes without resorting to retention. In Denmark, Slovenia, and Sweden, students themselves are involved in the decision-making process regarding grade repetition, ensuring that their perspectives are considered in academic planning.

Equity in education is closely linked to grade repetition policies. Socioeconomically disadvantaged students, particularly those from immigrant backgrounds, are disproportionately affected by grade repetition. According to PISA data, disadvantaged students are more likely to repeat a grade than their more advantaged peers, even when they achieve similar academic results. This trend contributes to persistent socioeconomic inequalities and lower completion rates for marginalized student groups (OECD 2023b).

Efforts to mitigate these disparities include targeted financial support, remedial education programs, and early intervention strategies. In countries such as the United States and Germany, policies are increasingly focused on addressing the root causes of academic underperformance rather than relying on grade repetition as a corrective measure.

In sum, the decline in grade repetition rates across OECD countries reflects a shift toward more inclusive and effective educational policies. While some countries still maintain relatively high repetition rates, many have adopted alternative strategies to support struggling students without requiring them to repeat a grade. The long-term effectiveness of these policies remains a subject of ongoing research, but trends suggest that early intervention and personalized support systems may offer more sustainable solutions to improving educational outcomes.

4.2 Performance in International Primary Assessments: PIRLS and TIMSS

The *Progress in International Reading Literacy Study* (PIRLS) is an international reading assessment conducted every five years for fourth-grade students. The latest results, published in May 2023 by the IEA, an international education organization based in the Netherlands with government participation, indicate that many countries have experienced declines in reading proficiency between 2016 and 2021. The PIRLS assessment uses a standardized scale with a central reference point of 500 (established in 1995) and a standard deviation of 100 to measure reading proficiency across countries (IEA, PIRLS 2021). The COVID-19 pandemic played a significant role in the decline in reading performance observed in several countries. Table 13 shows that OECD countries participating in PILRS lost on average, 7 points (533 versus 540) between 2016 and 2021. Among the 32 nations with comparable PIRLS data for 2016 and 2021, 21 recorded lower reading scores, with the drop largely attributed to school closures and disruptions to traditional learning. Research by Patrinos et al. (2023) found that, on average, school closures led to learning losses equivalent to 0.17 standard deviations—approximately half a school year of learning. However, some countries, such as England, conducted their assessments one year later than scheduled, allowing for partial recovery from the pandemic's impact. Despite these challenges, a few countries managed to maintain or even improve reading proficiency levels. France, for instance, showed an increase in its PIRLS scores between 2016 and 2021. Other countries, including Germany and Italy, recorded a greater impact of the pandemic on struggling students, affecting the proportion of students achieving at the highest levels. In contrast, England experienced a decline in top-performing students while maintaining the proportion of lower-achieving students.

Gender differences in reading performance vary significantly across countries. In Spain, for instance, the gender gap in reading proficiency is among the smallest, with only a two-point difference between boys and girls in 2021. This represents a narrowing of the gap from 2016, but it was primarily driven by a larger decline in girls' scores rather than an improvement in boys' performance. By contrast, in most OECD countries, girls continue to outperform boys in reading by a larger margin.

Another key factor influencing early reading proficiency is the effectiveness of early childhood education programs. Several countries with high participation rates in early childhood education show varying results in PIRLS. While countries like Finland and the Netherlands tend to sustain early learning advantages, others, including Spain and Italy, have seen their initial advantages diminish by fourth grade.

Table 13 PIRLS results in 2006, 2011, 2016, and 2021 in selected OECD countries

Country	2006	2011	2016	2021
France	522	520	511	514
Germany	548	541	537	524
Italy	551	541	548	537
Spain	513	513	528	521
England	539	552	559	558
United States	540	556	549	548
OECD Average	533	538	540	533

Source IEA, *Progress in International Reading Literacy Study* (PIRLS 2021)

This suggests that the quality of early education programs, including teacher qualifications, curriculum structure, and student–teacher ratios, plays a critical role in maintaining early academic gains. For instance, in terms of child-to-educator ratios in early education, Spain has a ratio of 12.1 children per educator, above the EU-22 average (11.7) but below the OECD average (12.7). Research by Araujo et al. (2016) indicates that higher-quality early education environments, enriched with effective pedagogical practices, contribute to better learning outcomes.

The decline in reading scores has been particularly pronounced at the lower end of the performance distribution in several countries. The percentage of students scoring at the lowest proficiency level increased in Spain, Germany, and Italy between 2016 and 2021 (Table 14). Meanwhile, in England, the pandemic had a more significant impact on high-achieving students rather than struggling readers.

The Trends in International Mathematics and Science Study (TIMSS) is a large-scale international assessment conducted by the International Association for the Evaluation of Educational Achievement (IEA). It evaluates students' mathematics and science proficiency at two key educational stages: fourth grade (primary education) and eighth grade (lower secondary education). We will focus on the fourth-grade assessment because it provides a broader basis for international comparisons, as a larger number of countries participate at this level compared to the eighth-grade assessment.

TIMSS 2023 marks the eighth cycle of the assessment since its inception in 1995. More than 650,000 students from 64 countries and six benchmarking systems worldwide participated, providing valuable insights into student achievement across different education systems. The TIMSS International Benchmarks offer a structured way to evaluate performance, going beyond simple average scores to provide a detailed breakdown of student achievement levels.

TIMSS 2023 results confirm the well-established global trends in mathematics achievement. East Asian countries, including Singapore, Taiwan, South Korea, Japan, and Hong Kong, continue to lead the rankings, not only in terms of average scores but also in the proportion of students reaching the highest achievement levels. Meanwhile, European countries such as Finland, the Netherlands, and Germany maintain

Table 14 Trends in PIRLS International Benchmark Achievement Levels (2021 vs. 2016)

	During the COVID-19 pandemic (2021)					Before the COVID-19 pandemic (2021)				
	2021					2016				
	Advanced (>625)	High (550–625)	Intermediate (475–550)	Low (400–475)	Very Low (<400)	Advanced (>625)	High (550–625)	Intermediate (475–550)	Low (400–475)	Very Low (<400)
France	5	27	40	22	6	4	26	42	22	6
Germany	8	31	36	19	6	11	36	34	14	5
Italy	8	36	39	14	3	11	41	35	11	2
Spain	6	29	41	19	5	6	33	41	17	3
England	18	39	29	11	3	20	37	29	11	3
United States	18	34	29	14	5	16	37	30	13	4

Source IEA, *Progress in International Reading Literacy Study* (PIRLS 2021)
[1]England was assessed one year later than originally scheduled, reflecting a six-year trend from PIRLS 2016. Data extracted from pirls2021.org/results

strong results but have seen their relative advantage decline in recent assessment cycles.

Across Europe, mathematics achievement has varied. Some countries have maintained or improved their performance, while others have faced stagnation or slight declines. The OECD average score in mathematics was 525 in TIMSS 2023, with most European countries positioned around this benchmark. Germany, for example, scored 524 points, maintaining relative stability over time, whereas France experienced a slight decline, reaching 484 points. Italy also showed minor fluctuations, scoring 513 points in 2023. In contrast, England has consistently outperformed the OECD average, with a score of 552, while the United States saw a decline from 535 points in 2019 to 517 in 2023.

Beyond average scores, TIMSS categorizes student performance across five benchmark levels: Advanced (above 625 points), High (550–625 points), Intermediate (475–550 points), Low (400–475 points), and Very Low (below 400 points). The proportion of students reaching the Advanced benchmark varies significantly across nations. In England, 22% of students achieved scores above 625 points in TIMSS 2023, a slight increase from 21% in 2019. The United States, another high-performing nation, reported 13% of students at the Advanced level, a small decline from 14% in the previous cycle. By contrast, in many European countries, the percentage of students achieving at this highest level remains relatively low. For example, Germany reported that only 8% of students reached the Advanced level, while Italy and Spain had 7% and 4%, respectively. France, at 3%, had one of the lowest proportions of students achieving this benchmark among the assessed countries. At the lower end of the achievement scale, TIMSS 2023 also highlights concerns about the proportion of students scoring below 400 points, indicating serious difficulties with foundational mathematical concepts. France recorded the highest percentage of students in this category among the major European nations, with 15% of students scoring below 400 points. Similarly, Spain and Italy reported 10% and 9% of students in the Very Low category, respectively. In contrast, Germany had a relatively lower proportion, with 6% of students falling into this category. Meanwhile, England had comparatively fewer students at the lowest level, with 6%.

Science achievement in TIMSS 2023 follows similar patterns to those observed in mathematics, with East Asian countries continuing to lead global rankings, while European nations present a more diverse range of results. Some countries, such as England, have improved their science performance, while others, including France and Germany, have seen slight declines.

The OECD average in fourth-grade science remained stable at 526 points, reflecting overall consistency in international performance. However, individual country results varied. Germany scored 515 points in 2023, down slightly from 518 in 2019. Italy's performance remained stable, with a score of 511 points, while France held steady at 488 points. In contrast, England is one of the top-performing European nations. Meanwhile, the United States saw a decline, dropping from 539 points in 2019 to 532 in 2023.

The TIMSS International Benchmarks also reveal significant disparities in science achievement across countries. The proportion of students reaching the Advanced benchmark remains relatively low in many European nations. In England, 19% of students scored above 625 points, a significant improvement from 10% in 2019. Similarly, the United States maintained a relatively high proportion, with 15% of students at the Advanced level. By contrast, countries such as France, Germany, Spain, and Italy reported much lower percentages of students reaching this level, ranging from 2 to 9%.

At the lower end of the achievement scale, TIMSS 2023 highlights concerns regarding the proportion of students scoring below 400 points in science, indicating significant gaps in scientific understanding. France recorded 12% of students in this category, while Germany, Spain, and Italy reported 9%, 8%, and 6%, respectively. In comparison, England had lower proportions of students in the Very Low category, at 4%. These figures suggest that, while some countries have successfully maintained high levels of science achievement, others continue to face challenges in closing performance gaps.

In sum, East Asian countries continue to lead global performance in mathematics, maintaining a significant advantage over other regions. While some European nations, such as England, have improved their performance, others, including France, Germany, Italy, and Spain, are stagnated below the OECD average. The TIMSS benchmarks indicate that a significant proportion of students across various countries struggle with fundamental concepts in mathematics and science. TIMSS 2023 also provides insights into how countries have managed learning recovery following the disruptions caused by the pandemic. Some nations have successfully mitigated learning losses, while others still face challenges in restoring pre-pandemic achievement levels. Research suggests that students with higher confidence in their mathematical abilities tend to achieve better results. Fostering positive attitudes toward STEM subjects may contribute to improved performance over time.

The TIMSS 2023 results indicate a widening gender gap in mathematics achievement compared to TIMSS 2019, with boys outperforming girls across all OECD countries. On average, the gender gap in mathematics increased to 16 points in the OECD and 18 points in the EU, with significant disparities in countries like France, Italy, and Portugal, where the difference exceeded 20 points. In Spain, the gap has grown steadily, reaching 18 points in 2023, while Germany, the UK, and the US also show persistent but varying gender differences in mathematics performance.

Table 16. Trends in TIMSS International Benchmark Achievement Levels Maths (2023 vs. 2019) (Tables 15, 16, and 17).

4.3 *Performance in International Secondary Assessments: PISA*

The OECD publishes the PISA results every three years, assessing the skills of 15-year-old students in Reading, Mathematics, and Science. The most recent data corresponds to PISA 2022, released in December 2023. In this assessment, the OECD's

Table 15 TIMSS results in mathematics and Science (2011, 2015, 2019 and 2023)

Country	2011	2015	2019	2023
Mathematics				
France	–	488	485	484
Germany	528	522	521	524
Italy	508	507	515	513
Spain	482	505	502	498
England	542	546	556	552
United States	541	539	535	517
OECD Average	522	525	527	525
Science				
France	–	487	488	488
Germany	528	528	518	515
Italy	524	516	510	511
Spain	505	518	511	504
England	529	536	537	556
United States	544	546	539	532
OECD Average	523	528	526	526

Source IEA, *Trends in International Mathematics and Science Study* (TIMSS, 2023)

average score was set at 500 points in the first edition of each competency (2000 for Reading, 2003 for Mathematics, and 2006 for Science). Each edition focuses on one of the three competencies, meaning that about two-thirds of the test concentrate on that area, making the estimation of its results more precise than those of the other two secondary subjects. In 2018, the main focus was Reading, in 2022, it was Mathematics, and in 2025, it will be Science. PISA 2022 included Creative Thinking, and PISA 2025 will assess foreign language proficiency, as outlined in the chapter on bilingualism of this book.

The PISA 2022 assessment in mathematics, reading, and science for 15-year-old students included participation from 37 OECD countries and 44 additional countries and economies that, while not OECD members, also conducted the tests. Table 1 presents the evolution of results from 2009 to 2022. We begin with mathematics, which was the main focus of PISA 2022, as it was in 2012. This means that students answered more mathematics questions than reading and science questions, making the results more precise. Specifically, 94% of students took a 60-minute mathematics test and then spent another 60 minutes on one of three subjects: reading, science, or creative thinking. The remaining 6% of students took reading and science tests instead.

The most recent cycle, PISA 2022, highlights a significant decline in student performance across many countries, a trend that predates the COVID-19 pandemic but has likely been exacerbated by learning disruptions caused by school closures.

Table 16 Trends in TIMSS International Benchmark Achievement Levels Maths (2023 vs. 2019)

	During the COVID-19 pandemic (2023)					Before the COVID-19 pandemic (2019)				
	2023					2019				
	Advanced (>625)	High (550–625)	Intermediate (475–550)	Low (400–475)	Very low (<400)	Advanced (>625)	High (550–625)	Intermediate (475–550)	Low (400–475)	Very low (<400)
France	3	17	36	29	15	3	18	36	28	15
Germany	8	30	37	19	6	6	30	39	21	4
Italy	7	27	35	22	9	4	26	43	22	5
Spain	4	21	37	28	10	4	23	38	26	9
England	22	31	27	14	6	21	32	30	13	4
United States	13	26	29	19	13	14	32	31	16	7

Table 17 Trends in TIMSS International Benchmark Achievement Levels Science (2023 vs. 2019)

	During the COVID-19 pandemic (2023)					Before the COVID-19 pandemic (2019)				
	2023					2019				
	Advanced (>625)	High (550–625)	Intermediate (475–550)	Low (400–475)	Very low (<400)	Advanced (>625)	High (550–625)	Intermediate (475–550)	Low (400–475)	Very low (<400)
France	2	18	39	29	12	3	19	37	27	14
Germany	9	27	34	21	9	7	30	35	21	7
Italy	4	26	41	23	6	3	24	44	24	5
Spain	4	23	40	25	8	3	27	41	23	6
England	19	36	30	11	4	10	34	37	15	4
United States	15	31	29	16	9	15	33	31	15	6

Source IEA, *Trends in International Mathematics and Science Study* (TIMSS 2023)

The overall decline in mathematical competencies is evident across most OECD countries. In PISA 2022, the OECD average in mathematics fell to 472 points, marking a significant drop from 494 points in 2012. Several countries, including France (474), Germany (475), Italy (471), and Spain (473), saw notable declines compared to previous cycles. The United Kingdom (489) and United States (465) also recorded lower scores than in earlier assessments.

Historically, in PISA 2003, when mathematics was first assessed as the primary domain, the OECD set the average score at 500 points, with a standard deviation of 100. The results of PISA 2022 indicate that 15-year-old students across OECD countries now have weaker mathematical competencies than their counterparts in 2003. The OECD (2023a) estimates that a 20-point difference in PISA scores corresponds to one academic year of learning. Hanushek and Woessmann (2020) further estimate that students typically gain about one-third of a standard deviation per school year. The 28-point decline from 2003 to 2022 is therefore close to the 33-point threshold equivalent to a full school year of learning.

Throughout two decades of PISA history, the OECD average in mathematics had never dropped by more than four points between consecutive assessments. However, the 17-point drop between 2018 and 2022 suggests that the COVID-19 pandemic had a major impact on student learning worldwide. The learning loss of 17 points (from 489 to 472) is comparable to the 14% standard deviation loss due the school closures estimated by Betthäuser et al. (2023), the 17% found in the survey by Patrinos et al. (2023), and the 18% loss found by Sanz and Tena (2023).

Despite the pandemic-related disruptions, PISA trend analysis reveals that the decline in mathematics performance started before 2020. In PISA 2018, the OECD average in mathematics had already fallen to 489 points, 11 points lower than in PISA 2003, suggesting structural challenges in global education systems. The decline in student performance extends beyond mathematics, with reading and science scores also showing downward trends before the pandemic. The highest reading scores in the OECD were recorded in 2012, while science performance peaked in 2009, followed by a steady decline.

Between 2018 and 2022, most OECD countries experienced a sharp decline in reading scores, with the OECD average dropping from 487 to 476 points. In science, the OECD average declined from 489 points in 2018 to 485 in 2022.

In sum, Mathematics performance has declined significantly across OECD countries, with many nations losing the equivalent of nearly a full academic year of learning since 2003. Reading and science scores also declined before the pandemic, reinforcing concerns about long-term educational trends. Between 2018 and 2022, most OECD countries recorded a sharp drop in reading performance. Science scores saw a smaller decline between 2018 and 2022 compared to reading and mathematics. The decline in student competencies in mathematics, reading, and science is not solely a result of the COVID-19 pandemic. Instead, it reflects broader, long-term structural challenges in education systems worldwide.

Given that mathematical competence is a strong predictor of future wages, as shown by Hanushek et al. (2015), addressing these educational challenges is critical for long-term economic and social development. In OECD studies such as PIAAC, individuals with higher mathematical skills earn significantly higher salaries—an effect observed across multiple countries. Furthermore, PISA 2022 data reveals widespread student anxiety about mathematics, particularly among female students. This perception of mathematics as a difficult subject may be exacerbating performance gaps. Encouraging a growth mindset, increasing confidence in mathematics, and enhancing teacher training in numeracy skills are potential strategies to mitigate this decline.

Failure to address these challenges could result in continued declines in STEM-related skills, negatively affecting future workforce productivity, innovation capacity, and economic competitiveness. Countries that implement targeted education policies to strengthen numeracy skills, reduce student anxiety, and enhance learning environments will be better positioned to reverse these trends and improve future PISA results (Table 18).

The results from PISA 2022 (Table 19) confirm that Japan (536) and South Korea (527) lead the OECD rankings in mathematics, followed by Estonia (510 points) and Switzerland (508 points). In total, 19 countries scored significantly above the OECD

Table 18 Results in PISA 2009, 2012, 2015, 2018, and 2022

		2009	2012	2015	2018	2022
Mathematics	France	497	495	493	495	474
	Germany	513	514	506	500	475
	Italy	483	485	490	487	471
	Spain	483	484	486	481	473
	United Kingdom	492	494	492	502	489
	United States	487	481	470	478	465
	OECD	495	494	490	489	472
Science	France	498	499	495	493	487
	Germany	520	524	509	503	492
	Italy	489	494	481	468	477
	Spain	488	496	493	483	485
	United Kingdom	514	514	509	505	500
	United States	502	497	496	502	499
	OECD	501	501	493	489	485
Reading	France	496	505	499	493	474
	Germany	497	508	509	498	480
	Italy	486	490	485	476	482
	Spain	481	488	496	477*	474
	United Kingdom	494	499	498	504	494
	United States	500	498	497	505	504
	OECD	493	496	493	487	476

Source OECD, PISA (2023b)

average (472 points), ranging from Estonia (510) to New Zealand (479). The gap between the highest- and lowest-performing OECD countries in mathematics is 153 points, highlighting substantial disparities in student achievement across education systems.

Within the European Union (EU), Estonia has established itself as the top performer, being the only EU country to compete with leading Asian education systems. In PISA 2022, Estonia scored 510 points in mathematics, compared to Japan (536) and South Korea (527). The Netherlands (493) and Ireland (492) ranked second and third within the EU, while the EU average in mathematics was 474 points.

In reading, Ireland (516) led the entire EU and even topped the OECD rankings, alongside Japan (516) and South Korea (515). Estonia followed as the second-highest EU performer with 511 points. The EU average in reading (475 points) lags behind Ireland and Estonia, suggesting significant differences in literacy performance within the bloc. For science, Estonia again ranked first within the EU, scoring 526 points, followed by Finland (511) and Ireland (504)—all well above the EU average of 484 points. These results highlight that Estonia and Ireland consistently outperform their EU peers across all three subjects (mathematics, reading, and science). However, Ireland's results carry a cautionary note in the PISA 2022 report, indicating potential comparability issues with other countries.

On average, Estonia and Ireland outperform the EU average by 30 points across all three domains—equivalent to nearly one additional year of learning. In practical terms, 9th-grade students in Estonia and Ireland (equivalent to Year 3 of lower secondary education) possess the same skills as 10th-grade students (Year 4 of lower secondary education) in many other EU and OECD countries. Given their consistent success, Estonia and Ireland have emerged as the "new Finland"—a reference to Finland's dominance in PISA rankings in the 2000s, which set a benchmark for quality and equity in education.

The success of Estonia and Ireland in PISA has been attributed to several key education policies that have shaped their strong student performance (OECD 2020b, 2020c). Some of the key strategies that other countries could adopt include:

- School Autonomy and Decentralized Governance: Estonia grants significant autonomy to schools, allowing them to design curricula and teaching methods tailored to local needs. This was reinforced by Estonia's 2014 curriculum reform.
- Teacher Professional Development: Both Estonia and Ireland prioritize continuous professional development for teachers and school leaders. Estonia introduced a competency-based career structure for teachers in 2013, while Ireland has focused on ongoing training, particularly in disadvantaged schools.
- Technology Integration and Digital Skills: Estonia is a leader in technology-enhanced education, with initiatives such as "E-Schoolbag" and the "Digital Mirror" program, which promote the use of digital tools in teaching.
- Adapting to Demographic and Social Changes: Ireland has responded to changing demographics with policies like "First 5," which expanded investment in early childhood education, providing free preschool education and enhancing early learning opportunities.

Table 19 Mathematics scores by country in PISA 2022

Country	Average score	95% Confidence interval	OECD rank
Japan	536	530–541	1
South Korea	527	520–535	1
Estonia	510	506–514	3
Switzerland	508	504–512	3
Canada	497	494–500	5
Netherlands	493	485–500	4
Ireland	492	488–496	5
Belgium	489	485–494	5
Denmark	489	485–493	5
United Kingdom	489	485–493	5
Poland	489	485–493	5
Austria	487	483–492	5
Australia	487	484–491	6
Czech Republic	487	483–491	5
Slovenia	485	482–487	6
Finland	484	480–488	6
Latvia	483	479–487	6
Sweden	482	478–486	6
New Zealand	479	475–483	7
Lithuania	475	472–479	16
Germany	475	469–481	8
France	474	469–479	15
Spain	473	470–476	18
Hungary	473	468–478	16
Portugal	472	467–477	17
Italy	471	465–477	16
Norway	468	464–472	19
United States	465	457–473	18
Slovakia	464	458–470	20
Iceland	459	456–462	26
Israel	458	451–464	23
Turkey	453	450–456	28
Greece	430	426–435	33
Chile	412	408–416	34
Mexico	395	391–399	35
Costa Rica	385	381–388	35
Colombia	383	377–389	35

Source OECD, PISA 2022 Database, Table I.B1.2.1 & I.B2.1

- Continuous Assessment and Constructive Feedback: Ireland has improved education quality through ongoing student assessments and feedback mechanisms aimed at supporting both teachers and students.
- School Network Consolidation: Estonia has restructured its school network, particularly in rural areas, by merging small schools and establishing secondary education centers in each county capital under specific national programs.

Beyond Estonia and Ireland, Poland and the United Kingdom have also achieved strong results in mathematics, reading, and science. Poland, which had similar scores to Spain in the early 2000s, has significantly improved over time. In PISA 2022, Poland ranked among the top EU performers, with 489 points in mathematics and reading, and 499 in science. However, school closures during the pandemic had a severe impact on Polish students' learning outcomes. The United Kingdom, on the other hand, maintained strong PISA results, scoring 489 in mathematics, 494 in reading, and 500 in science. These results align with the UK's top-tier performance in PIRLS 2021, the international reading assessment for primary school students, published in May 2023. Unlike Estonia and Ireland, Poland and the UK are large countries, where education management can be more complex. However, their strong PISA results demonstrate that well-implemented education policies can yield significant improvements even in large-scale education systems.

Two countries that have historically received significant attention in European education discussions—Finland and Portugal—recorded sharp declines in PISA 2022. Their latest scores reflect a continued downward trend from previous editions. Between PISA 2012 and PISA 2022, Finland's scores dropped by more than 33 points across all three domains. The decline was particularly steep among the lowest-performing students and those from lower socioeconomic backgrounds, widening the achievement gap between advantaged and disadvantaged students.

PISA 2022 reveals a clear pattern in student performance distribution across OECD countries. The assessment categorizes students into six proficiency levels in mathematics, reading, and science, with Level 2 considered the minimum required for students to successfully transition into upper secondary education or higher education. It also serves as a critical threshold for future employability and social integration. Between 2012 and 2022, the proportion of students scoring below Level 2 increased in multiple countries.

PISA 2022 highlights notable disparities in student performance across OECD countries, revealing significant variations in the distribution of students across different proficiency levels in mathematics, reading, and science. The framework defines six proficiency levels, with Level 2 considered the minimum benchmark necessary for students to transition successfully into upper secondary education or higher education. This level also serves as a critical threshold for ensuring future employability and social integration. Over the decade between 2012 and 2022, the share of students failing to reach Level 2 has increased in many countries, raising concerns about declining educational standards.

The results show that some of the largest OECD economies have experienced a decline in the proportion of students achieving at least Level 2 competency. In

France, Germany, Italy, and Spain, for example, the percentage of students failing to reach this threshold has grown considerably, particularly in mathematics, where low performance has become a pressing issue. Germany and Italy saw their share of low-achieving students in mathematics climb to 30% in 2022, while in France, this figure reached 29%, an eight-percentage-point increase compared to 2015. In reading and science, the trends are similar but less pronounced, though France has seen a substantial increase in low-performing students in reading, reaching 27% in 2022.

Across the OECD, 31% of students do not reach Level 2 in mathematics, a significant increase from previous assessments. At this level, students should be able to perform basic mathematical tasks, such as comparing distances between two different routes or converting prices from one currency to another. In reading, 26% of students across the OECD fall below Level 2, indicating difficulty in identifying the main idea of a moderately long text or reflecting on the structure and purpose of a passage when explicitly asked to do so. In science, 24% of students in the OECD do not meet the Level 2 benchmark, meaning they struggle to recognize fundamental scientific explanations and apply them to basic real-world situations.

The distribution of high-achieving students, those scoring at Levels 5 and 6, also highlights critical differences among OECD countries. While countries such as Germany, France, and the United Kingdom maintain a relatively high proportion of top performers, other major economies like Italy, Spain, and the United States consistently underperform in the highest categories. In Germany, 9% of students reach Level 5 or 6 in mathematics, while France has seen a similar decline to 7% over the same period. In the United Kingdom, 11% of students in mathematics achieved high scores in 2022, showing stability compared to previous cycles, while in the United States, only 7% reached these top levels.

Reading and science results paint a similar picture. The United Kingdom outperforms many OECD countries in reading, with 10% of students classified as top performers, compared to the OECD average of 7%. In contrast, France, Germany, and Italy have seen a drop in their share of high-achieving students in reading, with figures now ranging between 5 and 8%. In science, Germany, France, the United Kingdom, and the United States hover around 8–11% of students reaching Levels 5 and 6. One of the most striking concerns emerging from PISA 2022 is the growing gap between top-performing and low-achieving students, which is particularly visible in France and Germany. In these countries, while the proportion of students at Levels 5 and 6 has declined, the share of those failing to reach Level 2 has grown significantly. This trend suggests a widening performance gap, exacerbating educational inequality. By contrast, the United Kingdom and the United States exhibit a more balanced distribution, maintaining a significant proportion of high-achieving students while keeping the share of low-performing students relatively stable—except in mathematics, where the United States continues to struggle, with 34% of students failing to meet basic proficiency in 2022, the highest among the major OECD economies.

These trends have significant long-term implications for human capital development, workforce competitiveness, and innovation. Countries that struggle to cultivate a strong pipeline of high-achieving students may face challenges in research, development, and technological advancement, as STEM-intensive industries rely heavily on advanced mathematical and scientific competencies (Table 20).

4.3.1 Student Performance and Socioeconomic Status in PISA 2022

The PISA index of economic, social, and cultural status (ISEC) provides a standardized way to compare the socioeconomic background of students across countries. This allows for a meaningful analysis of student performance based on socioeconomic status, independent of the country in which they are assessed. The results of PISA 2022 highlight significant disparities in educational outcomes based on students' socioeconomic backgrounds, with some countries demonstrating stronger educational equity than others.

Across OECD countries, there are notable differences in how students are distributed among socioeconomic quintiles (Table 21). In countries like the United Kingdom (40.0%) and the United States (39.0%), a large proportion of students belong to the highest international socioeconomic quintile, indicating a higher concentration of students from privileged backgrounds. By contrast, countries such as Germany (30.9%), Italy (29.5%), and France (34.2%) have a more balanced socioeconomic distribution among students. These differences impact overall educational performance, as students from higher socioeconomic backgrounds typically achieve better results in mathematics, reading, and science.

The performance gap between students from different socioeconomic backgrounds is particularly evident in mathematics (Table 22). On average, students from the highest international socioeconomic quintile in the OECD scored 517 points in mathematics. However, there is considerable variation across countries. Germany (534 points) and the United Kingdom (529 points) had significantly higher scores for their wealthiest students, whereas Italy (512 points) and Spain (511 points) were closer to the OECD average. The results suggest that in countries like Germany and the United Kingdom, wealthier students have access to stronger educational resources or more effective teaching methods, giving them a competitive advantage.

At the other end of the spectrum, students from the lowest international socioeconomic quintile face considerable challenges in achieving strong academic performance. The OECD average for this group was 396 points in mathematics, with notable variations across countries. France (395 points) and Italy (400 points) scored very close to the OECD average, suggesting that their education systems struggle to provide adequate support for the most disadvantaged students. In contrast, Germany (406 points) and the United Kingdom (422 points) performed significantly above the OECD average, indicating a more effective approach to mitigating the negative impact of socioeconomic disadvantage.

One of the most striking findings from PISA 2022 is the educational equity seen in the United Kingdom. Despite having only 1.9% of students in the lowest international socioeconomic quintile—far below the OECD average—the performance of this group in mathematics (422 points) was significantly higher than the OECD average

Table 20 Distribution of students in PISA by performance levels

Country	2009 (%)	2012 (%)	2015 (%)	2018 (%)	2022 (%)
France	–	–	–	–	–
Reading—Low Level	20	19	21	21	27
Reading—High Level	10	13	13	9	7
Mathematics—Low Level	22	22	23	21	29
Mathematics—High Level	14	13	11	11	7
Science—Low Level	19	19	22	21	24
Science—High Level	8	8	8	7	8
Germany	–	–	–	–	–
Reading—Low Level	19	15	16	21	25
Reading—High Level	8	9	12	11	8
Mathematics—Low Level	19	18	17	21	30
Mathematics—High Level	18	18	13	13	9
Science—Low Level	15	12	17	20	23
Science—High Level	13	12	11	10	10
Italy	–	–	–	–	–
Reading—Low Level	21	20	21	23	21
Reading—High Level	6	7	6	5	5
Mathematics—Low Level	25	25	23	24	30
Mathematics—High Level	9	10	11	10	7
Science—Low Level	21	19	23	26	24
Science—High Level	6	6	4	3	4
Spain	–	–	–	–	–
Reading—Low Level	20	18	16	23	24
Reading—High Level	3	6	6	5	5
Mathematics—Low Level	24	24	22	25	27
Mathematics—High Level	8	8	7	7	6
Science—Low Level	18	16	18	21	21
Science—High Level	4	5	5	4	5
United Kingdom	–	–	–	–	–
Reading—Low Level	18	17	18	17	20
Reading—High Level	8	9	9	12	10
Mathematics—Low Level	20	22	22	19	24
Mathematics—High Level	10	12	11	13	11
Science—Low Level	15	15	17	17	20
Science—High Level	11	11	11	10	10
United States	–	–	–	–	–
Reading—Low Level	18	17	19	19	20

(continued)

Table 20 (continued)

Country	2009 (%)	2012 (%)	2015 (%)	2018 (%)	2022 (%)
Reading—High Level	10	8	10	13	14
Mathematics—Low Level	23	26	29	27	34
Mathematics—High Level	10	9	6	8	7
Science—Low Level	18	18	20	19	22
Science—High Level	9	8	9	9	11
OECD	–	–	–	–	–
Reading—Low Level	20	19	20	22	26
Reading—High Level	7	8	8	8	7
Mathematics—Low Level	24	24	25	24	31
Mathematics—High Level	12	12	10	11	9
Science—Low Level	19	19	22	22	24
Science—High Level	8	8	7	7	7

Source OECD (2023b). PISA 2022 Results (Volume I). Figure I.3.1, Figure I.3.4, and Figure I.3.5

Table 21 Proportion of students by international socioeconomic quintiles

	Lowest quintile	Second quintile	Middle quintile	Fourth quintile	Highest quintile
	% (S.E.)	% (S.E.)	% (S.E.)	% (S.E.)	% (S.E.)
France	3.2 (0.3)	11.7 (0.4)	22.5 (0.8)	28.5 (0.6)	34.2 (1.0)
Germany	6.0 (0.4)	15.2 (0.6)	21.7 (0.5)	26.2 (0.7)	30.9 (1.1)
Italy	4.2 (0.3)	13.6 (0.5)	24.9 (0.6)	27.8 (0.6)	29.5 (1.0)
Spain	6.3 (0.4)	10.7 (0.3)	20.2 (0.5)	26.5 (0.5)	36.2 (0.8)
United Kingdom	1.9 (0.3)	9.7 (0.4)	21.7 (0.8)	26.7 (0.7)	40.0 (1.0)
United States	3.9 (0.5)	11.5 (0.8)	20.7 (1.0)	24.8 (0.6)	39.0 (1.9)
OECD	4.9 (0.1)	11.8 (0.1)	20.4 (0.1)	25.7 (0.1)	37.1 (0.2)

Source OECD, PISA 2022, Tables I.B1.4.6 & I.B1.4.8. https://www.oecd-ilibrary.org/education/pisa-2022-results-volume-i_53f23881-en

(396 points). This suggests that the UK education system is particularly effective in providing support mechanisms that help disadvantaged students succeed.

Germany also demonstrated relatively strong equity, with students from the lowest quintile scoring 406 points, well above the OECD average. The German education system provides strong vocational pathways and targeted interventions, which may explain this higher performance. In contrast, France and Italy appear to struggle more with educational equity, as students from the lowest socioeconomic quintile in these countries scored at or below the OECD average, indicating potential gaps in support for disadvantaged students.

Table 22 Mathematics performance by international socioeconomic quintiles

	All Students	Lowest quintile	Second quintile	Middle quintile	Fourth quintile	Highest quintile
	Score (S.E.)	Score (S.E.)	Score (S.E.)	Score (S.E.)	Score (S.E.)	Score (S.E.)
France	474 (2.5)	395 (6.7)	421 (3.7)	441 (2.7)	474 (2.7)	526 (2.9)
Germany	475 (3.1)	406 (5.9)	435 (3.9)	458 (3.4)	482 (3.5)	534 (3.4)
Italy	471 (3.1)	400 (6.3)	432 (3.4)	454 (3.4)	476 (3.1)	512 (4.9)
Spain	473 (1.5)	412 (3.9)	440 (2.3)	448 (1.8)	473 (1.8)	511 (1.8)
United Kingdom	489 (2.2)	422 (11.9)	452 (4.5)	469 (3.5)	484 (3.0)	529 (3.7)
United States	465 (2.5)	413 (8.9)	423 (6.3)	430 (3.5)	456 (4.5)	507 (4.2)
OECD	472 (0.4)	396 (1.5)	427 (0.7)	449 (0.6)	474 (0.5)	517 (0.5)

Source OECD, PISA 2022, Tables I.B1.4.6 & I.B1.4.8. https://www.oecd-ilibrary.org/education/pisa-2022-results-volume-i_53f23881-en

Another key insight from PISA 2022 is the performance of middle-quintile students across different countries. While countries like Germany (458 points) and the United Kingdom (469 points) had strong results for students in this socioeconomic bracket, Italy (454 points) and Spain (448 points) performed below these levels. This suggests that educational systems in Germany and the UK provide a more consistent level of quality across different socioeconomic groups, whereas in countries like Italy and Spain, middle-class students may not be receiving the same level of support and opportunities.

A relevant issue highlighted by PISA 2022 is the gap between students from the highest and lowest socioeconomic quintiles within each country. Germany had one of the largest gaps (128 points), indicating that while its education system is highly effective for disadvantaged students in relative terms to other countries it is even more effective for wealthier students. In comparison, Spain (99 points), the United Kingdom (107 points), and Italy (112 points) exhibited gaps that, while still significant, were smaller than those observed in Germany.

Overall, PISA 2022 reinforces the importance of policies aimed at improving educational equity. Countries that provide targeted support for disadvantaged students—such as early childhood education, additional resources for low-income schools, and financial assistance for students—tend to achieve better results in terms of reducing inequality.

4.3.2 Socioeconomic Disparities and Academic Performance in PISA 2022

PISA 2022 provides several indicators of educational equity, highlighting how socioeconomic background influences academic performance across different countries. One of the key measures used to assess equity is the strength of the relationship between the PISA index of economic, social, and cultural status (ESCS) and student performance in mathematics. Ideally, there would be no correlation between socioeconomic background and educational outcomes, meaning that all students—regardless of their economic circumstances—would have equal opportunities to succeed. However, in reality, the strength of this relationship varies considerably across countries.

Among the analyzed countries, France and Germany exhibit the strongest correlation between socioeconomic background and mathematics performance. In both countries, a significant portion of the variance in student performance is explained by socioeconomic status, suggesting that students from disadvantaged backgrounds face greater educational barriers. These results are consistent with findings from previous PISA cycles, where Germany and France consistently showed lower levels of educational equity. By contrast, the United Kingdom, Italy, and Spain demonstrate greater equality of opportunity, with a weaker relationship between socioeconomic status and academic performance. In these countries, students from disadvantaged backgrounds are relatively more likely to achieve strong results, indicating that their education systems provide more robust support structures to mitigate socioeconomic disparities. These findings align with the results of PISA 2018, where the same countries displayed higher levels of educational equity.

Another key indicator of equity is the gap in mathematics scores between students from the highest and lowest socioeconomic quartiles. On average, across OECD countries, students from socioeconomically advantaged backgrounds scored 93 points higher than their disadvantaged peers. However, this gap varies significantly by country. France (113 points) and Germany (111 points) exhibit the largest disparities, reinforcing their position as two of the least equitable education systems among OECD countries. Conversely, the United Kingdom, Italy, and Spain display smaller gaps, with a difference of 86 points in both the UK and Spain, and 85 points in Italy. This suggests that students from disadvantaged backgrounds in these countries have better access to quality education and support mechanisms compared to their peers in less equitable systems.

One of the most insightful indicators of educational resilience is the proportion of disadvantaged students who perform in the top quartile of mathematics within their respective countries. These students, often referred to as academically resilient, demonstrate strong academic achievement despite coming from disadvantaged backgrounds. The OECD average for academically resilient students stands at 10.2%, meaning that roughly one in ten disadvantaged students across OECD countries manages to achieve top-quartile performance.

However, some countries perform significantly better than this benchmark. The United Kingdom stands out with 15.2% of its disadvantaged students reaching top performance levels in mathematics, the highest among the analyzed countries. This confirms previous findings that the UK education system, despite its reputation for elitism, provides robust pathways for disadvantaged students to succeed. Italy (11.3%) and Spain (11.7%) also outperform the OECD average, further reinforcing their relatively strong performance in terms of educational equity.

On the other hand, France (7.4%) and Germany (9.5%) show lower levels of academic resilience, consistent with their overall weaker equity indicators. These results suggest that fewer disadvantaged students in these countries are able to break through socioeconomic barriers and achieve strong academic outcomes. The United States (10.6%) is close to the OECD average, indicating a moderate level of resilience among disadvantaged students. Germany's high level of educational inequality may be partially explained by its early tracking system, which sorts students into different academic pathways as early as age 10. This system can create significant barriers for students from disadvantaged backgrounds, as early tracking decisions often determine whether a student follows an academic route leading to university or a vocational track with fewer academic opportunities (OECD 2023a). This may contribute to the large performance gap between advantaged and disadvantaged students in Germany.

By contrast, countries with more flexible and comprehensive education systems, such as the United Kingdom and Nordic countries like Finland and Denmark, tend to exhibit stronger educational equity. These countries delay academic tracking until later stages of secondary education, allowing all students more time to develop their potential before being placed in different educational streams.

In addition to socioeconomic disparities, PISA 2022 also highlights performance gaps related to gender and immigration status. Across OECD countries, girls outperform boys in reading by an average of 24 points, while boys outperform girls in mathematics by 9 points. In science, the gender gap is negligible. These results suggest that gender-related differences in performance are consistent across most OECD countries, although the underlying causes—such as societal expectations, educational approaches, and subject confidence—may vary. When considering immigrant status, native-born students scored 29 points higher in mathematics than their immigrant peers on average across OECD countries. However, after adjusting for socioeconomic status and language spoken at home, this gap shrinks to only 5 points, indicating that language barriers and socioeconomic disadvantages are the primary drivers of performance differences rather than immigration status itself.

4.3.3 Conclusion: The Long-Term Impact of Mathematics Proficiency

Mathematics proficiency is a key determinant of future economic success, with significant implications for labor market outcomes. Research by Hanushek et al. (2015) demonstrates that individuals with higher mathematical competencies earn significantly higher wages. Findings from PIAAC (the OECD's equivalent of PISA for adults aged 15–65) reveal that individuals with one standard deviation higher mathematical proficiency earn 17.8% more in the OECD. This highlights the strong correlation between quantitative skills and earnings potential. Further studies by Hernández

Table 23 Socioeconomic disparities and academic performance indicators

	Average PISA 2022 reading score	Strength of relationship between ESCS & math performance (R^2)	Score gap between highest & lowest socioeconomic quartiles	% of Disadvantaged students who are academically resilient
France	474	21.5	113	7.4
Germany	475	18.7	111	9.5
Italy	471	13.5	85	11.3
Spain	473	14.2	86	11.7
United Kingdom	489	11.0	86	15.2
United States	465	14.9	102	10.6
OECD	472	15.5	93	10.2

Source PISA 2022 Database, Tables I.B1.4.1, I.B1.4.3 y I.B1.5.19. https://www.oecd-ilibrary.org/education/pisa-2022-results-volume-i_53f23881-en

and Serrano (2013) using PIAAC data for Spain confirm that cognitive skills, particularly in mathematics, have a direct impact on wages. While literacy skills also influence earnings, the impact of mathematical proficiency is more substantial. Each additional PIAAC point in mathematics corresponds to a 0.27% wage increase, compared to only 0.13% for literacy. These findings reinforce the importance of strong mathematical skills for career success in modern economies (Table 23).

4.4 *Students with Bellow Upper Secondary Education Level*

Between 2016 and 2023, significant progress has been made in educational attainment among younger adults (25–34 years old) across OECD and EU countries. The share of individuals without an upper secondary qualification has decreased in almost all countries, reflecting broader efforts to expand access to education and align with labor market demands. On average, across OECD countries, the percentage of younger adults who had not attained an upper secondary education declined from 17% in 2016 to 14% in 2023. Within the EU-25, the decline was from 15 to 12%. This trend highlights ongoing improvements in education policies and access to secondary education, which have helped ensure that a greater proportion of young people complete at least an upper secondary qualification.

Some countries have seen particularly strong reductions in the share of individuals without upper secondary attainment. Spain experienced one of the largest improvements, reducing the percentage of 25–34-year-olds without an upper secondary qualification from 35% in 2016 to 26% in 2023. Similarly, Italy saw a decline from 26 to 20%. These reductions indicate that fewer young adults in these countries are leaving the education system without the minimum credentials needed to compete in the labor market. However, in some cases, these improvements have been accompanied by a shift in the distribution of educational attainment levels, with more individuals pursuing tertiary education rather than stopping at upper secondary qualifications.

At the same time, the share of younger adults with upper secondary or post-secondary non-tertiary education as their highest level of attainment has remained relatively stable or declined slightly. Across OECD countries, this figure fell from 41% in 2016 to 40% in 2023, while in the EU-25, it decreased from 46 to 44%. This shift reflects a growing trend of young people continuing their education beyond secondary school and obtaining tertiary qualifications. The decline is particularly noticeable in countries such as Germany, where the share of younger adults with upper secondary or post-secondary non-tertiary education dropped from 56% in 2016 to 45% in 2023. Similarly, in France, the share fell from 43 to 37%, and in the United Kingdom, it declined from 36 to 28%. These figures suggest that an increasing number of young people in these countries are opting to pursue higher education instead of entering the labor market immediately after secondary education.

The most significant trend observed in the past seven years has been the steady increase in tertiary education attainment among younger adults. On average, the share of 25–34-year-olds with a tertiary qualification rose from 42% in 2016 to 47% in 2023 across OECD countries, while in the EU-25, the increase was from 40 to 44%. In some countries, the rise in tertiary education attainment has been particularly striking. In Spain, the percentage of younger adults with a tertiary degree surged from 41% in 2016 to 52% in 2023, a remarkable 11-percentage-point increase. Similarly, in France, tertiary attainment grew from 44 to 52%, and in the United Kingdom, it increased from 52 to 60%. The United States also saw an increase, from 48 to 52%, while Italy's tertiary education attainment rose from 26 to 31%.

These trends highlight the growing importance of higher education in today's labor market. The demand for highly skilled workers has increased, prompting more young adults to pursue tertiary qualifications to enhance their job prospects and career advancement opportunities. This shift has been supported by government policies aimed at expanding access to higher education, increasing funding for universities, and promoting lifelong learning initiatives. Additionally, the growing participation of women in higher education has contributed to the overall rise in tertiary attainment. Women now outpace men in tertiary education in almost all OECD countries, with the exception of Mexico. On average, across OECD countries, 54% of younger women now have a tertiary degree compared to 41% of younger men. This gender gap has continued to widen in some countries but has also narrowed in others, such as Costa Rica, Finland, Ireland, and Portugal.

Despite these positive trends, challenges remain in ensuring equitable access to education across different regions and social groups. National-level data often obscure significant regional disparities in educational attainment. In countries such as Brazil, Canada, Colombia, Mexico, Portugal, Spain, and Türkiye, the differences between the regions with the highest and lowest shares of adults without an upper secondary qualification exceed 30 percentage points. Such disparities highlight the need for targeted education policies that address regional inequalities and ensure that all young people, regardless of their geographic location, have access to quality education.

Moreover, the educational attainment gap between native-born and foreign-born populations remains an important issue. On average, foreign-born adults are more likely than native-born adults to have either below upper secondary attainment (by 4 percentage points) or a tertiary qualification (by 3 percentage points). However, the differences vary widely across countries. In some nations, foreign-born adults have considerably higher attainment levels than their native-born counterparts, while in others, they are more likely to lack formal qualifications. Addressing these disparities requires policies that facilitate the recognition of foreign qualifications, provide language support programs, and improve access to education and vocational training for immigrant populations.

Overall, the trends observed between 2016 and 2023 reflect a shift toward higher educational attainment among younger adults, with more individuals completing secondary education and an increasing number pursuing tertiary qualifications. These improvements suggest that many countries are successfully expanding access to education and creating opportunities for young people to succeed in the labor market. However, ongoing efforts are needed to address regional disparities, support under-represented groups, and ensure that the benefits of higher education are accessible to all (Table 24).

Table 24 Trends in the educational attainment of 25–34 year-olds, by gender (2016 and 2023). Percentage of 25–34 year-olds with a given level of education as the highest level attained

	Bellow upper secondary		Upper secondary or post-secondary non-tertiary		Tertiary	
	2016	2023	2016	2023	2016	2023
	(1)	(2)	(3)	(4)	(5)	(6)
France	13	11	43	37	44	52
Germany	13	16	56	45	31	39
Italy	26	20	48	50	26	31
Spain	35	26	24	22	41	52
United Kingdom	12	12	36	28	52	60
United States	9	6	44	42	48	52
OECD average	**17**	**14**	**41**	**40**	**42**	**47**
EU-25 average	**15**	**12**	**46**	**44**	**40**	**44**

5 Education and Employment

Table 25 shows that in all countries, including the OECD and EU averages, the unemployment rate is higher among those with lower levels of education. For instance, in France, the unemployment rate for young people aged 25–34 with only lower secondary education is 19.5%, while it is 9.7% for those who completed upper secondary education and 6.1% for those with tertiary education. In Germany, these rates are 8.7%, 2.9%, and 2.9%, respectively. In Italy, the unemployment rate is 16.3% for those with lower secondary education, 10.1% for those with upper secondary education, and 7.3% for those with tertiary education. In Spain, the rates are 22.2%, 15.9%, and 9.2%, respectively. In the United Kingdom, the rates are significantly lower: 6.2% for lower secondary education, 4.1% for upper secondary education, and 2.9% for tertiary education. In the United States, the rates are 8.9%, 5.7%, and 2.9%, respectively.

The OECD and EU averages also reflect this trend. The OECD average shows an unemployment rate of 13.2% for those with lower secondary education, 7.0% for those with upper secondary education, and 4.7% for those with tertiary education. In the EU-25, the rates are 16.7%, 7.4%, and 4.5%, respectively.

These data indicate that higher education significantly reduces the likelihood of unemployment. In the EU-25, the unemployment rate of 4.5% among young people with tertiary education is almost four times lower than among those with only lower secondary education (16.7%). In comparison, in Spain, the unemployment rate for young people with tertiary education is less than half that of those with only lower secondary education (9.2% compared to 22.2%).

Another interesting aspect of Table 25 is how education provides some protection in the labor market during economic crises. In several countries, the unemployment rate increased more among young people with only lower secondary education compared to those with higher levels of education.

Table 25 Unemployment rates for individuals aged 25–34, by education level (2023). *Unemployment rates measured as a percentage of 25–34 year-olds in the labor force*

	Below upper secondary	Upper secondary	Tertiary
	(1)	(2)	(3)
France	19.5	9.7	6.1
Germany	8.7	2.9	2.9
Italy	16.3	10.1	7.3
Spain	22.2	15.9	9.2
United Kingdom	6.2	4.1	2.9
United States	8.9	5.7	2.9
OECD average	**13.2**	**7.0**	**4.7**
EU-25 average	**16.7**	**7.4**	**4.5**

Source OECD. Education at a Glance (2024), Page 93

Additionally, younger women face a higher risk of unemployment than their male counterparts, but tertiary education significantly reduces this gender gap. On average across OECD countries, 11.8% of younger men with below upper secondary attainment are unemployed compared with 16.4% of their female peers. The unemployment rate falls to 6.3% among younger men with upper secondary or post-secondary non-tertiary attainment and 8.3% for their female counterparts. Among tertiary-educated younger adults, the unemployment rates are roughly equal, at around 4.5% for both men and women.

Higher levels of educational attainment generally lead to higher earnings. The foundational skills, knowledge, and competencies provided by upper secondary education are essential in the labor market, ensuring that individuals have achieved a minimum level of literacy and numeracy, which are fundamental for most jobs. Without these basic skills, individuals are often limited to low-paying jobs. Tertiary education is key in achieving upward economic and social mobility, enabling individuals to improve their socioeconomic status through higher earnings. The in-depth knowledge and specialized skills provided by tertiary programs make individuals more competitive in the job market. A tertiary degree also opens up a wider range of job opportunities, including those in professional and managerial roles, which typically offer higher salaries. Universities and colleges also provide opportunities for students to network with their peers, professors, and industry professionals, which can lead to better job prospects and higher earnings.

Among tertiary-educated workers, the earnings advantage tends to increase with the level of tertiary attainment. In most OECD, partner, and accession countries, full-time full-year workers with a master's or doctoral or equivalent degree earn more than those with a bachelor's or equivalent degree, who in turn earn more than those with a short-cycle tertiary degree.

Earnings differences by educational attainment tend to widen among older workers. On average across OECD countries, 25–34 year-olds without upper secondary education earn 15% less than their peers with upper secondary attainment, while 45–54 year-olds earn 20% less. Among tertiary-educated adults, 25–34 year-olds earn 39% more than those with upper secondary attainment, and the average earnings advantage reaches 68% among 45–54 year-olds.

Table 26 reveals that individuals with higher education in Spain earn 45% more than those with at most upper secondary education, a wage premium that is 39% in the OECD average and 35% in the EU-25. In France, individuals with higher education earn 27% more than those with upper secondary education, while in Germany, the wage premium is 30%. In Italy, the premium is 35%, and in the United Kingdom, it is 25%. The United States stands out with a wage premium of 63% for higher education.

The differences in returns across countries stem from both higher vocational training and university degrees, including master's degrees. Compared to the EU-25, labor incomes for the first two educational levels vary, with some countries showing higher or lower returns. For example, the income gap between workers with only compulsory education and those with intermediate education is notable in several countries, reflecting the varying economic benefits of educational attainment.

Table 26 Relative earnings of workers, by education level (2022). Individuals aged 25–34 with employment income (full-time workers throughout the year); upper secondary education = 100

	Below upper secondary	Upper secondary	Tertiary			
			Short-cycle tertiary	Bachelor's or equivalent	Master's, doctoral or equivalent	Total
	25–34 year-olds	25–34 year-olds	25–34 year-olds	25–34 year-olds	25–34 year-olds	25–34 year-olds
	(1)	(2)	(3)	(4)	(5)	(6)
France	78		102	112	149	127
Germany	79	100	114	127	147	130
Italy	95			112	147	135
Spain	93	100	117	137	168	145
United Kingdom	60		98	126	134	125
United States	85	100	120	159	199	163
OECD average	**85**	**100**	**111**	**131**	**156**	**139**
EU-25 average	**87**	**100**		**123**	**150**	**135**

Source OECD. *Education at a Glance* (2024), Page 92

Chapter 4 of this book explores the evolution, causes, and consequences of the wage premium by education level in various countries. One possible hypothesis to explain the varying wage premiums for university degrees across countries could be the differing quality of education provided by these degrees. In other words, the amount of "real" human capital contained in a higher education degree may differ, influencing the wage premium. This variation highlights the importance of considering both the level and quality of education when analyzing economic outcomes.

PISA 2018 included, alongside reading, mathematics, and science, the assessment of "Global Competence" (OECD Education at a Glance, 2022). This competence includes students' attitudes toward immigrants through their responses to the following statements: "Immigrant children should have the same educational opportunities as other children in the country," "Immigrants who have lived in a country for several years should have the opportunity to vote in elections," "Immigrants should have the opportunity to continue their own customs and lifestyle," and "Immigrants should have all the same rights as everyone else in the country." Responses were given on a four-point scale: "strongly disagree," "disagree," "agree," and "strongly agree." Student responses are reflected in an index measuring overall attitudes toward immigrants, where a positive value indicates that students have more positive attitudes toward immigrants than the average student in OECD countries.

Table 27, reveals that in the OECD and EU-22, the index of attitudes toward immigrants is more positive the higher the education level of the student's mother, although the association is less conclusive when examining some components, such as those related to identity or political rights. For example, in Germany, the index of attitudes toward immigrants is 0.21 for students whose mothers have higher education, compared to 0.09 for those whose mothers have up to lower secondary education. In Italy, the index is negative across all education levels, with -0.23 for higher education. In Scotland (UK), the index is 0.42 for higher education, showing a positive attitude. The OECD average is 0.07 for higher education, while the EU-22 average is -0.08.

The PISA 2018 Global Competence assessment also asked students to what extent they agreed ("strongly disagree," "disagree," "agree," or "strongly agree") with the following statements: "I see myself as a global citizen," "When I see the poor conditions in which some people live, I feel responsible to do something about it," "I believe my actions can affect people in other countries," "It is right to boycott companies known to offer poor working conditions to their employees," "I can do something about the world's problems," and "Taking care of the global environment is important to me" (OECD, Education at a Glance 2022). Positive values on this index indicate that students have a greater sense of global mindedness than the average student in OECD countries.

In all countries except Italy, students with mothers who have higher education have a greater sense of global mindedness. For instance, in Germany, the global mindedness index is -0.10 for students whose mothers have higher education, compared to -0.35 for those whose mothers have up to lower secondary education. In Scotland (UK), the index is 0.01 for higher education, showing a slight positive attitude. The OECD average is 0.08 for higher education, while the EU-22 average is -0.01.

Table 27 Social tolerance of students, by mother's education level (2018). PISA; based on responses from 15-year-old students

	Attitude toward Immigration				Global mindedness			
	Mother's education level				Mother's education level			
	Compulsory secondary	Upper secondary	Tertiary	Total	Compulsory secondary	Upper secondary	Tertiary	Total
	(1)	(2)	(3)	(4)	(5)	(6)	(7)	(8)
France	–	–	–	–	–	–	–	–
Germany	0.09	0.05	0.21	0.12	−0.35	−0.32	−0.10	−0.27
Italy	−0.20	−0.22	−0.23	−0.22	−0.13	−0.09	−0.11	−0.10
Spain	0.37	0.44	0.40	0.39	0.15	0.20	0.29	0.24
Scotland	0.18	0.27	0.42	0.34	−0.03	−0.08	0.01	−0.05
United States	–	–	–	–	–	–	–	–
OECD average	**−0.02**	**0.00**	**0.07**	**0.03**	**−0.10**	**−0.03**	**0.08**	**0.01**
EU-25 average	**−0.15**	**−0.15**	**−0.08**	**−0.12**	**−0.20**	**−0.12**	**−0.01**	**−0.08**

Source OECD, (2022) and PISA 2018 Results (Volume VI) https://www.oecd.org/pisa/publications/pisa-2018-results-volume-vi-d5f68679-en.htm

Table 28 provides insights into the transition from education to the labor market for young people aged 25–29 across various countries, including Spain, France, Germany, Italy, the United Kingdom, the United States, and the OECD and EU-22 averages. Among individuals with at most compulsory education, employment rates vary significantly. For example, in France, 46% are employed, while 50.5% are not in the labor market (13% unemployed and 37.5% inactive). Similarly, in Germany, 51% are employed, and 39.2% are not in the labor market. In Spain, 48% are employed, while 48.1% are either unemployed (27.9%) or inactive (20.2%). The OECD average shows that 49% of individuals with compulsory education are employed, while 42.2% are not in the labor market.

For those with upper secondary education, the patterns shift. In France, 68% are employed, and 22.8% are not in the labor market. In Germany, 68% are employed, with only 11.3% not in the labor market. Spain shows a lower employment rate (51%) and a higher share of individuals neither studying nor working (27.3%). The OECD average indicates that 63% of individuals with upper secondary education are employed, while 20% are not in the labor market.

For individuals with higher education (tertiary education), employment rates are generally higher. In France, 76% are employed, and only 11.6% are not in the labor market. In Germany, 68% are employed, with 6.7% not in the labor market. Spain shows an employment rate of 59% for this group, with 18.4% neither studying nor working. The OECD average reveals that 70% of individuals with higher education are employed, while 12.1% are not in the labor market.

Table 28 Percentage of young people aged 25–29 in education/not in education, by education level and labor market status (2021, quarterly data)

	Compulsory education					
	In education	Not in education				
		Employed	Not in education nor employed			Total
			Unemployed	Inactive	Total	
	(1)	(2)	(3)	(4)	(5) = (3) + (4)	(6) = (2) + (5)
France	3	46	13.0	37.5	50.5	97
Germany	10	51	8.4	30.8	39.2	90
Italy	3	41	18.5	37.5	55.9	97
Spain	4	48	27.9	20.2	48.1	96
United Kingdom	5	57	6.1	32.1	38.3	95
United States	7	50	7.8	35.1	43.0	93
OECD	**10**	**49**	**11.0**	**31.8**	**42.2**	**92**
EU-22	**10**	**48**	**12.4**	**32.7**	**44.4**	**92**
	Upper secondary education					
	In education	Not in education				
		Employed	Ni en educación ni en el mercado de trabajo			Employed
			Unemployed	Inactive	Total	
	(7)	(8)	(9)	(10)	(11) = (9) + (10)	(12) = (8) + (11)
France	9	68	10.7	12.1	22.8	91
Germany	21	68	3.7	7.6	11.3	79
Italy	16	50	11.0	22.9	33.9	84
Spain	22	51	18.9	8.4	27.3	78
United Kingdom	11	76	4.2	9.4	13.6	89
United States	10	63	8.2	19.2	27.4	90
OECD	**17**	**63**	**7.7**	**12.5**	**20.0**	**83**
EU-22	**16**	**66**	**7.7**	**11.2**	**18.9**	**84**

(continued)

Table 28 (continued)

	Tertiary education					
	In education	Not in education				
		Employed	Ni en educación ni en el mercado de trabajo			Employed
			Unemployed	Inactive	Total	
	(13)	(14)	(15)	(16)	(17) = (15) + (16)	(18) = (14) + (17)
France	12	76	6.9	4.7	11.6	88
Germany	26	68	2.2	4.5	6.7	74
Italy	27	51	7.7	14.1	21.9	73
Spain	22	59	11.8	6.6	18.4	78
United Kingdom	15	79	2.7	3.7	6.4	85
United States	14	75	3.8	7.2	11.0	86
OECD	**18**	**70**	**6.0**	**6.1**	**12.1**	**82**
EU-22	**18**	**70**	**5.9**	**5.5**	**11.4**	**82**

Source OCDE. Education at a Glance (2022) Page 59

These trends highlight the protective effect of higher education in the labor market, with tertiary-educated individuals experiencing significantly lower rates of unemployment and inactivity compared to those with only compulsory or upper secondary education. The data also underscores the variability across countries, with some nations like Germany and the United Kingdom showing stronger labor market outcomes for young people across all education levels.

References

Araujo, M. C., P. Carneiro, Y. Cruz-Aguayo, and N. Schady. 2016. Teacher quality and learning outcomes in kindergarten. *Quarterly Journal of Economics*. 131 (3): 1415–1453. https://doi.org/10.1093/qje/qjw016.

Betthäuser, B. A., A. M. Bach-Mortensen, and P. Engzell. 2023. A systematic review and meta-analysis of the evidence on learning during the COVID-19 pandemic. *Nature Human Behaviour* 7: 375–385. https://doi.org/10.1038/s41562-022-01506-4.

Cabrales, A., M. Güell, R. Madera, and A. Viola. 2019. Income contingent university loans: Policy design and an application to Spain. *Economic Policy*. 34 (99): 479–521. https://doi.org/10.1093/epolic/eiz010.

Duncan, G., A. Kalil, M. Mogstad, and M. Rege. 2022. Investing in early childhood development in preschool and at home. In *Handbook of the economics of education*, ed. S. J. en Machin, L. Woessmann, E.A. Hanushek, Vol. 7. Amsterdam (en prensa).

European Commission. 2024. Education and training monitor 2024: Comparative report. Publications Office of the European Union. https://doi.org/10.2766/815875.

Flisi, S., and Z. Blasko. 2019. A note on early childhood education and care participation by socio-economic background. JRC Research Reports, JRC117663. Joint Research Centre, Sevilla. https://publications.jrc.ec.europa.eu/repository/handle/JRC117663.

García-Montalvo, J. 2020. El impacto de la introducción de subvenciones progresivas en la educación superior el caso de Cataluña. *Papeles De Economía Española.* 166: 123–142.

Hanushek, E.A., G. Schwerdt, S. Wiederhold, and L. Woessmann. 2015. Returns to skills around the world: Evidence from PIAAC. *European Economic Review* 73(C): 103–130. https://doi.org/10.1016/j.euroecorev.2014.10.006.

Hanushek, E., and L. Woessmann. 2020. The economic impacts of learning losses, OECD Education Working Papers, No. 225, OECD Publishing, https://doi.org/10.1787/21908d74-en.

Heckman, J. J., S. H. Moon, R. Pinto, P. A. Savelyev, and A. Yavitz. 2010. The rate of return to the highscope Perry preschool program. *Journal of Public Economics.* 94 (1–2): 114–128. https://doi.org/10.1016/j.jpubeco.2009.11.001.

Hernández, L., and Serrano, L. 2013. Efectos económicos de la educación en España: una aproximación con datos PIAAC. In: INEE, OCDE (Eds.) *PIAAC 2013. Programa Internacional para la Evaluación de las Competencias de la Población Adulta,* Vol. II. Ministerio de Educación, Cultura y Deporte, Madrid.

IEA. (2023). PIRLS 2021 International Results in Reading. Boston College, TIMSS & PIRLS International Study Center. https://doi.org/10.6017/lse.tpisc.tr2103.kb5342.

IEA. (2024). TIMSS 2023 International Results in Mathematics and Science. Boston College, TIMSS & PIRLS International Study Center. https://doi.org/10.6017/lse.tpisc.timss.rs6460.

Patrinos, H., E. Vegas, and R. Carter-Rau. 2023. An analysis of COVID-19 student learning loss. *Oxford Encyclopedia Research of Economics and Finance.* https://doi.org/10.1093/acrefore/9780190625979.013.893.

OECD. 2020a. *Education at a glance 2020: OECD indicators.* OCDE Publishing, Paris. https://doi.org/10.1787/69096873-en.

OECD. 2020b. *Education policy outlook in Estonia, OECD education policy perspectives, No. 13.* OECD Publishing. https://doi.org/10.1787/9d472195-en.

OECD. 2020c. *"Education policy outlook in Ireland", OECD education policy perspectives, No. 18.* OECD Publishing. https://doi.org/10.1787/978e377b-en.

OECD. 2022. *Education at a glance 2022: OECD indicators.* OCDE. https://doi.org/10.1787/3197152b-en.

OECD. 2023a. *Education at a glance 2023: OECD indicators.* OCDE. Publishing, Paris. https://doi.org/10.1787/e13bef63-en.

OECD. 2023b. *PISA 2022 results (volume I): The state of learning and equity in education.* PISA, OECD Publishing. https://doi.org/10.1787/53f23881-en.

OECD. 2024. *Education at a glance 2024: OECD indicators*, OECD Publishing, Paris. https://doi.org/10.1787/c00cad36-en

Sanz, I., and J.D. Tena. 2023. The impact of the COVID-19 pandemic on education learning. In *Addressing inequities in modern educational assessment*, J. Sainz, and I. Sanz. Springer. https://doi.org/10.1007/978-3-031-45802-6_2.

Empirical Methods: A Brief Introduction to Causal Inference

Jesus M. Carro

1 Introduction

This chapter is intended to help those not trained in econometrics in general and, in particular, in the econometric techniques used to estimate causal effects and evaluate public policies. The goal is to enable readers to understand the subsequent chapters with a clear grasp of how the discussed effects have been identified and even to discuss the scope and limitations of those effects. I have aimed to explain at a rather intuitive but rigorous level how these effects are identified and the potential biases that may arise when using data without entering into technical details. Additionally, I have not attempted to cover the more statistical aspects, such as standard errors, which, although essential in the scientific work from which the results are derived, are not central to the discussion regarding the validity and interpretation of the results and potential biases. Given this, this chapter is by no means a substitute for a good general course in econometrics and a specific course on all these econometric techniques. However, I hope it will make the rest of the chapters easier (or, if you wish, more profound) to read for those lacking such a background.

Some particularities of this chapter:

- I have tried to reduce the mathematical notation and equations to a minimum. That is why there are hardly any equations in the main text of this chapter. But, I have not avoided it altogether because a bit of notation often can greatly enhance the clarity of explanations. To compensate for this lack of mathematical expressions, the penultimate section intended to summarize the whole chapter but written only in mathematical expressions.
- Since this work is intended to be educational rather than a comprehensive literature review, I have opted not to include bibliographical sources or references at every step, nor to constantly indicate where more details can be found. To compensate

J. M. Carro (✉)
Departamento de Economía, Universidad Carlos III de Madrid, GETAFE (Madrid), Spain
e-mail: jcarro@eco.uc3m.es

A. Cabrales and I. Sanz (eds.), *Economics of Education*,
https://doi.org/10.1007/978-3-031-90911-5_2

for this and to assist readers who want to know more or look up something specific, the final section has a distinct structure. It is not just an alphabetical list of references. Instead, the bibliography is organized by topics and includes everything from introductory textbooks to the most recent articles on the latest advances in some of the estimators presented here.

I am grateful to Antonio Cabrales and Ismael Sanz for the initiative to make this book and for inviting me to participate. I also have to thank José Montalban for reading a first draft and providing comments and materials that have helped to improve this chapter, Jennifer Ruiz-Valenzuela for her suggestion for some of the illustrations I use, and the participants in the Workshop in which we presented the chapters of this book. Of course, any errors or limitations that remain are my sole responsibility.

2 What Effect Do We Want to Know?

2.1 Definitions

2.1.1 That Whose Effect We Want to Know

The first two things to define are (i) the variable whose effect we want to know, and (ii) the variable over which we want to measure its effect, known as the outcome variable. For example, we want to know the effect of reducing class size on students' academic performance. The variable whose effect we want to know is usually, a priori, relatively clear (for the previous example, "reduce class size"). However, there can be difficulties in measuring or observing it. If we want to know the effect of an educational policy, as it has been implemented, it may be clearer what we need to observe. We will need to know where and when it has been implemented and what the policy has consisted of. This policy may consist of several interventions, or affect several aspects that determine an educational outcome. An example is to know the effect of an educational policy that implements a bilingual education system in schools. The policy may involve pedagogical changes in the way classes are taught, changes in the teachers who teach those classes and their training, changes in the resources available to the school, and so on. If the objective is to know the effect of this policy, we can do so without the need to have a separate measure of each of these variables. Something similar happens if we want to know the effect of studying in a specific school or type of school versus studying in other schools, such as a public versus a private school. To know the overall effect, we do not need to observe and measure all the characteristics of the schools.

If, however, we want to know the effect of changing the magnitude of a variable that represents an input in the production of education—see the following chapters of the book for more details on the education production function—such as the effect of reducing class size, we need to define the measure we want to use; or choose from the available measures the one that best approximates our variable of interest. In the example of class size, we can use the number of pupils in a class (group of pupils) when these are built in a stable way throughout the school year and day. If the groups of pupils, in particular their size, are different for different subjects, it may be more convenient to use the pupil/teacher ratio at the school. The two are related but not the same (see Chaps. 1 and 3a by Ismael Sanz in this book for more details on the differences and relationship between the two measures). If both measures are available, we will have to decide which one best reflects what we want to know. Other variables on which we would like to know the effect may be unobservable, such as the teaching quality of each teacher, and we will have to try to find proxies or, better, use methods that allow us to identify (indirectly) what we do not observe/ measure directly.

We will call D the variable whose effect we want to know. We want to know the effect of changing the value of D from a value D_0 to a value D_1. In the example of class size (D), we might want to know the effect of reducing it from 30 (this would be D_0) to 25 (this would be D_1) pupils per class.

2.1.2 The Outcome Variable

Defining on which variable or outcome measure we want to know the effect can be more difficult in Education. How do we measure what is produced in education?

How is the quality of the education received measured? Two types of measures are commonly used in the literature:

- Measures internal to the education system: results in standardized tests taken by all pupils, academic progress, etc.
- Assessment by the labour market, or society in general, of the human capital acquired through the education system: wages, probability of unemployment, criminality, etc.

We will call Y the outcome measure on which we want to know the effect of D. An example of this Y is the result of an exam that all pupils in a region have to take at the end of an educational level.

2.2 *Causal Effect*

A causal relation or causal effect tells us what the value of Y would be in an alternative or counterfactual world in which the value of D is changed. That counterfactual world consists of the same individuals as the factual one, and occurs at the same time, that is, in the same circumstances, but the value of D has been changed from D_0 to D_1. The causal effect is the difference between the value of Y when D takes the value

D_1 and the value of *Y* when *D* takes the value D_0. This is the difference due only to that change in the value of *D*. This is the effect that tells us what would happen if we implement an intervention that allows us to change the value of D in that world.

2.2.1 Total or Reduced-Form Effect, Direct or Structural Effect, and Mechanisms Producing These Effects

Given that there are usually more variables than just *D* affecting *Y*, and that there may be causal relationships or cross-effects between these variables and *D*, we can distinguish between two types of causal effects of interest: (i) a direct causal effect defined within the context of a structural model, and (ii) the total or reduced-form causal effect. The primary difference between these is whether we are interested in understanding a causal relationship through a specific mechanism within an economic model, or if we want to determine the total effect on *Y* of altering *D*, irrespective of the mechanisms through which changes in *D* lead to changes in *Y*.

The former usually focuses on a single direct mechanism, leaving the rest of the ways by which *D* can affect *Y* invariant. This means that this effect tells us the change in *Y* when we leave constant anything else that can affect *Y*. The second effect includes also indirect effects, that is, it includes any other change in another variable affecting *Y* that has occurred as a consequence (and only for this reason) of the change in *D*.

For example, suppose we want to know the effect of reducing the number of students in a class (*D*) on the results of an exam taken by students at the end of the year (*Y*). The total effect might not only stem from each student receiving more individual attention from the teacher due to smaller class sizes but also from how the parents of these students react to this change. The time and resources that parents dedicate to helping students with their studies (*X*) may change because students now receive more attention from the teacher. Therefore, the change in *D* has a direct (positive) effect on *Y*. However, the change in *D* may also cause a change in another determinant of *Y*, such as the time parents spend with their children. Thus, the total effect of changing *D* (the reduced-form effect) would be the sum of the direct effect of *D* on *Y* plus the indirect effect through the reduction in X caused by the change in *D*. This total effect, without distinguishing between the different mechanisms, may be the causal effect of interest if we want to understand the impact of an educational policy aimed at reducing class size. The interest would be on knowing the total effect, without needing to separate the mechanisms, to assess the policy's effectiveness on the outcome.

We are interested in the direct causal effect of *D*, excluding the effect of *X* (and consequently the effect of *D* through *X*), when we aim to understand the contribution of each factor determining *Y* and/or the mechanisms by which the policy of changing *D* produces its overall effect. The scientific value of understanding and distinguishing the various mechanisms that contribute to the total causal effect is greater than merely knowing the overall effect. This is because the reduced-form effect can be derived from the individual mechanisms, but not vice versa. Even if identifying the mechanisms behind different policy effects is not the primary goal, understanding them can be important. Only with this knowledge can we design alternative policies that may be more effective than the one we have evaluated.

3 Main Difficulties in Obtaining the Causal Effect

3.1 The Counterfactual Situation Is Not Observed

The first and great difficulty to know the causal effect is unavoidable and almost obvious: we cannot observe at the same time an individual with a value D0 and with a value D1. At the same moment in time an individual can only have one of these two values of *D*. We can only observe the factual world; never the counterfactual, as their names indicate. Given this physical impossibility, the challenge becomes to find a group of individuals that we observe having the alternative value of *D*, D_0, and that is comparable (equal in everything except the value of *D*) to individuals with *D* equal to D_1.

Potential and observed outcomes For every individual there are a priori two potential outcomes or values of *Y*: 1) the one that will be obtained if $D = D_0$, which we call $Y(D_0)$, and 2) the one that will be obtained if $D = D_1$ which we call $Y(D_1)$. The causal effect for this individual is $Y(D_1) - Y(D_0)$. The problem is that for the same individual only one of these two potential outcomes is observed. Depending on the value of *D* for this individual, the *Y* we observe will be equal either to $Y(D_1)$ or to $Y(D_0)$. However, we cannot observe both simultaneously for the same individual.

Observing *Y* for the same individual with different values of *D* at different moments in time does not resolve this difficulty either, because there may be factors that determine *Y*, other than *D*, that change from one period to another. This would mean that the difference between those two observed outcomes would not be the causal effect of *D*, but would also include the effect of other things that may change over time.

Taking the terminology from the literature on the evaluation of medical treatments, the group with D1 is called the treated group, and the group with D0 is called the control group. Using this terminology, given the physical impossibility of being treated and control at the same time, the difficulty lies in finding a good control group that can tell us what the value of *Y* would have been if they had not been treated. Or, similarly, that allows us to say that the value of *Y* that the control group would have had if they had been treated is the value of *Y* that we observed for the treated group.

The search for these two comparable groups, i.e., the search for a good control group, leads us to the next important difficulty, which the methods we are going to review attempt to solve: selection bias.

3.2 Selection Bias

A selection bias occurs when the group of individuals with D_1 has (observable and unobservable) characteristics different from the group of individuals with D_0. Importantly, those characteristics have to be relevant in determining (affecting) Y. There is no problem for the two groups to be different in aspects that are irrelevant for Y. For example, if Y is a measure of academic performance, such as a standardized test score, the age of the student is a relevant variable. We do not want to compare treated and controls of a different age, because we would wrongly attribute to the treatment what is due to a difference in age. But the intensity with which the stars of Alpha Centauri are seen in the sky on the day of the pupil's birth is not a relevant variable and it does not matter that it is different between treatments and controls.

Note that when discussing and comparing groups, rather than a single individual, we are interested in an informative measure of causal effect for the whole group. The most frequent is the average causal effect. Although there are other possible measures describing the causal effect in the population, for simplicity, I will mostly refer to the average effect. Given this, another important qualification is that we do not need every treated individual to have someone exactly the same (in relevant characteristics) in the control group. Selection bias arises when the two groups are different on average, and would still be different even if they had the same value of D. In Sect. 11.1 the average causal effects and the problem of selection bias are defined mathematically.

Example 1 Suppose we want to know the quality of one school versus another, measuring it through the students' results in the university entrance exam (Y) and how this changes if they study at one school versus the other. It is common to observe that in order to decide the quality of one school versus another, the average mark of the pupils of these two schools is compared. Moreover, rankings of schools are often drawn up, ordered by the average mark of the pupils in each school, interpreting the differences in average marks as being due to (caused by) the different educational quality each school provides for its pupils. Under this interpretation, this difference would be what the same student would improve on average if he or she went from studying at one school to another with a better average mark for its students in the university entrance exam. However, there is clearly no guarantee that this gives us the causal effect. It suffers from a potential problem of selection bias. The students in one school and the other are different, with different characteristics, and different socio-economic contexts. The differences in Y would be mostly due to different characteristics and conditioning factors of the student. These characteristics and factors would not change even if he/she went to another school. It may even be that the causal effect is of the opposite sign to the difference in the average results observed. It may be that schools that, because of their geographical location, for example, have pupils with greater educational difficulties may have better teaching staff who bring greater added value to pupil learning. On average, however, their pupils perform somewhat worse. Although the other school is of poorer quality (adds little value to the learning of its pupils), the characteristics of its pupils are other learning inputs that more than compensate for the shortcomings of the school. Examples of such other inputs are pupils' efforts or the educational reinforcement and support that their families can give them outside the school. Due to selection bias in the composition of the student body, comparing observed results could lead us not only to estimate an effect of a different quantity, but also to estimate a causal effect of the school with the opposite sign to what it actually is. This could result in the incorrect inference that the school with the better average mark is the one with higher quality, when in fact, it might not be.

Selection bias as part of the endogeneity problem: Selection bias is part of a problem known in econometric terms as endogeneity. There is endogeneity when, at the same time that D changes, other things change that also affect Y and we are not controlling for them. The three sources of endogeneity are:

1. Omitted variables (characteristics) that affect Y and are related to D. Example 1 is a case of omitted variable bias. In the comparison between schools, student characteristics have been omitted, leading to the appearance that one school is better than another. In reality, this is due to differences in the characteristics of the students and their families.
2. Simultaneity: both Y and other factors that we do not observe are determined at the same time; they affect each other and are related to, or even affected by, D. An example of simultaneity would be when we want to determine the effect of an intervention D on the price Y of a market. Among the determinants of Y would be the quantity demanded in this market. But price and quantity sold are determined simultaneously (jointly), and the intervention D that may affect price would also affect quantity sold. We would have a bias in the estimation of the effects. Another example of simultaneity arises when we want to study peer-effects. The Y of each student affects and is determined simultaneously with the Ys of the peers, whose effect on this student we would like to know. See José Montalbán Castilla's chapter, "The Effects of Classmates (Peer Effects)," in this book for more details on this situation.
3. Measurement error in D. The variable we observe is an imprecise measure of D. The difference between that measure and the true value of D that determines Y is the measurement error. Even in the case where the measurement error is a completely exogenous thing this will generate a bias. Part of the variation in D that we observe is given by variation in measurement error. But that variation will not imply a change in Y because it is determined by the true value of D, not by the measurement error. This means that we will associate changes in D with Y not changing, estimating an effect of D smaller than there is. This is known as an attenuation bias. If, in addition, the measurement error were correlated with some factor affecting Y, the bias could go in either direction.

4 Randomized Controlled Trials (RCTs)

The first solution to selection bias is to prevent individuals from self-selecting or being selected based on factors that affect the outcome. In this method, assignments are made randomly and independently of any relevant characteristics or potential outcomes. This guarantees that the treatment and control groups are comparable by design. By comparable, I mean that their characteristics are similarly distributed in a statistical sense, not that they are identical. This includes, for example, that both groups have the same mean for relevant characteristics.

In the example of comparing two schools to determine their relative quality, if students are randomly assigned to each school, the average income level of families will be statistically the same in both schools. Therefore, if a difference is observed in the mean score of students in each school on a test taken after being at that school, it cannot be attributed to differences in family income, as this characteristic is the same in both schools. Randomization ensures comparability between the treated and control groups, allowing us to interpret the difference in average results between the two schools as being due to the school itself.

This method is considered the gold standard in evaluating public policies. Testing a policy by first implementing it through a randomized controlled experiment, or RCT, will allow us to know its causal effect, separated from other factors whose effect we could erroneously attribute to the outcome, thus solving the selection bias problem. However, it has its limitations, which are described in the following subsections.

4.1 Limitations on Practical Implementation

These limitations may arise in any experiment and may lead to situations where this solution for finding the causal effect cannot be implemented:

- Difficulties to implement them due to ethical and/or physical considerations. For example, it is neither ethically nor feasible to randomly decide who will have university studies and who will not, as a way of knowing the causal impact that university studies have on people's labour income. First, it would not be considered ethically acceptable to prevent people who are academically prepared and who want to go to university from doing so by an experiment. The lifetime cost of such an experiment for these people would be too great. Nor would it be very easy to force someone who does not want to study to get a university education even if this person is randomly assigned to go to college. This is why the (important) literature that tries to know the returns (or impact on productivity) to education uses other methods.

- High cost of the experiment. It requires a lot of new financial means, not only because of the policy to be tested, but also because of the requirements to implement and follow up the experiment. This sometimes means that it is only implemented on a sample that is too small, which leads to unreliable or inaccurate results.
- Difficulty in complying with randomized assignments: self-selection after randomization. Two possible deviations from random assignment: (i) some of the individuals assigned to the treatment group do not want to be treated and are not treated; (ii) some of the controls manage to receive the treatment even though they are not supposed to receive it. Deviation from random assignment breaks comparability between treated and controls because it may be due to self-selection. Even so, if everyone is observed, and we know who has actually been treated and their initial allocation, this data can still be used to obtain a causal effect. However, another method will have to be used to compare the treated and controls and estimate the causal effect. We will see this in the Instrumental Variables solution. Our ability to estimate causal effects of interest will be greater when only one of these two deviations is present, and the smaller the number of individuals who deviate.
- Difficulty in obtaining information on individuals over time (attrition). The trial usually requires implementing the policy over a period of time, and treated and controls must be followed and observed before, during, and after. In particular, information must be collected on the variability of outcomes for all individuals after the policy has been implemented. Given the random selection of treated and controls, some of them may have lost interest in continuing to collaborate with the experiment, or moved away and become unreachable. As long as this does not affect a large proportion and, above all, occurs independently of the potential results of the experiment, it does not pose a threat to the validity of the method. However, whenever there is attrition, we should always ensure that we still have comparable, representative, and sufficiently large groups of treated and control subjects to make accurate estimates. The trial will not yield valid results if, for example, individuals of a certain income level are the ones who most frequently fail to cooperate with the trial.

4.2 Problems of External Validity

If the randomized trial has been implemented correctly, it will tell us the causal effect of the policy or treatment that has been tested on the target group and at the time of the trial. This is called internal validity of the estimate. And no method will give us greater internal validity. But that is not our goal. Our objective is to know the causal effect of a policy that we are going to apply on the entire population of interest and to know it not only at the time of the trial but in other periods as well. Consider a trial that is a pilot project of a policy that is applied to a small group of people in order to evaluate its extension to the whole population in subsequent years. In addition, we often seek to use results from past experiments in another part of the world to find out the causal effect of a similar policy in other places and at other times.

All these objectives refer to the so-called external validity of the trial. External validity is not guaranteed no matter how many of the circumstances that guarantee the internal validity of the causal effect estimate are in place. Without additional assumptions, one can only know the effect of the program as it was implemented, and only at the time the experiment was implemented. Another program, at another time, or for another population may give different results.

The main threats to external validity are:

1. The experiment is not sufficiently similar to the policy to be implemented and whose effect we want to know.
2. The sample on which the experiment is applied is different (non-representative) from the population over which it is to be extended. The causal effects are potentially heterogeneous, ie., different between individuals, and therefore the policy will have different causal effects from those estimated in the group of individuals in the trial.
3. Existence of externalities (in this context, treatment affects people other than those treated). In this situation, the comparison of Y between treated and controls will not tell us the full causal effect of the treatment on the population, since it will not take into account these external effects. If, in addition, these external effects also affect the control group, the control group will not be valid to tell us what would have happened to the treated in the absence of treatment. Therefore, the trial will not correctly estimate the causal effect, even on the treated. The conditions necessary for internal validity of the estimate would not even be satisfied.
4. Whether there are general equilibrium effects once one moves from the experiment to the universalization of the policy. General equilibrium effects occur when market equilibria are affected as a consequence of implementing the program on a large scale. The supply and/or demand for some goods are being altered. To explain this better with an example, let us consider that we want to know the total effect of reducing class size on academic outcomes. We run a trial on some groups in some schools and estimate a positive effect. If we then apply this reduction in class size as a general policy to all classes and schools in the country or region, we will find that we need to recruit a large number of new teachers to cover the new classes that are generated in all schools by the reduction in the number of pupils in each class. The need to recruit a few teachers in a few schools in the trial does not alter the market for teachers. However, by extending it to the whole country, many new teachers are needed, and the requirements and quality demanded of teachers recruited in the new market equilibrium could be lower. This would generate a negative policy effect that could not be detected in the trial.

External validity is even more of an issue when one wants to learn about the effects of a new policy with the same objectives as the one tested because the one tested has been found not to work. This method reliably estimates the total causal effect 'internal' to the experiment. However, since we learn nothing about the mechanisms that produce the observed outcome, we cannot use it to think about what other policy might be applied that would be more effective or to learn the reason for the observed (failed) outcome.

Some of these limitations are common to many of the methods discussed below since they are intrinsic to the estimation of a full or reduced-form causal effect, but others are specific to RCTs. The following methods will continue to address the problem of selection bias in situations where we cannot use data from an RCT to estimate the causal effect of a variable.

5 Control for Observable Variables: Regression with Controls and Propensity Score Matching Method

The goal is still to have a control group that tells us what would have happened to the treated in the absence of treatment, solving the selection bias that makes treated and controls differ in more (relevant) dimensions than in receiving the treatment. If we do not have an experiment that guarantees this and we observe that both groups have different characteristics, a possible solution is to control for those observable characteristics.

Suppose that the selection bias in comparing the mean Y of two schools is due to students in one school having more educated parents than in the other school. If we compare all students in one school with all students in the other, we erroneously attribute differences in family characteristics to school quality. Instead, we can compare students from both schools who have parents with the same educational level. This way, we match treated students with controls who have exactly the same observable characteristics, thus controlling for differences that arise from varying family backgrounds between the schools.

When there are several characteristics to control for and/or they take many possible values, matching groups with exactly the same characteristics will not be possible. However, the same idea can be applied with two econometric methods: the regression method and the propensity score matching. The following two subsections summarize them, and the third relates them.

Key assumption: Controlling for observables (X) will provide an estimate of the causal effect if the selection, which differentiates treated and control groups, is based exclusively on those observables. In other words, if both groups are equal (on average) in unobservable characteristics. For practical purposes, unobservables include everything that we do not control for and that determines Y. The formal expression of this assumption, as well as its role in the estimation methods described below, can be found in Sect. 11.2.

5.1 Regression with Controls

Linear regression is one of the most widely used methods for finding relationships between variables. It has several interesting properties, including simplicity of application. The problem lies in being able to interpret these relationships as causal relationships. The key assumption to have a causal effect is the above assumption of non-selection on unobservables. But, in addition to that, an assumption is made about the (functional) way in which controls X affect Y. This functional form assumption implicitly extrapolates the effect of these X on Y for all possible values of the X. This may give us a false idea of the effect of the X on Y. This can give us a false sense of comparability between treated and controls. For example, if one of these Xs is parental income, the linear regression will assume the same relationship with Y for all the values of X, as

$$Y = \beta_0 + \beta_1 \ln(X) + \tau D + \varepsilon. \tag{1}$$

and estimate it by Ordinary Least Squares using the available data. The problem may arise when the values of X in the treated group are very different from those in the control group. For instance, income levels may only be present in one of the two groups. In the example, there may be no one with higher income levels in the control group, but only in the treated group. In this situation, we assume that the relationship in (1) indicates what would happen to those treated with a higher income level (X) in the absence of treatment, even though we do not observe anyone with those levels who has not been treated. We are extrapolating the effect for values of X that are not present in the control group. If the extrapolation is correct, there is no issue. However, if it is incorrect, we are misestimating the causal effect. The last subsection discusses how to avoid this extrapolation.

Endogeneity in the regression: Although our interest is in the effect of D, when introducing X, we must ensure that X is not endogenous and does not capture part of the effect of D. If any of the X variables are endogenous or capture part of the effect of interest, we need to use a different estimation method. This creates a situation where including X is necessary due to selection bias, but it also introduces new problems. Thus, we cannot simply use this method to estimate the causal effect. In some contexts, such regressors are called '*bad controls*', suggesting they should be excluded, but this is rarely the solution. Only when controls are not necessary to obtain a causal effect can we exclude them. When controls are used to address selection bias in observables, we cannot do without them. If they are endogenous or capture part of the effect of interest, we must find a way to address these problems without excluding them.

5.2 Propensity Score Matching

The matching method is to match treated with controls that can inform us about the value of Y that the treated would have had in the absence of treatment. The idea is that treated and matched controls have the same X values. When X takes a large set of possible values (for example, by having several X's), we use the following result: If matching based on the observable variables X allows us to estimate a causal effect, then the matching based on $P(X)$ also does so. $P(X)$ gives us the probability that an individual with characteristics X will be treated, i.e., $P(X) = \Pr(D = 1|X)$, called propensity score.

The intuition behind this result is that the problem comes because those X variables make treated and controls non-comparable insofar as they affect who is treated and who is control. If there were no selection in X (and hence would not need to be matched by value of X), the probability of being treated would be the same for any value of X. That is, $\Pr(D = 1|X) = \Pr(D = 1)$. This helps to understand why if an individual in the control group has characteristics such that his $\Pr(D = 1|X)$ is the same as that of another individual in the treated group, they will be a good match, without needing to require that the X's are all exactly the same.

In addition to the above, it will be necessary in practice to define what it means to have the same $\Pr(D = 1|X)$. The implementation details are beyond the scope of this chapter. It suffices to say that there are several criteria and methods, available in different software, to estimate $\Pr(D = 1|X)$, to decide how to match according to the closeness of the value of $\Pr(D = 1|X)$, and to estimate the average treatment effect from that matching.

A step prior to matching and estimating the causal effect, emphasized in the matching literature to avoid the extrapolation problem mentioned during regression, is the verification/imposition of the common support condition. This requires checking that the range of values of $\Pr(D = 1|X)$ is the same in treated and control groups. If not, we must limit our estimate to using only those treated and control units within the same value range. Of course, the average causal effect we estimate will not apply to the entire population or all treated units, but only to those that meet the common support condition. For instance, if we have high-income individuals in the treatment group but none in the control group, we cannot determine the effect of D for high-income individuals, as we lack control units to provide a counterfactual (without assuming how the treatment effect changes with income). However, recognizing this limitation and imposing the common support condition allows us to determine the causal effect for the rest.

5.3 Comparison Between Regression and the Matching Method

Both share the most important assumption: deciding which variables I have to control for and assuming that given these X there is no selection on unobservables. On the basis of this fundamental assumption for the identification of a causal effect neither method represents an advantage over the other. The advantages come from other assumptions and are mainly practical.

- In both, some functional form assumptions have to be made. The difference is on what object they are made. In regression, the relationship of Y to X and D is assumed. In matching, that relationship is not specified or constrained, but a functional form on $\Pr(D = 1|X)$. is assumed.
- In the pairing an arbitrary decision has to be taken on the matching criterion.
- The estimation of the correct standard errors is much more difficult in propensity score matching than in regression.
- The big disadvantage of regression with respect to matching is that traditionally regression has ignored the common support condition and extrapolated to X values not contained in both groups when it is not satisfied. But there is no reason why the common support condition cannot be imposed prior to regression estimation, as it is done in matching.

Given the above, running a linear regression in-sample that satisfies the common support condition, and using a flexible functional form with respect to how D and X enter (polynomials, interactions, etc.), may be just as good as matching and much easier to implement.

5.4 When the Selection on Observables Assumption Is Not Satisfied

When there is concern about selection on unobservables, and not just observables, the estimators in this section will not provide a good estimate of the causal effect. However, they can still help gauge the severity of the selection problem. By comparing how the estimated effect of D changes when X is included versus excluded, we can, under some assumptions, assess the severity of the selection issue and refine the effect estimate if needed. For instance, if we have a rich set of X variables and the effect estimate remains stable, it is reasonable to assume that the selection problem is not very large and we are close to an accurate estimate. See the reference list for more details.

6 Difference-in-Difference Method (DiD)

The main problem with the above method is that it is difficult to think of situations where the selection problem is due solely to observable variables. Unless we observe a very large set of relevant characteristics, it is likely that observable differences between treated and controls will also reflect differences in unobserved characteristics. The larger these differences, the greater the challenge of addressing selection bias with observables alone. The method in this section allows us to control for differences between the control and treatment groups, whether observed or unobserved, provided that, in the absence of treatment, these differences would have remained constant or the groups would have evolved in parallel.

If there is selection bias, we cannot compare treated and control outcomes at the same point in time to see the effect of the treatment. By examining results from a period before and after the treatment, we can consider comparing the outcomes of treated individuals before and after the treatment. Since they are the same individuals, it is reasonable to assume that their characteristics remain constant. However, factors affecting the outcome may change over time. By taking the temporal difference in outcomes, we might attribute to the treatment effects that are actually due to changes in other factors over time. The following method aims to address this issue.

6.1 Plain DiD and Identification Assumption

To solve the two problems that prevent us from estimating by making a single difference (that treaties and controls are different, and that there are changes from one period to another), we can make a double difference. This double difference, and the identification assumption required to identify the causal effect with DiD, can be expressed in two ways (which, by the commutative property of addition, are equivalent):

1. [(mean Y of treated after)—(mean Y of controls after)]—[(mean Y of treated before)—(mean Y of controls before)]. Here, the differences inside the square brackets account for factors that make the treated different from the controls, causing selection bias. The identification assumption in this formulation is that pre-existing differences between treated and control groups would have remained constant in the absence of treatment. We assume that any change in the pre-existing difference is due to the treatment.
2. [(mean Y number of treaties after)—(mean Y number of treaties before)]—[(mean Y number of controls after)—(mean Y number of controls before)]. Here, the differences inside the square brackets deal with factors that change from one period to another. The identification assumption in this formulation means assuming that the changes that would have occurred from one period to the next for the treated group, if they had not been treated, are the same as the changes

observed in the control group. We use the control group to discount the period-to-period changes that are not due to the treatment. In Sect. 11, we formally state this identification assumption and its implications for the DiD estimator.

Strictly speaking, the identification assumption cannot be tested and can only be assumed, argued, and evidenced for or against its validity. Part of the evidence required involves checking if the assumption holds during periods when no one has received the treatment. This can be done by examining several periods before the treatment. If treated and control groups do not evolve in parallel during these periods, the assumption that they would evolve in parallel just during the treatment period becomes not credible. This check, often called a parallel trend test, is not a formal test of the hypothesis. The fact that the assumption holds in earlier periods does not guarantee it will hold during the treatment period. However, such a test is necessary as a prerequisite for considering these results valid.

One of the situations in which the identification assumption is most plausible is when a **natural event** beyond the control of individuals has produced the change in D. For example, an earthquake may generate a change in the wealth of individuals and be used to find out the impact of a change in wealth on an outcome variable of interest. Any control group we look for is likely to be different from those affected, but, if they exhibit parallel past trends, it becomes more likely that in the absence of the earthquake the evolution would have remained parallel. For this reason the DiD method is also known as natural experiments or quasi-experiments.

The simplest way to obtain the DiD estimator, $\widehat{\tau_{DiD}}$, is through the following linear regression.

$$Y = \beta_0 + \beta_1 D + \beta_2 Post + \tau_{DiD}(D * Post) + \varepsilon, \tag{2}$$

where D denotes whether it is an observation of the group to be treated, *Post* denotes whether it is an observation from the post-treatment period, and thus the interaction between the two, $(D * Post)$, indicates whether it is an observation that has received the treatment.

6.2 *Extensions of the Plain DiD Approach*

6.2.1 Several Periods: Different Effects Over Time and Different Trends

When several post-treatment periods are available, it is possible to study how the treatment effect changes over time. If several pre-treatment periods are available, in addition to testing for parallel trends, one could, if considered more realistic, allow, instead of parallel trends, a parallel growth rate, e.g., by doing a triple difference, or other more parametric ways of allowing for some differences in trends between treated and controls.

6.2.2 DiD also Controlling for Observable Differences

DiD can be combined with methods that control for observable differences between treated and control groups. The assumption of parallel trends does not need to hold for the comparison of all treated with all controls; it suffices that it holds conditional on having the same value of the observables. For instance, students with parents of different educational levels may not only have different levels but also follow different evolutions in the absence of treatment. This different evolution would invalidate the DiD if the distribution of parents' educational levels differs between treated and control groups. However, parallel evolution (in the absence of treatment) could occur if we compare students whose parents have the same educational level.

Since the DiD estimator can be obtained through regression (2), the simplest way to control for observables is to include the observable variables, X, as additional regressors in (2). The drawback is that this imposes functional form restrictions, requiring a stronger parallel trend assumption, so its validity does not depend on that functional form (see the references at the end of the chapter for more details).

Another way to control for observables is to combine DiD with the matching method: matched double differences. The matching method is applied not to the Ys of the two groups, but to the double differences, so that a double difference is made for each value of the observables, or of $P(X)$ if the treatment probability is used for matching.

6.3 *Importance of Falsification and Placebo Tests*

Given that the identification assumption in the DiD is not testable and that many factors, in addition to treatment implementation, can change from period to period, affecting treated and control groups differently, it is important to test for falsification. Passing these tests does not prove the assumption is true, but failing them proves it is not. It is also possible and desirable to perform these falsification tests on other methods mentioned in this chapter, such as estimators based solely on selection on observables.

There are two types of falsification evidence:

- A placebo is used as treatment indicator. A treatment that never existed would be considered as if it did. For example, if we are evaluating the effect of a bilingual educational program on educational achievement, this falsification test would take a group of students and schools that have not been treated and would (falsely) consider that some of them have been treated and have $D = 1$. If an effect of this false D is found in this sample, where no one is actually treated, it would indicate that our estimation method is capturing the effect of factors other than the treatment.
- Use as the outcome of interest, Y a variable that cannot be affected by the treatment. For example, parents' years of education should not be influenced by the class size

of their children's schools. If, instead of using students' educational attainment as Y, we use parents' years of education, we should not find any effect of D. If there is an effect, our estimation method is incorrectly attributing to D what is actually due to other factors (such as the different educational levels of parents between treated and control groups).

7 Instrumental Variables

In cases where there is selection bias in unobserved variables, and either because we do not have the necessary data for DiD or because the assumption of parallel trends or selection on observables is not credible, we cannot apply any of the previous methods. An alternative solution is the use of instrumental variables. If we have a variable, which we call an instrument and denote by Z, that meets the following assumptions (the formal expression of which can be found in Sect. 11.4), it can be used to address these issues:

Assumption 1 (*S.1. Independence of the Instrument*) The instrument is independent of potential outcomes and potential treatment assignments.

Assumption 2 (*S.2. Exclusion restriction*) The outcome Y, given a treatment indicator value, is only a function of the treatment and is not a function of the instrument. That is, given a treatment status (treated or untreated), the value of Y does not depend on the value of the instrument. The instrument is related to the outcome Y only and exclusively through the effect that Z has on being treated.

Assumption 3 (*S.3. Rank or relevance condition of the instrument*) The instrument affects the proportion of treated units. That is, the proportion of treated changes with the values of the instrument.

Assumption 4 (*S.4. Monotonicity assumption*) The instrument affects the likelihood of being treated in the same direction for all individuals. Under this assumption, some individuals may not be affected in their decision (or assignment) to be treated by the instrument. However, for those who are affected, the instrument influences all of them in the same direction. $\Pr(D = 1|Z)$ increases with Z for all or decreases with Z for all, but there is no situation where it increases for some and decreases for others.

To discuss the plausibility of these assumptions and the causal effect we identify, I will use an example. Suppose we want to assess the effect of private language academies (D) on English language learning (Y). We have not conducted any experiment to randomly decide who attends these academies and who does not, so the comparison between treated and control groups will capture the effect on Y not only of the academies but also of the many characteristics that differentiate those who attend from those who do not. However, suppose we have provided grants (Z) to cover the full cost of these academies, and these grants can only be spent on academy fees. One year later, we measure the English proficiency of a representative sample of the population, which will be our measure of Y, in addition to knowing who attended the academy (D) and who received the scholarship (Z).

If we allocate the scholarship based on income (i.e., only to families below a certain income threshold), assumption S.1 will not hold since receiving the scholarship ($Z = 1$) will not be independent of potential values of Y. If we compare the Y of those who receive the grant with those who do not, we compare the English proficiency of lower-income families with higher-income families, who may have higher proficiency due to more resources for language learning. We would measure the effect of income and not solely the effect of the academies. Assumption S.1 is satisfied if, for example, we allocate the scholarship using a lottery. In this case, recipients and non-recipients would have, on average, the same characteristics, allowing us to determine the causal effect of the scholarship on language learning, known as ITT (Intention To Treat effect). However, our aim is to understand the effect of the academies, and for this, assumption S.1 is insufficient.

Assumption S.2 implies that the scholarship has no direct impact on language learning, which is plausible since merely receiving the scholarship does not change students' English proficiency. It also assumes the scholarship does not affect any other variable influencing Y, which is less clear. Assumption S.2 requires that the only relationship between Z and Y is through Z's impact on D, with D being the only causal effect on Y. However, if the scholarship ($Z = 1$) causes some families to spend saved income (which they would have spent on academies without the scholarship) on language courses abroad, the observed effect is not solely due to the academies. We can estimate the total effect of Z on Y well because assumption S.1 is satisfied, but we cannot isolate the effect of D.

To estimate the effect under assumption S.2, we must assume the aforementioned mechanism does not occur and that the only effect of the grant is to increase the probability of $D = 1$. The relevance condition is not an assumption but a requirement that can be tested with data. If the scholarship does not make people more likely to attend academies, we cannot use it as an instrument to determine the effect of D. The instrument must induce variation in D to identify the effect.

The monotonicity assumption in this case assumes that no one will be less likely to join academies due to receiving the grant. For everyone, receiving the scholarship should either leave their decision unchanged or increase their likelihood of attending the academy. This estimator compares the Y of those who receive the scholarship with those who do not, correcting for how the scholarship increases the proportion attending the academy. We need the scholarship to have a monotonic effect on D so the estimator provides an average causal effect, not a difference in causal effects.

A limitation of the instrumental variables method is that, under these four assumptions, the estimated causal effect is not the average effect for the entire population or the average effect for those treated (academy attendees), which is typically more interesting. Instead, it provides the average effect for those whose D value changes due to the instrument, weighted by how much the instrument affects D. This effect does not apply to those who would attend the academy regardless of the scholarship or indicate the effect on those who do not attend. To know these, we need to estimate the average treatment effect for the treated or for all. What is estimated under assumptions S.1 to S.4 is a local average treatment effect, known as LATE. A further problem is we do not know who in the population is affected by the instrument since the counterfactual decision regarding D is unobserved. The advantage is that we at least have an estimate of a causal effect free from the selection bias that complicates the estimation of educational policy effects and school comparisons.

There is a stronger version of assumption S.4 that is credible in certain contexts and would allow us to know the average treatment effect on the treated (ATT). Suppose that instead of providing a grant, we randomly decide which students from a municipality will attend the only academy in the municipality. The allocation is free of charge, equivalent to a scholarship. This experiment aims to directly assess the effect of D, as D is what we are trying to assign.

The problem is that we cannot force any student who does not want to attend the academy, so the decision of whether or not to go is not implemented as determined by randomization. Some students assigned to the treated group may decide not to go to the academy and effectively become part of the control group, breaking randomization and comparability. However, we can ensure that no student assigned to the control group is admitted to the academy, even if they request it. In this situation, the assignment (Z) can be a good instrument for D (actually attending the academy). It would fulfill assumptions S.1, S.2, and S.3, and additionally, a stronger version of S.4.

With the monotonicity assumption, it is possible that some students are unaffected by Z because they would attend the academy ($D = 1$) regardless. However, this situation is excluded here because those not selected are not allowed to attend the academy. In this case, the instrumental variables estimator will provide the average causal effect of attending the academy for those who actually go (the treated). Importantly, even when a strict trial implementation is not possible, randomized experimentation of some policies allows us to generate, at least, valid instruments to estimate the causal effect of policies for some population groups.

8 Regression Discontinuity Design (RDD)

Let us consider a high school deemed to be of excellence that receives many applications and admits its students based on their entrance exam scores. If we want to know the quality of this educational institution, i.e., the causal effect of studying here (D) on students' learning, measured by their results in the university entrance exams (Y) they take at the end of high school, we cannot simply compare the results of those who have been admitted to this institution with those who have not. As previously explained, such a comparison would have selection bias because these students have been selected precisely due to their better starting results. We would not know whether the differences are due to the school's quality or to the students' prior knowledge before attending that school. However, this selection system, which makes treated and control groups non-comparable, creates a discontinuity that this method will exploit to identify two groups of treated and control students that are comparable.

To continue with the same example, let us suppose that the threshold, the cut-off mark in the entrance exam that determines who is admitted, is 8.20 (on a scale of 0 to 10). Those admitted (treated) with a 9.4 are very different from those not admitted (controls) who scored 6.1. This is why we cannot compare them. However, those with scores between 8.20 and 8.30 have a level of prior knowledge (almost) the same as those with scores between 8.10 and 8.19. This difference of one-tenth of a point around the threshold, which has led to some being admitted and others not, can only be due to chance, meaning that that, despite having the same underlying knowledge, some scored slightly higher than others.

The difference in knowledge is negligible or irrelevant, but there is a significant difference in their D value: some are treated and some are not. Thus, we have a treated group comparable to a control group, and the differences in Y can be attributed to the causal effect of D, not to the difference in prior knowledge. If there is a jump in Y from one side of the threshold to the other, it is due to the treatment.

In the case where all those on one side of the threshold receive the treatment and all those on the other side do not, we speak of Sharp RDD. In the case where being on one side of the threshold does not completely determine the treatment assignment, but only serves to change the probability of being treated, we speak of Fuzzy Regression Discontinuity Design (fuzzy RDD). This can happen, for example, because the access score is only one of the criteria taken into account and only serves to increase the probability of being admitted. However, some of those with somewhat lower scores are eventually admitted, and some of those with higher scores, even though they are admitted, decide not to attend the school. The two accompanying graphs show these two situations: the sharp case and the fuzzy case.

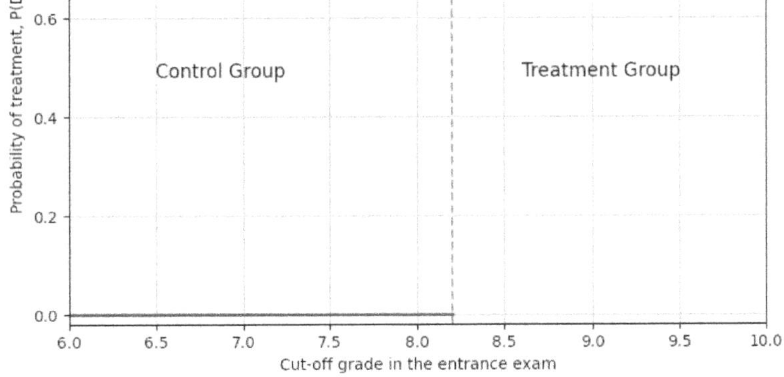

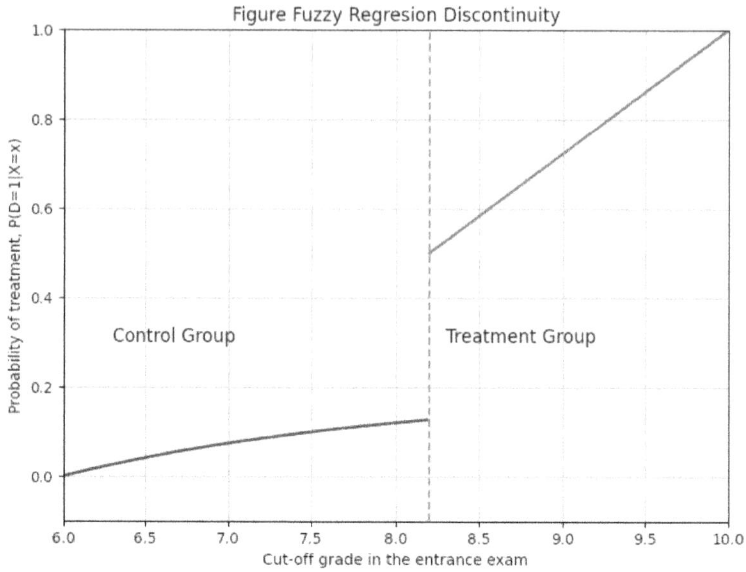

In the fuzzy case, the estimator is as intuitive as comparing the mean outcome of those who are very close to the threshold on either side. The fuzzy case estimator can be seen as an instrumental variables estimator, where the instrument is an indicator of being above the threshold. This means we not only compare the result in intervals close to both sides of the threshold but also account for the fact that some individuals' D value does not strictly correspond to their side of the threshold.

To explain this graphically, I will use a real application of the method. Specifically, the paper by Machin, McNally, and Ruiz-Valenzuela (2020) studies the effect of passing (versus failing) a set of tests that English students must take at the end of compulsory education at age 16. Practically, passing requires, among other things, a C grade in English. The authors analyse the effect of passing this subject in the exam (variable D). One of the outcome variables (Y) they use is whether or not, at the age of 18, the students are still studying (at any level or type of study).

The variable that determines the assignment to the treatment (passing the test) is the original score on the English test. The first graph below, which is Fig. 4 in Machin, McNally, and Ruiz-Valenzuela (2020), shows the proportion of students who pass (get a C) for each English score. As can be seen, the allocation is blurred because some students who do not reach 180 points (the cut-off for a C) finally manage to pass the exam. Some of those who come very close may request a revision of the original grade in some of the various aspects that make up the original grade. The details of all this can be found in the article by Machin, McNally, and Ruiz-Valenzuela (2020). What is important is that there is a discontinuity in the pass rate. The pass rate does not rise continuously with the original grade; it jumps from around 30% for those with a score almost equal to, but less than, 180 to 100% for those with 180 or more points on the exam.

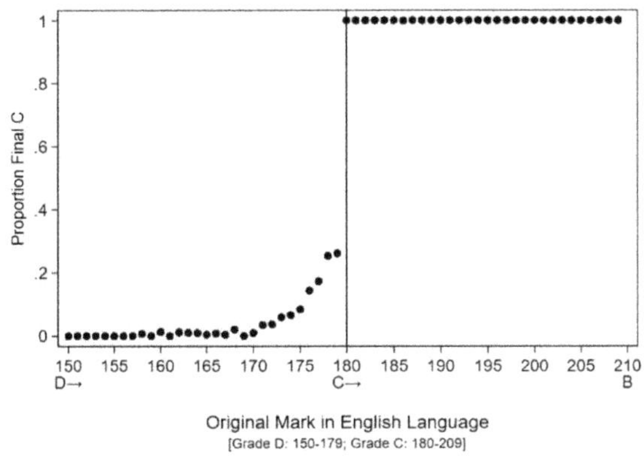

The two graphs below this paragraph, part of Fig. 6 in Machin, McNally, and Ruiz-Valenzuela (2020), show how the mean of Y, i.e., the proportion of people who at 18 are not studying, evolves for each level of English score. It is very interesting to observe a negative correlation in this graph between higher marks and the proportion of those who at 18 are not studying at all. This is why we cannot simply compare all those who have passed with all those who have not passed to determine the effect of passing. These students differ significantly in their level of knowledge at the end of compulsory education.

The RD method compares those with practically the same score but, by a very small margin, some are below and others above the pass mark. If the proportion of Y evolves similarly around the threshold as it does around any other value, we would conclude that there is no effect of passing. However, as seen in the graph, at the 180 mark, there is a jump, a discontinuity in the evolution of Y. The estimate of the effect is derived by comparing the levels of Y around 180. This comparison reveals a jump from around 14% to around 11%, discounting the fact that some students below 180 eventually pass.

Of course, the concrete estimate is not obtained merely by looking at a graph. Numerical procedures and estimators are employed to provide standard errors for that estimate. These details are available in the tables of the article. Nonetheless, the graphs are very useful for understanding how RDD identifies the causal effect.

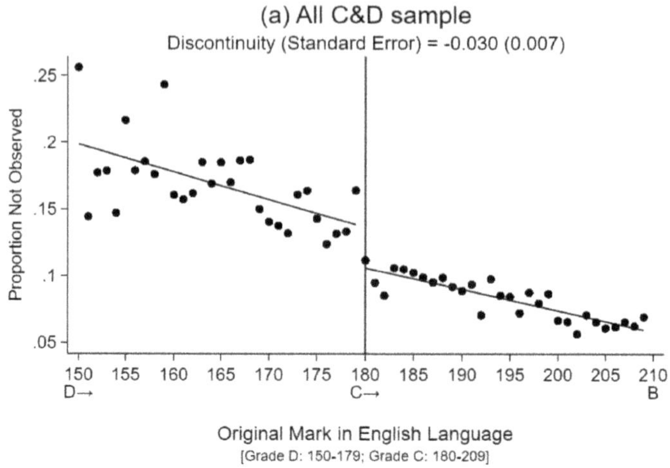

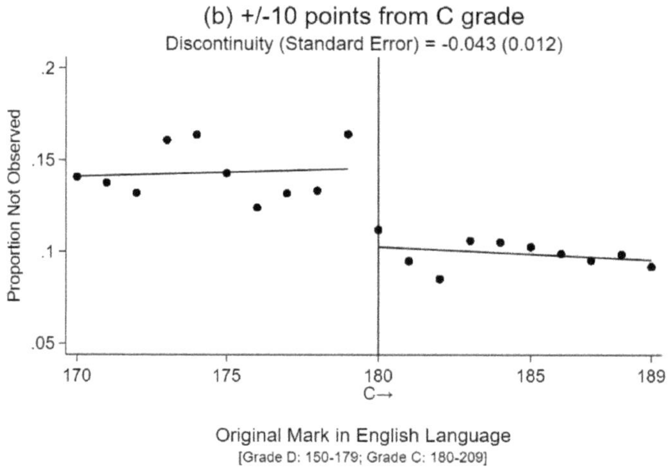

In any case, the main practical complication will come because we will normally not be able to stay in a very small interval around the threshold due to lack of sufficient observations. The comparison will include a not so small interval and this may introduce noise/bias in the estimation. There are different methods as to how to do this, including deciding the width of the interval, and the properties of the intervals, the description of which is beyond the scope of this chapter. More relevant to the purpose of this chapter is to discuss the assumptions necessary for this method to give us an estimate of a causal effect and its limitations.

In addition to the condition that there is such a discontinuity, it is necessary to assume that everything else, namely the potential outcomes, in the absence of the treatment change continuously around that threshold. This is known as the local continuity assumption. Ways of looking for evidence for or against such a continuity assumption are as follows:

1. Student characteristics or student outcomes prior to treatment should change continuously around the threshold. It is not surprising if they change; for example, students with higher initial levels may have more resources at home. However, what must not happen is a discontinuous change around the threshold. The treatment cannot affect this pre-existing characteristic. In the following graph, taken from Fig. 5 of Machin, McNally, and Ruiz-Valenzuela (2020), we see the continuity in the relationship between the marks students obtain at age 16 ("Original Mark In English Language" on the x-axis) and the marks they obtained on a test taken at age 11 ("Key Stage 2 Points" on the y-axis). There is a positive correlation, indicating that students who score higher at age 16 tend to have scored higher at age 11. However, as students move from just below to just above the 180-point threshold, there is no jump; the evolution is continuous. This makes sense, as passing or failing at 16 cannot causally affect the results of an examination taken at age 11.

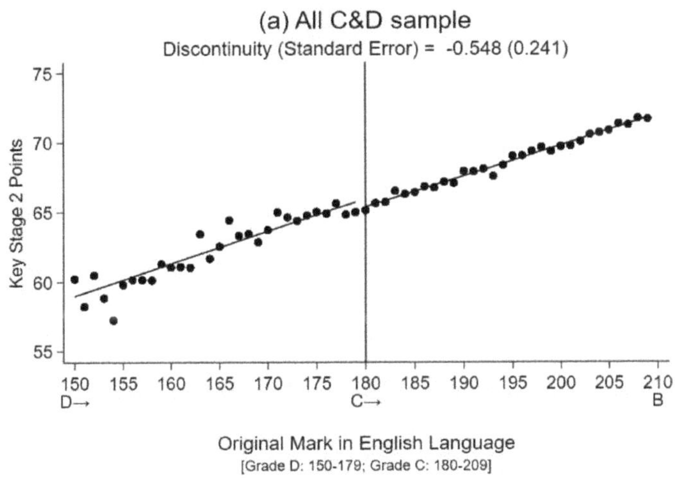

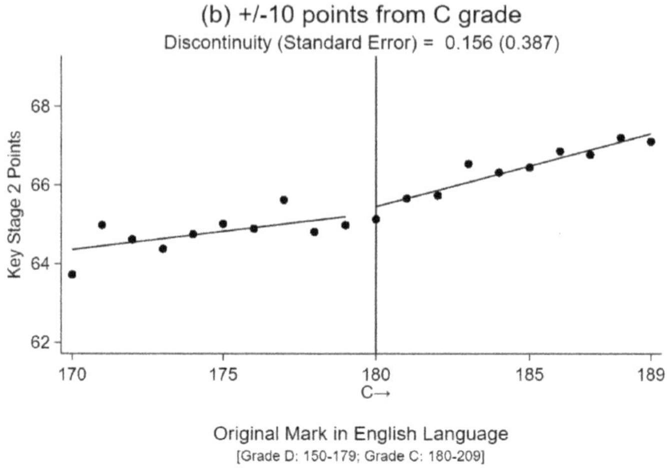

2. Perform falsification tests as described in Sect. 6.
3. Examine the distribution of students on either side of the threshold. If we find a concentration of students just above the threshold and a void just below it, this would be evidence of endogenous manipulation or possible selection bias. A common example of this is in academic grades when a threshold marks a dichotomous situation, such as promoting to the next grade or repeating the course. There is often a much higher proportion of students who pass just above the threshold compared to those who fail just below the threshold. These groups are not usually comparable because teachers consider more characteristics and information when deciding which students with similar grades close to the passing mark finally end up above the threshold. This issue prevents using such grades in the regression discontinuity method to evaluate the impact of repeating a course on future academic performance. Repeaters and non-repeaters, although they may have grades close to the threshold, will differ in other characteristics considered by the evaluation board when deciding who stays above and below the threshold.

Another threat to validity would be the existence of contamination in the control group, where the treatment also affects the untreated individuals, as noted in the case of experiments in the Sect. 4. In the example where the aim is to study the causal impact of a policy that mandates grade repetition on students' academic performance, it may happen that the threat of having to repeat a grade serves as a strong incentive for students who do not repeat, encouraging them to study and learn more. This effect would count as a negative effect of the policy when comparing repeaters with non-repeaters, even though it is actually a positive effect that disappears if the policy is eliminated and all students are automatically promoted.

Estimated causal effect: The estimated causal effect is valid for those around the threshold, but need not be valid for those far from the threshold. This is also a local effect. The mathematical expressions of the assumptions and the causal parameter that identifies the RDD are given in Sect. 11.

9 Structural Models: Investigating the Mechanisms That Explain the Overall Effects of a Policy

A structural model is an economic model that describes how the agents under study (such as students, families, or households) behave, how they make decisions, and the time, budgetary, and/or technological constraints they face. For example, the economic models presented in the next chapter of this book describe how students and families make decisions regarding education. By extending these models to incorporate more variables, including unobservable and dynamic elements, we can create a structural model that accurately describes a set of real observations. These real data will be used to estimate the values of the parameters that characterize this model, which are initially unknown.

The methods discussed above allow us to determine the total or reduced-form effect on Y of changing D from a value D_0 to a value D_1 without needing to specify how Y is determined, which other variables affect Y, or the nature of those effects. However, as explained in Sects. 2 and 4, these methods do not provide insights into the mechanisms causing this effect, nor do they allow us to separate the direct effect of D from the effect that occurs through other variables that also influence Y. Additionally, these methods may have issues with external validity and general equilibrium. In contrast, estimating a structural model to determine the effect of D offers the following advantages:

1. Behavioural models enable the **study of the mechanisms** through which policy affects the outcome variable, allowing us to separate direct effects from those mediated by other variables. As described in the next chapter of this book, students decide how much effort to invest in their studies, and families decide how much time and resources to allocate to their children's education. Both can respond to changes in school inputs, creating an additional mechanism through which these changes affect students' academic progress.
2. **External validity**: By capturing the mechanisms and the effects and interactions with other determinants of the decision, the impacts of a policy can be understood beyond the individuals to whom the policy has been applied. In a structural model, it is possible to consider how the varying characteristics and circumstances of different groups of individuals, on whom we now want to understand the policy effects, modify the impact of D on Y.
3. They allow the evaluation of both **long- and short-term effects** of an education policy, as these models consider the dynamic and expectation-based nature of individuals' decisions.
4. Structural models allow the simulation of **counterfactual policy**. To determine the causal effect of a policy using the method described in Sect. 4, we need to test the policy. If, after the trial, we want to know what would happen if we changed any aspect of that policy, no matter how small, we need to conduct another trial. The same applies if the results are not as expected and we want to know what would have happened with a different policy. Without another trial, it is impossible to know. However, once we have a structural model that

accurately characterizes the decisions, constraints, and restrictions of individuals, it allows us to simulate and understand the effects of a policy different from the one previously implemented without the need for further trials.

Among the disadvantages, the most significant is that validating the chosen model is not easy. Estimation requires a large amount of data and is not straightforward. Additionally, there are functional and parametric assumptions selected by the researcher that need to be validated. To demonstrate that the model is plausible, one must:

- Validate (explain decisions we observe) within the sample.
- Validate out-of-sample.
- Use regime changes and see if it is able to predict their effects well.
- Compare with experimental results: the estimate of the total impact of a tested policy should be equal to the total impact given by the RCT with the method described in Sect. 4.

10 Heterogeneous Effects

Implicit in everything written in this chapter is the fact that there are heterogeneous effects, meaning the effect varies for each student. The objective has been to estimate the average effect for the entire population of interest. This is why in instrumental variables we estimate the LATE (Local Average Treatment Effect) instead of the causal effect for all, and why in Regression Discontinuity Design (RDD) we obtain the effect only for those close to the cut-off point, but not for others. If the effect were homogeneous, estimating it well for a subgroup of the population would mean estimating it well for everyone, since everyone would experience the same effect.

We are not normally interested in knowing the effect for each student (or in generic terms, for each unit of observation, be it students, workers, households, etc.). We want to know an informative measure of that effect for our population of interest. The average effect is the most commonly used informative measure, and for this reason, all the above methods are interesting and, in principle, sufficient. However, if there are sufficiently different heterogeneous effects across individuals, we have two new problems to face.

1. This is one of the main reasons for questioning the external validity of the causal effect estimated by an experiment. We know the mean for that group of individuals. But if the effects are very heterogeneous, a different group of individuals may have a very different mean effect. For some, there may even be a positive and significant effect, and for others, a zero effect.
2. We will also want to be able to use various measures to characterize these heterogeneous effects in order to determine, for example, on which groups the education policy in question has a more positive effect.

One way to estimate, at least in part, heterogeneous effects is to calculate average effects for several subgroups of individuals, defined by observable variables where we expect the effects to differ. For example, we could analyse the different effects of reducing class size for students with differently educated parents. This is, in principle, straightforward to do with any of the methods described in the previous sections. For instance, with experimental data, one compares the treated and control groups on a subgroup-by-subgroup basis. The challenge often lies in the lack of sufficient data. Splitting the sample into several sub-samples requires a large enough sample size. A trial with 500 treated students and 500 controls may suffice to estimate the average effect. However, if we need to account for heterogeneous effects by the educational level of the mother, father, and gender of the students, we may end up with over 15 subgroups, each with fewer than 40 treated and control students.

Another approach is to use econometric techniques aimed at estimating the distribution or parts of it, such as various quartiles, of the heterogeneous effects. This method is most effective in a structural estimation context or when we incorporate more observable variables into the other estimation methods.

11 Formal Expressions of Some of the Parameters and Estimators

11.1 Potential Outcomes, Causal Effect, Selection Bias and RCTs

D_i is the value of the variable whose effect we want to know for individual i; i can represent students, households, workers, schools, companies, etc. At each case it will represent those units on which the effect of D on Y. Y_i represents the value of the outcome variable for the individual i. We are interested in knowing the effect on Y of increasing the value of D from a value D_0 to a value D_1.For every individual there are a priori two potential outcomes or values of Y_i: 1) the one that will be obtained if Di = D0 that we call Y (D)0i and 2) the one that will be obtained if Di = D1 that we call Y (D)1i . The (total) causal effect for this individual is $Y(D_1)_i - Y(D_0)_i$. Simplifying to the binary situation, treated $D_1 = 1$, controls $D_0 = 0$, we have,

Mean effect for the whole population: $\mathbb{E}(Y(1)_i - Y(0)_i) \equiv \tau_{ATE}$

Mean effect for those treated: $\mathbb{E}(Y(1)_i - Y(0)_i|D_i = 1) = \mathbb{E}(Y(1)_i|D_i = 1) - \mathbb{E}(Y(0)_i|D_i = 1) \equiv \tau_{ATT}$

We observe $\mathbb{E}(Y_i|D_i = 1) - \mathbb{E}(Y_i|D_i = 0) = \mathbb{E}(Y(1)_i|D_i = 1) - \mathbb{E}(Y(0)_i|D_i = 0)$. This would be equal to τ_{ATT} if

$$\mathbb{E}(Y(0)_i|D_i = 0) = \mathbb{E}(Y(0)_i|D_i = 1) \tag{3}$$

The difference between $\mathbb{E}(Y(0)_i|D_i = 0)$ and $\mathbb{E}(Y(0)_i|D_i = 1)$ is the selection bias. Condition (3) is going to occur when we have a well implemented randomized experiment. If this condition is met, the estimation would consist in obtaining the sample counterpart of $\mathbb{E}(Y_i|D_i = 1) - \mathbb{E}(Y_i|D_i = 0)$.

11.2 Selection on Observables Only

The regression which adds observable controls

$$Y = \beta_0 + \beta_1 X + \tau D + \varepsilon. \tag{4}$$

will give the causal effect if $\mathbb{E}(\varepsilon|X, D) = 0$. This is so because

$$\begin{aligned} &\mathbb{E}(Y|X, D = 1) - \mathbb{E}(Y|X, D = 0) \\ &\quad = \mathbb{E}(\beta_0 + \beta_1 X + \tau + \varepsilon|X, D = 1) \\ &\quad - \mathbb{E}(\beta_0 + \beta_1 X + \varepsilon|X, D = 0) \end{aligned} \tag{5}$$

$$= \beta_0 + \beta_1 X + \tau + \mathbb{E}(\varepsilon|X, D = 1) - (\beta_0 + \beta_1 X) - \mathbb{E}(\varepsilon|X, D = 0) \tag{6}$$

$$= \tau + \mathbb{E}(\varepsilon|X, D = 1) - \mathbb{E}(\varepsilon|X, D = 0) \tag{7}$$

with τ being the average causal effect:

$$\mathbb{E}(Y(1)_i - Y(0)_i) = \mathbb{E}(\beta_0 + \beta_1 X + \tau + \varepsilon - (\beta_0 + \beta_1 X + \varepsilon)) = \tau. \tag{8}$$

Mean treatment effect on treated, ATT estimated with matching based on $P(X)$:

$$\tau_{ATT}^{PSM} = \mathbb{E}_{P(X)|D=1}\{\mathbb{E}(Y|P(X), D = 1) - \mathbb{E}(Y|P(X), D = 0)\} \tag{9}$$

The assumption of conditional independence, or selection on observables only, can be expressed in general form as

$$\{Y(0), Y(1)\} \perp D|X, \forall X \tag{10}$$

11.3 Basic DiD and Identification Assumption

Identifying assumption:

$$\begin{aligned} &\mathbb{E}(Y(0)|D = 0, despues) - \mathbb{E}(Y(0)|D = 0, antes) \\ &\quad = \mathbb{E}(Y(0)|D = 1, despues) - \mathbb{E}(Y(0)|D = 1, antes) \end{aligned} \tag{11}$$

DiD:

$$\begin{aligned}\tau_{DiD} &= \left[\mathbb{E}(Y|D=1, despues) - \mathbb{E}(Y|D=1, antes)\right] \\ &\quad - \left[\mathbb{E}(Y|D=0, despues) - \mathbb{E}(Y|D=0, antes)\right] \\ &= \left[\mathbb{E}(Y(1)|D=1, despues) - \mathbb{E}(Y(0)|D=1, antes)\right] \\ &\quad - \left[\mathbb{E}(Y(0)|D=0, despues) - \mathbb{E}(Y(0)|D=0, antes)\right] \end{aligned} \tag{12}$$

Under the identifying assumption τ_{DiD} is equal to

$$\begin{aligned} &= \left[\mathbb{E}(Y(1)|D=1, despues) - \mathbb{E}(Y(0)|D=1, antes)\right] \\ &\quad - \left[\mathbb{E}(Y(0)|D=1, despues) - \mathbb{E}(Y(0)|D=1, antes)\right] \\ &= \mathbb{E}(Y(1)|D=1, despues) - \mathbb{E}(Y(0)|D=1, despues) = ATT \end{aligned} \tag{13}$$

11.4 Instrumental Variables: Wald Estimator, Assumptions and LATE

In the simplest case where D is binary, and Z is also binary, the VI estimator is known as the Wald estimator and is the sampling equivalent of the following ratio:

$$\tau_{VI} = \frac{\mathbb{E}(Y_i|Z_i=1) - \mathbb{E}(Y_i|Z_i=0)}{\mathbb{E}(D_i|Z_i=1) - \mathbb{E}(D_i|Z_i=0)} \tag{14}$$

The 4 assumptions set out in Sect. 7 are:

1. S.1. Independence of the Instrument

$$\{Y(D(1), Z=1)_i, Y(D(0), Z=0)_i, D(1)_i, D(0)_i\} \perp Z_i$$

2. S.2. Exclusion restriction

$$Y(d, Z=1)_i = Y(d, Z=0)_i$$

para $d = 0, 1$.

3. S.3. Rank or relevance condition of the instrument

$$\mathbb{E}(D|Z=1) \neq \mathbb{E}(D|Z=0)$$

4. S.4. Monotonicity assumption

$$D(1)_i \geq D(0)_i, \forall i.$$

or

$$D(1)_i \leq D(0)_i, \forall i.$$

Under these 4 assumptions τ_{VI} in (14) is equal to $\mathbb{E}(Y(1)_i - Y(0)_i|D(1)_i > D(0)_i) \equiv \tau_{LATE}$.

11.5 Regression Discontinuity

Let Z be the variable on the basis of which it is decided who is treated, and z be the threshold at which the probability of being treated changes (say, increases). Identification condition or discontinuity in the Probability of being treated:

$$\lim_{\Delta\to 0} \Pr(D = 1|Z = \overline{z} + \Delta) \neq \lim_{\Delta\to 0} \Pr(D = 1|Z = \overline{z} - \Delta) \tag{15}$$

Local continuity assumption necessary to identify a causal effect:

$$\lim_{\Delta\to 0} \mathbb{E}(Y(j)|Z = \overline{z} + \Delta) = \lim_{\Delta\to 0} \mathbb{E}(Y(j)|Z = \overline{z} - \Delta) \text{ for } j = 0, 1 \tag{16}$$

Definition, in population terms, of the parameter that gives rise to the Discontinuous Regression estimator (fuzzy, generic case):

$$\tau_{RDB} = \frac{\lim_{\Delta\to 0} \mathbb{E}(Y|_i Z_i = \overline{z} + \Delta) - \lim_{\Delta\to 0} \mathbb{E}(Y_i|Z_i = \overline{z} - \Delta)}{\lim_{\Delta\to 0} \Pr(D_i = 1|Z_i = \overline{z} + \Delta) - \lim_{\Delta\to 0} \Pr(D_i = 1|Z_i = \overline{z} - \Delta)} \tag{17}$$

Notice that If the discontinuity were sharp, then $\lim_{\Delta\to 0} \Pr(D_i = 1|Z_i = \overline{z} + \Delta) = 1$, and $\lim_{\Delta\to 0} \Pr(D_i = 1|Z_i = \overline{z} - \Delta) = 0$, and the denominator would be 1.

It can be shown that

$$\tau_{RDB} = \mathbb{E}(Y(1)_i - Y(0)_i|Z_i = \overline{z}) \tag{18}$$

which is the treatment effect for individuals at threshold $\overline{z}$.

12 Bibliography to Learn More

12.1 Books Covering Most of the Methods Described:

- Angrist, J. & J. Pischke (2009): "Mostly Harmless Econometrics". Princeton University Press.
- Cunningham, S. (2021): "Causal Inference. The Mixtape". Yale University Press.

12.2 Econometrics Textbooks

They contain materials necessary for a good understanding of the estimation techniques used. In addition, some chapters deal specifically with methods described here:

- Cameron A. & P. Trivedi (2005): "Microeconometrics: Methods and Applications". Cambridge University Press.
- Greene, W. (2003): "Econometric Analysis", 5th edition. Prentice Hall.
- Stock. J. H. & M. K. Watson (2012): "Introduction to Econometrics". Pearson.
- Wooldridge, J. W. (2010): "Econometric Analysis of Cross Section and Panel Data", 2nd edition. The MIT Press.

12.3 Article on RCTs

Article on the use of RCTs and their limitations:

- Deaton, A. (2009): "Instruments of Development: Randomisation in the Tropics, and the Search for the Elusive Keys to Economic Development" The Keynes Lecture in Economics, *NBER Working Paper 4690.*

12.4 Articles on Matching

- Caliendo, M. & S. Kopeinig (2005): "Some Practical Guidance for the Implementation of Propensity Score Matching", *IZA Discussion Paper No. 1588.*
- Dehejia, R. (2005): "Practical Porpensity Score Matching: A Reply to Smith and Todd", *Journal of Econometrics*, 125: 355-364.
- Heckman, J, H. Ichimura & P. Todd (1997): "Matching as an Econometric Evaluation Estimator", *Review of Economic Studies*, 64: 605-654.

Article demonstrating that if the causal effect can be identified by matching on observables, it can also be identified by matching on the probability of being treated:

- Rosenbaum, P. &D. Rubin (1983): "The central role of the Propensity Socore in Observational Studies for Causal Effects", *Biometrika*, 70: 41-50
- Smith, J. & P. Todd (2005): "Does Matching Overcome LaLonde's Critique of Non-Experimental Estimators?", *Journal of Econometrics*, 125: 305-353.

12.5 Use of Observables to Try to Bound the Selection Bias

- Altonji, J., T. Elder & C. Taber (2005): "Selection on Observed and Unobserved Variables: Assessing the Effectiveness of Catholic Schools", *Journal of Political Economy*, 113 (1): 151-184.

12.6 Articles on DiD

Recent advances regarding the assumption of parallel trends and functional form restrictions when controlling for observables:

- Rambachan, A. & J. Roth (2023): "A More Credible Approach to Parallel Trends", *Review of Economic Studies,* 90: 2555–2591
- Roth, J. & P. Sant'Anna (2023): "When is parallel trends sensitive to functional form?", *Econometrica,* 91(2): 737–747.
- Sun, L. & S. Abraham (2021): "Estimating dynamic treatment effects in event studies with heterogeneous treatment effects", *Journal of Econometrics*, 225(2): 175-199.

Recent articles on testing parallel trends:

- Jaeger, D., T. Joyce & R. Kaestner (2020): "A Cautionary Tale of Evaluating Identifying Assumptions: Did Reality TV Really Cause a Decline in Teenage Childbearing?", *Journal of Business & Economic Statistics,* 38: 317-326.
- Roth, J. (2022): "Pretest with Caution: Event-Study Estimates after Testing for Parallel Trends", *American Economic Review Insights*, 4(3): 305-322

Recent articles on estimation when several post-treatment periods are available:

- Callaway, B. & P. Sant'Anna (2021): "Difference-in-Differences with multiple time periods.", *Journal of Econometrics*, 225: 200-230
- Chaisemartin, C. & X. D'Haultfoeuille (2020): "Two-Way Fixed Effects Estimators with Heterogeneous Treatment Effects", *American Economic Review.* 110(9): 2964–2996

Beyond DiD:

- Arkhangelsky, D., S. Athey, D. Hirshberg, G. Imbens, & S. Wager (2021) "Synthetic Difference-in-Differences", *American Economic Review.* 111(12): 4088–4118

Article summarizing the latest relevant developments in DiD:

- Roth, J., P. Sant'Anna, A. Bilinski & J. Poe (2023): "What's trending in difference-in-differences? A synthesis of the recent econometrics literature", *Journal of Econometrics*, 235 (2): 2218-2244.

12.7 Articles on Instrumental Variables

- Imbens, G. & J. Angrist (1994): "Identification and Estimation of Local Average Treatment Effects", *Econometrica,* 62: 467–476.

Article that goes beyond LATE and relates instrumental variables to structural literature:

- Heckman, J & E. Vytlacil (2005): "Structural Equations, Treatment Effects, and Econometric Policy Evaluation", *Econometrica,* 73(3): 669–738.

Critical revision of modern IV literature with heterogenous treatment effects:

- Mogstad, M. and A. Torgovitsky (2024): "Instrumental Variables with Unobserved Heterogeneity in Treatment Effects", NBER Working Paper No. 32927.

12.8 Articles on Regression Discontinuity

- Hahn, J., P. Todd & W. van der Klaauw (2001): "Identification and Estimation of Treatment Effects with a Regression-discontinuit Design", *Econometrica,* 69: 201–209.
- Imbens, G. & Lemieux (2008): "Regression Discontinuity Designs: A Guide to Practice", *Journal of Econometrics,* 142 (2): 615-635.
- Lee, D. & T. Lemieux (2010): "Regression Discontinuity Designs in Economics", *Journal of Economic Literature* 48(2): 281-355

Example of an application used in this section:

- Machin, S., S. McNally, y J. Ruiz-Valenzuela (2020): "Entry through the narrow door: The costs of just failing high stakes exams", *Journal of Public Economics,* 90: 104224. https://doi.org/10.1016/j.jpubeco.2020.104224

12.9 Articles on Structural Estimation and Causal Inference

This article is a good example of how to use structural estimation to understand the causal effects of a policy and similar alternative policies:

- Todd, P. & K. Wolpin (2006): "Assessing the Impact of a School Subsidy Program in Mexico: Using a Social Experiment toValidate a Dynamic Behavioral Model of Child Schooling and Fertility", *American Economic Review,* 96(5): 1384–1417

More general articles on causal inference:

- Heckman, J. (2000): "Causal Parameters and Policy Analysis in Economics: A Twentieth Century Retrospective.", *Quarterly Journal of Economics*, 115(1): 45–97.
- Rosenzweig, M. & K. Wolpin (2000): "Natural "Natural Experiments" in Economics", *Journal of Economic Literature* 38(4): 827–874

Evaluating Educational Policies in Practice

Vedant Bhardwaj, María Valkov, and Alejandro Puerta-Cuartas

1 The Effect of Accessing Selective Colleges on Education and Labor Market Outcomes

There is an inherent trade-off associated with selective college admission. On the one hand, admitting a student to a high-quality institution can be beneficial, as it can improve student graduation and earnings outcomes (Hoekstra 2009; Zimmerman 2014), and boost the economic outcomes of low-income and underrepresented racial minorities (Kozakowski 2020). On the other hand, admitting one student means rejecting another, so selective rules can be detrimental to those rejected, as they lose access to the benefits of attending a high-quality institution. Accordingly, evaluating an admissions policy change requires assessing its positive and negative impacts.

In this section, we replicate the results in Black et al. (2023), who study the effect of the Texas Top Ten Percent rule- hereafter "TTP"– that guaranteed admission to any Texas public university to anyone in the top ten percent of their high school class. The introduction of this policy had positive and negative effects arising from the enrollment dynamics of the Texas higher education system. While it increased the chances for top students from disadvantaged high schools, it also reduced access to the flagship campuses for some students from "feeder" high schools who were

Supplementary Information The online version contains supplementary material available at https://doi.org/10.1007/978-3-031-90911-5_3.

V. Bhardwaj · A. Puerta-Cuartas (✉)
Department of Economics, Universidad Carlos III, Madrid, Spain
e-mail: alpuerta@eco.uc3m.es

V. Bhardwaj
e-mail: vbhardwa@eco.uc3m.es

M. Valkov
Bank of Spain, Madrid, Spain
e-mail: maria.valkov@bde.es

A. Cabrales and I. Sanz (eds.), *Economics of Education*,
https://doi.org/10.1007/978-3-031-90911-5_3

not in the top ten percent. Accordingly, the authors exploit the introduction of TTP to identify the positive and negative effects of access to a selective institution on education and labor market outcomes.

As previously discussed educational policies benefit some students, while potentially harming others (Pushed Out students). The authors find positive effects of the TTP on the benefited students, for whom they find an improvement in enrollment and graduation, while earnings either stay the same or increase. Furthermore, they find no substantial harm to the students that could have been negatively affected by the educational policy.

We first briefly describe institutional details on the Texas higher education system and the Top Ten Percent rule. We then present the setting the authors use to evaluate the educational policy. Subsequently, we describe the available data, and finally, we present their empirical strategy and main results.

1.1 The Texas Higher Education System and the Introduction of the Top Ten Percent Rule

Texas has a large public higher education system consisting of over 30 four-year universities and over 60 two-year colleges. Among them, the two most selective institutions are the University of Texas at Austin (UT) and Texas A&M University, which constitute the focus of analysis of Black et al. (2023). Most students attend public universities since only 18.8 percent of Texas students attend private colleges, and 9.8 percent attend out-of-state colleges.

Until 1997, admission to UT was mainly determined by continuous high school class rank and SAT or ACT scores, with affirmative action preferences for students from underrepresented groups. The SAT is a standardized test widely used for college admissions in the United States. It is a multiple-choice, computer-based test created and administered by the College Board. Conversely, the ACT is a curriculum-based education and career planning test for high school students that evaluates the mastery of college readiness standards.

In May 1997, the Texas legislature created the TTP, which guaranteed admission to any public university in Texas for students in the top decile of their high school class. The student's performance is calculated by each high school and measured at the end of the junior year. Except for the UT, the vast majority of top decile students would have been admitted in the absence of the TTP rule. Thus, this educational policy mainly concerned admission to the UT. For students outside the top decile, an Academic Index (AI), and Personal Achievement Index (PAI) were used as an admission rule. However, given the large number of top-ten-percent applicants, UT admissions were very competitive for non-TTP applicants. Accordingly, the TTP rule ensured entrance to high-performing students who otherwise would not have been admitted to the UT, while raising the bar considerably, albeit without racial preferences, for the lower-performing students that would have been admitted before the law.

The main purpose of this educational policy was to maintain diversity among students without the need to explicitly consider race in the admission process. The rationale is that basing admissions on SAT or ACT scores disproportionately favored students from high-income, and primarily white high schools. Moreover, explicitly considering race in admission decisions, permitted applicants to take advantage of the substantial racial and economic segregation.

Admission by high school yields a more diverse class than statewide admissions. In their sample, while the average student before the TTP attends a school that is 30 percent Hispanic and 12 percent Black, the average Hispanic student attends a school that is 60 percent Hispanic, and the average Black student attends a school that is 37 percent Black. Furthermore, although 22 percent of students get free or reduced-price lunches, the average student who receives free lunches goes to a school where this percentage is 42 percent. Thus, if the top decile of each high school is demographically representative of the school as a whole, admission by high school yields a more diverse class than statewide admissions, due to the presence of segregation across high schools.

The TTP had a substantial impact on the students' perceived admission chances. Since students had information regarding their high school rank, they could assess their prospects more easily than in the previous regime. This was enhanced by the fact that the TTP law mandated that every high school post a sign explaining the law and that a letter be sent to every parent of a qualifying student. Furthermore, this policy was widely covered in the media.

The top ten percent rule transformed the enrollment dynamics of the most selective campus in Texas. In the year of its introduction, 41 percent of freshmen from Texas high schools were admitted under the TTP. This number rose to 70 percent by 2003. More importantly, the composition of the admitted students became less concentrated at traditional feeder schools. Therefore, this educational policy gave access to high-performing students who, before the new regime, would not have been admitted (or even applied) to the UT.

1.2 The Setting

Our object of interest is the effect of the TTP on students' education and labor market outcomes. Due to the inherent trade-off associated with selective college admission, we are interested in both TTP's positive and negative effects. While some students were "Pulled In" by this educational policy since they became more likely to attend UT Austin, others were "Pushed Out", as they became less likely to attend a high-quality institution. To estimate the effect of the TTP, the authors compare these two treatment groups with a control group.

Figure 1 illustrates how the "Pulled In", "Pushed Out", and control groups were defined. The left panel depicts that, before the TTP, students admitted to the two

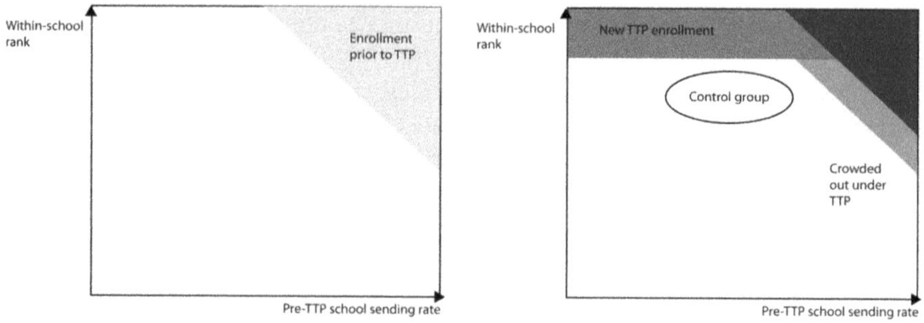

Fig. 1 Schematic description of top ten percent plan effect on enrollment

most selective campuses were the top students from feeder schools. After the TTP (see the right panel in Fig. 1), the students in the top ten percent of a school that had traditionally sent few if any students to the University of Texas flagship campus in Austin were "Pulled In". Conversely, students from "feeder" schools that do not qualify for the top ten percent, but performed above average in their schools were "Pushed Out". Finally, the control group consists of students who were above average in achievement but unlikely to be admitted to UT Austin under both regimes.

Ideally, we would like to know what the impact of the TTP for each student who was either pulled in or pushed out by the policy. Setting the time when the TTP took place at $t = 0$, we can express these individual effects as

$$\tau_{i,t}^{PI} = Y_{i,t}^{PI}(1) - Y_{i,t}(0), \quad t > 0, \tag{1}$$

$$\tau_{i,t}^{PO} = Y_{i,t}^{PO}(1) - Y_{i,t}(0), \quad t > 0, \tag{2}$$

where $Y_{i,t}^{PI}(1)$ is an education or labor market outcome at time t for a student i who was pulled in by the TTP, $Y_{i,t}(0)$ is the same education or labor market outcome for the student if the TTP had not taken place, and $Y_{i,t}^{PO}(1)$ is the outcome for the $i - th$ pulled out student at time t. Accordingly, we can express the observed outcomes for the pulled in students as $Y_{i,t} = Y_{i,t}^{PI}(1)\text{PulledIn}_{i,t} + Y_{i,t}(0)\big(1 - \text{PulledIn}_{i,t}\big)$, and those of the pulled out students as $Y_{i,t} = Y_{i,t}^{PO}(1)\text{PushedOut}_{i,t} + Y_{i,t}(0)\big(1 - \text{PushedOut}_{i,t}\big)$, where $\text{PulledIn}_{i,t} = 1$ for the students that were "Pulled In" by the TTP at time t and 0 for the control group, and $\text{PushedOut}_{i,t} = 1$ for the students that were "Pushed Out" by the TTP at time t and 0 for the control group.

In our context, $\tau_{i,t}^{PI}$ and $\tau_{i,t}^{PO}$ provide the causal effect of the TTP at time $t > 0$ on the $i - th$ student who was pulled in and pushed out by the educational policy, respectively. Thus, the former object provides the positive effect of the TTP, while the latter its negative effect.

The main limitation to estimate Eqs. (1) and (2) is that we do not observe the counterfactual $Y_i(0)$ for any student affected (treated) by the TTP. In other words, we do not observe the education or labor market outcome if the TTP had not taken place for any student who was either pulled in or pushed out by this policy. However, we observe a control group, whose likelihood of attending a high-quality campus remained unchanged with the TTP. Accordingly, we can exploit this information to estimate the average treatment on the treated (ATT) of the TTP at time t, which can be expressed as

$$\tau_t^{PI} = \mathbb{E}\left[Y_{i,t}^{PI}(1) - Y_{i,t}(0)|\text{PulledIn}_{i,t} = 1\right], \quad t > 0, \tag{3}$$

$$\tau_t^{PO} = \mathbb{E}\left[Y_{i,t}^{PO}(1) - Y_{i,t}(0)|\text{PushedOut} = 1\right] \quad t > 0. \tag{4}$$

On the one hand, τ_t^{PI} measures how much the pulled in students' outcomes changed on average due to the TTP.[1] On the other hand, τ_t^{PO} measures how much the pushed out students' outcomes changed on average because of the TTP. Accordingly, we will henceforth refer to τ_t^{PI} and τ_t^{PO} as the causal positive and negative effects of the top ten percent rule, respectively.

A natural approach to estimate these causal effects would be to compare the average outcomes of pulled in and pushed out students to those of the control group in the subsequent years

$$\mathbb{E}\left[Y_{i,t}|\text{PulledIn}_{i,t} = 1\right] - \mathbb{E}\left[Y_{i,t}|\text{PulledIn}_{i,t} = 0\right], \quad t > 0, \tag{5}$$

$$\mathbb{E}\left[Y_{i,t}|\text{PushedOut}_{i,t} = 1\right] - \mathbb{E}\left[Y_{i,t}|\text{PushedOut}_{i,t} = 0\right], \quad t > 0. \tag{6}$$

For instance, if our object of interest (Y) is post-college earnings, Eq. (5) corresponds to the difference between average post-college earnings of the pulled in students and the average of the control group. However, as we now show, Eqs. (5) and (6) do not identify the causal effects of the TTP. In other words, they are not equivalent to τ_t^{PI} and τ_t^{PO}

$$\begin{aligned}
\tau_t^{PI} &= \mathbb{E}\left[Y_{i,t}^{PI}(1) - Y_{i,t}(0)|\text{PulledIn}_{i,t} = 1\right] \\
&\neq \mathbb{E}\left[Y_{i,t}|\text{PulledIn}_{i,t} = 1\right] - \mathbb{E}\left[Y_{i,t}|\text{PulledIn}_{i,t} = 0\right] \\
\tau^{PO} &= \mathbb{E}\left[Y_{i,t}^{PO}(1) - Y_{i,t}(0)\text{PushedOut}_{i,t} = 1\right] \\
&\neq \mathbb{E}\left[Y_{i,t}|\text{PushedOut}_{i,t} = 1\right] - \mathbb{E}\left[Y_{i,t}|\text{PushedOut}_{i,t} = 0\right].
\end{aligned}$$

To see why, consider the case of the pulled in students

$$\begin{aligned}
&\mathbb{E}\left[Y_{i,t}|\text{PulledIn}_{i,t} = 1\right] - \mathbb{E}\left[Y_{i,t}|\text{PulledIn}_{i,t} = 0\right] \\
=&\mathbb{E}\left[Y_{i,t}^{PI}(1)|\text{PulledIn}_{i,t} = 1\right] - \mathbb{E}\left[Y_{i,t}|\text{PulledIn}_{i,t} = 0\right] \\
=&\mathbb{E}\left[Y_{i,t}^{PI}(1)|\text{PulledIn}_{i,t} = 1\right] - \mathbb{E}\left[Y_{i,t}(0)|\text{PulledIn}_{i,t} = 1\right]
\end{aligned}$$

[1] For instance, if Y is post-college earnings, τ_t^{PI} corresponds to the average change in post-college earnings of the students who were pulled in by the educational policy.

$$
\begin{aligned}
&+\mathbb{E}\big[Y_{i,t}(0)|\text{PulledIn}_{i,t}=1\big]-\mathbb{E}\big[Y_{i,t}|\text{PulledIn}_{i,t}=0\big]\\
&=\mathbb{E}\big[Y_{i,t}^{PI}(1)-Y_i(0)|\text{PulledIn}_{i,t}=1\big]\\
&\qquad+\mathbb{E}\big[Y_{i,t}(0)|\text{PulledIn}_{i,t}=1\big]-\mathbb{E}\big[Y_{i,t}|\text{PulledIn}_{i,t}=0\big]\\
&=\tau_t^{PI}+\underbrace{\mathbb{E}\big[Y_{i,t}(0)|\text{PulledIn}_{i,t}=1\big]-\mathbb{E}\big[Y_{i,t}|\text{PulledIn}_{i,t}=0\big]}_{\text{Selection Bias}},
\end{aligned}
\tag{7}
$$

where in the first equality we have used the definition of $Y_{i,t} = Y_{i,t}^{PI}(1)\text{PulledIn}_{i,t} + Y_{i,t}(0)\big(1 - \text{PulledIn}_{i,t}\big)$, and in the second we have added and subtracted the term $\mathbb{E}\big[Y_{i,t}(0)|\text{PulledIn}_{i,t} = 1\big]$.

Equation (7) shows that the difference in average outcomes of the pulled in and control group students in a subsequent year $\big(\mathbb{E}\big[Y_{i,t}|\text{PulledIn}_{i,t} = 1\big] - \mathbb{E}\big[Y_{i,t}|\text{PulledIn}_{i,t} = 0\big]\big)$ can be expressed as the sum of two objects, i.e., the average treatment on the treated (ATT) and the selection bias. While the former is our object of interest, the latter term captures that students who were pulled in by the TTP are systematically different from those who were not.

The selection bias in Eq. (7) would be zero if

$$
\mathbb{E}\big[Y_i(0)|\text{PulledIn}_{i,t} = 1\big] = \mathbb{E}\big[Y_i|\text{PulledIn}_{i,t} = 0\big],
$$

that is, if the average counterfactual outcome[2] of the pulled in students were the same as that of the students in the control group. In our framework, the treated students are the top performers in schools that had traditionally sent few if any students to the University of Texas flagship campus in Austin. Conversely, the control group consists of students who were above average in achievement who studied at high school with a high sending rate. Furthermore, these two groups of students are systematically different since Texas is highly segregated based on socioeconomic status. Since both academic performance and socioeconomic status affect expected earnings, it is likely that, had the TTP not taken place, the average educational and labor market outcomes of the treated students would be different from those of the control group. Thus, the selection bias is different from zero, so we cannot estimate the causal effects by comparing the outcomes of pulled in and pushed out students to those of the control group (see Eq. (7)). This gives rise to the question of how can we estimate the causal effects of the TTP? The answer lies in making reliable assumptions.

Assumptions are what allow us to learn from the data. For instance, if we assume that the counterfactual average outcome of the pulled in students is the same as that of the students in the control group, the selection bias is zero. Thus, we could estimate the causal effects of the TTP by comparing the outcomes of pulled in and pushed out students to those of the control group. However, we have argued that this assumption is not plausible in our setting.

[2] The average counterfactual outcome refers to the average outcome of the pulled in students if the TTP would not have taken place.

What reliable assumption can we make that allows us to estimate the causal effects of the TTP? In our framework, we can assume that outcomes for the three groups of students (pulled in, pushed out, and control) would have evolved similarly between the 1996 and 2002 cohorts had admissions policies been held stable. This is called a parallel trend assumption. We now illustrate the meaning and implication of this assumption in our framework, and how it allows us to estimate the causal effects of the TTP.

Figure 2 illustrates the effect of the TTP on college enrollment under the parallel trends assumption. The solid lines depict the evolution of college enrollment before and after the TTP of the pulled in students and the control group, respectively. The dotted line indicates the unobserved counterfactual college enrollment for the pulled in students. In other words, the outcome of these students if the TTP would not have taken place. According to Fig. 2 and Eq. (3), the causal effect of the intervention (average treatment on the treated) corresponds to the difference between the observed college enrollment of the pulled in students (A) minus its counterfactual outcome (B). However, we do not observe B, so we cannot estimate the causal effect without further assumptions.

The parallel trends assumption states that outcomes for the pulled in and control groups would have evolved similarly between the 1996 and 2002 cohorts had the TTP would not have been implemented. This can be formalized as

$$\begin{aligned} &\mathbb{E}\left[Y_{i,2002}(0)|\text{PulledIn}_{i,t}=1\right]-\mathbb{E}\left[Y_{i,1996}|\text{PulledIn}_{i,t}=1\right] \\ &\quad=\mathbb{E}\left[Y_{i,2002}|\text{PulledIn}_{i,t}=0\right]-\mathbb{E}\left[Y_{i,1996}|\text{PulledIn}_{i,t}=0\right]. \end{aligned} \tag{8}$$

To see how this assumption allows us to express the counterfactual outcome B in terms of observables, notice that according to Fig. 2, point A corresponds to the expected

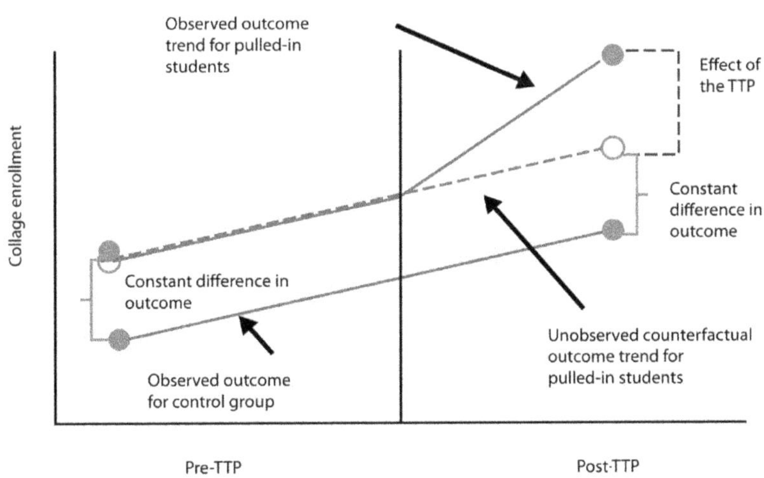

Fig. 2 The effect of the TTP under the parallel trends assumption

value of college enrollment of pulled in students evaluated at time $t = 2002$, which can be expressed as $A = \mathbb{E}\big[Y^{PI}_{i,2002}(1)|\text{PulledIn}_{i,t} = 1\big]$. Similarly, we have

$$\begin{aligned}
B &= \mathbb{E}\big[Y_{i,2002}(0)|\text{PulledIn}_{i,t} = 1\big] \\
C &= \mathbb{E}\big[Y_{i,2002}|\text{PulledIn}_{i,t} = 0\big] \\
D &= \mathbb{E}\big[Y_{i,1996}|\text{PulledIn}_{i,t} = 1\big] \\
E &= \mathbb{E}\big[Y_{i,1996}|\text{PulledIn}_{i,t} = 0\big].
\end{aligned}$$

Thus, Eq. (8) can be expressed as

$$\begin{aligned}
B - D &= C - E \\
B - C &= D - E,
\end{aligned}$$

which corresponds to the constant difference in outcomes in Fig. 2. Finally, the last display can be expressed as

$$B = C + D - E,$$

so that the counterfactual outcome (B) can be expressed in terms of objects we observe, which are the college enrollment of the control group in 2002 and 1996 (C and E, respectively), and the college enrollment of the pushed in students in 1996 (D). Thus, the parallel trends assumption allows us to write what we do not observe (B) in terms of objects we do observe (C, D, and E), so the causal effect of the TPP (A–B) can be computed with observables (A–(C+(D–E)).

We have illustrated that under the parallel trends assumption, the positive causal effect of the TTP in Eq. (3) can be computed (is identified) as

$$\begin{aligned}
\tau^{PI}_t &= \mathbb{E}\big[Y^{PI}_{i,t}(1) - Y_{i,t}(0)|\text{PulledIn}_{i,t} = 1\big] \\
&= \mathbb{E}\big[Y^{PI}_{i,t}(1)|\text{PulledIn}_{i,t} = 1\big] - \mathbb{E}\big[Y_{i,t}(0)|\text{PulledIn}_{i,t} = 1\big] \\
&= A - B \\
&= A - (C + (D - E) \\
&= \mathbb{E}\big[Y^{PI}_{i,2002}(1)|\text{PulledIn}_{i,t} = 1\big] - \mathbb{E}\big[Y_{i,2002}|\text{PulledIn}_{i,t} = 0\big] \\
&\quad - \mathbb{E}\big[Y_{i,1996}|\text{PulledIn}_{i,t} = 1\big] + \mathbb{E}\big[Y_{i,1996}|\text{PulledIn}_{i,t} = 0\big].
\end{aligned} \tag{9}$$

Similarly, the ATT for the pushed out is identified as

$$\begin{aligned}
\tau^{PO}_t &= \mathbb{E}\big[Y^{PI}_{i,t}(1) - Y_{i,t}(0)|\text{PushedOut}_{i,t} = 1\big] \\
&= \mathbb{E}\big[Y^{PI}_{i,2002}(1)|\text{PushedOut}_{i,t} = 1\big] - \mathbb{E}\big[Y_{i,2002}|\text{PushedOut}_{i,t} = 0\big] \\
&\quad - \mathbb{E}\big[Y_{i,1996}|\text{PushedOut}_{i,t} = 1\big] + \mathbb{E}\big[Y_{i,1996}|\text{PushedOut}_{i,t} = 0\big].
\end{aligned} \tag{10}$$

The main challenge to estimate τ_t^{PI} and τ_t^{PO}, is identifying which students were pulled in and pushed out by the policy. This arises from the fact that the student's class rank is not measured in the statewide pre-TTP data and only limited information is available after TTP. Thus, we now turn to describe the ideal data one would require to estimate the causal effects of the TTP, how the available data differs from it, and the challenges this issue poses to assessing the causal effect of the TTP.

1.3 Data

To evaluate the effect of a policy, practitioners need information before and after its introduction. In the case of the TTP, the ideal dataset would consist of the universe of students who graduated from Texas public high schools before and after 1997. The more years available for each pre- and post-treatment period, the better. In particular, data availability for several years after the policy took place allows the assessment of the policy's short and long-term effects. Moreover, information on students for several years before the implementation of the policy provides a solid benchmark and accounts for potential confounders. For instance, if some other policy was implemented the year before the TTP, its impact could be underestimated.

To estimate the effect of the TTP, the ideal dataset set will comprehend information on class rank or high school GPA before and after this educational policy took place. This way, we would identify the pulled in and pushed out students, along with the students serving as a control group. Furthermore, since the objective is to assess the effect on education and labor market outcomes, the ideal dataset will comprehend information on them as well.

The available data usually differs from the ideal one, which poses a significant challenge in assessing the effect of policies. In this case, the main data limitation is that the student's class rank was not measured in the statewide pre-TTP data and only limited information is available after TTP. Thus, the authors can not deterministically identify the pulled in and pushed out students. We now turn to describe the data available to the authors for estimating the impact of the TTP, and how they circumvent not observing the ideal one.

The authors draw from administrative data covering the entire State of Texas, which consists of students who graduated from Texas public high schools between 1996 and 2002 for whom they have grade scores in the TAAS. This is a standardized test constituting the Texas high school exit exam, which is taken in 10th grade. It is offered several times, so that students failing the test or being absent when it is taken, could re-take the exam at later dates.[3] The main limitation of the available data is that before the TTP took place, data on class rank were not systematically collected. However, beginning with the graduating class of 1999, they observe for each student

[3] The authors use the student's first recorded score.

who applied to any Texas public higher education institution whether he/she was in the top ten percent of his/her high school class. The authors exploit this information to impute each student's probability of being in the top ten percent, before and after TTP, regardless of whether he or she applied to college (a thorough discussion of the imputation method is presented in the Empirical Approach section).

The available data also contains information on college enrollment in the year after high school graduation, college completion, and labor market outcomes. For the first measure, the authors distinguish between community colleges, four-year campuses, and the two most selective campuses, i.e., Texas A&M and UT Austin. College completion is measured as whether an individual graduated with a bachelor's degree from a Texas public institution within six years of high school graduation, and attainment of a bachelor's degree in a scientific (STEM) field. Finally, the data includes information on earnings nine to eleven calendar years after high school graduation, at ages roughly 27 to 29, as well as thirteen to fifteen years after graduation. They also have access to a variable indicating whether each individual ever appears on the data, which accounts for long-term unemployment and absence from the state. Andrews et al. (2020) find that, in Texas, wages of students who leave the state are not systematically different from students who do not. Thus, not observing income for students leaving Texas does not entail a concern for the validity of the results.

1.4 Empirical Approach

To estimate τ_t^{PI} and τ_t^{PO} simultaneously, we can run the following linear regression

$$\begin{aligned} Y_{i,t} = {} & \beta_0 + \beta_1 \text{PulledIn}_{i,t} + \beta_2 \text{PushedOut}_{i,t} + \beta_3 \text{PulledIn}_{i,t} \times \text{Post}_{i,t} \\ & + \beta_4 \text{PushedOut}_{i,t} \times \text{Post}_{i,t} \\ & + Z_{i,t}\theta + \delta_t + \epsilon_{i,t}, \quad \mathbb{E}\big[\epsilon_{i,t} | Z_{i,t}, \text{PulledIn}_{i,t}, \text{PushedOut}_{i,t}\big] = 0, \end{aligned} \tag{11}$$

where $Z_{i,t}$ is a vector of individual characteristics, $\text{Post}_{i,t}$ is an indicator for the cohorts affected by TPP, from 1998 onward, δ_t are year-fixed effects, and $\epsilon_{i,t}$ is an idiosyncratic shock. The rationale to control for Z_{it} in the regression is that some students could be pulled it because of factors such as race, gender, or ethnicity. Thus, if we do not include them, $\text{PushedOut}_{i,t}$ could be correlated with the unobserved component (idiosyncratic shock), entailing misleading (biased) estimates for the causal effects. Furthermore, the inclusion of covariates helps to estimate the causal effects more precisely (reducing the estimates' variance). On the other hand, the year-fixed effects are included to account for potential events that could affect the outcomes of the treatment and control groups, avoiding over- or under-estimating the causal effects of the TTP. Finally, the variable $\text{Post}_{i,t}$ enables us to identify the causal effects for a given t. We now turn to illustrate how the parameters of interest relate to Fig. 2, to motivate their inclusion.

Consider the hypothetical case in which there were no pushed out students by the TTP, and the students' characteristics do not affect their treatment status. Furthermore, we are only interested in the causal effect for the year 2002. This way, Eq. (11) boils down to

$$\begin{aligned} Y_{i,t} = \beta_0 + \delta_{2002} + \beta_1 \text{PulledIn}_{i,t} + \beta_3 \text{PulledIn}_{i,t} \times \text{Post}_{i,t} \\ + \epsilon_{i,t}, \quad \mathbb{E}\left[\epsilon_{i,t} | \text{PulledIn}_{i,t}\right] = 0. \end{aligned} \tag{12}$$

To map the parameters in Eq. (12) to the elements in Fig. 2, consider evaluating Eq. (12) in the following cases:

$$\begin{aligned} A &= \mathbb{E}\left[Y^{PI}_{i,2002}(1) | \text{PulledIn}_{i,t} = 1\right] = \beta_0 + \delta_{2002} + \beta_1 + \beta_3 \\ C &= \mathbb{E}\left[Y_{i,2002} | \text{PulledIn}_{i,t} = 0\right] = \beta_0 + \delta_{2002} \\ D &= \mathbb{E}\left[Y_{i,1996} | \text{PulledIn}_{i,t} = 1\right] = \beta_0 + \beta_1 \\ E &= \mathbb{E}\left[Y_{i,1996} | \text{PulledIn}_{i,t} = 0\right] = \beta_0. \end{aligned}$$

The constant β_0 captures common characteristics of the individuals in the sample and corresponds to point E in Fig. 2. By subtracting E from C, we get δ_t, which estimates the outcome trend for the control group, corresponding to the solid green line in Fig. 2. Conversely, β_1 estimates the difference in outcomes of the baseline period (1996), which is D-E in Fig. 2). Finally, β_3 estimates the causal effect of the policy, which is A-B, or equivalently A-(C+(D-E)) under the parallel trends assumption. Thus, the parameters β_3 and β_4 in Eq. (11) estimate τ_t^{PI} and τ_t^{PO}, respectively. Motivated by Eqs. (9) and (9), β_3 and β_4 are called difference-in-differences estimators, because they estimate the causal effects as the difference in differences of the outcomes for the treatment and control groups.

The main challenge in estimating Eq. (11) is that the authors do not identify which students were pulled in and pushed out by the policy, so that $\text{PulledIn}_{i,t}$ and $\text{PushedOut}_{i,t}$ are unobserved. Accordingly, the authors adopt a three-step procedure to estimate the effects of the TTP. First, they estimate the likelihood that each student is in the top 10 percent of his or her high school class. Subsequently, they define the tree comparison groups (pulled in, pushed out, and control group) based on this likelihood. Finally, they estimate Eq. (11) using the treatment status imputed in the previous step.

The limitation of this three step procedure is that the interpretation of the difference-in-difference estimators is not causal. The estimated Pulled In and Pushed Out indicators are imperfect proxies for the groups affected by TTP. In particular, they both include some students who were eligible for TTP guaranteed admission and some who were not. Furthermore, the estimated treatment groups also include students who would have been admitted to UT under both the pre-TTP and post-TTP admissions rules. Consequently, the estimates of β_3 and β_4 in their setting can be interpreted as the intention-to-treat (ITT) estimates of the effect of changes in access to selective colleges.

We now describe the three-step procedure and illustrate the concept of intention-to-treat and its relationship with the average treatment on the treated in Eqs. (3) and (4).

1.5 First Step

The purpose of this step is to estimate the probability of each student being in the top ten percent of their high school. Let W be an indicator for a student from the 1999–2002 cohorts who applied to at least one public college in Texas, and $T = 1(r > 0.9)$ an indicator for being in the top ten percent of the high school class. The main data limitation is that only T is observed for the $W = 1$ subsample. Finally, let X be a vector of student characteristics, that includes characteristics that are measured consistently throughout our sample period, which include (i) TAAS exit exam scores in reading, writing, and math, measured both in statewide percentiles and as the percentile within the school; (ii) indicators for math and science course-taking (e.g., advanced math in 11th grade); (iii) the number of foreign language courses taken in high school; (iv) the number of courses failed in high school; (v) the number and percentage of school days absent in 12th grade; (vi) an indicator for being 18 upon graduation; (vii) the school's racial, gender, and socioeconomic (free & reduced-price lunch) composition; and (viii) the share of students at the school who are classified as special education.

We want to estimate the probability[4] of being in the top 10 percent of an individual's high school given student characteristics

$$p(T = 1|X) = \mathbb{E}[T|X]. \tag{13}$$

As we mentioned earlier, reliable assumptions are what allow us to learn from the data. To impute (estimate) the conditional probability of being in the top 10 percent of an individual's high school, the authors assume that conditional on X, T is independent of W. That is, once we have taken into account student characteristics, applying to at least one public college in Texas is independent of whether the student was in the top ten percent of her high school. In doing so, we have

$$\mathbb{E}[T|X] = \mathbb{E}[T|X, W = 1].$$

This equation tells us that we can estimate the probability in Eq. (13) for the whole sample, using only the subsample of students from the 1999–2002 cohorts who applied to at least one public college in Texas.

Differences between applicants and non-applicants in the relationship between covariates and top 10 status would violate the assumption that conditional on X, T is

[4] Since T is a binomial variable, the probability of its occurrence equals its expected value.

independent of W. However, the authors argue that the evidence in Long and Tienda (2008) supports the validity of this assumption.

To estimate $\mathbb{E}[T|X, W = 1]$ the authors perform Random Forest Classification. The main appeal of this approach is allowing for non-linearities and interactions between student characteristics while reducing overfitting.[5]

After estimating the conditional probability of being in the top ten percent, the authors find that 23 percent of students have zero predicted probability of being in the top 10 percent of their high school. Accordingly, they construct a variable $\hat{q}$ that takes 40 different values. In particular $\hat{q}_{it} = 1$ if $\hat{p}_{it}(T_{it} = 1|X_{it}) \leq 0.23$, $\hat{q}_{it} = 12$ if $0.23 < \hat{p}_{it}(T_{it} = 1|X_{it}) \leq 0.24$, and the remaining 38 value are assigned according to sets of two percent of the sample, e.g., $\hat{q}_{it} = 13$ if $0.24 < \hat{p}_{it}(T_{it} = 1|X_{it}) \leq 0.26$,..., $\hat{q}_{it} = 50$ if $0.98 < \hat{p}_{it}(T_{it} = 1|X_{it}) \leq 1$.

1.6 Second Step

From the right panel in Fig. 1 we have that the treatment and control groups were defined according to the school rank and the school sending rate. The former object was estimated in the First Step, while the latter is measured as the share of students from each high school in the 1996 and 1997 (pre-TTP) cohorts who enrolled at UT Austin. Subsequently, high schools are categorized into deciles (s) according to their sending rate. Figure 3 depicts the share of students from schools in each decile attending UT Austin, pre- and post-TTP. While pre-TTP the bottom five deciles each send less than two percent of students, the top decile of schools sends thirteen percent of students to Austin. Even though post-TTP this pattern remains, the schools that previously sent few students to Austin send slightly more, while the share of students from the top-decile schools who attend Austin falls to eleven percent.

The authors use the estimated top-ten-percent probability categories from the First Step, and school sending rate deciles (s) to define the Pulled In, Pushed Out, and control groups. These three groups are defined according to the change in the sending rate of cells composed of ($\hat{q}$, s) pairs. In particular, any cell where the share attending UT Austin rose (fell) by more than 3 percentage points is included in the Pulled In (Pushed Out) group.[6] Thus, consistent with Fig. 1, the Pulled In students are those from schools with low s and high $\hat{q}$ (top-ranked students), whose school sending rate increased post-TTP. Conversely, the Pulled Out groups consist of students whose school has high s and moderately high $\hat{q}$, that is, students with a moderate likelihood of being in their school's top decile. As regards the control group, the authors use two blocks of cells that are close the the treated groups but present small changes in

[5] In this framework, overfitting occurs when the top 10 status is almost perfectly classified for $W = 1$, so that the Random Forest would not make accurate predictions for the $W = 0$ (see Hawkins (2004) for an overview on overfitting).

[6] cells $\hat{q} = 50$, $s \geq 9$ are excluded from the Pulled In group, since they correspond to students in the top ten percent, attending "feeder" schools.

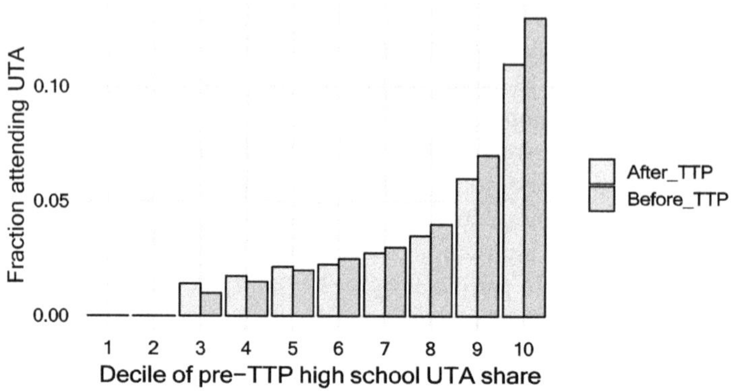

Fig. 3 Simulated histogram constructed to replicate the share of students from high school attending UT Austin, by school pre-TTP decile (s) in the dataset of Black et al. (2023)

the probability of enrollment at UT Austin. These two groups of cells are selected for $\hat{q} \in [25, 40]$, and $s \in [6, 8]$, and $\hat{q} \in [40, 45]$, and $s \in [3, 5]$.[7]

1.7 Third Step

The third step of the estimation approach consists of estimating Eq. (11) with the treatment status that was imputed in the Second Step. The treatment is defined in a multi-valued manner, which reflects each of the different colleges that students might attend, and that the TTP might affect it in complex ways. In some cases, the counterfactual of not being admitted to UT Austin is attending A&M, while for others it is a community college, a less selective UT campus, or no college at all. Furthermore, TTP may have affected students who do not attend UT Austin under either admissions policy, in their choices among other alternatives. For these reasons, along with the fact that the treatment status is not observed but imputed, the interpretation of β_3 and β_4 is not causal. Conversely, it can be interpreted as the intention-to-treat estimates of the effect of changes in access to selective colleges.

The intention-to-treat analysis considers every subject in the treatment and control groups ignoring noncompliance, protocol deviations, withdrawal, and anything that happens after the treatment status has been assigned (Gupta 2011). Accordingly, the setting to evaluate the TTP falls into this definition. Firstly, the imputed Pulled In and Pushed Out indicators are imperfect proxies for the groups affected by TTP. They both included some students who were eligible for TTP guaranteed admission and some who were not. Moreover, the estimated treatment groups also include students who would have been admitted to UT under both the pre-TTP and post-TTP admissions rules. Given their ITT interpretation, the estimated effect of the TTP will

[7] For a detailed selection of these three groups, see Fig. 2 in Black et al. (2023)

likely substantially understate the impact on students who were actually affected by TTP.

1.8 Main Results

Figure 4 reports the results of estimating Eq. (11) in an event study design. To study the dynamic effects of the TTP, the Post_{it} indicator is replaced with a set of Year_t indicators, where 1997 is the excluded category. This way, we can estimate β_3 and β_4 for different years. In Sect. 1 we discussed that the identifying assumption is the parallel trends. Notice that in every result in Fig. 4 the confidence intervals of estimates for 1996 cover the zero intercept. This lends evidence to the identifying assumption holding, as it suggests that the treated and control groups would have moved together absent the change in the admissions policy. Since in 1996, the TTP had not taken place yet, finding significant effects for the pulled in or pushed out would suggest that the parallel trend assumption does not hold. However, we find evidence it does.

The results suggest a positive effect on the pulled in students in educational and labor market outcomes, while the pulled out were only affected regarding enrollment at UT Austin. According to Fig. 4 pulled in students were more likely to enroll both at UT Austin and four-year colleges (see panels (a) and (b)). Furthermore, they were also more likely to have higher earnings 9-11 years after high school completion according to panel (e) in Fig. 4. In contrast, the authors find that Pushed Out students were less likely to enroll at UT Austin, meanwhile, the TTP did not have a significant effect on the remaining outcomes.

Table 1 reports the main results of estimating Eq. (11) for educational and labor market outcomes. According to column (1), we find that Pulled In students are 5.3 percentage points more likely to attend UT Austin due to the TTP, while there is no significant change in enrollment at Texas A&M. Moreover, these students are 6.6 percentage points more likely to attend a public four-year college in Texas. However, they are no more likely to enroll in community college. Finally, Pulled In students are 5.2 percentage points more likely to attend any college. It could have been that some students switched from no college to community college, and some others switched from community college to UT Austin. In any case, the results suggest that Pulled In students in the sample were more likely to enroll in college and more likely to attend UT.

Column (2) in Table 1 reports the results for Pushed Out students. After the TTP, these students were 3.6 percentage points less likely to enroll at UT Austin. However, such a decrease was compensated by a 2.2 percentage point increase in enrollment at other four-year schools, and a 1.1 percentage point increase in enrollment at community colleges. Meanwhile, both the net effect on total four-year enrollment and college enrollment overall is statistically insignificant.

Pulled In students were 3.9 percentage points more likely to graduate with a BA from UT Austin within 6 years after high school graduation relative to control

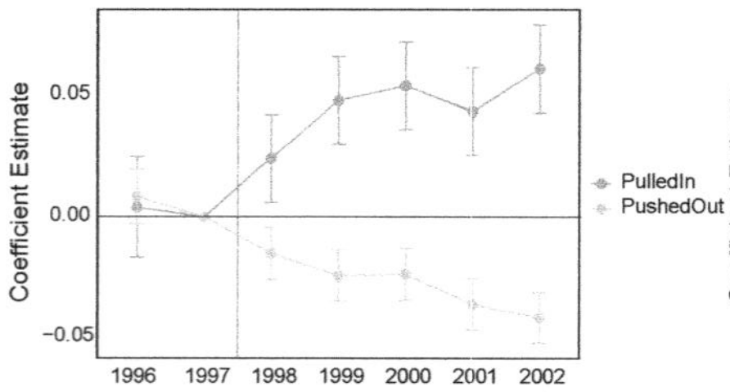

(a) UT Austin enrollment

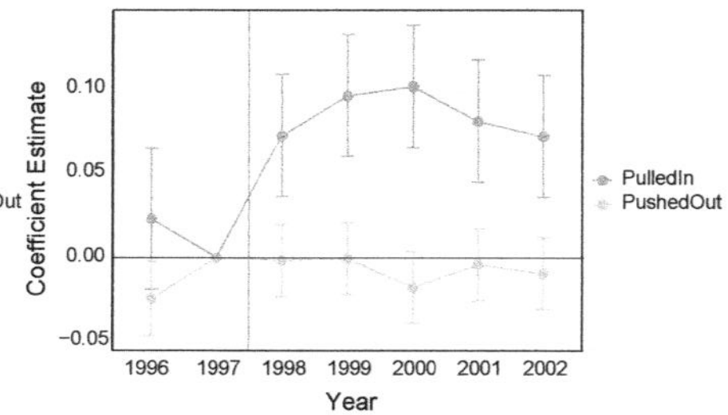

(b) 4-year college enrollment

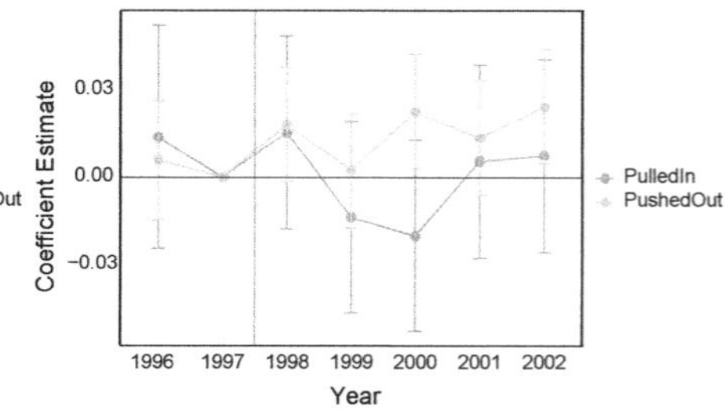

(c) 2-year college enrollment for students in Pulled In and Pushed Out groups

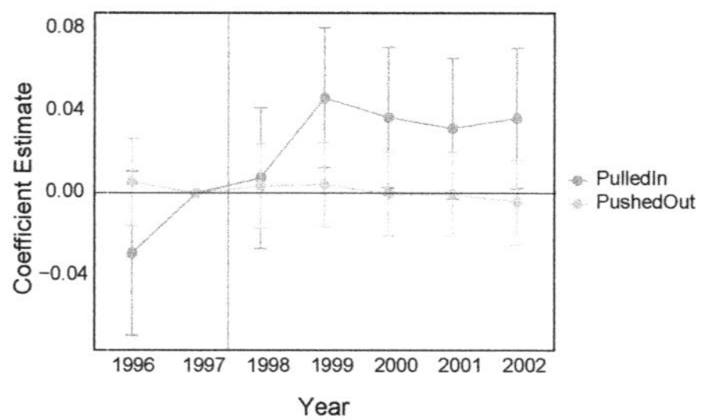

(d) college completion (BA attainment)

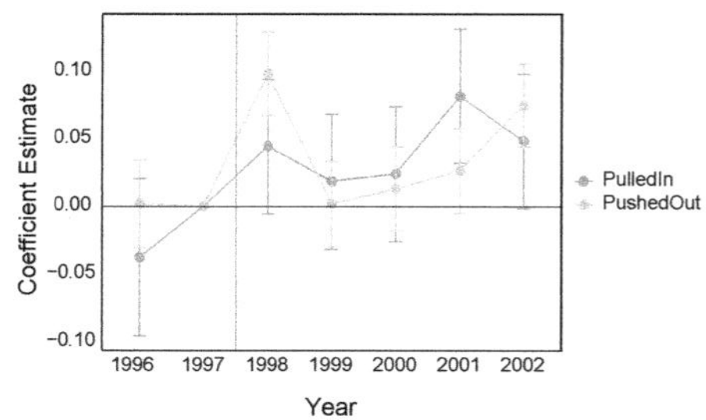

(e) earnings 9-11 years after high school completion

Fig. 4 Simulated event study constructed to replicate key results from Black et al. (2023). *Note* Figures show point estimates and 95% confidence intervals for simulated data corresponding to β_3 and β_4 interactions in an event study version of Equation (11) that replaces the Post_{it} indicator with a set of Year_t indicators, where 1997 is the excluded category

Table 1 Baseline difference-in-difference analysis

	Pulled in	Pushed out
	(1)	(2)
Enrollment outcomes		
UT Austin	0.053	–0.036
	(0.005)	(0.004)
Texas A&M	–0.010	0.008
	(0.007)	(0.004)
Any college	0.052	0.000
	(0.011)	(0.007)
Any 4-year	0.066	–0.005
	(0.011)	(0.008)
Any community college	–0.004	0.011
	(0.008)	(0.005)
Any other 4-year	0.024	0.022
	(0.009)	(0.006)
Degree attainment within 6 years		
Bachelors from UT Austin	0.039	–0.021
	(0.004)	(0.003)
Bachelors from any institution	0.037	–0.001
	(0.010)	(0.006)
Associates or better	0.032	–0.006
	(0.010)	(0.007)
Bachelors with STEM major	–0.007	–0.001
	(0.006)	(0.003)

Note Results taken from Table 3 in Black et al. (2023)

students. Regarding any four-year college in Texas, this number was 3.7 percentage points. Conversely, the Pushed Out students were 2.1 percentage points less likely to graduate with a BA from UT Austin within 6 years after high school graduation relative to control students. However, the effect on bachelors from any institution was non-significant.

In summary, the authors find that Pulled In students were more likely to attend UT Austin and different four-year universities, were also more likely to graduate from college, and had either equal or higher earnings after the TTP. Furthermore, they find that the Pushed Out students were not substantially harmed. Even though these students were less likely to enroll at UT Austin, this was compensated by enrollment in other four-year schools and community colleges.

2 The Effect of School-Starting-Age Rule on Educational Outcomes

Evaluating the impact of educational policies, such as school-starting age (SSA) is not an easy task, especially when we are interested in establishing causality rather than mere correlation. Determining whether starting school at an older age leads to improved academic performance requires a robust method that separates this factor from other potential influences on educational outcomes. In this section, we utilize a regression discontinuity design to estimate the causal effect of school-starting-age rules on educational outcomes for two countries, Austria (OECD) and the United Arab Emirates (non-OECD). For this purpose, we use the PISA dataset for the period 2015-2022. A detailed step-by-step guide to reproduce the results is available in the replication file, available at https://doi.org/10.1007/978-3-031-90911-5_3.

Regression discontinuity design (RDD) is a quasi-experimental approach that allows researchers to identify causal effects by exploiting cutoffs or thresholds (see Chap. Empirical Methods: A Brief Introduction to Causal Inference). These cutoffs may occur naturally or be enforced by policies, such as age-based enrollment rules. This section offers comprehensive guidelines on applying RDD in the context of educational policy analysis.

The identifying assumption in our framework is that a substantial discontinuity jump in the average enrollment age for a given month and country is exogenous. Consequently, we suggest implementing a fuzzy regression discontinuity design to address the threat of endogeneity caused by omitted variable bias. Such a threat arises here due to unobservable factors, i.e., determinants of school entry decisions that may affect the outcomes among children who start school at different ages, such as red-shirting and strategic birth timing.

Our results suggest a positive effect of starting school at an older age on standardized test scores in reading and math, though this effect is not uniform across countries or survey waves. In Austria, individuals who are older when they start school get on average better test scores in both reading and math disciplines when considering the 2018 wave and when pooling data across all waves (2015, 2018, and 2022). Similarly, in the combined sample of Austria and the United Arab Emirates (U.A.E.), significant positive effects are also observed only in the 2018 wave and in the pooled analysis. This contrast highlights country-specific differences in the impact of school-starting age on educational outcomes.

2.1 Motivation: RDD in the Context of Educational Policies

Educational policies often involve eligibility criteria based on arbitrary thresholds, which makes them well-suited for RDD analysis. However, one must be very careful with the caveats and the limitations that the specific context may have. For this, we propose the following framework as an example of application: school-starting-age policy.

In many countries, there are specific cutoff dates for children to start school. In our setup, we use August 31st as the cutoff date. For example, if a child's birthday is just before the cutoff date, they have to wait an extra year to start school. But if their birthday is just after the cutoff, they can start right away. This situation creates a natural experiment where students born just before and after the cutoff are likely similar in observable and unobservable characteristics, except for their school-starting age.

In the proposed application, we evaluate the causal effect of school-starting-age (SSA) rules on educational attainment. For this purpose, we use PISA data from 2015 to 2022 for a selection of one OECD country, i.e., Austria, and one non-OECD country, i.e., United Arab Emirates. Based on documented starting age criteria PIRLS (2022) and empirical evidence, we choose these countries since they exhibit a substantial jump in the average enrollment age for a given month.

In this context, we can estimate the causal effect of starting school at an older age by comparing educational outcomes in our case, standardized test scores of students born just before and just after the cutoff date (e.g., August vs. September). However, this can be done under certain assumptions that will be discussed later. Therefore, the cutoff date serves as an exogenous factor, unaffected by individual characteristics or choices, since birthdate is random enough. This allows for isolating the effect of school-starting age on outcomes, providing a rigorous identification strategy for policy analysis.

2.2 Data

For our analysis, we use data from the 2015, 2018, and 2022 PISA waves. They contain individual-level information on educational variables, along with individual characteristics. Our main dependent variables consist of educational outcomes measured by standardized test scores in mathematics and reading. Furthermore, we also consider being a repeater (variable that takes value 1 if the individual i has repeated a grade at least once, and 0 otherwise) as an outcome variable to evaluate the effect of starting school age in the likelihood of being a repeater. We exploit the role of the socio-demographic characteristics to mitigate the threat of endogeneity. We have information on age, gender, family structure, migration, whether the student has repeated or not, educational and labor expectations, parents' occupations, home possessions, and index of socioeconomic and cultural status.

The rationale for using the PISA dataset arises from the fact that it intends to evaluate the acquisition of important knowledge and skills required for adult life, rather than the mastery of the school curriculum (Schleicher and Tamassia 2000). Therefore, their measuring approach for educational attainment is informative about the ability to use the school knowledge in real-life challenges (Fuchs and Wößmann 2008). As regards the dependent variables, we rely on plausible values for the scores in math and reading to measure performance. The so-called plausible values are generated through multiple imputations based on pupils' answers to the subset of test questions they were randomly assigned and their responses to the background questionnaires. The analysis of such plausible values is a bit more complicated, but for illustration purposes, we take the average score per student on each domain (mathematics and reading) as an outcome variable for the analysis based on the sampling weights available in the data. Notice that the PISA dataset is based on a sample, and not on the whole population of 15-year-olds, therefore we must use the provided sampling weights. Moreover, in the context of PISA, there is no theoretical minimum or maximum score. Instead, the outcomes are standardized to align with approximately normal distributions, with mean scores hovering around 500 points and standard deviations of approximately 100 points.

Our objective is to evaluate the causal effect of SSA rules on educational attainment. Our identification strategy relies on the presence of a discontinuity jump in the average enrollment age for a given month. Consequently, our analysis must be based solely on countries with a clear school-starting rule which depicts a discontinuity jump in the data. Following Oosterbeek et al. (2021),[8] we report in Fig. 5 the discontinuity at the cutoff month. It is worth noting that if children were born after this month, they must wait for the next year to start primary school. The cutoff month is August-September. Notice that both countries exhibit a substantial discontinuity jump in the average SSA around the cutoff date. Furthermore, we exploit the fact that countries vary substantially in their educational systems to evaluate how our estimation procedure performs.

In Fig. 5, we report both the average for relevant ages and for all ages. The relevant ages are those that might impede a student from starting school. That is, if the cutoff point is six years,[9] then the only relevant children for identification purposes are aged either six or seven. Accordingly, calculating the weighted average age including all ages, might introduce noise in the average age. Fortunately, we do not see systematical changes in the selected countries.

We document variation in math and reading scores between countries in Fig. 6 and within countries in Fig. 7 over time. Figure 6 suggests that between-country differences in math and reading scores between Austria and the U.A.E. are persistent across deciles, with Austria consistently outperforming the U.A.E. in all waves. Moreover, such differences are systematic across the student distribution. That is, they are maintained across deciles. This suggests that (i) the highest-performing students in Austria achieve better scores than their counterparts in the U.A.E. across all deciles, and (ii) the lowest-performing students in the U.A.E. score lower than

[8] Our analysis is slightly different because we miss the days of birth, which is an important constraint in the data to bear in mind. The constraint is that the running variable will be no longer continuous but discrete. Further analysis will be conducted in the next steps.

[9] For Austria and U.A.E., it is compulsory to start school from the first day of September following their sixth birthday.

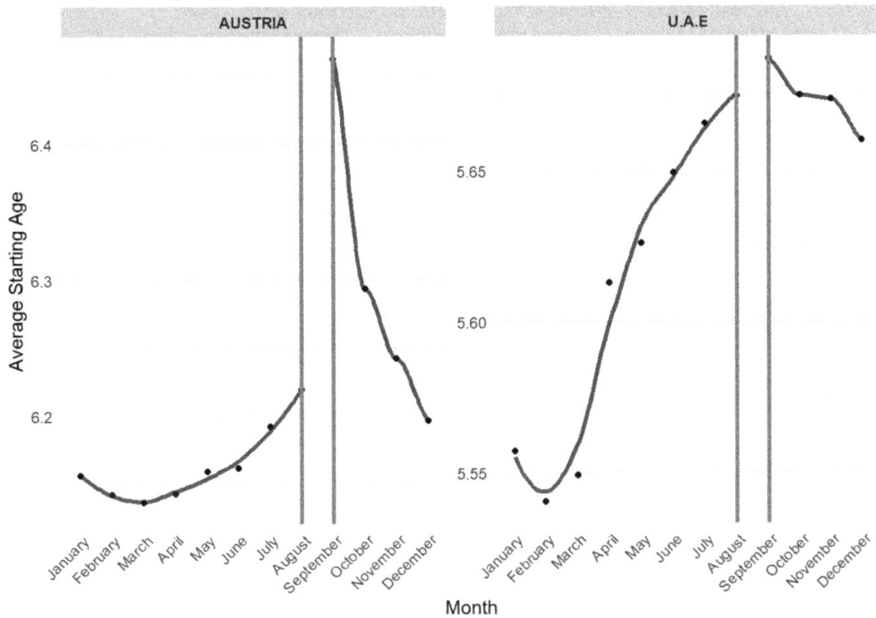

Fig. 5 Discontinuity at the cutoff

the lowest-performing students in Austria. In summary, a student from the U.A.E. is likely to have lower average test scores than a student from Austria within the same decile, regardless of the decile. On the other hand, Fig. 7, highlights how student performance has evolved over time within each country. In Austria, Math performance peaked in 2018 but declined by 2022, while Reading scores remained stable across all years. In contrast, the UAE saw consistent improvements in Math, with 2022 scores highest overall; however, gains were concentrated among students above the 4th decile. For Reading, UAE students below the 7th decile performed best in 2015, with little change over time among higher-performing students.

To assess variation in outcomes within countries, Fig. 8 shows the variation in outcomes (test scores) across different regions within countries. As one can see, there exists substantial variation in outcomes displayed by years, with the number of outliers either increasing or decreasing over time. This variation is important for several reasons. First, it highlights regional disparities within countries that might not be apparent when looking at national averages. Understanding these differences can help target interventions where students are most disadvantaged. Second, it provides valuable insight into how different regions or localities respond to the same national education policies, helping policymakers assess the effectiveness of reforms in specific contexts. Third, this variation underscores the need for tailored solutions rather than a one-size-fits-all approach, as educational needs may differ significantly

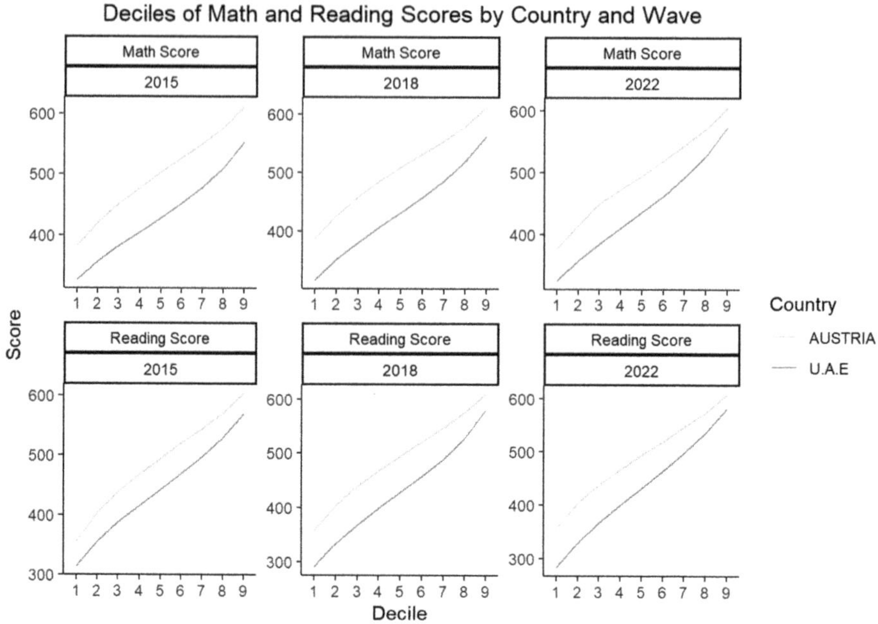

Fig. 6 Trend of test scores over time by countries

within a single country. However, in this exercise, we do not propose a policy evaluation, but a mere illustration of how starting school at a later age affects academic performance using a methodology that allows us to obtain causal estimates.

To identify the factors that contribute to these variations, Fig. 9 shows the differences between children with highly educated parents and those with low-educated parents. As expected, children with highly educated parents tend to perform better on average than children with low-educated parents. This finding, consistent with existing literature (Dubow et al. 2009), suggests that parental education plays a significant role in shaping educational outcomes. By incorporating this dimension into our analysis, we can better understand how family background contributes to the observed within-country variation.

Analyzing variation in outcomes within countries helps capture the influence of other demographic and socioeconomic factors. Alongside parental education, issues such as regional poverty levels, access to educational resources, and school quality all contribute to differences in outcomes. Regions with lower scores may face these cumulative challenges, which are often hidden when considering national averages alone.

In sum, understanding this variation allows for more precise, data-driven decisions. Regarding the relationship between SSA and test scores, our findings reveal a negative correlation between SSA and test scores, as presented in Fig. 10. On the left panel of Fig. 10, we find raw test scores, and on the right panel, we find standardized test scores, which will be our outcome variable. Moreover, to enhance the

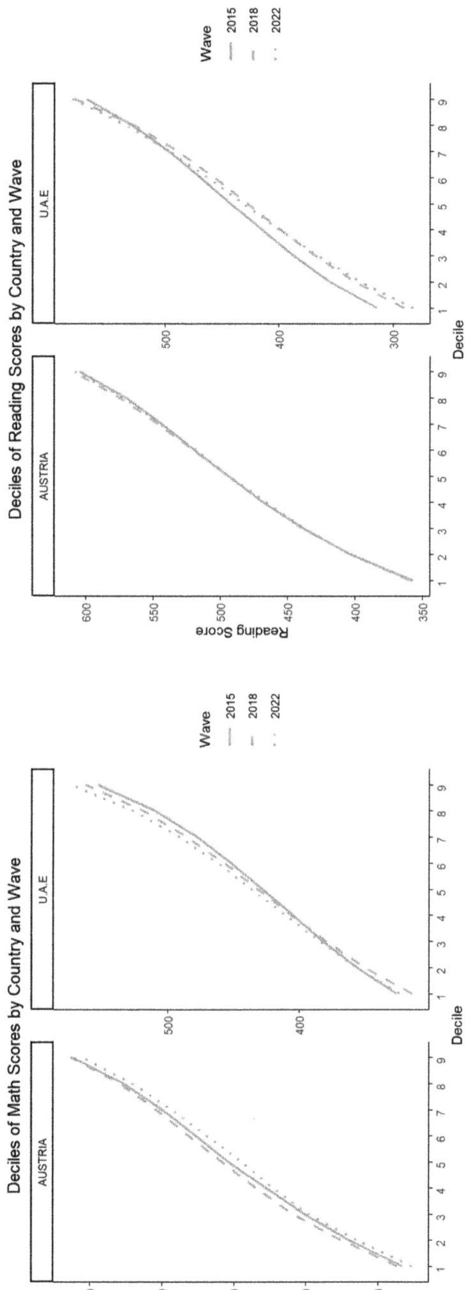

Fig. 7 Trend of test scores over time within countries

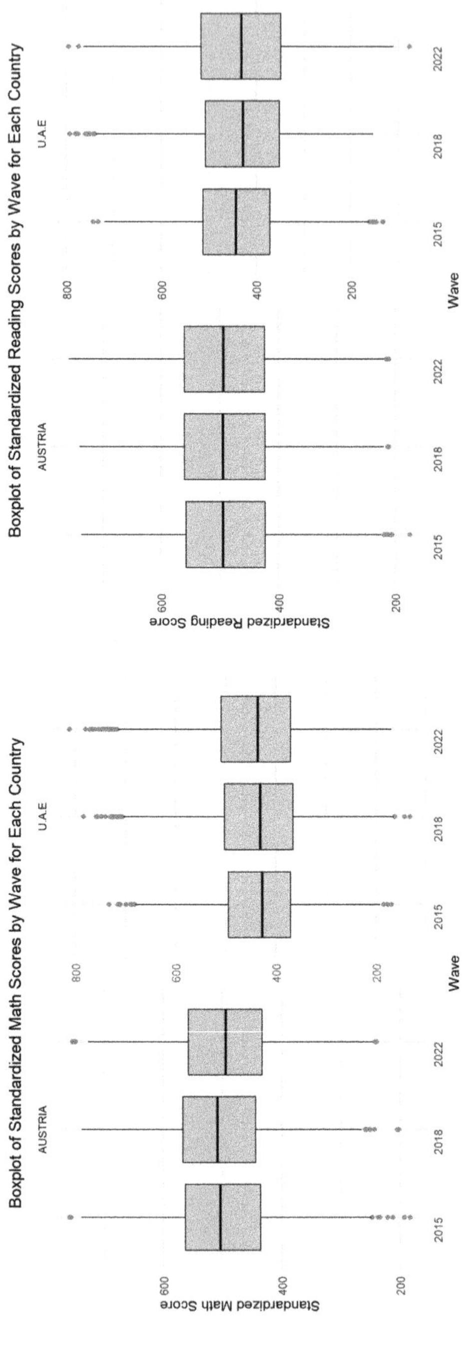

Fig. 8 Variation within countries

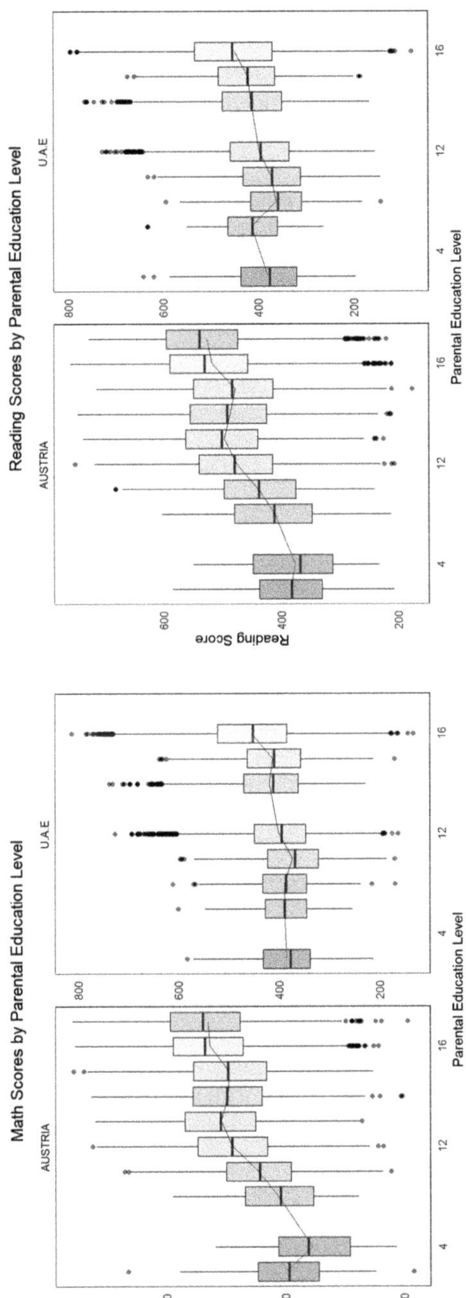

Fig. 9 Intergenerational mobility

comprehensiveness of our analysis, we considered the characteristics of students to assess the reliability of our correlation. This correlation suggests that students who start their academic journey at a later age tend to exhibit inferior performance in both math and reading. Our findings are in alignment with the existing literature, which emphasizes the significance of personal attributes (Van Bragt et al. 2011; Phelps 2006; Matthews et al. 2003). However, it is crucial to note that this correlation does not necessarily imply causation.

Moreover, we also provide further insight into the average starting age of schooling across countries and time. Specifically, Table 2 displays the average schooling starting age for each country in each wave. The results confirm our earlier findings and substantiate the average SSA of the country group as 6, making reasonable the choice of the cutoff playing a key role in the choice of the cutoff. Thus, we are comparing children who started school at the age of 6.

2.3 *Understanding the Regression Discontinuity Design Framework*

As previously introduced, the Regression Discontinuity Design is a quasi-experimental approach that uses cutoff-based rules to identify causal effects. In this context, we have to introduce a key concept: the *"running variable*". The running variable, denoted by Z, determines who gets the treatment (starting school) or not based on a cutoff. Usually, this variable is continuous. However, we will present a case in which the running variable is discrete. The idea behind this is to compare individuals just below and just above the cutoff, assuming that these observations are comparable except for their treatment status. In our exercise, individuals who were born in August and in September share the features to be compared, but their treatment statuses are completely different.

Broadly speaking, we can differentiate two types of RDD designs: sharp RDD and fuzzy RDD. In plain words, in a sharp RDD context, the treatment is perfectly determined by whether the running variable exceeds the cutoff or not. In our context, imagine that a student, Pepe, is born after August 31st. In his case, Pepe must start school the following year. Here, the assignment to treatment (e.g., delayed school entry) is a deterministic function of the running variable (birthdate).

On the other hand, we have the fuzzy RDD. As self-explanatory as it might seem, in this case, the probability of receiving the treatment is no longer perfectly determined by the cutoff (i.e., either 1 or 0), but it changes discontinuously at the cutoff. In our situation, imagine that Pepe's parents decide that Pepe is not starting school this year but the following (e.g., some parents delay their child's school start even if they qualify). In this case, there is partial compliance or exceptions, resulting in not all children who qualify starting school at the designated time.

In our example, our selection rule allows us to exploit such discontinuity jump to identify the causal effect of SSA rules on test scores. We employ a quasi-experimental

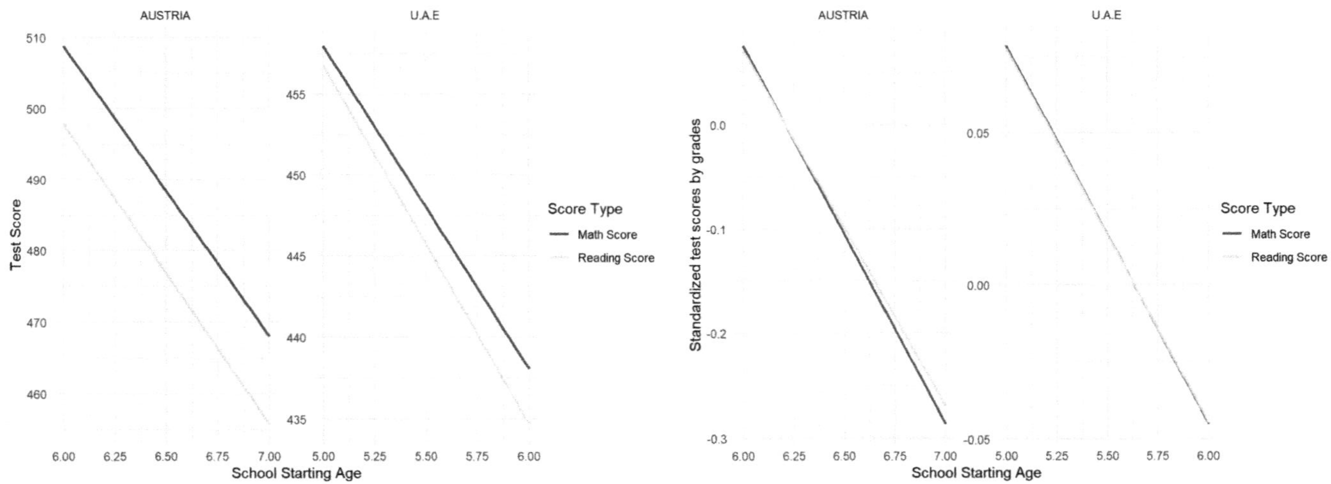

Fig. 10 Correlation between school-starting age and test scores

Table 2 Average school starting age by countries and waves

Country	2015	2018	2022
Austria	6.20	6.23	6.19
U.A.E.	5.59	5.65	5.65

approach implementing a fuzzy regression discontinuity design (Lee and Lemieux 2010) to address the threat of endogeneity caused by omitted variable bias. Such a threat arises here due to unobservable factors, i.e., determinants of school entry decisions that may affect the outcomes among children who start school at different ages, such as red-shirting (Dhuey et al. 2019) and strategic birth timing (Buckles and Hungerman 2013).

In particular, we exploit the exogeneity of the month of birth to elicit causal effects. Specifically, we aim to explore the differences in performance between individuals born in September, who are the eldest in their cohort, and those born in August, who are the youngest. We assume that there exists a linear association between an individual's outcome variable, designated by y_{it}, and their birth month, D_i, within a given cohort t:

$$y_{it} = \alpha_t + \tau D_i + \epsilon_{it}, \mathbb{E}[\epsilon_{it} D_i] = 0, \tag{14}$$

where ϵ_{it} is the unobserved component determining the test results orthogonal to the birth month, which gives rise to our first assumption.

Assumption 1

$$\mathbb{E}[\epsilon_{it} D_i] = 0. \tag{15}$$

Our parameter of interest is captured by τ and α_t denotes birth cohort fixed effects, with cohorts centered around August 31st. In particular, we consider a fuzzy regression discontinuity (RD) strategy that relies on birth dates.[10]

Before proceeding further, we just mentioned that RDD can provide a causal estimate under certain conditions. Let's see what are these and how they apply to our case:

- **Continuity Assumption:** Individuals just below and just above the cutoff are assumed to be similar in both observed and unobserved characteristics. This implies that any discontinuity in the outcome variable at the cutoff can be attributed to the causal effect of the treatment rather than pre-existing differences between the groups. In our case, we compare (within countries) students just below the threshold (being the youngest and therefore born in August) with students just above the threshold (being the oldest and therefore born in September). It seems reasonable to think that any jump in the outcome around that threshold is due to being born in either August or September. Assumption 2 ensures that there

[10] The probability of being treated depends on crossing the threshold, albeit it is not the only determinant.

is a clear discontinuity in the probability of receiving treatment at the threshold.
Assumption 2

$$\lim_{z \to z_0^+} Pr(D = 1|Z = z) \neq \lim_{z \to z_0^-} Pr(D = 1|Z = z) \tag{16}$$

$$Pr(D_i = 1|Z_i) = \begin{cases} g_1(Z) \text{ if } Z_i \geq z_0 \\ g_0(Z) \text{ if } Z_i < z_0 \end{cases}$$

The key assumption is that individuals right above and below z_0 are comparable since only the random variation is the reason why someone is put above z_0 or below, generating differences in treatment. As aforementioned, any difference in the outcome Y right at z_0 is due to treatment. Assumption 3 formalizes this requirement by stating that the distribution of potential outcomes should be continuous at the threshold. The RD design entails discontinuity in treatment assignment but continuity in potential outcomes.

Assumption 3

$$\lim_{z \to z_0^+} Pr(Y_j \leq r|Z = z) = \lim_{z \to z_0^-} Pr(Y_j \leq r|Z = z) \tag{17}$$

- **No Manipulation of the Running Variable**: The running variable (e.g., birthdate) should not be manipulated in anticipation of the treatment. For example, in the context of school enrollment rules, parents should not time births to ensure their child qualifies or not. If manipulation occurs, it can lead to biased estimates. In this case, the discontinuity arises due to arbitrary selection criteria used for school admissions. Hence the identification of average treatment only requires that there are no manipulation of running variables near the cutoff. In this framework, the discontinuity arises due to arbitrary selection criteria used for school admissions. We confirm no manipulation of the running variable using Fig. 11. Nevertheless, one may argue that the histogram is not uniform enough, implying a jump around the cutoff (month 0) for some cases. Since this is the number of students born either in August (month -1) or in September (month 0), this would imply that parents have some sort of strategical timing within a year when they decide to get pregnant, and this is unlikely since the process of getting pregnant is somewhat random. Accordingly, we assume that there is no manipulation of the running variable. However, one should notice that the inclusion of additional variables can cause downstream effects and cause issues in the estimation of the average treatment effect.
- **Local Randomization:** Near the cutoff, the treatment assignment is effectively random. Individuals just below and above the threshold should not differ systematically in other characteristics that might affect the outcome.

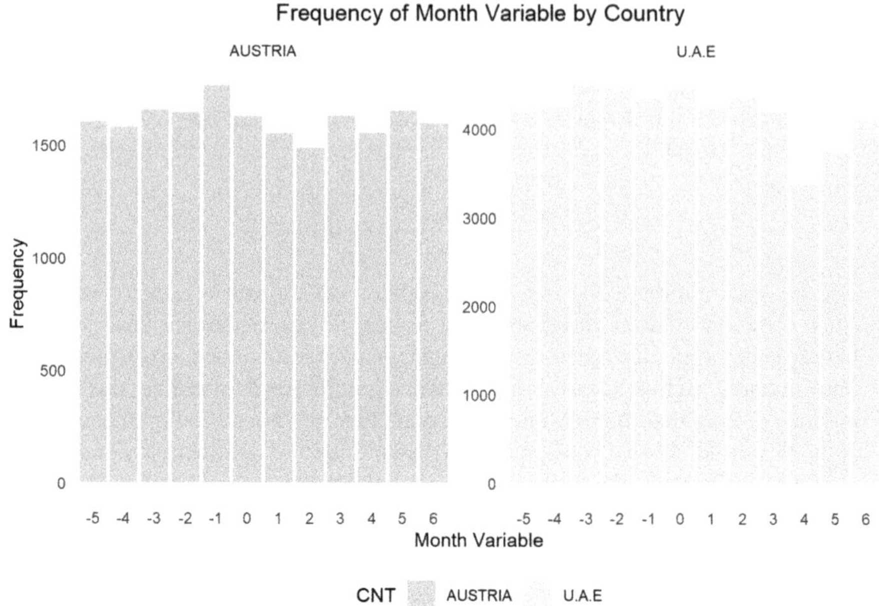

Fig. 11 Distribution of running variable near the cutoff for selected countries

The main identification strategy[11] is that individuals in the small neighborhood of the cutoff value will be similar to a randomized experiment at the cutoff point because they essentially have the same value of Z. Thus, a comparison of the average value of Y of those just above and below the cutoff z_0 will produce an estimate of the causal effect. An important limitation is that increasing the interval around the cutoff will bias the estimate of the treatment effect. In this application, individuals in the small neighborhood of the cutoff value (that is, being born close to 31st August) will be similar. Thus, a comparison of the average value of test scores of those just above and below (being born either before or after 31st August and therefore allocated in one course or another) will produce an estimate of the causal effect.

The rule used for students to present the PISA is the same for all countries: PISA sample represents all students between the age of 15 years and 3 months and 16 years and 2 months, and who are enrolled in an educational institution at grade 7 or higher, minus those that are excluded (OECD 2023). Thus, it does not matter in which academic course students are allocated but their age when taking the exam. However, there are three different effects regarding age and educational performance: *age-at-the-test*, *school-starting age*, and the *years of schooling at the time of the test.*

[11] The identification strategy allows us to elicit causal effects. In plain words, researchers use it to figure out if a relationship between two things is real or just coincidental. In our context, we figure out if X (age of school-starting) causes Y (better educational outcomes) without being fooled by other factors (like talent).

According to Avvisati and Givord (2021), in principle, it is not possible to disentangle these effects separately in a longitudinal study as PISA.

Since our goal is to isolate the impact of the age at which schooling starts, we need to control for the effects of both the age when taking the test and the years of schooling completed at the time of the test. In this regard, regression discontinuity is employed to address the effect of age when taking the test because we are comparing students whose ages on the test are less than one month apart. However, precisely because those in September start schooling when they are one year older than those born in August, they have one less year of schooling when taking the PISA test. Thus, in the RDD that we employ,[12] we cannot separate the effect of school-starting age from the effect of one more year of schooling. On this matter, to control for the effect of years of schooling, we standardize the PISA score by the grade in which the student is enrolled at the time of the test. Notice that standardization requires some extra assumptions to take care of the extra year of schooling. That is, we standardize the PISA score by the grade in which the student is enrolled at the time of the test assuming that this standardization approach reflects real-world comparisons, as student outcomes are generally assessed within their cohort. However, if one does not support this assumption, we might inadvertently reintroduce an age effect. On the other hand, the RDD does not need additional assumptions to make a same age-at-test comparison.

Another potential threat that prevents us from obtaining the causal effect and therefore affects the identification arises from heterogeneity in the distribution of other characteristics of individuals at the point of discontinuity. One way to check whether this is the case is by visualization. Nevertheless, the variables regarding individual characteristics are mostly discrete with many categories. Hence, including the visualization of these variables would be futile.

2.4 Estimation Procedure

2.4.1 Data Processing

Before proceeding to the estimation, it is crucial to conduct proper data processing to ensure reliability and accuracy across countries and waves. The steps involved are as follows:

1. **Selection of Starting Ages**: We limit the analysis to the two most common starting ages for each country, ensuring comparability across regions and time.
2. **Standardization by Country and Wave**:

[12] Other data and/or methodology will compare students with the same years of schooling but with different ages-at-the-test (in addition to different school-starting ages).

- All test scores (e.g., math and reading) are standardized within each country and survey wave by the grade in which the student is enrolled at the time of the test.
- Importantly, no weights are applied during this standardization process. Although we tested the impact of applying weights, the results indicated that their use did not significantly alter the estimates. Hence, we proceed without them in this step for the sake of simplicity.

3. **Restriction to Boundary Months**: To focus on the discontinuity in the running variable (birthdate), we restrict the dataset to individuals born in the months of August and September. These months represent the cutoff points on either side of the discontinuity, ensuring that the analysis captures the immediate effect of the birthdate threshold.

2.4.2 Estimation Procedure

Once the data is preprocessed, the estimation proceeds as follows:

1. **Country and Wave-specific Estimation**: We conduct separate estimations for each country and each survey wave. This allows for flexibility in capturing country-specific and temporal heterogeneity in the impact of the birthdate cutoff on educational outcomes.
2. **Generation of the Running Variable (Z)**: The running variable, denoted as Z, is discrete in this context and represents the birthdate of the individual. Specifically, Z is a binary variable that indicates whether an individual i was born before August 31st ($Z = 1$) or after ($Z = 0$). This variable serves as the threshold for identifying individuals who are likely to have started school in different cohorts.
3. **Regression Model**: We estimate the effect of the running variable Z on the standardized educational outcomes (e.g., math and reading scores) using a simple linear regression model. The model is specified as follows:

$$Y_i = \alpha + \beta Z_i + \epsilon_i$$

where Y_i represents the standardized score of individual i, Z_i is the binary indicator for birthdate, and ϵ_i is the error term.

- Robust standard errors are used to account for potential heteroskedasticity in the data.
- We also include sample weights in this step to correct for any potential survey design or sampling biases that might affect the representativeness of the sample, ensuring that our estimates reflect the underlying population accurately.

2.5 Results

Table 3 suggests that starting school at an older age has a positive and statistically significant causal effect on standardized test scores in both reading and math. Columns (1)–(3) and (5)–(7) report the results separately for each PISA wave—2015, 2018, and 2022—for reading and math, respectively. Specifically, Columns (1) and (5) correspond to the 2015 wave, Columns (2) and (6) to 2018, and Columns (3) and (7) to 2022. Columns (4) and (8) present the pooled estimates across all three waves. The results show that significant positive effects are concentrated in the 2018 wave and in the pooled specifications, both for Austria and the combined sample. For example, Column (6) shows that in Austria, being one year older at school entry increases a student's math score by approximately 0.10 standard deviations, on average. These findings highlight that while the effect is not uniform across all years and contexts, there is robust evidence of benefits in certain periods—particularly in 2018 and in the pooled analysis, where the effect remains statistically significant.

This gives us a glimpse that the age at which children start school seems to impact their performance later on in several ways. However, our estimates capture the aggregate effect of age-at-test school-starting age, and years of schooling at the time of the test rather than the effect of a policy. Firstly, older students at the beginning of their primary education will be older at the time of evaluation, giving them an advantage over younger students. Secondly, their readiness for the class, as indicated by factors such as whether they had to repeat a grade, can also influence their performance down the line. However, we find no evidence in the latter case.

The estimates in Table 3 are in line with previous results in the literature (Givord 2020; Oosterbeek et al. 2021), which, combined with the use of a regression discontinuity design, allows us to give them a causal interpretation. The RDD design, by exploiting the cutoff date for school entry, offers a clear strategy to address endogeneity and selection bias, thereby reinforcing the validity of our findings. However, it is still important to acknowledge several limitations in this analysis.

The external validity of these findings warrants attention. The aggregated results may mask important country-specific differences although we have incorporated into our analysis a normalization by country and year. Austria and U.A.E have distinct educational systems, curricula, and cultural expectations. The fact that positive or no effects were found for Austria and the U.A.E. suggests that factors such as policy changes or cohort effects could influence the results. Concerning this, we again accentuate that this exercise is not aiming to evaluate educational policies themselves but the aggregate of age-at-start and starting-school-age on educational outcomes. Thus, while the pooled analysis gives a broad picture, a deeper look into these cross-country variations is necessary to understand how different contexts shape the impact of school-starting age.

Additionally, the fact that the results for Austria are significant in only one wave (2018) and in the pooled estimates, but not consistently across all individual waves, raises questions about the robustness of the age-at-entry effect. This concern is further reinforced by the lack of statistically significant effects in the U.A.E. across all specifications. These results could indicate that the influence of school-starting age is not stable over time and may be affected by external factors. A closer investigation of changes in educational policies or assessment methods during the periods where no significant effects were observed could shed light on these variations. However, we remain agnostic about the mechanisms behind our causal estimates.

Another limitation is the lack of analysis of the mechanisms driving the age effect. Although older students may perform better due to their cognitive and emotional maturity, the data does not empirically support these hypotheses. Investigating specific channels, such as cognitive readiness, emotional development, or even peer interactions, could provide a clearer understanding of why being older at school entry positively impacts educational outcomes.

Moreover, cultural norms surrounding school-starting age differ significantly between countries. In some countries, delaying school entry might be an accepted practice, while in others, it might be less common. These norms could influence the magnitude and direction of the effect. Exploring within-country regional differences or conducting qualitative analyses could reveal how societal expectations shape the decision to delay school start and its educational outcomes.

Another key limitation is the focus on test scores as the primary outcome, which only provides a snapshot of students' abilities at a specific point in time. Longitudinal data tracking students throughout their educational journey could reveal whether the positive effects of starting school later persist into higher educational attainment, career success, or lifelong learning outcomes.

As an additional exercise, we conduct regressions that take grade repetition into account to determine whether it may influence our findings. This stems from the fact that older students might be more likely to have repeated a grade, which could affect their performance and taint the perceived benefits of being older.

To address this, we propose two approaches. First, we include a dummy variable in the regression equation to capture the differences between students who have

Table 3 Estimation results

Country	Standardized reading score				Standardized math score			
	(1)	(2)	(3)	(4)	(5)	(6)	(7)	(8)
Austria	0.032	0.198***	0.073	0.104***	0.099	0.185***	0.095	0.129***
	(0.069)	(0.068)	(0.071)	(0.040)	(0.070)	(0.067)	(0.072)	(0.040)
U.A.E	-0.061	0.004	0.019	-0.009	0.031	0.027	0.050	0.038
	(0.055)	(0.055)	(0.050)	(0.031)	(0.058)	(0.052)	(0.049)	(0.031)
All countries	-0.001	0.128***	0.054	0.064**	0.075	0.127***	0.079	0.097***
	(0.049)	(0.047)	(0.049)	(0.028)	(0.050)	(0.046)	(0.050)	(0.028)

Note *p<0.1; **p<0.05; ***p<0.01
Eicker-Huber-White (EHW) heteroskedasticity-robust standard errors in parenthesis. Columns (1) and (5) report results only considering wave 2015. Columns (2) and (6) report results only considering wave 2018. Columns (3) and (7) report results only considering wave 2022. Columns (4) and (8) report results considering the three waves

repeated a grade and those who have not. Second, we consider being a repeater as an outcome variable to evaluate whether starting school at an older age impacts the likelihood of repeating a grade. However, we must be cautious in interpreting this coefficient, as students who repeat a grade may differ significantly from those who do not.

Figure 12 illustrates that controlling for students who have repeated at least once yields consistent results regarding the advantages of starting school later when we pool the data for all waves. Specifically, older students tend to perform better on the PISA assessments compared to younger starters in the case of Austria, but not in the case of the United Arab Emirates. Nevertheless, we cannot determine whether repeating a grade earlier or later affects academic performance, as our analysis only accounts for students who have repeated at least once.

Moreover, we regress a dummy that takes value 1 if the individual repeated at some point or 0 otherwise on being born either in August or September (that is, our running variable). Figure 13 shows that those students who are older are less likely to be repeaters in the case of Austria, and no evidence was found for U.A.E. Again, we show the results pooling all waves. This finding is consistent with our earlier results that older students generally perform better.

Lastly, it is important to consider sample size and statistical power, especially in the puzzling cases where significant results were only observed for one wave (or none). Keeping the window for one month (before and after) gives us less statistical power than using for instance a larger window such as two months. In this regard, smaller sample sizes could limit the power to detect significant effects in certain years. Future studies could benefit from pooling waves for specific countries to assess whether larger sample sizes would reveal more consistent effects.

2.6 Conclusion

In this exercise, we attempt to find the effect of school-starting age on academic performance by using a regression discontinuity design framework. We consider data for 2 countries, Austria which is a OECD country, and U.A.E. as a non-OECD using PISA data for waves 2015, 2018, and 2022. The identifying assumption in our project is that the arbitrary criteria for enrolling students in primary school create a discontinuity in the age of students enrolled in a class.

We observe positive effects of age on academic performance at the aggregate level and results do not change much including country-level fixed effect. However, the effect varies widely across countries and waves. These results are in line with current literature. The procedure had some limitations. The running variable (birth month of the students) is discrete in nature, hence one cannot exploit the information further away from cutoff points. For this reason, we use the mean difference in mathematics and reading scores on either side of the cutoff.

To sum up, the findings indicate that a later school start time positively and significantly influences test scores for Austria, whereas for U.A.E. we do not find any

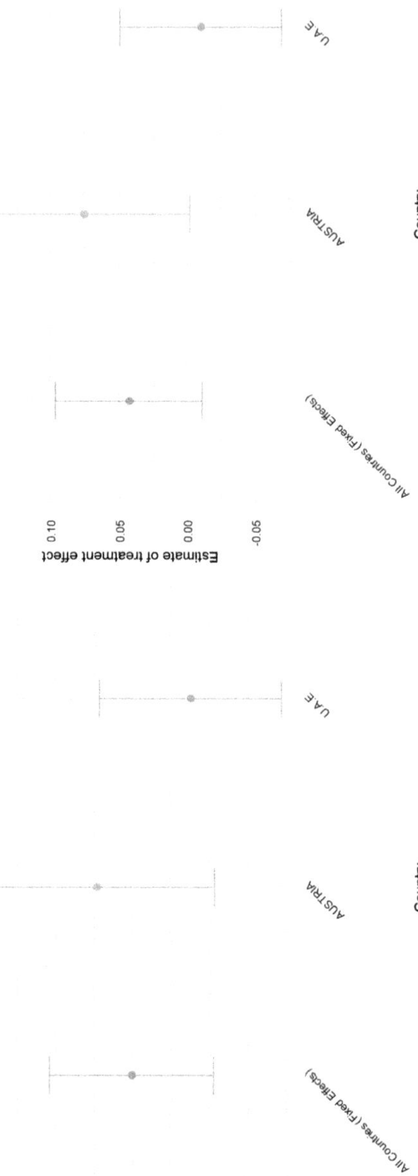

(a) Math (b) Reading

Fig. 12 Effect of school-starting age on educational outcomes (controlling for grade repetition)

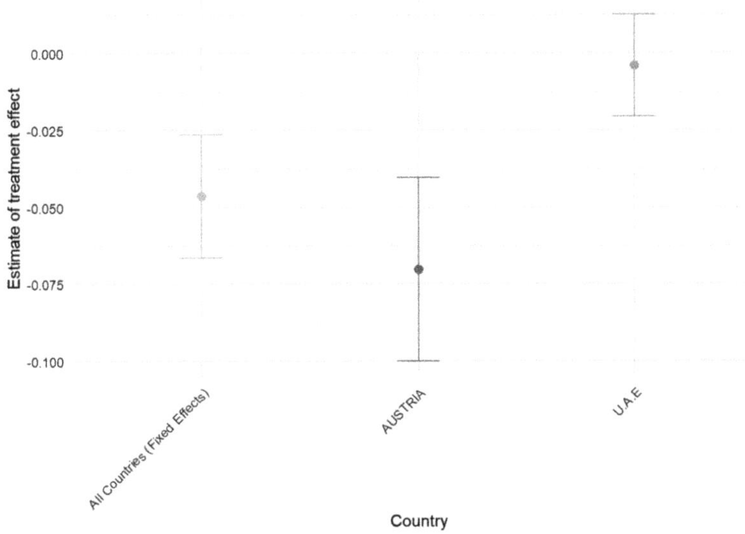

Fig. 13 Effect of school-starting age on grade repetition

effect. However, to comprehensively understand the underlying mechanisms and ensure the robustness of these effects, further research is necessary. Future studies should explore differences across countries, examine causal relationships, and evaluate the long-term effects of school-starting age on broader educational and life outcomes.

References

Andrews, R. J., S. A. Imberman, and M. F. Lovenheim. 2020. Recruiting and supporting low-income, high-achieving students at flagship universities. *Economics of Education Review* 74: 101923.

Avvisati, F., and P. Givord. 2021. How much do 15-year-olds learn over one year of schooling? an international comparison based on pisa.

Black, S. E., J. T. Denning, and J. Rothstein. 2023. Winners and losers? the effect of gaining and losing access to selective colleges on education and labor market outcomes. *American Economic Journal: Applied Economics* 15 (1): 26–67.

Buckles, K. S., and D. M. Hungerman. 2013. Season of birth and later outcomes: Old questions, new answers. *Review of Economics and Statistics* 95 (3): 711–724.

Dhuey, E., D. Figlio, K. Karbownik, and J. Roth. 2019. School starting age and cognitive development. *Journal of Policy Analysis and Management* 38 (3): 538–578.

Dubow, E. F., P. Boxer, and L. R. Huesmann. 2009. Long-term effects of parents' education on children's educational and occupational success: Mediation by family interactions, child aggression, and teenage aspirations. *Merrill-Palmer quarterly (Wayne State University. Press) 55*(3), 224.

Fuchs, T., and L. Wößmann. 2008. *What Accounts for International Differences in Student Performance? A Re-Examination Using PISA Data*. Springer.

Givord, P. 2020. How a student's month of birth is linked to performance at school: New evidence from pisa.

Gupta, S. K. 2011. Intention-to-treat concept: A review. *Perspectives in Clinical Research* 2 (3): 109–112.

Hawkins, D. M. 2004. The problem of overfitting. *Journal of Chemical Information and Computer Sciences* 44 (1): 1–12.

Hoekstra, M. 2009. The effect of attending the flagship state university on earnings: A discontinuity-based approach. *The Review of Economics and Statistics* 91 (4): 717–724.

Kozakowski, W. 2020. Are four-year public colleges engines for mobility? Evidence from statewide admissions thresholds. In *2020 APPAM Fall Research Conference*. APPAM.

Lee, D. S., and T. Lemieux. 2010. Regression discontinuity designs in economics. *Journal of Economic Literature* 48 (2): 281–355.

Long, M. C., and M. Tienda. 2008. Winners and losers: Changes in Texas university admissions post-hopwood. *Educational Evaluation and Policy Analysis* 30 (3): 255–280.

Matthews, G., I. J. Deary, and M. C. Whiteman. 2003. *Personality Traits*. Cambridge University Press.

OECD. 2023. *PISA 2022 Results (Volume I)*.

Oosterbeek, H., S. ter Meulen, and B. van Der Klaauw. 2021. Long-term effects of school-starting-age rules. *Economics of Education Review* 84: 102144.

Phelps, R. P. 2006. Characteristics of an effective student testing system. *Educational Horizons* 85 (1): 19–29.

PIRLS. 2022. National policies on age of school entry and promotion.

Schleicher, A., and C. Tamassia. 2000. *Measuring Student Knowledge and Skills: The PISA 2000 Assessment of Reading. Mathematical and Scientific Literacy. Education and Skills*. ERIC.

Van Bragt, C. A., A. W. Bakx, T. C. Bergen, and M. A. Croon. 2011. Looking for students' personal characteristics predicting study outcome. *Higher Education* 61: 59–75.

Zimmerman, S. D. 2014. The returns to college admission for academically marginal students. *Journal of Labor Economics* 32 (4): 711–754.

Inputs and Agents in the Education Production Function

The Impact of Class Size on Academic Performance

Ismael Sanz

1 Introduction

The association between the number of students per classroom and academic performance is a central aspect of the debate on the quality and allocation of educational resources. In the field of economics of education, articles addressing this relationship are known as the literature on class size. The number of students per classroom is one of the most common metrics used to evaluate resources in the educational field. Its measurement is straightforward and less subjective than improving quality. Among the advantages of reducing class size is its ease of implementation and, above all, its popularity with strong support among stakeholders in the educational system (parents and teachers). Class size variation is observable to parents as a measure of investment in education. Teachers also prefer classes with fewer students. Smaller classes are often seen as beneficial because they allow teachers to devote more time, attention, and support to students and focus on the needs of each one. In contrast, in larger classes, teachers need more time to deal with disruptions, while some students may disengage from instruction. Lazear (2001) develops a theoretical model in which optimal class sizes are higher for well-behaved students. Students with behavioral problems interrupt teaching more, negatively affecting learning (this education production model is detailed in Box 4 of this chapter). Lazear's (2001) model is non-linear, as the probability of disruption increases at a faster rate for small classes than for large ones, where disturbances are already more common.

The greatest disadvantage of reducing class size is that it is an extremely expensive measure. Creating new classes implies hiring new teachers, constructing additional classrooms, purchasing new classroom materials, additional administrative staff, and a series of other associated costs (Handel and Hanushek 2023). Class size has a considerable impact on the level of current education spending through teacher

I. Sanz (✉)
London School of Economics (LSE), Universidad Rey Juan Carlos (URJC), Madrid, Spain
e-mail: Ismael.Sanz@urjc.es

A. Cabrales and I. Sanz (eds.), *Economics of Education*,
https://doi.org/10.1007/978-3-031-90911-5_4

salaries. An increase in labor costs in education strains the already limited education budget, where 58% in the OECD of spending on non-university public institutions is allocated to teacher salaries (OECD, Education at a Glance 2022, Table C6.3).

The student-to-class ratio is an input, not an output, meaning it does not guarantee higher learning or better education quality. To examine whether reducing class size is an effective public policy, its cost must be determined, its benefits to students (in the short and long term) evaluated, and this cost–benefit compared with that of other educational measures that, for the same or lower budget, could have equally or more positive effects on learning. Lower student-to-class ratios must be weighed against other interventions, such as increasing teacher salaries, investing more in their professional development, increasing technology in teaching, or more widespread use of teaching assistants, to name a few examples. Any effect of reducing class sizes needs to be compared in terms of efficiency with other alternative educational interventions (Green and Iversen 2022).

Class size is calculated by dividing the number of students by the number of classes and measures the average number of students grouped in a classroom. The student-to-teacher ratio, on the other hand, is computed in terms of full-time equivalent students relative to full-time equivalent teachers, reflecting the level of teaching resources available in a country in relation to its student population (see Box 1 for differences between student-to-class and student-to-teacher ratios).

Box 1 The Relationship Between Class Size and the Student-to-Teacher Ratio. OECD Education at a Glance (2012, 2020, 2021)

Class size measures the number of students following the same curriculum, considered as the largest number of common courses and without accounting for class divisions (OECD 2020a). The calculation is done by dividing the total number of students by the number of existing classes. In contrast, the student-to-teacher ratio is computed by dividing the number of full-time equivalent students by the number of full-time equivalent teachers at each educational level. The two indicators are related but also measure different characteristics of the educational system. The student-to-teacher ratio provides information about the human resources available in a country relative to its student population, while class size reflects how those resources are used by measuring the average number of students grouped per classroom. That is, class size is affected not only by the student-to-teacher ratio but also by factors such as the number of classes or students a teacher is responsible for, the amount of instructional time that teachers must provide, the number of class hours students receive, or the possible existence of elective courses or class divisions. For example, a greater number of elective courses or class divisions will lead to larger common class sizes. The relationship between the estimated class size, which is not the same as the actual size due to the existence of elective courses and possible tracks, can be approximated by the student-to-teacher ratio multiplied by the ratio of student class hours to teacher instructional hours:

Table 1 Average class size, by type of institution and level of education (2013 and 2019)

	Primary 2019					Compulsory Secondary 2019					2013	
	Public	Private owned			Total Primary	Public	Private owned			Total Compulsory Secondary		
		Total Private	Charter	Private			Total private	Charter	Private		Total Primary	Total Compulsory Secondary
	(1)	(2)	(3)	(4)	(5)	(6)	(7)	(8)	(9)	(10)	(13)	(16)
France	22	25	25	–	23	25	26	27	12	25	23	25
Germany	21	21	–	–	21	24	23	–	–	24	21	24
Italy	19	19	–	19	19	21	21	–	21	21	19	22
Spain	21	24	25	20	22	25	27	27	21	25	22	25
United Kingdom	27	24	28	12	26	25	23	25	12	23	25	19
United States	21	16	–	16	20	26	18	–	18	25	21	27
OCDE Average	**21**	**20**	**21**	**18**	**21**ara>	**23**	**21**	**22**	**19**	**23**	**21**	**23**
European Union-22	**20**	**18**	**19**	**15**	**19**	**21**	**20**	**20**	**17**	**21**	**19**	**21**

Source OCDE/UIS/Eurostat (2021, p. 326) https://www.oecd-ilibrary.org/education/education-at-a-glance-2021_b35a14e5-en
More information and Annex 3 for notes https://www.oecd.org/education/education-at-a-glance/EAG2021_Annex3_ChapterD.pdf

Estimated class size ≈ Student-to-teacher ratio * (Student class hours)/ (Teacher instructional hours) (1)

Equation 1 shows that two countries with the same student-to-teacher ratio can have different estimated class sizes. For instance, if we focus on secondary education, Spain has more student instructional hours per year, 1,057 hours as shown in the OECD's Education at a Glance 2023, than the OECD average (916) or the EU-22 average (876). Spain also has fewer teacher instructional hours per year in secondary education (669) than the OECD average (723), though very similar to the EU-22 average (660). The result is that a student-to-teacher ratio in Spain similar to that of the OECD and EU-22 (12, compared to 13 and 11, respectively), but with a higher ratio of student class hours to teacher instructional hours, leads to a larger estimated class size.

Exercise 1

Calculate the estimated class size for three countries, A, B, and C:

- Country A (real data from France in Primary Education, 2019)
  - Student-to-Teacher Ratio: 19
  - Student Class Hours per Year: 864
  - Teacher Instructional Hours per Year: 900
- Country B (real data from the EU, 2019)
  - Student-to-Teacher Ratio: 13
  - Student Class Hours per Year: 766
  - Teacher Instructional Hours per Year: 769
- Country C (real data from the OECD, 2019)
  - Student-to-Teacher Ratio: 15
  - Student Class Hours per Year: 766
  - Teacher Instructional Hours per Year: 804

Now suppose that the data for teacher instructional hours per year changes in Country B. What would then be the estimated class size?

- Country A (real data from France in Primary Education, 2019)
  - Student-to-Teacher Ratio: 19
  - Student Class Hours per Year: 864
  - Teacher Instructional Hours per Year: 900
- Country B (real data from the EU-22, 2019)
  - Student-to-Teacher Ratio: 13
  - Student Class Hours per Year: 766

   - Teacher Instructional Hours per Year: 900

- Country C (real data from the OECD, 2019)
   - Student-to-Teacher Ratio: 15
   - Student Class Hours per Year: 766
   - Teacher Instructional Hours per Year: 804

Exercise 2
Refer to Table V.B1.4.9 and Table V.B1.4.11 of the PISA 2018 OECD Report at https://doi.org/https://doi.org/10.1787/888934132241, obtain the data for Student–Teacher Ratio and Language-of-Instruction Class Size. Calculate the correlation coefficient between the student-to-teacher ratio and student-to-class ratio for the 37 OECD countries, and check the position of England, France, Germany, Italy, Spain, and United States among the 37 countries in both variables.

Exercise 3
Access Tables II.B1.5.11, II.B1.5.12, II.B1.5.15, II.B1.5.13, and II.B1.5.16 of the most recent PISA 2022 OECD Report https://stat.link/pyhr6e. Compare the student–teacher ratio and class size for a selected set of OECD countries, such as England, France, Germany, Italy, Spain, and the United States. If you are from a different country, also include data from your own country.

1. **Rank Comparison:** Using the data from PISA 2022, rank the selected countries based on their student–teacher ratio and average class size.
2. **Trend Analysis:** Analyze the trend between 2018 and 2022 in both student–teacher ratio and class size for these countries.
3. **Spearman Rank Correlation:** To quantify the relationship between the student–teacher ratio and class size rankings across these countries, perform a Spearman rank correlation test.
4. **Interpretation:** Discuss the implications of your findings. What does the correlation (or lack thereof) tell us about the relationship between student–teacher ratio and class size in these countries?

2 The Association Between Class Size and Educational Performance: The First Generation of Non-Causal Studies

Box 2 The Non-Causal Association Between Class Size and PISA Outcomes
PISA analyses reveal that some of the highest-performing education systems, nevertheless, have large class sizes. The table at the end of this box shows data from Volume V of the PISA 2018 Report (OECD 2020b, Table V.B1.4.11). The information on average class size is based on data provided by the principals of secondary schools participating in the sample from each country in

this evaluation, focusing on classes where 15-year-old students are present. In contrast, the previous Table 1 was based on administrative data provided by the Ministries of Education of each country, also collected by the OECD. Despite the different data sources, the conclusions are consistent, offering a similar ranking of countries by student-to-class ratio. The table shows that in the OECD, class sizes in the subject of Language—the central subject of PISA 2018—are smaller in schools with lower economic, social, and cultural levels.

As shown in the table of this box, Germany (with 25.0 students per class) and the United Kingdom (24.9) achieve better results in PISA 2018 in reading, mathematics, and science than Italy, despite Italy having a smaller average class size (22.9). Comparisons in the opposite direction can also be found, as Germany and the United Kingdom also outperform countries with higher student-to-class ratios, such as France (29.8) or the OECD average (26.1). The OECD analysis in column 3 shows a positive, non-causal association, contrary to expectations, between class size and reading performance, even after accounting for the average socioeconomic level of schools and the individual socioeconomic level of students' families. Specifically, across the OECD, an increase of one student in the student-to-class ratio is associated with a one-point increase in PISA reading scores, and up to four points in the case of France. This counterintuitive association between class size and educational performance in the PISA report is affected by possible biases due to omitted variables and the endogeneity of resources. In their recent survey, Handel and Hanushek (2023) point out that this type of correlational and non-causal analysis only shows limited relationships between school resources—in this case, the student-to-class ratio—and student outcomes. Recent evidence offers a new perspective, paying much more attention to identifying key policy parameters. For the remainder of this chapter, we will summarize evidence from what Handel and Hanushek (2023) have called the "credibility revolution" in modern empirical analysis, which we will refer to as "second-generation" studies in this chapter, with studies that exploit exogenous variation in student-to-class ratios and show an inverse or null relationship between the two, but never a positive one.

For decades, it has been argued that spending on education, including the investment required to reduce class size, was not correlated with academic performance (see Box 2). Hanushek and Woessmann (2011), for example, concluded that the general evidence on the effect of class size on student performance, as measured by external and standardized tests, was mixed or at least did not identify significant benefits from reducing the number of students per classroom.

Class Size in Language, School Characteristics, and Reading Performance. PISA Report for 15-Year-Old Students. Results Based on School Principals' Reports

	All students (1)		By socioeconomic level (2)		After accounting for socioeconomic level of students and schools (3)		PISA 2018 results (4)		
	Average	Standard deviation	Lowest	Highest	Change in Reading Score per One-Student Increase in Class Size		Reading	Maths	Science
France	29.8	4.9	26.0	33.2	4	(0.5)	493	495	493
Germany	25.0	4.5	22.0	26.8	2	(0.9)	498	500	503
Italy	22.9	5.1	21.5	23.9	1	(0.7)	476	487	468
Spain	29.4	9.7	28.9	30.6	–	–	–	–	–
England	24.9	4.3	24.8	23.1	0	(0.5)	504	502	505
United States	26.2	5.4	26.9	26.4	1	(0.4)	505	478	502
OECD	26.1	5.6	23.8	27.4	1	(0.1)	487	489	489

1. The socioeconomic profile is measured by the PISA index of economic, social, and cultural status. Bold values are statistically significant

Sources OECD (2020c). PISA 2018 Results (Volume V). Table V.B1.4.11 https://doi.org/10.1787/888934132241
https://doi.org/10.1787/888934028140

More recent findings from PISA 2022 provide a new perspective. The new report highlights that education systems with lower student–teacher ratios and class size exhibited higher mathematics scores, even after accounting for per capita GDP (Table II.B1.5.101, PISA 2022, OECD 2023). Additionally, the change in class size between 2018 and 2022 was negatively associated with the change in performance during this period, indicating that systems where average class sizes increased tended to experience greater declines in mathematics performance (Table II.B1.5.104). Furthermore, across all countries and economies, smaller classes and fewer students per teacher were correlated with a stronger sense of belonging at school, emphasizing the importance of class size and student–teacher ratios in shaping educational outcomes and student well-being (see Exercise 5).

Exercise 4

Refer to Table V.B1.4.11 of the OECD at https://doi.org/10.1787/888934132241 and download the data on the student-to-class ratio in OECD countries into an Excel file. Retrieve information on each country's PISA 2018 results in reading, mathematics, and science (https://doi.org/10.1787/888934028140, PISA. Volume I). Using Excel's correlation function, calculate the association between the student-to-class ratio and the results in reading, mathematics, and science.

Exercise 5

Access Table II.B1.5.11, Table II.B1.5.12, and Table II.B1.5.15 of the more recent PISA 2022 OECD Report (https://stat.link/pyhr6e). Compare class size and mathematics scores for a selected set of countries (e.g., England, France, Germany, Italy, Spain, and the United States). If you are not from one of these countries, also choose data from your own country. PISA 2022 (Table II.B1.5.101 and Table II.B1.5.104 in https://stat.link/pyhr6e) presents a different conclusion regarding the impact of class size compared to PISA 2018. Create a scatter plot in Excel to visually represent the correlation between the student–teacher ratio and mathematics scores for these countries.

Exercise 6

Refer to Table II.B1.5.101 and Table II.B1.5.104 of the PISA 2022 OECD Report (https://stat.link/pyhr6e). Examine the relationship between the change in class size and the change in mathematics performance between 2018 and 2022 for the 37 OECD countries. Based on the data, discuss how changes in class size may have impacted educational outcomes and the potential policy implications for countries facing increasing class sizes.

These "first-generation" analyses, which typically do not find a relationship between class size and educational performance, generally fail to account for the non-random nature of class size. They do not consider the possibility that educational agents assign the number of students per classroom based on factors such as student ability or that families choose a school based on the expected class size. However, in practice, we see that some changes in the educational inputs that students experience result from decisions made by their parents, teachers, school principals, or education administrators. Some of these "first-generation" studies use observational data that is often cross-sectional or aggregated rather than individual-level data. Even in studies that use longitudinal datasets, it cannot be assured that all relevant variables are included, making it difficult to establish firm causal relationships (Cabrales 2010). As Angrist and Pischke (2014) conclude, the observed correlation between class size and student outcomes should not be taken as rigorous evidence. For example, if some students with learning difficulties are assigned to smaller classes to provide more individualized attention, empirical evidence using Ordinary Least Squares (OLS) would detect a positive impact of class size on student performance that is not real. Another endogenous factor in determining class size is the case where schools with smaller student-to-class ratios achieve better academic performance because they are highly selective or have more financial resources, which directly influences student learning (Graves and Zucchelli 2022).

3 The Causal Impact of Class Size on Educational Performance

Establishing a causal relationship between class size and student learning is a challenging task. "Second-generation" studies address the endogeneity problems that bias OLS estimates by using exogenous sources of variation, which are essential for a credible identification of the effect of reducing the number of students per classroom. The studies we will examine starting from this section employ convincing identification methods. They consider variations in class size that are unrelated to factors that could influence academic performance. These are studies that can attribute their estimated effects to the number of students per classroom. To determine the causal effect of class size, the following analytical methods have been used, which we will review below.

3.1 Randomized Controlled Trials

As mentioned earlier, the non-random assignment of students to classes, such as assigning students with learning difficulties to smaller support classes, generates spurious relationships between class size and educational performance. Randomized controlled trials (RCTs) solve this problem. This method randomly assigns different class sizes to estimate causal effects, avoiding selection bias. A group of students is randomly selected to benefit from a reduced class size, and their performance is compared with that of a control group that remains in classes with the usual number of students. The STAR (Student/Teacher Achievement Ratio) project, developed in Tennessee in the 1980s, is the most famous experiment in this area. Between 1985 and 1989, the STAR program randomly assigned 11,571 kindergarten students in Tennessee to either small classes (15 students) or large classes (22 students). The students from the 79 schools that volunteered to participate remained in their original treatment and control groups from kindergarten through third grade and were evaluated at the end of each school year. Krueger's (1999) analysis of the Tennessee STAR class size randomized controlled trial shows strong and robust causal effects of reduced class size on learning. Specifically, Krueger (1999) concluded that a reduction of 7 students (from 22 to 15) in the student-to-class ratio improves results by 22% of the standard deviation, equivalent to what a student learns in six months (Hanushek and Woessmann 2020). The effects are more positive for minority students or those eligible for free lunch, an indicator of poverty in the U.S. Krueger's (1999) estimate based on the STAR Project data has one of the highest estimated impacts of all those we will see in this chapter. Krueger and Whitmore (2001) show that the effect of the intervention diminishes over time. By the year following the experiment, the difference between students in the treatment and control groups is reduced to between half and three-quarters of the initial difference. Most of the improvements found in the small classes occurred in kindergarten, with much smaller benefits in first grade and almost non-existent in second and third grades.

Chetty et al. (2011) also analyze the same STAR project and conclude that being assigned to small classes increases the likelihood of attending higher education at age 20 by 1.8 percentage points, a significant improvement given the average was 26.4%. Additionally, the authors show a considerable impact of attending small classes in kindergarten on the quality of the university attended and on earnings at age 27. Specifically, each percentage point improvement in grade distribution is associated with an increase in annual earnings at age 27 of $94. Students from smaller classes also have other positive long-term outcomes, such as a higher likelihood of owning a home or having savings in retirement plans.

Since the STAR, there have been few other randomized trials large enough to make significant inferences, largely due to the high costs involved in such experiments. Among the more recent trials is Duflo et al.'s (2015) study in western Kenya, where an additional teacher was randomly assigned to 70 schools, effectively reducing the average class size from 82 to 44 students. These authors did not find positive effects on the learning of students whose teachers were already previously employed, despite the reduction in the student-to-class ratio. However, results improved by 0.24 standard deviations for students assigned to newly hired teachers. A possible explanation is that these newly hired teachers had low absenteeism rates, while the older teachers in the treatment group's schools reduced their efforts endogenously.

Exercise 7
Esther Duflo and Michael Kremer, two of the authors of this article, Duflo, E., Dupas, P., and Kremer, M. (2015). *School governance, teacher incentives, and teacher–pupil ratios: Experimental evidence from Kenyan primary schools. Journal of Public Economics,* 123, 92–110, https://doi.org/https://doi.org/10.1016/j.jpubeco.2014.11.008, won the Nobel Prize in Economics in 2019. In this exercise, we ask you to read the article, freely accessible at https://web.stanford.edu/~pdupas/DDK_ETP.pdf, and develop other possible interpretations that explain why these researchers did not find an effect of class size reduction on students of already employed teachers while finding a significant impact on the students of newly hired teachers.

Andersen et al. (2020) evaluate the effects of two treatments in Denmark in primary schools. In the first treatment group, students have an additional assistant with a teaching certificate, while in the second group, the assistant does not have this qualification. Both treatments have a positive and significant effect on students' reading comprehension but not on mathematics. In general, in the economics of education, the opposite conclusion is usually found, that interventions tend to be more effective in increasing mathematics performance compared to reading performance, as shown by Fryer's (2017) analysis of 196 randomized controlled trials. Students assigned to the intervention with a co-teacher with a teaching degree improved their reading scores by 0.086 standard deviations, while students who benefited from an additional assistant without a certificate increased their reading proficiency by 0.131 standard deviations, due to the ability to hire more assistants with the same budget (Andersen et al. 2020). The impact persists over time for disadvantaged and socioeconomically disadvantaged students. A deeper analysis of the mechanisms indicates that incorporating an uncertified teaching assistant is not simply a reduction in class size but is particularly effective when sharing instructional responsibility in the classroom and groups with students with behavioral problems. In the case of co-teaching, good coordination, with well-defined functions and roles, is key to the success of this intervention, with one of the two working in small groups.

Another related RCT to Andersen et al. (2020) is the analysis conducted by Haaland et al. (2024), who provides additional insights into the effects of increasing the teacher-student ratio, having two teachers working collaboratively in the same class. Haaland et al. (2024) carried out a large-scale field experiment in Norway, investigating the impact of an additional teacher in the classroom, specifically targeting literacy instruction during the first and second grades. This study involved nearly 6000 students across 300 classrooms, making it comparable in scale to the STAR project. The key innovation in this study was the focus on having two teachers in the same classroom, rather than reducing class size by splitting classes. The experiment randomly assigned one of the two classrooms in each school to have an additional teacher present during all literacy lessons, while the other classroom continued with the standard single-teacher setup.

The results from this study indicate that, on average, the presence of an additional teacher did not lead to significant improvements in literacy outcomes for the entire sample. However, the study revealed that boys, particularly those with low skills at baseline, showed significant improvements. The treatment effects for this subgroup included increases of 0.12 standard deviations on the national literacy assessment and 0.09 standard deviations in reading self-concept by the end of second grade. For boys with the lowest initial skills, the impacts were even more pronounced, with gains of 0.23 and 0.22 standard deviations, respectively. The findings from Haaland et al. (2024) emphasize the importance of tailoring educational interventions to the needs of specific subgroups within the student population.

MacKinnon et al. (2023) re-estimate the effect of reducing class size on academic performance using data from the STAR project as a practical application of the tests they propose to determine the correct level of clustering in regression models. These authors find that small classes lead to better reading outcomes in first grade and show that if fixed effects by school are included, clustering at the school level is more appropriate than at the classroom level. By including additional control variables such as student and teacher gender, race, free lunch status, teacher experience and qualifications, prior student performance, and birth quarter, in addition to school fixed effects, the dummy variable for whether the student attended a small class (15 students) instead of 22, has a positive and significant effect on student performance in first grade using the same STAR project data analyzed by Krueger (1999).

Adusumilli et al. (2024) introduce a novel empirical framework to evaluate the effects of class size reduction, building on data from the Tennessee STAR experiment. Their study emphasizes the significance of heterogeneity in the effectiveness of class size reductions across different schools and the role of endogenous compliance in shaping these outcomes. By employing the Grouped Random Effects (GRE) methodology—an approach that accounts for both heterogeneous treatment effects and endogenous class size determination—Adusumilli et al. (2024) reveal that the benefits of smaller class sizes are not uniformly distributed across schools. Specifically, they find that only 29% of the schools in the STAR experiment experienced substantial gains from class size reduction, with an average increase of 0.09 standard deviations in test scores per one-student decrease in class size. In contrast, the remaining 71% of schools showed minimal to no improvement, highlighting the variability in how different educational environments respond to class size interventions.

Adusumilli et al. (2024) underscores the complexity of scaling educational interventions like class size reduction policies. The authors argue that traditional econometric models, such as the two-stage least squares (2SLS) estimator, often used in earlier analyses of the STAR data, may be poorly aligned with the realities of the experiment's implementation, thereby limiting their utility in predicting the success of large-scale policy applications. Their findings suggest that a one-size-fits-all approach to class size reduction may not be effective and that more targeted interventions could yield better results. For example, by identifying and focusing resources on schools that are more likely to benefit from smaller class sizes, policymakers could achieve more significant improvements in student performance while also enhancing the cost-effectiveness of such initiatives. The study also highlights the importance of designing pilot programs that can reveal the extent of treatment effect heterogeneity before attempting to scale interventions across different contexts and populations.

3.2 Regression Discontinuity

The randomized controlled trials discussed in the previous section are not always easy to implement due to the high financial cost they entail and ethical reasons, as students assigned to large classes may have fewer educational and future employment opportunities. Chetty et al. (2011) show that being in smaller classes at a young age has long-term positive effects on academic development in higher education and entry into the labor market. Hanushek et al. (2015) also find that the skills measured by external test scores are closely related to subsequent economic outcomes, including individual earnings in the labor market.

The difficulty of conducting randomized trials has led to the development of a body of research that seeks to exploit natural variations in class size—changes not influenced by the choices of educational agents. One approach has been to use administrative rules regarding maximum class sizes as a source of quasi-random exogenous variation (see European Commission 2023: National Education Systems on regulations in EU Member States regarding maximum class size https://eurydice.eacea.ec.europa.eu/national-education-systems). This method uses rules on maximum class size to compare courses where additional classes are opened when the limit is exceeded (reducing the average class size) with those that remain at the threshold but have a very similar total number of students per course. For example, if the rule sets the maximum number of students per class at 30, and a course increases to 31 students, a second class will need to be opened, with an average class size of 15.5, compared to the previous 30. The same would happen if the enrollment of a course increases from 60 to 61 students, with a change in the student-to-class ratio from 30 to 20.3. The studies reviewed in this section use these discontinuities in class size as an instrument that does not reflect the choices of schools or parents.

Angrist and Lavy (1999) focus on 4th and 5th grade students in primary schools in Israel in the years 1991 and 1992, where Maimonides' rule is used, which specifies that classes should not have a ratio higher than 40. This rule leads to discontinuities in class size when enrollment in a course exceeds 40, 80, 120, and generally multiples of 40. In schools with 40 students in the same course, students will be in a single class. If one more student enrolls, making a total of 41, the cohort would be divided into two smaller classes. In practice, the division of classes is not always strictly followed, leading to an instrumental variable approach, where the actual class size is instrumented with the predicted class size derived from the class division rule. Identification only comes from contexts where these rules are binding. Using this methodology, Angrist and Lavy (1999) show that an increase of 8 students in class size causes a reduction of 0.29 standard deviations in scores. Under the assumption of linearity, this would be an approximate effect of 0.035 standard deviations per increase of one student in class size.

Fredriksson et al. (2013) use the exogenous variation generated by the maximum limit of 30 students per class in primary schools in Sweden, using different thresholds as points of discontinuity where class size jumps as an instrument. Compliance with the rule is high, but not perfect, leading to an instrumental variable approach. These authors also conduct reduced form estimates of the "fuzzy RD" design (fuzzy regression discontinuity, see Chapter 2 on empirical methods and the introduction to causal inference), using the discontinuities at different cut-off points as an instrument for class size. The class size rule is a very strong predictor of actual class size, so the instrumental variable estimates and the regression discontinuity estimates do not differ qualitatively. Fredriksson et al. (2013) find that an increase of one student in class size causes a reduction of between 0.032 and 0.047 standard deviations in student performance in cognitive skills (verbal and logical skills). Argaw and Puhani (2018) take advantage of the rule of a maximum ratio of 25 students per class in the German state of Hesse to examine the effect of class size on outcomes at the end of primary education. These authors find that, although only in the case of boys, an increase in class size of 10 students reduces the opportunity to attend the most academic track in secondary education by 3 percentage points, a choice that has significant effects throughout life.

Angrist et al. (2019) re-examined the impact of class size on academic performance in Israel, a study already conducted by Angrist and Lavy (1999), but with more recent data from the period 2002–2011. They again used Maimonides' rule of 40 students per class to carry out instrumental variable estimates of the impact of class size on test scores. In addition, Angrist et al. (2019) observed that there is some evidence of enrollment manipulation in some schools in Israel, in the sense that there are too many classes with the exact number of students that triggers the division. Using a strategy that employs students' birthdates to calculate enrollment and avoid manipulation bias, they concluded that there is no significant effect of class size on standardized and external test scores. In other words, Angrist et al. (2019) find that with more recent data, the positive effect that Angrist and Lavy (1999) found of reducing the number of students per classroom on academic outcomes disappears.

Exercise 8 Explain the reasons why the article by Angrist et al. (2019, https://doi.org/10.1257/aeri.20180120) does not find the same result as Angrist and Lavy (1999, https://www.jstor.org/stable/2587016) despite analyzing data on class size in Israel, albeit during different periods.

Connolly and Haeck (2022) estimate the impact of reducing class size on student performance by exploiting regulations that limit the maximum student-to-class ratio to 20 in kindergarten in Quebec. These authors differ from Angrist and Lavy (1999) in that they do not directly use the class size rule as an instrument due to the problems posed by possible classroom clustering around the thresholds and class composition. Their approach is closer to the "fuzzy RD" (fuzzy regression discontinuity) design of Fredriksson et al. (2013). In analyzing kindergarten, Connolly and Haeck (2022) focus on a level of education that reduces the likelihood that the school could in some way classify students since very little is known about the child before they start school. These authors find that reducing the number of students per class increases cognitive development by 0.014 standard deviations, approximately half the impact found by Krueger (1999). They also find that children living in disadvantaged geographic areas benefit more from reducing the student-to-class ratio, while the effect for other students is not significant. Connolly and Haeck (2022) also find a positive, though smaller, impact of reducing class size on non-cognitive skills (such as social competence, self-confidence, sense of responsibility, autonomy, work habits, and respect for peers) of children from disadvantaged families. These authors conclude that the impact of class size on student performance is non-linear since the marginal effect of reducing the student-to-class ratio is higher in smaller classes. This work concludes that focusing on reducing the student-to-class ratio in schools located in vulnerable areas would achieve a higher educational improvement than a generalized reduction in ratios.

In summary, regression discontinuity analyses based on maximum classroom size rules generally find a positive effect of reducing class size on educational outcomes. In their survey, Green and Iversen (2022) also note some exceptions to this conclusion of positive effects from class size reduction. Leuven et al. (2008) use the rule of a maximum of 30 students per class in lower secondary education in Norway, where this rule is a strong predictor of actual class size, and find no effects of reducing the student-to-class ratio on educational performance in language or mathematics for students in 2002 and 2003.

Clark et al. (2024) also employ the empirical strategy that leverages natural discontinuities in class size regulations, specifically employing the Maximum Classroom Size Rule that requires the division of classes when the number of students reaches 30 in the Region of Madrid (Spain). The impact of this first stage on the actual class size is estimated using a regression model, where various factors such as administrative district effects, year fixed effects, and alternative functions of the running variable are taken into account. Clark et al. (2024) conduct a comprehensive study using data from the Madrid region that expands the scope of class size research beyond the traditional focus on academic performance, providing one of the first thorough investigations into how these changes affect classroom environment, teaching practices, parent involvement, and family satisfaction. These authors reveal that while smaller class sizes may not universally lead to significant gains in standardized test scores, they have a profound impact on reducing classroom disruptions, which in turn creates a more conducive learning environment. This reduction in disruptions allows teachers to engage in more effective instructional practices, such as personalized attention and differentiated instruction, which are often difficult to implement in larger, more chaotic classroom settings. The study also sheds light on how families respond to class size changes, showing that in larger classes, there is often a compensatory increase in educational support provided at home, as parents seek to mitigate the potential drawbacks of a less individualized learning environment.

Furthermore, this research underscores the importance of considering the context-specific nature of class size effects. Clark et al. (2024) emphasize that the benefits of smaller class sizes are particularly pronounced in schools and classrooms where behavioral issues and disruptions are more prevalent. In these settings, the reduction in class size can lead to substantial improvements not only in academic performance but also in the overall quality of the educational experience.

3.3 Instrumental Variables

One of the problems with using rules for the maximum number of students per classroom is that for some schools, these thresholds are not binding because they are far from the discontinuity (Hoxby 2000). An alternative approach to class size rules is to use changes in enrollment per grade within the same school due to demographic variation, which is also less influenced by the choices of educational agents. Parents cannot predict year-to-year variation in enrollment size for a particular grade at a given school. Longitudinal data is used to exploit the random annual variation in school cohort sizes, which induces changes in class size. An additional advantage is that this methodology leads to estimates of changes in class size by one student without the need to make linearity assumptions based on larger changes in the student-to-class ratio. The within-school design is widely applicable and allows for the study of class size effects even if there are no such class size rules or when the correct class size threshold cannot be easily identified because different thresholds are in effect depending on characteristics that are not observable to the researcher (Bach and Sievert 2024). Within-school designs allow for the estimation of heterogeneous effects of class size across the entire class size distribution, enabling the testing of non-linear effects.

However, using year-to-year variation in enrollment by grade and school implies requirements for longitudinal data that are not always available and a loss of statistical precision due to both the lack of large changes in enrollment and a higher potential for error in measuring enrollment numbers (Green and Iversen 2022). The seminal article using this method is by Hoxby (2000). This author uses deviations from enrollment trend data in primary schools in Connecticut as an instrument. Hoxby (2000) finds no significant effects of class size variation on student performance and rules out effects as small as 0.04 standard deviations for a 10 percent reduction in class size. Heinesen (2010) examines the effect of the student-to-class ratio on the academic performance of students in Denmark in the subject of French. The variation in this case comes from both enrollment by grade and school and student language choice between French or German over time. This author finds that a reduction in class size by one student increases academic performance by 0.029 standard deviations. Cho et al. (2012) use variation in total enrollment within schools to examine the outcomes of 3rd and 5th grade students in Minnesota. They find that a decrease of ten students in class size would lead to an increase in test scores between 0.04 and 0.05 standard deviations.

More recently, Kedagni et al. (2021) also use Hoxby's (2000) approach of general enrollment variations as exogenous shocks to analyze the impact of the student-to-class ratio on secondary school student learning in Greece. In this country, the vast majority of students attend the nearest school, and high schools must admit all eligible students. Therefore, variations between cohorts at the same high school are exogenous to parents and schools. Kedagni et al. (2021) find that a decrease in class size by one student in 10th grade in Greece increases academic performance by 0.017 standard deviations. Kedagni et al. (2021) also provide evidence of a non-linear relationship between the student-to-class ratio and academic outcomes. Initially, class size increases academic performance, as students learn from both the teacher and each other. Students learn from peers with a similar skill level. The larger the class, the more likely they are to have students with similar academic outcomes. However, once a limit in the student-to-class ratio is reached, class size begins to harm student learning because the effects of crowding and congestion forces start to prevail. Additionally, Kedagni et al. (2021) develop a dynamic structural model with teacher hiring and firing costs. Reducing firing costs to zero has a direct effect by facilitating teacher turnover, which increases class size compared to the status quo. However, reducing teacher firing costs also has an indirect effect, as it makes hiring more likely, which reduces class size. The counterfactual results show that reducing teacher firing costs to zero increases the average class size by 5–6 students and reduces academic performance by approximately one point on a 1–20 scale. Lowering hiring costs reduces class size by 4–5 students, as more teachers are hired, and increases academic performance by 0.3 points. Bach and Sievert (2024) summarize the evidence from articles using cohort size variation within each school as an instrument in estimating the effects of class size and conclude that of the 11 articles summarized, five do not find that smaller student-to-class ratios improve learning (Table E.1, Bach and Sievert 2024). In Box 3, we analyze in more detail the article by Bach and Sievert

(2024) and the problems that instrumental variable analyses may have in estimating the causal effect of class size on student outcomes.

An important difference between studies using regression discontinuity or instrumental variables and the randomized controlled experiment study of the STAR (Student/Teacher Achievement Ratio) project is that the schools participating in the STAR experiment received additional resources to reduce class size. In contrast, in cases analyzed using regression discontinuity or instrumental variables, resources were likely diverted from other educational areas when natural population variation led to smaller classes. Therefore, one possible interpretation of the divergent results is that the positive effects found in the STAR experiment were achieved, at least in part, thanks to the additional resources.

Box 3. Bach and Sievert (2024) in More Detail

A large part of the quasi-experimental literature takes advantage of within-school variation in cohort size over time to analyze the impact of class size on student learning (see, for example, Hoxby 2000; Leuven et al. 2008; Cho et al. 2012). These studies generally find small or null effects of class size, which contrasts with the available experimental evidence showing substantial effects of class size (see, for example, Krueger 1999; Krueger and Whitmore 2001). Bach and Sievert (2024) find an explanation for this difference in results regarding the effect of class size on student learning. These two authors show that in educational systems with grade repetition or "redshirting" (delaying a student's entry into primary school by one year), cohort size is negatively related to the proportion of repeating students. Intuitively, in larger cohorts, students retained from the previous (smaller) cohort mechanically constitute a smaller proportion of students in the given (larger) cohort. This negative association causes a positive relationship between birth cohort size and test scores at the grade level, as students who have repeated in the past are negatively selected. The conclusion is that there is a spurious positive effect of class size on learning, leading to an upward bias (making the effect less negative) in class size estimates based on within-school cohort size variation. In terms of instrumental variables, this is a violation of the exclusion restriction of birth cohort size as an instrument.

Bach and Sievert (2024) illustrate this with a situation where there is generally a constant number of births each year, but in a specific year (t), there is an increase in enrollment for first grade. Due to this increase in enrollment in year t, more students move on to second grade the following year (t + 1). Therefore, students who repeated from the previous year represent a smaller percentage in second grade in t + 1. Additionally, due to the increase in first grade enrollment in year t, more students repeat. These students move on to second grade a year later (t + 2), increasing the percentage of repeat students in that cohort. That is, an unexpected increase in first grade enrollment in year t is related to a decrease in the percentage of repeat students in second grade the following year (t + 1). If there are fewer repeat students, who typically have lower competencies, the average skill level of the group will be higher. The conclusion is that even if the initial cohort size is unrelated to academic skills and repetition thresholds, the net effect of the bias will reduce the estimated negative effect of class size.

Using data from all primary schools in the German federal state of Saarland, Bach and Sievert (2024) demonstrate that birth cohort size is systematically related to the composition of students at the grade level. By correcting the resulting bias, controlling for whether a student has previously repeated a grade, they find that not only are smaller classes beneficial for exam results, but also for reducing grade repetition.

Bach and Sievert (2024) conclude that a decrease in class size by one student from 1st to 3rd grade improves test scores in language and mathematics at the end of 3rd grade by 0.019 and 0.014 standard deviations, respectively. Repetition rates also decrease by 0.15 percentage points (7%) when class size is reduced by one student. Additionally, the effects of class size are non-linear, with large effects in larger classes and no effects in smaller classes. It is estimated that a reduction of one student in classes with more than 20.5 students improves language and mathematics test scores by 0.048 and 0.038 standard deviations, respectively. At the same time, Bach and Sievert (2024) find no evidence to suggest that reducing class size improves student outcomes in classes with fewer than 20.5 students. Disadvantaged students, due to lower proficiency in German or learning disabilities, benefit more from attending smaller classes, with a positive effect of about 0.050 standard deviations in language and mathematics per one-student reduction in class size. This impact is of a similar magnitude to the STAR Project experiment.

3.4 Class Size Reduction Laws

The studies discussed in the previous sections isolate the causal effect of the number of students per classroom by analyzing class size variations unrelated to factors that might affect academic performance. These investigations can attribute the estimated effects to the number of students per classroom. However, in the real-world application of such policies, it is highly unlikely that all other educational factors remain constant. A growing body of research uses real variations in student-to-teacher ratios generated by changes in educational policies, specifically mandates to reduce class size. These analyses have the advantage of examining the general equilibrium effects of widespread class size reductions in an educational system, including their associated indirect impacts (Green and Iversen 2022). For example, reducing class size requires hiring many teachers, which could result in lower quality among newly hired teachers. In the previous sections, analyses focused on class size reductions in isolation without considering the broader effects of these measures.

Exercise 9

Based on the survey by Green and Iversen (2022) and the article by Gilraine et al. (2018), identify the possible indirect effects of class size reduction, beyond changes in learning, on students, teachers, and parents.

The Class Size Reduction (CSR) initiative in California, implemented in 1996, reduced the number of students in grades from kindergarten through third grade from 30 to 20 students per classroom. Jepsen and Rivkin (2009) report that this initiative required the rapid hiring of large number of teachers, resulting in the inclusion of educators who were often undertrained or inexperienced. As a result of this measure, only a small increase in math and reading performance was observed. Additionally, Jepsen and Rivkin (2009) indicate that California's CSR program created a high concentration of inexperienced teachers in schools with lower socioeconomic status students, where teacher recruitment was more challenging. Chingos (2012) also examines the class size reduction mandate (CSR) in Florida, approved in 2002, which decreased the student-to-class ratio to 18 students from kindergarten to 3rd grade, 22 from 4 to 8th grade, and 25 from 9 to 12th grade. Chingos (2012) leverages the fact that the degree of compliance with the new class size limits varied among schools, with some already close to these limits while others were far from them. Specifically, this author estimates the impact of reducing the student-to-class ratio by comparing deviations from previous performance trends in districts that had to reduce class size with deviations in districts that received equivalent resources but were not required to reduce ratios because they were already low. This author finds small to no effects of class size reductions on student learning. Jepsen and Rivkin (2009) and Chingos (2012) conclude that hiring a large number of teachers all at once, rather than gradually, can diminish the potential benefits of reducing the student-to-class ratio. This is because it often results in the employment of less experienced and less well-prepared teachers, particularly if teacher salaries are not increased. Moreover, a significant reduction in class size on a large scale can impact the distribution of teachers across schools. For instance, the availability of new positions in more affluent areas may draw experienced teachers away from schools in disadvantaged communities.

Han and Ryu (2017) analyze the average reduction from 44 to 35 students per class implemented in secondary schools in Seoul in 2002. Their identification exploits both the variation generated by this measure and the differences in when and how it was implemented in each school. These authors also find small effects on students' academic performance. Gilraine et al. (2018) reanalyzed the effects of California's class size reduction mandate on students' academic performance. These authors use a difference-in-differences strategy that takes advantage of the gradual implementation of the reform by grade, focusing, unlike Jepsen and Rivkin (2009), on the differential impact of the measure in public and private schools.

Jackson et al. (2016) studied the effect of changes induced by school finance reforms implemented in the United States starting in the early 1970s, which accelerated in the 1980s. These authors use the timing of court-mandated reforms and changes in the funding formula as an exogenous shock to school spending. Taking advantage of the fact that those born between 1955 and 1985 were exposed differently to school finance reforms depending on their place and year of birth, they show that a 10% increase in per-student spending each year over twelve years of schooling results in an additional 0.27 years of education completed, a 7.25% increase in wages, and a 3.67% reduction in the annual incidence of adult poverty. Moreover, the effects are much more significant for children from low-income families. The increases in school spending induced by the reform were associated with a reduction in the student-to-teacher ratio, more school days per year, and increased teacher salaries. Jackson et al. (2016) conclude that the positive effects of increased education funding are driven, at least in part, by the reduction in class size.

Gilraine et al. (2018) find direct positive effects of reducing the student-to-class ratio on student outcomes. The reduction in class size in public schools also reduced the competitive advantage of private schools in California. The entry of higher socioeconomic status students from private to public schools increases the potential for the "peer effect" discussed in Chapter 6 of this book, as well as providing the opportunity for public schools to hire private school teachers, who now have fewer students, to meet the new class size ratios. Gilraine et al. (2018) analyze the long-term benefit of California's CSR law using estimates from Chetty et al. (2011). The analyzed CSR cost is around $1100 per student (in 2009 dollars). The increase in individual present value income created by California's class size reduction law—based on Chetty et al.'s (2011) research on the relationship between class size, learning, and future wages—is $18,300 (in 2009 dollars). Therefore, the net benefit of the CSR analyzed by Gilraine et al. (2018) implies a substantially positive cost–benefit ratio.

Another related area of research that explores changes in the allocation of educational resources is the study of co-teaching, which public education authorities have promoted as a strategy to improve inclusion and academic outcomes for students with disabilities. Co-teaching is among a potential class of reforms, such as reducing class size, that alter the allocation of resources in a way that could better leverage current teachers' abilities. Notably, co-teaching has been widely endorsed by state departments of education, including the Massachusetts Department of Elementary and Secondary Education (MADESE) and New York State Education Department, which strongly encourages schools to adopt this practice as a way to promote the inclusion of students with disabilities (SWDs) in general education classrooms.

Jones and Winters (2024) conducted a comprehensive analysis of co-teaching, where a general education teacher and a special education teacher collaboratively instruct students with and without disabilities within the same classroom. Their study leveraged longitudinal administrative data from Massachusetts to measure the causal effect of co-teaching on student test scores. This analysis is particularly relevant as it provides empirical evidence on a reform that has been widely recommended by public education authorities as a means to enhance the educational experience of SWDs.

The empirical strategy employed by Jones and Winters (2024) is designed to address potential biases arising from non-random assignment of students to co-taught classrooms. Specifically, they use a regression model that controls for both student and school fixed effects, effectively isolating the impact of co-teaching by holding constant factors that do not change over time within students and schools. To further ensure the robustness of their findings, Jones and Winters (2024) conducted specification tests to evaluate potential threats to their identification strategy. One such test involved comparing their primary results with estimates from a regression model that includes a control for the student's prior test score, allowing them to assess whether the effects of co-teaching are consistent when accounting for previous academic performance. This helps to mitigate concerns about dynamic selection, where students might be assigned to co-taught classrooms based on time-variant characteristics such as prior academic achievement.

The results from this study reveal that co-teaching has either no effect or a small positive effect on math scores. However, the impact on English language arts (ELA) is more complex: co-teaching has a positive effect for students with disabilities in elementary grades, but a negative effect for both students with and without disabilities in secondary grades. These findings suggest that while co-teaching may offer benefits in certain contexts, particularly for younger students with disabilities, it may also present challenges in older grades.

In summary, the papers analyzing the introduction of laws that reduce maximum student-to-class ratios and examine the direct and indirect general equilibrium effects of these measures find less positive effects of class size reductions than previous methodologies, except the most recent article by Gilraine et al. (2018).

Exercise 10

The article by Banerjee et al. (2017) (co-authored by two Nobel laureates in Economics, Abhijit Banerjee and Esther Duflo, https://pubs.aeaweb.org/doi/pdfplus/https://doi.org/10.1257/jep.31.4.73) states that "However, as critics have pointed out, this credibility applies to the interventions studied—at that time, on that population, implemented by the organization that was studied—but does not necessarily extend beyond. Some pilot studies these days are enormous, covering many millions of people (we will discuss one such study below). But in the more typical case, critics say, it is not at all clear that results from small 'proof-of-concept' studies run by nongovernment organizations can or should be directly turned into recommendations for policies for implementation by governments on a large scale" (for example, see Deaton 2010). After discussing the possible problems, this paper traces the transition from the original concept to the design and evaluation of a scalable policy. Banerjee et al. (2017) illustrate their analysis using a randomized controlled trial of the "Teaching at the Right Level" methodology, implemented by the non-governmental organization Pratham in Indian primary schools. Summarize the key challenges encountered in scaling up an educational policy, drawing on insights from this significant article.

3.5 Comparison of Student-to-Class Ratios and Performance by Country Based on PISA, TIMSS, or PIRLS

Some studies have analyzed the effect of class size using the international standardized tests discussed in Chapter 1 of this book, such as PISA, TIMSS, or PIRLS. These analyses approach causality more closely than those in Box 1, though they may involve identification assumptions that are more restrictive than those in the four previous sections. Using large-scale international assessment data like PISA, TIMSS, or PIRLS potentially introduces measurement errors that could lead to an underestimation of the effects of class size reduction. These articles instrument the student-to-class ratio with the average class size across the entire course or educational stage, but this instrument is not sufficiently strong for some countries or is not applicable if the school does not have more than one group per course (Green and Iversen 2022). Woessmann and West (2006) use TIMSS data from 18 countries and within-school variation by grade, similarly to the studies initiated by Hoxby (2000) that use population variation in instrumental variable models. Additionally, they include fixed effects by school to control for selection among institutions. These authors find heterogeneous effects of class size in different countries: in particular, smaller class sizes are associated with better outcomes in Iceland and Greece, while the effect is essentially null in most of the other countries.

Exercise 11 Analyze the effect of class size on math and science outcomes as reported by Woessmann and West (2006) for each of the 18 countries they studied. Then, compare these findings with the effects identified in the countries that are also included among the 47 countries analyzed by Altinok and Kingdon (2012).

Altinok and Kingdon (2012) use variation in math and science results from TIMSS across 47 countries for a given student. Specifically, these authors relate the difference in the student-to-class ratio for the same student in their math and science classes with the difference in performance of that same student between the two subjects, math and science. This difference-in-differences approach avoids the problem of non-random matching of children with schools and classes within schools. The results show a significant negative effect of the student-to-class ratio on student performance in 14 countries, but of limited magnitude in most cases. Additionally, Altinok and Kingdon (2012) find that class size effects are smaller in countries with higher teacher quality. Altinok and Kingdon (2012), Denny and Oppedisano (2013) use PISA data from the United States and United Kingdom, instrumenting with variation in the size of adjacent cohorts. These authors do not find a negative effect of the student-to-class ratio on student math outcomes and even suggest a positive impact in the case of the United Kingdom. Overall, this literature demonstrates more mixed evidence and less negative effects of class size on student learning compared to randomized experiments, and even compared to regression discontinuity designs or instrumental variables.

4 Empirical Estimates of the Impact of Class Size Reduction: Long-Term Effects and Heterogeneity

Figure 1 presents a summary of the findings from the literature on the relationship between class size and educational achievement. The figure is based on the survey by Leuven and Oosterbeek (2018) and updated by Montalbán (2021). One new study has been incorporated since Montalbán (2021), the article by Kedagni et al. (2021) published in the European Economic Review. The articles included in the review meet the following criteria: (a) they are published in an international peer-reviewed journal; (b) they use European data; and (c) their research design is valid for estimating causal effects.

Based on Leuven and Oosterbeek (2018) and Montalbán (2021), with the incorporation of an additional article (Kedagni et al. 2021). "SD" refers to standard deviations. The coefficients indicate the change in academic performance, measured in standard deviations, caused by the increase of one student per class. Negative coefficients indicate positive effects of reducing class size. The dots represent the coefficients, while the horizontal black lines show the 90% confidence intervals.

Overall, the estimates in Fig. 1 indicate that reducing class size increases student learning. On average, an increase of one student in class size is associated with a decrease of −0.009 standard deviations in learning (with the median article showing an impact of −0.0099). However, the size of the effects is relatively small, equivalent to what a student learns in a week, and only half of them is statistically significant. The range of estimated coefficients varies from −0.044 in Fredriksson et al. (2016) to 0.065 in Denny and Oppedisano (2013). Out of 35 estimated coefficients: 18 are statistically significant and negative, 8 are not significant and negative, 8 are not significant and positive, and 1 is significant and positive.

Based on Leuven and Oosterbeek (2018) and Montalbán (2021), with the incorporation of an additional article (Kedagni et al. 2021). "SD" refers to standard deviations. The coefficients indicate the change in academic performance, measured in standard deviations, caused by the increase of one student per class. Negative coefficients indicate positive effects of reducing class size. The dots represent the coefficients, while the horizontal black lines show the 90% confidence intervals.

Figure 2 shows that reductions in class size are slightly more effective in primary education, with 65% of the studies finding statistically significant effects, compared to 53% in secondary education. The median coefficient in primary education is −0.0123, while in secondary education it is −0.0078. These results align with the greater cost-effectiveness of early interventions (Heckman 2006) and with studies that also conclude that effects are stronger and estimated more precisely for younger students (Iversen and Bonesrønning 2013; Nandrup 2016; Green and Iversen 2022).

We compare the cost-efficiency of reducing class size versus allocating that investment to other educational measures. For this purpose, Table 2 includes Table 11 and Table 16 from Handel and Hanushek (2023). The top part shows the revised estimates by these two authors on the impact of reducing class size by one student on student exam performance. In this case, and unlike Figs. 1 and 2, the effect is

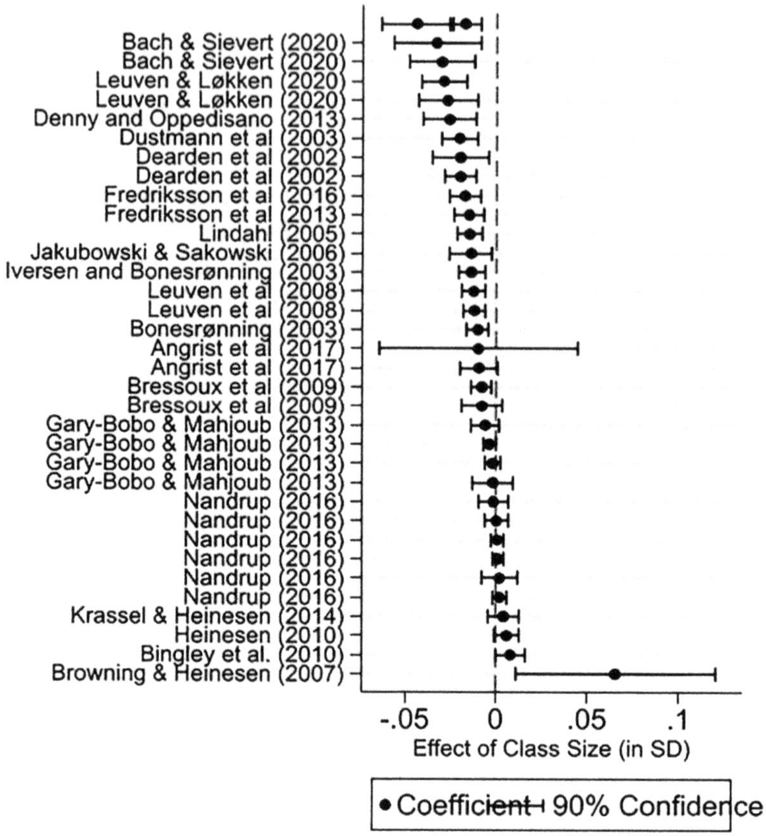

Fig. 1 Estimates on the effect of class size

positive since Handel and Hanushek (2023) analyze a decrease (not an increase) in the student-to-class ratio. The presented estimates, with an average impact of 0.003 standard deviations (one-third in absolute terms of what we presented in Fig. 1), have been standardized by the two authors to make the estimates comparable. Table 2 also shows the estimates collected and standardized by Handel and Hanushek (2023) on the effect of a 10% increase in education spending on student exam performance. The average impact of an increase in spending on exam scores is 0.069 standard deviations. Reducing class size by 10% would imply reducing the student-to-class ratio by up to 2.5 students (see Table 1), which would lead to an impact on learning (assuming linearity) of about 0.01 standard deviations. Handel and Hanushek (2023) conclude that the estimated positive impact on learning from reducing class size is significantly smaller than the impact of allocating those funds to general education spending. If instead of assuming an average effect of reducing the student-to-class ratio of 0.003, as Handel and Hanushek (2023) do, we use the one shown in Fig. 1 of 0.009, the comparison would still favor allocating public funds to educational

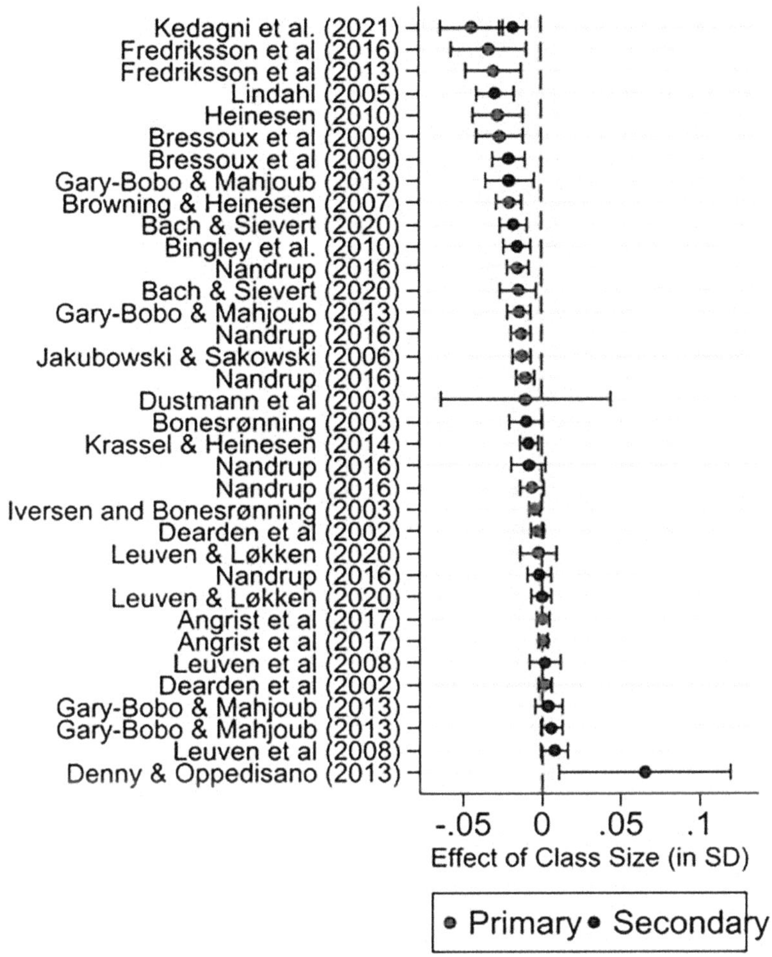

Fig. 2 Estimates on the effect of class size by education level

measures other than reducing class size, but the difference would be much smaller (0.069 versus 0.027 standard deviations). This conclusion aligns with Carneiro and Heckman (2003), who noted that although smaller classes increase students' earnings as adults, the wage gains received by students do not offset the costs of hiring additional teachers.

Bettinger et al. (2017) analyze the effects of increasing class size on the outcomes and persistence of college students in online courses, a common mode of instruction in many higher education institutions. A quasi-random experiment, where students at DeVry University were assigned to regular-sized classes with 31 peers or slightly larger ones (10% more), concluded that small changes in the number of students in online classes do not lead to differences in student performance or university

Table 2 The effect of a class size reduction compared to a 10% increase in education spending (Extracted from Handel and Hanushek 2023)

	Median	Minimum	Maximum	Number of studies
Distribution of estimates of the effect of reducing class size by one student. Effect on external test results				
Effect on external test results	0.003	−0.066	0.036	29
Distribution of estimates of the impact of a 10% increase in education spending				
Effect on external test results	0.069	−0.244	0.543	23

Source Handel, D. V. Hanushek, E.A., 2023. U.S. School Finance: Resources and Outcomes, en Machin, S.J., Woessmann, L. Hanushek, E.A. (Eds.), Handbook of the Economics of Education. Volume 7. North Holland, Amsterdam

persistence. Bettinger et al. (2017) also do not find heterogeneity in effects based on the academic discipline studied by the students. The large sample size analyzed by these authors allows for precise estimates that rule out significant effects.

The education young people receive is intended to have lifelong effects, so it is important to assess the impact of educational measures in the long term, beyond their effect on test results. It could be that reducing class size has benefits that are valued in the labor market. Conversely, the effects of class size may diminish over time. As mentioned at the beginning of this chapter, Krueger and Whitmore (2001) found that the impact of class size reduction decreases by half to three-quarters one year after the intervention, even after maintaining the new and smaller student-to-class ratio. Chetty et al. (2011) also find that the effect of class size on students' academic performance fades quickly in the short term. However, this seminal work also finds that a smaller student-to-class ratio does significantly affect the likelihood of pursuing higher education. The empirical evidence from Chetty et al. (2011) presents a paradox, as it indicates that reducing the student-to-class ratio does not have substantial short-term effects, but it does have significant medium- and long-term effects. One hypothesis that could explain this puzzle is that studying in smaller classes may not significantly impact cognitive skills but may be beneficial for non-cognitive skills such as perseverance, motivation, effort, or determination. The limited impact of smaller classes on improving cognitive skills would explain why the impact of class size on academic performance is, at most, modest and disappears over time. On the other hand, studying in small classes improves non-cognitive skills, an effect that does not manifest in external and standardized tests but has a long-term impact by increasing the likelihood of reaching higher education and enjoying a more stable financial situation in adulthood (Chetty et al. 2011). Chingos (2012) also did not find a significant impact of Florida's Class Size Reduction (CSR) mandate, but he did find evidence of effects on non-cognitive outcomes, including higher class attendance in primary school and fewer disciplinary problems in secondary school. Fredriksson et al. (2013) also found a significant effect of smaller classes on students' acquisition of non-cognitive skills. A smaller student-to-class ratio in grades 4–6 improves perseverance, educational aspirations, and self-confidence by age 13. The effects of smaller classes in primary school on non-cognitive skills persist until age

18, measured in this case by perseverance, social character, emotional stability, willingness to take responsibility, and initiative. In fact, Fredriksson et al. (2013) found that smaller class sizes in the last years of primary school significantly increase the likelihood of completing higher education and raise labor income between ages 27 and 42, particularly for individuals in the middle of the wage distribution. Overall, the effects on students' non-cognitive skills seem more consistent (Sevilla et al. 2020).

As discussed in Chapter 9, the Perry Preschool Project and the Abecedarian Project are two early childhood intervention programs that have followed participants for over half a century, showing promising results along the way. These are two early childhood interventions evaluated using the randomization method with long-term follow-up. The Perry Preschool Project (PPP) was carried out in Michigan starting in 1962, providing a preschool program for children aged 3–5 with up to 3 hours a day throughout the school year, as well as parental guidance with weekly teacher visits to homes. Highly qualified teachers were hired, maintaining a ratio of less than 6 children per teacher. The Abecedarian Project (ABC) was developed in North Carolina starting in 1972, from birth to age 5, with an intensive program of more than 6.5 hours a day, applying a specific curriculum that included both educational activities and a health and nutrition component. The eligibility of both programs (PPP and ABC) was based on an indicator of socioeconomic disadvantage in the children's households, though the specific criteria and emphasis varied between the two interventions. Decades of follow-up have shown encouraging results in non-cognitive skills such as self-control or motivation, with long-term positive effects on education, income, health, and lower participation in crime (Conti et al. 2016).

The direct effect of class size varies among different types of students, resulting in heterogeneous effects (Lazear 2001; Albornoz et al. 2018). Green and Iversen (2022) summarize the evidence that the effects of class size are more positive for students from low-income or low-education families, minority groups, or previously underperforming students, although in some cases the differences are not significant (Leuven and Løkken 2020). These heterogeneous patterns have important policy implications. It would be efficient for maximum class sizes to be smaller as the proportion of disadvantaged children in a course increases (Bach and Sievert 2024).

Variations in the student-to-class ratio may have complementarities or be substitutes for other educational inputs such as family support and teacher effort. For example, parents whose children have been assigned to larger classes might react by providing more educational support, helping with homework, or arranging external tutoring. Chapter 5 on family discusses the theoretical model by Albornoz, Berlinski, and Cabrales (2018), in which student effort and learning outcomes, parental behavior, and public resources devoted to education are jointly determined within an integrated theoretical framework. The conclusions of the Albornoz et al. (2018) model predict that when classes are larger, parents spend more time helping students with homework, but teachers tend to place more responsibility on their students—a hypothesis confirmed by Fredriksson et al. (2016). Teachers can take advantage of class size reduction by changing their methodologies to conduct more interactive teaching practices between teachers and students, and among students themselves. Green and Iversen's (2022) review does not find clear and conclusive evidence of parental response to changes in class size. Bonesrønning et al. (2020) do show that reducing the student-to-class ratio leads to substantial increases in teacher effort, motivation, or job satisfaction. In contrast, as highlighted earlier, Clark et al. (2024) demonstrate that reducing class sizes can markedly improve teacher effectiveness by creating a more manageable classroom environment. This enhancement not only leads to better student behavior but also empowers teachers to implement more engaging and student-centered instructional practices.

Box 4: The Theoretical Model of Lazear (2001)

Lazear (2001) presents an educational production model in which, when a student disrupts the class, learning decreases for the other students. The optimal class size is larger for students with better classroom behavior, which helps explain why it is difficult to find effects related to class size in the data. The basic structure begins with the recognition that education in a classroom setting is a public good. As with most public goods, learning in the classroom has congestion effects, which are negative externalities created when one student hinders the learning of their classmates.

Lazear's (2001) theoretical model starts by defining p as the probability that a particular student is not hindering his own learning or that of others at any given time. Therefore, the probability that all students in a class of size n are behaving well is p^n, so that disruptions occur $1 - p^n$ of the time. Neither the student nor their classmates can learn much when a student misbehaves, which forces the teacher to spend time addressing the disruption. Lazear (2001) points out that p will be relatively high because even with $p = 0.98$in a class of 25 students, there will still be disruptions 40% of the time $1 - (0.98)^{25} = 0.40$. To determine the actions of schools under different conditions, Lazear (2001) begins by asking how much a family would pay for a student to be in a class of size n. It is assumed that the value of one unit of learning is given by V, which is determined by the market value of human capital and the probability that a student is focused on learning at any given moment. To determine the optimal class size, Lazear (2001) considers a school with Z students, m teachers, and m classes. It is assumed that the cost of a teacher and the associated capital rent for their classroom is given by W, which is assumed to be independent of p and other working conditions. A private school seeking to maximize profits can sell each moment of school time for ZVp^n, with a total cost of Wm. Profit maximization would mean choosing m to maximize (Lazear, 2001):

$$Profit = ZVp^{\frac{Z}{m}} - Wm \tag{1}$$

$$Profitperstudent = ZVp^n - \frac{W}{n} \tag{2}$$

Given that

$$n = \frac{Z}{m} \tag{3}$$

The first-order condition is then:

$$-V\frac{Z^2}{m^2}p^{\frac{Z}{m}}\ln(p) - W \tag{4}$$

And using (2).

$$Vp^n\ln(p) - \frac{W}{n^2} = 0 \tag{5}$$

.

Variations in V may result either because the market for educated individuals relative to less educated individuals changes, or because the amount of learning that takes place during an uninterrupted moment of schooling changes (as a result, for example, of variations in teacher quality or student skills).

Market equilibrium is achieved in two ways, given the existence of positive profits. Competitive entry of firms into the education industry drives W up through demand pressure on teacher salaries. At the same time, the supply of educated graduates to the labor market reduces V. Equilibrium is achieved when profit maximization results in zero total profits for the competitive education provider.

Class size is a choice variable, and the optimal class size varies inversely with students' ability to stay focused. It is efficient to use fewer teachers and a higher student-to-teacher ratio when students behave better. The negative effects of class size are greater for students who behave poorly in class.

Exercise 12: Based on the basic model in Eq. (2), demonstrate Proposition 1 from Lazear's (2001) paper (page 782 and page 799, https://www.jstor.org/stable/2696418). The optimal class size increases with teacher salary, decreases with the value of a unit of education, and, most importantly, increases with the probability that students behave well. It is optimal to reduce class size when students behave worse.

Exercise 13: Suppose that the ratio of W to Vp^n is 5. The teacher's time is five times more valuable than what any student gets from the class. $Z = 100$ and $p = 0.99$, meaning that 99% of the time, any student is not causing a disruption significant enough to prevent learning in the classroom. Using the first-order condition (3), calculate the optimal m and the optimal class size n.

a. Calculate the optimal number of classes m and the class size n, if $p = 0.98$, that is, if there are more class interruptions than when $p = 0.98$.
b. Calculate the optimal number of classes m and the class size n, if $p = 0.995$, that is, if there are fewer class interruptions than when $p = 0.99$.

c. Calculate the educational production per student (p^n), with the optimal n when $p = 0.98$; $p = 0.99$; and $p = 0{,}995$. Check how a class with fewer students n may have lower educational production if class engagement p drops sufficiently.
d. Explain why the relationship between n and p results in optimal early childhood education classes being smaller than those at the university level.

5 Small-Group Tutoring

In Sects. 3 and 4, it has been shown that reducing class size improves cognitive skills in the short term and has a longer-term effect on non-cognitive skills. However, even with the highest estimates of the impact of reducing the student-to-class ratio, such as that of Krueger (1999), a widespread reduction in class size is not a very efficient policy given the enormous investment it requires (Carneiro and Heckman 2003). Bonesrønning et al. (2022) provide evidence that more flexible and less costly approaches, such as small-group tutoring, can focus on certain subjects and support struggling students by allowing for more individualized instruction from tutors. Causal empirical evidence has been found demonstrating the effectiveness of small-group tutoring. In their meta-analysis, Nickow et al. (2023) review 96 articles that analyze the effects of this measure based on randomized controlled trials and conclude that the average impact is significant, amounting to 0.37 standard deviations, equivalent to what a student learns in a school year. The effects for reading and math interventions are similar. However, reading tutoring tends to produce larger effect sizes in the early grades, while math tutoring tends to produce larger effect sizes in later grades. Besides academic support, these interventions can also improve students' socio-emotional development and increase school attendance. The COVID-19 pandemic had an uneven impact on disadvantaged children (Betthäuser et al. 2023), placing small-group tutoring programs in a prominent position as an efficient policy to reduce the educational gaps that widened during the pandemic.

The effectiveness of small-group tutoring decreases as the group size increases, with a more pronounced drop when the group exceeds six students (Burgess 2020). The impact will also be greater the more intensive the program is. For example, Burgess (2020) notes that a half-hour daily tutoring session over 12 weeks results in additional progress for students equivalent to four months of school learning. Kraft and Falken (2021) highlight the factors that contribute to the success of small-group tutoring programs, including a rigorous selection process for tutors, full-time employment throughout the academic year with the same group of students, ongoing training in best teaching practices, and coordination with teachers at the school where the student is enrolled. Tutoring programs are more effective when delivered by teachers or, in general, education professionals, rather than by volunteers or parents. Tutoring provided by volunteers often does not produce good educational outcomes because it does not run throughout the school year and because volunteers lack specific training for teaching struggling students. The challenge of providing high-quality tutoring across a wide range of subjects and grades becomes even more complex when addressing the needs of students with disabilities (Kraft 2015). The result of volunteer tutoring is generally low student participation rates and little improvement in academic performance. The lack of coordination between tutors and regular teachers and a high turnover of the former has also led to the failure of some interventions. Kraft and Falken (2021) also point out that tutoring carried out during school hours tends to have greater impacts than those conducted after school. In conclusion, the implementation of well-designed and coordinated small-group tutoring programs could offer significant opportunities for improving education. However, it is vital to ensure their success by considering careful planning, meticulous selection of tutors, ongoing commitment from them, and their adaptation to the diverse needs of students. White et al. (2023) also show that the educational support provided by small-group tutoring is more meaningful when tutors foster positive relationships with students, focusing on their strengths and needs. Reviewing 33 articles on the implementation of educational support, these authors conclude that the environment and timing of support, recruitment, and training, and the curriculum significantly affect whether individual or small-group tutoring constitutes quality instruction for students.

Among the most recent causal studies on the effect of small-group tutoring is Bonesrønning et al. (2022), which conducted a large-scale randomized controlled trial in Norway. Primary school students who were randomly assigned to small-group math tutoring left their regular classes, so this initiative had the additional effect of reducing the size of the main math group. Bonesrønning et al. (2022) show that smaller classes lead to substantial increases in a variety of teacher effort, motivation, and job satisfaction measures. The intention-to-treat estimates show that students in the treated schools increased their performance by 0.06 standard deviations in national tests (equivalent to two months of learning), with no heterogeneous effect based on prior achievement, parental education, or gender.

Gortázar et al. (2024) provide evidence from a randomized controlled trial on the effectiveness of an online math tutoring program aimed at secondary school students aged 12–15 from disadvantaged areas in Spain. This was an intensive eight-week program held during after-school hours in groups of two students from the same class. The tutoring was provided by qualified and paid secondary school teachers in collaboration with Empieza por Educar (ExE), the Spanish branch of Teach for All, an NGO specializing in training young teachers who work in schools attended by vulnerable and low-income students. The intervention increased standardized math test scores by 0.26 standard deviations and reduced the likelihood of repeating the school year by 9.4 percentage points, equivalent to a 78% decrease compared to the control group, which had a repetition rate of 12%. Gortázar et al. (2024) provide evidence that the program's positive effects persist one year later. The intervention also improved some non-cognitive outcomes, such as aspirations: students in the treatment group were 13.6 percentage points more likely to express a desire to continue academic studies in high school, equivalent to a 33.2% increase compared to the control group average. The authors find no impact on students' perceived math competence, interest in math, locus of control, perseverance, or overall well-being.

Gortázar et al. (2024) find evidence supporting Kraft and Falken's (2021) hypotheses about the importance of qualified and paid tutors, as 96.6% of the students in the treatment group completed the program, with very low turnover during the program. These authors conducted this randomized controlled trial several months after Spanish schools fully reopened after the pandemic. The positive evidence they find shows that small-group tutoring programs can be considered a complement rather than a substitute for regular classroom teaching. The intervention costs approximately 300 euros per student, indicating that the cost–benefit ratio is an increase of 0.087 standard deviations (0.26/3) per 100 euros.

6 Conclusions

Identifying the causal relationship between class size and students' educational outcomes through correlations or ordinary least squares (OLS) estimates leads to spurious associations. Causal studies show that reducing class size by one student improves students' external test results by approximately 0.01 standard deviations, which is equivalent to what is learned in one week of school. Estimates of the impact of reducing the student-to-teacher ratio vary widely, with some studies finding no impact and others finding a significant effect of up to 0.044 standard deviations. Reducing class size has a positive impact on learning, but the effect is limited for a measure that comes with a very high budgetary cost. As Chingos (2011) already concluded, large-scale class size reductions "are also extremely costly and represent a missed opportunity to make smarter educational investments" (page 2). Other educational measures could have a better cost–benefit ratio than reducing the student-to-teacher ratio. The median of the studies reviewed by Handel and Hanushek (2023) shows that a 10% increase in spending on other educational policies leads to a learning improvement that is seven times greater than the effect of a 10% reduction in class size.

An alternative approach could be to implement class size reductions in a more targeted manner, focusing on the early educational levels, such as preschool and primary education. As shown in the early childhood education chapter of this book (Chapter 9), empirical evidence consistently supports the benefits of high-quality early interventions. Many good habits are established very early. The positive impact of class size reduction appears to be concentrated within primary education, particularly in the subject of mathematics (Handel and Hanushek 2023).

Class size reduction benefits students from disadvantaged or low-education families, those from unstable family environments, minority groups, or those lagging in academic performance to a greater extent (Green and Iversen 2022). Consequently, it is more efficient to focus class size reductions in schools located in disadvantaged areas or with a higher proportion of students with learning difficulties, as these students can benefit more from increased teacher attention. This conclusion reinforces the idea that a teacher's ability to control and manage the classroom is more challenging when students are disruptive or need additional support (Lazear 2001), making the effects of class size reduction more noticeable in environments with a higher number of students who struggle to keep up with classes or have behavioral issues. Public policies such as small-group tutoring and academic recovery programs have a much higher benefit–cost ratio than generalized class size reduction.

As for future research directions, the interaction between class size and teaching practices, classroom environment, and the expectations, incentives, constraints, and behaviors of students, parents, and teachers could be explored. The study of the impact of the student-to-teacher ratio has focused on conventional instructional approaches. However, in the current era, the introduction of modern technologies and pedagogical innovations in schools has led to substantial changes. Finally, the study of the effect of class size reduction could focus on specific areas or cognitive processes where more learning obstacles are identified (Connolly and Haeck 2022).

References

Adusumilli, K., F. Agostinelli, and E. Borghesan. 2024. Heterogeneity and endogenous compliance: Implications for scaling class size interventions. National Bureau of Economic Research. Report No. w32338. http://www.nber.org/papers/w32338

Altinok, N., and G. Kingdon. 2012. New evidence on class size effects: A pupil fixed effects approach. *Oxford Bulletin of Economics and Statistics* 74 (2): 203–234. https://doi.org/10.1111/j.1468-0084.2011.00648.x.

Albornoz, F., S. Berlinski, and A. Cabrales. 2018. Motivation, resources, and the organization of the school system. *Journal of the European Economic Association* 16 (1): 199–231. https://doi.org/10.1093/jeea/jvx001.

Andersen, S.C., L. Beuchert, H. Skyt Nielsen, and M.K. Thomsen. 2020. The effect of teacher's aides in the classroom: Evidence from a randomized trial. *Journal of the European Economic Association* 18 (1): 469–505. https://doi.org/10.1093/jeea/jvy048.

Angrist, J.D., E. Battistin, and D. Vuri. 2017. In a small moment: Class size and moral hazard in the Italian Mezzogiorno. *American Economics Journal: Applied Economics* 9 (4): 216–249. https://doi.org/10.1257/app.20160267.

Angrist, J.D., and V. Lavy. 1999. Using Maimonides' rule to estimate the effect of class size on scholastic achievement. *Quarterly Journal of Economics* 114 (2): 533–575. https://doi.org/10.1162/003355399556061.

Angrist, J.D., V. Lavy, J. Leder-Luis, and A. Shany. 2019. Maimonides' rule redux. *American Economic Review: Insights* 1 (3): 309–324. https://doi.org/10.1257/aeri.20180120.

Angrist, J., and J. Pischke. 2014. *Mastering 'metrics: The path from cause to effect*. Princeton: Princeton University Press.

Argaw, B.A., and P.A. Puhani. 2018. Does class size matter for school tracking outcomes after elementary school? Quasi-experimental evidence using administrative panel data from Germany. *Economics of Education Review* 65: 48–57. https://doi.org/10.1016/j.econedurev.2018.06.005.

Banerjee, A., R. Banerji, J. Berry, E. Duflo, H. Kannan, S. Mukerji, M. Shotland, and M. Walton. 2017. From proof of concept to scalable policies: Challenges and solutions, with an application. *Journal of Economic Perspectives* 31 (4): 73–102. https://doi.org/10.1257/jep.31.4.73.

Bach, M., and S. Sievert. 2024. Birth cohort size variation and the estimation of class size effects. *Journal of Human Resources* (in Press). https://doi.org/10.3368/jhr.0919-10430R2.

Betthäuser, B.A., A.M. Bach-Mortensen, and P. Engzell. 2023. A systematic review and meta-analysis of the evidence on learning during the COVID-19 pandemic. *Nature Human Behaviour* 7 (3): 375–385. https://doi.org/10.1038/s41562-022-01506-4.

Bettinger, E., C. Doss, S. Loeb, A. Rogers, and E. Taylor. 2017. The effects of class size in online college courses: Experimental evidence. *Economics of Education Review* 58: 68–85. https://doi.org/10.1016/j.econedurev.2017.03.006.

Bingley, P., V.M. Jensen, I. Walker. 2010. The effect of class size on education and earnings: Evidence from Denmark. Unpublished Working Paper. https://www.bristol.ac.uk/media-library/sites/cmpo/migrated/documents/bingley.pdf

Bonesrønning, H. 2003. Class size effects on student achievement in Norway: Patterns and explanations. *Southern Economic Journal* 69 (4): 952–965. https://doi.org/10.1002/j.2325-8012.2003.tb00542.x.

Bonesrønning, H., C. Green, J.M.V. Iversen, O.H. Nyhus. 2020. How do teachers respond to changes in class size? Evidence from a randomised trial. Norwegian University of Science and Technology. Unpublished Working Paper.

Bonesrønning, H., H. Finseraas, I. Hardoy, J.M.V. Iversen, O.H. Nyhus, V. Opheim, K.V. Salvanes, A.M.J. Sandsør, and P. Schøne. 2022. Small-group instruction to improve student performance in mathematics in early grades: Results from a randomized field experiment. *Journal of Public Economics* 216: 104765. https://doi.org/10.1016/j.jpubeco.2022.104765.

Bressoux, P., F. Kramarz, and C. Prost. 2009. Teachers training, class size and students' outcomes: Learning from administrative forecasting mistakes. *The Economic Journal* 119 (536): C540–C561. https://doi.org/10.1111/j.1468-0297.2008.02247.x.

Browning, M., and E. Heinesen. 2007. Class size, teacher hours and educational attainment. *Scandinavian Journal of Economics* 109 (2): 415–438. https://doi.org/10.1111/j.1467-9442.2007.00492.x.

Burgess, S., 2020. How we should deal with the lockdown learning loss in England's schools. Voxeu. https://cepr.org/voxeu/columns/how-we-should-deal-lockdown-learning-loss-englands-schools. Accessed on August 16, 2024.

Cabrales, A., 2010. El tamaño de la clase y el experimento STAR a largo plazo. Nada es Gratis. https://nadaesgratis.es/cabrales/el-tamano-de-la-clase-y-el-experimento-star-a-largo-plazo. Accessed on August 16, 2024.

Carneiro, P., and J.J. Heckman. 2003. Human capital policy. In *Inequality in America: What role for human capital policy?*, ed. J. Heckman and A. Krueger, 77–240. Cambridge: MIT Press. https://www.nber.org/system/files/working_papers/w9495/w9495.pdf

Chetty, R., J.N. Friedman, N. Hilger, E. Saez, D.W. Schanzenbach, and D. Yagan. 2011. How does your kindergarten classroom affect your earnings? Evidence from Project STAR. *Quarterly Journal of Economics* 126 (4): 1593–1660. https://doi.org/10.1093/qje/qjr041.

Chingos, M.M. 2011. The false promise of class-size reduction. Center for American Progress. Accessed on August 16, 2024. https://files.eric.ed.gov/fulltext/ED536071.pdf

Chingos, M.M. 2012. The impact of a universal class-size reduction policy: Evidence from Florida's statewide mandate. *Economics of Education Review* 31 (5): 543–562. https://doi.org/10.1016/j.econedurev.2012.03.002.

Cho, H., P. Glewwe, and M. Whitler. 2012. Do reductions in class size raise students' test scores? Evidence from population variation in Minnesota's elementary schools. *Economics of Education Review* 31 (3): 77–95. https://doi.org/10.1016/j.econedurev.2012.01.004.

Clark, D., J. Montalbán, A. de Gendre, and P. Deschamps. 2024. The impact of class size reduction on classroom dynamics and instructional practices: Evidence from the Madrid region. University of Stockholm (mimeo).

Cohen-Zada, D., M. Gradstein, E. Reuven. 2013. Allocation of students in public schools: Theory and new evidence. *Economics of Education Review* 34 (C): 96–106.

Connolly, M., and C. Haeck. 2022. Nonlinear class size effects on cognitive and noncognitive development of young children. *Journal of Labor Economics* 40 (S1): 341–382. https://doi.org/10.1086/718328.

Conti, G., J.H. Heckman, and R. Pinto. 2016. The effects of two influential early childhood interventions on health and healthy behaviour. *Economic Journal* 126 (596): 28–65. https://doi.org/10.1111/ecoj.12420.

Deaton, Angus. 2010. "Instruments, randomization, and learning about development." *Journal of Economic Literature* 48 (2): 424–55. https://doi.org/10.1257/jel.48.2.424.

Dearden, L., J. Ferri, and C. Meghir. 2002. The effect of school quality on educational attainment and wages. *Review of Economics and Statistics* 84 (1): 1–20. https://doi.org/10.1162/003465302317331883.

Denny, K., and V. Oppedisano. 2013. The surprising effect of larger class sizes: Evidence using two identification strategies. *Labour Economics* 23: 57–65. https://doi.org/10.1016/j.labeco.2013.04.004.

Duflo, E., P. Dupas, and M. Kremer. 2015. School governance, teacher incentives, and teacher-pupil-ratios: Experimental evidence from Kenyan primary schools. *Journal of Public Economics* 123: 92–110. https://doi.org/10.1016/j.jpubeco.2014.11.008.

Dustmann, C., N. Rajah, and A. van Soest. 2003. Class size, education, and wages. *Economic Journal* 113: F99–F120. https://doi.org/10.1111/1468-0297.00101.

European Commission. 2023. National Education Systems. Eurydice, Luxemburgo. https://eurydice.eacea.ec.europa.eu/national-education-systems.

Fredriksson, P.B. Öckert, and H. Oosterbeek. 2013. Long-term effects of class size. *Quarterly Journal of Economics* 128 (1): 249–285. https://www.jstor.org/stable/26372498.

Fredriksson, P., B. Öckert, and H. Oosterbeek. 2016. Parental responses to public investments in children: Evidence from a maximum class size rule. *Journal of Human Resources* 51 (4): 832–868. https://doi.org/10.3368/jhr.51.4.1114-6779R1.

Fryer, R.G. 2017. The production of human capital in developed countries: Evidence from 196 randomized field experiments. In *Handbook of Economic Field Experiments*, vol. 2, ed. A.V. Banerjee and E. Duflo, 95–322. Amsterdam: North-Holland. https://scholar.harvard.edu/sites/scholar.harvard.edu/files/fryer/files/handbook_fryer_03.25.2016.pdf

Gary-Bobo, R.J., and M.B. Mahjoub. 2013. Estimation of class-size effects, using Maimonides' rule and other instruments: The case of French junior high schools. *Annals of Economics and Statistics* 111–112: 193–225. https://doi.org/10.2307/23646331.

Gilraine, M., H. Macartney, and R. McMillan. 2018. Education reform in general equilibrium: Evidence from California's class size reduction. National Bureau of Economic Research. Report No. w24191. https://www.nber.org/system/files/working_papers/w24191/revisions/w24191.rev0.pdf

Gilraine, M. 2020. A method for disentangling multiple treatments from a regression discontinuity design. *Journal of Labor Economics* 38 (4): 1267–1311. https://doi.org/10.1086/706740.

Gortázar, L., C. Hupkau, and A. Roldán-Monés. 2024. Online tutoring works: Experimental evidence from a program with vulnerable children. *Journal of Public Economics* 232: 105082. https://doi.org/10.1016/j.jpubeco.2024.105082.

Graves, J. and E. Zucchelli. 2022. Consecuencias no intencionadas de las medidas de política pública: ejemplos de sanidad y educación. *Papeles de Economía Española* 172, 30–42. https://www.funcas.es/articulos/consecuencias-no-intencionadas-de-las-medidas-de-politica-publica-ejemplos-de-sanidad-y-educacion/

Green, C., and J.M.V. Iversen. 2022. The effect of class size in schools on student outcomes. In *Critical perspectives on economics of education*, ed. S. Mendolia, M. O'Brien, A.R. Paloyo, and O. Yerokhin, 166–181. Abingdon: Routledge. https://doi.org/10.1080/02188791.2023.2224634

Han, J., and K. Ryu. 2017. Effects of class size reduction in upper grades: Evidence from Seoul. *Korea. Economics of Education Review* 60: 68–85. https://doi.org/10.1016/j.econedurev.2017.07.004.

Handel, D.V., and E.A. Hanushek. 2023. U.S. School finance: Resources and outcomes. In *Handbook of the Economics of Education*, vol. 7, ed. S.J. Machin, L. Woessmann, E.A. Hanushek, 143–226. Amsterdam, North Holland. https://doi.org/10.1016/bs.hesedu.2023.03.003.

Hanushek, E.A. 1997. Assessing the effects of school resources on student performance: An update. *Educational Evaluation and Policy Analysis* 19 (2): 141–164. https://doi.org/10.3102/01623737019002141.

Hanushek, E.A., G. Schwerdt, S. Wiederhold, and L. Woessmann. 2015. Returns to skills around the world: Evidence from PIAAC. *European Economic Review* 73: 103–130. https://doi.org/10.1016/j.euroecorev.2014.10.006.

Hanushek, E., and L. Woessmann. 2011. The economics of international differences in educational achievement. In *Handbook of the economics of education*, vol. 3, ed. S. Machin and L. Woessmann, 89–200. Amsterdam, North Holland. https://www.sciencedirect.com/handbook/handbook-of-the-economics-of-education/vol/3/suppl/C

Hanushek, E., and L. Woessmann. 2020. The economic impacts of learning losses. OECD Education Working Papers. No. 225. OECD Publishing, Paris. https://doi.org/10.1787/21908d74-en.

Haaland, V.F., M. Rege, and O.J. Solheim. 2024. Do students learn more with an additional teacher in the classroom? Evidence from a field experiment. *The Economic Journal* 134 (657): 418–435. https://doi.org/10.1093/ej/uead074.

Heckman, J.J. 2006. Skill formation and the economics of investing in disadvantaged children. *Science* 312 (5782): 1900–1902. https://doi.org/10.1126/science.1128898.

Heinesen, E. 2010. Estimating class-size effects using within-school variation in subject-specific classes. *Economic Journal* 120 (545): 737–760. https://doi.org/10.1111/j.1468-0297.2009.02301.x.

Hojo, M. 2013. Class-size effects in Japanese schools: A spline regression approach. *Economics Letters* 120 (3): 583–587. https://doi.org/10.1016/j.econlet.2013.06.027.

Hoxby, C.M. 2000. The effects of class size on student achievement: New evidence from population variation. *Quarterly Journal of Economics* 115 (4): 1239–1285. https://doi.org/10.1162/003355300555060.

Iversen, J.M., and H. Bonesrønning. 2013. Disadvantaged students in the early grades: Will smaller classes help them? *Education Economics* 21: 305–324. https://doi.org/10.1080/09645292.2011.623380.

Jackson, C.K., R.C. Johnson, and C. Persico. 2016. The effects of school spending on educational and economic outcomes: Evidence from school finance reforms. *Quarterly Journal of Economics* 131: 157–218. https://doi.org/10.1093/qje/qjv036.

Jakubowski, M., and P. Sakowski. 2006. Quasi-experimental estimates of class size effect in primary schools in Poland. *International Journal of Educational Research* 45: 202–215. https://doi.org/10.1016/j.ijer.2006.11.003.

Jepsen, C., and S. Rivkin. 2009. Class size reduction and student achievement: The potential tradeoff between teacher quality and class size. *Journal of Human Resources* 44 (1): 223–250. https://doi.org/10.3368/jhr.44.1.223.

Jones, N., Winters, M.A., 2024. Are two teachers better than one? The effect of co-teaching on students with and without disabilities. *Journal of Human Resources* 59 (4). https://doi.org/10.3368/jhr.0420-10834R3

Kedagni, D., K. Krishna, R. Megalokonomou, and Y. Zhao. 2021. Does class size matter? How, and at what cost? *European Economic Review* 133 (C): 103664 https://doi.org/10.1016/j.euroecorev.2021.103664

Kraft, M. A. (2015). How to make additional time matter: Integrating individualized tutorials into an extended day. *Education Finance and Policy*, 10 (1), 81–116.

Kraft, M. A., and Falken, G. T. (2021). A blueprint for scaling tutoring and mentoring across public schools. *Aera Open*, 7 (1), 1–21. https://doi.org/10.1177/23328584211042858

Krassel, K.F., and E. Heinesen. 2014. Class-size effects in secondary school. *Education Economics* 22 (4): 412–426. https://doi.org/10.1080/09645292.2014.902428.

Krueger, A.B. 1999. Experimental estimates of education production functions. *Quarterly Journal of Economics* 114 (2): 497–532. https://doi.org/10.1162/003355399556052.

Krueger, A.B., and D.M. Whitmore. 2001. The effect of attending a small class in the early grades on college-test taking and middle school test results: Evidence from project STAR. *The Economic Journal* 111 (468): 1–28. https://doi.org/10.1111/1468-0297.00586.

Lazear, E.E. 2001. Educational production. *Quarterly Journal of Economics* 116 (3): 777–803. https://doi.org/10.1162/00335530152466232.

Leuven, E., H. Oosterbeek, and M. Rønning. 2008. Quasi-experimental estimates of the effect of class size on achievement in Norway. *Scandinavian Journal of Economics* 110 (4): 663–693. https://doi.org/10.1111/j.1467-9442.2008.00556.x.

Leuven, E. and Oosterbeek, H. 2018. Class size and student outcomes in Europe. European Expert Network on Economics of Education Analytical Report, 33. Publications Office of the European Union, Luxemburgo. https://doi.org/10.2766/59709

Leuven, E., and S.A. Løkken. 2020. Long-term impacts of class size in compulsory school. *Journal of Human Resources*. 55 (1): 309–348. https://doi.org/10.3368/jhr.55.2.0217.8574R2.

Lindahl, M. 2005. Home versus school learning: A new approach to estimating the effect of class size on achievement. *Scandinavian Journal of Economics*. 107 (2): 375–394. https://doi.org/10.1111/j.1467-9442.2005.00413.x.

MacKinnon, J.G., M.O. Nielsen, and M.D. Webb. 2023. Testing for the appropriate level of clustering in linear regression models. *Journal of Econometrics* 235 (2): 2027–2056. https://doi.org/10.1016/j.jeconom.2023.03.005.

Montalbán, J. 2021. ¿Es realmente efectiva la política educativa más popular?. Nada es Gratis. https://nadaesgratis.es/jose-montalban/es-realmente-efectiva-la-politica-educativa-mas-popular. Accessed on August 16, 2024.

Nandrup, A.B. 2016. Do class size effects differ across grades? *Education Economics* 24 (1): 83–95. https://doi.org/10.1080/09645292.2015.1099616.

Nickow, A., Oreopoulos, P., and Quan, V. (2023). The promise of tutoring for preK–p2 learning: A systematic review and meta-analysis of the experimental evidence. *American Educational Research Journal* 61 (1): 74–107. https://doi.org/10.3102/00028312231208687

OCDE. 2012. Education at a glance 2012: OECD Indicators. OCDE, Paris. https://doi.org/10.1787/eag-2012-en.

OCDE. 2014. PISA 2012 results: Students and money (Volume VI): Financial literacy skills for the 21st century. OCDE, Paris. https://doi.org/10.1787/9789264208094-en.

OCDE. 2020a. Education at a glance 2020: OECD indicators. OCDE, Paris. https://doi.org/10.1787/69096873-en.

OCDE. 2020b. PISA 2018 Results (Volume I): What students know and can do, annex A9. A note about Spain in PISA 2018: Further analysis of Spain's data by testing date (updated on 23 July 2020). PISA, OCDE, Paris. https://www.oecd.org/pisa/PISA2018-AnnexA9-Spain.pdf

OCDE. 2020c. PISA 2018 results (Volume V): Effective policies, successful schools. OCDE, Paris. https://doi.org/10.1787/ca768d40-en.

OCDE. 2021. Education at a glance 2021: OECD indicators. OCDE, Paris. https://doi.org/10.1787/b35a14e5-en.

OCDE. 2022. Education at a glance 2022: OECD indicators. OCDE, Paris. https://doi.org/10.1787/3197152b-en.

Sevilla, A., J. Sainz, and I. Sanz. 2020. La reducción en un 7,7% de la ratio alumnos por clase podría compensar parte del impacto negativo de la COVID-19 en la educación: Maimónides nueve siglos después (II). Nada es Gratis. https://nadaesgratis.es/admin/la-reduccion-en-un-77-de-la-ratio-alumnos-por-clase-podria-compensar-parte-del-impacto-negativo-de-la-covid-19-en-la-educacion-maimonides-nueve-siglos-despues-ii. Accessed on August 16, 2024.

Urquiola, M., and E. Verhoogen. 2009. Class-size caps, sorting, and the regression discontinuity design. *American Economic Review* 99 (1): 179–215. https://doi.org/10.1257/aer.99.1.179.

White, S., Groom-Thomas, L., and Loeb, S. (2023). A systematic review of research on tutoring implementation: Considerations when undertaking complex instructional supports for students (EdWorkingPaper No. 22–652). *Annenberg Institute at Brown University.*

Woessmann, L., and M. West. 2006. Class-size effects in school systems around the world: Evidence from between-grade variation in TIMSS. *European Economic Review* 50 (3): 695–736. https://doi.org/10.1016/j.euroecorev.2004.11.005.

The Impact of Families on Education

Antonio Cabrales

1 Introduction

The goal of this chapter is twofold. On the one hand, we intend to continue the study of the different factors that affect the performance of students and the educational system. In particular, we will examine the effect of families on this system. On the other hand, we want to introduce students to game-theoretic modeling methods for educational problems. These methods may prove useful and applicable beyond this chapter.

Families are clearly crucial to the outcomes of the educational system. On the one hand, parents provide the genetic inheritance and an important part of the environment in which students grow up. And this has a direct, albeit passive, influence on student performance. In this chapter we want to focus primarily on another, more active, influence of parents as providers of incentives and other elements to improve their children's performance.

As for modeling, many types of agents operate simultaneously in education. Students, their families, teachers, school managers, citizens who benefit from, and often finance, the system, and their political representatives who are elected in part to make it work. This complexity of decision-makers interacting with each other, and whose interests are not always perfectly aligned, is what makes the use of game theory appropriate to understand how these decisions are made.

The chapter does not claim to be exhaustive, and we prefer to give a few examples of highly relevant contributions in some detail and depth, rather than a simple listing of all relevant academic contributions. First, we will describe some evidence on the impact of parental effort on their children's educational outcomes in Sect. 2 and in Sect. 3 an article describing the impact of a specific intervention to improve parental involvement in education.

A. Cabrales (✉)
Universidad Carlos III de Madrid, Getafe (Madrid), Spain
e-mail: antonio.cabrales@uc3m.es

A. Cabrales and I. Sanz (eds.), *Economics of Education*,
https://doi.org/10.1007/978-3-031-90911-5_5

We then go on to describe in detail three models that describe and explain parental involvement in education. In Sect. 4 we explain the Doepke and Zilibotti (2017) model on why different parenting styles exist and how they are decided. This model is important because it explains the economic motives that influence parents' choice of different ways to focus their educational efforts. Then, in Sect. 5 we study the model of Bisin and Verdier (2000, 2001) which, in contrast to the previous one, focuses more on the transmission of cultural values in education. This serves to point out that economists are well aware that education is more than just the formation of human capital and that cultural issues are very important and subsequently generate crucial feedback for the economy.

Finally, in Sect. 6 we use the model of Albornoz et al. (2018) to clarify how the interactions of multiple decision-makers—families, students, schools, and political authorities—are crucial to understanding student performance and the allocation of resources and efforts in education.

Finally, the Sect. 7 collects other studies, which we do not describe in detail, but which may be useful for the student of this volume to continue his or her exploration of this topic.

2 Evidence on Parents and Their Influence on Education

In this section we discuss in detail some representative articles on the influence of parents on education. In Sect. 7 we provide additional evidence on this impact in a more summarized manner.

A first relevant reference is an article by De Philippis and Rossi (2021) that uses PISA data. The question the authors ask is how much of the difference in educational attainment between countries can be attributed to the characteristics or actions of parents. A first approximation can be obtained from a standard regression that attempts to explain individual student performance based on characteristics of the student, the family, and the country. When this is done, the variables observed for parents (education, profession, whether they are employed, number of books at home, and whether the language spoken at home is not the official language) explain a modest proportion of the differences.

The problem with this approach is that focusing on socioeconomic status (which is basically what these variables measure) is reductionist. We know that there are other things that parents do. For example, here we are going to talk about parenting styles Doepke and Zilibotti (2017) and also that the transmission of cultural values is important Bisin and Verdier (2000, 2001).

And this is why De Philippis and Rossi (2021) use a different strategy. What the authors do is compare, within the same country, students who are children of natives and immigrants with different nationalities, for the same socioeconomic level. Obviously this is not perfect, because the emigrants may be systematically selected, and because there may be difficulties of assimilation for immigrants that vary between countries of origin. In the article, the average PISA scores by country of a student who is the child of immigrants from country A are related to the averages of students from country A. A positive correlation close to 1 can be observed. In other words, if the average PISA scores of the country of origin are a percentage higher than the average, in the destination country the children of immigrants from that country improve the average of that country by the same percentage. The fact that these differences between countries are preserved even though students in the host country enjoy material, school and institutional conditions, similar to those of natives suggests that parental influence is important.

The regression analysis shows that this observation is robust to the inclusion of many controls. And the effect is not primarily due to East Asian mothers, because it persists when students of these nationalities are excluded. The study has many checks for robustness of the results, including the use of data from the American census, which has more observations on family characteristics. A serious concern is that parents of immigrants are selected (either positively or negatively, although recent immigration research, such as Albornoz et al. (2018) suggests positive selection), but since what matters are relative comparisons across immigrant groups, this only matters if there is differential selection across countries. One way to see that this is not a problem can be seen in Figure 3 of the paper. In it, the relative educational level of migrants compared to natives of their country of origin is associated with the average grade of the host country and it can be observed that there is no correlation.

Although these results by De Philippis and Rossi (2021) are interesting, we still have to understand what are the mechanisms by which parents affect the instruction of their children. And for this we go to another article, by Chen, Cunha et al. (2023). The question in this case is how does the presence of children of powerful parents (in this case senior officials of the Chinese Communist Party) affect the academic performance of the classmates of these children.

The authors use a survey, the China Educational Panel Survey. And they exploit an important feature of the Chinese school system. The assignment of students to classes, when there is more than one class per grade, is random. Thus, the number of children of senior officials per class is, within the school, random. And because they use school and grade fixed effects, they are isolating the effect of receiving some more children of party cadres in the setting for which this assignment is random.

The first relevant result is that having one more child of a senior official in the class increases the performance of his or her classmates by 2%. In contrast, having a father who is a senior official does not improve the performance of his or her own child. This is not to say that parents do not influence their children. In schools where parental interference in class assignment is observed (via a check of computerized assignment reports and actual assignment) and which are extracted from the general sample, there is indeed a significant effect of public servant parents on their own children. This latter observation suggests that public servant parents' influence on their children arises through influence in the social environment (better resources in class, or better social networks), and not through increasing their human capital directly.

But what is most interesting is where the effect of the children of party official of their peer arises. This effect is practically the same if we control for their personal characteristics, in particular their own school academic results. Remember that public officials have no direct effect on their children. This, together with the fact that the impact of the children of public officials is independent of their school results, indicates that this impact must be explained in another way.

A reasonable explanation is that the presence of these children induces the parents of the peers to increase their efforts with them. The most likely reason is that the parents of the peers want to benefit from contact with the public official through their children. And in China, a child's good academic performance is a good way to get him/her noticed by his/her peers, and especially his/her parents. Evidence in favor of this hypothesis (which can be obtained from the wealth of data from the survey) is that as the number of children of public servants in the class increases, the parents of the classmates become more involved in the friendships that their children choose, increase their communication with them about what happens at school, and help more with the children's homework.

It is not easy to know whether these results would be applicable outside China, in the sense of the influence of the parents of classmates on the students' effort. What is clear is that getting parents involved in their children's school is a crucial factor in improving their children's outcomes, and policy measures that make this involvement more likely could achieve this objective. This is what we turn to in the next Sect. 3.

3 Policy Interventions to Increase Parental Involvement

The previous Sect. 2 contains some evidence about the effect of parents on their children's education with their active intervention, beyond providing a good material and affective environment. In this section, we explain a representative intervention that has recently been proposed in the literature to enhance parental involvement in education. In the Sect. 7 we briefly discuss more evidence on interventions.

An article by Barrera-Osorio et al. (2020) describes two randomized trials (see Chapter 2 to understand what randomized trials are) conducted by the Mexican government related to the Apoyo a la Gestión Escolar (AGE) program. The randomized trials were conducted in four states (Chiapas, Guerrero, Puebla, and Yucatán) with a significant indigenous population, which has suffered historical discrimination.

The first intervention provided funding to parent associations (AMPAs). The standard grant is between \$500 and \$700 per year depending on the size of the school and cannot be used for infrastructure, materials, or activities. It cannot be used for salaries for principals or teachers. The treatment doubled this grant to between \$1,000 and \$1,400. This covers approximately 83% of the extra costs parents have to contribute to education beyond what the state contributes. The experiment was conducted in approximately 250 schools. The experiment began in 2007, when baseline data were collected, and continued in 2008, 2009, and 2010 when outcome data were collected.

The other intervention provided information to parents on how to become more involved in school and how to help their children in school. The core of the intervention consisted of five sessions led by a community advisor who facilitated the discussion. The first session introduced the AGE program, and explained the importance of parental involvement. The second explained to parents how to become involved in school and help with decision making. The third informed about education and health resources in the community. The fourth explained milestones in child and adolescent development and introduced age-appropriate activities to support learning. The fifth encouraged parents to create an action plan on how to improve their child's education. This intervention was conducted in approximately 180 schools. The intervention began in 2009 when baseline data were collected and continued through 2010 when outcomes were collected.

Researchers relied on data from standardized tests of participants in the experiment as well as from student questionnaires. (from third to fifth grade), parents and teachers. In the first experiment, the largest expenditure item was related to school supplies (books, blackboards, writing materials, 38% in the third year of intervention) and sanitary supplies (first aid, 16% in the third year). Repairs and improvements to infrastructures became more important over time, going from 35% in the first year to 44% in the third year. The informative treatment was carried out in 95% of the treatment group.

In terms of results, they first looked at parental involvement. For the first treatment, there did not seem to be a significant impact on involvement in school activities, or in meetings with teachers. Instead, there was an increase in participation in school decision-making bodies (votes, meetings) of around 18%. But this effect disappeared in the following years. In contrast, the informative intervention increased participation in activities by 16.9%. This increase occurred mainly among parents who were already members of the association because the number of members of these did not change.

They then observe the outcomes related to behavior of parents at home. For the first experiment, no changes were observed. Neither in knowledge of homework, nor in helping with homework. Nor did teachers change, neither in terms of their absences from class, nor in making education more personalized. For the information experiment, there were significant changes. Parents were 5.7% more likely to be aware of homework and 8.8% more likely to help with their children's homework. That is, this information not only increased participation within schools, but also improved parents' behavior outside schools. An important observation is that these effects were much stronger for indigenous parents. For example, the percentage of these parents who helped with homework rose from 20.5% to 31.9%, which represents an increase of 50%.

Finally, they studied the school outcomes themselves. For the first experiment, perhaps not surprisingly given the previous results, no differences were found in school results of any kind. For the informational intervention, a 1.2% decrease in school dropouts and a 6% decrease in disciplinary actions were observed (something that has a greater impact on families with a lower socioeconomic level). However, there did not appear to be any difference in school grades. Although the authors were slightly pessimistic about this lack of impact on grades, it is possible to argue that the results are in fact positive. We know from the literature on early school interventions described in Chap. 9 that sometimes an intervention affecting non-cognitive skills does not have immediate effects on grades, but has an important impact on the likelihood of graduating, having a good job, and living a fulfilling life. The results here point in that direction as well. Note that the results on Perry Preschool and Abecedarian experiments that we referred to in Chap. 9 do reduce dropout, and that one mechanism was improved student behavior, as is observed here as well.

Finally, the authors looked at the impact of the interventions on parents' trust in teachers. Here they saw a significant improvement in teacher trust from the second intervention, which is probably the mechanism for improving engagement at home.

Although the results themselves are not spectacular, these are not very expensive interventions either. So for me the message is optimistic. It is possible to design low-cost interventions that convince some parents to increase their attention to education.

4 Parenting Styles and Education: Doepke and Zilibotti (2017)

This section presents a simplified version of Doepke and Zilibotti (2017) model, hereafter referred to as DZ17, to understand how parents and their children interact in making decisions about the effort students devote to education.[1] The original perspective of DZ17 is that families want to have an influence on the dedication of their children, because they do not have a sufficiently formed perspective of the future. For this reason, students may make decisions that do not consider in a sufficiently deep way the long-term impact of the acquisition of knowledge, human capital.

The model is very useful for understanding the frictions that make the desires of parents and children not coincide, and the strategies that parents use to guide their children in the direction they prefer. At the same time the model sheds light on how the conditions of the economic environment make it more or less likely that one strategy or another will be used. DZ17 describes four parenting styles, taken from the psychological literature, which we will call: authoritarian, authoritative, permissive, and neglectful. The authoritarian style directly influences the actions that the student can take, the authoritative style tries to affect the student's preferences, and the permissive and neglectful styles simply do not intervene in these decisions, although they differ in that the permissive styles care about the students and their decisions, and the neglectful styles simply show no interest in what happens to them. In DZ17 the neglectful style is not explored because in their way of modeling it is confused with the permissive style, but extensions are proposed where the difference between permissive and neglectful styles is important.

[1] The simplification is adapted from a version of the model derived in Cabrales and Hauk (2024).

We will first see how students make decisions, and then we will see what influences parents' decisions. Finally, we will describe some evidence consistent with the results of the model.

4.1 The Student's Decision

The student's total time is normalized to one unit. The student has to decide the proportion of that total time devoted to educational effort. Let us denote that proportion as the variable x. Each unit of time spent in education has a cumulative future return that we denote R. Therefore, educational effort has a total return of Rx.The rest of the time $1 - x$ is devoted to other activities, which we generally call leisure. Each unit of time devoted to leisure has a return aK, that depends on a preference parameter a and a marginal return K, and therefore the total time devoted to leisure yields $aK(1 - x)$. The total utility of the student is simply the sum of the two returns, that of educational effort and that of leisure, and can be expressed as:

$$U_E(x) = aK(1 - x) + Rx. \tag{1}$$

This can be rewritten as

$$U_E(x) = aK + (R - aK)x.$$

Note that this utility function is linear, and therefore the value of the variable x that is maximized (1) is:

$$x = \begin{cases} 1 \text{if} R > aK \\ 0 \text{if} R \leq aK \end{cases} \tag{2}$$

This corner solution is typical of a linear function, and is very unrealistic. Naturally, students do not spend all their time either studying or at leisure. But this specification makes the derivations that follow very simple, and they reveal some important factors in decisions, which is what theoretical models are for. In particular, as can be seen, if the return to education R is very high compared to the "enjoyment" derived from leisure aK, students will spend a lot of time studying, and the opposite happens if R is low. The following exercise will help the reader deduce what happens for more realistic utility functions.

Exercise 1 What would be the student's decision if the utility function were:

$$U_E(x) = aK(1 - x) + Rx^{\alpha} \tag{3}$$

where $0 \leq \alpha \leq 1$.

4.2 *The Choice Between Authoritativeness and Permissiveness*

Authoritative parents (those who decide to change the student's a) are more frequent, as we will see in Sect. 4, in places where income is distributed more unequally. These parents are aware that educational effort has very high returns in adult life compared to not making that effort. One way to model this perspective of the world is to assume that these parents have a utility function like the one we now present, where $\mu \in (0, 1)$ represents the weight that the family gives to the enjoyment of the child's leisure. That is, these families do not value the child's leisure as much as the child itself, which is equivalent to saying that they realize the large future value of education.

$$U_P(a) = \mu a K(1 - x) + Rx. \tag{4}$$

These parents have an important power/strategy. They can influence the value of a that the students have. Specifically, they can choose any value of $a \in [\underline{a}, \overline{a}]$. This is what it means that they can be authoritative. The wider this interval is, the greater the parents' potential persuasive power. And vice versa if the interval is small. We will interpret the choice of a as a choice between authoritativeness and permissiveness. If the parents choose to influence a, they are authoritative. Otherwise they are permissive.

Using the student's optimal response (2) the family's utility can be written as:

$$U_P(a) = \begin{cases} R\text{if}\frac{R}{K} \geq a \\ \mu a K\text{if}\frac{R}{K} < a \end{cases} \tag{5}$$

Let's examine this expression in more detail, taking into account the limits on parental choice (keeping in mind that authortative parents are those who decide to influence the a, and permissive parents are those who do not).

1. If $\frac{R}{K} > \overline{a}$ then students will use $x = 1$ for all values of a. In this case parents do not change the students' choice for any value of their choice variable.
2. If $\frac{R}{K} < \underline{a}$ The boys always choose $x = 0$, so í the parents cannot change the boys' choice either.
3. If, on the other hand, $\underline{a} < \frac{R}{K} < \overline{a}$ the parents' choice of a can determine whether the student chooses $x = 1$ or $x = 0$.

Exercise 2 Show that the following statements are true:

1. The family prefers $x = 1$ if $\overline{a} \leq \frac{R}{\mu K}$. Therefore the condition for $x = 1$ is $\frac{R}{K} \leq \overline{a} \leq \frac{R}{\mu K}$.
2. The family prefers that the boys use $x = 0$ if $\overline{a} > \frac{R}{\mu K}$.

Given what is shown in the exercise it is easy to see that the optimal response of the family in terms of their choice of a is as follows:

$$(1) a = \min\left[\overline{a}, \frac{R}{K}\right] \text{ when } \max\{\underline{a}, \overline{a}\mu\} < \frac{R}{K} \text{ which implies } x = 1 \tag{6}$$

$$(2) a = \overline{a} \text{ for } \frac{R}{K} < \max\{\underline{a}, \overline{a}\mu\} \text{ which implies } x = 0 \tag{7}$$

Let us now interpret these results. When *R*/*K*, the relative return on investment in human capital with respect to the intrinsic value of leisure, is high, before being affected by parental influence, the family wants to exert more influence. This makes the family want to use its authority. This is the type of result that allows us to explain, as we will see in Sect. 4, why in unequal countries, where the premium on a college degree is higher, there are more authoritative parents and less permissive ones.

Something similar happens for different relative values given by parents to student leisure. If μ is high (leisure is considered important), parents decide not to intervene in a, and become permissive. If μ is low, they will decide to intervene, and become authoritative. This predicts that in an environment where creativity is important, permissiveness will increase.

4.3 The Choice Between Authoritarianism and Permissiveness

Authoritarian parents wish to directly choose the value of effort that the student uses. That is, they do not use a as an influence variable, but rather directly x. This is possible in an environment where students can be directly monitored by parents and can supervise the learning process. Therefore, this is more reasonable to occur in the initial educational stages, but certainly not in the more advanced ones, where precisely because they are not compulsory, the decisions are more crucial. On the other hand, authoritarianism, as we will see, is more reasonable when the parental authoritativeness is low. This is more frequent in environments where parents have a lower level of education. As a consequence of this, they understand in a more confused way the working world that the children will face students, and therefore they are not able to convey the importance of education.

Now let's see how to model these parental choices. We assume that the family can choose a lower bound to x, ($\underline{x}$). But this supervision has a cost, which we assume to be quadratic. For this type of influence to be optimal, it has to be true that persuasion does not work, and controlling preferences is difficult, which as we have seen happens when:

$$\frac{R}{K} < \max\{\underline{a}, \overline{a}\mu\}.$$

In that case we can write

$$U_P(\overline{a}, \underline{x}) = \mu\overline{a}K(1 - \underline{x}) + R\underline{x} - \frac{b}{2}\underline{x}^2 \tag{8}$$

Ejercicio 3 If the parents' utility is as represented in Sect. 8 the optimal choice of parents is:

$$\underline{x} = \frac{R - \mu\overline{a}K}{b}$$

Note that $\underline{x}$ is higher, and therefore the degree of parental control is greater, when $R - \mu\overline{a}K$ is higher. That is, when the difference between professional performance and the value of student leisure perceived by the family is large, the latter wants to intervene. This would also explain the positive relationship that DZ17 finds between authoritarianism and inequality and that we review in Sect. 4. The reason why this relationship is not as strong as with authoritativeness has to do with other factors that are guessed here. Note for example that if parental control technology is good ($\underline{a}$ low) or the cost of direct parental control is high (b high), one does not want to intervene as much in x. That is, b is high in more advanced countries where students have a high degree of freedom. In those same countries, parents have a high power of persuasion, meaning that $\underline{a}$ is low, parents can convince their children that it is worth the effort for future returns, and they get them to place a lower value on leisure.

4.4 Evidence on Cultural Styles and Their Relationship to Economic Environments

A first important piece of evidence concerns parents' time use in various countries. Doepke, Zilibotti, and Sorrenti (2019) document using the Multinational Time Use Study survey for all countries for which there are sufficient data, such as Canada, Italy, the Netherlands, Spain, the United Kingdom, and the United States, that parents have increased the time they spend with their children in the last decades, while inequality has also increased within countries. In a couple of countries, the United States and the Netherlands, for which the data series is longer, parents with a college education have shown to have greatly increased the amount of time they spend on their children's education compared to those with lower levels of education. From virtually no difference in 1970, to a difference of more than three hours per week today.

To identify the types of parenting styles in the data, DZ17 uses the World Values Survey, which has questions about the values that parents think are important in their children's behavior. These authors think that one question that identifies the authoritarian style well is whether parents think that an important value is obedience. The persuasive style is identified with parents who think that hard work is important. The permissive style is identified with parents who think that imagination is important.

Table 1 World values survey wave 7—2017-2022. Questions: Q17, Q9, Q11

Value/País	France	Germany	Italy	Spain	Sweden	UK	US
Obedience (authoritarian)	25.9	11.8	23.3	40.4	7.3	22.2	20.5
Hard work (persuasive)	41.3	40.4	29	23.7	8.2	47.3	67.9
Imagination (permissive)	21	23.8	17.9	36	43.8	35.5	29.8

In the following table we observe the comparison of some of these data for several countries (Table 1).

What is relevant about these data is that they vary greatly between countries, and DZ17 shows that there are very interesting correlations, for example with inequality. The permissive style is much more frequent in countries with little inequality, and much less in more unequal countries. The authoritative style has the opposite pattern, it is very frequent in unequal countries and much less frequent in the most egalitarian ones. The authoritarian style has a similar pattern, although less strong, to that of the authoritative.

In fact, Table 2 of Doepke, Zilibotti and Sorrenti (2019), reproduced below, shows associations between variables at the individual level, not just at the country level. The table presents logistic regressions where the dependent variable is an indicator that receives a value of 1 if the parenting style is intensive (authoritative or authoritarian). The coefficients shown are probability ratios ("odds-ratios") and therefore a number greater than one means that the variable increases the probability of the intensive parenting style, and a number less than one indicates that the variable decreases the probability of that style. All models include survey wave fixed effects. Models in columns 2, 3, 5, and 6 include controls for gender, age, age squared, and log GDP per capita (based on chained real GDP in purchasing power parity from Penn World Table 9.0). Models in columns 3 and 6 also include country fixed effects. Inequality is defined as the ratio of the 90th to the 10th percentile of gross earnings of individuals in full-time employment. Tax progressivity is taken from Andrew Young School Policy Studies (2010). Social expenditures are expressed as a percentage of GDP. As can be seen, inequality is a very strong factor in favor of the most intensive parenting styles, the authoritative and authoritarian. And, on the other hand, fiscal progressivity or social spending decrease the probability of these parenting styles.

5 Cultural transmission: Bisin and Verdier 2000 and 2001

Economists tend to talk about education because of its importance in the formation of a factor of production, labor. That is, we think of education as an input into the creation of "human capital". But we are also aware that education is much more than that, because it has an influence on the creation of values, preferences and social norms. One can say, stretching the metaphor, that in addition to "human capital" it influences the creation of "cultural capital".

Table 2 Inequality, redistribution, and parenting styles

	(1)	(2)	(3)	(4)	(5)	(6)
	Logit	Logit	Logit	Logit	Logit	Logit
	Intensive	Intensive	Intensive	Intensive	Intensive	Intensive
Inequality	2.38***	2.50***	2.12**	1.74***	1.74***	27.22**
	(0.44)	(0.29)	(0.72)	(0.37)	(0.28)	(35.21)
Progressivity of taxation				0.20**	0.24**	5.35
				(0.13)	(0.17)	(5.88)
Social spending				0.70	0.58	0.21**
				(0.29)	(0.25)	(0.14)
Controls	No	Sí	No	Sí	No	Sí
Fixed effect country-wise	No	No	Sí	No	No	Sí
Observations	45482	45482	45482	32196	32196	32196

Standard errors (in parentheses) are clustered at the country level. *, **, *** indicate statistical significance at the 10%, 5%, and 1% levels, respectively

And this leads us to a potential conflict between parents' preferences and social preferences. To give a concrete example, about 20% of American adults reject the theory of evolution, meaning that they think humans have always existed in our present form. This percentage rises to 38% among evangelical Protestants (Masei 2023). These parents are not very happy that the theory of evolution by natural selection is taught in a school. And their political representatives have tried in many states to ban this teaching in schools, although fortunately the courts have prevented this.

The articles by Bisin and Verdier (2000, 2001) inaugurate a very interesting literature that attempts to model this tension between parental desires and those of society as a whole. The model is related to a literature in anthropology that studies cultural transmission in dynamic models of preference evolution that was started by Cavalli-Sforza and Feldman (1981) and Boyd and Richerson (1988).

We will first present a very simple version of the model, adapted from Cabrales and Hauk (2023) where we also connect with the DZ17 model from the previous section and then in Sect. 5, we discuss the evidence consistent with the model.

5.1 *Human Capital Cultures and Cultural Evolution*

Suppose there are two "human capital cultures" like those in the Sect. 4 in which one group gives more weight than the other to the future return on education and therefore $\mu_1 < \mu_2$. The proportions of the population that have each of these cultures are q_1 and q_2.

Student socialization combines a vertical dimension" by the family and a horizontal one" by the rest of society. This means that the probability that the student " inherits" the cultural value of his family is d_i, and with probability $1 - d_i$ he will be like the rest of society. Therefore the probabilities of each type of student are:

$$\begin{aligned} P_{ii} &= d_i + (1 - d_i)q_i \\ P_{ij} &= (1 - d_i)(1 - q_i) \end{aligned}$$

5.2 The Student's Decision

The utility of the student with cultural style i is

$$U_i^E(x) = \mu_i K(1 - x) + Rx.$$

Therefore, the optimal decision about how much to study is

$$x_i = \begin{cases} 1 \text{ si } R \geq \mu_i K \\ 0 \text{ si } R < \mu_i K \end{cases}$$

To make the problem interesting, let's assume that the two types of students have different choices. This means that we assume that

$$\mu_2 K > R > \mu_1 K,$$

and therefore

$$U_1^E(x_1^*) = R;\ U_2^E(x_2^*) = \mu_2 K.$$

5.3 Family Decisions

Families have "imperfect empathy", that is, they do not fully internalize the utility of the student. Therefore a family of cultural style i with a student of style j has a utility

$$U_i^P\left(x_j^*\right) = \mu_i K\left(1 - x_j^*\right) + Rx_j^*.$$

If $i \neq j$ the utility of the parents is lower than if the children had the same cultural style. That is, $U_i^P\left(x_j^*\right) < U_i^P\left(x_i^*\right)$. To see that this is true, notice that:

$$U_1^P\left(x_2^*\right) = \mu_1 K < R = U_1^P\left(x_1^*\right)$$

and

$$U_2^P\left(x_1^*\right) = R < \mu_2 K = U_2^P\left(x_2^*\right).$$

Under these conditions, it seems clear that the family would want to invest in changing their child's type. For example, if increasing d_i (the probability that the student is like his parents) had a quadratic cost, the total utility of family type i would be:

$$\begin{aligned} U_i^P =& P_{ii} U_i^E\left(x_i^*\right) + P_{ij} U_i^E\left(x_j^*\right) - \frac{b}{2} d_i^2 \\ =& (d_i + (1 - d_i) q_i) U_i^E\left(x_i^*\right) + (1 - d_i)(1 - q_i) U_i^E\left(x_j^*\right) - \frac{b}{2} d_i^2 \end{aligned} \tag{9}$$

Exercise 4 Show that if the parent utility is as represented in Sect. 9 the optimal choice of the parents is:

$$d_i^* = \frac{(1 - q_i)}{b}\left(U_i^E\left(x_i^*\right) - U_i^E\left(x_j^*\right)\right)$$

$$d_1^* = \frac{(1 - q_1)}{b}(R - \mu_1 K),\ d_2^* = \frac{(1 - q_2)}{b}(\mu_2 K - R)$$

As can be seen, investment in[2] (d_i) depends (inversely) on the size of the group, and on the extra profitability perceived by the family of the student being in their group.

Exercise 5 Discuss the economic intuition of this result and its empirical implications.

5.4 Evidence on Cultural Transmission

Although there is a large literature on the importance of cultural factors in economic issues, the literature on cultural transmission is scarcer. In sociology, Ozorak (1989) and Hayes and Pittelkow (1993) document the importance of the family in the transmission of religious beliefs. In economics, Patacchini and Zenou (2004) find that in

[2] It is not a frequent word, but it is very appropriate here. The RAE dictionary defines it as "Process of integration of an individual or group into the culture and society with which they come into contact".

the United Kingdom the family is important for the transmission of attitudes towards education for students with parents with a high educational level, while the community is crucial for the attitudes of students from families with a low educational level. On the other hand, Cohen-Zada (2006) found that in the United States religious parents decide to send their children to religious or private schools to protect them from external influences and thus preserve their religious identity as suggested by the model we have just presented. Fernandez et al. (2004) show that the presence of men raised in a family in which the mother worked has been a significant factor in the increase in female labor force participation over time, thus showing the importance of the cultural transmission of attitudes regarding this participation. Finally, Bisin et al. (2004), using data from the GSS (General Social Survey) for the United States during the period 1972-1996, estimate the structural parameters of the Bisin and Verdier (2000) model applied to the socialization of married couples and their children with a religious orientation in the United States. The observed rates of intermarriage and socialization are consistent with the fact that Protestants, Catholics, and Jews have a strong preference for their children to identify with their own religious beliefs and that they make costly decisions to influence their children's religious beliefs.

6 Families and Resources: Albornoz et al. (2018)

The motivation for this model arises from the fact that the implementation and evaluation of educational policies often ignores that these reforms can generate behavioral changes in the actors involved in the educational process. For example, when discussing the role of school resources in student learning, there is often no consideration of how parents and school administrators will respond. If teacher resources are increased, parents may decrease their involvement in school. An extreme case is boarding schools where parental involvement is nonexistent. Or they may increase it. Similarly, school voucher proposals often ignore their influence on parental involvement in education.

To enhance this discussion, Albornoz et al. (2018), which we will call ABC18, study a model of education in which student effort and learning outcomes, parent and school behavior, and public resources devoted to education are jointly determined in an integrated theoretical framework. Then, in section ABC18 evidence, we discuss some evidence relevant to the model.

6.1 Student, Family, and Teacher Utility

Student i's human capital, H_i, is a linear function of his/her effort, e_i, and a productivity parameter, υ_i.

$$H_i = \upsilon_i e_i. \tag{10}$$

Students internalize only imperfectly the effect of their effort on human capital. Parents and teachers spend some of their time inducing students to exert costly effort using different motivational tools. In particular, students' short-term utility is given by:

$$U_{S_i} = c_{1i}e_i + c_{2j}e_i - \frac{1}{2}e_i^2. \tag{11}$$

Effort e_i has quadratic cost. Parent and teacher participation enters positively into the child's utility, $c_{1i}e_i + c_{2j}e_i$ with the subscript j denoting the school attended by child i. The variable c_{1i} (c_{2j}) expresses the strength of parents' (teachers') incentives for each unit of child effort. Thus, $c_{1i}e_i + c_{2j}e_i$ is the child's total reward for his effort. In other words, the role of parents (teachers) is to help children internalize the value of e_i (and ultimately H_i) in their utility function.

The **family's utility** depends on the child's human capital and its own well-being:

$$U_{P_i} = H_i + W_i.$$

Parents' well-being W_i depends on the time spent at work or doing leisure activities. This is the total time (T) available minus the time spent with the child as a result of the reward scheme (t_i). The effective reward ($c_{1i}e_i$) depends on time (t_i) and parental efficiency (υ_{P_i}) to generate a given effective reward, such that $c_{1i}e_i = 2t_i\upsilon_{P_i}$[3]. The parameter υ_{P_i} captures the fact that some parents are better at motivating than others, and therefore generate a greater reward for any given amount of time spent with their children. That is, we associate the productivity of parental involvement with some innate attribute, such as talent or persuasiveness. Implicitly, we are imposing that the time spent inducing effort, for a given effective reward, decreases with the parent's ability to generate it. Therefore, if ψ_i is the opportunity cost of the family i

$$W_i = (T - t_i)\psi_i = \left(T - \frac{c_{1i}e_i}{2\upsilon_{P_i}}\right)\psi_i,$$

and therefore,

$$U_{P_i} = \upsilon_i e_i + \left(T - \frac{c_{1i}e_i}{2\upsilon_{P_i}}\right)\psi_i. \tag{12}$$

The **utility of teachers**, is very parallel to that of parents, except that they have more students in their charge. It depends on the average human capital their students obtain and their own well-being. This welfare is determined by the difference between the time for the teacher and the effective time for the students, which as for the parents

[3] The 2 is not necessary, but it helps save notation in what follows.

is inversely related to an efficiency parameter υ_{T_j}. If γ is the opportunity cost of teachers,

$$U_{Tj} = \frac{1}{N_j}\sum_{i\in j}\upsilon_i e_i + \left(T - \frac{n_j}{N_j}\sum_{i\in j}\frac{c_{2j}e_i}{2\upsilon_{T_j}}\right)\gamma, \tag{13}$$

where N_j is the total number of students in school j and n_j is the number of students per classroom.

The policymaker's objective function (and its control variable, class size) maximizes the utility of the family (median voter $\bar{P}_i$) taking into account the cost of the policy, which depends on the number of total classes: N/n. That is, the cost is higher the fewer students there are in each classroom.

$$U_D = U_{\bar{P}_i} - \frac{1}{N}\frac{\omega'}{2}\left(\frac{N}{n}\right)^2, \tag{14}$$

To simplify notation we denote $\omega = \omega' N$, so that

$$U_D = U_{\bar{P}_i} - \frac{\omega}{2}\frac{1}{n^2}, \tag{15}$$

6.2 The Structure and Equilibrium of the Educational Policy Game

The policymaker acts first and announces the school resources, which in this case is simply the class size (n). Next, families decide c_{1j} and schools decide c_{2j}, the strength of the student incentives, simultaneously. Finally, students decide their optimal level of effort, e_i.

Since we are dealing with a sequential game, we will solve the game using backward induction. That is, we solve the decision of the last player to decide first, taking as given the actions of the previous movers. And then we proceed for each previous player, taking as given the decisions of earlier movers, but taking into account the effect of their decisions on subsequent movers.

Thus, we first derive the students' optimal decision.

Exercise 6 Show that since the students' utility is (11), their optimal reaction to the parents' and teachers' decisions is:

$$e_i = c_{1i} + c_{2j}. \tag{16}$$

The next step is to derive the optimal decisions of parents and teachers, taking into account the impact of their decision on the students. Note that, in fact, this subgame between parents and teachers is similar to a Cournot game between the two decision-makers.

Excercise 7 Show that by substituting the student's decision (16) into the family's utility (12) we obtain that the family's optimal choice is:

$$c_{1i} = \max\left\{\frac{\upsilon_{P_i}\upsilon_i}{\psi_i} - \frac{c_{2j}}{2}, 0\right\}. \tag{17}$$

To simplify the notation in what follows, we define the parameter of relative parental motivation efficiency:

$$\Upsilon_{P_i} \equiv \frac{\upsilon_{P_i}}{\psi_i}.$$

For teachers, the solution is quite symmetrical to that of parents.

Exercise 8 Show that by substituting the student's decision (16) into the teachers' utility (13) their optimal choice is:

$$c_{2j} = \frac{\upsilon_{M_j}\overline{\upsilon}_j}{\gamma n_j} - \frac{\overline{c}_{1j}}{2}. \tag{18}$$

We also define the parameter of *relative efficiency of motivation of teachers:*

$$\Upsilon_{T_j} \equiv \frac{\upsilon_{T_j}}{\gamma}.$$

And, therefore, $\Upsilon_{T_j}\overline{\upsilon}_j$ measures the quality of the school.

Finally, we characterize the politician's optimal decision:

Exercise 9 Show that by substituting the decision ón of the student (16), teachers (18) and parents (17) in the utility of the politician (15) their optimal decision is:

$$n = \frac{\omega - \frac{4\upsilon^2}{9\,\upsilon_P}\Upsilon_T^2}{\frac{4\upsilon^2}{9}\Upsilon_T}. \tag{19}$$

6.3 Comparative Statics and Policy Implications of the Model

The first implication of the model that we are going to explore has to do with one of the most important political and academic debates of our time. We know from Chap. 4 that most of the studies where a good causal inference can be made indicate that educational resources, and specifically (a reduction in) the size of the classes has a positive impacts on the performance of the students. And yet, in most developed countries, resources, including those devoted to reducing the size of classrooms, have increased significantly in the last decades without any significant improvement in student performance being observed. How can this phenomenon be explained? Comparative statics gives us a reasonable explanation.

From the optimal decision of the politician, expressed in the equation (19) the following proposition can be deduced immediately.

Proposition 1 (Comparative class size statics) The class size:

- increases with the cost of the teaching staff (ω) and the *relative motivational efficiency of the teachers* (Υ_T).
- decreases with student ability (υ) and the *relative effectiveness of parental motivation:* (Υ_P).

This allows us to understand a few important things. To begin with, the apparent paradox of resources. The time that parents can devote to their children's learning process has a direct (and observable) effect on school resources. Recall that Υ_{P_i} increases as υ_{P_i} (parental talent) and decreases in ψ_i (opportunity cost of parents' time). The decades following World War II were characterized by a large increased female participation in the labor force. This is compatible with an increase in ψ_i. But at the same time it also implies an increase in υ_{P_i}, the efficiency of the parents. Hence the effect on Υ_{P_i} may be ambiguous. This would result in a decrease in n in this model (probably moderated because the general economic improvement led to a concomitant increase in the cost of teachers γ). Indeed, Flyer and Rosen (1997) find a connection between the rapid growth in public spending on primary and secondary education in the U.S. and the increasing value of women's time. Between 1960 and 1990, the real costs of primary and secondary education increased by 300 percent. The main cause of the increase in per-pupil spending was the increase in school staff, with the number of students per teacher falling by half between 1950 and 1990. Flyer and Rosen study the connection between female labor force participation and student-to-teacher ratios using a panel of 50 U.S. states over 4 decades. They observe that increases in female labor force participation rates explain a significant portion of both the level and decline in states' student-teacher ratios. In addition, the findings are robust to other plausible explanations, such as increases in unionization and changes in fertility patterns.

The ω effect is economically obvious: higher teacher salaries result in larger class sizes. Note that in universities, for example, main lectures, normally taught by professors (senior, higher-paid teachers), have more students than tutorials, often taught by PhD students or external lecturers. The influence of teachers on school resources is subtle. Recall that Υ_{T_j} increases by υ_{T_j} (teaching talent) and decreases by γ (the opportunity cost of teachers' time). The γ effect connects teacher commitment to government investment in school resources. If it is harder for teachers to devote their time to school activities, the benefits of reducing class size are marginally smaller. On the other hand, teacher talent (υ_{T_j}) reinforces the benefits of investing in smaller classes. To our knowledge, these channels that influence public investment in school resources have not been empirically explored.

We also find that resources increase with student ability. This is a natural consequence of the fact that in this model, the marginal benefits to both parents and schools of strengthening teacher incentives increase with student talent.

Other comparative statics results can be observed by substituting n into the equilibrium optimal values of c_1, c_2 and e.

$$c_1 = \frac{2\Upsilon_P \upsilon}{3}\left(\frac{2\omega - 3\left(\frac{2\upsilon\Upsilon_T}{3}\right)^2 \frac{1}{\Upsilon_P}}{\omega - \left(\frac{2\upsilon\Upsilon_T}{3}\right)^2 \frac{1}{\Upsilon_P}}\right), \tag{20}$$

$$c_2 = \frac{2\Upsilon_P \upsilon}{3}\left(\frac{3\left(\frac{2\upsilon\Upsilon_T}{3}\right)^2 \frac{1}{\Upsilon_P} - \omega}{\omega - \left(\frac{2\upsilon\Upsilon_T}{3}\right)^2 \frac{1}{\Upsilon_P}}\right), \tag{21}$$

which implies:

$$e = \frac{\frac{2\Upsilon_P \upsilon}{3}\omega}{\omega - \left(\frac{2\upsilon\Upsilon_T}{3}\right)^2 \frac{1}{\Upsilon_P}}. \tag{22}$$

We assume that

$$\omega - \left(\frac{2\upsilon\Upsilon_T}{3}\right)^2 \frac{1}{\Upsilon_P} > 0 \tag{23}$$

From these three equations, (20), (21), and (22), we can deduce the following proposition.

Proposition 2 *(Comparative statics of motivation and effort.)*

1. (c_1): increases by υ, ω and Υ_P decreases in Υ_T
2. (c_2): increases in Υ_T and υ, decreases in ω and Υ_P
3. (e): increases in Υ_T and υ, decreases in ω, and is ambiguous with Υ_P.

Comparative statics with respect to Υ_T is simple to understand. An improvement in teacher ability increases school involvement (c_2) which in turn increases student effort (e) and reduces parent activity (c_1), which it "replaces". The effect of student ability υ is obvious if we look at (20) and (22). However, this expression hides some more subtle behavioral responses between parents and schools. For example, we know that the sign of $\partial c_1/\partial \upsilon$ is negative. This means that student talent reduces parental motivation in equilibrium. But a lower value of c_1 induces greater school motivational effort (c_2) because parents' and schools' efforts are substitutes for each other, compensating for lower levels of c_1.

The effect on effort (e) of a drop in Υ_P (which may arise, for example, from an increase in parental opportunity cost ψ) is ambiguous. First, a lower Υ_P translates into a higher parental opportunity cost in providing motivational activities to students. Thus, c_1 decreases with lower Υ_P. The educational system reacts by decreasing n and increasing c_2. The main driver of this result on c_2 and n is that the policymaker devotes more resources to education, and this decreases the cost of inducing effort by teachers. Conversely, smaller class sizes and higher teacher dedication reduce the gain to parents from inducing high effort at home.

The student's optimal effort decision is equal to the sum of parent and school incentives. When the opportunity cost to parents increases, the resulting drop in parental incentive is not always fully offset by the school system. Therefore, the net effect of a decrease in Υ_P on student performance may be negative. To see that this is true observe that:

$$\frac{\partial e}{\partial \Upsilon_P} = \frac{\frac{2}{3}\upsilon\omega\Upsilon_P\left(9\omega\Upsilon_P - 8\upsilon^2\Upsilon_T^2\right)}{\left(3\omega\Upsilon_P - 3\left(\frac{2\upsilon\Upsilon_T}{3}\right)^2\right)^2}$$

which implies that the effort decreases with the decrease of Υ_P when

$$\omega < \frac{8\upsilon^2\Upsilon_T^2}{9\Upsilon_P} = 2\left(\frac{2\upsilon\Upsilon_T}{3}\right)^2\frac{1}{\Upsilon_P}.$$

.

Note that from (23) we have,

$$3\left(\frac{2\upsilon\Upsilon_T}{3}\right)^2\frac{1}{\Upsilon_P} > \omega > \frac{3}{2}\left(\frac{2\upsilon\Upsilon_T}{3}\right)^2\frac{1}{\Upsilon_P},$$

so effort and academic performance can be both increasing and decreasing with respect to Υ_P within our parametric range.

Exercise 10 Discuss some empirical or educational policy implications that the results of this section suggest to you.

6.4 Evidence on Families and Educational Resources

A simple implication of the model is that a decrease in class size, for example because of a decrease in cost, leads to an unequivocal increase in student effort and improvement in student performance. As we saw in Chapter 4, most credible studies of the class size effect (Angrist and Lavy 1999, Jackson et al. 2016) find that lower class sizes generally lead to better student outcomes.

However, there are few credible estimates of teacher and parent reactions to smaller class sizes. An exception is the work by Fredriksson et al. (2016) who, in line with ABC18 predictions, find that when class sizes are larger, parents spend more time helping students with homework, but teachers tend to place more responsibility on their students. This evidence suggests that, as the ABC18 model indicates, the responses of all educational actors should be taken into account in the design of public policy interventions.

Another interesting implication of ABC18 is that an improvement in the average ability of school peers leads to greater school effort. However, parents of children in schools with better peers reduce their involvement. Under the parameter assumptions of the ABC18 model, parent reactions are not strong enough to offset the effort a student puts into a better school. Therefore, the ABC18 model predicts a positive effect for a student going to a higher quality school, although this will be attenuated by parent responses.

There is a large body of research on the effect of going to a school with better peers as we see in Chap. 6. Cullen et al. (2006) and Pop-Eleches and Urquiola (2013) find that parents of students who go (are randomly assigned) to schools with better peers spend less time helping their children with homework than parents whose children go to schools with worse peers. This is consistent with the ABC18.

Regarding the final outcome in terms of learning, there are some studies that find positive effects of better peers on student outcomes Pop-Eleches and Urquiola (2013), Deming et al. (2014), or Dobbie and Fryer (2011). There are, however, others that find no effects, such as Cullen et al. (2006), Abdulkadiroğlu et al. (2014) or Clark (2010). This discrepancy may be due to the parametric and functional form restrictions of the ABC18 model, which if removed may lead to much stronger compensatory effects of parents. Therefore, the general and robust message is that to interpret the reduced-form effect on outcomes of attending better schools, it is necessary to consider the behavioral responses of the different actors. This will help to understand the contexts in which the results found in a particular article translate to other contexts.

Finally, ABC18 suggests a connection between the opportunity cost of parents' time, schoolmates, teacher characteristics, and the cost of the time spent by parents. and the determination of school resources. A related argument appears in Besley abd Case (2000) who argue that educational policies are not exogenous to the political process. However, in the literature we find no credible empirical estimates of how these factors may affect the choices that politicians make about the allocation of school resources.

7 Additional Evidence on Families and Education

In Sect. 4.2. In Chap. 4 of Volume 3 of the Handbook of Economic Education by Hanushek and Woessmann (2011), there is a very extensive summary of the evidence, especially from international standardized tests (PISA, TIMMS, and PIRLS), about the influence of the family on school performance. Given the type of data, this is what we have called passive influence. That is, how the characteristics of the family affect the result, and not so much the effect of active involvement. Among these influences, it is worth highlighting, due to its importance in Spain, the impact of parental unemployment on the education of their children. This is extensively documented in Ruiz-Valenzuela (2020b, 2021) for international contexts, and specifically for Spain in Ruiz-Valenzuela (2020a). Another important aspect has to do with gender roles. The influence of mothers' labor market participation on daughters' choice of technical studies is well documented (Cheng et al. 2019; De San Román et al. 2016; Anaya et al. 2022) or for non-cognitive skills (Mendez et al. 2018).

In the same volume 3 of the Handbook of Economic Education cited above, Chap. 3 by Björklund and Salvanes (2011) offers a more in-depth study of parental influences. On the one hand, it focuses on presenting more plausibly causal evidence (Sect. 3.2.) than the international evidence offered by Hanushek and Woessmann (2011), and on the other hand, Sect. 4.3. illuminates the mechanisms of parental influence, both money (in some sense what we call passive influence) and time (active influence). The chapter pays special attention to the importance of the dedication in the earliest years of students' lives. Likewise, Sect. 5 studies different policy options, such as maternity leave or preschool education. In this same sense, about the early years, where the family is particularly important, Chap. 3 of volume 6 in the Handbook of Economic Education, by Duncan et al. (2023), offers a very detailed treatment.

There is a lot of experimental evidence (RCT) on programs to stimulate parental intervention, similar to what we discuss in the Sect. 3. A very exhaustive review of the literature is found in Fryer (2017). The chapter studies human capital formation in general, but Sect. 3.2.1 describes experiments where parents are provided with information or incentives. Section 3.2.2 studies interventions where resources for home education are given, such as computers, for example. Section 3.2.3 describes programs to reduce family poverty. And Sect. 3.2.4 describes other types of aid to improve the family environment, helping them to change neighborhoods. In general, the programs have an interesting impact and a low cost. Another summary of this evidence, somewhat more recent, is from the Education Endowment Foundation (2023). An advantage of this source is that they have very well-constructed technical appendixes to organize the articles (as of my last reading, 97). Readers may find it interesting to choose some and go deeper into them.

A recent article that we find important is by Cunha et al. (2023) who studied, through an RCT, the effectiveness of a program to reduce bullying in classrooms. The intervention was led by mothers and fathers, it lasted four months, and attempted to foster empathy in high school students in China. The intervention increased empathy and reduced bullying incidents. Furthermore, the authors measure the cost and observe that it costs \$12.50 on average to reduce a bullying incident. That low cost is a virtue of this type of intervention.

When we talked about the ABC18 article we discussed in a generic way the resources allocated to education, and we specified it in the number of students in the classroom. But another way to increase resources when parents cannot devote as much time to students is through a longer school day (or school year). Ferrero et al. (2022) review the literature on school hours in relation to the labor supply of parents. Another important aspect in this direction is that of private lessons and extracurricular activities. A good review of the literature on the impact of private lessons is found in Nickow et al. (2020), and a description of the situation in Spain in Moreno and Martínez (2023).

References

Abdulkadiroğlu, A., J. Angrist, and P. Pathak. 2014. The elite illusion: Achievement effects at Boston and New York exam schools. *Econometrica* 82 (1): 137–196.

Albornoz, F., S. Berlinski, and A. Cabrales. 2018. Motivation, resources, and the organization of the school system. *Journal of the European Economic Association* 16 (1): 199–231.

Albornoz, F., A. Cabrales, P. Calvo, and E. Hauk. 2018. Immigrant children's school performance and immigration costs: Evidence from Spain. *Economics Letters* 170: 27–30.

Anaya, L., F. Stafford, and G. Zamarro. 2022. Gender gaps in math performance, perceived mathematical ability and college STEM education: The role of parental occupation. *Education Economics* 30 (2): 113–128.

Andrew Young School Policy Studies. 2010. *Andrew Young School World Tax Indicators*. Atlanta, GA: Int. Stud. Progr.

Angrist, J. D., and V. Lavy. 1999. Using Maimonides' rule to estimate the effect of class size on scholastic achievement. *The Quarterly journal of economics* 114 (2): 533–575.

Barrera-Osorio, F., P. Gertler, N. Nakajima, and H. Patrinos. 2020. *Promoting parental involvement in schools: Evidence from two randomized experiments (No. w28040)*. National Bureau of Economic Research.

Besley, T., and A. Case. 2000. Unnatural experiments? Estimating the incidence of endogenous policies. *The Economic Journal* 110 (467): 672–694.

Bisin, A., G. Topa, and T. Verdier. 2004. Religious intermarriage and socialization in the United States. *Journal of political Economy* 112 (3): 615–664.

Bisin, A., and T. Verdier. 2000. "Beyond the melting pot": cultural transmission, marriage, and the evolution of ethnic and religious traits. *The Quarterly Journal of Economics* 115 (3): 955–988.

Bisin, A., and T. Verdier. 2001. The economics of cultural transmission and the dynamics of preferences. *Journal of Economic theory* 97 (2): 298–319.

Bisin, A., and T. Verdier. 2023. Advances in the economic theory of cultural transmission. *Annual Review of Economics*, 15.

Björklund, A., and K.G. Salvanes. 2011. Education and family background: Mechanisms and policies. In *Handbook of the Economics of Education*, Vol. 3, 201–247. Elsevier.

Boyd, R., and P.J. Richerson. 1988. *Culture and the Evolutionary Process*. University of Chicago Press.

Cabrales, A., and E. Hauk. 2024. Parenting styles with externalities.

Cavalli-Sforza, L. L., and M.W. Feldman. 1981. *Cultural Transmission and Evolution: A Quantitative Approach (No. 16)*. Princeton University Press.

Chen, L., B. W. Chung, and G. Wang. 2023. Exposure to socially influential peer parents: Evidence from cadre parents in China. *China Economic Review* 78: 101943.

Cheng, A., K. Kopotic and G. Zamarro. 2019. Parental Occupational Choice and Children's Entry into a Stem Field.

Clark, D. 2010. Selective schools and academic achievement. *The B.E. Journal of Economic Analysis Policy* 10 (1 (Advances)): 9.

Cohen-Zada, D. 2006. Preserving religious identity through education: Economic analysis and evidence from the US. *Journal of Urban Economics* 60 (3): 372–398.

Cullen, J. B., B. A. Jacob, and S. Levitt. 2006. The effect of school choice on participants: Evidence from randomized lotteries. *Econometrica* 74 (5): 1191–1230.

Cunha, F., Q. Hu, Y. Xia and N. Zhao. 2023. *Reducing Bullying: Evidence from a Parental Involvement Program on Empathy Education (No. w30827).* National Bureau of Economic Research.

De Philippis, M., and F. Rossi. 2021. Parents, schools and human capital differences across countries. *Journal of the European Economic Association* 19 (2): 1364–1406.

De San Román, A. G., and S. de La Rica. 2016. Gender gaps in PISA test scores: The impact of social norms and the mother's transmission of role attitudes. *Estudios de Economía Aplicada* 34 (1): 79–108.

Deming, D. J., J. S. Hastings, T. J. Kane, and D. O. Staiger. 2014. School choice, school quality, and postsecondary attainment. *American Economic Review* 104 (3): 991–1013.

Dobbie, W., and R. G. Fryer Jr. 2011. Are high-quality schools enough to increase achievement among the poor? Evidence from the Harlem Children's Zone. *American Economic Journal: Applied Economics* 3 (3): 158–187.

Doepke, M., and F. Zilibotti. 2017. Parenting with style: Altruism and paternalism in intergenerational preference transmission. *Econometrica* 85 (5): 1331–1371.

Duncan, G., A. Kalil, M. Mogstad, M, Rege. 2023. Investing in early childhood development in preschool and at home. In *Handbook of the Economics of Education*, Vol. 6, 1–77. Elsevier.

Education Endowment Foundation (14 de agosto 2023). *Parental engagement.* https://educationendowmentfoundation.org.uk/education-evidence/teaching-learning-toolkit/parental-engagement

Fernandez, R., A. Fogli, and C. Olivetti. 2004. Mothers and sons: preference formation and female labor force dynamics. *Quarterly Journal of Economics* 119: 1249–99.

Ferrero, M., L. Gortazar, and Á. Martínez. 2022. Jornada escolar continua: Cómo la pandemia está acelerando un modelo social y educativo regresivo. EsadeEcPol Brief #26.

Flyer, F., and S. Rosen. 1997. The new economics of teachers and education. *Journal of labor Economics* 15 (1, Part 2): S104–S139.

Fredriksson, P., B. Öckert, and H. Oosterbeek. 2016. Parental responses to public investments in children: Evidence from a maximum class size rule. *Journal of Human Resources* 51 (4): 832–868.

Fryer Jr, R.G. 2017. The production of human capital in developed countries: Evidence from 196 randomized field experiments. In *Handbook of Economic Field Experiments*, Vol. 2, 95–322. North-Holland.

Hanushek, E. A., and L. Woessmann. 2011. The economics of international differences in educational achievement. *Handbook of the Economics of Education* 3: 89–200.

Hayes, B., and Y. Pittelkow. 1993. Religious belief, transmission, and the family: an Australian study. *Journal of Marriage and the Family* 55: 755–66.

Jackson, C. K., R. C. Johnson, and C. Persico. 2016. The Effects of School Spending on Educational and Economic Outcomes: Evidence From School Finance Reforms. *Quarterly Journal of Economics* 131: 157–218.

Masey, D. 2023. *For Darwin Day, 6 facts about the evolution debate.* Pew Research Center. https://www.pewresearch.org/short-reads/2019/02/11/darwin-day/

Mendez, I., and G. Zamarro. 2018. The intergenerational transmission of noncognitive skills and their effect on education and employment outcomes. *Journal of Population Economics* 31: 521–560.

Moreno, J.M., and Á. Martínez. 2023. Educación en la Sombra en España. EsadeEcPol Brief #35.

Nickow, A., P. Oreopoulos, and V. Quan. 2020. The impressive effects of tutoring on prek-12 learning: A systematic review and meta-analysis of the experimental evidence.

Patacchini, E., and Y. Zenou. 2011. Neighborhood effects and parental involvement in the intergenerational transmission of education. *Journal of Regional Science* 51 (5): 987–1013.

Pop-Eleches, C., and M. Urquiola. 2013. Going to a better school: Effects and behavioral responses. *American Economic Review* 103 (4): 1289–1324.

Ruiz-Valenzuela, J. 2020. Job loss at home: children's school performance during the Great Recession. *SERIEs* 11 (3): 243–286.

Ruiz-Valenzuela, J. 2020. Intergenerational effects of employment protection reforms. *Labour Economics* 62: 101774.

Ruiz-Valenzuela, J. 2021. The effects of parental job loss on children's outcomes. In *Oxford Research Encyclopedia of Economics and Finance*.

The Effects of Classmates (*Peer Effects*)

José Montalbán Castilla

1 Introduction

Understanding and measuring the processes by which individuals influence our behavior—whether inspiring us to improve our performance or encouraging unproductive activities—is considered a key factor in social sciences to comprehend various problems and opportunities. In education, student performance and aspirations are simultaneously influenced by interactions with classmates, family dynamics, and neighbors in their residential communities. Peer effects (PE), as they are commonly called, refer to an externality where the context, behaviors, and outcomes of peers impact an individual's educational achievements (Sacerdote 2001).

If the composition of a social group, such as a classroom or neighborhood, significantly affects individuals' outcomes through social interactions, then peer effects hold substantial implications for public policy. These impacts can be positive, negative, or neutral, often lacking a straightforward answer. For instance, key public policy questions related to PE include:

- Should schools be integrated or segregated based on students' ethnic or social composition?
- Is it better to form highly heterogeneous groups where students exhibit varying academic levels, or should students be placed in homogenous groups?
- At what age should students be separated into different academic levels?

Answers to these questions are not ideological but require rigorous theoretical and empirical studies, as they depend on several factors. These include econometric methodologies to identify causal impacts, the chosen objective function (e.g., academic performance, aspirations, or subjective well-being), and the observed time horizon (e.g., short- or long-term).

J. M. Castilla (✉)
Swedish Institute for Social Research (SOFI), Stockholm University, Stockholm, Sweden
e-mail: jose.montalban@sofi.su.se

A. Cabrales and I. Sanz (eds.), *Economics of Education*,
https://doi.org/10.1007/978-3-031-90911-5_6

The clear advantage of PE from a public policy and social planning perspective is their relatively low cost compared to other policies. It merely involves redistributing student groups to improve outcomes, theoretically making this approach simple and cost-effective. In contrast, other policies, such as reducing class sizes, require hiring additional teachers—a costly measure given that 72% of education budgets are typically allocated to salaries (see Chapter 4). Ambitious PE-related policies include programs like Moving to Opportunity (Chetty et al. 2016), a randomized social experiment implemented in the United States during the 1990s to analyze the effects of offering low-income families the opportunity to move to different neighborhoods, or Bussing (Angrist et al. 2022), a policy in the United States that transported students to schools in different districts to increase racial diversity. A critical challenge in implementing such policies lies in defining the counterfactual. Estimating the efficacy of these policies is not straightforward, as they may provoke strategic reactions from families choosing schools or influence public and private school incentives, ultimately affecting school segregation. Empirical evidence on this topic remains underdeveloped (see Chapter 12 on school choice).

Exercise 1: Why should we observe PE? Consider your particular context: Which individuals influence you, and whom do you influence? In what ways do these dynamics manifest in your life?

From a theoretical standpoint, there are several reasons to expect PE:

1. **Homophily**: People within close proximity often exhibit similar behavior, which can be attributed to shared traits or circumstances. For instance, individuals tend to associate with others who share similar values or socioeconomic backgrounds (*ex-ante* similarity).
2. **Shared Environments**: Proximity leads to shared experiences, whether in neighborhoods, homes, or schools, resulting in similar behaviors among individuals exposed to the same environment.
3. **Social Interaction**: Individuals influence one another through direct interactions, such as classmates, friends, or neighbors, creating mutual behavioral impacts.
4. **Human Capital Technologies**: Through interactions, students learn from their peers, collaborate on projects, or adopt their peers' negative behaviors.
5. **Sociological Externalities**: Students from differing socioeconomic backgrounds often choose role models based on their social environment.

From an empirical perspective, identifying PE requires considering which group characteristics are relevant. Imagine an extreme case: measuring PE on a student's academic performance while isolated on a deserted island. Initially, the student is alone, but their academic performance is measured before and after the arrival of a second student. Group characteristics—such as the new student's academic abilities or socioeconomic background—would be pivotal. However, this scenario is unrealistic, as students typically interact within larger social groups such as classes, schools, neighborhoods, and households. Thus, determining which group characteristics—e.g., mean academic level, heterogeneity, or outliers such as a high-performing student—are most impactful becomes essential.

Hoxby and Weingarth (2005) classify PE into seven categories, based on different assumptions:

1. **Linear-in-Means Model**: Only the group's average characteristics matter.
2. **Bad Apple**: A disruptive student negatively impacts others.
3. **Shining Light**: A brilliant student inspires peers.
4. **Invidious Comparisons**: High-performing students lower group outcomes.
5. **Boutique/Tracking**: Students perform better when surrounded by peers like themselves.
6. **Focus:** Homogeneous classes improve outcomes regardless of relative group performance.
7. **Rainbow**: Classroom heterogeneity benefits all students.

Exercise 2: What other configurations of PE do you find missing in Hoxby and Weingarth's (2005) taxonomy? Discuss

2 Estimating the Effects of Classmates

Measuring the magnitude and nature of PE is notably difficult due to the non-random nature of student, neighbor, or coworker groupings. Parents often invest significant effort in selecting neighborhoods or schools to benefit from specific peer groups, teachers, and school resources. Similarly, highly productive firms attract highly productive workers.

This self-selection complicates distinguishing between the causal effect of PE and self-selection into a particular social group. For example, Christakis and Fowler (2007) found that the probability of becoming obese increases by 57% if a friend is obese. However, how much of this effect stems from the friend's influence versus shared ethnic, socioeconomic, or lifestyle similarities? Cohen-Cole and Fletcher (2008) show that controlling for selection variables substantially reduces the estimated effect.

To identify causal PE, two primary challenges arise, as detailed by Manski (1993):

1. **Endogeneity or Reverse Causality (Reflection/Simultaneity):** It is difficult to separate the effect of the group on an individual from the individual's effect on the group, as outcomes are jointly determined.
2. **Unobserved Correlated Variables:**
   - **Self-Selection (Endogenous Sorting):** Individuals self-select into desired groups, complicating isolation of PE.
   - **Shared Environment:** Common group environments, such as shared teachers or neighborhood conditions, impact individual outcomes.

Manski's classic linear-in-means model (1993) illustrates these identification issues. The model seeks to estimate how the average academic performance of classmates impacts an individual's outcomes:

$$y_{ig} = \alpha + \beta x_{ig} + \phi \overline{y}_{(-i)}g + \delta \overline{X}_{(-i)}g + \mu_g + \varepsilon_{ig}$$

where:

- $\overline{y}_{(-i)}g$: Group mean excluding the individual's outcome (leave-out mean).
- $\overline{X}_{(-i)}g$: Observable group characteristics (e.g., age, gender, socioeconomic status).
- μ_g: Group's shared environmental factors.

1. **Endogenous effects** (ϕ): This parameter indicates the direct effect that the behavior (or performance) of peers has on my own behavior (or performance). This is the parameter of interest for estimating how my peers' grades affect mine.
2. **Exogenous or contextual effects** (δ): This parameter indicates how the exogenous characteristics of my peers affect my behavior (or performance). This is the parameter of interest for estimating how the context or characteristics of my peers influence my own outcomes. For example, if my classmates' parents have low incomes, this may result in observing a lower reward for education.
3. **Correlated effects** (μ_g): This parameter indicates how the shared environment or context with my classmates affects my performance.

The linear-in-means model has strengths and weaknesses. Its primary strength is its simplicity, offering an intuitive way to explain the world. However, this simplicity may not provide a compelling or nuanced description of reality. Policymaking based on this model often yields unexciting conclusions, as reconfiguring groups under this framework typically results in zero-sum outcomes. In other words, improving the performance of some students comes at the expense of others.

In contrast, non-linear models, which have recently gained traction, present more intriguing public policy applications. As noted by Hoxby and Weingarth (2005), non-linear models allow for scenarios where certain group configurations can enhance the outcomes of some students without negatively impacting others. For example, a new grouping arrangement might leave high-performing students unaffected while significantly boosting the performance of low-performing students. Hoxby and Weingarth (2005) propose a coherent framework for estimating PE beyond the linear-in-means model. Their suggestion involves calculating the fraction of peers within a given decile of past academic performance and interacting this with a binary variable indicating an individual's own decile. Using deciles, this approach generates 100 interactions (10 binary variables for peer academic ability multiplied by 10 for individual ability levels). Results can be graphically represented, as shown in Fig. 1 for quintiles. While this is just one example, the non-linear model's added flexibility and transparency have made it a common choice for PE estimations.

Exercise 3: Model Exploration. What other non-linear PE models can you propose? Discuss

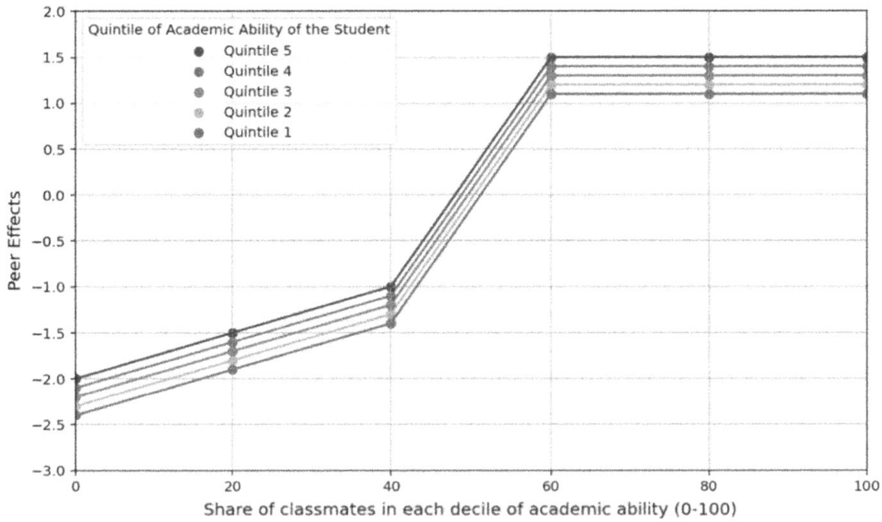

Fig. 1 Quintile of academic ability of the student. *Note* Own elaboration

3 Methods for Estimating Peer Effects

Economists and other social scientists have tackled some of these identification challenges by identifying or creating contexts where peers are randomly assigned to each other (e.g., through randomized grouping).

3.1 Non-Experimental Variation

3.1.1 Exogenous Population Movements

Social scientists have utilized various natural or controlled experiments that generate exogenous shocks in location or school assignment—and, consequently, in group configurations—to study the causal impact of PE. These studies often consider the effects of movers themselves and the influence of migrants on incumbent residents in the areas they join. Both perspectives offer valuable insights.

For example, a court order aimed at reducing school segregation is an event that may exogenously alter peer characteristics in schools receiving new students. Such an intervention is considered exogenous because it does not result from direct family decisions but rather from an external entity, like a court. Another example involves using natural disasters as exogenous shocks. If a hurricane forces families to relocate, this displacement creates new peer groups without being a direct choice of the affected individuals.

Angrist and Lang (2004) study the effects of bussing students from Boston public schools to Brookline schools on the academic outcomes of Brookline residents. They exploit variations in the percentage of bused students over different years and school cohorts within the same institutions. Their findings reveal no significant PE on local students' academic performance. Another example is Imberman et al. (2012), who examine changes in group composition due to the evacuation of students following Hurricane Katrina in schools across Houston, Texas, and Louisiana. While these authors find no evidence that the arrival of evacuees reduced local students' academic performance on average, they identify significant effects when considering non-linear interactions. A 10-percentage-point increase in the fraction of low-performing evacuees reduces local students' performance by 17% of a standard deviation. Conversely, a 10-percentage-point increase in high-performing evacuees improves local students' outcomes by 9% of a standard deviation.

3.1.2 Random Variation Across Cohorts

The concept of identifying PE by comparing cohort characteristics within the same school is not limited to migration, natural disasters, or asylum policies. In fact, one of the earliest applications of this method is Hoxby (2000), which leverages natural variation in gender and racial composition across small school cohorts over time. Girls tend to achieve better reading outcomes and commit fewer infractions than boys. Therefore, natural variations in cohort gender composition can provide exogenous variation in peer characteristics, enabling researchers to observe how this impacts academic outcomes.

Two notable studies employing this approach are Hoxby (2000) and Lavy and Schlosser (2011). Hoxby (2000) finds that the academic performance of both boys and girls increases by approximately 2% of a standard deviation when a cohort has 10 percentage points more girls. Lavy and Schlosser (2011) extend this strategy by investigating the mechanisms behind these results using Israeli educational data. They find that increasing the proportion of girls in a cohort by 10% raises boys' probability of earning a high school diploma by 0.5% and girls' by 1%.

3.1.3 Asignación aleatoria de compañeros de cuarto

An alternative strategy involves systematic processes where students are randomly assigned to roommates or classmates within a specific school or university. Although these studies focus on a very particular context, they offer a significant advantage in identifying tightly connected groups of students. That is, they can closely examine the relevant group dynamics (e.g., the influence of one's roommate).

Examples of studies utilizing this design include Sacerdote (2001), Zimmerman (2003), and Carrell et al. (2009). Sacerdote (2001) was the first to analyze PE in academic performance among college roommates randomly assigned at Dartmouth College in the United States. Sacerdote finds no significant effects on average but demonstrates substantial impacts using a more flexible non-linear model. High-achieving students benefit academically from having high-achieving roommates, especially when both students are high-achievers. Conversely, low-performing roommates most significantly reduce the performance of students at similar achievement levels. Carrell et al. (2009) exploit the random assignment of cadets to different squadrons at the U.S. Air Force Academy. The design of this study creates an ideal environment for estimating PE, as new cadets are randomly assigned to squadrons with limited interaction across them. Carrell et al. (2009) find squadron-level PE, where a one standard deviation increase in the average academic ability of a squadron increases grades by 5% of a standard deviation.

Exercise 4: Case Study Analysis. Read the work of Carrell et al. (2009) and discuss: Which matters more—mean academic levels or non-linear peer effects within squadrons? Explain the differences and potential public policy implications.

3.2 Experimental Variation

3.2.1 Random Experiments

Randomized controlled trials (RCTs) represent the gold standard for estimating causal effects and are widely used in social science to identify peer effects. By randomly assigning individuals to treatment or control groups, researchers ensure that the observed differences in outcomes can be attributed to the treatment itself and not to pre-existing differences among participants. This methodology has been employed extensively in educational settings to understand peer dynamics.

For instance, the Tennessee STAR experiment randomized students and teachers into classrooms of varying sizes, allowing researchers to investigate the impact of class size on academic performance. Though the primary focus was not on peer effects, the random assignment of students created exogenous variation in classroom composition, enabling the estimation of peer influences. Results indicate significant peer effects: the average ability level of classmates positively affected individual performance, particularly for low-performing students.

Another example is a study by Duflo et al. (2011), which evaluated tracking in Kenyan primary schools. Students were randomly assigned to homogenous or heterogeneous classrooms based on prior achievement levels. The findings revealed that tracking improved outcomes for all students, with high-performing peers exerting positive influences on their classmates.

In another seminal study, Carrel et al. (2013) conducted a randomized controlled experiment in which they assigned soldiers from the U.S. Air Force Academy into three groups: (i) **Treatment 1 (Bimodal Squadrons):** mixing students with high academic levels with those with low levels; (ii) **Treatment 2 (Homogeneous Squadrons):** students with medium academic levels; (iii) **Control:** half of the students were randomly assigned to squadrons mixing academic levels. The goal of this study was to design optimal group structures so that, above all, students with low academic levels could benefit more from those with high levels. The results of the study were not what the authors initially expected. Dividing groups into three modes had a negative effect on the academic performance of low-level students, positive effects for those in the middle of the distribution, and a neutral effect for high-level students. The mechanisms identified in the study suggest that the negative outcomes for low-level students occurred because they did not interact with high-level students, segregating into their respective subgroups, which harmed the performance of the former.

This study teaches an important lesson: endogenous responses to behavior are a clear obstacle to predicting the effects of manipulating groups to achieve a socially desirable outcome. Endogenous behavioral responses can pose a critical challenge for social planners, as these responses increase the likelihood of serious unintended consequences.

3.2.2 Partial Population Approach

In line with the findings of Carrell et al. (2013), the Partial Population Approach (PPA) leverages pre-existing friendship networks and connections, which are often robust as they are naturally formed, to carry out a randomized intervention within a fraction of the network. This involves identifying distinct friendship networks, randomly implementing a treatment for a percentage of individuals within the network, and then estimating the externalities of the treatment on untreated peers, yielding the Peer Effect (PE). This approach, first proposed by Moffitt (2001) and highlighted by Sacerdote (2014), is ideal in many ways. In the real world, opportunities to randomly assign groups are rare, whereas the feasibility of implementing a randomized intervention is much higher.

An example of this is Babcock and Hartman (2010), who applied this strategy in the context of gym exercise at UC Santa Barbara. Instead of randomly assigning peers to a group, the authors implemented a randomized intervention—in this case, an incentive to exercise more—within a fraction of the friendship networks. The study found that the friends of students who received the treatment exercised more if a larger portion of their network received the treatment. Thus, friends influenced each other to engage in more exercise.

Avvisati et al. (2014) provides another excellent example of this method. The authors conducted a large-scale controlled experiment in schools within a low-income area of Paris, France. The program provided parents with information about how schools function, along with advice on how to support and monitor their children's schoolwork. In each school and class, families were identified as volunteers or non-volunteers for the program before its implementation. Half of the school-classes were randomly selected to participate in the program. By comparing volunteer families in treated classes with volunteer families in control classes, the authors captured the direct effect of the program on treated parents and their children. By comparing non-volunteer families in treated and untreated classes, the authors captured the indirect effect (or PE) of having treated families in the class.

The program yielded very positive outcomes. By the end of the academic year, treated families significantly increased their involvement in their children's schoolwork. Students in treated classes demonstrated improved behavior and attitudes toward school, along with an additional positive indirect impact on their classmates' outcomes.

3.3 Reconciling Experimental with Natural Variation

Natural variation, which typically exploits continuous variation in group composition, has both advantages and limitations. The primary advantage is its flexibility in estimating the peer response function, enabling researchers to better predict outcomes under alternative group configurations. However, it has two main limitations. The first is that this variation almost always occurs in a very limited way. For instance, fortunately, natural disasters, immigration shocks, or political asylum events are not very frequent in developed countries, and situations where group members are randomly assigned are rare. The second is that these studies have clear support problems. When certain group configurations are not represented in the data, extrapolation relies solely on the functional form and risks being invalid. For example, in schools, a typical class might have about 50% boys and 50% girls. Hoxby (2000) leverages slight deviations from this rule (e.g., 48% vs. 52% of one gender). However, classes with extreme imbalances, such as 90% boys and 10% girls, are rare, leaving insufficient data to confidently extrapolate outcomes for such scenarios. This issue is clearly illustrated in Fig. 2 of Booij et al. (2017), where 99% of the randomly formed groups do not vary significantly from one another.

Randomized experiments, which typically explore the effect of discrete (random) interventions rather than continuous variations, also have pros and cons. The key advantage is their ability to provide highly credible estimates for a specific group configuration. However, their main limitation is that discrete treatments clearly restrict the scope of extrapolation, making it difficult to predict outcomes for group configurations different from the one tested. For example, Carrell et al. (2013) credibly estimate the effects of grouping students from the bottom third of the academic distribution with those from the top third, compared to mixing students with varying academic levels. Duflo et al. (2011) credibly estimate the effects of grouping students from the bottom half with those from the top half of the academic distribution, compared to a mixed configuration. However, neither study can estimate the impact of the other's group configuration within their specific context. Carrell et al. (2013) cannot estimate the effect of grouping the bottom half with the top half in their population of U.S. Air Force Academy cadets, nor can Duflo et al. (2011) estimate the effect of grouping the bottom third with the top third in their population of primary school students in Kenya.

Booij et al. (2017) explicitly designed an experiment to address these limitations. They conducted a randomized experiment manipulating the composition and skills of student groups in first-year Economics at the University of Amsterdam, ensuring group configurations spanned the entire possible distribution. The randomness of this setup solved the selection and reflection problem, while the variation in group composition (illustrated by the blue points in Fig. 2 of Booij et al. 2017) allowed them to estimate the impact of different scenarios on students' overall performance.

In peer effects (PE) research, there is a trade-off between external validity and the robustness of empirical identification. Most PE studies are based on highly specific contexts, where exogenous variation is creatively and robustly exploited. For instance, the random assignment of college roommates in a specific U.S– university. However, this specificity comes at the cost of potential difficulty in generalizing findings to broader contexts. Broader, more generalizable contexts are often studied at the cost of less clear identification strategies. Therefore, when interpreting the results of different studies and drawing public policy conclusions, it is crucial to account for these dynamics. Balancing the trade-off between context specificity and generalizability is key to advancing both research and practical applications in this field.

4 What Do We Know About the Effects of Classmates in Education?

This section summarizes the main findings of peer effects (PE) research in education. In all subsections, distinctions are made between the PE exerted by classmates, family, and neighbors.

4.1 Academic Achievement

4.1.1 Classmates

Most studies investigating the influence of peer effects (PE) on academic performance focus on classmates. Numerous studies aim to capture the effect of peer characteristics (e.g., academic ability, gender, race, socioeconomic background). These studies typically find insignificant effects, or, if significant, they are modest in magnitude. Most research exploring heterogeneous effects concludes that certain groups of students are more influenced by peer characteristics than others.

Among the studies examining the effect of varying proportions of peers by gender are the previously mentioned Hoxby (2000) and Lavy and Schlosser (2011), along with Black et al. (2013). Black et al. (2013) find that the IQ of boys is unaffected by exposure to female classmates during high school in Norway. Furthermore, they show that characteristics such as the average age, education, and parental income of classmates have little to no effect on the IQ of their peers. There is also research focused on whether the race of classmates impacts academic performance. Angrist and Lang (2004) is a previously mentioned example. Additionally, Figlio and Özek (2019) conducted a study leveraging the large influx of Haitian migrants, who were non-native English speakers and low-income, into Florida's public schools following the 2010 earthquake. These authors found virtually no effects on the academic performance of Floridian students, regardless of socioeconomic status, age, race, or place of birth.

Another area of research focuses on the effects of being exposed to peers with varying academic levels. Similar to the findings on student characteristics, these studies yield mixed results. The previously mentioned Imberman et al. (2012) is an example. Abdulkadiro˘glu et al. (2014) exploit quasi-experimental variation generated by admission thresholds at the most selective schools in Boston and New York. Despite these thresholds providing significant variation in student academic levels, their research finds that the academic level of classmates does not significantly affect students' academic performance. The previously mentioned Booij et al. (2017) found that students at the highest academic levels were not affected by group composition. However, students in the lower and middle ranges of academic ability improved their performance by 19% of a standard deviation and reduced university dropout rates by 12 percentage points when grouped with peers of similar academic levels.

Additionally, there are other ways in which students' academic levels may impact the performance of their peers. For instance, Murphy and Weinhardt (2020) use data from the universe of English students to demonstrate that, independent of absolute academic ability, a student's relative academic ranking within their primary school class has medium-term consequences for academic performance in secondary education. That is, for the same absolute academic ability, the relative position a student held in their former class has long-term implications. These effects are particularly pronounced for males and include impacts on students' confidence levels and additional effects on the decision to pursue an academic track.

Exercise 4: What public policy implications do these results have? If you were the Minister of Education in Spain, discuss whether you would implement any specific educational policy derived from this work, explain the reasoning behind your decision, and highlight the potential costs and benefits of such a policy.

4.1.2 Family

There is also another body of research focused on studying how siblings affect academic performance. These studies typically find larger effects than those documented for classmates. However, evidence suggests that depending on the general and family context, the direction of the effects may vary. This is an important factor to consider, especially when attempting to incorporate these types of peer effects into cost–benefit analyses and the design of new public policies. See Chapter 5 on Families.

Qureshi (2018b) finds that younger siblings benefit when their older siblings have more experienced teachers in North Carolina. According to this study, greater experience in a language teacher improves the language academic outcomes of older siblings by 4.2% of a standard deviation, and subsequently those of younger siblings by 1%. However, this effect is not symmetrical, as older siblings are not affected by the experience of their younger siblings' teachers. Nicoletti and Rabe (2019) study sibling externalities in public schools in England. Their research finds that an increase of one standard deviation in the academic performance of older siblings improves the performance of younger siblings by 11% of a standard deviation.

4.1.3 Neighbors

The third type of peer effect (PE) presented in this chapter involves neighbors, a relatively recent area of research. Identifying the effect of neighborhoods is challenging because people who live close to one another often share characteristics correlated with academic performance in school. Furthermore, identifying immediate neighbors, who are presumed to have the strongest effects, is difficult because most datasets with neighborhood information define this category too broadly. There is robust evidence that exposure to a better neighborhood from an early age improves future income, increases the likelihood of attending university, and reduces the probability of teenage pregnancy (Chetty et al. 2014, 2016; Chetty and Hendren 2018a, b). However, these studies leave open the question of whether the effects of neighborhoods stem from greater exposure to neighbors with higher educational levels or from access to higher-quality local resources (e.g., schools, healthcare services, infrastructure, or safety). The public policy implications differ greatly depending on which factor is dominant.

Exercise 5: Detail and discuss the public policy implications depending on which effect is dominant in the paragraph above.

Some examples of neighbor PEs include Goux and Maurin (2007) and Åslund et al. (2011). Goux and Maurin (2007) is one of the earliest studies to investigate PEs among neighbors. The authors leverage unique characteristics of France, finding that a teenager's performance at the end of high school is strongly influenced by the academic level of other adolescents in the neighborhood. According to this study, the birthdate distribution of nearby neighbors and the proportion of families assigned to social housing significantly impact academic performance during adolescence. Åslund et al. (2011) examine how exposure to highly educated adults in the neighborhood affects academic performance. To identify this effect, the authors use a quasi-experimental analysis based on the locations where recently arrived refugees are assigned in Sweden.

4.2 Educational Trajectory

There is evidence focusing on the influence that other people have on our educational trajectories. This is an important area of study, particularly in contexts with high levels of segregation, where the influence of others may underlie persistent inequalities between different social groups. Other people can influence our educational trajectories by transmitting relevant information, providing support with applications to various schools or universities, helping in preparation for competitive exams, or even shaping our preferences.

4.2.1 Classmates

The aforementioned study by Black et al. (2013) also finds that a higher proportion of girls in a cohort improves long-term labor market outcomes for girls. However, a greater presence of girls appears to harm boys' outcomes by reducing the likelihood of choosing an academic track and completing fewer years of education. Carrell et al. (2010, 2018) explore the "bad apple" hypothesis, or the influence of disruptive students on their classmates (previously mentioned in Sect. 1). In this study, disruptive students are approximated as those who have experienced domestic violence at home, as these students are more likely to exhibit behaviors related to violence and difficulties in peer relationships (Carlson 2000). This research finds that being exposed to one additional disruptive student in a class of 25, particularly if the disruptive peer is male, reduces college enrollment and graduation rates for classmates, as well as lowers their future earnings between the ages of 24 and 28.

Bursztyn and Jensen (2015) and Bursztyn et al. (2019) take a different angle by studying how peer pressure and social norms influence students' investment in education. Both studies use randomized controlled experiments. These studies show that classmates exert an amplifying externality on social pressure and norms, influencing students' individual choices. In another recent study, Barrios-Fernández et al. (2022) demonstrate that university peers can have intergenerational effects on educational trajectories. Using a regression discontinuity approach, this study shows that Chilean parents' university peers significantly influenced the type of high schools and social circles their children later belonged to.

4.2.2 Family

Several studies have focused on the influence of siblings on the years of education completed. Qureshi (2018a) studies the effect that older sisters have on younger siblings in Pakistan. This study finds that the more years of education the older sister has, the younger sibling follows her lead by increasing their own. Gurantz et al. (2020) also document positive externalities of siblings on the likelihood of taking advanced exams, which are often required for university admission in the

United States. Joensen and Nielsen (2018) exploit quasi-experimental variation in a pilot study at the school level in Denmark and show that greater enrollment of older siblings in advanced math and science courses during high school increases the probability of younger siblings enrolling in those same courses. Dahl et al. (2020) show that the educational field chosen by older siblings during high school has a significant impact on the field chosen by younger siblings in Sweden. This indicates that older siblings not only impact the quantity of education attained but also the type of education that younger siblings seek to pursue. Altmejd et al. (2021) investigate the impact of siblings on the transition from high school to university in an analysis using administrative data from Chile, Croatia, Sweden, and the United States. The authors find that older siblings greatly influence the decision to enroll in university as well as the decision about which university to attend.

Exercise 6: Discuss which mechanisms are most relevant in leading to the effects shown in this section. Based on the results presented, which one(s) do you believe dominate?

4.2.3 Neighbors

Research focusing on the impact of neighbors on educational trajectories is quite limited and relatively recent, meaning much more evidence is still needed.

Bobonis and Finan (2009) study the impact of neighbors on secondary school enrollment in rural areas of Mexico, using the quasi-random assignment of the conditional cash transfer program Progresa. These authors find that Progresa increases secondary school enrollment for the children of families who received the program as well as for the children of those who did not. This latter result indicates the influence of neighbors on the decision to enroll in secondary education.

Barrios-Fernández (2022) documents similar effects but in the decision to enroll in university. This study exploits the variation generated by the rules governing the allocation of student loans in Chile. It shows that high school seniors are more likely to attend and complete a university degree when their closest neighbor (defined as the person living nearest who applied to university a year earlier) obtained a loan and enrolled in university. This increase in enrollment occurs through a higher likelihood of taking the final admission exam and applying to a university program.

Michelman et al. (2022) study peer effects in university by exploiting the random assignment of students to dormitories at Harvard between the 1920s and 1930s. These authors find that individuals of high social status benefit from interacting with roommates of high social status—specifically, they increase their likelihood of joining exclusive clubs and achieving successful careers in finance—while individuals of low and middle social status do not benefit at all. This study shows that peer effects do not necessarily influence our trajectories for academic reasons. In fact, the effects documented in this work are more closely related to social dimensions than academic ones.

4.3 Non-Academic Outcomes

The two previous sections focus on the impact of peer effects (PE) on academic performance and educational trajectories. However, classmates, family, and neighbors can also influence other variables of interest.

4.3.1 Classmates

There is a large number of studies dedicated to investigating the influence of classmates in school and university on outcomes beyond academics.

Gaviria and Raphael (2001) is perhaps the study that examines the greatest number of non-educational variables such as drug use, alcohol and tobacco consumption, church attendance, or dropping out of school. They use a sample of 15-year-old students in the United States and find a very strong relationship in the influence that school peers exert on the five variables mentioned.

Other studies analyze peer effects on misbehavior in school. For example, Bennett and Bergman (2021) use administrative data from the state of West Virginia in the United States and develop a new method to identify friendship networks based on students who engage in truancy together. This study shows that implementing an intervention for parents, in which they are given information about their children's absenteeism, has an additional positive externality on the untreated children's peers since, as friends, they interact, creating a multiplier effect. The authors show that ignoring this externality underestimates the cost-effectiveness of the program by 43%. Carrell et al. (2008)also investigate peer effects on the likelihood of cheating in exams at the three largest military academies in the United States. These authors find that the more classmates cheat, the higher the probability that a student will end up cheating as well.

On a more dramatic level, there is also available evidence that school peers can influence participation in criminal activities. Deming (2011) studies the effect of the school and high school attended on future adult crime in Charlotte-Mecklenburg in the United States. The study presents suggestive evidence that, while in elementary school the influence of peers is a decisive factor in the effect on crime, in high school, the most important factor is the quality of education received. Eren et al. (2022) exploit grade repetition thresholds for 13-year-old students, finding that grade repetition increases the likelihood of committing a violent crime by 1 percentage point (58%). As in Deming (2011), peers seem to have a decisive influence on explaining these results.

Exercise 7: Do you believe this case is generalizable to Spain? Base your answer on multiple concrete data points regarding criminality, grade repetition, and the quality of education in Spain compared to other countries.

4.3.2 Family

Multiple studies document the high correlation of risky behaviors among siblings, suggesting that habits may be influenced by siblings. Altonji et al. (2017) investigate whether the correlations in drug use and sales among siblings are at least partially explained by a causal effect. They conclude that, although tobacco, alcohol, and marijuana use appear to be influenced by the example set by older siblings, most of the observed correlations between siblings arise from shared influences (i.e., correlated effects). Bingley et al. (2021) document peer effects among siblings in the selection of employment sectors in Denmark. They find that the random assignment of the older sibling to serve in the military increases the probability of the younger sibling serving as well by 7%. Heissel (2017) shows that siblings with sisters who became teenage mothers exhibit lower academic performance in school, are more likely to drop out of high school, and have higher chances of interacting with the juvenile justice system after the birth of their nephew or niece. The increased need for parental support, attention, and resources following the birth of a new child in the family may explain the negative externalities documented in this study.

4.3.3 Neighbors

There are studies that consistently document neighborhood effects on crime and delinquency. Kling et al. (2005), for example, examine the Moving to Opportunity (MTO) initiative in the United States and its effects on juvenile crime and delinquency. The MTO program randomly assigned housing vouchers to families, which they could use to move to better neighborhoods in five U.S. cities. The study shows that relocating to lower-poverty areas reduces arrests for property theft and violent crime among young girls. It also reduces participation in violent crime among boys but increases participation in property theft. Billings et al. (2019) demonstrate that neighborhoods and school segregation increase crime levels by fostering social interactions among at-risk youth. The study finds that concentrating more disadvantaged students in the same school increases overall crime. Moreover, these disadvantaged students are more likely to become "crime partners" and eventually commit crimes together.

Neighbors can also affect other variables. Corno and Burns (2022) exploit the random assignment of university roommates in South Africa, showing that being assigned to an interracial room reduces prejudice and improves attitudes among students of different races. Additionally, it increases the likelihood of forming interracial friendships.

5 Conclusion and Discussion

The evidence discussed in this article highlights the importance of the many ways in which other people—whether classmates, family, or neighbors—influence student outcomes. When all the evidence on peer effects (PE) is analyzed together, four fundamental conclusions emerge:

1. As Sacerdote (2014) points out, only half of the studies using a linear-in-means model to explain the reality of PE find modest effects on academic performance, while the other half find no significant effects.
2. The effect of classmates increases in magnitude and statistical power when the assumptions of the linear-in-means model are relaxed, and a non-linear model is applied to describe reality.
3. The results of PE on non-academic and social variables show much larger effects compared to those found in academic performance. That is, it is easier for classmates to influence variables like classroom behavior, drug use, or physical activity than academic performance (see also Chapter 9 on Early Childhood Education).
4. We still do not know enough about the nature of PE to engage in social engineering experiments (Sacerdote 2014), as: (i) Results are inconsistent across studies; (ii) They vary greatly depending on the context; (iii) There are clear endogenous responses to group manipulation, as seen, for example, in Carrell et al. (2013).

Exercise 8: How do you think the limitations mentioned in point (4) can be addressed?

Empirically confirming the existence of PE is important because it affects the cost–benefit analysis of different public policies and can be incorporated into the design of new programs to maximize their impact. In the educational context, as Barrios-Fernandez (2023) points out, they can help explain the persistence of inequality across different social groups. However, making general public policy recommendations in this regard is complicated, as the size of the effects documented in this chapter varies substantially across contexts and depending on how influential individuals are characterized and defined. Understanding what drives this heterogeneity is key to drawing broader policy lessons and gaining a more comprehensive understanding of the nature and importance of social interactions in educational contexts.

A first step involves identifying the mechanisms behind PE, where much work remains to be done. For example, the positive effects on academic performance associated with having a higher proportion of girls in a class have been attributed to the improved learning environment associated with this—fewer classroom disruptions, better relationships between students, between students and teachers, and less teacher fatigue. If an improved classroom environment is indeed the main mechanism behind these results, this could explain why, in some contexts, a higher proportion of female classmates appears to have no effect (e.g., Black et al. 2013). There are other reasons why peers may impact student outcomes differently. For instance, high-performing peers may enhance the classroom learning environment by causing fewer disruptions and helping other students, but at the same time, they may make it more difficult for lower-performing students to ask questions and participate actively in class. Evidence supports the existence of both mechanisms, but it is unclear what makes one mechanism more relevant than the other in different contexts. A student's relative academic position in the class has been shown to affect their confidence and future performance (e.g., Murphy and Weinhardt 2020). Thus, being surrounded by high-achieving peers can both improve and worsen classmates' academic outcomes.

Understanding the mechanisms behind the results, in addition to helping us rationalize differences in PE that arise in different contexts, is key to making public policy decisions. If improving the classroom learning environment is a fundamental mechanism of PE, then we should try to assign students to groups in ways that minimize classroom disruptions (see Chapter 4, which outlines Lazear's model on the effects of classroom disruptions) and maximize positive interactions. However, another alternative is to create a better learning environment by modifying school culture or reducing class sizes. Another example is the substantial evidence documenting PE in educational trajectories, which has not yet been able to conclude which mechanism is most relevant: information transmission, direct academic support, or preference changes (e.g., changes in aspirations or motivation). Understanding this is key to knowing which policy tools should be used. For example, if the primary mechanism is information transmission, governments could design strategies to compensate for the absence of such information from peers and provide it directly to students, though designing effective interventions of this kind is not easy (e.g., Dynarski et al. 2021). Thus, understanding the mechanisms behind PE is essential for identifying which alternative or complementary policies could help improve student outcomes.

Regardless of the mechanisms, the existence of social externalities in education is a relevant fact for understanding inequalities in educational performance. This implies that the consequences of barriers and challenges disproportionately affecting certain groups of students are amplified through social interactions. However, from a more optimistic perspective, these social externalities imply that programs designed to expand access to educational opportunities for disadvantaged students are likely to have larger effects than those that only measure their impact on specific students and ignore the effects on the broader social group (e.g., Bennett and Bergman 2021).

All these findings have implications for the public policies that should be implemented. As Sacerdote (2014) suggests, public policies that implement interventions such as those by Duflo and Saez (2003) or Avvisati et al. (2014), in which only part of the peers in a friendship network are targeted (hoping that these individuals influence untreated peers), but do not actively attempt to manipulate who is in the network or how much the individuals interact, are safer and more likely to achieve the intended goal. In other words, the Partial Population Approach is potentially the safest method for implementing policies aimed at influencing peers through the multiplier effects of interventions.

In general, there is no doubt that significant progress has been made in PE research, and it has been demonstrated that these effects exert a powerful influence on human behavior. Despite the limitations and identification challenges, solid progress has been made toward understanding in which domains peers matter most and how large these effects are. What remains to be discovered about this topic in the future is exciting.

References

Abdulkadiro˘glu, A., J. Angrist, and P. Pathak. 2014. The elite illusion: Achievement effects at Boston and New York exam schools. *Econometrica* 82 (1): 137–196.

Altmejd, A., A. Barrios-FernÅLandez, M. Drlje, J. Goodman, M. Hurwitz, D. Kovac, C. Mulhern, C. Neilson, and J. Smith. 2021. O brother, where start thou? Sibling spillovers on college and major choice in four countries. *The Quarterly Journal of Economics* 136 (3): 1831–1886.

Altonji, J.G., S. Cattan, and I. Ware. 2017. Identifying sibling influence on teenage substance use. *Journal of Human Resources* 52 (1): 1–47.

Angrist, J.D., and K. Lang. 2004. Does school integration generate peer effects? Evidence from Boston's Metco Program. *American Economic Review* 94 (5): 1613–1634.

Angrist, J., G. Gray-Lobe, C.M. Idoux and P.A. Pathak. 2022. Still worth the trip? School busing effects in Boston and New York. No. w30308. National Bureau of Economic Research.

Åslund, O., P.-A. Edin, P. Fredriksson, and H. GrÅNonqvist. 2011. Peers, neighborhoods, and immigrant student achievement: Evidence from a placement policy. *American Economic Journal: Applied Economics* 3 (2): 67–95.

Avvisati, F., M. Gurgand, N. Guyon, and E. Maurin. 2014. Getting parents involved: A field experiment in deprived schools. *Review of Economic Studies* 81 (1): 57–83.

Babcock, P.S., and J.L. Hartman. 2010. Networks and workouts: Treatment size and status specific peer effects in a randomized field experiment. No. w16581. National Bureau of Economic Research.

Barrios-Fernández, A. 2022. Neighbors' effects on university enrollment. *American Economic Journal: Applied Economics* 14 (3): 30–60.

Barrios- Fernández, A., C. Neilson, and S. Zimmerman. 2022. Elite universities and the intergenerational transmission of human and social capital.

Barrios- Fernández, A. 2022. Peer effects in education.

Barrios-Fernandez, Andrés. 2023. Peer effects in education. In *Oxford Research Encyclopedia of Economics and Finance.*

Billings, S.B., D.J. Deming, and S.L. Ross. 2019. Partners in crime. *American Economic Journal: Applied Economics* 11 (1): 126–150.

Bennett, M., and P. Bergman. 2021. Better together? Social networks in truancy and the targeting of treatment. *Journal of Labor Economics* 39 (1): 1–36.

Bursztyn, L., and R. Jensen. 2015. How does peer pressure affect educational investments? *The Quarterly Journal of Economics* 130 (3): 1329–1367.

Bursztyn, L., G. Egorov, and R. Jensen. 2019. Cool to be smart or smart to be cool? Understanding peer pressure in education. *The Review of Economic Studies* 86 (4): 1487–1526.

Black, S.E., P.J. Devereux, and K.G. Salvanes. 2013. Under pressure? The effect of peers on outcomes of young adults. *Journal of Labor Economics* 31 (1): 119–153.

Booij, A.S., E. Leuven, and H. Oosterbeek. 2017. Ability peer effects in university: Evidence from a randomized experiment. *The Review of Economic Studies* 84 (2): 547–578.

Bobonis, G.J., and F. Finan. 2009. Neighborhood peer effects in secondary school enrollment decisions. *The Review of Economics and Statistics* 91 (4): 695–716.

Bingley, P., P. Lundborg, and S.V. Lyk-Jensen. 2021. Brothers in arms spillovers from a draft lottery. *Journal of Human Resources* 56 (1): 225–268.

Carlson, B.E. 2000. Children exposed to intimate partner violence: Research findings and implications for intervention. *Trauma, Violence, & Abuse* 1 (4): 321–342.

Carrell, S.E., R.L. Fullerton, and J.E. West. 2009. Does your cohort matter? Measuring peer effects in college achievement. *Journal of Labor Economics* 27 (3): 439–464.

Carrell, S.E., and M.L. Hoekstra. 2010. Externalities in the classroom: How children exposed to domestic violence affect everyone's kids. *American Economic Journal: Applied Economics* 2 (1): 211–228.

Carrell, S.E., M.L. Hoekstra, and E. Kuka. 2018. The long-run effects of disruptive peers. *American Economic Review* 108 (11): 3377–3415.

Carrell, S.E., F.V. Malmstrom, and J.E. West. 2008. Peer effects in academic cheating. *Journal of Human Resources* 43 (1): 173–207.

Carrell, S.E., B.I. Sacerdote, and J.E. West. 2013. From natural variation to optimal policy? The importance of endogenous peer group formation. *Econometrica* 81 (3): 855–882.

Chetty, R., and N. Hendren. 2018a. The impacts of neighborhoods on intergenerational mobility I: Childhood exposure effects. *The Quarterly Journal of Economics* 133 (3): 1107–1162.

Chetty, R., and N. Hendren. 2018b. The impacts of neighborhoods on intergenerational mobility II: Childhood exposure effects. *The Quarterly Journal of Economics* 133 (3): 1163–1228.

Chetty, R., N. Hendren, P. Kline, and E. Saez. 2014. Where is the land of opportunity? The geography of intergenerational mobility in the United States. *The Quarterly Journal of Economics* 129 (4): 1553–1623.

Chetty, R., N. Hendren, and L.F. Katz. 2016. The effects of exposure to better neighborhoods on children: New evidence from the moving to opportunity experiment. *American Economic Review* 106 (4): 855–902.

Christakis, N.A., and J.H. Fowler. 2007. The spread of obesity in a large social network over 32 years. *New England Journal of Medicine* 357 (4): 370–379.

Cohen-Cole, E., and J.M. Fletcher. 2008. Is obesity contagious? Social networks vs. environmental factors in the obesity epidemic. *Journal of Health Economics* 27 (5): 1382–1387.

Corno, E.L.F., and J. Burns 2022. Interaction, stereotypes, and performance: Evidence from South Africa. *American Economic Review* 112 (12): 3848–3875.

Dahl, G.B., D.-O. Rooth, and A. Stenberg. 2020. Family spillovers in field of study.

Deming, D.J. 2011. Better schools, less crime? *The Quarterly Journal of Economics* 126 (4): 2063–2115.

Duflo, E., P. Dupas, and M. Kremer. 2011. Peer effects, teacher incentives, and the impact of tracking: Evidence from a randomized evaluation in Kenya. *American Economic Review* 101 (5): 1739–1774.

Dynarski, S., C.J. Libassi, K. Michelmore, and S. Owen. 2021. Closing the gap: The effect of reducing complexity and uncertainty in college pricing on the choices of low-income students. *American Economic Review* 111 (6): 1721–1756.

Eren, O., M.F. Lovenheim, and H.N. Mocan. 2022. The effect of grade retention on adult crime: Evidence from a test-based promotion policy. *Journal of Labor Economics* 40 (2): 361–395.

Figlio, D., and U.Å.N. Özek. 2019. Unwelcome guests? The effects of refugees on the educational outcomes of incumbent students. *Journal of Labor Economics* 37 (4): 1061–1096.

Gaviria, A., and S. Raphael. 2001. School-based Peer effects and juvenile behavior. *The Review of Economics and Statistics* 83 (2): 257–268.

Goux, D., and E. Maurin. 2007. Close neighbours matter: Neighbourhood effects on early performance at school. *The Economic Journal* 117 (523): 1193–1215.

Gurantz, O., M. Hurwitz, and J. Smith. 2020. Sibling effects on high school exam taking and performance. *Journal of Economic Behavior & Organization* 178: 534–549.

Imberman, S.A., A.D. Kugler, and B.I. Sacerdote. 2012. Katrina's children: Evidence on the structure of peer effects from hurricane evacuees. *American Economic Review* 102 (5): 2048–2082.

Joensen, J.S., and H.S. Nielsen. 2018. Spillovers in education choice. *Journal of Public Economics* 157: 158–183.

Heissel, Jennifer A. 2017. Teenage motherhood and sibling outcomes. *American Economic Review* 107 (5): 633–37. https://doi.org/10.1257/aer.p20171130

Hoxby, C.M. 2000. Peer effects in the classroom: Learning from gender and race variation.

Hoxby, C.M., and G. Weingarth. 2005. Taking race out of the equation: School reassignment and the structure of peer effects. No. 7867 Working Paper.

Karbownik, K., and U.Å.N. Ozek. 2019. Setting a good example? Examining sibling spillovers in educational achievement using a regression discontinuity design.

Kling, J.R., J. Ludwig, and L.F. Katz. 2005. Neighborhood effects on crime for female and male youth: Evidence from a randomized housing voucher experiment. *The Quarterly Journal of Economics* 120 (1): 87–130.

Lavy, V., and A. Schlosser. 2011. Mechanisms and impacts of gender peer effects at school. *American Economic Journal: Applied Economics* 3 (2): 1–33.

Manski, C.F. 1993. Identification of endogenous social effects: The reflection problem. *The Review of Economic Studies* 60 (3): 531–542.

Michelman, V., J. Price, and S.D. Zimmerman. 2022. Old boys' clubs and upward mobility among the educational elite. *The Quarterly Journal of Economics* 137 (2): 845–909.

Murphy, R., and F. Weinhardt. 2020. Top of the class: The importance of ordinal rank. *The Review of Economic Studies* 87 (6): 2777–2826.

Moffitt, R.A. 2001. Policy interventions, low-level equilibria, and social interactions. *Social Dynamics* 4 (45–82): 6–17.

Nicoletti, C., and B. Rabe. 2019. Sibling spillover effects in school achievement. *Journal of Applied Econometrics* 34 (4): 482–501.

Qureshi, J.A. 2018a. Additional returns to investing in girls' education: Impact on younger sibling human capital. *The Economic Journal* 128 (616): 3285–3319.

Qureshi, J.A. 2018b. Siblings, teachers, and spillovers on academic achievement. *Journal of Human Resources* 53 (1): 272–297.

Sacerdote, B. 2001. Peer effects with random assignment: Results for Dartmouth roommates. *The Quarterly Journal of Economics* 116 (2): 681–704.

Sacerdote, B. 2014. Experimental and quasi-experimental analysis of peer effects: Two steps forward? *Annual Review Economy* 6 (1): 253–272.

Vigdor, J., and T. Nechyba. 2007. *Peer effects in North Carolina public schools*, 73–101. Cambridge: Schools and the equal opportunity problem.

Zimmerman, D.J. 2003. Peer effects in academic outcomes: Evidence from a natural experiment. *Review of Economics and Statistics* 85 (1): 9–23.

Teachers: Much More than a Profession

Lucas Gortazar

1 Introduction: The Most Important Profession in the World

Teachers are the architects of future societies and economies. They transmit knowledge, skills, and values at school to the next generations: they are the basis of human capital and the future knowledge of economies. Countries that are able to make the teaching profession much more than a job are those that have achieved great changes in education and in the accumulation of human capital and knowledge and, therefore, in the generation of wealth and jobs. And this is no easy task. Being a teacher is not only about being academically prepared and, therefore, having been a good student. It is much more than that: it involves observing, diagnosing, communicating, organizing, setting an example, facilitating, managing, and leading. According to research from the 1960s that was very popular, teachers make an average of 1200 to 1500 decisions a day, understanding decisions as non-routine and improvised choices (Jackson 1968). Being a teacher is above all a profession associated with a form of social vocation and transcendence beyond oneself.

The teaching profession has been a growing focus of interest in the field of educational economics over the past few decades. A review of what has happened in the United States allows us to understand why that focus has increased, why it has strengthened economic research, and why it sheds light and relevant results on the importance of teachers to the education of millions of children.

In 1983, a commission appointed by Secretary of Education Terrel Bell, in Ronald Reagan's administration, published "*A nation at risk: the imperative for education reform*" (National Commission on Excellence in Education 1983). The report is considered one of the most relevant documents in the history of education in the United States because of its subsequent repercussions. The report, which challenged

L. Gortazar (✉)
Esade Center of Economic Policy, Madrid, Spain
e-mail: lucas.gortazar@esade.edu

A. Cabrales and I. Sanz (eds.), *Economics of Education*,
https://doi.org/10.1007/978-3-031-90911-5_7

the sense of urgency of educational administrations as if it were a situation of war and national threat, focused on several issues, but one of them was the teaching profession. It talked about salaries, careers and incentives, and how those incentives were key to improving the school system as a whole. A few years later, the federal government and several states were already beginning to implement incentive programs to attract, evaluate, and improve teacher performance in schools across the country.

The year 2001 marked a turning point with the passage of the "No Child Left Behind" law, supported by Republicans and Democrats and promoted by George Bush's administration. This reform was the definitive backing to promote stronger incentives for schools and teachers, one of the historical priorities of the Republican party, then in the federal government. But it also focused on the fact that these changes would improve student outcomes, especially for minorities and lower-income students, one of the Democratic Party's historic priorities, which also led it to sign the bill into law. It also gave a boost to the measurement of learning with rigorous tools, to the promotion of educational research and, more generally, to the use of educational research based on causal empirical methods for decision-making by schools and administrations.

The United States is the paradigmatic example of what has happened, but it is not the only place to focus on. In other countries such as the United Kingdom, Canada, the Netherlands, Nordic countries such as Finland or Asian countries such as Japan, China, Singapore, or Vietnam, something similar has happened. More and more eyes are on the teaching profession and more and more economists are studying it. In 2007, the prestigious American consulting firm McKinsey published a report (Barber and Mourshed 2007) on international education systems that caused a great impact on the media and governments. It was entitled "*How the world's best performing education systems achieved their goal*" and pointed to the experience of some of these countries: all of them had a common denominator, and that is to have bet on the teaching profession as a profession of excellence and as a pillar of change in their school systems. A phrase of a South Korean governor, quoted in the report, had enormous repercussions and became a mantra for many: "*the quality of a school system cannot exceed the quality of its teachers*". The ceiling of a school system is set by its teachers. Although this is a phrase that we will question in the chapter with some recent research (Is the sum greater or not than the parts?), it did leave a message that resonated with many. The report conveyed to companies, multilateral agencies, large foundations and governments the total priority of focusing on teachers. And it was another example of the push to put the teaching profession at the center of economic research.

Unfortunately, economic research on teachers in Spain is practically non-existent. This is due to the lack of tradition in the economics of education in Spain, with a research community still incipient, which this book will try to help grow. But also because of the lack of access to administrative and survey data related to teachers, which would often be framed in projects of unification of databases not prepared for research: this also increases entry costs (and makes research more expensive and costly), costs that are difficult to reduce until the data become accessible, processable, and easy to manipulate for research purposes.

This chapter will try to show the importance of the teaching profession from the point of view of economics. Some might ask: Why should economics be concerned with studying and thinking about the teaching profession and not leave it to other disciplines, such as pedagogy, psychology, or sociology? There are powerful reasons for doing so.

The first, which is the subject of this entire book, is that education is a factor that impacts the economy, the labor market and inequalities; if the teaching profession is one of the factors (if not the most important factor) in the production function of education, then it deserves to be addressed in all its depth. And this is not just a phrase or slogan, but is reflected in the use of public and also private resources (from families and companies). In particular, a large part of the public budget allocated to education goes to pay teachers' salaries. In developed countries, 91% of public spending on education goes to recurrent spending, 74% of which goes to pay salaries (i.e., almost 70% of public spending on education goes to teachers). This figure is even higher (81% of recurrent spending, when it accounts for 95% of total spending, i.e., 77% of the total) in the case of Spain (OECD 2022), an issue also mentioned in Chapter 3 of this book. And it is even higher in the countries, easily exceeding 80% of public educational spending. Therefore, there are economic reasons to think of teachers as a central part of the long-term future of the economy.

The second is that school systems are a source of public and private employment that can reach 5% of the labor market in developed countries and even more in developing countries: according to the most recent data from the Ministry of Education and Vocational Training, in the 2022/23 school year there were 811,049 teachers hired between public and private centers in non-university education, which represents 4.3% of the entire Spanish labor market that year. Understanding this labor market and its characteristics is key. If economists deal with the labor market as one of their areas of greatest interest for understanding the workings of the economy, then the labor market of the teaching profession takes on enormous importance.

The third reason has to do with the political economy of educational reforms. Teachers are a usually organized collective (both union and professionally), with the capacity to mobilize and influence and, therefore, with significant scope to influence educational policies and outcomes (Lovenheim et al. 2019; Biasi and Sarsons 2022). Understanding their incentives, as well as their beliefs, forms of organization, and political participation is key when crafting public policies. They are always necessary in any ambitious educational reform; and, likewise, they have the power and ability to slow down policy changes in education if they so deem.

The chapter reviews all the recent economic research that has been dealing with teachers. The examples used are mostly from developed countries, although an incipient literature is also being conducted in developing countries. The structure of the chapter is as follows. Chapter 2 situates teachers as a central element in building and creating human capital through education, showing their effect on the cognitive and socioemotional skills of students (and schools) and, more prospectively, on the future of the labor market and the economy. Chapter 3 addresses the question of what it is to be a good teacher and how we can identify it through social sciences in general and economic research in particular; it also tries to understand why some teachers are more effective than others and finally addresses the question of how we can potentially better select, attract, train, and develop teachers in schools. Chapter 4 briefly discusses the role of school leadership teams and principals in student learning

2 Faculty and Human Capital

2.1 Teachers from a Human Capital Perspective

Thinking about teachers from a human capital perspective makes economic sense. Since Becker's model (Becker 1962; Becker and Chiswick 1966), a large field of research and economic thinking has developed to study human capital as a factor of production in the economy, usually measured through educational attainment, academic credentials, and professional experience.

In education, econometric models related teaching characteristics as an input or explanatory variable and student learning as an output or outcome. Much of the research in the second part of the twentieth century and the beginning of the twenty-first century in the field of economics of education tried to identify the relationship between teaching skills and student learning: it clearly showed that, in the context of a developed country with universal and free education such as the United States, the usual characteristics (university degree, for example) that measure the human capital of teachers were not able to explain differences in learning outcomes and graduation among students. This was despite the fact that causal models were gaining strength in the field of econometrics and in a context in which researchers had increasing access to better longitudinal administrative data.

2.1.1 Einstein: Added Teaching Value

For example, Rivkin et al. (2005) conducted a value-added model (then already becoming popular in economics) of student learning for the first time with a large database of just over 80,000 observations of students in the state of Texas that included rich and accurate information on schools and teachers matched to these students. These models typically take the following form (Eq. 1):

$$A_{ijgs} = A_{ij(g-1)s} + X_i\beta_X + T_{ij}\beta_T + S_{si}X_S + f_i + \varepsilon_{cijgs}$$

where, the learning A_{ijgs} of the student i, with the teacher j, in the school s and the course g depends on the learning of the same student in the course $g-1$, a vector X of socioeconomic and personal characteristics of the student, a vector T of characteristics of the teacher j of the student i, a vector S of characteristics of the school s of the student i, a parameter f reflecting the inherent abilities and unobservable characteristics of the student i and an error ε_{cijgs}. The possibility of applying differences between present and past learning allows us to eliminate the biases introduced by the unobserved characteristics of student i, which is a significant methodological improvement: this makes it possible, for example, to control for differences in effort, predisposition to learning, prior learning, or factors such as genetic or cultural capital transmitted by the family.

The authors identify significant variation in teaching quality as measured from the model, but that such variation does not appear to be due to educational level (in particular, having a Master's degree compared to having only a Bachelor's degree) or years of experience in the profession (with only the effect of the first few years being slightly significant). Using more recent data from the OECD's Proficiency Assessment of Adult Skills (PIAAC), Hanushek et al. (2019) introduced metrics of cognitive skills (measured by standardized tests of mathematics and reading comprehension) into the estimation of the relationship between teacher human capital and student learning for 31 countries: they found that these measures explained some of the variation in student learning levels across countries and that part of these skill differences were due to access to high-skill occupations in the labor market by women.

2.1.2 Beyond Cognitive Skills

To some extent, the results may seem obvious. Teachers' human capital is not just about diplomas, certificates, or years in the profession. It is also about what one knows and can teach. But is it just cognitive knowledge or is there more to it? In recent years, access to individual and anonymized student and teacher information has multiplied in many countries, especially in the United States. In particular, student learning outcomes have been joined by other types of outputs or results such as behavior, absences or truancy, absenteeism, and also, through subsequent data, graduation, and continuation in post-compulsory studies and finally participation in the labor market. Several recent studies have highlighted the importance of non-cognitive skills in teachers (something that is included in chapter 5d of the book, signed by Ildefonso Mendez and Gemma Zamarro) and their ability to transmit them to students, and how this has an impact in the long term.

The reflection to better understand the role of non-cognitive skills in teachers arose from recent studies that showed that even the correlation between cognitive skills and teaching effectiveness (measured as the added value we have previously explained) was also weak. For example, Zamarro and Cheng (2018) show that teachers' non-cognitive skills such as effort, leadership, or resilience also have an impact on learning. They conduct this study from the Measures of Effective Teaching (MET) project of the Bill and Melinda Gates Foundation, another large Foundation supported research on teachers, in which thousands of teachers and students were randomly matched and monitored over time. In other contexts, for example Sweden, Grönqvist and Vlachos (2016) found that behind a null impact of teaching skills on student learning, there were very disparate results by student type: while teachers with high cognitive skills had a higher academic impact among students with higher academic skills, teachers with high social skills had a higher academic impact on students with poorer academic skills. For the case of Finland, Izadi (2019) shows, from an administrative database of all university students entering the teaching profession, that teachers' academic results are not related to other (non-cognitive) skills that also impact on students. In conclusion, this set of results makes it necessary to depart from the premise that, as we anticipated in the introduction, a good teacher is not only a good student, but that cognitive skills seem to be a necessary, but not sufficient condition. Reducing, therefore, the measurement of teacher quality to their academic results in high school or university seems to be insufficient to capture their performance in school and in the classroom and their impact on students in the short and long term.

2.2 *Why Is Faculty So Important to Student Achievement?*

We have seen that teachers matter for learning, that the manner in which they do so is manifold, and that the skills required are varied. The next question is to know how important this effect is in relation to other factors of the educational production function and what the effect materializes in the **short** (learning and development of social and emotional skills), **medium** (graduation and continuation of studies), and **long** (participation in the labor market, health, or crime indicators) term for students.

In this section we have presented both the new teaching quality metrics and value-added metrics. What is their ability to predict future impact on the student body? Recent studies show that they have an economically large effect on future learning and labor market returns. In an original paper, Chetty et al. (2014), using measures of teaching quality, find a relevant and positive long-term impact, i.e., on graduation, college access, and labor market returns. The authors measure the impact of value-added metrics (from learning at age 14) on long-term indicators: they find that one standard deviation of teaching value-added increases the probability of being in college at age 20 by 0.82 percentage points (relative to an average of 37 percent). They also increase future earnings since, at age 28, an increase in one standard deviation of value-added increases annual earnings by 1.3 percent, the equivalent of $39,000 in aggregate lifetime earnings. There is also a positive impact on reducing the probability of having a child in adolescence, an increase in the quality of the neighborhood in which one lives in adulthood, and participation in pension savings plans.

In a real case in the District of Columbia in Washington, a teacher evaluation system was implemented based on value-added estimates: teachers with lower value-added were replaced by other teachers if they failed to improve their performance. This policy resulted in an improvement of between 0.14 (reading) and 0.21 (mathematics) standard deviations of learning (Adnot et al. 2017). As Hanushek (2011) explains, this size is higher than what can be achieved with usual alternatives, much more costly in terms of public budget, such as, for example, class size reduction.

Three very recent research articles have complemented the commonly used value-added metrics on learning: they have done so with teacher value-added metrics on non-cognitive, i.e., social and emotional outcomes, and have been able to show that this leads to enormous effects in adult life. For example, Jackson (2018) causally shows that teacher influence also occurs on non-standardized indicators, such as absenteeism, truancy, class grades, or grade repetition. Moreover, teacher effects on these indicators in secondary school (at age 15) predict later outcomes, such as secondary school completion (at age 18), and do so more strongly than value-added on learning outcomes. Incorporating into the teacher effect not only test scores but other types of outcomes such as those presented in the study implies a long-term predictive ability greater than double the predictive ability when only test scores are taken into account in the measurement of teacher value-added.

In an even more recent study, Petek and Pope (2023), answer a similar question using administrative data on more than 100,000 students in Los Angeles City Public Schools, with very specific information on non-cognitive skills of teachers and students. They find something similar to what Jackson (2018) contributed, but add three more results: teacher effectiveness on learning tests does not correlate with teacher effectiveness on behavioral and non-cognitive outcomes, so they posit a much more accurate metric of teacher effectiveness (via greater long-term impact) than those that only used tests: they point to the importance of policies to favor teachers with a mix of skills, not just those who are able to get the best out of their students academically. They also find that value-added models for the subjects of reading and mathematics are much better predictors of future outcomes, compared to other subjects. Finally, they find that secondary teachers with high value-added (both test and non-cognitive outcomes) are much more decisive than elementary teachers in terms of long-term outcomes. Graduation and labor market outcomes are not the only ones through which teachers impact their students. For example, Rose et al. (2022) find a positive effect of teachers on crime reduction (associated with less absenteeism and more graduation), an effect unrelated to the effect in cognitive terms, again pointing to complementarities in teacher effectiveness and their disparate long-term effects.

This complementarity of effects can also be observed when we transfer the argument of teacher effectiveness to the school. We highlight here, because of its relevance for this book, the work of Loviglio (2019) that shows, with administrative data from the city of Barcelona, that indeed, there seems to be such specialization in added value (albeit at the school level): schools capable of improving students' academic performance (conditional on them graduating from compulsory secondary school) are those that receive high-income students; in contrast, schools that maximize the probability of graduation and continuing studies usually serve low-income students. These results show that evaluating and comparing schools using only external exam and test results is not sufficient to identify and improve the school success of lower-income students.

2.3 *Teachers, Schools and Their Impact Beyond the Classroom*

So far we have identified the impact of teachers on students' learning and socioemotional development and tried to understand how this affects long-term outcomes, including economic outcomes. Behind this approach we have assumed that the impact of teachers materializes in the physical space of the class or classroom and that the usual school organization is that of a teacher in a classroom with a group of students ("*egg-crate classroom*" in English—see Corbett (1982)-, "*aula huevera*" in Spanish—see Fernandez Enguita (2018)), rather than as an individual in an institution (the school) where their impact goes beyond their own classroom.

While sociology and pedagogy studies have addressed the question of the teaching profession as a networked phenomenon, this question reached the field of economics not so long ago. However, the contributions of the last decade have been decisive, this being especially relevant in Spain, a country where, as we see in Fig. 1, interaction and collaboration among teachers is very low compared to other countries.

2.3.1 Einstein: Impact of Teachers on Their Peers

The work, again by Jackson, this time with Bruegmann (2009), is the most important study in the field of economics addressing the impact of teachers beyond students (but with an important indirect impact). Following the value-added example, how can the teaching impact on peers be measured? In particular, how can we control for the endogenous fact that teachers do not interact with their peers randomly? To avoid incurring such self-selection errors, the authors incorporate information from peer teachers into an equation like the one we have described above (Eq. 1), but calculate

$$A_{ijgs} = A_{ij(g-1)s} + X_i\beta_X + T_{ij}\beta_T + S_{si}X_S + \mu P_{ij} + f_i + \varepsilon_{cijgs}$$

where P_{ij} is a measure of peer teaching quality. Therefore, they propose the following model:

$$A_{ijgs} = A_{ij(g-1)s} + X_i\beta_X + T_{ij}\beta_T + S_{si}X_S + f_i + \xi_{js} + \varepsilon_{cijgs}$$

where ξ_{js} is a teacher and school fixed effect, which eliminates potential biases and disappears when calculating the effect of peer change on the change in student outcomes. Using the above, the authors identify, from North Carolina administrative data, causally **positive externalities in teacher value-added** when their schools receive effective teachers. They also find that these effects are larger for inexperienced teachers, explaining as much as 20% of a teacher's effect in the long run. While this question had been extensively studied in the economics of agglomerations and cities, this paper changed the perspective and broadened the view of the teaching profession to something much larger than what a teacher does with his or her students. Again,

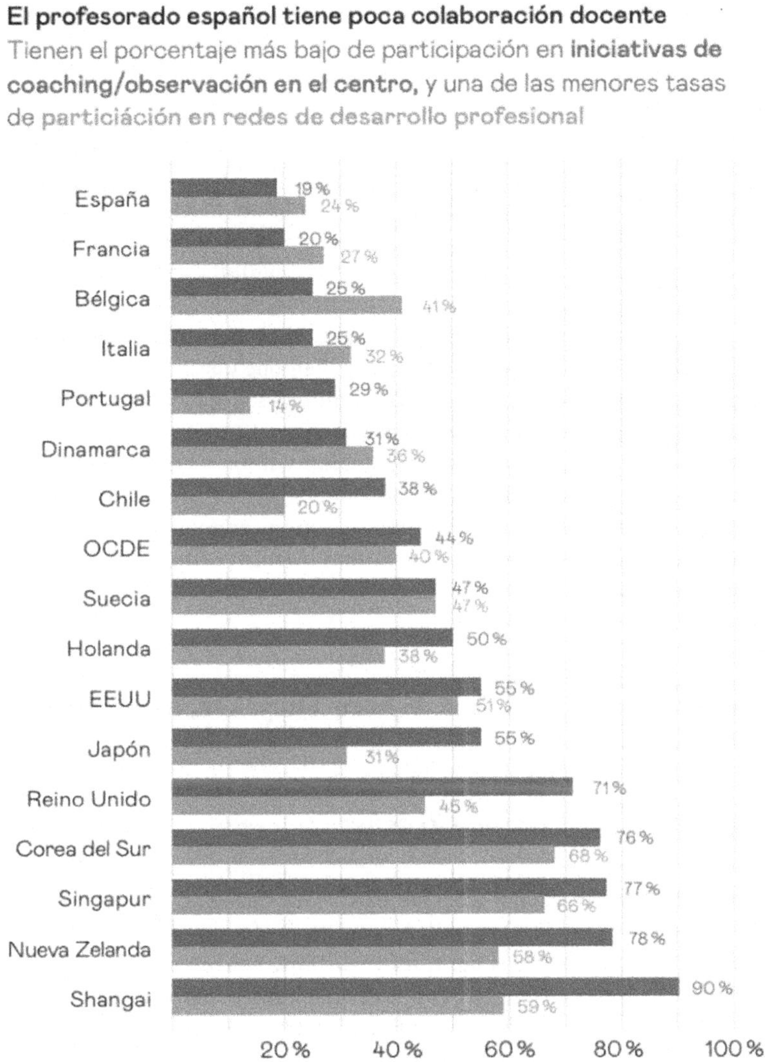

Fig. 1 Collaboration among faculty (*Source* OECD (2019a), Table 1.5.7 from TALIS 2018)

back to the beginning: we are talking about a high value-added profession, a value that is transmitted when there is peer-to-peer interaction.

We said in the introduction that the evidence from economics would refute the South Korean politician's statement about teachers being the ceiling of education systems. Perhaps the results of this study force us to refute the phrase and complement it in such a way that "*the quality of a school system cannot exceed the quality of* ***sum of*** *its teachers in* ***a school***". Following this article has come a whole line of research to expand upon. Sun et al. (2017) find something similar to Jackson and Bruegmann's results in the city of Miami.

In an experimental project where high—and low-performing (value-added) teachers were paired to work together, Papay et al. (2020) find a positive impact by 0.12 standard deviations for low-value-added teachers, associated with improvement in the specific skills in which the teacher performed worst. For their part, Burgess et al. (2021) explore the mechanisms of such interaction in a randomized controlled experiment where teachers observe and are observed by their peers: they find that students improved by 7% of a standard deviation, with the effects being larger for low-performing teachers. In a similar study, Murphy et al. (2021) find a null effect, but when disaggregated by school characteristics, they show that the effect is heterogeneous by school size: in schools with more than one class per grade, the effect is positive (and similar to Burgess et al. 2021), while in schools with only one class per grade, the effect is negative and significant: these results make sense from a **supply-side point of view**, as size correlates with higher within-school variance in teacher quality, which would be associated with higher chances of peer learning on average. In summary, it seems that the teachers' field of action cannot be circumscribed to the classroom, but that they can have an important impact on their peers through their interactions, and this can increase their own quality with students.

3 Teachers: Who They Are, Where They Are, and The Role of Public Policies

3.1 *How to Identify a Good Teacher*

It is said that the perfect teacher does not exist. That each teacher has his or her own book. And that trying to measure such a complex profession is daring and probably reductionist. Perhaps there is some truth in all this, but research, and in particular economic science, has tried to contribute and shed light to improve our understanding of who is and how to identify a good teacher. The results of the last few years are truly important. What follows is a review of what we have learned about how teacher effectiveness can be measured with different instruments, what specific information and nuances each instrument provides, and how they complement each other.

i. **Cognitive and non-cognitive teacher value-added**: in the previous section, we have seen the different ways of estimating value-added (i.e., progress from a particular learning point and other indicators, controlling for student, teacher, and school factors) from longitudinal data on cognitive and non-cognitive student performance and individual characteristics. More recent value-added metrics from the work Chetty et al. (2014) have been extended, as we have explained, to non-cognitive outcomes (Jackson 2018) and have also been conducted in developing countries, for example, with the case of Pakistan (Bau and Das 2020). They have the statistical property of being unbiased estimators

(Chetty et al. 2017). Despite being accepted as a metric in the field economics, its application for teacher evaluation has had some difficulties that we will discuss below.

ii. **Classroom observation**: while value-added metrics provide precise estimates of teacher-derived learning outcomes, they say nothing about the process inside the classroom to explain them. This absence of information has popularized the term "the black box of education", i.e., the entire relationship between inputs and outputs of the educational production function. From the field of pedagogy and research methods in education, in recent decades **reliable** (the instrument gives the same results regardless of the observer) and **valid** (the instrument is associated with good results of students in a given learning competency) instruments have been developed. The best known are the Classroom Assessment Scoring System (CLASS), focused on interactions between teachers and students, the Framework For Teaching (FFT), inspired by a constructivist view of learning, or the specific instruments for reading (PLATO) or mathematics (MQI). More recent research has shown that these methods are able to predict future learning and correlate positively with value-added measures (Tyler et al. 2010; Araujo et al. 2016) although they are expensive to implement. All of these instruments have the enormous advantage of unpacking what is happening in the classroom and translating what is observed into changes in teaching through teacher training.

iii. **Student surveys**: these surveys, completed by students, collect information on their opinions about the work of their teachers. They have the advantage of being cheaper than observation instruments. However, when evaluated and compared with value-added measures, they show that they do not have a strong correlation with these metrics (Bacher-Hicks et al. 2019).

iv. **Impact on peers and the school**. As we have explained above, teacher quality should not only be reduced to the classroom, as evidence shows that effective teachers are also able to have an indirect impact on other students through their peers in the school (Jackson and Bruegman 2009; Papay et al. 2020).

How can we construct comprehensive, reliable, and highly predictive measures of teacher quality? Studies by Kane and Staiger (2012) and Bacher-Hicks et al. (2019) show that combining measures, especially classroom observations and value-added metrics, would allow us to increase the predictive ability of separate instruments and in turn help increase accuracy by understanding what happens inside the classroom. In turn, continuing to explore the impact teachers have on their peers and their schools should be in the equation for defining "what it is to be a good teacher".

3.2 What Is the Impact of Teachers' Working Conditions on Their Effectiveness?

In the previous subsection we explored what defines a good teacher and how to identify him or her. In this part we focus on contextual factors of the teaching profession independent of its individual qualities and characteristics. In particular, we review the structure of the labor market for teachers, the working conditions they have in schools, and the bargaining power of teachers' unions: the aim is to understand how they affect teacher effectiveness, their professional development, and ultimately promote greater student learning.

3.2.1 The Labor Market for Teachers

As we noted at the beginning of the chapter, the teacher labor market is large in volume and usually comprises between 4 and 5% of employment in developed countries, and may be higher in developing countries. One of the most obvious indicators for understanding the labor market is teacher salaries in public schools, which are usually set by governments through negotiation with teachers' unions. In Spain, teachers' salaries are comparatively higher than those of other workers with higher education, as can be seen in Graph 1 below (see also Chapter 1 of Indicators), from the entry salary to the profession, although it is true that the maximum salary to which they can gain access does not grow much, which reflects a rather flat professional career in comparison with other countries. But the flip side of this reality, as Fig. 3 shows, is that Spanish teachers have experienced a loss of purchasing power since the Great Recession, as a result of a moderation of their salaries below inflation and without ever recovering the levels of 2010. Added to this is the addition of price increases in 2022 due to the Ukrainian War, something that may continue in 2023 and 2024 (Graph 2).

What does the research on teacher labor markets say about salaries? From the supply side, it seems clear that since it is a case of an equal career path for all teachers, and therefore with similar starting working conditions, those conditions are going to influence the supply of employment by workers entering the labor market. This is what Leigh (2012) and Gjefsen (2020) find. Leigh's (2020) work with data on teachers in Australia is very relevant, as it allows us to separate supply and demand effects when identifying the effect of wages on teacher quality (as measured by the test scores of those admitted to Australian universities and in particular university programs to enter the teaching profession). The author finds that a 1% increase in the entry salary of teachers improves the academic aptitude of teachers by 0.6 percentiles. He also finds that the greater the variation in the labor market outside of teaching, the lower the quality of potential teachers. In a study for the city of Oslo (Norway), the work of Gjefsen (2020) shows again through a Differences-in-Differences methodology that, after a 5% increase in salaries, there was an increase in the entry of teachers with higher academic credentials (Master's degree) but above

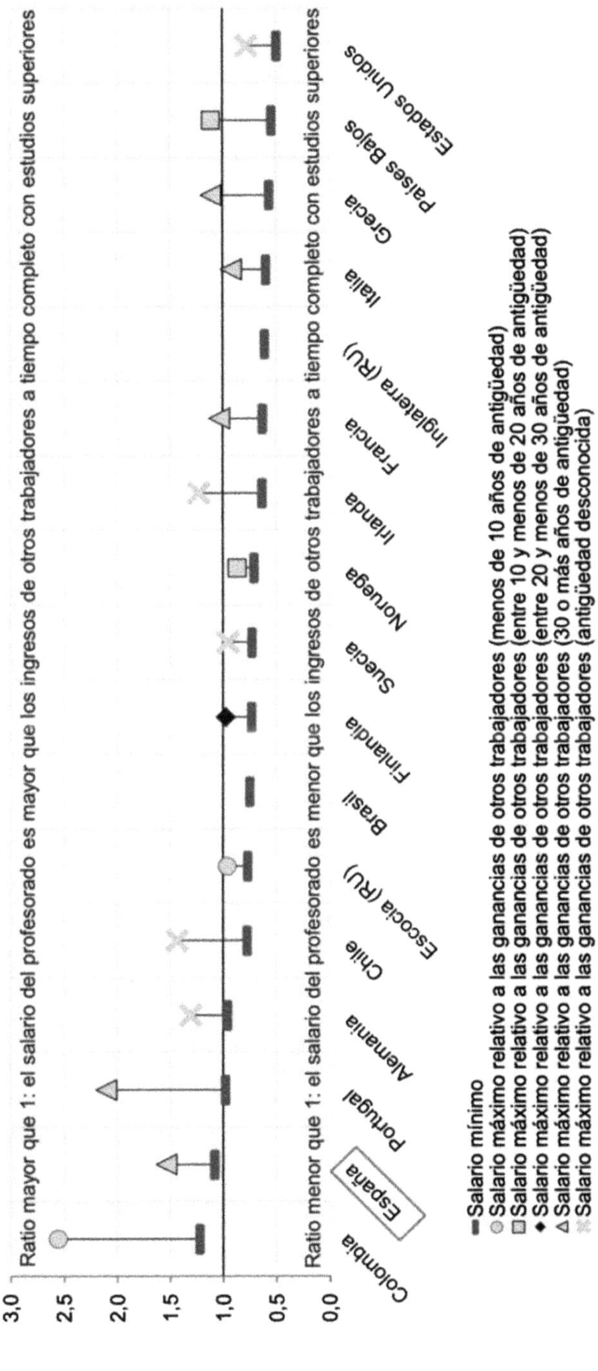

Graph 1 Ratio of teachers' salaries to those who work full time with higher education (*Source* Ministry of Education and Vocational Training [2023]. Starting salaries and relative statutory maximums of upper secondary education teachers and years required to reach the maximum of the scale [2022])

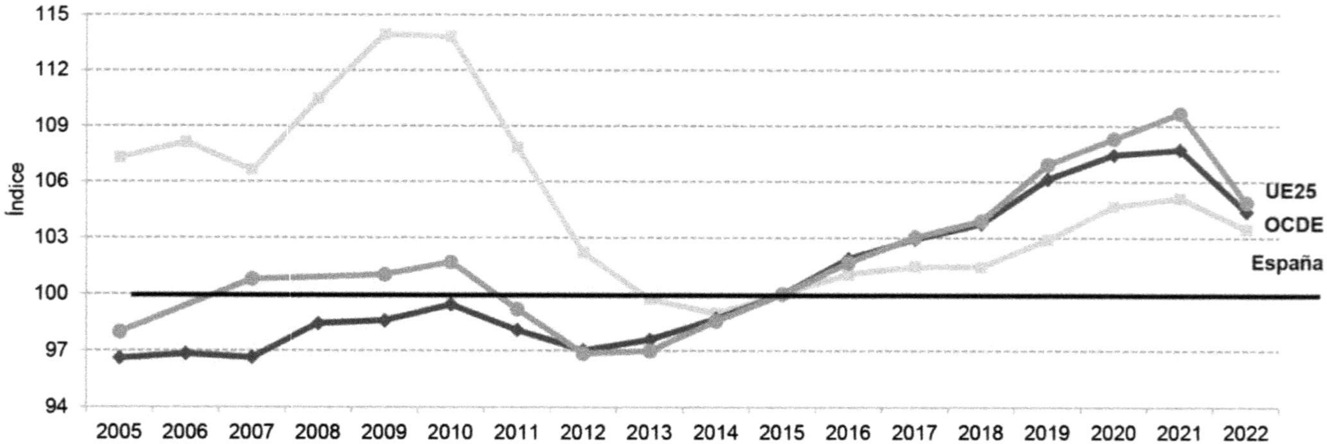

Graph 2 Salary evolution (discounting inflation) of secondary school teachers with the most frequent qualification, between 2005 and 2022 (*Source* Ministry of Education and Vocational Training [2023]. Index of change between 2005 and 2022 of the statutory salary of upper secondary education teachers with 15 years of experience [2015 = 100], converted to constant prices using deflators for private consumption)

all, and more importantly, an improvement in students' academic results: the latter suggests that the new teachers had higher effectiveness as well as higher academic credentials.

Entry salary seems to be an important factor, although it is likely that the effect on teacher supply has diminishing returns and other factors come into play once a certain salary level is reached. What other factors matter? As the study by Leigh (2012) pointed out, salaries should not be analyzed in absolute terms, but in relative terms. The labor market context is relevant: for example, Bacolod (2017) documents, based on Roy's (1951) model of self-selection into occupations, the drop in teaching quality in the United States of young women entering the profession due to increased opportunities in high value-added jobs. Under the same logic, Nagler et al. (2020) find, using data from the case of the state of Florida, and exploiting business cycle variation as a source of exogeneity that alters potential teachers' alternatives, that teachers who enter the profession during recessions are significantly more effective at improving their students' outcomes. Marchand and Weber (2020) point to the same argument with another example: the positive shock that the state of Texas experienced with oil and gas drilling reduced learning outcomes and classroom attendance, the mechanism being the higher teacher turnover and lower experience of new teachers, whose salaries (in relative terms) were not improved by the positive shock to the economy, unlike other sectors.

Other elements of the labor market also influence learning outcomes and teaching quality. Lack of liquidity for students from lower-income households can be a disincentive to join the profession. The study by Coffman et al. (2019) shows that barriers to entry into a profession that pays less than others means in the short term a lack of liquidity that is impossible for some candidates to overcome. Finally, working conditions at the center have an influence. The study by Ronfeldt et al. (2013) shows that excessive teacher turnover in schools is detrimental to learning.

Finally, it is worth asking about the determinants of working conditions, since to the extent that the latter influence academic results, they are relevant. In recent years, the research framework has been broadened to incorporate the role of bargaining between government, schools, and unions on salaries and working conditions. For example, Biasi (2021) finds that decentralizing the ability to set working conditions to the school level attracts better teachers and improves student outcomes. In addition, evidence presented by Lovenheim and Willem (2019) shows that collective bargaining (i.e., wage setting by unions and government) has a long-term impact on students (especially racial minorities and men) through a worsening of their non-cognitive skills and a reduction in their long-term labor market participation and earnings (a reduction they estimate at $213 billion per year in the United States). But other research also identifies negative externalities, such as higher teacher turnover in schools (Baron 2018) and a wider gender gap among teachers (Biasi et al. 2022).

3.3 The Teaching Career Continuum: From Selection to Retirement

We have already learned what good teachers look like, what impact they have on their students, and how the economic and political context affects their performance and their interest in the profession. Next, we turn to what is probably the most important question in this chapter: What policies work to make teachers better? When and how should we intervene to attract, select, empower, develop, improve, and evaluate the best teachers? Next, we review what is called the "continuum" of the professional teaching career, which includes selection, initial training, induction, continuing professional development, and retirement.

Selection: To the question of how to select teachers, the answer must obviously be answered taking into account what we have learned about "what makes a good teacher" in the previous section. And that is precisely what all the research regarding teacher selection has shown, which speaks of a selection with varied criteria that value both the academic record and by other skills, something found by both Izadi (2019) for the case of Finland (known for its teaching policies of excellence) and Jacob et al. (2018) in the case of the United States. Finally, the study by Schaede and Mankki (2023) for Finland is relevant, where they find that removing a minimum threshold of 40% of male teachers in primary school had a negative impact on the long-term student body of both genders, suggesting the importance of combining talents and skills (in this case, gender complementarity in the classroom) not necessarily captured in selection processes, usually based on cognitive and non-cognitive indicators.

Initial experience: To what extent is experience relevant in improving teaching effectiveness? How many years are necessary to reach optimal effectiveness? And how does this experience develop and what does it depend on to reach it? A summary of what economic research has provided in recent years invites us to conclude the following: experience is relevant, but it is especially so in the early years and has a diminishing marginal effect. Compared to other factors, it seems to be a less relevant factor than the starting point (initial teacher quality) or other factors (Rockoff et al. 2011; Kane et al. 2008), although other studies show that returns to teaching may continue to grow (Kraft and Papay 2014). In any case, and perhaps this is most relevant, the experience does not automatically impact all places equally, but is associated with the quality of the school's organizational and professional development context: the work of Kraft and Papay (2014) is illustrative, as they show that depending on the school's professional development context and how these support teachers (through measures that capture disciplinary climate, teacher collaboration, principal leadership, professional development, professional respect and trust among teachers, and the existence of teacher evaluation) the differences in teacher effectiveness growth between a teacher at the 25th percentile of initial effectiveness and a teacher at the 75th percentile can be almost 40%.

Continuous training, peer learning, and coaching. As we have already noted, one way to improve teacher performance is by encouraging interaction between teachers, something that requires adequate space and time for this to occur, but which undoubtedly has the capacity to bring about significant improvements in schools and classrooms. Similarly, teacher coaching programs, in which an experienced teacher accompanies another teacher for several sessions and observes and provides feedback on his or her classroom strategies, have enormous potential, although the costs are significant, as the programs are usually highly individualized. The meta-analysis by Kraft et al. (2018) finds an effect of 0.18 standard deviations on learning, albeit with small-scale studies that have not been replicated on a large scale.

Teacher expectations and biases. How teachers view, diagnose, and observe their students matters and has a huge impact, which is promising, as these are changes that have more to do with beliefs and biases than with costly, resource-intensive programs. For example, the work of Papageorge et al. (2020) shows that the elasticity of college completion with respect to teacher expectations is 0.12. In addition, more recent research has studied the existence of gender biases by income or origin that unequally affect the student body: studies show the existence of significant gender biases in Italy and France (Carlana 2019; Terrier 2020). In Spain there are three studies that show very similar results in Andalusia (Marcenaro-Gutierrez et al. 2015), Catalonia (Calsamiglia and Loviglio 2019) and the Basque Country (Gortazar et al. 2022): all three show how teachers evaluate their students with respect to external evaluations and evidence the induced biases to the detriment of boys, low income and immigrants.

Incentives and teacher motivation. One of the questions that the field of microeconomics has tried to answer most in recent decades is how individual agents respond to incentives. In education, logically, this has been transferred with particular intensity to understanding whether and how incentives work on teachers. In this sense, it is important to return to what we discussed in the introduction: the complexity of the teaching profession cannot be ignored when we talk about incentives (monetary and non-monetary) and their impact on teachers. If teachers have the capacity and skills to react to incentives in a positive way, it makes sense that incentives can work; but on many occasions, it is not only a matter of putting the right incentives in place, but also of ensuring that these incentives take into account teachers' capacities to react to them: sometimes the complexity of the profession means that teachers do not react to incentives, not because they do not want to, but because they do not know how to. It is therefore central to understand the question: what incentives work and what role does teacher motivation play? Below, we review the main results of the question:

1. *Informing teachers about* their own performance can be an incentive in itself by activating motivation. Reporting on performance can provide an incentive through intrinsic motivation (Taylor and Tyler 2012).
2. *Economic incentives* for performance (paying teachers for their results) work in some contexts, positively affecting graduation rates and long-term labor market outcomes through improvements in teaching, more hours of reinforcement and adaptation to student needs (see Lavy 2009 and Lavy 2020 for the case of Israel). But other programs have been little or not at all effective in this regard: for example, school reforms in the United States that have promoted greater teacher accountability and evaluation through economic incentives to teachers based on

their performance in the United States show mixed evidence (Dee and Wyckoff 2015; Dee et al. 2021) being politically very costly (because of their unpopularity) while reducing teacher satisfaction and supply in the teacher labor market (Kraft 2020). In developing countries, evaluation by results can work in contexts of low performance (Ganimian and Murnane 2014; Muralidharan et al. 2011) especially to prevent teacher absenteeism.

Matching teachers to schools and students ("Matching policies"). A central question in thinking about teachers and their effects on students is how we should match and assign teachers to schools and students. Research has shown that the sociodemographic characteristics of teachers influence and impact students differently depending on student characteristics. For example, a common finding in the literature is that gender influences outcomes: Lim et al. (2020) show that for the case of South Korea, female teachers have a positive impact on girls, both in the short term (academic results) and in the long term (increasing their probability of choosing science subjects in secondary education). In turn, as we have seen, the study by Schaede and Mansski (2023) for Finland speaks of the importance of gender balance among teachers, since from 60% of female teachers the results may suffer. Finally, there is evidence of improved results when teacher and student share race, something that occurs especially with students of low socioeconomic level (Dee 2005). In the same direction point to policies that promote bringing experienced teachers to schools serving low-income students (Steele et al. 2010; Swain et al. 2019; Bobba et al. 2021) in remote areas or in subjects with low teacher supply (Bueno et al. 2018; Feng et al. 2018). These programs are articulated through *ex-ante* financial incentives for working in these types of schools.

4 Management Teams and Their Impact on the School

In this last section we look at the work that some teachers end up doing throughout their careers: leading schools. What does the research on school management say from an economic perspective? Do principals have an impact and make a difference? In what ways do they do so? Reading this chapter and understanding that the school and its context explain a part of teacher effectiveness, then those who are ultimately responsible for it (the management teams) should have something to do with everything we have discussed in these pages.

What evidence do we have and how do we measure that management? What does good management consist of? Does it refer to the economic and financial management of the institution or do we also refer to the educational impact that principals have? An important study published by Bloom et al. (2015) adapted the business economics methodology on organizational management to apply it to education: the authors conducted 1800 telephone interviews with school principals in 8 countries to construct a school management indicator based on 20 dimensions of school management focusing on operations, monitoring, goal setting, and people management. They show that these indicators are associated with better academic results.

Some channels under which good principals operate is that of stability: two recent studies show that the impact of good principals (measured through various evaluation systems) is high on students and is also associated with stability in schools (Grissom et al. 2019; Miller 2013). However, even being a very important issue from a research and public policy point of view, it is a field in the process of exploration with recent methodological criticisms (Bartanen 2022).

On the other hand, there are two more dimensions about school principals that deserve special attention: how they are selected and how we can improve their performance. Regarding the former, the work of Akhtari et al. (2022) shows that a school management model too dependent on political power has a negative impact on learning: based on a regression model in discontinuity with the results of local elections in Brazil, they find that in municipalities with a change of party in the mayor's office, the replacement of principals and teachers in schools that depend on local power increases, and this, in turn, causes a drop in learning outcomes of between 5 and 8% of a standard deviation. On the other hand, the work of De Hoyos et al. (2021) in Argentina shows an important avenue of research, which links with what we have already seen about how information and feedback on their own performance improves teacher effectiveness: in this case, through a randomized controlled experiment, the authors randomly assign school principals to three groups: one where they received information on the performance of their schools, another where principals received training and visited the schools, and a control group. The authors show that schools where principals received feedback and information about their performance had better results one year and two years later, in a relevant magnitude: principals in these schools were more likely to use data to make decisions and their students reported that their teachers used effective learning strategies.

5 Conclusions

This chapter has tried to contribute to one of the most important questions to be answered by economists interested in education: How much do teachers matter in education? In particular, we have reviewed the relevance of teachers from an economic point of view, i.e., both from the public budget side and their impact on the economy through the creation and building of human capital. If a school system and a school is able to translate schooling into learning and human capital, this is due, above all, but not only and not always in isolation, to the role played by teachers.

This chapter benefits from the revolution in causality that has occurred over the last 20 years in economics, since a large part of the results presented and the questions answered are due to it. It is also due to the increased availability of administrative data, as well as collaboration with other disciplines such as sociology and psychology. It is striking how economic research is becoming enormously sophisticated and multiplying its questions and models to understand the universe of teachers, such as the importance of the school factor, the incorporation of non-cognitive factors in learning or the study of the key policies of teachers and management teams.

The expansion of available data and surveys, the application of new econometric methodologies, as well as the increased relevance of the questions to major economic issues (such as the role of unions, the functioning of the teachers' labor market or the functioning of incentives to motivate effectively) show that we are facing a central issue in the economics of education and labor economics, which will certainly contribute to the improvement of knowledge in the coming decades and to the decisions taken by governments. At the global level, issues such as the lack of attractiveness of the profession and the shortage of teachers, teachers' preferences in the labor market and their working conditions, and the gender imbalances seem to be gaining importance and will continue to do so in the coming years.

All this must reach and extend to the Spanish case where, as we have seen throughout the chapter, the challenges are important, but research is still very scarce, due to lack of data, lack of financial support for complex projects, and the still scarce research community in the economics of education. Research on teachers requires three key ingredients: first, to make administrative data related to teachers accessible and tractable; second, to prioritize this issue in public and private funding agencies, as we speak key to the accumulated knowledge and the long-term economic growth model for Spain; third, to collaborate more actively with faculties of education, in charge of teacher training; fourth, to promote greater interest in the issue in faculties of economics, something that this book and this chapter aim to achieve.

The Spanish educational system is not exempt from challenges, being the teaching profession a space where few changes have taken place in the last decades. Some important questions should be answered by our discipline and include, among others, the lack of teacher accountability, the measurement of added value, collaboration, and peer learning, the existence of biases or the role of expectations on students. Another avenue of work should incorporate the effect of the post-crisis teacher labor market and teacher assignment systems, taking into account the high intermittency and turnover and its impact on learning, the role of other systems of teacher assignment to schools, and the progressive aging of the profession. Finally, from the point of view of teacher selection, it is necessary to understand, through panel data, the predictive capacity of selection systems (and their possible alternatives) in Bachelor's, Master's and competitive teaching examinations on future job performance. It is also necessary to better understand the effectiveness of continuous teacher training programs, as well as the role that incentives for teachers to work in rural areas or in schools with students of low socioeconomic status can and are playing, both of which are very relevant for the Spanish case.

References

Adnot, M., T. Dee, V. Katz, and J. Wyckoff. 2017. Teacher turnover, teacher quality, and student achievement in DCPS. *Educational Evaluation and Policy Analysis* 39 (1): 54–76.

Akhtari, M., D. Moreira, and L. Trucco. 2022. Political turnover, bureaucratic turnover, and the quality of public services. *American Economic Review* 112 (2): 442–493.

Araujo, M.C., Carneiro, P., Cruz-Aguayo, Y., and Schady, N. (2016). Teacher quality and learning outcomes in kindergarten. *The Quarterly Journal of Economics* 131 (3): 1415–1453.https://academic.oup.com/qje/article-abstract/131/3/1415/2461200

Bacher-Hicks, A., M. J. Chin, T. J. Kane, and D. O. Staiger. 2019. An experimental evaluation of three teacher quality measures: Value-added, classroom observations, and student surveys. *Economics of Education Review* 73: 101919.

Barber, M., and Mourshed, M. 2007. *How the world's best-performing school systems come out on top*. McKinsey & Company.

Bacolod, M. P. 2007. Do alternative opportunities matter? The role of female labor markets in the decline of teacher quality. *The Review of Economics and Statistics* 89 (4): 737–751.

Bardach, L., and R. M. Klassen. 2020. Smart teachers, successful students? A systematic review of the literature on teachers' cognitive abilities and teacher effectiveness. *Educational Research Review* 30: 100312.

Baron, E. J. 2018. The effect of teachers' unions on student achievement in the short run: Evidence from Wisconsin's Act 10. *Economics of Education Review* 67: 40–57.

Bartanen, B., Husain, A.N., and Liebowitz, D.D. 2022. *Rethinking principal effects on student outcomes*. Ed Working Paper: 22–621. Retrieved from Annenberg Institute at Brown University, Providence, RI, USA. https://doi.org/10.26300/r5sf-3918.

Bau, N., and J. Das. 2020. Teacher value added in a low-income country. *American Economic Journal: Economic Policy* 12 (1): 62–96.

Becker, G.S. 1962. Investment in human capital: A theoretical analysis. *Journal of political economy* 70 (5, Part 2): 9–49.

Becker, G. S., and B. R. Chiswick. 1966. Education and the distribution of earnings. *The American Economic Review* 56 (1/2): 358–369.

Biasi, B., and H. Sarsons. 2022. Flexible wages, bargaining, and the gender gap. *The Quarterly Journal of Economics* 137 (1): 215–266.

Biasi, B. 2021. The labor market for teachers under different pay schemes. *American Economic Journal: Economic Policy* 13 (3): 63–102.

Bloom, N., R. Lemos, R. Sadun, and J. Van Reenen. 2015. Does management matter in schools? *The Economic Journal* 125 (584): 647–674.

Bobba, M., Ederer, T., Leon-Ciliotta, G., Neilson, C., and Nieddu, M.G. 2021. *Teacher compensation and structural inequality: Evidence from centralized teacher school choice in Peru* (No. w29068). National Bureau of Economic Research.

Bueno, C., and Sass, T.R. 2018. The effects of differential pay on teacher recruitment and retention. *Andrew Young School of Policy Studies Research Paper Series* (18–07).

Burgess, S., S. Rawal, and E. S. Taylor. 2021. Teacher peer observation and student test scores: Evidence from a field experiment in English secondary schools. *Journal of Labor Economics* 39 (4): 1155–1186.

Calsamiglia, C., and A. Loviglio. 2019. Grading on a curve: When having good peers is not good. *Economics of Education Review* 73: 101916.

Carlana, M. 2019. Implicit stereotypes: Evidence from teachers' gender bias. *The Quarterly Journal of Economics* 134 (3): 1163–1224.

Cheng, A., and G. Zamarro. 2018. Measuring teacher non-cognitive skills and its impact on students: Insight from the measures of effective teaching longitudinal database. *Economics of Education Review* 64: 251–260.

Chetty, R., J. N. Friedman, and J. E. Rockoff. 2014. Measuring the impacts of teachers II: Teacher value-added and student outcomes in adulthood. *American Economic Review* 104 (9): 2633–2679.

Chetty, R., J. N. Friedman, and J. E. Rockoff. 2017. Measuring the impacts of teachers I: Evaluating bias in teacher value-added estimates. *American Economic Review* 104 (9): 2593.

Coffman, L. C., J. J. Conlon, C. R. Featherstone, and J. B. Kessler. 2019. Liquidity affects job choice: Evidence from teach for America. *The Quarterly Journal of Economics* 134 (4): 2203–2236.

Corbett, H. D. 1982. To make an omelette you have to break the egg crate. *Educational Leadership* 40 (2): 34–35.

Dee, T. S. 2005. A teacher like me: Does race, ethnicity, or gender matter? *American Economic Review* 95 (2): 158–165.

Dee, T. S., and J. Wyckoff. 2015. Incentives, selection, and teacher performance: Evidence from impact. *Journal of Policy Analysis and Management* 34 (2): 267–297.

Dee, T. S., J. James, and J. Wyckoff. 2021. Is effective teacher evaluation sustainable? Evidence from district of Columbia public schools. *Education Finance and Policy* 16 (2): 313–346.

Escardíbul, J.O. 2015. ¿ Is it advisable to implement teacher salary incentives linked to student academic performance. *Alegre, MÀ, and Escardíbul, JO¿ What works in education.*

Feng, L., and T. R. Sass. 2018. The impact of incentives to recruit and retain teachers in "hard-to-staff" subjects. *Journal of Policy Analysis and Management* 37 (1): 112–135.

Fernández Enguita, M. 2018. More school and less classroom: Innovation in the perspective of an epochal change.

Ganimian, A. J., and R. J. Murnane. 2016. Improving education in developing countries: Lessons from rigorous impact evaluations. *Review of Educational Research* 86 (3): 719–755.

Gjefsen, H. M. 2020. Wages, teacher recruitment, and student achievement. *Labour Economics* 65: 101848.

Gortazar, L., D. M. de Lafuente, and A. Vega-Bayo. 2022. Comparing teacher and external assessments: Are boys, immigrants, and poorer students undergraded? *Teaching and Teacher Education* 115: 103725.

Grissom, J. A., and B. Bartanen. 2019. Principal effectiveness and principal turnover. *Education Finance and Policy* 14 (3): 355–382.

Grönqvist, E., and J. Vlachos. 2016. One size fits all? The effects of teachers' cognitive and social abilities on student achievement. *Labour Economics* 42: 138–150.

Hanushek, E. A. 2011. The economic value of higher teacher quality. *Economics of Education Review* 30 (3): 466–479.

Hanushek, E.A., Piopiunik, M., and Wiederhold, S. 2019. The value of smarter teachers international evidence on teacher cognitive skills and student performance. *Journal of Human Resources* 54 (4): 857–899.

Izadi, R. 2019. Teacher selection in Finland. Does academic ability predict teacher aptitude? IZA *Working Paper*.

Jacob, B. A., J. E. Rockoff, E. S. Taylor, B. Lindy, and R. Rosen. 2018. Teacher applicant hiring and teacher performance: Evidence from DC public schools. *Journal of Public Economics* 166: 81–97.

Jackson, P.W. 1968. *Life in classrooms*. Teachers College Press.

Jackson, C. K., and E. Bruegmann. 2009. Teaching students and teaching each other: The importance of peer learning for teachers. *American Economic Journal: Applied Economics* 1 (4): 85–108.

Jackson, C. K. 2018. What do test scores miss? The importance of teacher effects on non-test score outcomes. *Journal of Political Economy* 126 (5): 2072–2107.

Kane, T. J., J. E. Rockoff, and D. O. Staiger. 2008. What does certification tell us about teacher effectiveness? Evidence from New York City. *Economics of Education Review* 27 (6): 615–631.

Kraft, M. A., and J. P. Papay. 2014. Can professional environments in schools promote teacher development? Explaining heterogeneity in returns to teaching experience. *Educational Evaluation and Policy Analysis* 36 (4): 476–500.

Kraft, M. A., D. Blazar, and D. Hogan. 2018. The effect of teacher coaching on instruction and achievement: A meta-analysis of the causal evidence. *Review of Educational Research* 88 (4): 547–588.

Kraft, M. A., E. J. Brunner, S. M. Dougherty, and D. J. Schwegman. 2020. Teacher accountability reforms and the supply and quality of new teachers. *Journal of Public Economics* 188: 104212.

Lavy, V. 2009. Performance pay and teachers' effort, productivity, and grading ethics. *American Economic Review* 99 (5): 1979–2011.

Lavy, V. 2020. Teachers' pay for performance in the long-run: The dynamic pattern of treatment effects on students' educational and labor market outcomes in adulthood. *The Review of Economic Studies* 87 (5): 2322–2355.

Leigh, A. 2012. Teacher pay and teacher aptitude. *Economics of Education Review* 31 (3): 41–53.

Lim, J., and J. Meer. 2020. Persistent effects of teacher-student gender matches. *Journal of Human Resources* 55 (3): 809–835.

Lovenheim, M. F., and A. Willén. 2019. The long-run effects of teacher collective bargaining. *American Economic Journal: Economic Policy* 11 (3): 292–324.

Loviglio, A. 2019. Schools and their multiple ways to impact students: A structural model of skill accumulation and educational choices. Mimeo.

Marcenaro-Gutierrez, O., and A. Vignoles. 2015. A comparison of teacher and test-based assessment for Spanish primary and secondary students. *Educational Research* 57 (1): 1–21.

Marchand, J., and J. G. Weber. 2020. How local economic conditions affect school finances, teacher quality, and student achievement: Evidence from the Texas shale boom. *Journal of Policy Analysis and Management* 39 (1): 36–63.

Miller, A. 2013. Principal turnover and student achievement. *Economics of Education Review* 36: 60–72.

Muralidharan, K., and V. Sundararaman. 2011. Teacher performance pay: Experimental evidence from India. *Journal of Political Economy* 119 (1): 39–77.

Nagler, M., M. Piopiunik, and M. R. West. 2020. Weak markets, strong teachers: Recession at career start and teacher effectiveness. *Journal of Labor Economics* 38 (2): 453–500.

National Commission on Excellence in Education. 1983. A nation at risk: The imperative for educational reform. *The Elementary School Journal* 84 (2): 113–130.

OECD. 2022. Education at a Glance 2022: OECD indicators. *OECD Publishing, Paris,.* https://doi.org/10.1787/3197152b-en.

Papageorge, N. W., S. Gershenson, and K. M. Kang. 2020. Teacher expectations matter. *Review of Economics and Statistics* 102 (2): 234–251.

Papay, J. P., E. S. Taylor, J. H. Tyler, and M. E. Laski. 2020. Learning job skills from colleagues at work: Evidence from a field experiment using teacher performance data. *American Economic Journal: Economic Policy* 12 (1): 359–388.

Petek, N., and N. G. Pope. 2023. The multidimensional impact of teachers on students. *Journal of Political Economy* 131 (4): 1057–1107.

Rivkin, S. G., E. A. Hanushek, and J. F. Kain. 2005. Teachers, schools, and academic achievement. *Econometrica* 73 (2): 417–458.

Ronfeldt, M., S. Loeb, and J. Wyckoff. 2013. How teacher turnover harms student achievement. *American Educational Research Journal* 50 (1): 4–36.

Rose, E.K., Schellenberg, J.T., and Shem-Tov, Y. 2022. The effects of teacher quality on adult criminal justice contact (No. w30274). *National Bureau of Economic Research.*

Rockoff, J. E., B. A. Jacob, T. J. Kane, and D. O. Staiger. 2011. Can you recognize an effective teacher when you recruit one? *Education Finance and Policy* 6 (1): 43–74.

Roy, A. D. 1951. Some thoughts on the distribution of earnings. *Oxford Economic Papers* 3 (2): 135–146.

Steele, J. L., R. J. Murnane, and J. B. Willett. 2010. Do financial incentives help low-performing schools attract and keep academically talented teachers? Evidence from California. *Journal of Policy Analysis and Management* 29 (3): 451–478.

Schaede, U., and Mankki, V. 2022. Quota vs quality? Long-term gains from an unusual gender quota. Working Paper

Sun, M., S. Loeb, and J. A. Grissom. 2017. Building teacher teams: Evidence of positive spillovers from more effective colleagues. *Educational Evaluation and Policy Analysis* 39 (1): 104–125.

Swain, W. A., L. A. Rodriguez, and M. G. Springer. 2019. Selective retention bonuses for highly effective teachers in high poverty schools: Evidence from Tennessee. *Economics of Education Review* 68: 148–160.

Terrier, C. 2020. Boys lag behind: How teachers' gender biases affect student achievement. *Economics of Education Review* 77: 101981.

Taylor, E. S., and J. H. Tyler. 2012. The effect of evaluation on teacher performance. *American Economic Review* 102 (7): 3628–3651.

Tyler, J. H., E. S. Taylor, T. J. Kane, and A. L. Wooten. 2010. Using student performance data to identify effective classroom practices. *American Economic Review* 100 (2): 256–260.

Wiswall, M. 2013. The dynamics of teacher quality. *Journal of Public Economics* 100: 61.

Foreign Language Knowledge

Brindusa Anghel

1 Introduction

Learning and knowing a foreign language is a fundamental part of an individual's education in today's society and is essential for individuals to carry out their activities in an increasingly globalized and interconnected world. Additionally, it is becoming more common for foreign language learning to occur from very early ages. According to Foreign Language Statistics (Eurostat), in 2021, more than 80% of primary school students were studying English as a foreign language, and in many European Union (EU) countries, learning English is mandatory at the primary education level (see Chart 1). Nearly all primary school students (99–100%) in countries such as Austria, Cyprus, Spain, or Malta were studying English. Regarding secondary school students in the EU, 98.3% of lower secondary students and 88% of upper secondary students were studying English[1] (see Chart 2). Besides English, the most studied languages in EU countries are French (30.5% and 19% of lower and upper secondary students, respectively), German (approximately 20% of lower and upper secondary students), and Spanish (approximately 18% of lower and upper secondary students).

Data from the 2018[2] Programme for International Student Assessment (PISA) international test show that secondary school students' expectations regarding graduating from university or pursuing a career as a manager or specialist in a field are higher among those students who speak more than one language compared to monolingual students. These expectations are also higher among students who are

[1] See Foreign Language Statistics (Eurostat): https://ec.europa.eu/eurostat/statistics-explained/index.php?title=Foreign_language_learning_statistics&oldid=379813

[2] The last year available at the publication of this book.

B. Anghel (✉)
Banco de España, Madrid, Spain
e-mail: brindusa.anghel@bde.es

A. Cabrales and I. Sanz (eds.), *Economics of Education*,
https://doi.org/10.1007/978-3-031-90911-5_8

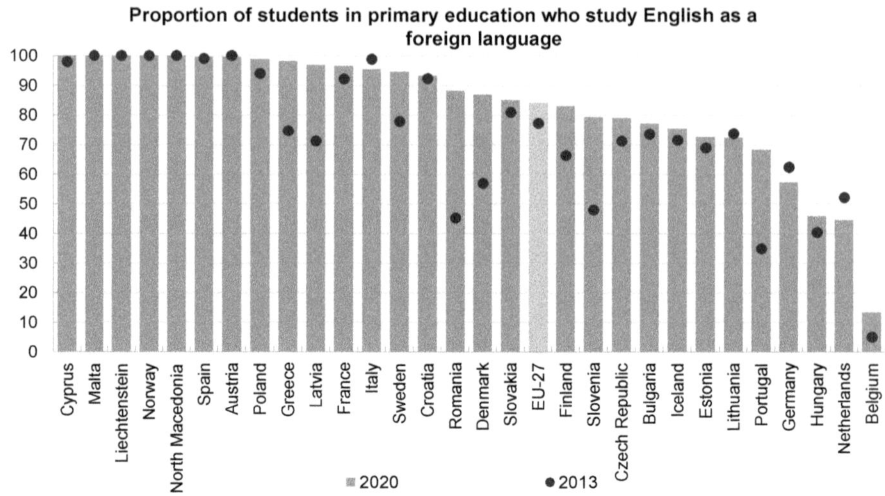

Chart 1 Proportion of students in primary education who study English as a foreign language

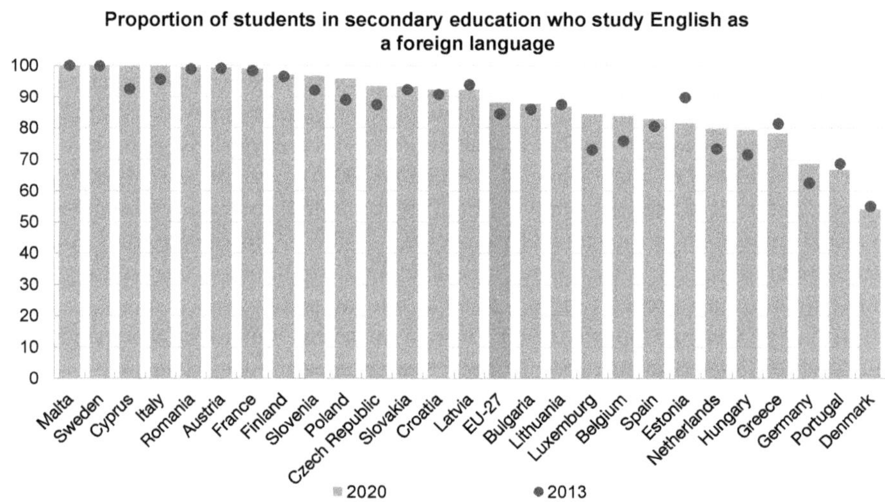

Chart 2 Proportion of students in secondary education who study English as a foreign language

learning a foreign language at school compared to those who are not. These associations are observed even when considering students' academic performance, gender, immigrant status, as well as the socio-economic level of the students and schools. This result can be interpreted in two ways: knowledge of another language could lead students to have higher expectations for their educational or professional development, or students with high expectations simply choose to study more foreign languages. Qualitative information collected through personal interviews in some

OECD countries that participated in PISA[3] indicates that both mechanisms might be at play.

Learning one or more languages can occur in very different contexts (Costa and Sebastián-Gallés 2014). Individuals can learn two languages simultaneously from birth (simultaneous bilinguals). Alternatively, individuals can learn a second language later in life within a formal educational system, for example, as a foreign language in school or in a linguistic immersion environment where the foreign language is used as the language of instruction (bilingual education programs). Additionally, an important social context that could lead to learning a language different from the mother tongue is immigration (sequential bilinguals). This chapter will focus mainly on language learning within formal educational programs (such as subjects in the school curriculum or bilingual education programs), but it will also briefly analyze the case of bilingual individuals as a result of immigration.

Firstly, the chapter presents the economic benefits derived from foreign language knowledge for individuals, companies, and countries, and provides a review of the most prominent academic articles that analyze this issue in different countries. Theoretically, foreign language knowledge would improve an individual's human capital, thus potentially having a positive impact on their productivity and, consequently, on their labor market outcomes.

Secondly, the chapter describes several programs that implement learning of a foreign language through its use as the language of instruction (sometimes referred to as bilingual education programs) in Spain and other European countries, as well as in the USA.

Thirdly, the chapter emphasizes the importance of research on second language acquisition and the evaluation of these programs and policies, given that both teaching and learning another language have not only benefits but also costs that must be considered when implementing such policies. Regarding teaching, the most obvious costs are financial: for example, schools need to hire specialized teachers for those languages, provide them with training in the foreign language, or hire native assistant teachers for conversation classes. Regarding learning, for the case of children, it requires investing time in school at the expense of instruction in other subjects in their native language, and for the case of adults, it requires investing financial resources as well as time at the expense of other work or training activities. Therefore, a significant part of the chapter will be dedicated to thoroughly studying some academic papers that have evaluated programs and policies that promote foreign language learning.

As will be seen throughout the chapter, the results of existing studies differ depending on many factors such as the country, the language, the legislation, the educational system, etc. According to Hulstijn (1997), one of the biggest limitations in research on second language acquisition is that there are many variables that affect the comparability of the groups involved in different learning experiences and that can be confounding when analyzing these experiences. According to this author,

[3] Within the framework of the 2018 PISA test, the OECD organized qualitative personal interviews with students from some of the participating countries, one of them being Spain (for more information, see Covacevich and Vargas, 2021).

"One of the biggest methodological challenges is to keep these variables constant. This is almost impossible in 'normal' classes with real students learning a second language. Therefore, it is no surprise that the results of studies conducted in natural learning environments are very often the subject of considerable discrepancies."

The structure of the chapter is as follows: the second section analyzes the benefits of foreign language knowledge, the third section describes several programs that implement the use of a second language as the language of instruction in schools in Spain and other countries, the fourth section analyzes some academic articles that evaluate these programs and policies, and the fifth section examines other examples of programs or reforms that have implemented the use of a foreign language as the language of instruction in schools. The final section contains the conclusions.

2 The Economic Benefits of Foreign Language Knowledge

From a worker's perspective, the skills derived from knowing a foreign language are part of their human capital, and therefore, could improve their situation in the labor market in terms of finding better job opportunities, having more geographical mobility, having more opportunities for promotion, or earning higher salaries. From the perspective of companies and countries, the foreign language knowledge of their workers would be an essential element for opening markets, marketing products, or investing in other countries.

2.1 Economic Benefits at the Individual Level

A study by the European Commission conducted by Araújo et al. (2015) finds that in 25 EU member states, individuals who know one or more foreign languages are more likely to be employed than monolingual individuals, regardless of their skill level. Several studies using data on immigrants in Germany or the United Kingdom (Aldashev et al. 2009; Dustmann and Fabbri 2003) find that employment opportunities for immigrants increase with proficiency in the country's language. Specifically, in the case of Germany, a high use of the German language reported by immigrants increases the likelihood of being employed, while in the United Kingdom, English proficiency of immigrants is associated with a 22% increase in the probability of being employed.

Regarding salaries, existing empirical evidence shows different results in various countries. In the United States (USA), estimates indicate that the wage returns for skills in languages other than English are relatively modest, approximately 2–3% (Saiz and Zoido 2005). Fry and Lowell (2003) argue that the higher wages of workers who know a language other than English actually reflect their higher educational level, and once they control for observable socio-economic characteristics, there does not seem to be a statistically significant wage return for foreign languages.

In Europe, the wage returns for foreign languages are considerably higher than in the USA, with English being a language that has an undeniable economic value in the labor market. For example, Ginsburgh and Prieto-Rodriguez (2011) show that in nine European countries, proficiency in a foreign language used at work has a positive impact on workers' wages. Thus, knowledge of English increases wages very heterogeneously in the different countries analyzed: in Austria by 11%, in Italy by 18%, in Finland by 23%, in France by 29%, and in Spain by 39%. In some countries, the impact on wages is even greater when it comes to languages other than English: knowing French increases wages in Spain by 49% and in Portugal by 34%, knowing German in France increases wages by 46%, and knowing Spanish in Portugal by 45%. Furthermore, in half of the countries analyzed, the effects are larger in the upper deciles of the wage distribution, where the most qualified occupations are found and where foreign languages are more likely to be used.

Williams (2011) estimates the labor return of using foreign languages at work for samples of workers in fourteen Western European countries and obtains results similar to those of Ginsburgh and Prieto-Rodriguez (2011): returns between 5 and 20%, depending on the country. The most significant impact is for the English language, while French, Italian, or German also yield wage returns in some countries. Similar results are obtained for a sample of immigrants in Spain in the work of Isophording (2013): very high wage returns for English, but also for French.

Hahm and Gazzola (2022) estimate the relationship between skills in English as a foreign language of individuals and their labor incomes in Germany. They find that, for native Germans, English proficiency can yield a wage return of up to 13%. Additionally, the authors analyze the impact on wages of different levels of English proficiency using the instrumental variables estimation method and find that each additional level of improvement in English proficiency increases wages by 11% on average.

2.2 *Economic Benefits at Company and Country Level*

The economic benefits of foreign languages go beyond the impact on wages or the labor market situation of an individual. At the company level, foreign language skills of employees could be associated with an increase or decrease in export revenues. In 2006, the European Commission conducted a study called ELAN[4] ("The Effects on the European Economy of Shortages of Foreign Language Skills in Enterprise", European Commission 2006) which collected information on the foreign language skills of workers in 2000 small and medium-sized enterprises. The results indicate that the lack of foreign language skills in companies of this size could be associated with a loss of business opportunities. The study also shows that a very large proportion of recruiting companies choose candidates who are native speakers of a foreign language or have foreign language skills; that many companies offer language

[4] https://ec.europa.eu/assets/eac/languages/policy/strategic-framework/documents/elan_en.pdf.

training courses to their employees; that besides English, French, German, or Russian are also used in the European business environment; and that candidates with work experience outside their home country are considered more competitive due to their language skills and broader business culture. Another conclusion of the study is that small and medium-sized companies with exports capacity that do not have employees with foreign language skills could lose a significant amount of business, to the point that some companies may have lost contracts worth more than 8 million euros.

At the country level, languages are an important determinant of bilateral trade. Hutchinson (2002) analyzes the role of English in the trade relations of 33 countries with the USA and concludes that the proportion of the population that speaks English in those countries is a significant factor for both exports and imports between the USA and those 33 countries. Melitz (2008) and Melitz and Toubal (2014) analyze, apart from official languages, the role of indigenous or established languages spoken by 4% of the population and find that both categories of languages increase bilateral trade. Fidrmuc and Fidrmuc (2016) demonstrate through a gravity model of trade and using data from 29 European countries that the foreign language skills of a country's population are an important determinant of its foreign trade, with English playing an especially important role.

3 Programs that Implement the Use of a Foreign Language as the Language of Instruction (Bilingual Programs) in Spain and Other Countries

Teaching a language different from the native language is currently a fundamental part of national education systems. Bilingual education programs in schools (in the language of the country and a second language, usually English), the introduction of one or more foreign languages into school curricula from early ages, student exchange programs abroad, private schools for teaching foreign languages, etc., are some examples of educational tools that can help in learning other languages. Below, the characteristics and design of some programs that implement the use of a foreign language as the language of instruction in Spain and other countries are described. Understanding these characteristics is very important for later evaluating these programs.

3.1 Bilingual Education in Spain

In Europe, supporting linguistic diversity and language learning has been a consistent policy line. Bilingual education began to be offered in public schools through programs generally known as Content and Language Integrated Learning (CLIL). The goal is to learn a foreign language simultaneously with the native language and within the curriculum of each grade. These are language immersion programs where some subjects, such as geography, natural sciences, physics, music, etc., are taught in a language different from the language of schooling. These programs have proliferated in Spain in recent decades for at least two reasons: first, Spain is a territory where other languages besides Spanish (Catalan, Basque) are spoken, so these types of programs could be suitable for promoting trilingualism; and second, there is a great need in Spain to improve foreign language skills, especially in English, after this was identified as one of the weaknesses of the Spanish education system. According to Eurobarometer 386 (European Commission 2012) or Eurydice data on language teaching in schools (Eurydice 2023), Spain consistently ranks behind other European Union countries in terms of foreign language proficiency.

An example of such a program is the bilingual and bicultural education offered by the Ministry of Education jointly with the British Council through an agreement signed in 1996, which follows the model of the British Council School in Madrid, called the Bilingual Education Program[5] (*Programa Educativo Bilingüe—PEB*). The program currently reaches 90 early childhood and primary schools and 58 secondary education schools across 10 autonomous communities. The PEB dedicates approximately 40% of the weekly teaching time to instruction in English for various subjects such as Science, History, or Geography.

Another example of a program, which is one of the most ambitious in Spain, was launched in the Community of Madrid in 2004. It involved the introduction of bilingual education (in Spanish and English) in the first year of primary education in selected public schools. Subsequently, this program was also extended to secondary education (during the first four years). In these so-called bilingual schools, it is mandatory that at least one-third of the classes are conducted in English and that English classes are held five times a week. Additionally, it is mandatory that Spanish language and mathematics classes are taught in Spanish.

To enter the bilingual program, a school must apply and meet certain requirements: (i) have the support of the school's teachers and the school council (composed of the principal and some teachers and parents); (ii) the feasibility of the application, which takes into account the school's previous experience, the teachers, particularly those specialized in English, the school's resources, and the number of classes and students; (iii) the existence of a balanced distribution of selected schools across different geographical areas. Within this program, students learn English as a foreign language, but they also study other subjects (science, history, geography, physical education, arts, religion, or values) in English. In this way, at least one-third to 40% of the teaching is conducted in English (between 10 and 12 hours out of a total of 25 hours of classes per week).

[5] For more details, see the webpage of the program: https://www.britishcouncil.es/programas/educacion/educacion-bilingue.

3.2 *Bilingual Education in Other Countries*

3.2.1 The Netherlands

In the Dutch educational system, bilingual education consists of partial immersion in the foreign language, which is usually English, with approximately 50% of the subjects taught in English. The content of some subjects is taught in the foreign language, but the focus of the teaching is on the subject knowledge rather than the language in which it is taught (Admiraal et al. 2006). The first school to use English as the language of instruction for some subjects started in 1989, and currently, there are about 120 schools. These programs are typically offered at the lower secondary education level, corresponding to the age group of 12–15 years. Schools have some freedom to design their curriculum, but they must meet important requirements from the Dutch Ministry of Education: 50% of the classes can be taught in English, they must follow the Dutch pre-university curriculum, and these programs must not affect the students' proficiency in Dutch. The subjects taught in English are mostly history, geography, and biology. Additionally, to reach 50% of the curriculum in English, schools can offer other subjects in English such as drama, drawing, crafts, physical education, mathematics, and in more advanced courses, economics, physics, and chemistry. In the last two years of upper secondary education, Dutch is the most used language in classes, as the final secondary exams are in Dutch.

3.2.2 United States

A particular case of bilingual education is that of the U.S., where a significant proportion of the population is made up of immigrants. A considerable number of immigrant children with low English proficiency have to attend classes in public primary and secondary schools where they are taught in English. As a result, this language barrier often translates into low educational outcomes for these students. Therefore, in several U.S. states, schools offer programs that fall into the following two categories: those that partially use the native language of the student as the language of instruction (bilingual education) and those where English is used as the language of instruction and is also taught as a second language.

The vast majority of bilingual education programs in the U.S. are available mainly for Spanish-speaking immigrants, as they represent a significant proportion of immigrants in this country. Therefore, a student's participation in a bilingual program is not random and depends on many factors such as their native language, grade level, English proficiency, parents (income level, education, whether they accept the bilingual program offered), the district of residence (sometimes the availability of these programs in a district requires the presence of a sufficient number of students with the same native language and the same level of English and who are in the same academic year), the state (in some states bilingual education is mandatory, while others prohibit it). All these variables can affect the academic performance, so when evaluating these programs, if they are not taken into account in the estimates, they generate an omitted variable bias. Therefore, estimating the causal impact of a bilingual program with these characteristics is a challenge for academic research (Chin 2015).

3.2.3 Latin American countries

Many schools in Spanish-speaking Latin American countries have also started offering bilingual education to their students. Banfi and Day (2004) document this process in the case of Argentina, where the vast majority of bilingual schools belong to the private sector. In these schools, the content of some subjects is taught in the foreign language (mostly English), but unlike previous examples of bilingual education, bilingual schools in Argentina represent a very diverse group in terms of size, curriculum, age and traditions, resources, or connections with the country of the foreign language. Therefore, the task of evaluating bilingual programs is very complicated, and in fact, there are no academic studies that analyze or evaluate these schools in Argentina.

A similar example is the case of Colombia. The acquisition of a foreign language, particularly English, is a very important part of the educational system in Colombia (Ordoñez 2004). There is a lot of political and social pressure for early access, and learning English is widespread through immersion programs in this language. Bilingual schools belong to the private sector and offer approximately 50% of the teaching time in English and the other 50% in Spanish. In these programs, students use English from the age of four or five in subjects such as science, mathematics, or arts. Extracurricular activities can be conducted in both languages, depending on the availability of English-speaking teachers. In the vast majority of these schools, reading skills are first taught in Spanish and then extended to English after the first year of primary school. Ordoñez (2004), using a very qualitative approach and without establishing any causal relationship, analyzes the oral narrative competence of 15-year-old students who have been studying in these schools in Colombia for ten years and finds that bilingual students perform worse in these skills than monolingual students, both in Spanish and in English. However, the author of this study acknowledges the need for more research to support these results. She concludes that, although it cannot be expected that bilinguals have the same competencies as monolinguals in both languages, a careful analysis of the costs that acquiring a second language in school from an early age might have on the first language (the native language) is necessary. This could help teachers design teaching methods to minimize these costs.

4 The Evaluation of Bilingual Education Programs

All the programs described in the previous section involve significant economic and human resources, both public and private, which is why it is important to evaluate their impact. This section presents in detail some examples of evaluations of bilingual education programs. The main objectives of these evaluations are usually to analyze, on the one hand, the students' language competencies in the foreign language of the program, and on the other hand, the knowledge of students in the subjects that are studied in the foreign language.

There is a considerable lack of studies evaluating bilingual education programs, and those that do exist use data from a specific region or country where such programs have been implemented. When evaluating the success of these programs, it is important to consider the social, political, and economic environments being analyzed. For example, in the case of Spain, students hardly need to use English in their daily lives outside of school. In contrast, in other countries like the Netherlands, children are exposed to the English language from a very young age and in many settings, similar to children of immigrants in countries like the USA. Therefore, the results obtained from evaluating these programs in a specific country or region cannot be easily generalized or extrapolated to other countries.

4.1 Methodology and Results from the Evaluation of a Bilingual Education Program in Spain

4.1.1 Description of Data and Estimation Methodology

A database widely used in various research studies on the economics of education in Spain contains the results of a standardized test for 6th-grade students (12–13 years old) in the Community of Madrid, called the Essential Knowledge and Skills test (*Conocimientos y Destrezas Indispensables (CDI)*). This test evaluates the skills considered essential for 6th-grade students. The exam was administered from the 2004/2005 academic year until the 2014/2015 academic year and was mandatory for all schools in the Community of Madrid (public, charter, and private). Similar to the OECD's PISA test, the results of the exam have no academic consequences for the students; its purpose is to provide additional information to teachers, students, and parents.

The exam consists of 2 parts, each lasting 45 minutes: the first part includes dictation, reading, and general knowledge tests (natural and social sciences), and the second part includes math exercises. The tests are conducted in Spanish for all students, regardless of whether they are attending a school with a bilingual program or not.

Before taking the exam, students must fill out a brief questionnaire, where they are asked about themselves, their parents, and the socio-economic environment in which they live. The answers to these questions provide information about various characteristics of the students: gender, age, country of birth, parents' educational level, parents' occupation, composition of the household where the student lives, age at which the student started school (early childhood education), and whether the student has any special needs or disabilities.

With the help of this data, Anghel et al. (2016) evaluate the implementation of the bilingual program in the region of Madrid as follows: the results of students from schools where the bilingual program was implemented are compared with the results of students from schools without such a program. Additionally, since it is known that the first year the program was implemented was 2004/2005, it is possible to compare the cohorts of students who entered school that year and later took the CDI test in sixth grade, with the cohorts who entered school a year earlier and are not part of the bilingual education program.

Anghel et al. (2016) start from the following econometric model of the education production function (see also chapter 2 of this book). For an academic year, the test score for a student i in school j is determined by:

$$y_{ij} = \delta bil_j + \beta x_i + v_j + u_i + \varepsilon_{ij} \tag{1}$$

where x_i includes observable characteristics of students and their parents, bil_j is a dummy variable indicating whether school j participates in the bilingual program, v_j are unobservable characteristics of the school (e.g., the quality of the teachers or the school principal), u_i are unobservable characteristics of the students (e.g., effort or innate ability), and ε_{ij} is a random error.

The parameter of interest is the coefficient δ, which measures the average impact of the bilingual program on y_{ij}. However, when estimating the regression of y_{ij} on bil_j and x_i with the available data, there could be an endogeneity bias due to two issues related to self-selection:

1. Students are not randomly distributed among schools (see also Chapter 5a of this handbook). That is, students, or rather their parents, choose the school. In the case of the region of Madrid, if there is no excess demand for places at the chosen school, all children are admitted. If there is excess demand, admission is based on criteria such as the proximity of the student's home to the school and the family's income. Neither of these variables is random and they are correlated with the students' academic performance.
2. Schools are not randomly assigned to implement the bilingual program. Section 3.2 explains that the program is implemented only in those schools that apply for it, and furthermore, the schools that apply for and access the program must meet certain requirements. The application to implement a bilingual program could be a positive signal of the quality of the principal and teachers at the school, as the program involves significant extra work on their part. But at the same time, it could be a signal that the school has low admission demand, possibly due to its low quality.

To control for endogeneity caused by the two self-selection problems, the article by Anghel et al. (2016) proposes using the difference-in-differences method[6]. In this context, this method involves comparing the grades of students in treated (bilingual) schools before and after the treatment—that is, the implementation of the bilingual program—with the control group of schools (untreated, i.e., non-bilingual) before and after the treatment. The treatment group consists of the first cohort of students in bilingual schools in the region of Madrid. These students started the first grade in the 2004/2005 academic year, and therefore took the CDI test six years later, when they were in the sixth grade, in the 2009/2010 academic year. This cohort of students is made up of 25 schools that were the first to implement the bilingual program.

Data from the CDI test for the academic years 2008/2009 and 2009/2010 are used, and the four groups of schools analyzed are as follows: the group of bilingual schools in 2008/2009 (the treatment group before the treatment), the group of non-bilingual schools in 2008/2009 (the control group before the treatment), the group of bilingual schools in 2009/2010 (the treatment group after the treatment), and the group of non-bilingual schools in 2009/2010 (the control group after the treatment).

This method solves the problem of self-selection bias of schools in the program since the academic performance in the CDI test of students from the same school is observed in the first year the bilingual program was implemented and also in the previous year. Another important aspect for the identification strategy is that it can be assumed that the only significant changes in material resources and school staff from one year to the next were related to the bilingual program.

Regarding the problem of self-selection bias of students in schools, the difference-in-differences method also helps to solve it, to the extent that it can be assumed that the differences between the first cohort of treated students and previous cohorts are not related to the introduction of the program. To this end, Anghel et al. (2016) conduct a very detailed analysis of the characteristics of students in the treatment and control groups. The authors observe a certain change in the characteristics of students in bilingual schools after the introduction of the program, not very large, but possibly endogenous. This change consists of an improvement in some characteristics of students in treated schools, such as parents' educational level, parents' occupation, or nationality, factors that the academic literature has identified as determinants of students' success (see Chapter 3b). To address this problem and control for these changes, the difference-in-differences method allows incorporating the observable characteristics of students in the estimation. Therefore, the authors estimate the following regression:

$$y_{ij} = \alpha_0 + \alpha_1 bil_j + \alpha_2 year2010 + \delta\left(year2010 * bil_j\right) + \beta x_i + \varepsilon_{ij} \qquad (2)$$

where the variable $year2010$ is a dummy variable for the 2009/2010 academic year, which is the first year in which children from the bilingual program are observed in the CDI test.

[6] See Chapter 2 of this book on econometric methods.

4.1.2 Empirical Results

In Eq. (2), the parameter δ associated with the interaction term $year2010 * bil_j$ indicates the effect of the bilingual program on the results of students in the three CDI test subjects: mathematics, reading, and general knowledge. When the regression from Eq. (2) is estimated without any control variable x_i, , the authors find that the impact of the program is not statistically significant (see Table 8 in Anghel et al. 2016). When control variables, which are student characteristics, are included, the impact of the program decreases, reflecting that there may be some self-selection of students in schools once the bilingual program is implemented. For mathematics and reading, the coefficient is not statistically significant, although it changes from positive to negative. However, for the general knowledge test results, the bilingual program has a negative and statistically significant impact. As explained in Sect. 3.1 in the description of the bilingual program in the region of Madrid, the general knowledge subject is the only one of the three evaluated subjects that is taught in English in bilingual schools but is assessed in Spanish in the CDI test. Therefore, this result would indicate, on the one hand, that teaching a subject in English in primary education could worsen students' performance. On the other hand, it could show that students possibly have the necessary knowledge but are simply unable to express it in Spanish since they learn it in English. Nonetheless, if this is the case, it would also be a negative impact of the program, given that students do not have the necessary level of English to overcome the language barrier.

The authors of this study conduct several robustness checks on their results, but all lead to the same conclusion: there is a clear and quantitatively significant negative effect of the bilingual program on the subject taught in English, and the effect is not statistically different from zero in math and reading skills in Spanish. Additionally, the authors highlight two aspects of this result that are very relevant for educational policy implications: first, the negative impact is concentrated in the group of students whose parents have a low educational level, and second, when they perform the same estimations for the group of schools that implemented the bilingual program in the second year (2005–2006), the negative impact is reduced and is no longer statistically significant, neither on average for the entire sample of students nor for the sample of students with less educated parents. A possible explanation for this second result is that the schools selected in the second year are possibly better and better prepared for the implementation of the program, as, for example, a higher level of English knowledge is required from the teachers in these schools. However, this is only a hypothesis that cannot be verified with the data used by these authors.

4.2 Methodology and Results of Evaluations of Bilingual Education Programs in Other Countries

4.2.1 The Netherlands

The study by Admiraal et al. (2006) evaluates the bilingual education program in secondary schools in the Netherlands, described in Sect. 3.2 of the chapter. Through several pilot studies, the authors construct a longitudinal evaluation study. Their main interest focuses on the effects of using English as the language of instruction on students' competencies in English as a foreign language, although they also analyze the impact of bilingual education on the subjects taught in English, as well as on competencies in Dutch.

Students' competencies in English are evaluated through the following measures: receptive vocabulary knowledge in English—a vocabulary test called the "English as a Foreign Language Vocabulary Test" (EFL vocabulary test)—reading comprehension—a national final exam in English for intermediate secondary education—and oral proficiency—an exam designed for the final year of intermediate secondary education.

Regarding knowledge in the subjects taught in English, the results of the final exams of upper secondary education in the subjects of geography and history, which are taught in English in bilingual schools, are used.

The authors also have information on student characteristics that could be correlated with the level of competencies and English acquisition: gender, results of a test at the end of primary education, language spoken at home, contact with the language outside of school, and motivation to learn English.

To estimate the impact of the program, they use a sample of students enrolled in schools with bilingual education programs (the treatment group) and another sample of students following regular secondary education courses in Dutch (the control group)—a total of 1305 students. The information covers a period of six academic years. The data have a hierarchical structure: students' grades in different exams, for four cohorts of students in nine schools. The data are analyzed using multilevel regression analysis that takes this structure into account. Additionally, given the limited number of observations, the study authors use the Restricted Iterative Generalised Least Squares (RIGLS) method (see Goldstein 2011).

The analysis of this paper shows that there is no significant difference between the group of students in the bilingual program and the control group regarding the average score in the vocabulary test, which measures receptive vocabulary knowledge. However, in both reading comprehension and oral proficiency in English, students in the bilingual program achieve better results than those in the control group attending the regular program, even when considering the observable and relevant characteristics of the students. Finally, regarding the subjects taught in English (history and geography) and the Dutch language, no impact of the bilingual program is found.

The authors of this study suggest that it is difficult to generalize the conclusions obtained for all schools offering bilingual programs in the Netherlands, as they analyze a small sample of students and schools that were pioneers in implementing this type of education. Like the study for schools in the region of Madrid (Anghel et al. 2016), Admiraal et al. (2006) point out that their research describes the effects of bilingual education in secondary schools in the early years of implementation, before it became a fully developed educational program with around 120 secondary schools. Therefore, it is not clear if the results would be the same for schools that implemented bilingual education later, as they might benefit from the experience and knowledge of the pioneering schools.

Finally, the authors also emphasize that their analysis focuses on the case of a country where English holds a very important position in society in general. Children are highly motivated to learn English, which is a prominent language in Dutch society, in the education system, and in the scientific world, and therefore, they are very exposed to the English language outside of their schools as well.

4.2.2 United States of America

An example of evaluating a bilingual program in the U.S. is a study from the state of Texas (Chin et al. 2013), where a school district[7] is required to offer bilingual education (BE) when 20 or more students with limited English proficiency (LEP students) are enrolled in the same grade and speak the same native language. Below this threshold of 20 students, school districts have the freedom to offer bilingual education or teach all subjects in English and offer English as a second language (ESL). In this situation, most choose the latter option as it is less costly.

Most bilingual programs in the U.S. are offered to native Spanish-speaking immigrants. In the case of Texas, Spanish is the native language of approximately 90% of immigrant students enrolled in ESL.

BE and ESL programs have both advantages and disadvantages for LEP students. For example, teaching in the student's native language might delay English learning, but at the same time, it could help students keep up with math and other subjects while they are learning English. On the other hand, an ESL program could improve learning both English and other subjects by redistributing the time that would be used to teach LEP students to read and write in their native language.

Additionally, when evaluating these programs, it is also important to consider the impact of the presence of LEP students on their non-LEP peers (see also Chapter 3c on the effect of classmates). This impact could occur through various mechanisms. For example, teachers with LEP students might need to pay more attention to them at the expense of time for other students. Furthermore, to the extent that the academic performance of LEP students is lower than that of non-LEP students, there could be a negative peer effect of LEP students on the results of non-LEP students. However, there could also be positive peer effects from LEP students because they might be

[7] In the U.S., most schools operate as units of a school district that typically manages several schools.

more advanced in other areas, such as knowledge of other subjects, non-cognitive skills, etc., which are relevant to academic performance, or there could be benefits from being in a more diverse class.

In this context, identifying the causal effect of bilingual education on student performance is complicated because the provision of BE in a school district is an endogenous variable. Districts that offer BE are not randomly assigned: they could be the ones with more LEP students, a greater increase in the number of LEP students, more wealth, LEP students with significantly low levels of English, etc.

To correct this endogeneity bias, the authors use the threshold of 20 students, which allows them to design a regression discontinuity.[8] Specifically, the effect of BE (relative to teaching English as ESL) on students' academic performance can be obtained by comparing the results of students in school districts just above this threshold (where BE is more likely to be offered) with the results in districts just below. For example, school districts with 19 LEP students should not be very different from school districts with exactly 20 LEP students, but given the policy, the latter are required to offer BE. Therefore, the difference in results between districts with 19 and districts with 20 students can be used to identify the effect of the provision of BE in a district.

Estimates using this methodology lead to the following conclusions. First, the provision of BE programs at the school district level generally has a positive but very small and statistically insignificant effect on students whose native language is Spanish. These students are the ones eligible to participate in a BE program, so these results indicate that the beneficiaries of LEP programs achieve similar outcomes in both BE and ESL programs.

Second, the provision of BE programs at the school district level has a statistically positive impact on the math and reading performance of students who are not LEP and whose native language is not Spanish. This indicates the presence of spillover effects from these programs.

5 Other Examples of Programs or Reforms that Affect the Language of Instruction in Schools

5.1 *Reforms that Change the Language of Instruction in Schools*

Several studies focus on some countries where, for historical reasons, the language of instruction in all (or some) subjects is different from the native language. Angrist and Lavy (1997) analyze the impact of a reform in Morocco in 1983 that replaced the language of instruction in secondary education from French to Arabic. Using the difference-in-differences method, they find a negative impact on the French

[8] See Chapter 2.

writing skills of individuals exposed to the reform. Additionally, this negative impact translates into a negative impact on the wages of the affected individuals.

In contrast, Angrist et al. (2008), in a study analyzing a reform in Puerto Rico that changed the language of instruction from English to Spanish in post-primary education, find no effect of the reform on English proficiency, measured through English-speaking skills. The authors suggest that this result demonstrates that intensive instruction in another language (English in this case) is neither sufficient to improve English skills nor necessary to have good English skills.

5.2 The Case of Countries with Multiple Official Languages

A particular case is that of countries or regions where two or more official languages coexist, and the use of multiple languages in the education system is very common. In this regard, South Africa is a very relevant example, as there are 11 official languages (nine African languages and two European languages—English and Afrikaans, the latter derived from Dutch). Most primary schools use native language instruction during the first three years and then switch to English in the fourth grade, while some schools use English as the language of instruction, although for most students this is not their native language. Additionally, final secondary education exams are conducted in English or Afrikaans, yet only 23% of South Africans speak one of these two languages (Taylor and von Fintel 2016). Given that there is significant inequality within the public education system in South Africa, the impact of language on children's educational outcomes could be very relevant.

To analyze this impact, Taylor and von Fintel (2016) use some changes in the norms on languages of instruction in certain schools, which provide exogenous variation used to identify the impact of these policies. The authors build a database covering the period 2007–2012 for the entire population of schools in South Africa. The results estimated using the OLS method indicate that early-age instruction in English is associated with better English performance in later school years. However, when they use a fixed-effects model for schools (which includes characteristics such as school quality), they find that being in schools where the native language is used as the language of instruction in the first three years leads to better English performance in subsequent years. According to the authors, this result is consistent with pedagogical theory that promotes the use of the first language as the language of instruction for approximately three to six years. During this period, children would reach a certain level of academic competence in their first language, which would allow for subsequent instruction to switch to a second language (Hakuta et al. 2000).

Ivlevs and King (2014) exploit a reform in Latvia in 2004, when the language of instruction in the schools of the Russian minority in this country changed from 100% Russian to 60% Latvian and 40% Russian. Specifically, they analyze the performance of Russian minority schools and Latvian majority schools on a standardized exam at the end of secondary education, which is identical for all schools in the country. The reform and the exam allow for the construction of a treatment group (the group of

Russian minority schools affected by the reform) and a control group (the group of Latvian schools not affected by the reform). The main result is that the performance of Russian minority schools deteriorated significantly after the reform, relative to the control group schools, especially in the years when the first treated cohorts graduated. However, preliminary results from their analysis show that in later years, in some subjects, the performance of Russian minority schools returns to pre-reform levels, indicating that the treated schools may have adjusted to the change. Nevertheless, the authors note that information from a larger number of years after the reform is needed to confirm this result.

The language of instruction is also relevant in tertiary education, as the international mobility of students is constantly growing. Bernhofer and Tonin (2022) use administrative data from the Free University of Bozen-Bolzano, which is located in a bilingual region of Italy, where 65% of the population uses German as their native language and 27% uses Italian as their native language. The university is trilingual—English, German, and Italian—meaning that students can learn and take exams in all three languages. The authors find a significant reduction in students' grades in exams conducted in a language different from their native language, which could indicate that studying a subject in a non-native language may entail certain costs.

6 Conclusions

This chapter analyzes the importance of foreign languages as a relevant input in the education production function of an individual. Language skills are fundamental for the progress of an individual in society in general, and in the labor market in particular. The importance of foreign languages is also reflected in the effort that the OECD will make within the PISA 2025 test, which will evaluate students' foreign language skills on a global scale.[9]

The chapter shows that there is sufficient empirical evidence in favor of the economic benefits of foreign languages, in terms of better salaries and better situation on the labor market. Given these benefits, in most countries, significant public and private resources are invested in language teaching, in some cases from an early age. The evaluation of some educational programs that implement the use of a second language of instruction in schools at different educational levels (primary, secondary) shows different results that depend greatly on the country or region, the social environment, the educational system, and the characteristics of the program. Therefore, generalizing the results of these studies is very complicated and must be done with great caution. To obtain comparable results between countries, standardized international tests should be available, where students are assessed on their proficiency in a foreign language studied at school (English, for example) in the same way. Additionally, socio-economic characteristics of the students and their families, as

[9] PISA 2025 will conduct an optional English test that will assess three skills: reading, listening, and speaking. See OECD (2021).

well as characteristics of schools and educational systems of the countries, should be available.

Additionally, to conduct a complete and rigorous evaluation of these programs, it would be necessary to have databases that track students in bilingual education programs throughout their academic and professional lives and obtain information about, for example, their university careers, if any, or their situation in the labor market (salaries, employment status, etc.). Having this information would truly allow for an assessment of whether these programs have achieved their objectives.

One limitation of the studies presented in this chapter is that they do not consider the quality of the teachers who teach in bilingual education programs. As explained in Chapter 3d on teachers, they are a determining factor in the academic performance of the students. In the case of programs that implement the use of a foreign language as the language of instruction, teachers must also meet additional requirements related to their proficiency in the foreign language, which would demand greater knowledge and effort on their part. This could be an indicator of their motivation and quality as teachers. Therefore, information about teachers and the quality of teaching would be essential to better explain the results on the impacts of this type of educational program found in the studies summarized in this chapter.

The chapter opens several avenues for future research topics, such as: (i) at what age and how should foreign languages be introduced into the education of children in schools, (ii) should a foreign language be used as the language of instruction for some subjects in schools? (iii) if the answer is yes, at what ages should this be done?

Appendix

List of Proposed Exercises

Exercise 1

On the PISA website (https://www.oecd.org/pisa/data/2018database/), download the microdata from PISA 2018 (you can also use data from other years, or the data from the latest available year), which are under the name "Student questionnaire data file." Use only the data from Spain (or any other country).

a) Identify in the database:

i. the variables that correspond to students' foreign language skills.

ii. the variables that correspond to students' expectations regarding pursuing a university degree and becoming a manager or specialist.

b) Using these variables, perform an OLS estimation where the dependent variable is: (i) students' expectations regarding pursuing a university degree, and (ii) students' expectations regarding becoming a manager or specialist, and the independent variables are: number of foreign languages, student's gender, student's socio-economic status (measured through the PISA index of economic, social, and cultural status), and immigrant status. In this way, verify the statement made in the Introduction of the book.

c) Using these variables, check if the number of foreign languages a student knows is related to their results in some of the PISA tests (math, reading, science, or global competencies), taking into account their socio-economic status, immigrant status, and gender.

Exercise 2

What are the methodological problems of estimating the wage returns of foreign language skills? Use the Mincer equation explained in Chapter 4b to support your answers.

Exercise 3

The study by Anghel, Cabrales, and Carro (2016) is detailed in Sect. 4.1 of this chapter. They find that when they perform the same estimations for the group of schools that implemented the bilingual program in the second year (2005/2006), the negative impact is reduced and is no longer statistically significant. Discuss what could be the explanations for this result and what data would be needed to test the proposed hypotheses.

References

Admiraal, W., G. Westhoff, and K. De Bot. 2006. Evaluation of bilingual secondary education in the Netherlands: Students' language proficiency in English. *Educational Research and Evaluation* 12 (1): 75–93.

Aldashev, A., J. Gernandt, and S. L. Thomsen. 2009. Language usage, participation, employment and earnings: Evidence for foreigners in West Germany with multiple sources of selection. *Labour Economics* 16 (3): 330–341.

Anghel, B., A. Cabrales, and J. M. Carro. 2016. Evaluating a bilingual education program in Spain: The impact beyond Foreign language learning. *Economic Inquiry* 54 (2): 1202–1223.

Angrist, J., A. Chin, and R. Godoy. 2008. Is Spanish-only schooling responsible for the Puerto Rican language gap? *Journal of Development Economics* 85 (1–2): 105–128.

Angrist, J.D., and V. Lavy. 1997. The effect of a change in language of instruction on the returns to schooling in Morocco. *Journal of Labor Economics* 15 (1), Part 2, S48–S76.

Araújo, L., P. Dinis da Costa., S. Flisi., and E. Soto Calvo. 2015. Languages and Employability. European Commission. https://crell.jrc.ec.europa.eu/sites/default/files/files/JRC97544.pdf

Banfi, C., and R. Day. 2004. The evolution of bilingual schools in Argentina. *International Journal of Bilingual Education and Bilingualism* 7 (5): 398–411.

Bernhofer, J., and M. Tonin. 2022. The effect of the language of instruction on academic performance. Labour Economics. 78.

Chin, A., N. M. Daysal, and S. A. Imberman. 2013. Impact of bilingual education programs on limited English proficient students and their peers: Regression discontinuity evidence from Texas. *Journal of Public Economics*. 107: 63–78.

Chin, A. 2015. Impact of bilingual education on student achievement. IZA World of Labor.

Comisión Europea. 2006. Effects on the European Union economy of shortages of foreign language skills in enterprise.

Comisión Europea. 2012. Europeans and their languages. Special Eurobarometer 386. https://europa.eu/eurobarometer/api/deliverable/download/file?deliverableId=40204

Comisión Europea, E. A. C. E. A., and Eurydice,. 2023. *Cifras clave de la enseñanza de lenguas en los centros escolares de Europa—Edición 2023*. Informe Eurydice: Oficina de Publicaciones de la Unión Europea, Luxemburgo.

Costa, A., and N. Sebastián-Gallés. 2014. How does the bilingual experience sculpt the brain? *Nature Reviews Neuroscience*. 15 (5): 336–345.

Covacevich, C., and J. Vargas. 2021. *How language learning opens doors*. OECD Publishing.

Dustmann, C., and F. Fabbri. 2003. Language proficiency and labour market performance of immigrants in the UK. *The Economic Journal* 113 (489): 695–717.

Eurydice. 2023. Key data on teaching languages at school in Europe—2023 edition. https://eurydice.eacea.ec.europa.eu/publications/key-data-teaching-languages-school-europe-2023-edition

Fidrmuc, J., and J. Fidrmuc. 2016. Foreign languages and trade: Evidence from a natural experiment. *Empirical Economics* 50: 31–49. https://doi.org/10.1007/s00181-015-0999-7.

Fry, R., and L. B. Lowell. 2003. The value of bilingualism in the U.S. labor market. *Industrial & Labor Relations Review* 57: 128–140.

Ginsburgh, V. A., and J. Prieto-Rodriguez. 2011. Returns to foreign languages of native workers in the European Union. *Industrial and Labor Relations Review* 64 (3): 599–618.

Goldstein, H. 2011. *Multilevel statistical models*. John Wiley & Sons.

Hahm, S., and M. Gazzola. 2022. The value of foreign language skills in the German labor market. *Labour Economics* 76: 102150.

Hakuta, K., Y. G. Butler, and D. Witt. 2000. *How long does it take English learners to attain proficiency? Policy Report 2000–1*. Santa Barbara, CA: The University of California Language Minority Research Institute.

Hutchinson, W. 2002. Does ease of communication increase trade? Commonality of language and bilateral trade. *Scottish Journal of Political Economy* 49: 544–556.

Hulstijn, J. H. 1997. Second language acquisition research in the laboratory: Possibilities and limitations. *Studies in Second Language Acquisition* 19 (2): 131–143.

Isphording, I. E. 2013. Returns to Foreign language skills of immigrants in Spain. *Labour* 27 (4): 443–461.

Ivlevs, A., and R. M. King. 2014. Minority education reform and pupil performance in Latvia. *Economics of Education Review*. 38: 151–166.

Melitz, J. 2008. Language and foreign trade. *European Economic Review* 52 (4): 667–699.

Melitz, J., and F. Toubal. 2014. Native language, spoken language, translation and trade. *Journal of International Economics* 93: 351–363.

OECD. 2021. PISA 2025 Foreign Language Assessment and Analytical Framework. OECD Publishing, Paris. Disponible en: https://www.oecd.org/pisa/foreign-language/PISA-2025-FLA-Framework-Learning-Another-Language.pdf

Ordóñez, C. L. 2004. EFL and native Spanish in elite bilingual schools in Colombia: A first look at bilingual adolescent frog stories. *International Journal of Bilingual Education and Bilingualism*. 7: 449–474.

Saiz, A., and E. Zoido. 2005. Listening to what the world says: Bilingualism and earnings in the United States. *Review of Economics and Statistics* 87: 523–538.

Taylor, S., and M. von Fintel. 2016. Estimating the impact of language of instruction in South African primary schools: A fixed effects approach. *Economics of Education Review* 50: 75–89.

Williams, D. R. 2011. Multiple language usage and earnings in Western Europe. *International Journal of Manpower* 32 (4): 372–393.

Educational Stages

Early Childhood Education

Álvaro Choi and Gabriela Sicilia

1 Introduction

Early childhood education (ECE hereafter) is the first level of educational systems and spans from the earliest months of age until the start of primary education, which in most countries is typically set between the ages of 5 and 7. Just like primary education, early childhood education can also be divided into different stages, depending on the institutional design of each country. For example, in most developed countries, ECE is divided into a first cycle from 0 to 3 years and a second cycle from 3 to 6 years.

Early childhood education expanded rapidly in developed countries from the 1960s, largely in response to the increasing participation of women in the labour market. Gradually, it moved away from its initial welfare-oriented conception and began to be progressively recognised as a vital stage in the human capital formation process. ECE promotes the development of physical, social, cognitive, emotional, and linguistic skills, and its significance is reflected in Sustainable Development Goal (SDG) 4, which aims to "*ensure that all children have access to quality early childhood development, care, and pre-primary education so that they are ready for primary education*" by 2030 (UN 2015). In fact, SDG 4 only partially captures the importance of ECE, as the benefits associated with early years schooling extend beyond mere educational outcomes.

Early childhood education has positive effects, as demonstrated by literature focusing on the impact of attendance (Duncan and Magnusson 2013), the age of enrolment (Duncan et al. 2022), and the quality (including structural factors—teacher-student ratios, teacher quality, length of the school day—as well as process factors—pedagogical approaches, teacher-student interactions—; see Ulferts et al. 2019, or

Á. Choi
Universitat de Barcelona, Barcelona, Spain
e-mail: alvarochoi@ub.edu

G. Sicilia (✉)
Universitat Autònoma de Barcelona, Barcelona, Spain
e-mail: gabriela.sicilia@uab.cat

A. Cabrales and I. Sanz (eds.), *Economics of Education*,
https://doi.org/10.1007/978-3-031-90911-5_9

Bowne et al. 2017), both in the short and long term (Heckman 2012). Although the evidence shows that ECE positively impacts student development, the effects are heterogeneous depending on the student's characteristics and the type of outcome evaluated, such as the teacher-student ratio (Duncan et al. 2023) and the optimal age to start schooling. The literature provides mixed results, partially explained by alternative care types, such as home care, which often serve as the counterfactual (Lubotsky and Kaestner 2016; Li et al. 2020), and the length of the school day—there are significant differences between part-time, half-day, or full-day enrolment (Felfe and Zierow 2018).

In the short term, ECE has the potential to enhance both cognitive skills (Blau 2021) and non-cognitive or socio-emotional skills (Joo et al. 2020), which facilitate later educational processes. On the other hand, these benefits are not evenly distributed among the population, being greater for students from more disadvantaged socioeconomic backgrounds (Van Huizen and Plantenga 2018).

Whether directly or indirectly, in the long term, participation in ECE reduces the likelihood of grade repetition and increases enrolment and graduation rates in subsequent educational levels (McCoy et al. 2017). Again, these positive effects of early childhood education are not uniformly distributed, making it a policy tool with the potential to promote the educational equality (Heckman 2011). This is even more evident when considering additional benefits linked to ECE, such as higher employment rates and better wages (De Haan and Leuven 2020), lower rates of teenage pregnancy (Barr and Gibbs 2022), and a reduced likelihood of committing crimes in adulthood (García et al. 2019). Therefore, the social benefits of early childhood education exceed individual gains, paving the way for potential public intervention (as it is a preferred good with positive consumption externalities). Indeed, analyses by Cascio (2023) and García et al. (2023) show that investment in ECE is cost-effective.

Despite this growing evidence of the individual and social returns on investment in early childhood education, its development at the international level has been highly uneven, even among relatively similar countries in terms of economic development (Fig. 1), due to the confluence of supply and demand factors. On the supply side, the extent of public sector intervention in the regulation and provision of ECE services is crucial, given the high cost of provision—requiring higher teacher-student ratios than in later educational stages. On the demand side, factors such as the level of female participation in the labour market, different family models, cultural differences, and geographical distribution of the population are relevant. The existence of work-life balance policies also affects these factors and family preferences.

As shown in Fig. 1, there are significant differences between countries in their levels of overall and cyclical early childhood education enrolment. Within each country, there are also inequalities in ECE enrolment based on geographical and socioeconomic variables, among others. Given the effects of ECE on later outcomes in various crucial areas, inequalities in access to quality early childhood education can exacerbate disparities in opportunities. Therefore, investment in ECE can be analysed—though not exclusively—from both the perspectives of effectiveness and efficiency, as well as equity.

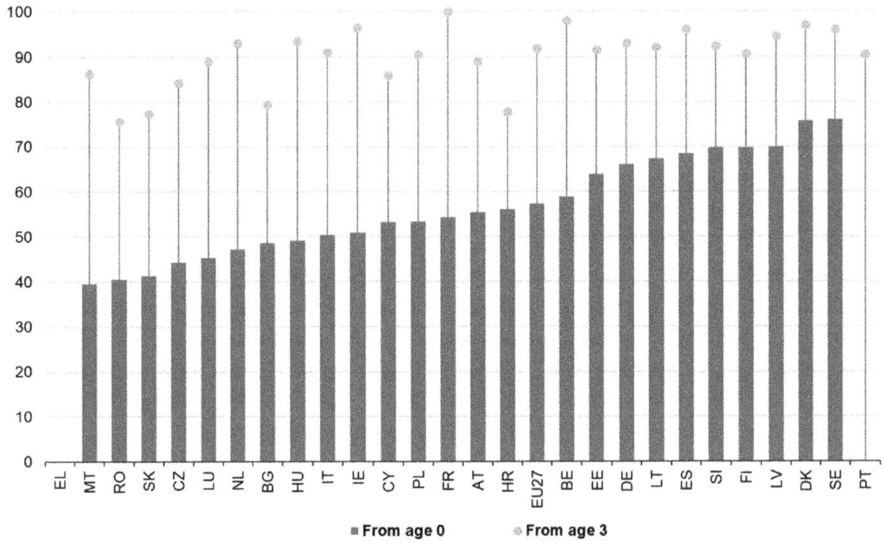

Fig. 1 Participation rate in early childhood education from 0 years and from 3 years until the age of primary school enrolment (in %), European Union, year 2021 (*Source* Elaborated from Eurostat database. Data for Greece and Portugal (from birth) not available)

This chapter reflects on various elements to consider when analysing the impacts of ECE. It does not aim to provide a literature review—in this regard, excellent works include those by Van Huizen and Plantenga (2018), Blau (2021), Cascio (2021), and Duncan et al. (2023)—but rather to serve as a starting point that helps the reader delve deeper into the analysis and evaluation, particularly of causal impact, of early childhood education. To this end, the chapter first (Sect. 2) provides a brief overview of the recent evolution of early childhood schooling in the OECD countries. In Sect. 3 presents the theoretical framework of early childhood education production and the family decision-making process, which underpins most impact evaluations. Section 4 describes different empirical approaches to evaluating the impact of early childhood education, distinguishing between experimental and quasi-experimental methods, and highlights key factors to consider when conducting these evaluations in practice. Finally, Sect. 5 presents the main conclusions of the chapter.

2 Early Childhood Education in the OECD Countries

In most developed countries, early childhood education is structured into two cycles: from birth to two years (ISCED level 01) and from three years until the start of primary education (ISCED level 02). In the majority of countries, both cycles are voluntary rather than mandatory, although there is greater heterogeneity regarding their funding and provision. The second cycle typically has more regulation in terms hours, educational curricula, and features (such as class size, teacher training, among other factors) to ensure a minimum level of quality across various institutions. Therefore, it is important when evaluating the effects of attending ECE, particularly at younger ages, to not only consider the number of years of attendance (or age of entry), but also to take into account the characteristics of the institution they attend (ratios, staff training, pedagogical processes, etc.) and, ultimately, the quality of the service. In any case, measuring the quality of institutions poses a challenge for evaluating early childhood education.

Over the last few decades, there has been a gradual increase in the enrolment rates in ECE, to the extent that nowadays most OECD countries have enrolment rates in the year prior to the start of primary education exceeding 95%. However, some heterogeneity persists, as shown in Fig. 2. For example, in countries like France or Britain, nearly all students are enrolled during the year before entering primary education, whereas in New Zealand this rate barely exceeds 80%.

Significant differences can be observed between countries in early childhood education (before age 3) enrolment rates. Figure 3 shows, for instance, that at the age of two, 95% of Norwegian children are enrolled in ECE centres, while in Turkey or Costa Rica, that rate is below 5%. The diversity of situations illustrated in Fig. 4 is striking, as it clearly depicts the variety of organisational models in early childhood education.

The degree of public sector intervention in the provision of educational services plays a very significant role in the expansion of early childhood education. Figure 4 presents the trend in public sector participation in educational services from the age of three until the beginning of primary education. In New Zealand and Ireland, the public sector has a minimal role in the direct provision of services, although it does intervene by funding private centres. In other countries, such as Japan, South Korea, or Australia, less than half of the students are enrolled in public centres, with the remainder in private centres receiving public funding. In countries like the Czech

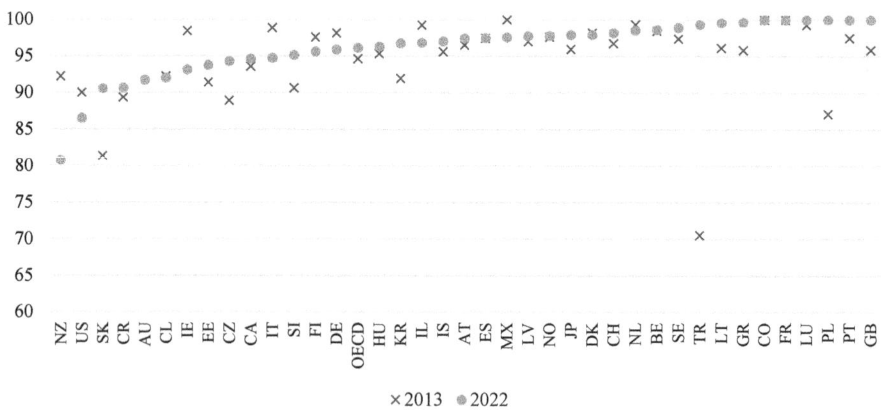

Fig. 2 Evolution of enrolment rates in early childhood schooling one year before the typical primary entry age. OECD countries, 2013–2022 (*Source* Elaborated from OECD (2024), Table B1.2)

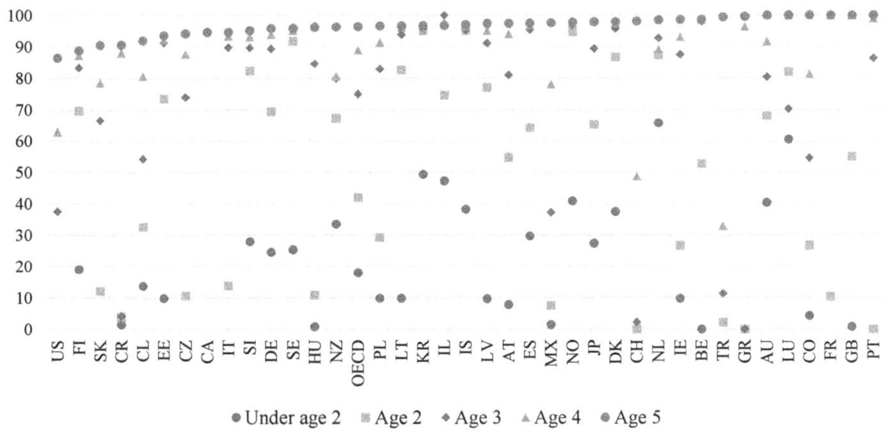

Fig. 3 Enrolment rates in OECD countries, 2022 (*Source* Elaborated from OECD (2024), Table B1.1. Data for some countries, especially during the first years of schooling, are non-available. In some countries, enrolment at ages 4 and 5 includes children enrolled in primary schooling)

Republic, Switzerland, or Slovenia, more than 95% of students in these age groups are enrolled in private publicly funded centres.

Figure 5 delves into the characterisation of different models of early childhood education, presenting by country the various forms of childcare for children during their early years, as well as the childcare gap, which can be defined as the amount of time between the end of paid parental leave and the start of free education. In Fig. 5, countries are ordered based on the duration of the childcare gap—from shortest to longest.

The duration of the maternity leave varies widely within the OECD. For example, compare the extreme situations of U.S. and Finland or Slovakia. As can be observed, free education at the early stages is a minority. Few countries guarantee free ECE for at least a duration of three years. Therefore, the childcare gap considerable differs between OECD countries. Seven countries have a childcare gap of five years during which households must independently find solutions for the care of their children. At the opposite end, seven countries have no childcare gap in the period from birth to the start of primary education. As seen in Fig. 4, participation rates in ECE are lower the younger the child is and significantly vary between countries. This is clearly linked to different models of early childhood care (Fig. 5) and means that whether a child is enrolled in school at a certain age in a specific country depends, to a greater or lesser extent, on the family income level (Fig. 6). Given the positive effects of early childhood education on a child's later development, this situation has important implications for equal opportunities, not only between countries but also within them.

Figure 6 ranks several OECD countries in descending order based on their enrolment rates for children aged 0 to 2 and compare them by families' income. Differences across countries are striking. In Scandinavian countries, for example, enrolment rates hardly differ based on family income level. In contrast, in countries like Switzerland

Panel A. 2013

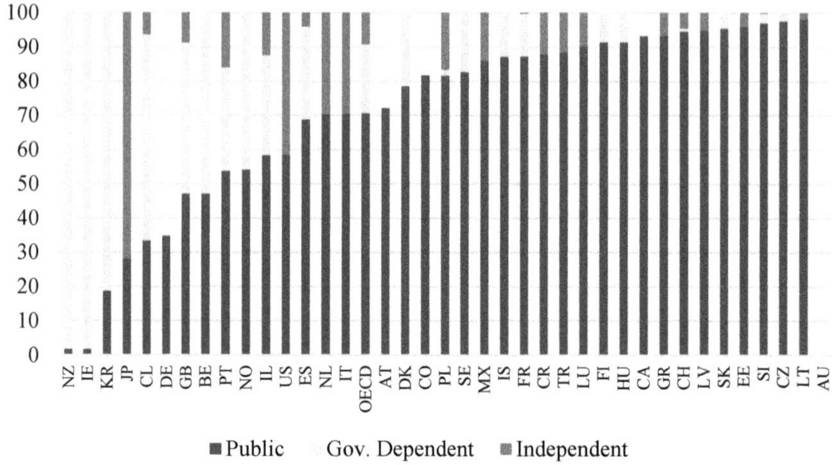

Panel B. 2022

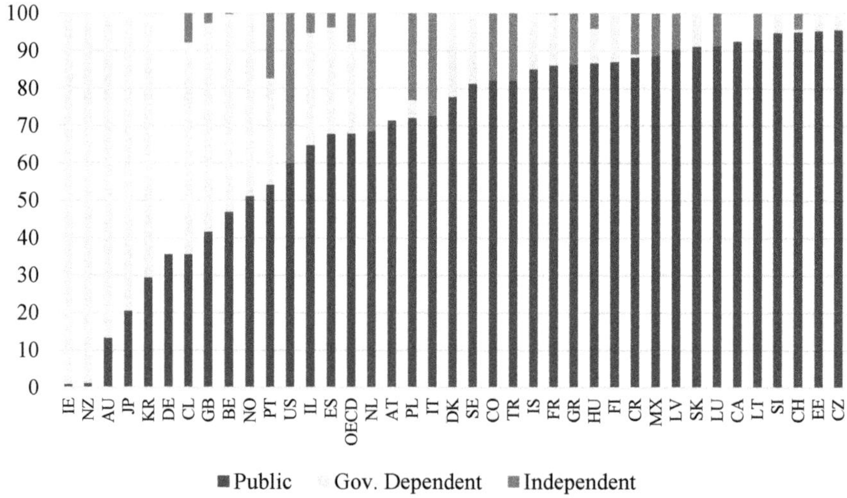

Fig. 4 Trends in the distribution of children enrolled in pre-primary education (ISCED 02) and type of institution (2013—Panel A and 2022—Panel B) in OECD countries (*Source* Elaborated from OECD (2024), Table B1.3. In 2013, data for Australia, not available; data for private institutions in Germany, Austria, Colombia and Canada not available. Data for Germany, Austria and Colombia, not available in 2022)

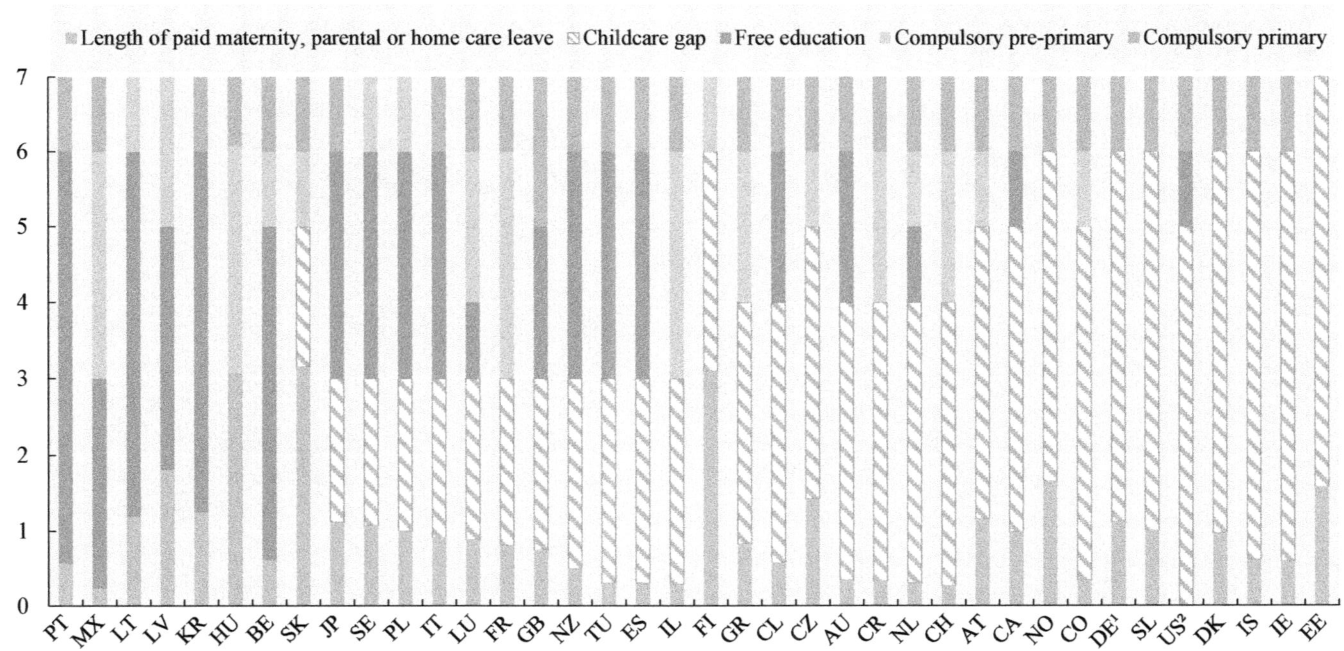

Fig. 5 Childcare gap in 2022, in OECD countries (*Source* Elaborated from OECD (2024), Figure B.1.3. *Notes* (1) Starting age and the extent of free ECEC vary by federal state. (2) Starting ages of free and compulsory education vary by state)

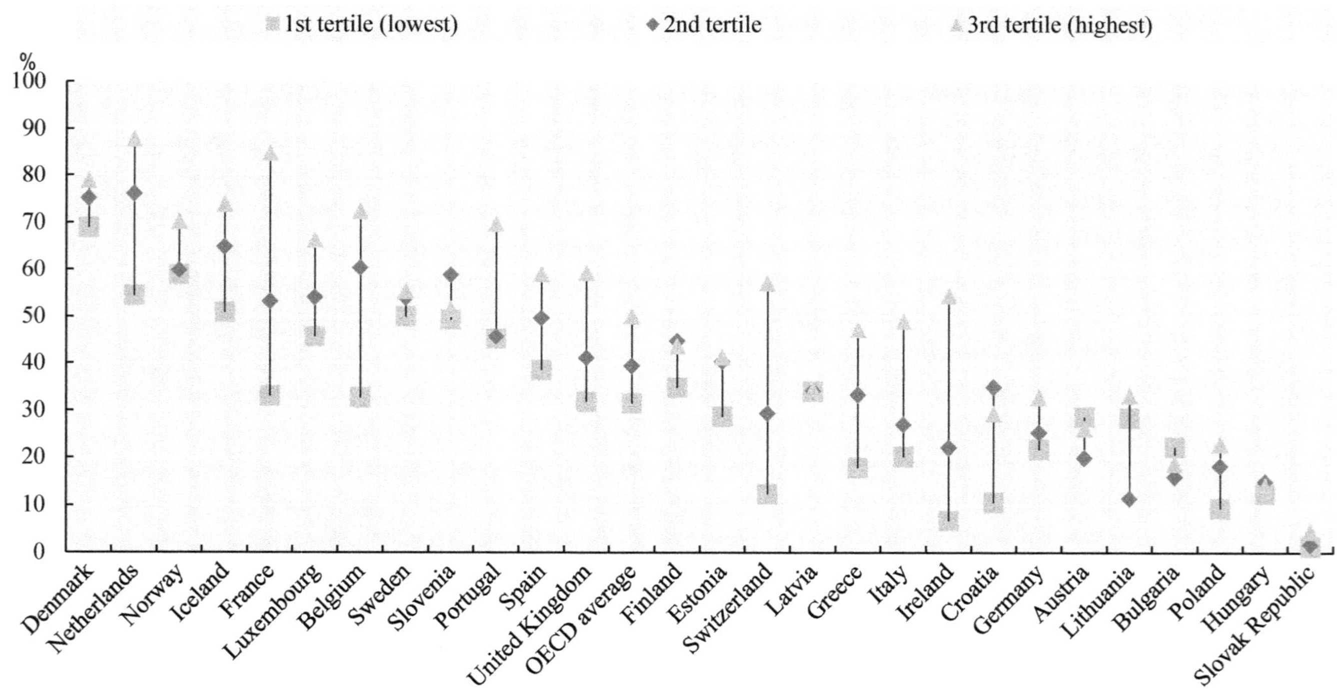

Fig. 6 Participation in early childhood education and care among 0–2-year-olds, by disposable income (2022) in OECD countries (*Source* Elaborated from OECD (2024), Figure B.1.5. Year of reference differs from 2022: 2018 for Iceland and United Kingdom, 2020 for Norway and 2021 for Switzerland)

or France, there are differences of over 50 percentage points between the enrolment rates of children from the lowest and highest income thirds. Remarkable differences based on income level are also observed in countries with low participation rates limited to two-year-olds (Fig. 3), such as Italy, Greece, or Ireland. It is worth noting, when comparing Figs. 5 and 6, that differences in enrolment based on income level are not necessarily linked to the duration of the childcare gap.

3 Conceptual Framework

The aim of this section is to provide a theoretical framework that facilitates understanding the underlying principles of empirical analyses measuring the impact of ECE on children's skills and well-being. To this end, the section first describes the educational production function (EPF) and details its main characteristics and implications for early childhood education. Subsequently, an economic model is presented to explain the determinants of family decisions regarding ECE, and to understand the mechanisms through which some public policies and programmes commonly evaluated in the literature might operate. This chapter introduces a simple model, but the Chapter 3b in this book discusses further extensions regarding the effect of parental models and the transmission of 'cultural' values in education. Finally, the main empirical challenges associated with the estimation of the impacts of ECE policies are briefly discussed, considering information limitations, and particularly the difficulty of identifying causal effects in practice.

3.1 The Educational Production Function

The educational production function is rooted in the human capital theory. According to this theory, the level of human capital results from investments made by individuals, which depend on their preferences and the expected benefits (Schultz 1960, 1961; Becker 1962). Within this framework, investment in education is considered the primary channel for acquiring human capital. Broadly speaking, the educational production function (EPF) establishes the productive relationship between educational resources (both familial and school-based) and educational outcomes (Hanushek 1979; Todd and Wolpin 2003). The primary precursor of the EPF—at least the most influential—is the well-known "Coleman Report" (1966), which, based on a survey of over half a million children from more than 3000 schools in the United States, examined the statistical association between educational outcomes and family socioeconomic characteristics, introducing the discussion about the role of school resources in the academic results. The report's main findings indicated that differences between schools had little to do with the student's achievements, with family background being the most significant determinant (see Chapter 3b, which presents different models that could explain the channels through which these backgrounds operate) as well as the characteristics of other students at the school (see Chapter 3c for a detailed discussion on peer effects). These conclusions and their implications for educational policy sparked considerable controversy and debate, as well as significant interest in studying the input–output relationship in the field of education economics (Hanushek 1986, 2003). This led to the development of various economic models based on the EPF to estimate causal relationships between resources and educational outcomes (see Todd and Wolpin 2003, for a detailed discussion of the main theoretical and empirical aspects of estimating the EPF).

The EPF applied to the context of early childhood education is closely related to the extensive and influential research conducted over the past two decades by James Heckman and his collaborators, focusing on the study of cognitive and non-cognitive skill formation, and combining multidisciplinary evidence from Economics, Neuroscience, and Psychology. In their seminal works, Cunha and Heckman (2007, 2008) propose an economic model to explain the "technology of skill formation" (TSF) for both cognitive and non-cognitive skills across multiple stages of childhood, aiming to systematise the available evidence on child development. Subsequently, various extensions have been carried out to propose alternative specifications or to impose identification assumptions in the economic model to address the most relevant challenges in estimating the TSF (see, for example, Cunha and Heckman 2008; Cunha et al. 2010; Attanasio 2015; Attanasio et al. 2022a).

While conceptually both approaches (the EPF and the TSF) share the same aim—studying the process of skill formation or educational outcomes in children—there are some nuances regarding their focus and assumptions. The TSF is primarily focused on studying the familial role and how the environment, characteristics, and family investments affect children's skill development. In this case, the focus is on family decisions, then the school resources—and public investment—are implicit in the model, included in the 'parental investment' component. That is, families decide to invest in one type of schooling (e.g., sending their children to private or public schools) based on their preferences, budget constraints, and available information, which, under the assumption of perfect information, would determine the level of school resources (we will revisit this point later). In contrast, the EPF is centred on the productive relationship between resources and educational outcomes (input–output relation), where school resources have an explicit role in the model and do not solely depend on family decisions but also on the decisions of the schools themselves and/or educational policy-makers (see Sect. 6 of Chapter 3b for a detailed discussion on how the interaction of multiple actors' decisions can affect student performance and the allocation of resources and efforts in education). Given that this chapter focuses on measuring the impact of early childhood education on children's skills, the EPF has been chosen as the main theoretical framework, incorporating some characteristics of the SFT proposed by Cunha and Heckman (2007).

In general terms, the EPF for early childhood education can be expressed as follows:

$$A_{it} = f_t\left(X_i, F_i, I_{i,1\ldots t}, S_{i,1\ldots t}\right) \tag{1}$$

where A_{it} represents the educational outcome of child i at the end of period t; X_i encompasses individual characteristics (including innate ability); the vector F_i represents exogenous family characteristics; the vector $I_{i,1...t}$ captures the family investments in educational resources and time accumulated up to period t; and finally, the component $S_{i,1...t}$ corresponds to the educational system resources accumulated up to period t. The function f_t indicates that the parameters of the EPF may vary over time, meaning that the impact of educational resources on children's skills can change with their age.

As can be seen from Eq. (1), the skill formation process is cumulative. Thus, skills produced at a certain stage accumulate with those obtained in subsequent stages, i.e., $\partial f_t(X, F_{1...t}, S_{1...t})/\partial A_{t-1} > 0$. This effect is what Cunha and Heckman (2007) refer to as *self-productivity* property. *Self-productivity* reflects the idea that skills reinforce and enhance each other. When multiple cognitive and non-cognitive skills are studied, this characteristic includes both intrinsic and cross-effects. For instance, acquiring non-cognitive skills like self-discipline at an early age enables higher levels of cognitive skills during later school stages (Duckworth and Seligman 2005).

Another feature of skill formation is what is known in the literature as *dynamic complementarity,* which refers to the fact that the level of skills acquired in period $t-1$, A_{it-1} (as a result of investments in $t-1$), makes investments in period t more productive in generating A_{it} (see, for example, Cunha and Heckman 2007; Cunha et al. 2010). In terms of the EPF in Eq. (1), the *dynamic complementarity* of family investments, F, would imply that $\partial^2 f_t(X, F_{1...t}, S_{1...t})/\partial A_{t-1}\partial F_{t'} > 0$. That is, investments in educational resources at an early age have effects not only in the period they are made but also in later ages. Additionally, *dynamic complementarity* also implies that for early investments to be productive in later periods, they must be followed by investments at later ages. Both characteristics—*self-productivity* and *dynamic complementarity*—create multiplier effects, which are the mechanisms through which the "skills beget skills" effect, popularised by Heckman and collaborators, occurs. These features are particularly relevant for understanding the mechanisms through which ECE impacts the level of skill development in children and, importantly, for interpreting medium and long-term effects. They are also highly useful for understanding why early investments in childhood education are particularly beneficial for economically disadvantaged students and, thus, for promoting equality of opportunity.

Exercise 1 *Assuming the following EPF:*

$$lnA_{it} = \beta_1 lnA_{it-1} + \beta_2 lnF_i + \beta_3 lnI_{it} + \beta_4 lnS_{it} + \varepsilon_{it}$$

Derive the effect of a policy to reduce class sizes in ECE at period t-1 on educational outcomes at t-1 and t. How does the result relate to the concepts of self-productivity and dynamic complementarity discussed earlier?

In Eq. (1), it is assumed that individual characteristics X_i and family characteristics F_i are exogenous components (the latter including family preferences and beliefs, parental education level, etc.), while family investments in educational resources $I_{i1...t}$ are endogenous. As for school investments $S_{i1...t}$, , one part is determined by the decisions of the families (e.g., the age at which schooling begins, hours of attendance, or the type of educational institution), and thus is endogenous; while another part is exogenous, as it depends on decisions made by the schools or educational authorities (decisions that families are unaware of when making their investment choices).

It is important to note that families can react (both in terms of home educational resources

$I_{i1...t}$ and child schooling $S_{i1...t}$) to changes in the other components of the EPF. Therefore, modelling the family decision-making process helps to understand the mechanisms through which early childhood education programmes or public policies can impact the skill development. For instance, if families anticipate a public policy or programme (such as the introduction of a subsidy for ECE services) and adjust their level of investment in home educational resources, the effect of the policy may be influenced by this reaction (either offsetting or amplifying the direct effect). Below we present an economic model that helps to understand the factors involved in family decisions on how much to invest in ECE for their children. As mentioned earlier, this chapter presents a simple model adapted to the case of early childhood education. Interested readers may refer to Chapter 3b for more specific models on the effects of parental models and the transmission of cultural values in education.

3.2 Determinants of Family Investment in ECE

One of the first decisions that families face regarding their children's education is how much to invest from a very young age. Specifically, families must decide when to start schooling, how many hours per day to allocate, and, most importantly, to choose the educational institution to send their children to. They consider various factors, such as the ability to balance work and family life (time constraints), their beliefs about the effectiveness of ECE for their child's development, the cost of the services, and the family's budgetary constraints, among other objective and emotional factors. Additionally, families need to determine how much time and money to invest in their children at home, considering the aforementioned factors.

On the other hand, educational authorities, also constrained by their own budgetary limitations, decide on the age from which ECE should be free and universal, as well as regulating the content and training of the teachers required to deliver this level of education, among other matters. These decisions can also impact the family's choices. In this context, having a conceptual framework helps to understand the mechanisms through which the effects of programmes and public policies operate (ideally facilitating their proper design). Moreover, modelling family behaviour can also be useful as a strategy for identifying the causal effects of educational resources, as will be discussed later.

Following Attanasio (2015), we present a model where the family's decision on investment in educational resources is based on optimising family's utility subject to a series of constraints. For simplicity, we will refer to $E_{i1...t}$ as the set of family investments in educational resources, which includes investments in home educational resources (materials and time)$I_{i1...t}$, , and investment in children's schooling (years of education, attendance time, type of institution, etc.), partly captured in the $S_{i1...t}$ component of the EPF (Eq. 1). Note that, if families were assumed to have perfect information about the quality and characteristics of educational institutions, as well as the importance of ECE, the $S_{i1...t}$ component would depend entirely on family decisions and, therefore, would be fully endogenous and could be included within the $I_{i1...t}$ component (see Cunha and Heckman 2007). In practice, families have a certain degree of information about the characteristics of educational institutions (some more than others), but this is far from being perfect. The model presented below is the simplest version in the literature, as the aim of this section is to discuss the most relevant factors that can affect family's decisions. For more complex specifications and the relaxation of various assumptions, see the works of Cunha et al. (2010) or Attanasio et al. (2020).

In general terms, the maximisation problem that families face when deciding how many educational resources to invest at early ages can be expressed as follows:

$$\max_{\{C_t, E_{i,t}\}} U\left(C_t, A_{i,t}\right) \tag{2}$$

$$s.a. C_t + P_t^E E_{i,t} = Y_t \tag{3}$$

$$A_{i,t} = f_t\left(X_i, F_i, E_{i,t}\right) \tag{4}$$

where C_t represents family consumption in period t; P_t^E reflects the vector of prices for educational investments $E_{i,t}$ (such as school fees, educational materials, etc.) in period t; and Y_t denotes the family's available economic resources in period t. Thus, investment decisions will depend on family preferences and tastes (U), the parameters of the EPF in Eq. 1 (f_t), the prices of the investments (P_t), , and the family's budgetary constraints (Y_t). Then, the educational investment function can be expressed as follows:

$$E_{i,t} = z_t(X_i, F_i, P_t, Y_t, f_t, U) \tag{5}$$

In other words, households maximise their utility based on their preferences and tastes, their budgetary constraints, and the level of information they have about the parameters of the EPF.

Exercise 2 *Assuming the same EPF as in Exercise 1 and taking into account the following educational investment function* $E_{i,t} = \delta_1 F_i + \delta_2 P_t + \delta_3 Y_t + \delta_4 S_{it}$, *derive the effect of the same classroom size reduction policy implemented in period t on* *educational outcomes in t, if families respond by reducing their level of investment* $E_{i,t}$. *What if they increased it?*

It is interesting to note that in the maximisation problem (2), it is assumed that there is no savings. Thus, family preferences and tastes depend on the utility they derive from consumption and the level of skills their children develop. Factors such as the level of altruism or paternalism explain why some families place a higher value on skill development and, therefore, invest more in educational resources for their children. Likewise, some families will place greater importance on the development of certain types of skills over others and will take their investments' decisions depending on its impact on each type of skill. Therefore, the parameters of the FPE are a determining factor in family investments.

Exercise 3 *Suppose families are unaware of the EPF and believe that classroom size does not affect their child's educational outcome* $A_{i,t}$. *How would the results from Exercise 2?*

The model presented assumes that there is only one child in the family, but if there are multiple children, parents will need to decide how much to invest in each child based on their characteristics (age, gender, perceived ability, etc.). Preferences regarding the allocation of investments within the household can be highly heterogeneous. For example, some families may choose to compensate for initial differences in abilities or, conversely, invest more in those children with higher abilities (Almond and Mazumder 2013). The literature on the allocation of educational investments within the home is extensive and exceeds the scope of this chapter, but Attanasio et al. (2022b) can be consulted for a broader discussion on this issue. Finally, societal changes and social preferences may also influence family tastes and preferences, which should be considered when interpreting the results in empirical analyses.

Another determining factor for families when choosing the optimal level of investment in early education is the budget constraint, which is determined by the investment price vector (given to families) and the family's economic resources. Higher investment prices or lower levels of resources lead to lower educational investments. In this sense, policies targeting low-income families that reduce investment prices (e.g., free ECE services, childcare vouchers, etc.) are often effective mechanisms for increasing early childhood education attendance in this population segment.

Finally, another highly relevant element in educational investment decisions is parents' knowledge and beliefs regarding their children's skill formation process and the importance of investments in educational resources. That is, the parameters of the EPF in Eq. 1. While initially standard economic models assumed that families were rational and had perfect information about the EPF, evidence from the last two decades has highlighted the importance of relaxing this assumption to consider the role of information imperfections in determining educational investments. The lack of information among families, both in terms of the quality of available early childhood education services and the impact of educational resources on their children's skill development, influences parental preferences and, consequently, the level of investments they make (Attanasio et al. 2022a; Cunha et al. 2022). This implies that, although families maximise their utility function (Eq. 2), the decisions they make regarding educational investment may be suboptimal as they are based on what parents perceive about the educational process and their children's developmental level.

Again, knowledge and information constraints are particularly relevant among low-income families, who tend to underestimate the returns on educational investments (Cunha et al. 2013; Attanasio et al. 2019). This fact, combined with beliefs about child-rearing, can be a key explanatory factor for the deficits in ECE investment among vulnerable families. In these contexts, public policies aimed at providing more and better information to parents can be effective mechanisms for promoting greater investment in ECE and thus enhancing children's skill development.

Exercise 4 *Discuss the pros and cons of the following mechanisms employed by households to obtain information about the importance and quality of early childhood education:*

1. *Word of mouth among family and friends.*
2. *Rankings appearing in several media.*
3. *Public information campaigns through advertising and media.*
4. *Public evaluations of the value-added by early childhood education centres.*

3.3 Challenges in Empirical Estimation of the Impact of ECE

Conducting impact evaluations to determine the effectiveness of ECE involves addressing several challenges. These include: (1) issues of endogeneity and self-selection; (2) challenges in defining and measuring the outcome of interest; and (3) a lack of sufficient data for conducting evaluations.

Let's begin with endogeneity and self-selection. In ECE, the non-random allocation of students across different centres—with different characteristics and quality, and a heterogeneous student body—is compounded by the complexity, typical of non-compulsory educational levels, that enrolled students have personal and family characteristics different from those who choose not to participate. For example, if we were interested in directly comparing the average outcomes between participants and non-participants in an ECE programme, the estimate might be biassed upwards if participants primarily come from favourable socioeconomic backgrounds. Even if we could control for a series of socioeconomic variables in our analysis, participants might fare better than non-participants simply due to having parents with more advantageous characteristics, regardless of their participation in the early childhood programme. The opposite would be true if the programme were primarily targeted at students with unfavourable personal and/or family circumstances.

It is also crucial to highlight the importance of choosing the appropriate counterfactual group, as evaluating the effectiveness of ECE can involve comparing participation to non-participation (e.g., staying at home with a family member or a babysitter) or comparing participation in an alternative programme to those participating in the programme being evaluated. In this case, participation by the control group in some form of alternative ECE might reduce the effect of the evaluated programme or explain the finding of diminishing effects over time. Naturally, this dynamic depends on the quality of the alternatives to the evaluated programme and the characteristics of the children both in the evaluated programme and in the counterfactual group.

Given the above, it is not surprising that studying causal relationships at the average population level (average treatment effects—ATE) is particularly challenging for this educational level, with more common analyses focusing on the effects of participation on specific subpopulations or the impact of specific policies on participants. Consequently, these are often impact evaluations with high levels of internal validity but very limited external validity. In any case, achieving internal validity involves correcting biases related to endogeneity and sample self-selection. Such correction can be achieved, as will be seen in Sect. 3.2, through experimental and quasi-experimental techniques.

A second challenge faced by impact evaluations in ECE is the difficulty in defining and measuring the outcome of interest. As mentioned earlier, this educational level has less structured curriculum content and objectives than compulsory education (especially in the first cycle of ECE), and the acquisition of non-cognitive skills, such as personal interaction, self-control, or attention, is central. Even if these skills are defined, measuring them is more complicated than, for example, measuring mathematics or language outcomes, which are usually quantified from primary school onwards through standardised tests, whether at the national or international level. Thus, short and medium-term evaluations of the impact of ECE outcomes often benefit from multidisciplinary approaches that incorporate psychometric elements—such as Peabody tests or SDQ from psychology—to accurately quantify non-cognitive outcomes.

However, much of the literature has focused on the impact of ECE on other types of adult outcomes, such as academic trajectory, employment, or criminal behaviour. In such cases, it is essential to track participants in ECE over decades and often to link early childhood education participation information with other administrative records.

This links to the third challenge in conducting impact evaluations in ECE: the scarcity of information on the educational trajectory and outcomes of the participants. This shortage, combined with the need for a temporal perspective to analyse outcomes over the life cycle, explains the relatively lower number of impact evaluations for ECE and the use of information from programmes implemented years or even decades earlier, with the limitations that this implies in countries with a less developed evaluation culture.

4 The Measurement of the Impact of ECE

To address the aforementioned challenges, the strategies used for impact evaluations in ECE—as in other education levels—can be divided into experimental and quasi-experimental approaches.

4.1 Experimental Evaluations

Experimental studies allow for precise estimation of the impact of ECE by randomly assigning participation in the evaluated programme. This intentional randomisation, which controls who participates and who does not, is known as *Randomised Controlled Trials* (RCTs). RCTs ensure comparability between the observable and unobservable characteristics of the treated group and the control group (see Chapter 2 for more detail on RCTs). Thus, if randomisation has been carried out properly, differences between the two subgroups can be only attributed to programme participation. It is noteworthy that in some situations, children do not receive the treatment they were assigned, leading to what is known in the literature as a *non-compliance* problem. For example, some children assigned to the ECE programme may not eventually participate due to family decisions, known as Never-Takers. Conversely, some children in the control group may end up participating in the programme, known as Always-Takers. In this case, comparing the treatment group to the control group would not allow for estimating the Average Treatment Effect (ATE) for the population but would identify the average effect of the intention to treat (Intention-to-Treat; ITT). In such a scenario, it is necessary to correct the estimates to estimate the Local Average Treatment Effect (LATE)—see Chapter 2 for a discussion on this—only for those children who adhere to the original programme assignment (compliers).

Despite being evaluations with high internal validity, most of the RCT-based evidence has focused primarily on analysing a series of programmes implemented locally in the United States for subpopulations with low socioeconomic status. Notable examples include the Perry Preschool Program (1962) in Michigan and the Carolina Abecedarian Project (1972) in North Carolina, which evaluated the impact of ECE on disadvantaged students; and the STAR (Student–Teacher Achievement Ratio 1985) project in Tennessee, which focused on analysing the impact of class size. Elango et al. (2016) provides a good summary of the findings from the first two experiments, while Chetty et al. (2011) and Dynarski et al. (2013) are prominent examples of impact evaluations conducted on the STAR project.

The impact of the Tennessee Voluntary Prekindergarten Program (TN-VPK), a programme for four-year-olds from low-income households, with disabilities, or non-English speakers, has also been evaluated through RCTs, leveraging the programme's excess demand (Lipsey et al. 2013). The results provide a less optimistic view of ECE participation compared to other programme evaluations, as positive effects—on cognitive and non-cognitive skills—identified one year after participating in TN-VPK diminish after a few years.

Lastly, another widely evaluated programme in the literature is the Head Start Impact Study in the U.S., the randomised evaluation of the federal Head Start programme, which provides, among other services, free ECE to children from low-income households. To do this, offers to participate in the programme were randomised in areas with excess demand, and this cohort was followed through to third grade. Lipsey et al. (2015a) and Kline and Walters (2016) are illustrative examples of evaluating the effectiveness of the Head Start on various educational and health outcomes.

In Europe, the use of RCTs for evaluating ECE programmes is notable in the United Kingdom and Denmark. In the UK, the Hackney Day Care Study evaluated the effects of participating in high-quality public ECE on the behaviour and non-cognitive skills of low-income children aged between 6 months and three years in that London borough (Toroyan et al. 2004). In Denmark, Jensen et al. (2013) examined the impact of Action Competences in Social Pedagogical Work with Socially Endangered Children and Youth (ASP), a programme aimed at improving teacher training in ECE centres, on cognitive skills and wellbeing levels of low-income children aged between 3 and 6 years in two Danish municipalities.

In summary, despite their generally higher internal validity, the number of RCTs in ECE is limited due to their high cost—which affects sample size—the potential for sample attrition (such as programme drop-out or loss to follow-up), especially when analysing long-term outcomes, and the previously mentioned lack of external validity.

4.2 *Quasi-Experimental Evaluations*

The fact that participation is not typically assigned randomly complicates the attainment of causal evidence regarding the effects of ECE. However, the use of quasi-experimental techniques such as Difference-in-Differences (DD), Fixed Effects Models, Instrumental Variables (IV), and Regression Discontinuity (RD) has enabled the provision of such evidence under the conditions discussed below. The application of these techniques relies on having microdata available at various points in time to link participation in ECE with later life outcomes.

DD models exploit temporal and/or geographic differences in the implementation of programmes and have been widely used for the evaluation of early childhood education. One feature that makes this approach popular is that it does not require longitudinal databases—relatively scarce—but can be applied using microdata that follow the same cohort over time. The main idea is to construct the treatment and control groups for different years based on varying implementation rates of ECE programmes. Thus, two differences are exploited: the change over time or between cohorts in treated areas (cities, districts, regions, etc.), and the change over time or between cohorts in initially untreated areas. For example, Felfe et al. (2015)

and Bosque-Mercader (2022) leveraged disparities in the speed of adaptation of Spanish regional educational systems to the General Organisation of the Educational System Law (LOGSE in Spanish), which established free ECE for children aged 3 to 5 years, to evaluate the effects of ECE participation on grade repetition and cognitive skills at age 15, and on the likelihood of developing diseases in adulthood, respectively. Callaway and Sant'Anna (2021) and Goodman-Bacon (2021) provide methodological solutions for the challenges of estimating DD with gradually implemented programmes.

As in other fields, heterogeneous effects of ECE are often evaluated through Difference-in-Differences-in-Differences (DDD) analysis, and efforts to establish the internal validity of DD models focus on demonstrating parallel trends prior to programme implementation. A relevant issue to consider is the possible endogeneity of varying programme implementation rates, suggesting the need for sensitivity tests using data from the year before the programme implementation (Cascio 2021). It should also be considered that families might alter their behaviour to ensure their child accesses the programme (e.g., through geographic mobility or persistent attempts to secure admission). In such cases, using sensitivity tests excluding years close to the implementation date could complement classic placebo tests, where the programme is simulated in different years or territories to achieve statistically insignificant results.

Fixed Effects Models exploit the diversity of treatment (attendance at ECE) within a clustering unit. Typically, these models use the household as the clustering unit and compare outcomes between siblings. Pages et al. (2020) and Berlinski et al. (2008) are representative examples. The key to estimating these models is having longitudinal databases—which explains why such analyses are mainly concentrated in the U.S. and naturally, identifying households where only some children have been affected by an ECE reform over which households have no decision-making power. Under this assumption, the results obtained will have high internal validity but will be restricted to households with more than one child.

Some studies evaluating the impact of ECE, particularly in Europe and Asia, have used the IV method. This method starts with a main model based on the EPF detailed in Sect. 3, where a particular outcome depends on a set of variables, including participation in an ECE programme. These approaches aim to overcome the problems of endogeneity and self-selection associated with programme participation by calculating a first-stage model where the endogenous variable (participation in ECE) depends on a set of control variables (used in the second-stage model) and at least one exogenous variable (instrument) that: (a) must be strongly correlated with the endogenous variable (instrument validity); and (b) must only affect the outcome variable in the second-stage model (the outcome of interest) through its effect on the endogenous variable (instrument exogeneity)—Chapter 2 provides a more detailed description of IV techniques. In ECE, commonly sources of exogenous variation used as instruments include the child's birth date and local temporal variation in ECE coverage (Nguyen 2022; Zachrisson et al. 2023), which are good examples respectively.

Results obtained from IV in ECE face the same challenges as in other areas. It should be considered that the presented estimators measure the Local Average Treatment Effect (LATE), so they only measure the effect for those who had their participation altered because of the chosen instrument. On the other hand, the validity and exogeneity of the instruments must be tested. It is pertinent to verify that families have not altered their behaviour. For the two mentioned instruments, this would involve ensuring that ECE centres could not bypass age-related enrolment regulations, and that the assumption of no geographic mobility is credible.

Finally, RD models are frequently applied to evaluate programmes where design involves surpassing a certain threshold for participant admission. In ECE, two commonly used criteria for determining admission are the child's age (Berlinski et al. 2011) and family income level (Carneiro & Ginja 2014). RD evaluations provide evidence very similar to that obtained through experimental approaches, assuming that individuals close to the threshold are, on average, identical in all their characteristics (observable and unobservable), differing only in whether they were admitted to the ECE programme. However, several warnings must be noted. Firstly, the estimated effects will be LATE, not Average Treatment Effects (ATE). That is, the estimated effects will not be extrapolatable to the general population but only to those who want to participate in ECE and are close to the threshold. Secondly, as Lipsey et al. (2015b) highlight, using age as a decision variable is particularly delicate. For example, given the young age of children, a few months' difference can result in significant differences in maturation levels, so results may be especially sensitive when using age as a discontinuity, depending on the selected interval of days or months. On the other hand, the counterfactual, when using age as the decision variable (running variable), will be all the experiences and activities of the child during the year before they become eligible (exceed the threshold) for the programme. Finally, literature shows strong heterogeneous effects of ECE (Lee et al. 2022), so using RD for its estimation, focusing on a very specific part of the population (those close to the threshold), may not be the most advisable. In summary, as with RCTs, these evaluations have high internal validity but limited external validity.

Exercise 5 *Propose the most suitable method for evaluating the impact of the following public policies. Consider the impact of interest and the type of information required for the evaluation and discuss the scope and limitations of the results.*

1. *Implementation of a programme providing tuition fee waivers for early childhood education centres based on a family income threshold.*
2. *Reduction of the student-to-teacher ratio in schools within a region, with a ten-year period for centres to adapt to the new regulations.*
3. *Extension of compulsory early childhood education from age two across your country starting January 1st in five years.*

5 Conclusions

In recent decades, ECE has experienced significant expansion, covering increasingly younger age groups. This evolution is explained by multiple factors such as the increased participation of women in the labour market, changes in family structures, and the growing recognition of the positive effects of early schooling. Evidence has demonstrated substantial benefits, both at the individual and societal levels, from early interventions like full-day ECE, improved teacher training, and universal access starting at age 3. Moreover, these benefits are greater for children from more disadvantaged backgrounds. Although much of this evidence comes from the implementation of programmes targeted at economically disadvantaged families in the U.S., it has also been shown that universal policies, more common in European countries, are effective—e.g., generating greater peer effects and standardising the quality of the education received by all students when they enter primary school. However, the available evidence is not conclusive on other relevant aspects of ECE policy design, such as class size reduction, the age at which early schooling should start (before age 3), or the determinants of the persistence of skills acquired during ECE.

On the other hand, the external validity of results obtained through strategies like RCT, IV, or RD is limited, as they focus on estimating Local Average Treatment Effects (LATE) or, in the case of RCTs, on very specific population subgroups. Evidence has highlighted significant heterogeneity in the effects of policies based on various population profiles. These studies are useful for identifying programmes that work for specific groups but less so for understanding why these programmes work or for designing systemic policies. Therefore, an interesting avenue to explore is combining impact evaluations with the estimation of parameters from the models discussed in Sect. 3 of this chapter. For example, using social experiments to estimate parameters of the Family Production Function (FPE) or the function of family investment in ECE. Such exercises would not only estimate the impacts of interventions but also identify the mechanisms through which they operate.

Additionally, it is important to note that, at the early childhood level, accompanying impact evaluations with cost estimates is particularly crucial. This is because early education has alternatives outside of formal schooling (e.g., staying at home) and alternative interventions, such as programmes aimed at strengthening the family-child bond, which can be equally effective and less costly. Moreover, it is important to consider that at early ages, simply talking to the child, reading a book, or engaging in simple games can have significant effects on the child's cognitive development and can sometimes be more cost-effective than investing more resources in ECE.

References

Almond, D., and B. Mazumder. 2013. Fetal origins and parental responses. *Annual Review of Economics* 5 (1): 37–56.

Attanasio, O. P. 2015. The determinants of human capital formation during the early years of life: Theory, measurement, and policies. *Journal of the European Economic Association* 13 (6): 949–997.

Attanasio, O., F. Cunha, and P. Jervis. 2019. Subjective parental beliefs. Their measurement and role (No. w26516). National Bureau of Economic Research.

Attanasio, O., S. Cattan, E. Fitzsimons, C. Meghir, and M. Rubio-Codina. 2020. Estimating the production function for human capital: Results from a randomized controlled trial in Colombia. *American Economic Review* 110 (1): 48–85.

Attanasio, O., T. Boneva, and C. Rauh. 2022a. Parental beliefs about returns to different types of investments in school children. *Journal of Human Resources* 57 (6): 1789–1825.

Attanasio, O., S. Cattan, and C. Meghir. 2022b. Early childhood development, human capital, and poverty. *Annual Review of Economics* 14: 853–892.

Barr, A., and C. R. Gibbs. 2022. Breaking the cycle? intergenerational effects of an antipoverty program in early childhood. *Journal of Political Economy* 130 (12): 3253–3285.

Becker, G. S. 1962. Investment in human capital: A theoretical analysis. *Journal of Political Economy* 70 (5, Part 2): 9–49.

Berlinski, Samuel, Sebastian Galiani, and Marco Manacorda. 2008. Giving children a better start: Preschool attendance and school-age profiles. *Journal of Public Economics* 92: 1416–1440. https://doi.org/10.1016/j.jpubeco.2007.10.00.

Berlinski, S., S. Galiani, and P. J. Mc Ewan. 2011. Preschool and maternal labor market outcomes: Evidence from a regression discontinuity design. *Economic Development and Cultural Change* 59 (2): 313–344.

Blau, D. M. 2021. The effects of universal preschool on child and adult outcomes: A review of recent evidence from Europe with implications for the United States. *Early Childhood Research Quarterly* 55: 52–63.

Bosque-Mercader, L. 2022. *The effect of a universal preschool programme on long-term health outcomes: Evidence from Spain* (No. 2022–07). FEDEA.

Bowne, J. B., K. A. Magnuson, H. S. Schindler, G. J. Duncan, and H. Yoshikawa. 2017. A meta-analysis of class sizes and ratios in early childhood education programs: Are thresholds of quality associated with greater impacts on cognitive, achievement, and socioemotional outcomes? *Educational Evaluation and Policy Analysis* 39 (3): 407–428.

Callaway, B., and Sant'Anna, P. H. 2021. Difference-in-differences with multiple time periods. *Journal of Econometrics* 225 (2): 200–230.

Carneiro, P., and R. Ginja. 2014. Long-term impacts of compensatory preschool on health and behavior: Evidence from Head Start. *American Economic Journal: Economic Policy* 6 (4): 135–173.

Cascio, E. U. 2021. *Early childhood education in the United States: What, when, where, who, how, and why* (No. w28722). National Bureau of Economic Research.

Cascio, E. U. 2023. Does universal preschool hit the target? Program access and preschool impacts. *Journal of Human Resources* 58 (1): 1–42.

Chetty, R., J. N. Friedman, N. Hilger, E. Saez, D. W. Schanzenbach, and D. Yagan. 2011. How does your kindergarten classroom affect your earnings? Evidence from Project STAR. *The Quarterly Journal of Economics* 126 (4): 1593–1660.

Coleman, J. S. 1966. *Equality of educational opportunity* [summary report (Vol. 1). US Department of Health, Education, and Welfare, Office of Education.

Cunha, F., and J. Heckman. 2007. The technology of skill formation. *American Economic Review* 97 (2): 31–47.

Cunha, F., and J. J. Heckman. 2008. Formulating, identifying and estimating the technology of cognitive and noncognitive skill formation. *Journal of Human Resources* 43 (4): 738–782.

Cunha, F., J. Heckman, and S. Schennach. 2010. Estimating the technology of cognitive and noncognitive skill formation. *Econometrica* 78 (3): 883–931.

Cunha, F., I. Elo, and J. Culhane. 2013. *Eliciting maternal expectations about the technology of cognitive skill formation* (No. w19144). National Bureau of Economic Research.

Cunha, F., I. Elo, and J. Culhane. 2022. Maternal subjective expectations about the technology of skill formation predict investments in children one year later. *Journal of Econometrics* 231 (1): 3–32.

De Haan, M., and E. Leuven. 2020. Head start and the distribution of long-term education and labor market outcomes. *Journal of Labor Economics* 38 (3): 727–765.

Duckworth, A. L., and M. E. Seligman. 2005. Self-discipline outdoes IQ in predicting academic performance of adolescents. *Psychological Science* 16 (12): 939–944.

Duncan, G. J., and K. Magnuson. 2013. Investing in preschool programs. *Journal of Economic Perspectives* 27 (2): 109–132.

Duncan, G., A. Kalil, M. Mogstad, and M. Rege. 2022. Investing in early childhood development in preschool and at home. *NBER Working Papers*. 29985.

Duncan, G., A. Kalil, M. Mogstad, and M. Rege. 2023. Investing in early childhood development in preschool and at home. In *Handbook of the economics of education*, Vol. 6, ed. Stephen J. Machin, Ludger Woessmann, and Eric A Hanushek, 1–91. North Holland.

Dynarski, S., J. Hyman, and D. W. Schanzenbach. 2013. Experimental evidence on the effect of childhood investments on postsecondary attainment and degree completion. *Journal of Policy Analysis and Management* 32 (4): 692–717.

Elango, S., J. L. Garcia, J. J. Heckman, and A. Hojman 2016. Early childhood education. In *Economics of means-testing transfer programs in the United States*, Vol. 2, ed. Robert Moffitt, 235–297.

Felfe, C., N. Nollenberger, and N. Rodríguez-Planas. 2015. Can't buy mommy's love? Universal childcare and children's long-term cognitive development. *Journal of Population Economics* 28: 393–422.

Felfe, C., and L. Zierow. 2018. From dawn till dusk: Implications of full-day care for children's development. *Labour Economics* 55: 259–281.

García, J. L., J. J. Heckman, and A. L. Ziff. 2019. Early childhood education and crime. *Infant Mental Health Journal* 40 (1): 141–151.

García, J. L., J. J. Heckman, and V. Ronda. 2023. The lasting effects of early-childhood education on promoting the skills and social mobility of disadvantaged African Americans and their children. *Journal of Political Economy* 131 (6).

Goodman-Bacon, A. 2021. Difference-in-differences with variation in treatment timing. *Journal of Econometrics* 225 (2): 254–277.

Hanushek, E. A. 1979. Conceptual and empirical issues in the estimation of educational production functions. *Journal of Human Resources* 14 (3): 351–388.

Hanushek, E. A. 1986. The economics of schooling: Production and efficiency in public schools. *Journal of Economic Literature* 24 (3): 1141–1177.

Hanushek, E. A. 2003. The failure of input-based schooling policies. *The Economic Journal* 113 (485): F64–F98.

Heckman, J. J. 2011. The economics of inequality: The value of early childhood education. *American Educator* 35 (1): 31.

Heckman, J. J. 2012. Invest in early childhood development: Reduce deficits, strengthen the economy. *The Heckman Equation* 7 (1–2).

Jensen, B., A. Holm, and S. Bremberg. 2013. Effectiveness of a Danish early year preschool program: A randomized trial. *International Journal of Educational Research* 62: 115–128.

Joo, Y. S., K. Magnuson, G. J. Duncan, H. S. Schindler, H. Yoshikawa, and K. M. Ziol-Guest. 2020. What works in early childhood education programs? A meta–analysis of preschool enhancement programs. *Early Education and Development* 31 (1): 1–26.

Kline, P., and C. R. Walters. 2016. Evaluating public programs with close substitutes: The case of Head Start. *The Quarterly Journal of Economics* 131 (4): 1795–1848.

Lee, S. Y., J. Rodgers, R. Kim, and S. V. Subramanian. 2022. Distributional effects on children's cognitive and social-emotional outcomes in the Head Start Impact Study: A quantile regression approach. *SSM-Population Health* 18: 101108.

Li, W., G. J. Duncan, K. Magnuson, H. S. Schindler, H. Yoshikawa, and J. Leak. 2020. *Timing in early childhood education: How cognitive and achievement program impacts vary by starting age, program duration, and time since the end of the program* (Ed WorkingPaper No. 20-201). Annenberg Institute for School Reform at Brown University.

Lipsey, M. W., K. G. Hofer, N. Dong, D. C. Farran, and C. Bilbrey. 2013. *Evaluation of the tennessee voluntary prekindergarten program: End of pre-k results from the randomized control design.* Vanderbilt University. Peabody Research Institute.

Lipsey, M. W., D. C. Farran, and K. G. Hofer. 2015a. *A randomized control trial of a statewide voluntary prekindergarten program on children's skills and behaviors through third grade.* Research Report. Peabody Research Institute.

Lipsey, M. W., C. Weiland, H. Yoshikawa, S. J. Wilson, and K. G. Hofer. 2015b. The prekindergarten age-cutoff regression-discontinuity design: Methodological issues and implications for application. *Educational Evaluation and Policy Analysis* 37 (3): 296–313.

Lubotsky, D., and R. Kaestner. 2016. DoSkills Beget skills'? Evidence on the effect of kindergarten entrance age on the evolution of cognitive and non-cognitive skill gaps in childhood. *Economics of Education Review* 53: 194–206.

McCoy, D. C., H. Yoshikawa, K. M. Ziol-Guest, G. J. Duncan, H. S. Schindler, K. Magnuson, and J. P. Shonkoff. 2017. Impacts of early childhood education on medium-and long-term educational outcomes. *Educational Researcher* 46 (8): 474–487.

Nguyen, C. V. 2022. The effect of preschool attendance on children's health: Evidence from a lower middle-income country. *Health Economics* 31 (8): 1558–1589.

OECD. 2024. *Education at a glance 2024: OECD indicators.* OECD Publishing.

Pages, R., D. J. Lukes, D. H. Bailey, and G. J. Duncan. 2020. Elusive longer-run impacts of head start: Replications within and across cohorts. *Educational Evaluation and Policy Analysis* 42 (4): 471–492.

Schultz, T. W. 1960. Capital formation by education. *Journal of Political Economy* 68 (6): 571–583.

Schultz, T. W. 1961. Investment in human capital. *The American Economic Review* 51 (1): 1–17.

Todd, P. E., and K. I. Wolpin. 2003. On the specification and estimation of the production function for cognitive achievement. *The Economic Journal* 113 (485): F3–F33.

Toroyan, T., A. Oakley, G. Laing, I. Roberts, M. Mugford and J. Turner. 2004. The impact of day care on socially disadvantaged families: An example of the use of process evaluation within a randomized controlled trial. *Child: Care, Health and Development* 30 (6): 691–698.

Ulferts, H., K. M. Wolf, and Y. Anders. 2019. Impact of process quality in early childhood education and care on academic outcomes: Longitudinal meta-analysis. *Child Development* 90 (5): 1474–1489.

UN. 2015. *Transforming our world: The 2030 Agenda for Sustainable Development.* United Nations.

Van Huizen, T., and J. Plantenga. 2018. Do children benefit from universal early childhood education and care? A meta-analysis of evidence from natural experiments. *Economics of Education Review* 66: 206–222.

Zachrisson, H. D., E. Dearing, N. T. Borgen, A. M. J. Sandsør, and L. A. Karoly. 2023. Universal early childhood education and care for toddlers and achievement outcomes in middle childhood. *Journal of Research on Educational Effectiveness* 1–29.

Post-compulsory Education

Aitor Lacuesta, Brindusa Anghel, Marcel Jansen, and Ana Regil

1 Introduction

At the end of compulsory education stage, students can choose to start working, continue with vocational training, or pursue an academic education. This decision has significant consequences for their future well-being and labor market situation, as it affects their ability to gain further knowledge and higher academic degrees, which can lead to future income streams and better-quality jobs. Actually, this decision is made gradually and sequentially from the end of compulsory education, until individuals decide to finish their education, at least temporarily.

Figure 1 illustrates the percentage of individuals aged 25–34 who have attained at least upper secondary education (post-compulsory education) in OECD countries. This percentage ranges from nearly 100% in Korea to less than 50% in countries such as Costa Rica, Mexico, and India. On average, 86% of individuals in this age group across OECD countries have reached this level of education, indicating that a significant proportion of young adults choose to continue their education beyond compulsory schooling.

In most countries, upper secondary education prepares students either for further study in tertiary education or for entering the labor market with the relevant skills through vocational training and education programs. In this respect, Fig. 2 shows the share of individuals aged 25–34 whose highest level of education has a vocational orientation, by different levels of educational attainment, in OECD countries. There is considerable variation among countries, with this share exceeding 50% in countries like Austria and Germany which have strong vocational training systems, compared to 20–25% in countries like Korea, United Kingdom, and Portugal. On average, in

A. Lacuesta (✉) · B. Anghel · A. Regil
Banco de España, Madrid, Spain
e-mail: aitor.lacuesta@bde.es

M. Jansen
Universidad Autónoma de Madrid y FEDEA, Madrid, Spain

A. Cabrales and I. Sanz (eds.), *Economics of Education*,
https://doi.org/10.1007/978-3-031-90911-5_10

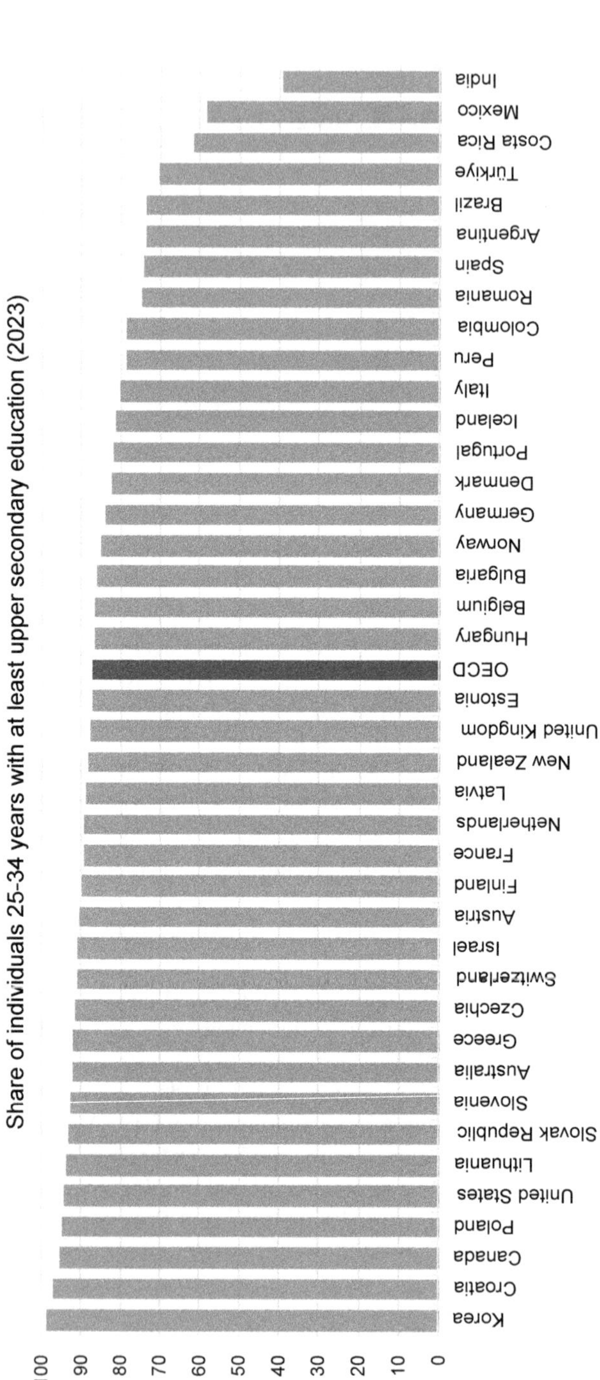

Fig. 1 Share of individuals 25–34 years with at least upper secondary education (2023) (*Source* OECD Education at a Glance 2024. *Note* Share of individuals 25–34 years with at least upper secondary education in total of individuals 25–34)

OECD countries, about 1 in 3 students 25–34 year-olds have a vocational training qualification as their highest level achieved.

Furthermore, integrating work-based learning into vocational education and training is a distinguishing element in such programs which has many benefits. It could help students acquire both technical and soft skills in real-world settings and it could reduce training costs for schools. Additionally, it strengthens connections between schools, individuals, and potential employers (see OECD 2023). Despite these recognized benefits, Fig. 3 shows that there are many differences across countries with respect to the share of vocational students who are enrolled in combined school- and work-based programs in which the work-based component is at least 25%. In some countries, this share is above 90%. These are basically apprenticeship programs (Denmark, Germany, Hungary, and Switzerland). Countries like Romania, Sweden, or Spain where this share is below 10% have made efforts in recent years to expand the use of such work-based learning.

This chapter will analyze how individuals select their post-compulsory education paths, distinguishing between the decision to continue studying into tertiary education or to follow vocational education and training, which facilitates early entry into the labor market.

The chapter is structured as follows: Sect. 2 explains the international classification of education levels in order to highlight differences in post-compulsory education attainments across countries, providing some examples. Section 3 outlines the theoretical and empirical framework for educational decisions and the returns on post-compulsory education. Section 4 discusses the theoretical framework for choosing between vocational or academic training. Section 5 explores into the decision-making process between traditional or dual vocational training. Finally, Sect. 6 concludes the chapter.

2 How to Compare Educational Systems Across Countries

Comparing educational systems at the international level is a complex issue. This chapter uses the International Standard Classification of Education (ISCED) by UNESCO, which classifies degrees based on the skills acquired at each education level, the degree of complexity and specialization, the age of entry, and the organization of each program. According to this classification, several levels lay within the compulsory education period:

- ISCED 1: Primary education provides fundamental skills in reading, writing, and mathematics with minimal specialization. The age of entry is between 5 and 7, and the education is usually delivered by one main teacher. It lasts between 4 and 6 years.

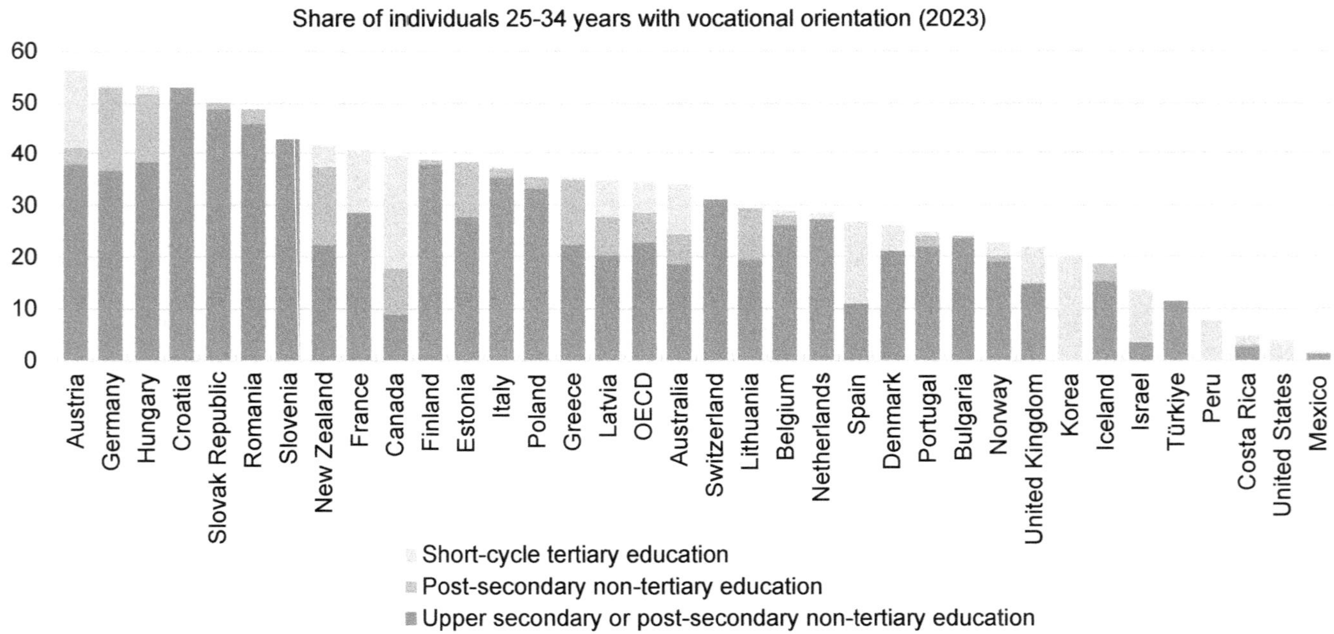

Fig. 2 Share of individuals 25–34 years with vocational orientation (2023) (*Source* OECD Education at a Glance 2024. *Note* Share of individuals 25–34 year-olds with vocational orientation at the level of at least upper secondary education in total of individuals 25–34)

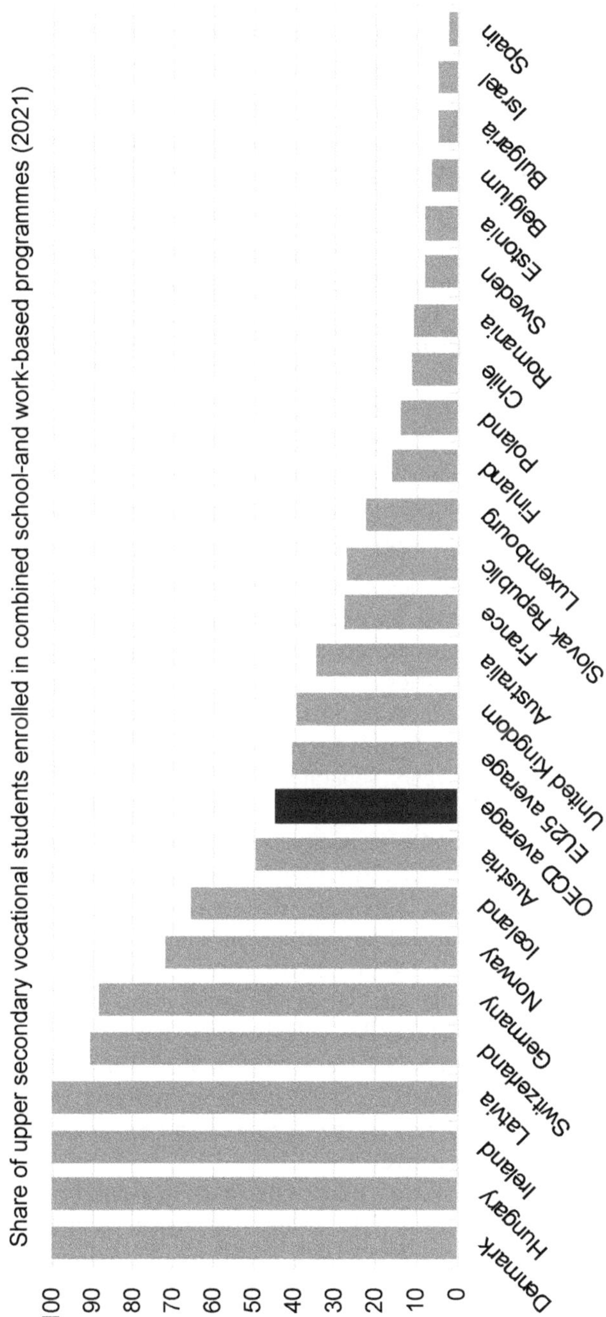

Fig. 3 Share of upper secondary vocational students enrolled in combined school- and work-based programmes (2021) (*Source* OECD Education at a Glance 2024. *Note* Share of individuals 25–34 year-olds with vocational orientation at the level of at least upper secondary education in total of individuals 25–34)

- ISCED 2: Lower secondary education lays the foundation for lifelong learning and human development. The age of entry is between 10 and 13, and it is organized around a more subject-oriented curriculum taught by several teachers with specialized knowledge. It lasts around 4 years.

The rest of educational levels are usually non-compulsory because individuals might decide to initiate them at an age when they are also legally allowed to work. Therefore, this makes labor market conditions at the age of entry to post-compulsory education very relevant to understand the decisions of individuals:

- ISCED 3 and 4: Upper secondary education prepares students for tertiary education or provides skills relevant to employment. The age of entry is between 14 and 16. These levels offer an increased range of options and streams, with teachers often highly qualified in their subjects or fields of specialization. These studies last between 2 and 4 years.
- ISCED 5 to 8: Tertiary education provides learning activities in specialized fields with a high level of complexity. There is a clear hierarchy between qualifications granted by tertiary education: short-cycle programs of around 2 years are considered ISCED 5; bachelor first degree programs are considered ISCED 6; masters are ISCED 7; and Ph.D. programs are ISCED 8.

The National Institutes of Statistics match their own country educational classifications to ISCED levels. That is, for example, how statistics like the European Labour Force Survey (LFS) can provide a homogeneous comparison of educational attainments across European countries. As an example, below it is compared the selection into post-compulsory education in the four major Euro Area countries (France, Germany, Italy and Spain). Figure 4 compares the educational attainment in 2023 of youth between 25 and 29 years, separately for males and females. The share of low educated (ISCED 0–2) males is the lowest in France (11.8%), followed by Germany and Italy (19.6% and 19.4% respectively). Spain has the highest share of young males with at most ISCED 2 (27.7%). Regarding post-compulsory education, Germany and Italy stand out with a high share of young men that achieved middle studies (ISCED 3–4)—48.6% and 54.2%—while France and Spain excel in tertiary education (ISCED 5–8)—48.2% and 47.3% respectively.

Females have a higher educational attainment than males in the four countries. The share of low educated (ISCED 0–2) females is the lowest in France (8.9%), followed by Germany and Italy (14.8% and 14.9% respectively). Spain has the highest share of youth females with at most ISCED 2 (18.8%). Again, Germany and Italy stand out in middle studies (45.8% and 47.1%), while France and Spain excel in tertiary education (55.8% and 59.9% respectively).

Figure 5 illustrates the evolution over time of the share of youth between 25 and 29 years with an education level of ISCED 2 or lower in France, Germany, Italy, and Spain. In 1993, France and Germany had a fairly low share of youth males with low education (26% and 10% respectively), while Italy and Spain had a high share (55% both). A similar picture emerged for females, with France and Germany standing out (25% and 13%) and Italy and Spain lagging behind (52% and 51% respectively).

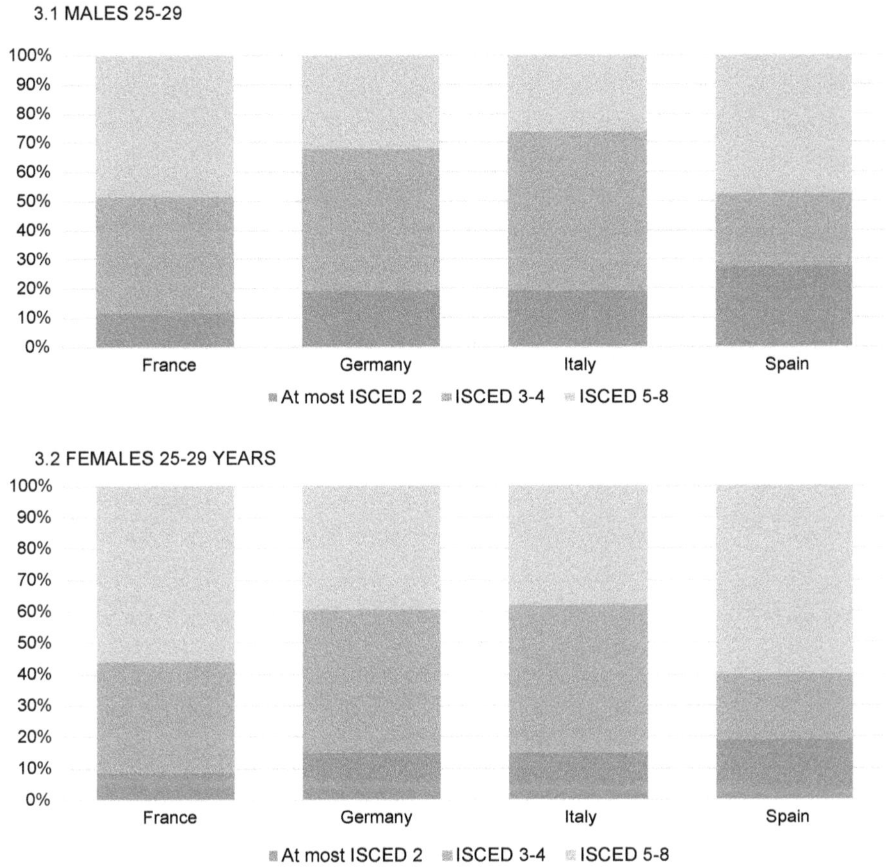

Fig. 4 Educational attainment distribution of 25–29 years old (2023) (*Source* Eurostat [Labor Force Survey 2023])

However, over the last 30 years, there has been a convergence in the proportion of individuals with at most ISCED 2 level of education among the four countries.

When interpreting those figures subtle differences on the structure of the educational system across countries and over time are crucial. Here are two examples:

German and French educational system: In Germany, specialization begins in ISCED 2, while in France it is postponed to ISCED 3. This different timing of specialization might affect transitions into vocational training and university in later stages.

Germany has a primary school level (4 or 6 grades) followed by an early tracking system with three streams: "*Hauptschule*" (low track leading to blue-collar apprenticeship training after 9th grade), "*Realschule*" (medium track leading to white-collar apprenticeship training after 10th grade), and "*Gymnasium*" (high track continuing until grade 12th-13th to enter college or university).

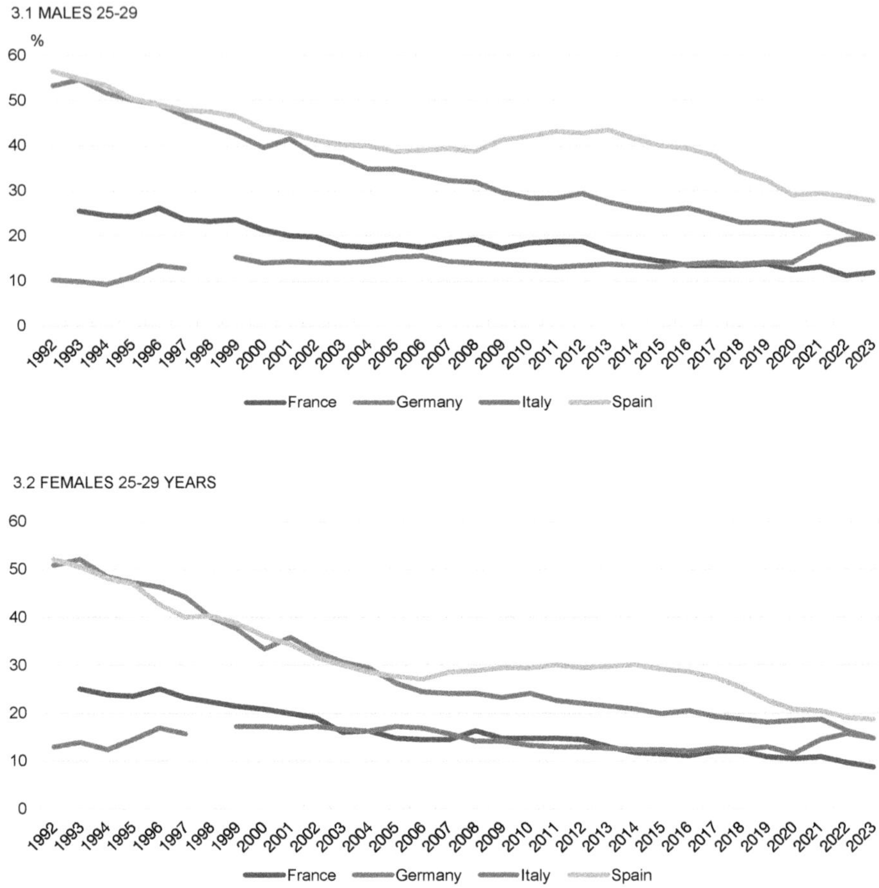

Fig. 5 Share of individuals 25–29 years with an education level of ISCED2 or below (2023) (*Source* Eurostat [Labor Force Survey, 2023])

In France, there is a primary degree (5 grades) followed by a common lower secondary degree called "*Collège*" that covers compulsory education up to 9th grade (ISCED 2). Afterward, students take the "*Lycée*" for the final three grades up to 12th grade (ISCED 3). The "*Lycée*" provides a "*Baccalaureat*" degree to proceed to university, with options for a "*Baccalaureat Professionnel*" through a "*Lycée professionnel*" or as an on-the-job apprentice, since one can leave school at the age of 16. This delayed specialization in France might decrease the willingness to pursue vocational training after completing the lower secondary level compared to Germany.

Italian and Spanish educational system: In Italy, ISCED 3 starts early (in 9th grade) and lasts up to 5 years. In Spain it starts later (in 11th grade) and lasts only 2 years, which makes students perceive this education level as a preparation for tertiary education rather than a final stage.

The Italian system is similar to the French one, with a primary degree (5 grades) followed by a common lower secondary degree called "*Scuola media*" up to 8th grade (ISCED 2). Afterward, students can choose among three types of "*Scuola superiore*" which lasts between 3 and 5 years (ISCED 3): "*Struzione e formazione professionale*" (blue-collar apprenticeship training, up to 11th grade), "*Instituto tecnico-professionale*" (blue and white-collar apprenticeship training, up to 13th grade), and 5 years of "*Liceo*" (in order to attend university, up to 13th grade).

In Spain, there is a common primary degree (6 grades) followed by a common lower secondary degree called "*Educación Secundaria Obligatoria (ESO)*" covering compulsory education up to 10th grade (ISCED 2). In 9th grade, one might enter "*FP básica*" (blue-collar apprenticeship training, also ISCED 2). After 10th grade, one might choose "*FP Media*" (blue or white-collar apprenticeship training, ISCED 3) or "*Bachillerato*" (high track continuing until grade 12th to attend college or university, ISCED 3).

On top of these general differences across countries, there might be regional issues that might affect the comparability of individuals even within a country. For example, in Germany the regulation of the education system belongs to the regions, which complicates homogenization of the education levels even further. In particular, "*Hauptschule*" is only offered in six federal states: Bayern, Hessen, Niedersachsen, Nordrhein-Westfalen, Rheinland-Pfalz, and Saarland.

3 Is it Worth Studying?

3.1 Theoretical Framework

To analyze the factors behind the decision to study after compulsory education, we can use a stylized version of the model in Altonji (1993). This model incorporates several interesting features like preferences for studying, the ability to pass grades, earning returns for the knowledge acquired and the possibility to continue studying implying even higher returns. The decision-making process is as follows:

- Initial Decision: After finishing lower secondary education, a student must decide what to do next (s_1): start working $(s_1 = l)$ or going to upper secondary school $(s_1 = a)$. If the individual starts working after the training period, she obtains the discounted present value of her income expectation throughout life, denoted as Y_0. On the other side, if she continues to study, she will obtain knowledge that will later be rewarded with a return r_1 above the previous income stream.
- Knowledge Acquisition: In school, general knowledge (k) is acquired, and a student will graduate from upper secondary school when this knowledge exceeds a certain threshold. The accumulation of knowledge depends on an initial level of knowledge (k_0), which is a function of ability, parental background, and other factors discussed in Chapter 5. It also depends on a random component that can be

related to various factors, such as the possibility of having a bad teacher or a bad class, discussed in Chapters 6 and 7. The accumulation of knowledge is crucial because completing a certain level of education requires that knowledge surpasses a specific threshold. The probability of success *(g) depends on the accumulation of knowledge and* is conditional on the student's initial level of knowledge:

$$k_1 = f(k_0, \varepsilon_1)$$

$$g = P\left(k_1 > \overline{k_1}|k_0\right)$$

- Preference Uncertainty: There is an additional source of uncertainty: the preference to study, which is revealed before initiating the academic year. This allows individuals to decide to abandon studies just before starting the course. One could be Θ_0 (a person who does not like to study) or Θ_1 (a person who has no preference restrictions).
- Return on Education: Completing upper secondary education provides a certain return (r1). Consequently, the decision to continue studying involves comparing:

$$\theta_0 Y_0 + \theta_1(1-g)\frac{Y_0}{(1+R)} + \theta_1 g\frac{Y_0(1+r_1)}{(1+R)} > Y_0$$

If people have neither preference restrictions nor chances of failing high school, the decision boils down to comparing earnings streams: $(1+r_1)/(1+R)>1$. In the particular case when $(r_1 = \text{R})$, both streams of earnings for low and high educated individuals are equal.

- Tertiary Education: Completing upper secondary education allows entrance to tertiary education. If this option exists, returns from higher degrees should be included in the previous expression, properly weighted by at least the probability of success.

Exercise 1

Altonji (1993) clearly shows the difference between ex-ante and ex-post returns. State two mechanisms within the Altonji model by which a student could decide to drop out of school even though the chosen option presents a high ex-post return (ra > R). Can you think of other mechanisms that might affect the decision of education and that are not in the previous model? [Hint: Once you have thought of some additional mechanism you can find some related ideas in Wiswall and Zafar (2015) or Coelli (2011)].

3.2 *Empirical Framework for Educational Decisions and Returns*

The common empirical framework correlates the decision to continue studying or the probability of obtaining a high degree with changes in the relative economic opportunities for both groups. If s represents the educational outcome dependent on the relative income of educational options $\left[\frac{W(s)}{W(0)}\right]$, along with other observable (z) and unobservable (u) variables for the econometrician, the regression used in these studies is as follows:

$$S(W(s)/W(0), z) = \beta_0 + \gamma\left[\frac{W(s)}{W(0)}\right] + \beta_1 z + u$$

As seen in the previous section, u can include variables such as innate abilities or family background that affect both the decision to pursue education and the labor market performance of the highly educated. Moreover, aggregate relative wages are related to changes in the relative supply of high and low educated. Consequently, the estimation of the previous equation using Ordinary Least Squares (OLS) would not be appropriate. To avoid this bias, researchers often seek for situations where an economic disturbance has exogenously increased the demand for job opportunities for a particular group. For example, a construction boom related to changes in financial conditions, growth of the agriculture sector related to weather or particular shocks in industries like mining or textile exports should disproportionately increase job opportunities for low-skilled workers without being related to changes in the supply of low skilled.

Many other studies do not focus on calculating the elasticity of continuing education relative to labor opportunities. Instead, they aim to directly estimate the internal rate of return (IRR) for an additional year of education (ρ). By conceptualizing education as an investment, this parameter determines whether further education is worth it. Continue studying provides an earning premium during someone life but this premium should be compared to what is foregone during the period of study. The return from completing s years of education is defined as the discount rate that equates the present value of earnings over years of experience x (up to retirement age $X(s)$, which may also depend on years of education) with both opportunity costs (the present value of foregone income from not being educated) and the monetary and non-monetary costs of education $C(s)$. Mathematically, in discrete time, it can be expressed as:

$$\sum_{x=0}^{X(s)} \frac{W(s,x)}{(1+\rho)^{x+s}} - \sum_{x=0}^{X(0)} \frac{W(0,x)}{(1+\rho)^{x}} - C(s) = 0$$

This return can be compared to the interest rate at which an individual can borrow or to the returns from alternative investments to determine whether continuing education is a “good” or “bad” investment.

From Mincer (1974), the term returns to education also applies to the coefficient of the variable "years of education" in a particular equation. Assume that *W(s,x)* represents the wage level given *s* years of education and *x* years of experience. Then, the logarithm of wage is represented as:

$$\ln(W(s,x)) = \alpha_0 + \rho s + \alpha_1 x + \alpha_2 x^2 + \varepsilon$$

The justification for this model comes from human capital theory, which suggests that investments in human capital occur primarily early in life, either through education or as a result of time spent in training during the initial years of work (Becker 1962). To account for diminishing learning over the lifespan, a quadratic term in experience is incorporated.

Heckman et al. (2006) detail the conditions necessary for the coefficient in the above regression estimated by Ordinary Least Squares (OLS) to be equal to the internal rate of return from the previous expression:

1) There should be no costs associated with education.
2) Active working years should increase one-to-one with years of education.
3) Salaries should increase linearly with years of education, without non-linearities across different educational levels.
4) There must be separability between education and years of experience, meaning that the slopes across the life cycle for different educational levels should be equal.
5) There should be no correlation between ε and s, i.e., no omitted variable in the regression that could affect both wages and the decision to pursue education.
6) Returns should be homogeneous across the population.

Exercise 2:
If we assume that labor earnings given an educational level remain constant throughout life and that the retirement age increases one-to-one with years of education, the present value of income, expressed in continuous time, for a given educational level (s) is:

$$V(s) = \int_{s}^{T+s} \frac{W(s)}{e^{rt}} dt$$

Demonstrate, as Heckman suggested, that in the absence of education costs, the internal rate of return on education (*V(s)* = *V(0)*) is equal to the coefficient in a Mincer regression.

A review of several articles conducted by Card (2018) suggests that, using European data, the coefficient per year of education in this regression would range from 5% for Sweden to 10% for the United Kingdom. In the United States, the coefficient would be close to 10%. This return is significantly higher compared to the returns on other investments and implies a strong incentive to pursue education.

However, some of the abovementioned conditions may not hold, potentially reducing educational returns for at least a significant portion of the population.

Heckman et al. (2006) demonstrated that in the case of the United States, monetary costs of education (point (1)) only slightly diminish the estimated returns, by one or two percentage points. Differences in the age of retirement (point (2)) should not affect much the estimated rate of return since earnings late in life are highly discounted. On the contrary, using a different functional form in estimation, rather than the traditional linear relationship between education years and returns (points (3) and (4)), significantly impacted the estimated returns. Specifically, Heckman et al. (2006) employed functional forms that allow for non-linearity in returns across education years and account for different interactions between education and experience. As a result, they obtained different returns compared to those estimated by the Mincer equation, but they were very high for completing a bachelor's degree (between 10 and 12 years) and a university degree (between 12 and 16 years). All this evidence together with the high returns to schooling in the United States made Heckman suggest that the fact that a big fraction of individuals stop schooling in early stages might be partially related to the presence of important non-monetary costs to continue studying.

Points (5) and (6) might also be important and must be taken into consideration when interpreting mincerian regressions. Card (2001) discusses how selection bias and heterogeneity of returns in the population can affect estimates. Selection bias should theoretically bias estimates upward. However, most studies that use changes in the educational system as instruments for educational decisions find coefficients larger than those obtained by OLS. According to Card, this discrepancy may arise because instrumental variables, while addressing endogeneity, have a challenging interpretation when there is substantial heterogeneity in returns across the population. In particular, an educational system reform, which serves as an instrument, likely aims to improve academic performance for disadvantaged groups. Consequently, if many individuals from these groups did not pursue education due to financial constraints rather than low expected returns, the instrumental variable coefficient would overestimate higher returns.

In summary, the estimation of mincerian regressions usually obtain large coefficients for the variable years of education, even when education is properly instrumented. However, the interpretation of those estimates as the internal rate of return in a specific economy and time period is not straightforward. Studies should discuss the underlying assumptions, including the chosen functional form for the estimation and potential heterogeneity in returns across the population.

Other practical considerations come into play when estimating mincerian regressions. First, some studies calculate wage differentials between higher and lower degrees without using the continuous variable of years of education. In such cases, the regression coefficient should not be directly interpreted as the internal rate of return, as the return must account for income earned after several years of study. Consequently, the internal rate of return will be lower than the coefficient estimated in the regression. Also, note that income can be either gross or net of taxes. In the latter case, progressive income tax schemes generally lead to lower educational returns.

Additionally, the regression can be conducted for hourly, monthly, or yearly income. Since individuals with more education tend to work more hours and days per month or year, the differentials will increase with the chosen unit of measurement. This is especially relevant for countries where unemployment rates and job insecurity are high for individuals with lower education levels. Finally, it should be noted that the performance estimated from a mincerian equation is the ex-post return of one year of education, something very different to the ex-ante return as pointed out in 3.1. Obviously, the estimation of these ex-ante returns requires a greater number of variables, in particular, data on educational transitions and probabilities of success. There are not many studies that calculate them (see Cunha y Heckman 2007, for more details and comparisons between ex-ante and ex-post returns).

3.2.1 Elasticity of Low-Skilled Labor Opportunities and Post-Compulsory Education

This subsection presents results of a group of studies which estimate the causal elasticity of economic opportunities for low-skilled workers regarding school dropout or educational attainment. These papers analyze how job opportunities for low-skilled individuals affect schooling decisions using particular events in the labor market of some countries. The tricky part of those studies is to ensure the exogeneity of those events with respect to educational developments. To exemplify this, we use two papers that relate the poor educational performance in Spain between 1994 and 2008 with the housing boom that took place during those years.[1] Let's go back to Fig. 5. Notice that between 1990 and 2023, Italy and Spain converged in terms of educational attainment with France and Germany. However, the convergence process in Spain stopped for the cohorts aged 25 to 29 between 2007 and 2016. Those young individuals had to decide whether or not to continue post-compulsory education between 1994 and 2008. Unlike other economies, Spain reduced the wage premium of education between 1995 and 2008. This fall in the wage differential by educational level has been corroborated by different authors and using different databases (Pijoan-Mas and Sánchez-Marcos, 2010; Izquierdo and Lacuesta 2012; Bonhomme and Hospido 2017). It also contrasts with what has been documented for other countries such as the USA (Autor et al. 2008), United Kingdom (Gosling et al. 2000), Canada (Fortin et al. 2012) and Germany (Dustmann et al. 2009). In particular, in these countries, it has been argued that, at the top of the distribution of wages, there was an increase in the demand for workers with higher education caused by changes in technology. Therefore, some authors have suggested the importance of the complementarity between education and information technology. However, Spain's growth in the late 90 s and early 2000s was caused by a real estate boom that increased the relative demand for construction workers. This boom in job opportunities for the less educated changed the incentives to continue in the education system. If we consider 1995 as the start of the real estate boom and 2008 as the start of the financial crisis and housing bust,

[1] See also the remarks at the end of Sect. 2.

this means that the cohorts born between 1978 and 1991 had to decide whether to enter the workforce or pursue further education to post-compulsory degrees, all while facing significant economic disruptions.

Using this period of falling returns to education derived from the real estate boom, several authors have causally linked the economic opportunities of the less educated to the slowdown in Spain's educational improvement.

Aparicio-Fenoll (2016) uses information from the Labour Force Survey (LFS) 2001–2006 for the population between 16 and 18 years old, wage information at the provincial level for the same period from the Continuous Sample of Working Histories 2007 and the value added of construction at province level from the regional accounts of the Spanish National Institute of Statistics (Instituto Nacional de Estadística). Her hypothesis is that the weight of construction at the provincial level correlates with the job opportunities of men with less training relative to women. On the other hand, she argues that the growth of construction activity at the provincial level was motivated by causes which are exogenous to the decision of individuals to pursue further education. Therefore, this makes it a good instrument for gender differences in the wage differential between trained and untrained individuals. In this way, she analyzes differences between men and women in the decision to pursue further education, according to variations in relative wage differentials motivated by construction activity at the provincial level. The article finds that a 10% decrease in the wage differential of educated and uneducated workers decreases the probability of enrollment in post-compulsory education by at least 2% of the average transition rate (from 80%) and decreases the proportion of those who complete the degree by at least 0.2% of the average degree completion rate (87%).

Lacuesta et al. (2020) confirms this result using a different empirical strategy. The authors use information from the Labour Force Survey 1993–2007 for the population of 17 and 25 years old, wage information at the provincial level for the same period from the different waves of the Continuous Sample of Working Histories and the register of collective agreements between 1990 and 2009. The starting hypothesis is that collective agreements for different professional categories correlate well with wage differentials by contribution group. Also, the authors argue that whoever negotiates the agreements does not take into account the job opportunities of young people so collective agreements are a good instrument for wage differentials by educational attainment. Thus, they analyze at the provincial level how changes in relative wages derived from what was negotiated in agreements affect educational decisions. They find that a 10% increase in the relative wages of unskilled workers for cohorts that turn 17 years old results in an increase of 2 to 6% points in the probability of remaining with only a degree of compulsory education. Their empirical specification goes further by distinguishing between workers with university education and those with technical training. This distinction allows them to argue that the increase in the proportion of young men with only basic schooling occurs at the expense of the proportion of young men who follow a secondary academic trajectory, rather than vocational training.

Comparable elasticities have been found in other studies analyzing similar events in other countries and contexts. Black et al. (2005) examine the decision to enroll in post-compulsory secondary courses in Kentucky and Pennsylvania in the 70 s and 80 s. This decision was affected after the embargo on oil shipments from OPEC to the United States in the early 70 s causing a boom in the coal mines of rural Appalachia. Thus, those municipalities with greater coal reserves experienced an increase in the wages of high school dropouts relative to graduates during the 70 s followed by a decline during the 80's. Estimates indicate that a 10% increase in the income of unskilled workers could decrease enrollment rates in post-compulsory secondary school by up to 5–7%. Also, Atkin (2016), documents that changes in training in Mexico derived from the growth of job opportunities for people with less education during a period of trade reforms that took place between 1986 and 2000. Specifically, those cohorts that at 16 years old experienced in their communities a greater increase in employment in export industries achieved a lower number of years of education. For every 25 new jobs, there would be a dropout of 1 ninth-grade student.

Exercise 3
In addition to changing the return on education, the real estate boom caused a change in asset prices, especially in housing. Argue to what extent this channel could affect the educational decisions of families distinguishing by the level of household income and the country of residence. [Hint: Once you have thought of some argument you can find some related ideas in Lovenheim (2011)].

3.2.2 Estimation of Internal Rates of Return of Education for the Four Major Euro Area Economies

This subsection illustrates how to calculate internal rates of return (IRR) for different schooling levels across different countries and over time. This exercise uses four waves of the Household Finance and Consumption Survey from the European Central Bank, HFCS from now onwards, from 2010 to 2020.[2] We continue providing evidence for the 4 major Euro Area economies. Consistent with the approach used in Figs. 5 and 6, we group education levels into three categories: ISCED 0, 1 and 2 form the first group; ISCED 3 and 4 form the second group; and ISCED 5 to 8 form the third group (tertiary education, encompassing from short-cycle degrees to Ph.D levels). The concept of earnings is gross annual labor income including in kind payments for all employees.[3] We calculate real annual earnings by adjusting nominal annual earnings using the Eurostat harmonized consumer price index (HICP) for each country.

We first estimate mincerian regressions separately for each country (c), schooling level (s) and gender (g). The regressions include experience (x) and experience squared (x^2). Experience is calculated by subtracting the estimated age of completing

[2] More details on the webpage of HFCS: https://www.ecb.europa.eu/pub/research-networks/html/researcher_hfcn.en.html#docs.

[3] Notice that we only consider labor income of employees and we do not consider income of self-employed.

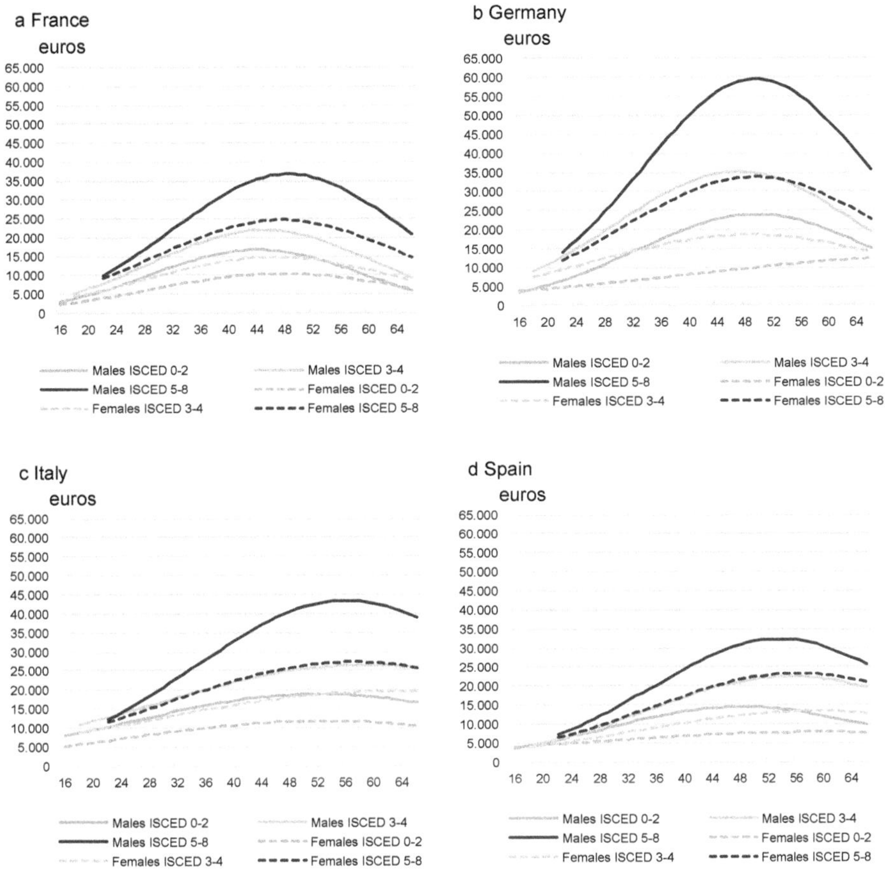

Fig. 6 Earnings profile over the working life, by gender and education level (*Source* Calculations using the microdata of the Household Finance and Consumption Survey [European Central Bank])

education for each level from the current age: age-16 for lower secondary education and less, age-18 for upper secondary education, and age-22 for tertiary education. By estimating separate regressions we avoid problems (3) and (4) abovementioned by Heckman et al. (2006).

$$\ln(W(x)|c, s, g) = \alpha_0^{c,s,g} + \alpha_1^{c,s,g} x + \alpha_2^{c,s,g} x^2 + \varepsilon^{c,s,g}$$

We could have used a different functional form than the quadratic to better capture the big raise in earnings that usually occurs in the first years of labor career (see Murphy and Welch (1990). In particular, we have checked that results do not change much when using a quartic on experience instead of a quadratic specification.

Given the coefficients $\left(\alpha_0^{c,s,g}; \alpha_1^{c,s,g}; \alpha_2^{c,s,g}\right)$ one can estimate labor earnings over the life cycle in each country and for each schooling level by gender. Figure 6 shows the estimated wage profiles which are used to calculate IRRs.

Table 1 computes IRR comparing the ex-post earnings stream of a tertiary degree and that of a lower secondary degree. Consistently with other international evidence, we obtain very high returns, above 10%. Spain and Italy face the lowest returns (13% and 11% for males and 14% for females, respectively), while France and Germany face the highest returns (19% and 24% for males and 23% for females, respectively). In general, returns for females are higher than those for males. These results are consistent with the relatively poor educational attainment in Spain and Italy described in Sect. 3.2.2.

In general terms, returns are diminishing across the hierarchy of degrees. This means that, except for Spain, returns are higher when comparing a lower and an upper secondary degree than when comparing a tertiary and an upper secondary degree. On the other hand, returns for tertiary education relative to an upper secondary degree are more similar across countries, Italy being the country with lower returns. It is noticeable that the premium for tertiary education in Spain is higher than in Italy and Germany.

Note also that the estimated earnings profiles over the life cycle were constructed with people belonging to different cohorts. Consequently, changes over time in the educational system of different countries might affect the estimation. The fact of having 4 different waves of the HFCS allows the construction of a synthetic cohort panel to check for possible changes in the quality of the education level of different cohorts. Cohorts are defined by birth year, grouped into 5-years intervals. Figures 7, 8, 9, and 10 show the average earnings profile of different cohorts by age. In most of the countries and educational levels there is no clear pattern of improvement by cohort with maybe the exception of tertiary education in Italy and Germany. This could be a potential explanation for the low tertiary education premium in these two countries which was estimated with the 4 waves.

Assuming that there were not changes of quality of cohorts, one could estimate returns to education over time. Figure 11 uses the 2010 and the 2020 waves of the HFCS to compare the evolution of returns over time, for upper secondary education relative to lower secondary education. On the one hand, in Spain, the IRR doubled for both males and females between 2010 and 2020. Italy also faced a slight increase for males. On the other hand, IRR in France and Germany remained unchanged,

Table 1 Internal Rates of Return for different countries and gender

	University vs. Lower secondary			
IRR	Spain	Italy	German France	France
Male	13%	11%	24%	19%
Female	14%	14%	23%	23%

Source Calculations with the Household Finance and Consumption Survey 2010–2020 (European Central Bank)

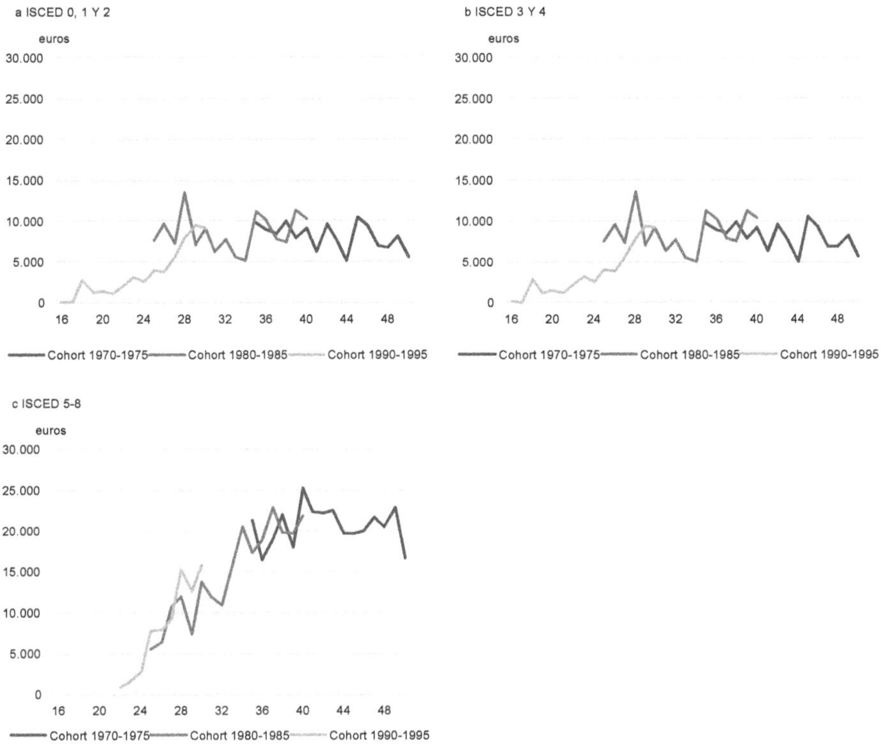

Fig. 7 Earnings profile over the working life, by level of education, for different cohorts. SPAIN (*Source* Calculations using the microdata of the Household Finance and Consumption Survey [European Central Bank])

except for males in Germany that suffered a big drop. Consequently, assuming no changes of quality of cohorts, during the last decade, there was a big convergence of IRR within the four major Euro Area economies.

4 Vocational or Academic Training?

4.1 Theoretical Framework

Altonji's model sketched in Sect. 3.1 could be enlarged by incorporating different streams in the upper secondary level (vocational and academic).

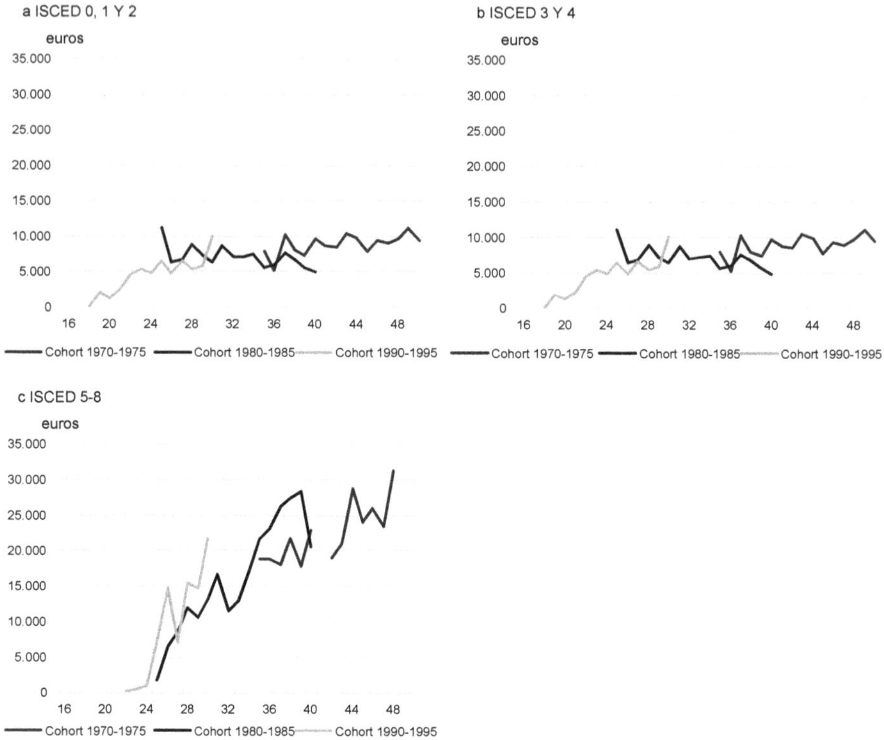

Fig. 8 Earnings profile over the working life, by level of education, for different cohorts. ITALY (*Source* Calculations using the microdata of the Household Finance and Consumption Survey [European Central Bank])

- Initial Decision: In this case, the student decides between: start working ($s_1 = l$), go to a medium vocational training degree ($s_1 = p$) or continue the academic path into high school ($s_1 = a$). Different streams can result in different returns throughout the lifetime span.
- Knowledge Acquisition: Vocational training offers professional knowledge (k_p) that differs from academic knowledge (k_a). It is typically more applied and focused at learning how to operate at the current technological level. Academic knowledge is usually more theoretical and useful for adapting to a changing world or for developing new technologies. The accumulation of knowledge will be stream dependent:

$$k_{1,p} = f\left(k_{0,p}, s_1, \varepsilon_1\right)$$

$$k_{1,a} = f\left(k_{0,a}, s_1, \varepsilon_1\right)$$

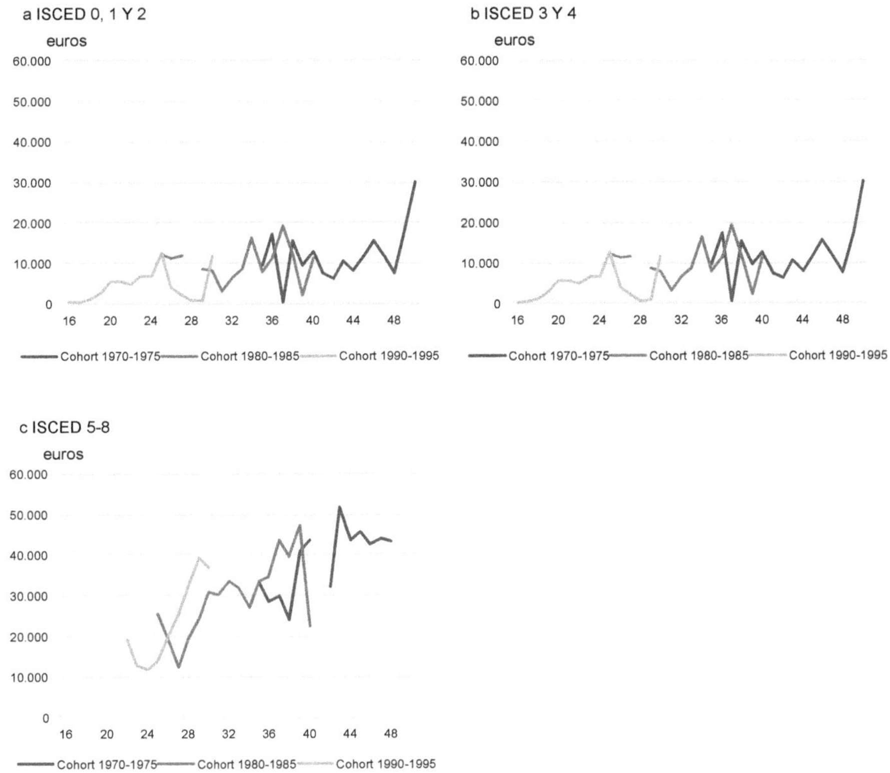

Fig. 9 Earnings profile over the working life, by level of education, for different cohorts. GERMANY (*Source* Calculations using the microdata of the Household Finance and Consumption Survey [European Central Bank])

The probabilities of success g_p, g_a on each stream are conditional on the ability of the student in that particular field of specialization and the stream chosen:

$$g_p = P\left(k_{1,p} > \overline{k_p} | k_{0,p}, s_1\right)$$

$$g_a = P\left(k_{1,a} > \overline{k_a} | k_{0,a}, s_1\right)$$

- Preference Uncertainty: Now, there could be an additional typology of person: One could be Θ_0 (a person who does not like to study at all), Θ_1 (a person who does not like to study but is willing to learn a profession) and Θ_2 (a person who has no preference restrictions).

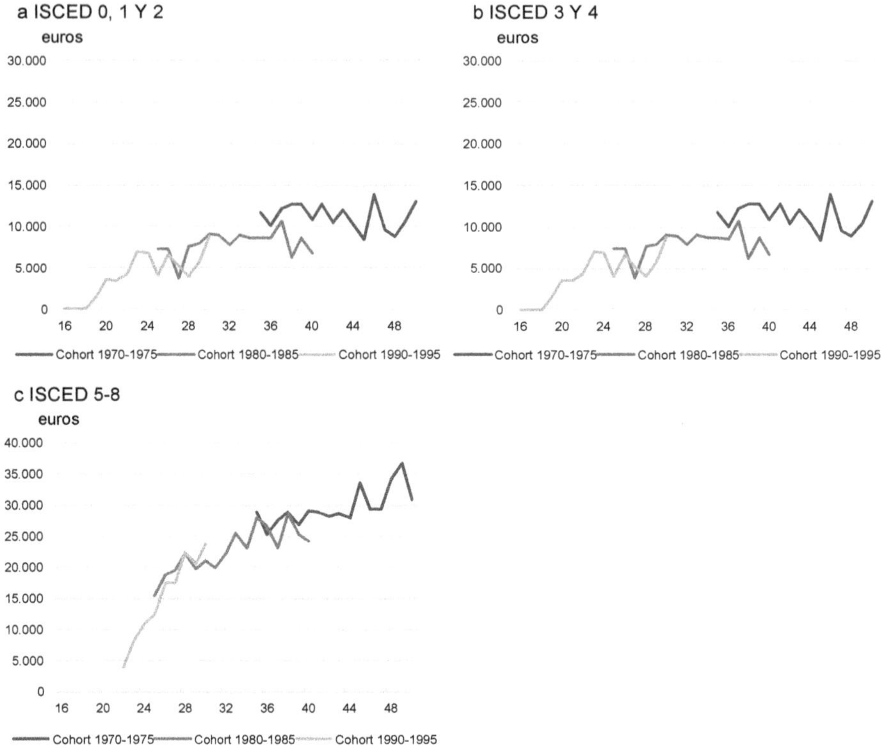

Fig. 10 Earnings profile over the working life, by level of education, for different cohorts. France (*Source* Calculations using the microdata of the Household Finance and Consumption Survey [European Central Bank])

- Return on Education: Completing the vocational training stream provides a certain return (r_p), while the academic stream offers a different return (r_a). Consequently, the decision to continue studying involves comparing ex-post and ex-ante returns of those two streams.

Some papers have used the difference between professional and academic skills across countries and individuals to explain differences in aggregate growth and life cycle earnings. As stated before, the skills acquired in the professional stream do not have to be the same as those learned in the academic one, so the labor income of the same number of years of education can be different depending on the chosen path. Krueger and Kumar (2004) suggest that academic education facilitates workers to operate with new production technologies, while professional studies are focused on teaching to operate established technologies. The authors use this idea to underline that vocational training policies in Europe facilitated its economic growth relative to the USA during the 60 s and 70 s, when technology was stable. However, at present, with a more changing technological context, they could be harming it. Following the same idea, Hanushek et al. (2017) suggest that vocational training degree holders

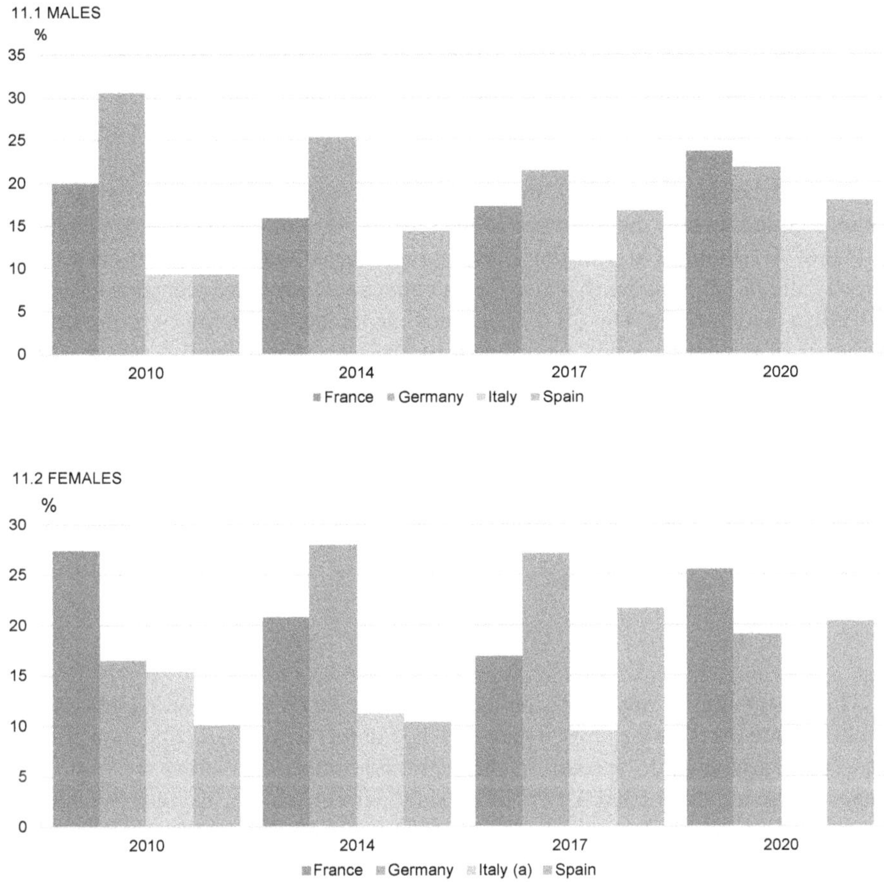

Fig. 11 Internal rates of return for upper secondary education relative to lower secondary education, by gender (2010 and 2020), for the four major European countries (*Source* Calculations using microdata of the Household Finance Consumption and Consumtpion Survey 2010–2020 [European Central Bank]. *Notes* a For Italy it was not possible to estimate precise internal rates of return for females for the year 2020)

might acquire skills that could facilitate the transition to the labor market in the short term, but could become obsolete at a faster rate than academics in the long term. As a consequence, they might face high earnings just after completing the formation period at the cost of having a flat slope over the lifetime span. The following section present some papers that tackle this question empirically.

4.2 Empirical Framework for Educational Decision and Returns from Vocational and Academic Training

The empirical framework in Sect. 3.2 might be used to compare vocational and academic training but with one key distinction: wage earnings over a lifetime should depend both on the years of education and the type of training. A good starting point for understanding how the inclusion of the type of curriculum affects wage equation estimates is Altonji et al. (2012). These authors argue that the type of curriculum directly affects labor income but also the incentives to study more years that indirectly will affect labor income. Thus, if C is a type of curriculum (academic or professional), the years of education S will be affected by the path that is finally chosen and by other observable (z) and unobservable (v) variables:

$$S(C, z) = \beta_0 + \gamma_0 C + \beta_1 z + v$$

In addition, ex-post labor income will also be affected by the type of skills acquired in each curriculum and the years of education that have finally been completed in the system:

$$\ln(W(C, S, x)) = \alpha_0 + \gamma_1 C + \rho S + \alpha_1(C, S)x + \alpha_2(C, S)x^2 +$$

This distinction is important for the interpretation of mincerian equations that might include together the chosen path and the number of years of education. Taking these two variables into account in the regression implies isolating the impact on wages of having completed a type of educational curriculum, beyond the number of years of education that have been completed. If they are not taken into account separately, the impact incorporates the ability of the curriculum to affect the years of education.

Additionally, one main problem of this type of regressions comes from the difficulty of dealing with biases that could arise from the self-selection of students between vocational and academic training. Hanushek et al. (2017) tries to avoid the problem of self-selection by proposing a difference-in-differences strategy. They use a cross-section of the International Adult Literacy Survey (IALS) with information for 11 countries comparing the labor outcomes of people of different ages with academic or vocational education. Under the assumption that the self-selection bias does not vary over time or over the individual's lifetime, the difference-in-differences approach eliminates it. For example, by subtracting the wage difference between vocational and academic training at age 50 from the difference at age 25, the selection bias, which is assumed to be the same for all cohorts, would be eliminated. In this way, the differences in the profile over the life of each curriculum are isolated. They find that people with academic training initially have worse labor outcomes than people with vocational training, but they experience an improvement as they age. These results are confirmed by Hampf and Woessmann (2017) using a different database (PIAAC) that allows them to include more controls for individual cognitive knowledge. The authors also use the same identification strategy of age differences in differences. The results seem more robust in countries with a strong system of professional practices (Austria, Denmark, and Germany).

These findings have been corroborated with longitudinal data that allow to follow the same cohort over time decreasing the bias that might be produced by potential unobserved quality changes across cohorts. Brunello and Rocco (2017) follow students born in the United Kingdom in 1958 between the ages of 23 and 55 and those born in 1970 between the ages of 26 and 42. In terms of employment, they find that individuals with higher vocational training experience an initial advantage at the beginning of their career. Although this advantage diminishes over time, it never becomes negative. For those with medium vocational training, they find no differences with respect to academic training. In terms of wages, they find a small initial advantage that becomes a disadvantage from the age of 30 for those with medium vocational training and born in 1958 and for those with higher vocational training and born in 1970. Similarly, Golsteyn and Stenberg (2017) identify the educational decisions of cohorts born in Sweden during the period 1955–1963, as well as their annual earnings for each year from 1978 to 2011. With these data they find a negative differential in favor of vocational students for the first years of career that becomes negative beyond 28 years.

The previous papers do not fully solve the problem of self-selection into vocational and academic training. People choosing one particular stream might have unobserved characteristics that might influence their schooling decisions and earnings over time. A more convincing way to eliminate the selection bias comes from those works that evaluate educational reforms that changed the percentage of academic versus professional training. In general, the results are quite different from the previous ones and the advantage in favor of academic training at older ages is less clear. For example, Malamud and Pop-Eleches (2011) analyze the impact of an educational reform in Romania in 1973. Prior to that year, the system began vocational training after 8 years of schooling. However, the reform required 2 additional years of academic studies before entering vocational studies. Using census data and discontinuity techniques, it is observed that students born from 1959 onwards were more likely to complete the academic high school curriculum compared to their counterparts who were born immediately before. This is especially important for students from poor and rural regions and from families with less education, who were a priori less likely to complete university. However, although these disadvantaged students became significantly more likely to be eligible for university after the reform, this did not translate into a relative increase in university graduation.

Similarly, Bertrand et al. (2021) studies a reform of vocational training in Norway in 1994, whose objective was to reduce the high dropout rates at that time. Previously, the professional system was characterized by a very early specialization of students decreasing the likelihood to enter university. After the reform, academic training was increased in the first two years, students having to complete a common core in language, mathematics, natural sciences, and social sciences, which allowed them to accumulate credits in order to be eligible to access university. Greater specialization was postponed to the last 2 years. Vocational training students could return to the academic line after the first two years and vocational training graduates could even be eligible for university after the four years of vocational training provided they completed an additional general course of 6 months. This reform was strictly enforced for individuals born on and after January 1st, 1978, which enables the authors to perform a discontinuity analysis. They find that the reform increased enrollment in both vocational training and academic training. In terms of training achieved there were differences by gender. The reform did not induce changes in the male high school dropout rate: there was an increase in the percentage of men with a vocational degree, which was equal in magnitude to the decline in the share of men with an academic degree. On the other hand, the reform increased the percentage of women who graduated both the vocational training track and the academic training track. Specifically, there were more women who did both degrees. Despite the increase in the percentage of women eligible for university, the percentage of women who completed a university degree did not increase. They can also follow students over time on the labor market and they find that males increased their annual income by 5% while females experienced no changes in their wages.

Finally, Silliman and Virtanen (2022) uses a discontinuity analysis motivated by the centralized admission process to secondary education in Finland. Specifically, the study focuses on applicants who apply for both professional and academic tracks and whose admission is determined by the excess of applications at some school. Compared to other identification strategies using reforms affecting educational decisions of entire cohorts and potentially changing the context, this strategy uses an excess of demand to compare outcomes of individuals from the same age cohort and labor market context. Their causal estimates suggest that enrollment in vocational training increases annual income compared to academic training and the differential persists until the age of 33 (6%). The authors incorporate an interesting idea which is that of heterogeneous returns according to the type of student. This would help explain the different results in different contexts and reforms. In particular, they observe that their positive results apply to students in the middle of the academic ability distribution, while enrolling in vocational training students with high academic ability would be detrimental and therefore could imply a loss of income in the long term.

5 Traditional or Dual Vocational Training

The design of VET programs varies considerably from country to country. A fundamental aspect that is subject to changes in many countries is the role assigned to firms through the introduction or strengthening of dual VET programs.

Dual VET programs offer a combination of workplace learning and classroom instruction. The students who enroll in these programs spend more time at firms and less time in school than their peers in traditional VET programs and undertake a substantial part of their formal training activities in firms. In this section, the advantages of dual VET programs and their impact on students' labor market outcomes are analyzed.

Dual apprenticeships are the standard option in upper secondary education in countries such as Germany, Switzerland, or Austria, which stand out also because of their comparatively low youth unemployment rates. In the rest of continental Europe, dual VET programs have gained in importance over the last two decades, often as part of attempts to improve the school-to-work transition of youth. It is important to distinguish these dual programs from the apprenticeship system in Anglo-Saxon countries like the United Kingdom. The former are firmly rooted in the education system, while the latter are entirely managed by the private sector.

Figure 3 from Introduction shows the percentage of upper secondary vocational students enrolled in combined school and work-based programs for a selection of OECD countries (OECD 2023). The weight of dual programs in the overall VET system varies widely across countries. In the top six countries, dual programs account for more than 80% of upper secondary VET students, while the corresponding figure is less than 10% for the bottom six countries.

School-to-work transition

There exists a broad consensus in the literature that dual VET improves the school-to-work transition in comparison to equivalent school-based degrees (European Commission (2013), Ryan (1998, 2001), Wolter and Ryan (2011)). In most cases, however, the differences between these two types of degree disappear and/or become statistically insignificant after a few years, as those who completed a school-based system tend to catch up with their peers from dual programs. A key explanatory factor for the better initial labor market outcomes is the high share of apprentices who remain with their training firm upon completion of their dual apprenticeship. In Germany, this share is around 60%. However, high retention rates do not appear to be the only explanation for the superior performance of the dual system. Non-retained graduates from the dual system also tend to obtain better initial outcomes than the graduates from school-based programs.

The improvements in average outcomes include employment rates, hours worked, the duration of the employment spells and the type of contract. On the contrary, in the case of salaries the evidence is mixed. To ensure that firms are willing to invest in the general skills of workers, participation in the apprenticeship system must be profitable for firms. Apprentices therefore need to pay a substantial share of their training costs, either by accepting low wages during or after their apprenticeship and/or by engaging in productive activities. Again, considerable cross-country differences are observed. The available evidence indicates that German firms tend to make a net-investment in apprentices during their training. To recover these costs, they retain a large share of their apprentices and pay them relatively low starting wages. On the contrary, in the Swiss system, apprentices generate profits as they devote a substantial share of their time to productive activities. Upon completion of their training, most apprentices move to a different employer and there is no need to recover costs through low starting wages. The above examples also serve to illustrate that training firms do not necessarily train their own future staff.

Channels

The literature has proposed a variety of explanations for the comparatively good performance of dual VET programs. The acquisition of occupation-relevant competencies and skills in a professional setting, rather than in a simulated setting in schools, is generally perceived to be an effective way to narrow the distance to the labor market. This includes the acquisition of non-cognitive skills, either as a by-product of the workplace training or as an explicit objective to the training activities in firms. Additionally, the dual system may help to reduce information asymmetries by allowing firms to monitor the performance of their apprentices and assess their suitability during longer time periods than in the school-based system. Both features tend to improve the school-to-work transition. However, these advantages must be weighed against potential drawbacks such as the risk of training being too company or technology-specific. Furthermore, the substitution of school-based training by company-based training may end up reducing the quality of instruction and the experience shows that it may be challenging to guarantee a sufficient supply of apprenticeships during economic downturs.

The available evidence

Despite the decades-long experience with dual VET in countries like Germany, there is remarkably little evidence on its *causal* effects. The literature highlights two identification problems. Firstly, constructing a reliable counterfactual is difficult when dual VET is the default option. Secondly, when students have a choice between school-based and dual programs, OLS estimates of the impact of dual VET on labor market outcomes tend to be biased as the best students may select into dual VET. As explained in Chapter X, this is a problem when the selection is based on unobservables that affect both the choice of track and the future labor market outcomes of the students.

Recent studies have followed two complementary approaches to overcome this selection problem. A small emerging literature employs field experiments to explore the impact of firm-based training in VET programs. While most research focus on brief interventions aimed at disadvantaged youth,[4] two studies delve into a comparison between firm-based and school-based VET. Cahuc and Hervelin (2024) set up a so-called correspondence experiment in which they submitted fictitious CVs of unemployed youth to actual job openings. The applicants differed solely with respect to the type of secondary-level VET. One group allegedly spent between one-half and two-thirds of their time in firms on a paid apprenticeship position, while the other group spent at most eight weeks in firms during an unpaid internship. Despite these differences, the estimates of Cahuc and Hervelin (2024) show no differences in the call back rates by pathway. The second experimental study is Alfonsi et al. (2020). It contrasts the labor market outcomes of young, low-skilled individuals who undergo six months of work-based versus school-based VET in Uganda. According to their results, the former achieve higher initial earnings and employment, but they

[4] Acevedo et al. (2020) examine the interplay of vocational and soft skill training's effects on employment outcomes for at-risk youth in the Domenican Republic. Katz et al. (2022) investigates the repercussions of sectoral employment initiatives outside formal education targeting low-wage workers in the United States.

are surpassed by the latter over time. The reversal is attributed to the fact that the individuals trained in schools exhibit higher exit rates out of unemployed than those trained in firms. In light of their findings, the authors underscore the importance of certified training, which in their experiment is only guaranteed in the case of school-based VET.

A second set of papers uses IV designs to control for selection effects. A recent example is Bentolila et al. (2023) which studies the causal effect of the introduction of dual VET in Spain, using matched administrative records for the first three cohorts of graduates in tertiary-level VET in the region of Madrid whose labor market outcomes are compared to graduates who completed the same studies in a school-based track. To deal with selection, the authors construct an IV based on the difference in commuting time from students' homes—proxied by their lower secondary school—to the nearest VET schools that offer a dual and a school-based track in their chosen fields. The exclusion restriction is that the differences in commuting distance only affect the labor market outcomes of the graduates through their choice of track.[5] The main results show that graduation in dual rather than school-based VET leads to an improvement of approximately 30% in the cumulative days of work and earnings during the first two years of labor market experience, while the authors find no effect on the quality of jobs. Two of the mechanisms that help to explain these effects are the higher retention rate and the favorable of the training firms in the dual system, but neither of them is strong enough to account for the entire difference in outcomes. In line with the literature, Bentolila et al. (2023) also estimate the effects for the sub-sample of non-retained apprentices who had to initiate their job search being unemployed. Also in that case the graduates from dual VET outperform the ones who completed a school-based degree. This result does not have a causal interpretation since retention is an endogenous decision. Nonetheless, the result clearly indicates that the skills acquired in dual VET are transferable to third firms.

The above evidence is suggestive. Nonetheless, more evidence is needed before we can draw unambiguous conclusions about the relative performance of dual and school-based VET beyond their short-run impact on the school-to-work transition. Given the enormous variety in the type of dual VET programs, it would be interesting to perform a meta-analysis to structure the evidence taking into account the differences in the duration and the level of the programs as well as the share of training activities undertaken in firms. Finally, the future research in this field should try to include objective measures of the cognitive and non-cognitive skills of the students to a better insight in the mechanisms behind the observed differences in labor market outcomes.

[5] The use of distance-based instruments has a long tradition in the estimation of the returns to education (e.g., Card, 1995), mostly to study college enrollment. On the contrary, in this study the authors use the difference in distances which depends on the entire offer distribution of VET, which is arguably more exogenous than the distance to a single school or university.

6 Conclusions

The chapter outlines the theoretical and empirical framework that analyzes the factors influencing the decision to pursue further education after compulsory schooling. It places particular emphasis on a set of studies that investigate how job opportunities for low-skilled individuals impact educational choices, using specific labor market events in various countries. A subsection is dedicated to explaining how to calculate the Internal Rate of Return (IRR) for different education levels across different countries and over time, focusing on the four major European countries. Following this, the chapter explores the theoretical and empirical framework for deciding between an academic career and a vocational training program. Finally, it describes traditional vocational training programs and dual VET programs, summarizing the findings of several studies that have estimated the impacts of these programs in different countries.

References

Alfonsi, L., O. Bandiera, V. Bassi, R. Burgess, I. Rasul, M. Sulaiman, and A. Vitali. 2020. Tackling youth unemployment: Evidence from a labor market experiment in Uganda. *Econometrica* 88: 2369–2414.

Altonji, J. 1993. The demand for and return to education when education outcomes are uncertain. *Journal of Labor Economics* 11(1): Part 1: Essays. Honor of Jacob Mincer, 48–83. https://www.journals.uchicago.edu/doi/abs/10.1086/298317.

Altonji, J., E. Blom and C. Meghir. 2012. Heterogeneity in human capital investments: High school curriculum, college major and careers. *Annual Review Economics* 4: 185–223. https://www.annualreviews.org/doi/abs/10.1146/annurev-economics-080511-110908.

Aparicio-Fenoll, A. 2016. Returns to education and educational outcomes: The case of the Spanish Housing Boom. *Journal of Human Capital* 10 (2): 235–265. https://www.journals.uchicago.edu/doi/abs/10.1086/686154.

Atkin, D. 2016. Endogenous skill acquisition and export manufacturing in Mexico, *The American Economic Review* 106 (8): 2046–2085. https://www.jstor.org/stable/43956906.

Autor, D., L. Katz and M. Kearney. 2008. Trends in U.S. wage inequality: Revising the revisionists. *The Review of Economics and Statistics* 90 (2): 300–323. https://www.jstor.org/stable/40043148.

Becker, G.S. 1962. Investment in human capital: A theoretical analysis. *Journal of Political Economy* 70: 9–49. https://www.jstor.org/stable/1829103.

Bentolila, S., A. Cabrales and M. Jansen. 2023. does dual vocational education and training pay Off?, *CEPR Discussion Paper* 18602.

Bertrand, M., M. Mogstad and J. Mountjoy. 2021. Improving educational pathways to social mobility: Evidence from Norway's Reform 94. *Journal of Labor Economics* 39 (4): 965–1010. https://www.journals.uchicago.edu/doi/epdf/10.1086/713009.

Black, D., T. McKinnish and S.G. Sanders. 2005. Tight labor markets and the demand for education: Evidence from the Coal Boom and Bust. *Industrial and Labor Relations Review* 59 (1): 3–16. https://www.jstor.org/stable/25063012.

Bonhomme, S. and L. Hospido. 2017. The cycle of earnings inequality: Evidence from Spanish Social Security Data. *The Economic Journal* 127 (603): 1217–1729. https://onlinelibrary.wiley.com/doi/epdf/10.1111/ecoj.12368.

Brunello, G. and L. Rocco. 2017. The labor market effects of academic and vocational education over the life cycle. *Journal of Human Capital* 11 (1): 106–166. https://www.journals.uchicago.edu/doi/full/10.1086/690234.

Cahuc, P. and J. Hervelin. 2024. The effect of workplace vs school-based vocationaleducation on youth unemployment: Evidence from France. *European Economic Review* 162: 104637.

Card. D. 1995. Using geographic variation in college proximity to estimate the return to schooling. In *Aspects of Labour Market Behaviour: Essays in Honour of John Vanderkamp*, ed. L.N. Christofides, E. K. Grant and R. Swidinsky, 201–222. University of Toronto Press.

Card, D. 2001. Estimating the return to schooling: Progress on some persistent econometric problems. *Econometrica* 69 (5): 1127–1160. http://links.jstor.org/sici?sici=0012-9682%28200109%2969%3A5%3C1127%3AETRTSP%3E2.0.CO%3B2-Q.

Card, D. 2018. *Returns to schooling. The New Palgrave Dictionary of Economics.* London: Palgrave Macmillan. https://doi.org/10.1057/978-1-349-95189-5_2574.

Cunha, F. and J. Heckman. 2007. Identifying and Estimating the Distributions of Ex Post and Ex Ante Returns to Schooling. *Labour Economics* 14 (6): 870–893. https://doi.org/10.1016/j.labeco.2007.06.002.

Dustmann, C., J. Ludsteck and U. Schönberg. 2009. Revisiting the German wage structure. *The Quarterly Journal of Economics* 124 (2): 843–881. https://www.jstor.org/stable/40506245.

European Commission. 2013. *The effectiveness and cost-benefits of apprenticeships: Results of the quantitative analysis.* DG Employment, Social Affairs and Inclusion.

Fortin N., D. Green, T. Lemieux and K. Milligan. 2012. Canadian inequality: Recent developments and policy options. *Canadian Public Policy* 38 (2): 121–145. http://www.sfu.ca/~pendakur/teaching/econ104/fortin%20et%20al%20CPP%202012.pdf.

Gosling, A., S. Machin and C. Meghir. 2000. The changing distribution of male wages in the U.K. *The Review of Economic Studies* 67 (4): 635–666. https://www.jstor.org/stable/2695942.

Hampf, F. and L. Woessmann. 2017. Vocational vs. General Education and Employment over the Life Cycle: New Evidence from PIAAC. *CESifo Economic Studies* 63 (3): 255–269. https://doi.org/10.1093/cesifo/ifx012.

Hanushek, E., G. Schwerdt, L. Woessmann, and L. Zhang. 2017. General education, vocational education, and labor market outcomes over the lifecycle. *Journal of Human Resources* 52 (1): 48–87. https://jhr.uwpress.org/content/52/1/48.

Heckman, J., L.J. Lochner and P.E. Todd. 2006. Earnings equations and rates of return: The Mincer equation and beyond. In *Handbook of the Economics of Education*, Hanushek, E.A. and Welch F. Capítulo 7, 307–458. North-Holland, Amsterdam. http://jenni.uchicago.edu/papers/Heckman_Lochner_etal_2006_HEE_v1_ch7.pdf.

Izquierdo, M. and A. Lacuesta. (2012). The contribution of changes in employment composition and relative returns to the evolution of wage inequality: The case of Spain. *Journal of Population Economics* 25: 511–543. https://link.springer.com/article/10.1007/s00148-011-0371-y.

Katz, L. F., J. Roth, R. Hendra, and K. Schaberg. 2022. Why do sectoral employment programs work? Lessons from WorkAdvance. *Journal of Labor Economics* 40: S249–S291.

Krueger, D. and K. Kumar. 2004. Skill-Specific rather than general education: A reason for US-Europe growth differences? *Journal of Economic Growth* 9 (2): 167–207. https://www.jstor.org/stable/40212697.

Lacuesta, A., S. Puente and E. Villanueva. 2020. The schooling response to a sustained increase in low-skill wages: Evidence from Spain 1989–2009. *SERIEs* 11: 457–499. https://doi.org/10.1007/s13209-020-00218-0.

Malamud, O. and C. Pop-Eleches. 2011. School tracking and access to higher education among disadvantaged groups. *Journal of Public Economics* 95 (11–12): 1538–1549. https://doi.org/10.1016/j.jpubeco.2011.03.006.

Mincer, J. 1974. *Schooling, experience and earnings.* New York: NBER (distributed by Columbia University Press). https://books.google.es/books/about/Schooling_experience_and_earnings.html?hl=es&id=9IGqAAAAIAAJ&redir_esc=y.

OECD. 2023. *Spotlight on vocational education and training: Findings from education at a Glance 2023*, https://doi.org/10.1787/acff263d-en, OECD Publishing, Paris.

Pijoan-Mas, J. and V. Sánchez-Marcos. 2010. Spain is different: Falling trends of inequality. *Review of Economic Dynamics* 13: 154–178. https://www.sciencedirect.com/science/article/abs/pii/S109420250900057X#:~:text=Our%20analysis%20shows%20that%20inequality,to%20understand%20this%20%20falling%20trend.

Ryan, P. 1998. Is Apprenticeship better? A review of the relevant literature. *Journal of Vocational Education and Training* 50: 289–329.

Ryan, P. 2001. The School-to-work transition: A cross-national perspective. *Journal of Economic Literature* 39: 34–92.

Silliman, M. and H. Virtanen. 2022. Labor market returns to vocational secondary education. *American Economic Journal: Applied Economics* 14 (1): 197–224. https://doi.org/10.1257/app.20190782.

Wolter, S. and P. Ryan. 2011. Apprenticeship. In *Handbook of the Economics of Education*, ed. E.A. Hanushek, S. Machin, and L. WÅNoessman, vol. 3, 521–576. Elsevier.

Tertiary Education: Access, Financing, and Cost-Effectiveness

José García Montalvo and Jorge Sainz

1 Introduction

Higher education cannot be analyzed in isolation from the educational system. Although the public and private profitability of the university system contributes to the accumulation of human capital by a country, adding years of education alone does not generate growth in a society, and its contribution to growth depends on the competencies that students have cemented from the knowledge accumulated in previous years (Hanushek 2016). Even so, Valero and Van Reenen (2019) show how a 10% increase in the number of university centers translates into an increase in GDP per capita of 0.4% through stimulating innovation and the supply of human capital, as well as playing a role in promoting democracy, social equity, and civic behaviors.

Figure 1 shows how tertiary education has spread to most of the countries around us. In some countries, such as Japan, Ireland, the United Kingdom, and the United States, more than half of the adult working-age population has passed through its classrooms. There has been a generalization of higher education, regardless of the structure of the different systems, which has affected different aspects of the university system. The main reasons for this are private profitability, the homogeneity of the centers, the cost of studies, and segregation within the university systems. For example, in the case of Spain, at the beginning of democracy in 1975, there were 26 public and four Catholic Church universities attended by some 540,000 students. Today, almost 50 years later, the number of university students is around 1,700,000 in 86 universities, including 50 public and 36 private or Catholic Church universities, six more in the process of being set up, in addition to hundreds of centers that

J. G. Montalvo (✉)
Department of Economics, Universitat Pompeu Fabra, Barcelona, Spain
e-mail: jose.garcia-montalvo@upf.edu

J. Sainz
Department of Applied Economics, Universidad Rey Juan Carlos, Madrid, Spain

A. Cabrales and I. Sanz (eds.), *Economics of Education*,
https://doi.org/10.1007/978-3-031-90911-5_11

offer non-university higher education (Higher Vocational Training) and dozens of international institutions that offer higher degrees in Spain (Fig. 1).

Let us look at the education level attained by the higher education population (Fig. 2). We can observe the heterogeneity of the composition of the population with tertiary studies in different OECD countries. As a general trend, an increasing number of students access higher education through short cycles (OECD 2023), while the percentage of PhDs rarely exceeds 2% of the population, and the rates of Master's studies are around 14% (see also Chapter 1 in this manual).

Another important aspect of the modern university is inclusion. Figure 3 shows that women represent a majority in tertiary education. Although there is still a long way to go, the greater academic preparation of women is a relevant factor in achieving equality in other professional fields and in the university itself. However, in many countries, there is still strong segregation in the university system, which benefits certain social groups. This reality should lead to the intervention of public administrations to prevent gaps from arising in terms of the possibility of equal access and use that will be pointed out throughout this chapter, as they were in previous chapters in the general education system.

Some of the functioning mechanisms of the university system are little known, probably due to the need for more transparency in higher education markets. Many of the areas of the production function of universities correspond to a public–private hybrid, to decisions conditioned by the preferences of students, their talent, their previous training, access systems, the socioeconomic characteristics of their families, the regulatory framework of each country, the structure of the university market in each country or region, the quality of the teaching staff, university financing, the professional expectations of the users of the system on completing their studies, or something as ethereal as the quality of university management. The contribution of each of these elements to the final product, the graduate, varies significantly in size and quality, mainly because of the complementarities between them, which can be decisive in the final result. For example, based on the structure of the university market, Aghion et al. (2010) causally demonstrate that an exogenous increase in the number of graduates can significantly impact the final result.

The assumption is that a university generates more patents or publications if it has greater autonomy or competition.

The same authors, in a previous document (Aghion et al. 2008), which is still current (unfortunately), propose reforms for Europe, such as increasing student mobility, making the curriculum more flexible, and selecting entry-level professors and researchers. To make European universities competitive, they must increase competition among themselves and with international universities, achieved through mobility and greater autonomy, accompanied by greater transparency. Finally, better financing of the system is also necessary.

Three decades later, some progress has been made in some of these areas. Programs such as the European universities are trying to make the European university system more mobile and competitive; in research, the Commission's Horizon funding schemes are creating the necessary incentives for better research. However,

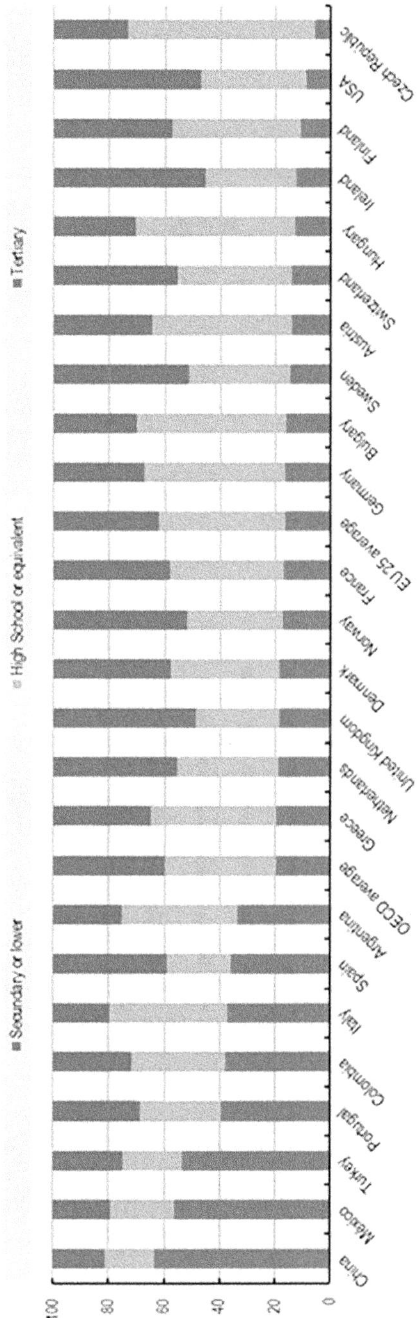

Fig. 1 Level of education between 25 and 64 years of age (2022) (*Source* Education at a Glance, OECD 2023)

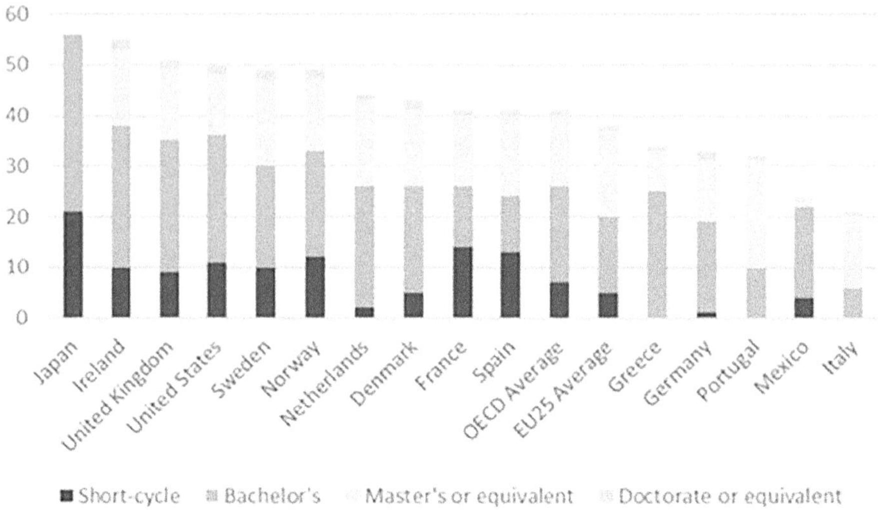

Fig. 2 Distribution of the adult population with tertiary education by level attained (25–64 years) (2022) (*Source* Education at a Glance, OECD 2023)

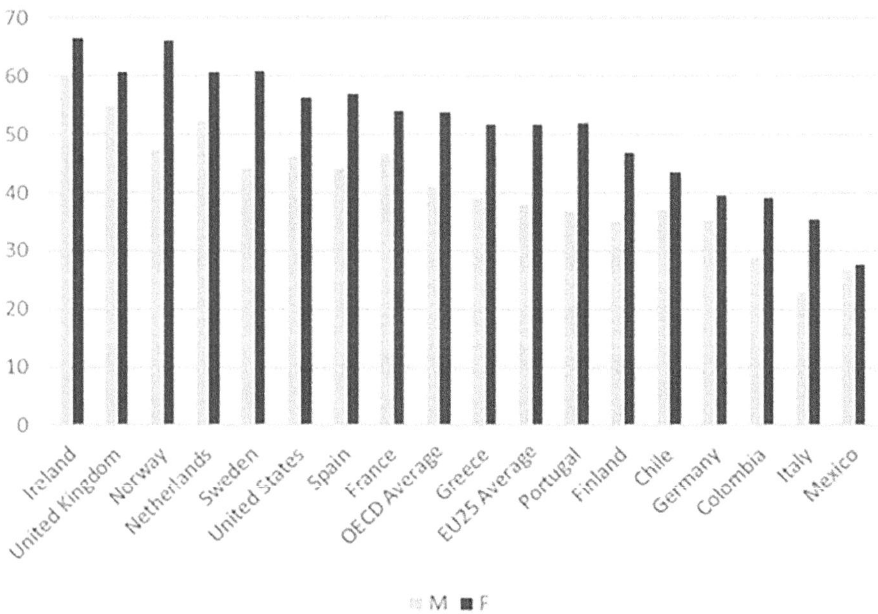

Fig. 3 Distribution by gender of the adult population (25–34 years old) in tertiary education (2022) (*Source* Education at a Glance, OECD 2023)

at the country level, heterogeneity is still dominant. These pages aim to provide managers and researchers with tools to further deepen this change.

2 Higher Education Markets and Educational Choice

The demographic structure of Western countries is leading to the paradox that the percentage of students attending higher education is reaching its maximum. At the same time, the installed capacity of universities continues to grow. For example, in Spain, the INE projections for the population of the typical university entrance age, 18 years old, have a clearly downward trend (see Fig. 4). Meanwhile, the ratio of the population attending university within this age group is at a maximum (for more detail, see Chapter 10 in this manual). Societies in our environment, in general, and Spain, in particular, may already be past the maximum population in the classroom.

In Spain, two aspects add to these factors: the irruption of non-university tertiary education (Higher Vocational Training) and, in contrast to the stability in the number of public universities (50 since the creation of the Polytechnic University of Cartagena in 1998), the growth of private centers (42 universities, including private, Catholic, and Concordat-Catholic chartered before 1975- universities, 26 of them in the last 25 years) that compete for a dwindling population (Kurban et al. 2015; OECD 2022b). The aim of the next sections is to provide a comprehensive, but not exhaustive, sketch of the existing literature on student behavior to support the analysis of why and where our young university students study.

Fig. 4 Evolution and projection of the Spanish population aged 18 (*Source* INE)

2.1 The Higher Education Market vs. VET

The various legislative changes, but especially the LOMCE (2013) and the Vocational Training Law (2022), have consolidated vocational Higher Education as a real option after Compulsory Education for a significant percentage of Spanish students (Fig. 5), increasing the diversity of options for acquiring the necessary skills to contribute to society (Durazzi 2019; OECD 2022a). The creation of an effective gateway system between VET and university, the generalization of duality and high employability have increased the percentage of young people choosing short-term higher education over traditional university studies, in a trend similar to other countries in our environment (Marginson 2016).

Therefore, we are no longer talking about Higher Education, yes or no, but about how, when, and where, since the decision raises issues related to social stratification, future salaries, and mobility between classes (Hoxby 2004; Marginson 2016). Figure 6 shows the evolution of the percentage of the population graduating from the different levels of higher education and the trend toward an increase in higher vocational training (short-cycle higher education), as discussed in the descriptive introduction to Chapter 1 and Chapter 10 in this manual, linked to the demand for

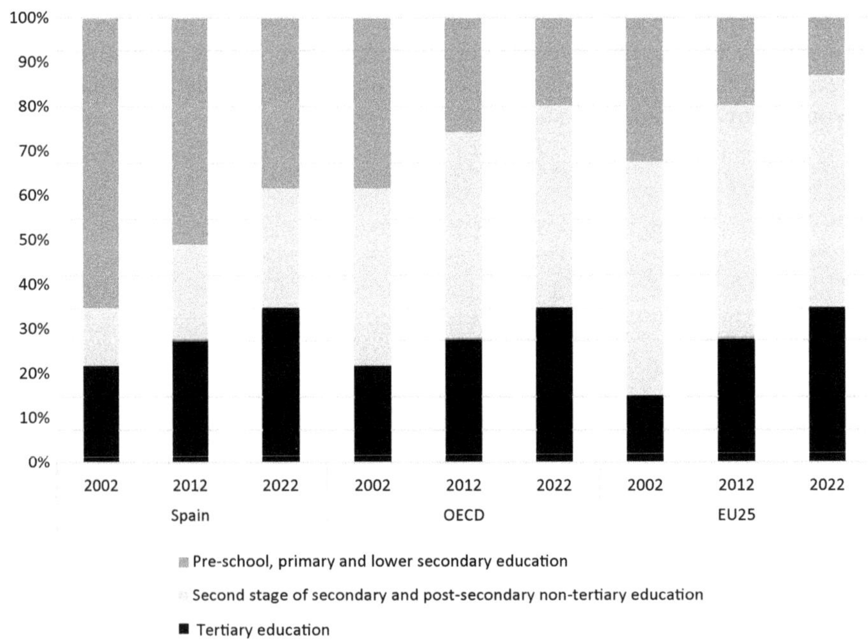

Fig. 5 Evolution of the level of education of the adult population (25–64 years old) (*Source* Education at a Glance, OECD 2023)

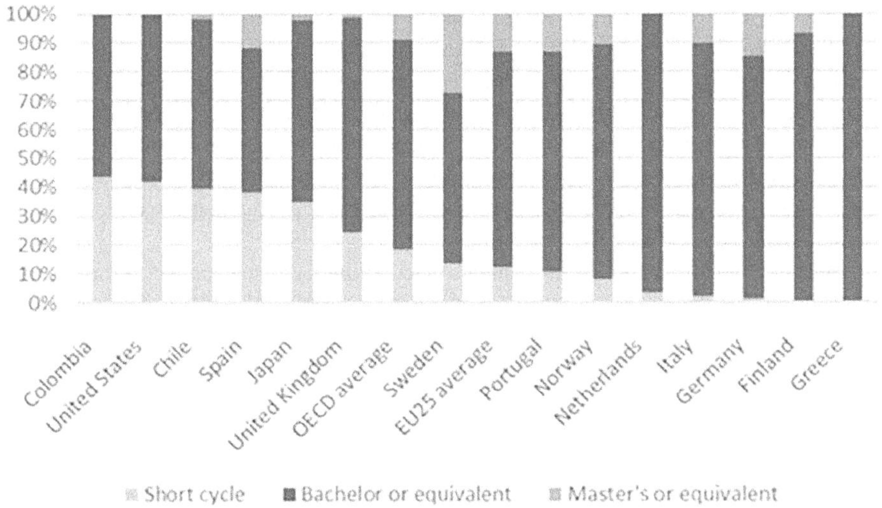

Fig. 6 Distribution of people accessing tertiary education for the first time by level of education (2021) (*Source* OECD, Education at a Glance 2023)

specific skills and the recovery of the prestige of vocational training, primarily due to greater employability (Martínez-Morales and Marhuenda-Fluixá 2020).

Although there are important differences, it is a good time to draw lessons from the U.S. Community Colleges (CC), transformed into a short-cycle option for professionalizing Higher Education, without abandoning their previous step as academic training leading to a bachelor's degree at a university. The system converged as there is a shift in educational demand for new skills and flexibility of short higher education (Kasper 2003; OECD 2018, 2022a) and the need for potential workers to correct the stigma of unemployment in many countries (Ayllón et al. 2022).

Triventi (2013) points out one of the problems linked to different levels of higher education: social stratification can be generated according to educational levels and reduce social mobility. Although the article does not present causality, it serves as a reference for the risk that higher vocational education may pose as an option for families with less academic training and lower incomes, at least in Spain.

Examples of causality in the United States are linked to this phenomenon. Mountjoy (2022) uses data on fee reductions at all levels of higher education in the state of Texas as an instrumental variable that resolves selection biases in university access to measure the academic success and earnings of four cohorts of students and their access or not to higher education and, where appropriate, short cycle or the equivalent of a bachelor's degree. Their results indicate that students who did not plan to go on to higher education but eventually attended CC increase their wages by 18% above the average, their average education by 1.7 years, and are 27% more likely to go on to a university degree. The remaining third group, those students who drop out of college to pursue a 4-year degree and focus on vocational studies, reduce their chances of earning a degree by 20%, resulting in a consequent drop in future earnings.

Other articles that analyze similar interventions obtain results that also show improvements in access to Higher Education, either directly through short cycles or using them as an intermediate step toward degrees. Denning (2017), using a difference-in-differences methodology, finds that a $1000 fee decrease increases participation in Higher Education by 5.1% without any reduction in graduation rates, while Carruthers et al. (2023), synthetically comparing cohorts, find that a fee elimination results in a 24% increase in graduation in the short cycle but has no effect on access to degrees and no effect on salaries.

Another exciting aspect of its translation to Spain, mainly because of the gap that unemployment generates among the youngest (Ayllón et al. 2022), is the relationship between the minimum wage and enrollment in vocational studies. Schanzenbach et al. (2023), using a stacked events strategy (Autor et al. 2006), find a 4% decrease in enrollment in short-cycle programs in the first year, which is also maintained over time, while in undergraduate programs, there are no significant variations. The result implies that despite being higher studies in both cases and, to a certain extent, substitutes, the demand for one and the other is different, generating different behaviors (Betts and McFarland 1995).

2.2 *Choice of Study Area*

For many young Spaniards, choosing a degree is the most complicated first moment of adult life. The decision, as shown by data from the Ministry of Universities study on the labor market insertion of Spanish graduates, impacts the young person's life throughout.

There are two aspects that must be taken into account when analyzing how students make this choice. First, in public universities, the highest quality private universities, and in general in all the most in-demand degrees, such as Medicine, by the university entrance exam, i.e., the choice depends exclusively on academic merit. This system risks excluding students with extraordinary abilities, which only translates into convincing academic results in some of the subjects evaluated, affecting the diversity of talent in the classroom (Kamis et al. 2023). In addition, there are criticisms of the diversity of educational levels by Autonomous Communities, consistent with the level gap shown in PISA (OECD 2019), which in a single district framework may affect the possibilities of some students to access degrees with higher demand, such as Health Sciences and some engineering (Ruiz-Lázaro 2021).

Figure 7 shows the evolution of the percentage of graduates according to fields of study. The consolidated trend in our country is an increase in Social Science degrees and a simultaneous reduction in Science degrees, a behavior consistent with the trends of other countries in our environment. However, Science degrees continue to be those with the highest level of employability and the best working conditions and salaries (Fig. 8), which poses a paradox between the future expectations of young people and the demand for degrees.

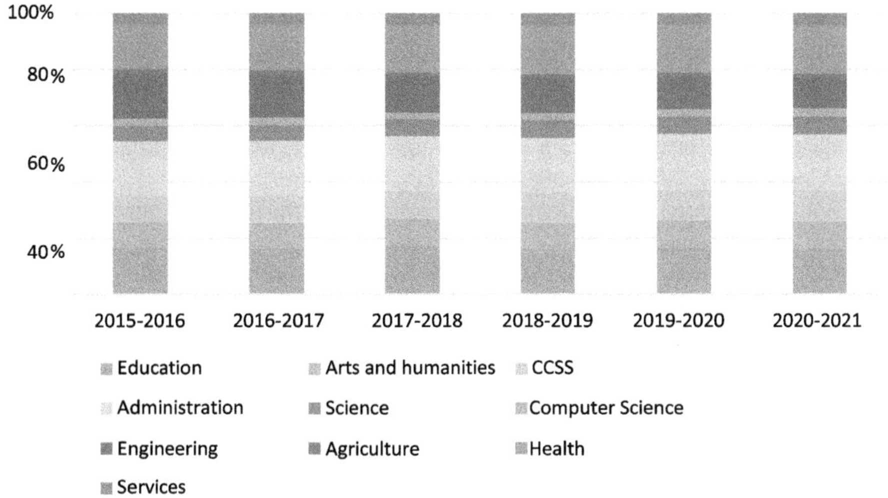

Fig. 7 Evolution of the percentage of graduates according to fields of study (*Source* INE)

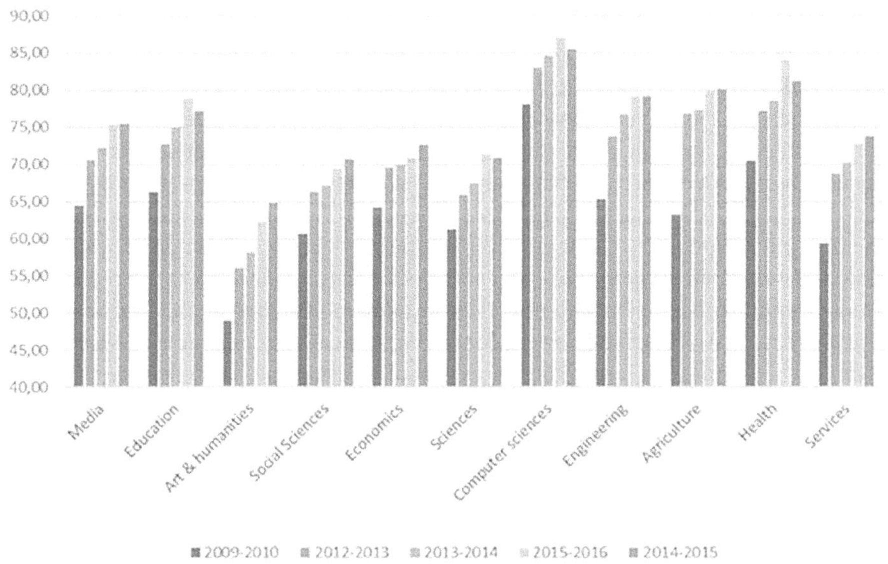

Fig. 8 Affiliation to Social Security four years after graduation according to fields of study (*Source* INE)

From an economic point of view, university access decisions often pose a choice under uncertainty where the different career direction options depend on the expectation of institutions and studies that maximize the expected utility from the available data and alternative choices, family experience, gender, and cognitive abilities of candidates to perform in certain areas (Anelli and Peri 2015; Arcidiacono et al. 2012; Coenen et al. 2021; Patnaik et al. 2021).

If not instrumented, the reality of the expectations of the possible outcomes in the different careers generates biases, such as the absolute advantage in an area (unobservable), which may not correspond to the wage remuneration in the estimation. These biases are difficult to deal with econometrically (Altonji et al. 2016; Cardoso et al. 2016).

Hastings et al. (2013) present the choice analysis in the Chilean model, which is similar to the Spanish model. It consists of a centralized system of university access based on an academic exam analogous to the EVAU that determines students' chances of accessing more than 1000 degrees offered in 2012 by Chilean universities. Students choose among eight of these degrees based on their grades. They are selected for a degree at a given university based on an algorithm similar to the one used by the different autonomous communities.

This allows us to apply discontinuity regressions on cut-off levels based on demographics and future earnings expectations. As a result, the difference in salary return between degrees in the lowest demand quartile (2%) and degrees in the highest demand quartile (9.2%) is noteworthy, specifically within the same quartile between Health Sciences and Social Sciences degrees. The difference between quartiles is much greater, with differences between the first and fourth quartiles reaching 24.7%. These results are consistent regardless of the social level of origin of the students. The only exception is the Business Administration degrees, whose employability in Chile is determined by belonging to a network of acquaintances and the presence of non-academic skills, generating results different from the rest of the analysis.

It also needs to be clarified how students' preferences are constructed. Wiswall and Zafar (2015), through a large panel of personal information, state that the expected salary and the student's skills play an essential role, while some family characteristics and aspects linked to the offer are also relevant. However, most decisions still correspond to heterogeneous characteristics linked to personal preferences that are difficult to describe, which may be innate or endogenously constructed throughout life, and where gender may have some weight.

Another aspect to consider is the access system. In countries such as Chile, China, Spain, France, and Norway, the choice of university and career occurs simultaneously. For this reason, the results of Bordon and Fu (2015) for Chile are intriguing. To analyze this, they contrast an equilibrium model where a planner distributes the places in the degree and university and compares the results with a Stackelberg game where the planner chooses the university and the student chooses the degree. The results show that in the latter, there is an increase in enrollment in the lower three quartiles, but especially for the lowest quartile, there is an increase in retention rates in all groups. As a corollary, the analysis shows that women and students from low-income families are more likely to benefit from the system change. These results are consistent with recent reforms in university access in China (Ma et al. 2023).

2.3 *University Dropout*

If, as we have seen in the introduction, completing higher education studies is advantageous for students, who and why do they leave the authorities behind? Figure 9 gives a first view of the latest available data from the Ministry of Universities (SIIU 2023). A strong gender and area of study component is observed with respect to the 11.7% of young people who drop out in the first year of study at university and a 22.85% dropout rate over the course of their studies.

(technically, those who, after having begun their degree, do not enroll in any official university studies at any Spanish university for two consecutive years and do not graduate).

There is also an important geographical component. Three years after starting studies, the dropout rate in communities such as the Canary Islands (20.5%) or the Balearic Islands (20.4%) is almost double that of Madrid (10.8%) or the Basque Country (11.8%). However, it is curious that while the most selective studies, which are currently Health and Sciences, have low dropout rates, education studies, with relatively low entry averages, are characterized by a relatively low dropout rate.

There is extensive literature on the causes of university dropout (e.g., Aina et al. 2018, 2022; Behr et al. 2020; Kehm et al. 2020). A brief summary of the literature

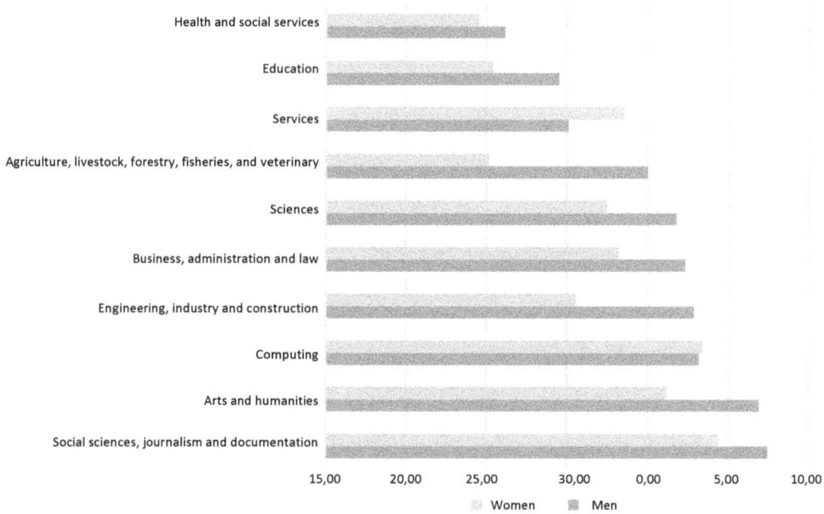

Fig. 9 SUE first-year dropout rate by gender (2019–2020) (*Source* SIIU 2023)

points out, among the main aspects that determine continuity or not: (a) conditions of study at the university; (b) academic and social integration at the university; (c) personal efforts and motivations to study; (d) information and admission requirements; (e) previous academic performance; (f) cost and financing of the university; (g) personal characteristics; (h) sociodemographic characteristics; and (i) external conditions. Part of these characteristics are subjective to the individual and pose difficulties in their estimation and evaluation. Altonji et al. (2016) and Braga et al. (2014) point out the importance of teacher quality for student performance, measured by performance in subsequent courses; however, their results also point out that student evaluations are not co-related to learning, as many aspects such as student selection bias, grade expectations in the subject, or grade inflation itself within different universities may influence.

For the Spanish case, Lassibille and Navarro Gómez (2008) estimate a logit model that establishes that the probability of dropping out of university studies is higher for Law or Sciences than for Health Sciences. The gender data are not statistically significant. However, they find a higher dropout rate for students who delay their studies after high school, have repeated a year during secondary school, or come from vocational training. The fact of receiving a scholarship, whether the student is pursuing his or her first choice of studies or the fact that the parents have a university degree, is also an important factor for continuing in the classroom, results consistent with the causal findings for Spain of Montalbán (2023) in a different context or those of Backes-Gellner et al. (2021) for Switzerland, Modena et al. (2018), or Vergolini and Vlach (2017) for Italy.

Finally, note the paradox of engineering and STEM careers and their high dropout rate despite being selective in the academic competencies that characterize their students (Lassibille and Navarro Gómez 2008). The demand for their skills in a digital society (Autor et al. 2003; Bresnahan et al. 2002) is linked to the need for more motivation of students despite high employability, high return, or entry grades (Tayebi et al. 2021).

2.4 Epitome: Markets that Do Not Exist but Should

Universities in Spain are incomplete markets. There is no recruitment market for academics as understood in most of the civilized world, and a market for hiring young professors and the mobility of senior professors is a rarity (García Hombrados 2022). The framework of the new Law on Universities passed in 2023 (LOSU) generates opportunities but also uncertainties about incentives, discrimination in hiring, stratification, hierarchy, and networks (Carlsson et al. 2021; Checchi et al. 2021; Ginther and Kahn 2021; Musselin 2009; Terviö 2011; Wapman et al. 2022; Williams and Ceci 2015).

Nor have we discussed the three-year university degrees, which, allowed as of 2015, disappear in a generalized manner in the LOSU unless they link to the program of European universities, as in the case of Italy. Cappellari and Lucifora (2009) find empirical evidence using a difference-in-differences methodology where the differences between cohorts are exclusively due to the implementation of Bologna, which in Italy meant moving to three years of studies in the bachelor's degree. After the change, students who graduated from secondary school were 15% more likely to attend university because of a decision to invest in human capital and not because of the underlying long-term trend in university attendance. There is also a social component: most of the increase is among bright students from low-income backgrounds, although they find a negligible dropout rate increase, consistent with previous results.

3 Elitism, Discrimination, and Access

In his 2020 book, "The Tyranny of Merit" (Sandel 2020), philosopher Michael Sandel harshly criticizes the system of access to American universities. Based on the scandal of the 33 families whose children gained access to universities in the top decile of the rankings,[1] he argues for the consideration of elites based on factors beyond the control of the individual, such as socioeconomic conditions and the market's valuation of certain skills and abilities over others. It is, therefore, crucial to understand that chance plays a vital role in the concept of "success."

The empirical antecedent of this type of approach corresponds to Dale and Krueger's (2002, 2014) articles that will be analyzed in detail in the following section when analyzing the profitability of university education, which demystified what until then had been a dogma: getting into an Ivy League university ensured a life of "success." The wage differentials between graduates of more selective universities and those of less selective ones seemed to justify the argument. However, Dale and Krueger argue that the existing differences do not correspond to attendance at one university or another but to unobservable prior characteristics that influence the admissions process and determine earnings after graduation (diligence, intelligence, initiative).

Hoxby (2009) criticizes their identification strategy and considers university selection more accessible for most students. However, due to technological change that has facilitated their mobility, the most able students compete for a relatively constant number of places at the best universities. This generates a dichotomy between students who want access to elite universities and those who simply want to go to university.

In the next section, Chetty et al. (2023) also analyzed why children of higher-income families are more likely to access the most selective private universities in the United States (Ivy League, Stamford, MIT, etc.). The data are conclusive: within the group of students who are in the 99th percentile for best results in the university

[1] In fact, the mechanisms used by these families to get their children into these universities show the need for more meritocracy rather than less. This could not happen in a system like the Spanish one.

entrance exam, more than 30% come from families that are in the upper-income bracket and end up in the most selective classrooms (9.3% more possibilities than they would have), and only 10% belong to the middle class (percentiles 70–80). The authors find that, even after correcting for entrance score, students with families in the 99–99.9 percentile are 43% more likely to be admitted to one of these institutions than those in the middle class, while, by comparison, admission rates to selective public universities are similar for the entire income distribution.[2]

However, what are the reasons for this higher participation in elite universities? The first is that the prospective student's parents have been former students at the university, and the second is the credentials they can present. Students in the 99th percentile do not have better academic credentials than middle-class students. However, they do extracurricular activities and have better letters of recommendation from their professors at school, especially if they are also selective. The admissions advantage explains that two-thirds of the higher attendance rates at selective schools in the top 1% relative to the middle class derive from college sports, preferences for children of alums, and higher extracurricular scores.

Grossman et al. (2023) analyze another controversial aspect of the U.S. admissions process, namely the discrimination of students of Asian (but U.S.) origin in access to universities, especially elite universities. Their findings indicate that individuals of Southeast Asian origin see a significant decrease in their chances of admission, 49%, compared to their white counterparts with comparable test scores, high school grade point averages, and participation in extracurricular activities. After controlling for early applications, the applicant's institution of origin, and parents' alums, they find that Southeast Asian students achieve admission rates similar to those of their white peers. In contrast, students of Indian and Pakistani descent experience a 10% decrease in their chances of admission compared to white students who pre-sit similarities on the variables, as mentioned earlier.

The above analysis leads us to the effect of affirmative action regulation on college access. Bleemer (2022) uses a difference-based research design and a longitudinal database of the University of California applicants from 1994 to 2002 and their subsequent educational trajectories and income levels, analyzing the impact of the discontinuation of affirmative action. Specifically, it demonstrates that the elimination of this policy in the state of California resulted in minority applicants enrolling in lower-tier academic institutions. The "mismatch hypothesis" conceptual framework suggests that this enrollment change would apparently confer net educational advantages to minority applicants. However, the analysis reveals an opposite result, as overall degree attainment by applicants from underrepresented groups with lower academic qualifications experienced a decline, particularly in STEM disciplines. The cessation of affirmative action also deterred a substantial number of qualified

[2] Hoekstra (2009), using a regression discontinuity methodology, finds that those students who gained borderline access to high-quality public universities versus those who missed the cutoff by tenths of a percentage point obtained wage differences of up to 21%.

minority students from applying to prestigious UC campuses. Complementary analyses, encompassing regression discontinuity and institutional value-added assessments, suggest that the net educational and wage benefits of affirmative action for minority applicants exceed the net costs to White and Asian applicants at the margin of admission.

In Europe, there is a distinction between the evidence from the United Kingdom, where attendance at elite universities (Oxbridge and, to a lesser extent, the Russell Group) form a group where gender, networks, social origin, and ethnicity are determinants of access (Richardson et al. 2020), and the growing heterogeneity in the quality of universities even in countries where relative homogeneity is considered, such as Italy (Pietro and Cutillo 2006) or in Spain (see Andreu and Casamiglia analysis on the effects of the EVAU in Chapter 5a).

4 The Private Profitability of University Education

In most countries, the employment situation of tertiary education graduates is substantially better than that of graduates from other lower levels of education. They have lower unemployment rates and higher salaries. In 2021, OECD tertiary graduates aged 25–64 had an employment rate 10 percentage points higher than upper-secondary or post-secondary non-tertiary education graduates. The rate of those who were neither studying nor working among 25–29-year-olds was 12%, clearly lower than the upper-secondary/post-secondary non-tertiary rate. They also have lower long-term unemployment rates than other educational levels. On average, tertiary graduates in the OECD with continuous full-time employment earn about 55% more than upper-secondary graduates.

However, there are large differences between countries. A simple way to analyze the cost-effectiveness of tertiary education is to compare the wages earned versus graduates of upper-secondary education. Figure 10 presents this comparison by country. The advantage is 50% on the EU average, somewhat lower than the OECD average. In the Spanish case, the advantage is 41%, somewhat below the EU average.

An alternative way is to calculate the internal rate of return on tertiary education. The OECD (2017) calculates the gross income from obtaining tertiary studies (taking into account the effect of unemployment spells in each country) minus income tax, Social Security contributions, and the effect of transfers. To this are added unemployment insurance benefits. The net benefits are subtracted from the costs that include direct costs (tuition fees for the number of years of study plus living expenses) and income foregone (the salary that the student could have obtained in the labor market considering the unemployment rate for that age group). In countries where it is customary to study and work, the opportunity cost is the difference between what could be earned in the labor market and what is earned by combining work and university studies. The difference between income and expenses is discounted at a rate of 2%, although applications for some countries have used rates between 2 and 5%. Figure 11 shows the result of calculating the internal rate of return of

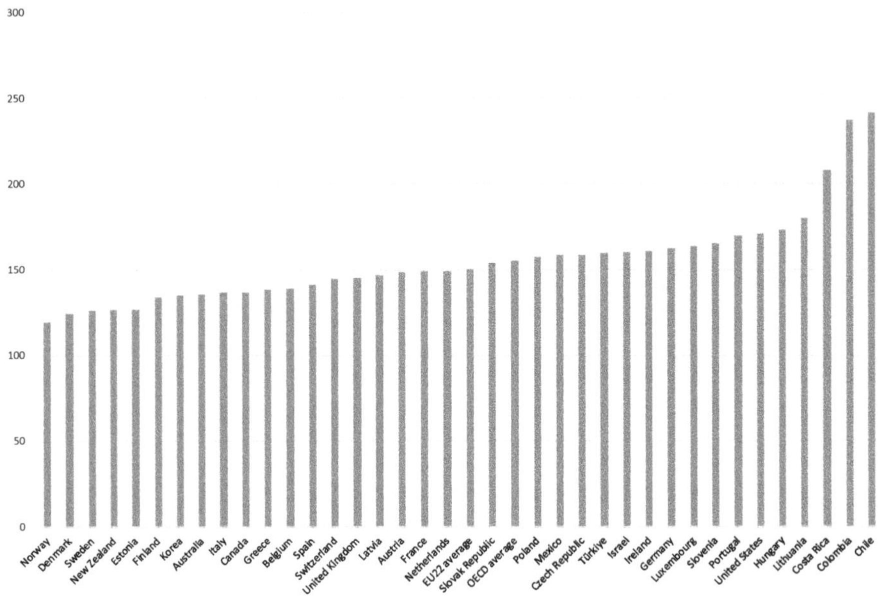

Fig. 10 Relative earnings of tertiary education graduates vs. higher secondary education (full-time). 2020 (*Source* Education at a Glance, OECD [2022b])

higher education in OECD countries. Specifically, the graph shows the private costs and benefits of a male tertiary education graduate compared to an Upper Secondary Education graduate in equivalent dollars converted using purchasing power parity.[3] The calculation shows that in countries where the direct cost of university education is low (Germany, Norway), the total cost of studies is high because of the high opportunity cost. On the other hand, in countries where university graduates receive high salaries, they also pay more taxes, which reduces the differences between countries when calculating net benefits. The average rate of return for both OECD and EU countries is 13%. In Spain, the profitability is lower (9%). In the case of women graduates with tertiary education, the average profitability of OECD and EU countries is lower, 11%. However, Spanish female graduates have a higher profitability than the average (13%).

Another way of calculating the private profitability of tertiary education is to use a Mincerian regression (Card 2001). The classic reference for this calculation for cross-country comparisons is the work of Psacharopoulos (1994), according to which each additional year of tertiary education provides a return of 8% in developed countries. Psacharopoulos and Patrinos (2018) updated those estimations and obtained a return of 9% for all 135 countries analyzed, although in developed countries, the return is

[3] Diris and Ooghe (2018) present a similar calculation, albeit with some change in assumptions. For example, the OECD uses minimum wages to calculate the opportunity cost of college years, while Diris and Ooghe (2018) use an estimate of the relationship between age and earnings to impute the average wage of workers in their 20 s.

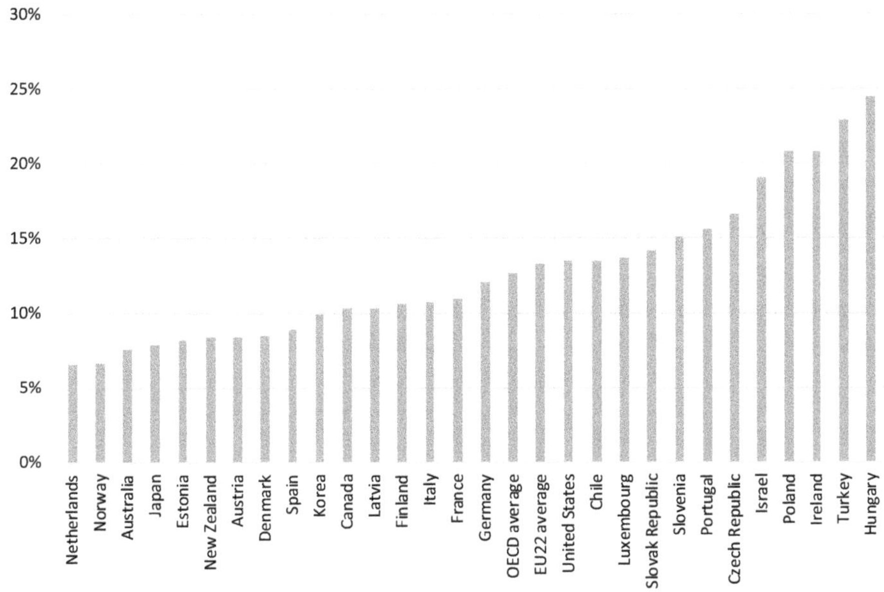

Fig. 11 Internal rate of return of tertiary education (*Source* Education at a Glance, OECD [2017])

still anchored at 8%. Bhuller et al. (2017) propose to overcome the limitations of Mincerian regressions due to the non-compliance with the key assumptions of this methodology. To overcome this, Bhuller et al. (2017) use three alternative procedures (discontinuity regression, instrumental variables, and difference-in-differences). The results show that the Mincer regressions underestimate the internal rate of return to education, which according to the preferred estimates of Bhuller et al. (2017), reaches 11%. The results show that the Mincer-type regressions underestimate the internal rate of return to education, which, according to the preferred estimates of Bhuller et al. (2017), reaches 11%. The authors wonder how, with rates much higher than the interest rate (even when considering progressive taxes and the pension system), individuals still need to acquire higher levels of education.

Most of the above calculations assume that the profitability of tertiary education is homogeneous and, in particular, does not depend on the university chosen for studies (as long as they are minimally selective), on the family's socioeconomic level, or the degree studied. Dale and Krueger (2002) analyze the profitability of studying at more selective universities versus comparable but less selective universities. Using a regression with variables observed by the researchers, the result is that the profitability of the more selective universities is higher. However, when Dale and Krueger (2002, 2014) correct admission decisions for students' latent skills and other factors, the results show that attending a more selective university in the United States has little impact on graduates' future earnings. Chetty et al. (2023) use a similar methodology and find results consistent with Dale and Krueger (2002): graduates of Ivy League universities do not have higher earnings than those who attended a good public university. However, they are likelier in the top 1% income distribution. Chetty et al.

(2023) find that there is no heterogeneity in the causal effect of attending an extended Ivy League university[4] versus a good university in terms of parental income, SAT scores, or other characteristics of applicants for admission.

In contrast, Dale and Krueger (2002, 2014) find that students from lower-income families earn superior returns at highly selective universities, even adjusting for unobservable student characteristics. Also, there are significant differences in the returns to tertiary education depending on the degree selected. Kirkeboen et al. (2016) use a very detailed database of the post-secondary Norwegian education system to analyze the effect of degree choice.

These authors conclude that different fields of study have very different labor market returns, even conditional on the institution and the quality of peers. Second, they show that the effect of attending a more selective university is small compared to the effect of selecting a field of study. Finally, Kirkeboen et al. (2016) conclude that the field of study chosen by students is consistent with the subjects in which students have comparative advantage.

As shown in the previous graphs, Spain's internal rate of return on university education is below the OECD and EU average but still quite high. Thus, in Spain, as in most countries, there are also high private incentives for students to invest in university education.

5 Financing of University Studies

Spending on higher education has increased substantially in recent years due to the expansion of demand for tertiary education. Between 2008 and 2019, growth in real terms in the OECD reached 22%, exceeding the growth of the budget of non-university education institutions by more than four points. In some countries, such as Chile, Mexico, Israel, and Norway, growth has exceeded 40% in this period.

There are two main ways of financing a university education. The first is using the tax system (either through general taxes or through taxes on university graduates[5]) to finance transfers to students (universal or income- or qualification-conditional scholarships) and to higher education institutions to keep tuition fees low.[6]

The second is direct payment. The university's public subsidies are paid either directly from the income of students and their families or through loans. These two modalities are not mutually exclusive since, in most cases, university financing comes from a combination of public subsidies and private payments. In contrast to pretertiary

[4] Ivy League (Harvard, Princeton, Yale, Cornell, Columbia, Pennsylvania, Brown, and Dartmouth College) plus MIT, Stanford, Duke, and Chicago.

[5] This procedure is known as the "graduate tax system" and involves a public subsidy to education that makes repayment contingent on income, but only when earnings exceed the cost of education. This difference is the public subsidy. In this case, therefore, the subsidy does not come from general taxation.

[6] There is a vast international academic literature on the effect of university prices and scholarships on enrollment and dropout rates. See summary in García-Montalvo (2020).

education, where approximately 90% of funding comes from public budgets, in the OECD average, private funding accounts for one-third of the resources of tertiary education institutions.

Each of these modalities may have different specialties. Subsidies derived from tax funding may depend on the income of students and their families, the level of student grades, or both. For example, the cost of tuition may be a function of the number of times a subject is failed, or the scholarship may be contingent on passing a minimum number of credits or obtaining an excellent grade. Credit financing also has different versions. The public sector could provide the loans directly, guaranteeing them, or they could be private loans. The loans could be unconditional or contingent on the income obtained after graduation (income-contingent loan or ICL).

The distribution between public and private funding of university studies is highly politically charged and is often used as an element of confrontation between political parties. This section analyzes the impact of the different university funding mechanisms on their efficiency and equity and discusses the political economy behind each option. The discussion in this section needs to consider funding distribution among various educational levels. For example, since the social profitability of 0–3 education is much higher than that obtained with university studies, public funding should be directed primarily to this educational segment to the detriment of the educational level where private profitability is dominant. This type of argument should be included in the discussion in this chapter.

The distribution between public and private funding of university studies changes over time and from country to country. In general, after the onset of the financial crisis of 2007–2008, there was an increasing strain on public budgets, which reduced public funding of universities and tended to shift a substantial part of the costs of these studies to the private sector.

Figure 12 shows how the proportion of private spending increased in most countries in the first years of the financial crisis. Since 2015, some countries that had reduced private participation have increased it, with the exception of Chile, which continues to reduce it. This trend moderated and even reversed in some countries at the end of the second decade of the twenty-first century.

The classification by country (Fig. 13) shows that there is a group that consistently has private financing above 60% (United States, United Kingdom, South Korea, Australia, Japan, and Chile) while other groups, mainly made up of Northern European countries, have levels below 15% (Finland, Norway, Iceland, Denmark, Austria, and Sweden).[7] Figure 14 shows no apparent relationship between tertiary education expenditure over GDP and the funding distribution between private and public.[8] Figure 15 breaks down the total cost of tertiary education, including public subsidies, public transfers to private institutions, and private spending. Figure 15 breaks

---

[7] It is important to note that the OECD, the source of these data, includes higher vocational training and other programs in tertiary education. For this reason, for example, the proportion of private financing in Spain is around 30%, while private university financing did not reach 20%.

[8] The correlation between Tertiary Education spending and the proportion of private funding is -0.13.

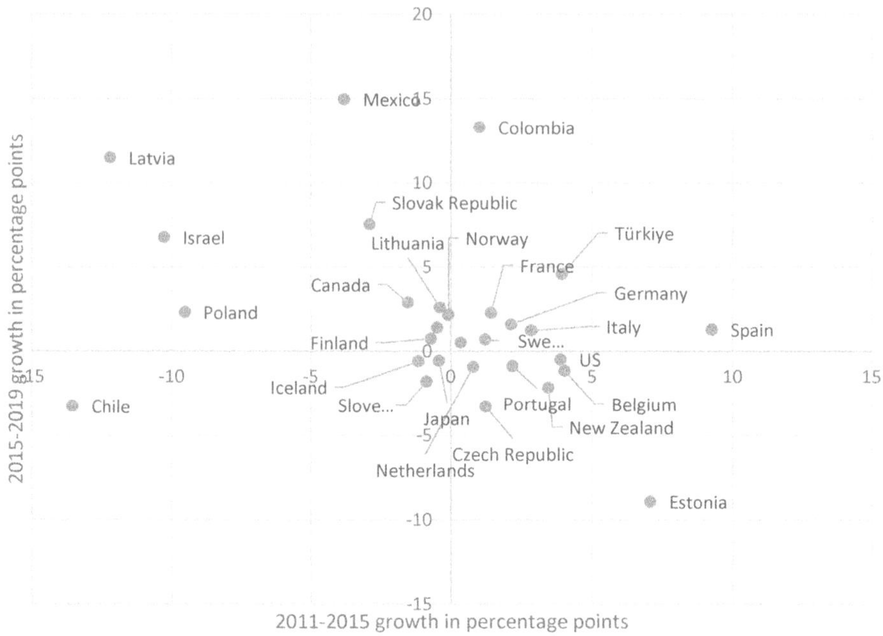

Fig. 12 Growth of private contribution 2011–2015 versus 2015–2019. (*Source* Education at a Glance [2023])

down the total cost of tertiary education, including public subsidies to institutions, public transfers to private institutions, and private spending.

The literature provides a multitude of reasons justifying an increase in private contributions to university funding. The private profitability of university education produces strong incentives for students in terms of improved salaries and reduced probability of unemployment, as discussed in the previous section. This profitability is private and may fulfill the graduate's expectations. The values are relatively high, which generates a strong incentive to pursue university studies. Second, tax-based financing in a society where students from the most disadvantaged classes have a lower propensity to go to university but pay income taxes implies a regressive transfer of resources from lower- to higher-income families.

Logically, there may be market failures that justify public intervention. An example in the university education sector is the existence of credit restrictions derived from imperfections in the capital market, which prevent bright students from low-income families from paying the price of the university. In this case, a high private cost could prevent access to university for students from families with liquidity restrictions, despite the fact that the studies could have high private profitability. Likewise, there are risks of investment in university education (increase in future income, study time, etc.) that are difficult to insure without state intervention.

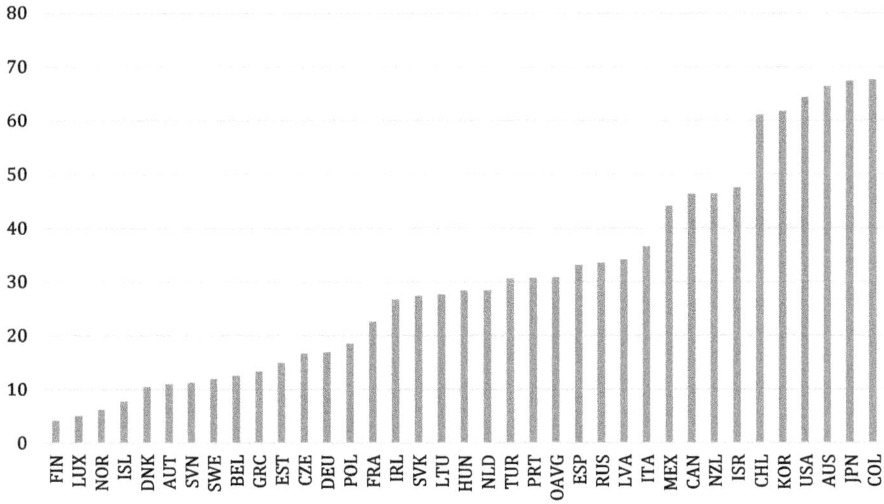

Fig. 13 Share of private spending on tertiary education (2019) (*Source* Education at a glance, OECD [2023])

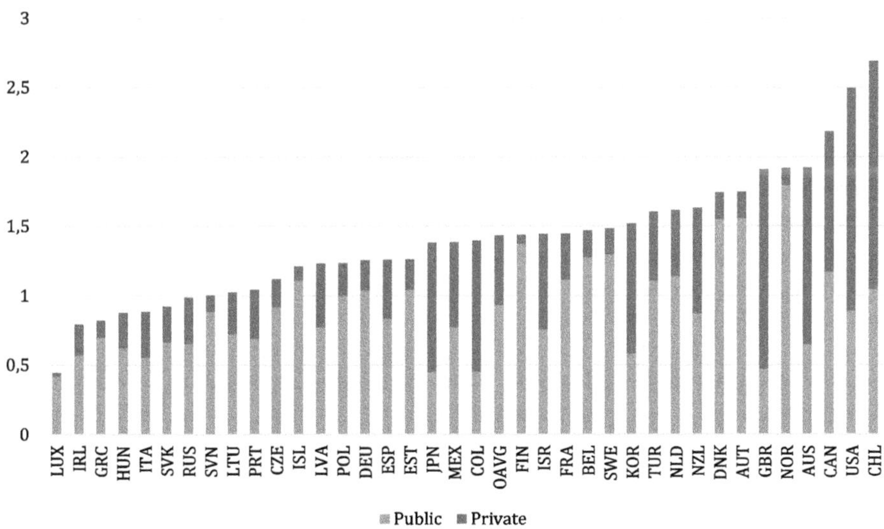

Fig. 14 Proportion of public and private financing over GDP (2019) [*Source* Own elaboration based on OECD [2023])

Another potential justification is the existence of externalities provided by the University that would lead to sub-optimal investment.[9] Lawson (2017) calculates the optimal tuition subsidy by balancing the impact of positive externalities due to the existence

[9] In fact, public policy should be based on the social marginal profitability provided by subsidies.

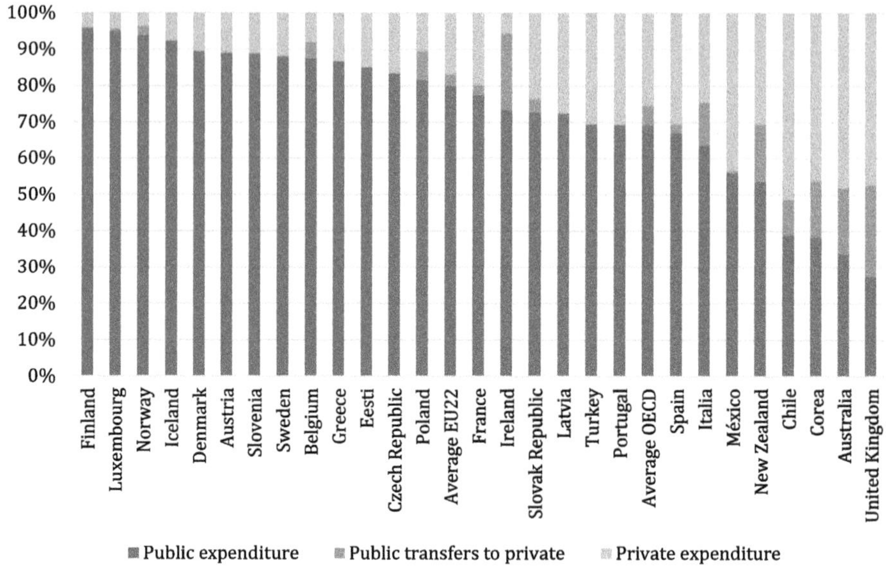

Fig. 15 Proportion of public and private spending and transfers (*Source* Education at a Glance, OECD [2022a, 2022b])

of a larger tax base (graduates earn higher salaries) with liquidity constraints.[10] The calibration of the model implies that the optimal subsidy at U.S. public universities should be $3000 higher per year. This result depends on the intensity of fiscal externalities and the insensitivity of the optimal subsidy to liquidity constraints.

In general, private benefits far outweigh pecuniary externalities. Some non-pecuniary externalities have been described as a higher propensity to vote or a higher level of trust. However, there is no evidence concerning criminal behavior. Diris and Oogher (2018) discuss the possibility of the existence of negative effects linked to the use of university education as a form of signaling (over qualification) or social pressure to pursue higher education when the most appropriate option would be a lower educational level. In any case, the effect of externalities has little empirical support.

The rest of the section discusses different factors that determine the optimal combination of public and private financing of university studies from the perspective of social profitability. Therefore, it combines elements of efficiency and equity.

[10] This trade-off does not take into account equity and redistribution considerations.

5.1 *Redistributive Elements of Financing Through General Taxation*

To analyze the redistributive effect of subsidies to tertiary education, it is necessary to analyze who pays for and benefits from them. It is clear that if the average taxpayer has a lower net lifetime income (sum net of future labor income minus taxes and private cost of education) than an average university graduate, a subsidy to tertiary education from general taxation results in a redistribution from the poor to the rich. Subsidies financed by regular taxation always generate a trade-off between efficiency and equity: the subsidy increases investment in human capital and generates reverse redistribution. Only in exceptional and counterfactual cases (for example, if workers without university education had such a low income that they did not pay taxes, or if all workers had university education, or if there were strong complementarities between low-skilled and high-skilled workers) could this trade-off be avoided.

García-Peñagolosa and Wälde (2000) build a model of successive generations with two types of workers (low-skilled and high-skilled) to analyze the impact of different forms of financing Higher Education. Subsidies financed by general taxation always imply a trade-off between efficiency and equity. The subsidy that allows an optimal number of workers to pursue university studies results in higher income for skilled workers than for unskilled workers. An increase in the subsidy increases the number of college students and tends to equalize lifetime incomes. However, workers are overqualified in that case, resulting in a loss of potential output. State student loans, the graduate tax, and income-contingent loan systems produce the same result if future income is certain. If uncertainty exists, non-contingent credits always assume repayment,[11] while contingent repayment systems only produce repayment if the student is successful in employment. The graduate tax increases the payoff for unsuccessful graduates. It decreases it for successful graduates, producing a partial insurance system that increases efficiency in the case of a risk-averse agent. Income-contingent loans produce a similar result to graduate taxes but involve some tax funding to subsidize students who were unsuccessful in their jobs. It thus generates a reverse redistribution that is absent in the graduate tax mode.[12]

Finding empirical analogs to study who benefits and who loses from subsidy funding from general taxes is complicated. Diris and Ooghe (2018) propose to calculate the net fiscal cost from a dual perspective: the parents' point of view (cross-sectional view) and the student's point of view (longitudinal view). From the students' perspective, there is regressivity by construction: high-skilled workers receive Higher Education subsidies while all future taxpayers pay those subsidies. Data from Diris and Ooghe (2018) show that the net fiscal cost from this perspective

[11] The issue of defaults on these types of loans is also a topic that has received some attention in the literature.

[12] Johnson (1984) uses a model with strong complementarities between skilled and unskilled workers to argue that there is no reverse redistribution problem. Using this argument, Borck and Wimbersky (2014) point out that the poor may prefer the tax and subsidy system to the other financing mechanisms.

is almost zero for high- and low-skilled workers in Chile because the earnings of the low-skilled workers are so low that they do not pay taxes. The net fiscal cost for Scandinavian countries is the highest. From the parents' perspective, the outcome depends on the intergenerational transfer of education (relative probability that the child of university-educated parents, as opposed to less educated parents, will go to university), the subsidy size, and the tax system's progressivity. Diris and Ooghe's (2018) calculations show that the Nordic countries (Sweden, Denmark and Norway) have the most regressive systems from the parental perspective (high subsidies and low tax progressivity), while the Netherlands, Ireland, and Chile have the least regressive systems.

5.2 *Credit Restrictions*

Another justification for the use of subsidies in Higher Education is the existence of imperfections in the capital market. The risk of uninsurable risks and credit restrictions can generate efficiency losses. Adverse selection and moral hazard can lead to underinsurance in private markets. Some risks are difficult to insure without government intervention. This is the case of the risk associated with lifetime income or credit default risk. The lack of insurance (due to the absence of collateral or guarantors) may result in the markets failing to produce enough credit, and students with few academically prepared resources may not be able to access university.

Empirically contrasting the impact of credit restrictions on access to tertiary education is complex. The evidence that there is a correlation between family income and access to university is not evidence of the existence of credit restrictions. Students from high-income families have better access to credit markets, better academic preparation, higher skills, and stronger preferences for attending college. For this reason, empirical contrasts based on indirect credit access measures have generated literature with often inconsistent results.

Solis (2017) presents the first causal analysis of the impact of access to credit on access to university education. Solis (2017) uses two university credit programs introduced in Chile that provide funding to students who score above a certain level on the national university admissions test. Comparing students who scored just above the eligibility level with those who scored just below, Solis (2017) proposes a discontinuity design that avoids the problems of omitted variables and sample selection that plague the vast majority of studies on the effect of credit restrictions on university access. The results show that the two credit programs increased the probability of immediate enrollment by 18 percentage points, doubling the enrollment rate of the group that fell just below the credit score. The improvement was greatest for students in the lowest quintile of the distribution (by 140%) versus 15% of students just below the cutoff for accessing loans. Finally, Solis (2017) shows that access to these programs (students above the score cutoff) eliminates the enrollment gap between families of different income levels, while in the group that fell just below the cutoff, the graduation rate of students in the highest income quintile is double that of students in the poorest income quintile.

Azmat and Simion (2020) analyze three reforms in the United Kingdom that involved an increase in public fees, an income-contingent loan system, and an increase in scholarships for students from low-income families. The evaluation by Azmat and Simion (2020) shows that, despite such a substantial change in university funding, it did not have a significant effect on enrollment, and the small effect observed resulted in a small reduction in the enrollment of students from more advantaged families, reducing the enrollment gap between different socioeconomic levels.

5.3 *Behavioral Effects on Decisions*

A relevant strand of the literature argues that part of the difference between the rate of access to higher education for high-income families versus lower-income families is explained by student choices that are not in line with the classic economic decision model. Lack of information about the cost of the university or the student's ability to follow courses in a highly selective institution may reduce the educational investment of students of low socioeconomic status. Present bias, debt aversion, or the excessive weight of routine and default options in decisions is particularly important among low-income students or in complex and uncertain decisions such as the admissions process or the functioning of the aid and scholarship system. In this situation, small changes can bring about large changes in decisions. Dynarski et al. (2021) use a randomized experiment to analyze whether reducing uncertainty about financial aid can modify the decisions of low-income students. The researchers identified 2000 high-achieving, low-income students in public high schools. The treatment was randomized at the school level, with half assigned to the treated group and half to the control group. The treatment consisted of sending personalized letters to encourage them to apply to the (highly selective) University of Michigan with the promise of four years of free tuition for those who were admitted. Thus, the HAIL scholarship provides an early and unconditional guarantee of free tuition.The conditional nature of the aid avoids having to fill out forms to verify that the student is qualified for the scholarship.

Dynarski et al. (2021) find a large impact of the intervention on application and enrollment rates at the University of Michigan. The application rate increased from 26% in the control to 68% in the treated group. The enrollment rate increased from 12% in the controls to 27% in the treated group. Twenty-five percent of the effect on enrollment was caused by students who would not have attended college. The remainder are students who would have gone to a community college or a less selective university without affecting universities as selective or more selective than Michigan.

5.4 The Political Economy of University Financing

The previous sections show that excessive public subsidies or high private prices can produce regressive effects or underinvestment in university education. In both cases, a shift of funding toward systems of contingent credits on future earnings or taxes for graduates would lead to improvements. For example, in case of the Nordic countries, whose high level of tax-financed subsidies for the population as a whole makes it a very regressive system, the move toward contingent credits on future salaries or graduate taxes reduces regressivity (prevents graduates who do not benefit from university education from financing those who do benefit) and provides insurance by reducing moral hazard during studies. In countries with very high private contributions, credit restrictions can leave good students from low-income families out of higher education. Again, a system of conditional credit or graduate taxes would provide clear advantages (e.g., insurance against the unknown impact of higher education on future income), although in some cases, these advantages have to be balanced against the potential regressive impact of the change.

Given the evidence of the advantages of increasing the weight of subsidized loans and graduate taxes over traditional procedures (subsidies and private financing), which implies efficiency improvements and equity, it is difficult to understand why so few countries have moved in this direction. Exceptions include the Netherlands, Hungary, New Zealand, the United Kingdom, and Australia. The latter two and an increase in tuition fees established a system of credits contingent on future income.[13] Azmat and Simion (2020) show that, in the case of the United Kingdom, the progressive shift from a tax-paid free tuition system to a system with high tuition fees supplemented by income-based scholarships and contingent credits had no negative effect on the participation of students from disadvantaged families, with a very limited effect on the choice of degree and university. In the case of Australia, Chapman and Ryan (2005) show that the move to the contingent credit system did not reduce participation in the higher education system, either overall or among students from less well-off families.

Although empirical evidence shows that the move toward credit-contingent systems does not lead to a drop in enrollment among the most economically disadvantaged groups of students, the political economy of university financing limits the extension of these systems. Many political parties in some countries that increased tuition costs after the financial crisis and its impact on public budgets are proposing a return to a system of near-total subsidization of university tuition. The seminal work of Fernandez and Rogerson (1995) shows how a coalition of the middle and upper classes may prefer to keep subsidies high so that the less advantaged classes cannot

[13] In the case of the United Kingdom, financial support for students from low−income families was also substantially increased, and repayment of loans among the poorest was even lower under the new system than under the lower tuition fees prior to the reform.

access university (due to credit restrictions) but pay, via taxes, the subsidies from which university student's benefit.[14]

5.5 University Financing in Spain

Spain belongs to the group of countries with a high public subsidy for university tuition. The system provides free tuition to students from disadvantaged families with an income ceiling that depends on the size of the family. Above that limit, students pay between 10 and 15% of the cost of university tuition. In 2012, in the face of market pressure on Spanish public debt, the Government made budgetary adjustments that affected the resources to finance public universities. The Ministry of Education, Culture, and Sports proposed an increase in university fees from the Autonomous Communities, limiting the maximum price to be paid by students to 25% of the cost of the university place. In addition, the price of second, third, and fourth enrollments was considerably increased. Each autonomous region decided on the proportion of increase in public prices. While some (Galicia and Asturias) increased them very little, Catalonia and Madrid opted for a very substantial increase. In the case of Catalonia, the price increase was progressive and graduated from the so-called equity grants. Full payment of tuition fees only occurred in the case of families with incomes above €67,000.[15] For those with lower incomes but higher than those who gave access to free tuition, the equity scholarships provided more significant discounts for the lower income. García-Montalvo (2020) analyzes the impact of this new system of financing university tuition and finds no evidence of any adverse impact of the policy change on the dropout rate. He also analyzes the distributional impact of the reform, showing that carefully designed progressive public prices can generate additional revenue for universities without any negative impact on the dropout rates of students from low socioeconomic backgrounds.[16] In this case, the subsidy reduction focused on students from families with higher purchasing power had no impact on enrollment rates and reduced the regressivity of the system from the student's perspective.

Beneito et al. (2018) focus on the increase in the cost of second and third enrollments and show that the increase in tuition increased student effort. Montalbán (2022) shows that need-based scholarships have no impact on academic outcomes if the requirements in terms of academic performance are standard in most countries. The provision of a small scholarship salary has a much greater impact on academic

[14] Borck and Wimbersky (2014) build a model with risk–averse consumers and income heterogeneity and argue that a majority support for a containing credit or graduate payment system is more likely if risk aversion increases or inequality is reduced.

[15] For a reference family of four.

[16] The need to apply for the general scholarship before applying for the equity scholarship meant that quite a few students who did not traditionally apply for the general scholarship because they considered their family income to be above the limits obtained the tuition waiver.

outcomes and the probability of completing university studies when they are associated with demanding minimum academic requirements, although this effect occurs only if the scholarship is communicated at the beginning of the academic year. Increasing the size of the aid does not improve academic results. On the other hand, increasing the academic requirements does not produce an increase in university dropout rates.

Cabrales et al. (2019) analyze the change from the current system of financing universities in Spain to a procedure based on credits contingent on future income (see also Chapter 1 in this manual). The simulations are based on a virtual laboratory where the distributional effect of the change in funding is analyzed. The analysis uses a simulation of university graduates' lifetime earnings that reproduces the employment dynamics and earnings calculated from Social Security administrative data. On this basis, the authors estimate the effect of introducing a contingent credit system on individuals in different positions of income distribution and the impact on the state. The results show that the structure is very progressive in all specifications: the top 25% of the income distribution ends up paying almost the entire cost of tuition and the bottom 10% pays practically nothing. Moreover, the share of the subsidy in the cost of university education is between 16 and 56 percentage points lower than in the current system.

6 University Governance

Managing the university is complicated. Most Western countries recognize, in one way or another, university autonomy in management, especially academic management. This generates the necessary freedom to create innovation on the part of professors and should be linked to a desirable funding framework.

In reality, this inevitably leads to competition for funds, allowing the regulator to generate incentives that optimize the provision of teaching and research (Del Rey 2001). As a consequence, more or less virtuous processes could occur, favoring the concentration of research in the most productive universities (De Fraja and Valbonesi 2012), the higher productivity of the most active academics (Checchi et al. 2021; De Fraja et al. 2019), or favoring the admission of students (Bouchard St-Amant et al. 2020). The aim of this section is to analyze who should lead this process and how.

6.1 Talent Management

Becker and Gerhart (1996) highlight the importance of personnel management and selection in institutions' economic performance and survival. In fact, the literature has evolved to consider the governance of the human resources of any company as a whole as a system that goes beyond the selection, remuneration, and behavior of the head of the organization, including the organization as a whole, and how this translates into its performance (Bloom and Van Reenen 2007; Boon et al. 2019).

This premise is not trivial. McCormack et al. (2014) use the methodology proposed by Bloom and Van Reenen (2007) and conclude that the quality of university management has a significant effect on performance in both teaching and research (which are not always correlated). From a pool of 248 English universities, the authors use a total of 17 characteristics of university management quality divided into four groups: operations, supervision, objectives, and incentives, evaluated through a questionnaire and contrasted against the Research Excellence Framework (REF), which assesses every five years the research of English departments, the student satisfaction survey, and academic rankings. The results are robust when controlling for the size of the departments, the number of students they serve, and other variables. The first result to note is that the individual characteristics of university leaders do not have a significant effect on the functioning of the university; on the contrary, they do find a positive relationship between the qualities of decentralized management which affects the less strategic tasks, such as those of Human Resources or academic departments, etc.

6.2 *The Manager's Talent*

In contrast to the previous holistic approach, Goodall (2009) focuses on university presidents. He provides empirical foundations through the analysis of a data set of 400 chancellors and principals from top U.S. and British business schools. His hypothesis argues that research-oriented universities experience substantial progress when individuals of renown in academia assume positions of responsibility. He also posits that academics should play leadership roles in other organizations, including governmental entities charged with funding educational institutions, to support and sustain themselves. Goodall (2009) finds a positive correlation between research excellence and organizational achievement, proposing that the appropriate level of academic competence in a president will vary according to the position of the university in terms of its research and its position in rankings, as well as its future goals. He also develops an empirical model using as a dependent variable the results of the REF of 55 British universities conducted in the years 1992, 1996, and 2001, and as an independent variable, the cumulative citations over the careers of 157 British university presidents in his sample. In short, extensive literature theoretically and causally supports the basis of their analysis; good managers generate good results that persist over time (Lazear et al. 2015; Manthei et al. 2023).

Gerashchenko (2022) uses the same methodology as Goodall (2009) for the universe of Russian universities but interestingly extends it with independent variables by taking into account some differential aspects; he improves the bibliometric variables, characterizes the universities according to their specialization, and differentiates between those rectors who are appointed for their management skills and those who are politically selected. His results, which do not contain causality, indicate that being a quality researcher has a long-term effect on the institutions and the productivity of the rector's own area. For Gerashchenko (2022), it is the quality of the rector and not the form of appointment that determines the final outcome.

The system implemented in the LOSU, which is far removed from professionalism or academic merit-based teaching, is far from the results seen in the previous articles and leaves room for further improvements in the field of governance in Spain.

Exercises

Exercise 1. *Why is funding university education through public subsidies regressive by construction on the student approach (longitudinal analysis)?*

Exercise 2. *Explain why, if there is a high degree of complementarity between the skills of low-skilled workers and university workers, the trade-off between efficiency and equity generated by the financing of tertiary education based on public subsidies can be broken.*

Exercise 3. *(García Peñagolosa and Wälde 2000). Imagine an economy with N individuals living in three periods. In the first period, all children complete compulsory education. In the second period, they choose whether to work immediately or to invest in tertiary education. tertiary education costs are E. All consumption occurs in the third period. Parents bequeath to their children an inheritance g with a distribution f(g). The economy produces a consumption good with technology* $Y = F(H, L)$ *where H are university workers and L are non-university workers. Therefore,* $N = H + L$*. There is perfect competition in product and factor markets. The government can only subsidize education and collect taxes while maintaining budget constraints.*

a) *If human capital cannot be used as collateral and education is not subsidized, who will be able to access university education?*
b) *If the capital market is perfect and there is no subsidization, what is the equilibrium number of college students? Describe the net lifetime income of a college student and a non-college worker. Use the principles discussed in the chapter to construct theinternal rate of return to education.*
c) *Suppose the government's objective is to achieve the optimal number of college-educated workers, H*, and for this, it uses public subsidies, but the capital market does not accept human capital as a co-side. Will it be able to achieve its objective? Explain the distributional impact of the equilibrium obtained.*

Exercise 4. *Use the data fromthe INE survey on job placement of university students (You can use the data corresponding to the surveys of your favorite country. The Spanish microdata can be obtained from the following link*https://www.ine.es/dyngs/INEbase/es/operacion.htm?c=Estadistica_C&cid=1254736176991&menu=results&idp=1254735976597#!tabs-1254736195339

a) *Calculate the internal profitability of university education. Use the assumptions you believe necessary to make the calculation.*
b) *Analyzes the results by field of study and gender.*
c) *Some studies*(e.g. https://www.fbbva.es/wp-content/uploads/2023/05/FBBVA-Ivie_U-ranking_Informe_Insercion_laboral_2023_def.pdf) *use Social Security data to analyze the labor market outcomes of university students. What are the*

advantages and disadvantages of Social Security data compared to INE in the analysis of university students' educational rentability?

Exercise 5. *Using the data catalog of the Spanish Ministry of Universities* (https://www.universidades.gob.es/catalogo-de-datos/)*:*

a) *In 2018, Andalusia started subsidizing 100% of the tuition fees to students who had passed. Analyze the effect on the demand for university studies in that Autonomous Community compared to the rest.*
b) *Does university entrance grade inflation exist in Spain? Analyze empirically and justify your position.*

References

Aghion, Philippe, Mathias Dewatripont, Caroline Hoxby, Andreu Mas-Colell, and André Sapir. 2008. *Higher Aspirations: An Agenda for Reforming European Universities.* (5; Bruegel Blueprint Series). Bruegel.

Aghion, Philippe, Mathias Dewatripont, Caroline Hoxby, Andreu Mas-Colell, and André Sapir. 2010. The governance and performance of universities: Evidence from Europe and the US. *Economic Policy* 25 (61): 7–59. https://doi.org/10.1111/j.1468-0327.2009.00238.x

Aina, Carmen, Eliana Baici, Giorgia Casalone, and Francesco Pastore. 2018. *Delayed Graduation: A Survey* (11421; Discussion Papers). https://www.iza.org

Aina, Carmen, Eliana Baici, Giorgia Casalone, and Francesco Pastore. 2022. The determinants of university dropout: A review of the socio-economic literature. In *Socio-Economic Planning Sciences* (vol. 79). Elsevier Ltd. https://doi.org/10.1016/j.seps.2021.101102

Altonji, Joseph G., Peter Arcidiacono, and Arnaud Maurel. 2016. The analysis of field choice in college and graduate school: Determinants and wage effects. In *Handbook of the Economics of Education* (vol. 5, pp. 305–396). Elsevier.

Anelli, Massimo, and Giovanni Peri. 2015. Gender of siblings and choice of college major. *CESifo Economic Studies* 61 (1): 53–71. https://doi.org/10.1093/cesifo/ifu028

Arcidiacono, Peter, V. Joseph Hotz, and Songman Kang. 2012. Modeling college major choices using elicited measures of expectations and counterfactuals. *Journal of Econometrics* 166 (1): 3–16. https://doi.org/10.1016/j.jeconom.2011.06.002

Autor, David H., John J. Donohue III, and Stewart J. Schwab. 2006. The costs of wrongful–discharge laws. *The Review of Economics and Statistics* 88 (2): 211–231.

Autor, David H., Frank Levy, and Richard J. Murnane. 2003. The skill content of recent technological change: An empirical exploration. *The Quarterly journal of economics* 118. https://doi.org/10.1162/003355303322552801

Ayllón, Sara, Javier Valbuena, and Alexander Plum. 2022. Youth unemployment and stigmatization over the business cycle in Europe. *Oxford Bulletin of Economics and Statistics* 84 (1): 103–129. https://doi.org/10.1111/obes.12445

Azmat, Ghazala, and Ştefania Simion. 2020. Charging for higher education: Estimating the impact on inequality and student outcomes. The B.E. *Journal of Economic Analysis & Policy* 21 (1): 175–239.

Backes-Gellner, Uschi, Holger Herz, Michael Kosfeld, and Yvonne Oswald. 2021. Do preferences and biases predict life outcomes? Evidence from education and labor market entry decisions. *European Economic Review* 134: 103709. https://doi.org/10.1016/j.euroecorev.2021.103709

Becker, Brian, and Barry Gerhart. 1996. The impact of human resource management on organizational performance: Progress and prospects. *The Academy of Management Journal* 39 (4): 779–801. https://about.jstor.org/terms

Behr, Andreas, Marco Giese, Herve D. Teguim Kamdjou, and Katja Theune. 2020. Dropping out of university: A literature review. *Review of Education* 8 (2): 614–652. https://doi.org/10.1002/rev3.3202

Betts, Julian R., and Laurel L. McFarland. 1995. Safe port in a storm: The impact of labor market conditions on community college enrollments. *The Journal of Human Resources* 30 (4): 741–765. https://about.jstor.org/terms

Bleemer, Zachary. 2022. Affirmative action, mismatch, and economic mobility after california's proposition 209. *The Quarterly Journal of Economics* 137 (1): 115–160. https://doi.org/10.1093/qje/qjab027

Bloom, Nicholas, and John Van Reenen. 2007. Measuring and explaining management practices across firms and countries. *The Quarterly Journal of Economics* 122 (4): 1351–1408. https://doi.org/10.1162/qjec.2007.122.4.1351

Boon, Corine, Deanne N. Den Hartog, and David P. Lepak. 2019. A systematic review of human resource management systems and their measurement. *Journal of Management* 45 (6): 2498–2537. https://doi.org/10.1177/0149206318818718

Bordon, Paola, and Chao Fu. 2015. College-major choice to college-then-major choice. *Review of Economic Studies* 82 (4): 1247–1288. https://doi.org/10.1177/0149206318818718

Borck, Rainald, and Martin Wimbersky. 2014. Political economics of higher education finance. *Oxford Economic Papers* 66 (1): 115–139.

Bouchard St-Amant, Pier-André, Alexis-Nicolas Brabant, and Éric Germain. 2020. University funding formulas: An analysis of the Québec reforms and incentives. *Canadian Journal of Higher Education* 50 (1): 1–27.

Braga, Michela, Marco Paccagnella, and Michele Pellizzari. 2014. Evaluating students evaluations of professors. *Economics of Education Review* 41: 71–88. https://doi.org/10.1016/j.econedurev.2014.04.002

Bresnahan, Timothy F., Erik Brynjolfsson, and Lorin M. Hitt. 2002. Information technology, workplace organization, and the demand for skilled labor: Firm-level evidence. *The Quarterly journal of economics* 117. https://doi.org/10.1162/003355302753399526

Cabrales, Antonio, Maia Güell, Rocio Madera, and Analía Viola. 2019. Income contingent university loans: Policy design and an application to Spain, *Economic Policy* 34 (99): 479–521.

Cappellari, Lorenzo, and Claudio Lucifora. 2009. The bologna process and college enrollment decisions. *Labour Economics* 16 (6): 638–647. https://doi.org/10.1016/J.LABECO.2009.08.009

Cardoso, Ana Rute, Annalisa Loviglio, and Lavinia Piemontese. 2016. Misperceptions of unemployment and individual labor market outcomes. *IZA Journal of Labor Policy* 5 (1). https://doi.org/10.1186/s40173-016-0069-6

Carlsson, Magnus, Henning Finseraas, Arnfinn H. Midtbøen, and Guðbjörg Linda Rafnsdóttir. 2021. Gender bias in academic recruitment? Evidence from a survey experiment in the Nordic region. *European Sociological Review* 37 (3): 399–410.

Carruthers, Celeste K., William F. Fox, and Christopher Jepsen. 2023. What knox achieved: Estimated effects of tuition-free community college on attainment and earnings. *Journal of Human Resources*, 11359R2. https://doi.org/10.3368/jhr.1220-11359R2

Checchi, Daniele, Gianni De Fraja, and Stefano Verzillo. 2021. Incentives and careers in academia: Theory and empirical analysis. *The Review of Economics and Statistics* 103 (4): 786–802. https://doi.org/10.1162/rest_a_00916

Chetty, Raj, David J. Deming, and John N. Friedman. 2023. Diversifying society's leaders? The causal effects of admission to highly selective private colleges. In *NBER Working Paper Series* (31492). https://doi.org/10.3386/w31492

Coenen, Johan, Lex Borghans, and Ron Diris. 2021. Personality traits, preferences and educational choices: A focus on STEM. *Journal of Economic Psychology* 84: 167–4870. https://doi.org/10.17632/vt5v7c27kw.1

Dale, Stacy Berg, and Alan B. Krueger. 2002. Estimating the payoff to attending a more selective college: An application of selection on observables and unobservables. *The Quarterly Journal of Economics* 117 (4): 1491–1527. https://doi.org/10.1162/003355302320935089

Dale, Stacy Berg, and Alan B. Krueger. 2014. Estimating the effects of college characteristics over the career using administrative earnings data. *Journal of Human Resources* 49 (2): 323–358. https://doi.org/10.3368/jhr.49.2.323

De Fraja, Gianni, Giovanni Facchini, and John Gathergood. 2019. Academic salaries and public evaluation of university research: Evidence from the UK research excellence framework. *Economic Policy* 34 (99): 523–583. https://doi.org/10.1093/epolic/eiz009

De Fraja, Gianni, and Paola Valbonesi. 2012. The design of the university system. *Journal of Public Economics* 96 (3–4): 317–330. https://doi.org/10.1016/j.jpubeco.2011.10.005

Del Rey, Elena. 2001. Teaching versus research: A model of state university competition. *Journal of Urban Economics* 49 (2): 356–373. https://doi.org/10.1006/juec.2000.2193

Denning, Jeffrey T. 2017. College on the cheap: Consequences of community college tuition reductions. *American Economic Journal: Economic Policy* 9 (2): 155–188. https://doi.org/10.1257/pol.20150374

Dynarski, Susan, Carmello J. Libassi, Katherine Michelmore, and Stephanie Owen. 2021. Closing the gap: The effect of reducing complexity and uncertainty in college pricing on the choices of low-income students. *American Economic Review* 111 (6): 1721–56.

Durazzi, Niccolo. 2019. The political economy of high skills: Higher education in knowledge-based labour markets. *Journal of European Public Policy* 26 (12): 1799–1817. https://doi.org/10.1080/13501763.2018.1551415

García Hombrados, J. 2022 December 7. *Limitaciones a la atracción de talento joven en las universidades públicas españolas.* Nadaesgratis. https://nadaesgratis.es/jorge-garcia/limitaciones-a-la-atraccion-de-talento-joven-en-las-universidades-publicas-espanolas

Gerashchenko, Daria. 2022. Academic leadership and university performance: Do Russian universities improve when they are led by top researchers? *Higher Education* 83 (5): 1103–1123. https://doi.org/10.1007/s10734-021-00732-5

Ginther, Donna K., and Shulamit Kahn. 2021. Women in academic economics: Have we made progress? *AEA Papers and Proceedings* 111: 138–142.

Goodall, Amanda H. 2009. Highly cited leaders and the performance of research universities. *Research Policy* 38 (7): 1079–1092. https://doi.org/10.1016/j.respol.2009.04.002

Grossman, Joshua, Sabina Tomkins, Lindsay C. Page, and Sharad Goel. 2023. *The Disparate Impacts of College Admissions Policies on Asian American Applicants* (31527; NBER Working Papers). National Bureau of Economic Research. https://doi.org/10.3386/w31527

Hanushek, Eric A. 2016. Will more higher education improve economic growth? *Oxford Review of Economic Policy,* 32. https://doi.org/10.1093/oxrep/grw025

Hastings, Justine S., Christopher A. Neilson, and Seth D. Zimmerman. 2013. *Are Some Degrees Worth More than Others? Evidence from college admission cutoffs in Chile* (19241; Nber Working Paper Series). http://www.justinehastings.com/images/downloads/HNZ_Chile_Appendix_2013a.pdf

Hoekstra, Mark. 2009. The effect of attending the flagship state university on earnings: A discontinuity-based approach. *Review of Economics and Statistics* 91 (4): 717–724. https://doi.org/10.1162/rest.91.4.717

Hoxby, Caroline M. 2009. The changing selectivity of american colleges. *Journal of Economic Perspectives* 23 (4): 95–118. https://doi.org/10.1257/jep.23.4.95

Hoxby, Caroline Minter. 2004. *College Choices: The economics of where to go, when to go, and How to Pay for it hasis>. University of Chicago Press.*

Johnson, George E. 1984. Subsidies for higher education. *Journal of Labour Economics* 2: 303–18.

Kamis, Rais, Jessica Pan, and Kelvin KC Seah. 2023. Do college admissions criteria matter? Evidence from discretionary vs. grade-based admission policies. *Economics of Education Review* 92. https://doi.org/10.1016/j.econedurev.2022.102347

Kasper, Henry T. 2003. The changing role of community college. *Occupational Outlook Quarterly*, 14–21.

Kehm, Barbara M., Malene Rode Larsen, and Hanna Bjørnøy Sommersel. 2020. Student dropout from universities in Europe: A review of empirical literature. *Hungarian Educational Research Journal* 9 (2): 147–164. https://doi.org/10.1556/063.9.2019.1.18

Kirkeboen, Lars J., Edwin Leuven, and Magne Mogstad. 2016. Field of study, earnings, and self-selection. *The Quarterly Journal of Economics* 131 (3): 1057–1111.

Kurban, Haydar, Ryan M. Gallagher, and Joseph J. Persky. 2015. Demographic changes and education expenditures: A reinterpretation. *Economics of Education Review* 45: 103–108. https://doi.org/10.1016/j.econedurev.2015.01.001

Lassibille, Gérard, and Lucía Navarro Gómez. 2008. Why do higher education students drop out? Evidence from Spain. *Education Economics* 16 (1). https://doi.org/10.1080/09645290701523267

Lazear, Edward P., Kathryn L. Shaw, and Christopher T. 2015. The value of bosses. *Journal of Labor Economics* 33 (4): 823–861. https://doi.org/10.1086/681097

Ma, Liping, Xin Li, Qiong Zhu, and Xiaoyang Ye. 2023. College-major choice to college-then-major choice: Experimental evidence from Chinese college admissions reforms. *Economics of Education Review* 94: 102380. https://doi.org/10.1016/J.ECONEDUREV.2023.102380

Manthei, Kathrin, Dirk Sliwka, and Timo Vogelsang. 2023. Talking about performance or paying for it? A field experiment on performance reviews and incentives. *Management Science* 69 (4): 2198–2216. https://doi.org/10.1287/mnsc.2022.4431

Marginson, Simon. 2016. The worldwide trend to high participation higher education: Dynamics of social stratification in inclusive systems. *Higher Education* 72 (4): 413–434. https://doi.org/10.1007/s10734-016-0016-x

Martínez-Morales, Ignacio, and Fernando Marhuenda-Fluixá. 2020. Vocational education and training in Spain: Steady improvement and increasing value. *Journal of Vocational Education & Training* 72 (2): 209–227. https://doi.org/10.1080/13636820.2020.1729840

McCormack, John, Carol Propper, and Sarah Smith. 2014. Herding cats? Management and university performance. *The Economic Journal* 124 (578): F534–F564. https://doi.org/10.1111/ECOJ.12105

Modena, Francesca, Enrico Rettore, and Giulia Martina Tanzi. 2018. *The effect of grants on university drop-out rates: Evidence on the Italian case* (1193; Temi Di Discussione). https://ssrn.com/abstract=3415672

Montalbán, José. 2023. Countering moral hazard in higher education: The role of performance incentives in need-based grants. *Economic Journal* 133 (649): 355–389. https://doi.org/10.1093/ej/ueac062

Montalvo, José García. 2020. El impacto de la introducción de subvenciones progresivas en la educación superior: El caso de Cataluña, *Papeles de Economía Española* 166: 123–142.

Mountjoy, Jack. 2022. Community colleges and upward mobility. *American Economic Review* 112 (8): 2580–2630.

Murphy, Richard, Judith Scott-Clayton, and Gill Wyness. 2019. The end of free college in England: Implications for enrolments, equity, and quality. *Economics of Education Review* 71: 7–22.

Musselin, Christine. 2009. *The Market for Academics*. Routledge.

OECD. 2018. The future of education and skills: Education 2030. *OECD Education Working Papers*, 1–23. http://www.oecd.org/education/2030/E2030PositionPaper(05.04.2018).pdf

OECD. 2022a. Pathways to professions: *Understanding Higher Vocational and Professional Tertiary Education Systems*. OECD. https://doi.org/10.1787/a81152f4-en

OECD. 2022b. *Education at a Glance 2022* (Education at a Glance). OECD. https://doi.org/10.1787/3197152b-en

OECD, O. for E. C. and D. 2019. *PISA 2018 Results (Volume I)*. OECD. https://doi.org/10.1787/5f07c754-en

Patnaik, Arpita, Matthew Wiswall, and Basit Zafar. 2021. College Majors 1. *The Routledge Handbook of the Economics of Education*, 415–457.

Pietro, Giorgio Di, and Andrea Cutillo. 2006. University quality and labour market outcomes in Italy. *Labour* 20 (1): 37–62. https://doi.org/10.1111/j.1467-9914.2006.00333.x

Psacharopoulos, George, and Harry Anthony Patrinos. 2004. Returns to investment in education: A further update. *Education Economics* 12: 2.

Psacharopoulos, George, and Harry Anthony Patrinos. 2018. Returns to investment in education: A decennial review of the global literature. *Education Economics* 26 (5): 445–458.

Richardson, John TE, Jenna Mittelmeier, and Bart Rienties. 2020. The role of gender, social class and ethnicity in participation and academic attainment in UK higher education: An update. *Oxford Review of Education* 46 (3): 346–362.

Ruiz-Lázaro, Judit. 2021. Evaluation of the academic performance of students entering university in Spain. *Edunovatic 2021*, 446.

Sandel, Michael J. 2020. *The Tyranny of Merit: What's Become of the Common Good?* Penguin UK.

Schanzenbach, Diane Whitmore, Julia A. Turner, and Sarah Turner. 2023. *Raising State Minimum Wages, Lowering Community College Enrollment* (31540; NBER working paper series). http://www.nber.org/papers/w31540

SIIU. 2023. *Indicadores Universitarios de Rendimiento Académico Curso.* 2021–2022.

Solis, Alex. 2017. Credit access and college enrollment. *Journal of Political Economy* 125 (2): 562–622.

Tayebi, Abdelhamid, Josefa Gómez, and Carlos Delgado. 2021. Analysis on the lack of motivation and dropout in engineering students in Spain. *IEEE Access* 9: 66253–66265. https://doi.org/10.1109/ACCESS.2021.3076751

Terviö, Marko. 2011. Divisions within academia: Evidence from faculty hiring and placement. *Review of Economics and Statistics* 93 (3): 1053–1062.

Triventi, Moris. 2013. Stratification in higher education and its relationship with social inequality: A comparative study of 11 European countries. In *European Sociological Review* (vol. 29, Issue 3). https://www.jstor.org/stable/24479990

Valero, Anna, and John Van Reenen. 2019. The economic impact of universities: Evidence from across the globe. *Economics of Education Review* 68: 53–67. https://doi.org/10.1016/j.econedurev.2018.09.001

Vergolini, Loris, and Eleonora Vlach. 2017. Family background and educational path of Italian graduates. *Higher Education* 73 (2): 245–259. https://doi.org/10.1007/s10734-016-0011-2

Wapman, K. Hunter, Sam Zhang, Aaron Clauset, and Daniel B. Larremore. 2022. Quantifying hierarchy and dynamics in US faculty hiring and retention. *Nature* 610 (7930): 120–127.

Williams, Wendy M., and Stephen J. Ceci. 2015. National hiring experiments reveal 2: 1 faculty preference for women on STEM tenure track. *Proceedings of the National Academy of Sciences* 112 (17): 5360–5365.

Wiswall, Matthew, and Basit Zafar. 2015. *Determinants of College Major Choice: Identification using an Information Experiment* 82 (2). https://www.jstor.org/stable/43551547

Cross-Cutting Issues

School Choice

Andreu Arenas and Caterina Calsamiglia

1 Introduction

School choice is a broad term that describes the process through which families attempt to choose a school for their children, as opposed to an assignment based solely on their residential neighborhood. The goal is to assign students to schools while taking their preferences into account, without considering their willingness to pay. One initial way to achieve this is through school vouchers. Instead of providing public education, the government transfers resources to families so they can spend them on the school of their choice. In such cases, the school admission process is usually decentralized (for example, in Chile or the United States). Another, more common form of school choice in Europe involves asking families to submit a ranked list of school preferences and attempting to satisfy them as best as possible through a centralized process based on predetermined criteria.

On one hand, these criteria often determine which types of families receive priority for different types of schools, for example, based on the parents' place of residence or work, the presence of siblings in the school, purchasing power, or students' educational needs. Among these possibilities, it is also possible to disregard any consideration of family circumstances and treat all potential students equally.

On the other hand, the allocation criterion also establishes how families' preferences are taken into account. This is an important aspect to consider. When families express their preferences, they must consider two key questions. The first concerns their true preferences—what is the school they would ideally want for their children? The second relates to the preferences they should strategically express. For example, strong emphasis is often placed on satisfying families' first preference. Imagine that

A. Arenas (✉)
Economics Department and IEB, University of Barcelona, Barcelona, Spain
e-mail: andreu.arenas@ub.edu

C. Calsamiglia
Barcelona Supercomputing Center, ICREA, Barcelona, Spain

A. Cabrales and I. Sanz (eds.), *Economics of Education*,
https://doi.org/10.1007/978-3-031-90911-5_12

our favorite school is far from our home, making admission difficult because families living closer are given priority. If we state that this school is our top choice, it is highly likely that we will not secure a spot. In that case, we then compete for admission to our second preference. However, if priority is given to first-choice satisfaction, we may find ourselves at a disadvantage compared to families who listed that school as their first choice. The final result could be that we receive our third choice. Conversely, if we decide not to list our favorite school and instead rank our second real preference as our first choice, we might secure it. This example illustrates how the method of satisfying families' preferences can impact—especially for more sophisticated families—the schools that are in demand. In general, it is useful to distinguish between allocation criteria that incentivize strategic preference revelation, as in the example above, and those that encourage the revelation of true preferences.

The school choice process operates through a centralized mechanism within a specific geographic area, which may correspond to the boundaries of a neighborhood, municipality, metropolitan area, or a region of similar size. A crucial aspect is the percentage of schools whose access is determined by the centralized school choice mechanism. Some private schools may assign spots based on families' willingness to pay, in a decentralized manner. The possibility of accessing these schools influences how the school choice mechanism functions. If a family has both the ability and willingness to pay for a private school, they will only enroll in the school resulting from the centralized school choice process if they consider it better than the private alternative.

Compared to purely residential assignment, the school choice process entails potential benefits and costs. Economic theory and market design help anticipate some of the key effects of different types of school choice. However, as we will see later, the significance and variability of implementation details in school choice worldwide have led to an ongoing dialogue between theory and empirical analysis.

2 Determinants of School Demand

One of the greatest potential benefits of school choice is the ability to better understand families' preferences. This is important because it allows the government to identify the most in-demand schools, learn from their successes, and provide them with resources to expand their capacity. This process can create a virtuous cycle that improves social and family welfare.

These hypothetical benefits rely on several assumptions. First, families must have sufficient information about schools to judge their quality. Additionally, school quality must be a central factor in families' demand. The credibility of these assumptions is fundamentally an empirical question. Moreover, whether these assumptions hold depends partly on the institutional context. For example, there may be room for public policies that provide information about schools and the importance of their quality, fostering an environment where these assumptions are more plausible and school choice works more effectively.

Understanding the determinants of school demand is therefore a crucial issue that shapes any analysis and interpretation of the process's outcomes. Empirical evidence shows that families have a preference for schools with high-achieving students. For example, Hastings and Weinstein (2008) conducted two experiments in which low-income families in North Carolina (United States) were randomly provided with direct information about the academic performance of various public schools. The results show that families who received this information ended up choosing higher-performing schools, which resulted in better academic outcomes for their children (which is not surprising, as discussed in Chapter 3c regarding peer effects).

In Spain, Vega-Bayo and Mariel (2018) analyze the probability that parents choose a particular school based on its characteristics (and family characteristics) using PISA (2012) data. The results indicate that the most explanatory factors in school choice are its ownership (public or private), location, and reputation (measured by the school's average grades). Other visible characteristics that might be important in choosing a school, such as size, infrastructure, extracurricular offerings, or socioeconomic composition, have less explanatory power, and their importance varies by autonomous community.

Another way to quantify to what extent families value school quality is by analyzing housing prices in school districts with better or worse schools. The intuition is simple: if living in a particular neighborhood provides preferential access to quality schools, and families value that quality, they should be willing to pay a higher price to live in that neighborhood. If we observe higher demand (and therefore higher prices) in those neighborhoods, we can quantify the price families are willing to pay for a greater probability of accessing a good school, which serves as a measure of its importance. The main challenge in making this calculation is that neighborhoods with better or worse schools often differ not only in the educational dimension but also in many others, such as demographic composition, social capital, or income level. A creative way to overcome this challenge is to compare housing prices between two sidewalks of the same street, which belong to the same *neighborhood* and where residents experience the same socioeconomic context but nonetheless have access to different school districts.

Fack and Grenet (2010) conduct this exercise using data from Paris, classifying school quality based on their average score in a national exam taken at the end of secondary school, the proportion of secondary students admitted to the general high school curriculum instead of vocational studies, and the proportion of students from privileged socioeconomic backgrounds. The results show that housing prices providing greater access to quality schools (with a one-standard-deviation higher performance) increase by around 2%. Moreover, this effect is particularly pronounced in areas with limited availability of private schools. The intuition is as follows: in areas without private schools, the only way to access a quality school is by purchasing a home in the district with better schools, which drives up prices. However, in areas with private schools, there is another way to access a good school: directly paying tuition for a quality private school. For this reason, the effect of school quality is smaller in these areas.

In summary, studies using data from countries around the world confirm that there is a preference for schools with higher academic performance.

2.1 Absolute Performance vs. Value-Added

Schools with better results, however, are not necessarily the best schools: they may simply be schools that manage to attract better students or those from more affluent backgrounds. In other words, a school having students with higher grades does not mean that students achieve better grades as a consequence of being enrolled in that school. In such a case, attending a school with higher average grades could have no effect on individual academic performance. A study by Gibbons et al. (2013) using data from England replicates the empirical analysis of Fack and Grenet (2010), but examining the relationship between housing prices and the value-added of schools, where value-added is measured as the average improvement in academic performance between ages 7 and 11. value-added is an important measure because it separates the school's productivity from the composition of its students, which should already be reflected in results at age 7. The study's findings show that housing prices respond both to the value-added of the school and to the initial characteristics of its students, and no alternative variable can explain the effect of value-added. This result is important because, if extrapolated, it would mean that family preferences respond to quality in a way that incentivizes schools to improve, rather than simply attracting better students (which is a zero-sum game, based on shifting good students from one school to another instead of improving them).

Exercise 1:

(a) Consider a family deciding between buying a house for €300,000 or another for €306,000. The €306,000 house is in a neighborhood with a school that has a one-standard-deviation higher value-added. What is the implicit return (i.e., the increase in expected salary due to higher-quality education) that justifies paying 2% more for housing?

(b) Suppose there is also the possibility of attending a private school, regardless of the neighborhood of residence. Attending private school results in an expected salary equal to that of the school near the €306,000 house. The tuition for private school (the sum over all schooling years) is €10,000. What decision will the family make?

Another interesting and more nuanced result is found in New York City. Abdulkadiroğlu et al. (2020) study the relationship between family preferences (based on applications), the quality of classmates, and measures of school value-added. The results show, once again, that families prefer schools that admit high-achieving students. In turn, these schools tend to have high value-added: they generate greater short- and long-term improvements in student academic performance. However, the data show that once preference for student quality is accounted for, preferences are not related to school effectiveness and academic quality. In this case, it could be that families use student quality as an indicator of value-added. Nonetheless, this suggests that school choice programs may create strong incentives for stricter student selection rather than for improving academic quality.

More studies show that family demand often responds very little to school value-added measures. Mizala and Urquiola (2013) examine Chile's National Performance Evaluation System (SNED). The SNED identifies high-value-added schools by comparing the progress of the same cohort's grades with progress in other schools with similar characteristics. Thus, the SNED identifies schools with the highest value-added within each comparison group, which usually have different levels of performance and socioeconomic status. The SNED results are widely publicized in the media and in the schools themselves. Teachers at *winning* schools also receive a salary bonus. This is an ideal scenario to understand this question better because SNED closely approximates the ideal setting: it is a rigorous measure of value-added compared to similar schools and includes the dissemination of information to improve choice and school effort.

To understand family reactions to the information that a school has high value-added, Mizala and Urquiola (2013) exploit the fact that earning that label from SNED depends on a score (which in turn is the average of six value-added sub-scores). SNED rewards the top 25% of schools within each group without revealing their exact score. Consequently, some schools (e.g., those between the top 24% and 26%) have very similar value-added but receive significantly different recognition due to randomness (as explained in Chapter 2, this follows a regression discontinuity design). The study compares demand for these schools the following year to assess the effects of providing information on value-added. The results show no reaction—parents seem indifferent to SNED recognition. In summary, these findings suggest that the preference for high-value-added schools is weaker than the preference for schools with students who generally achieve good academic results (even if those results are independent of the school).

What are the implications of these results for the benefits of school choice? MacLeod and Urquiola (2019) propose a theoretical model to shed light on this issue. The starting point is that one of the primary reasons for acquiring a good education is its subsequent economic return. A key consideration in the model is the existence of frictions, such as imperfect information, in the labor market. The intuition is as follows: if employers do not directly observe worker productivity but do observe the average productivity of the school they graduated from, this could explain why it is preferable to attend a high-average-performance school (and thus have better job prospects), even if it adds no value, rather than a loweraverage-performance school (with worse job prospects) but with higher academic valueadded. In such a case, school choice does not improve quality through competition, as schools compete for good students rather than improving them.

Exercise 2: Explain whether the model by MacLeod and Urquiola (2019) is more relevant for primary, secondary, or university admissions and justify your answer.

2.2 *Multidimensionality*

There are other mechanisms that might lead us to prefer schools that are not necessarily those with the highest academic value-added. It is enough to realize that the school we attend has effects on our lives beyond our exam results. For example, the school largely determines the social network we will have throughout our lives, including our chances of finding a satisfying partner or friends with similar values and interests. Parents often socialize us and transmit their preferences, motivated by a form of paternalistic altruism, evaluating our actions based on their own preferences (Bisin and Verdier 2001), as we explained in Chapter 3b regarding the family. The multidimensionality of schools, ultimately, emerges as a potentially important issue, where value-added is just one dimension. In such a case, we must be cautious when interpreting families' demands for certain schools as demands for educational quality that should be rewarded, replicated, or arise naturally in a competitive environment.

A study by Beuermann et al. (2023) using data from Trinidad and Tobago seeks to characterize the importance of multidimensionality in school demand, its effects, and their interrelation. First, they examine the causal effect of attending a particular school on a range of outcomes: various academic results, the probability of graduation, teenage pregnancy, being arrested, and participation in the labor market. For each school, they obtain the effect of enrollment on each of these outcomes. Many education policies, such as *No Child Left Behind* in the United States or *League Tables* in the United Kingdom, tend to assume that schools that improve students' academic performance are the best schools. An interesting finding is that the correlation between a school's academic value-added and its value-added in other dimensions is quite low. For instance, the correlation between academic value-added (in terms of standardized test scores) and value-added in graduation probability is only 0.12. This means that most schools that improve students' test scores have little effect on their likelihood of graduating, and vice versa. The correlation between academic value-added and employment probability is 0.12. The correlation with the probability of being arrested is 0.28, and there is no correlation with teenage pregnancies. Although this quantification refers to a very specific case—public schools in Trinidad and Tobago—it perfectly illustrates the importance of school multidimensionality.

The second step in Beuermann et al. (2023)'s study is to analyze the extent to which families understand each school's value-added and how it reflects in their preferences. Although families do not explicitly state their reasons for choosing a school, their preferences for attributes can be inferred from the list of preferred schools they submit with their application. The results show that families tend to choose schools with higher academic value-added, especially families of students with good academic performance, and particularly for female students. On the other hand, families also tend to choose schools that reduce the likelihood of teenage pregnancy, particularly families of students with lower academic performance. Similarly, there is a preference for schools that reduce the probability of arrest and increase labor market participation.

The interpretation of these results is interesting. Initially, we saw the observation (in previous studies) that families respond little to academic value-added as a significant problem for the realization of the potential benefits of school choice since schools would not strive to improve in that dimension. However, Beuermann et al. (2023)'s results nuance this conclusion because if families are not paying attention to academic value-added because they are focusing on value-added in other socially valuable dimensions, then school choice may lead schools to strive for improvements across these dimensions.

There is also evidence of the multidimensionality of school quality in Spain. The work of Loviglio (2023) studies the value-added of public secondary schools in Barcelona using a dynamic structural model of skill accumulation, distinguishing between value-added in academic performance and graduation probability. This is particularly important in this context, given that Spain's school dropout rate is 17%, and 35% do not enroll in upper secondary education. The results suggest that traditional measures of value-added should be complemented with effects on graduation probability, especially for disadvantaged students, once again highlighting the multidimensionality of what we understand as school quality.

3 Assignment Mechanisms

Regardless of the determinants of school preferences, competition is not the only potential benefit of school choice. In a world of heterogeneous preferences, assigning students to their most preferred schools can result in significant welfare improvements, even if school behavior does not change. To achieve this, it is essential to specify how preferences are translated into student-school assignments. School choice materializes through assignment mechanisms, which are algorithms that allocate students to schools based on (a) their preferences and (b) the criteria or priorities specified by the schools or the system.

The preferences of schools or the system are usually materialized through points (e.g., for residing in the neighborhood) and define the priority that each student has in obtaining a place at each school: in case of excess demand, only those with the highest points will be admitted. In practice, there are two major types of priorities, which are not mutually exclusive. First, priorities aimed at achieving a social objective. For example, points for having siblings at the school, proximity, or socioeconomic level. Second, priorities aimed at achieving an academic objective—these usually consider previous academic performance or special needs. Such priorities are more common in the later stages of the educational system. A school choice mechanism solves a school choice problem. Formally, a school choice problem consists of a finite set of students and a finite set of schools with a finite number of available seats for enrollment. Each student must be assigned a seat in one (and only one) school. We assume that each student has strict preferences regarding all schools and the possibility of remaining unassigned. Likewise, each school has strict preferences (different priorities) over students. A matching is a solution to a school choice problem, an assignment of students to school seats, such that:

- Each student is matched with a school or their reserve option.
- The number of students matched to a school does not exceed the school's capacity.
- A student a is matched with school e if and only if school e is matched with student a.

There are various mechanisms that assign students based on different criteria. For example, some mechanisms place greater or lesser emphasis on satisfying families' top preferences. To compare them, we will focus on the properties of the matchings generated by each mechanism. The main desirable properties of a matching are stability, Pareto efficiency, and non-manipulability.

Stability. A mechanism is stable if it selects a stable matching for each school choice problem. A matching is stable if it satisfies the conditions of individual rationality, no waste, and absence of justified envy.

- Individual rationality: Each student prefers their matching over their reserve option.
- No waste: If a student prefers another school over their assigned one, that school must be full.
- Absence of justified envy: If a student i prefers the school where student j is matched over their assigned school, then i must have lower priority in j's school than j.

Efficiency. A mechanism is Pareto-efficient if it selects a Pareto-efficient matching for each school choice problem. A matching μ' Pareto dominates another matching μ if all students prefer μ' to μ, and at least one student strictly prefers it without indifference. That is, in the context of school choice, only student welfare is considered. The notion of Pareto efficiency does not refer to total welfare but to the impossibility of improving one student's welfare without necessarily worsening that of another student.

Non-manipulability. A mechanism is non-manipulable if no student can ever benefit from misrepresenting their preferences. Declaring true preferences must be a weakly dominant strategy for each student in the preference revelation game induced by the mechanism. A weakly dominant strategy is one where the utility is at least as high as any other strategy, regardless of the strategies chosen by other players. This is a very restrictive but interesting requirement because playing optimally requires very little information about what others are doing.

The most popular school choice mechanisms are Boston, Gale-Shapley, and Top Trading Cycles.

Boston. In the Boston mechanism (also known as the immediate acceptance mechanism), in each round, students apply to their highest-ranked school where they have not been rejected in previous rounds. Schools accept applications in order of priority. Once available spots are filled, subsequent applications for that round and future rounds are rejected. For example, if a school receives more applications than spots in the first round, all subsequent applications are rejected. The algorithm ends when all students have been assigned a school.

Gale-Shapley. In the Gale-Shapley mechanism (also known as the deferred acceptance mechanism), in each round, students apply to their highest-ranked school where they have not been rejected in previous rounds. Each school provisionally (unlike Boston, where acceptance is final) accepts applications in order of priority, up to its capacity, rejecting the rest. In each round, previously accepted applications and new applications (from students rejected by higher-ranked schools) are considered. For example, if a school receives more applications than spots in the first round, all applications continue to be considered in later rounds. The algorithm ends when no school rejects an application in a round. The assignment in this round is final.

Top Trading Cycles. The Top Trading Cycles mechanism starts with an initial assignment where students are placed in the school where they have the highest priority. From this assignment, cycles of mutually beneficial exchanges are identified. The search for these cycles begins with a randomly selected student. Suppose this student is in school A. We examine the preferred schools of all students according to their submitted rankings. If a cycle exists, for example, if the student in school A prefers school B and a student in B prefers A, they are reassigned, and their assignment is considered final. The cycle does not need to be bilateral: if a student in A prefers B, a student in B prefers C, and a student in C prefers A, each moves to their preferred school, and their assignment is final. When no trading cycles exist, the assignment is final.

Exercise 3: Given 5 students and 3 schools (with their ranked preferences and priorities, ordered from highest to lowest), compute the resulting assignments for the three mechanisms. School 1 has one spot, while the others have two spots each.

• $P(i_1) = s_1, s_2, s_3$	• $P(i_5) = s_3, s_2, s_1$
• $P(i_2) = s_3, s_1, s_2$	• $P(s_1) = i_5, i_3, i_2, i_4, i_1$
• $P(i_3) = s_1, s_3, s_2$	• $P(s_2) = i_2, i_5, i_3, i_4, i_1$
• $P(i_4) = s_2, s_3, s_1$	• $P(s_3) = i_3, i_1, i_2, i_4, i_5$

4 Properties

What differences exist between the properties of assignments produced by different mechanisms? It is easy to see that the Boston mechanism is manipulable. This is because the assignments in the first round are final. Therefore, if a student's first preference is rejected in the first round, it may happen that their second or third preference, where they would have been accepted, is already full in the second round. In such a case, they would end up, for example, with their fourth preference. However, if the student (or their family) can anticipate the low probability of getting into their first preference, they may declare their second preference as their most preferred option, and in that case, they would secure enrollment in it. A central concern when implementing a Boston mechanism, therefore, is ensuring that all families equally understand the probabilities of successfully enrolling, so they can compete on equal terms.

On the other hand, in the Gale-Shapley mechanism, since assignments are provisional, if a student is rejected by their first preference, they compete with others for their second preference school without being penalized, and they have the same probability of being accepted as if they had listed it as their first preference. It is important to realize that this only holds if students can declare as many preferences as they wish. If a student or family could only list 3 schools (and would remain unassigned if they did not obtain a place in any of them), this would introduce strategic behavior, making Gale-Shapley manipulable.

In Top Trading Cycles, the best strategy is also to reveal true preferences. If there is a possible exchange for the second preference, it will still be viable if the student declares a more preferred school. If there is also a possible exchange for the most preferred school, it will take place. Otherwise, the same exchange that could exist when declaring the second choice as the first still exists.

We can also easily see that the assignment produced by the Boston mechanism is not stable. If a student's first preference is rejected in the first round, it may happen that their second preference is full in the second round, occupied by students with lower priority at that school who obtained the spot by declaring it as their first preference. Therefore, that school excludes students with higher priority who prefer it (compared to the assigned students).

In contrast, the Gale-Shapley assignment is stable. However, it is not Pareto-efficient. In the case of Top Trading Cycles, the situation is reversed. In summary, there is no mechanism that is simultaneously non-manipulable, Pareto-efficient, and stable.

Finally, in addition to the properties of the assignment, there are other implementation details that likely influence the quality of the assignments. Cantillon (2017) suggests considering, for example, the time between application and decision or the ease of use of the application system for parents and schools, among other factors.

Exercise 4: Based on the assignments from the previous exercise, explain whether they are stable, efficient, and manipulable.

Exercise 5:

(a) How do you interpret the absence of excess demand at any school if the assignment follows Gale-Shapley? And f it follows Boston?.
(b) How do you interpret an assignment where everyone receives their first preference if the assignment follows Gale-Shapley? And if it follows Boston?

4.1 Empirical Studies

Do theoretical predictions align with the data? A first useful approach to this question is through experiments. The experiment by Chen and Sönmez (2006) simulates a school choice problem with several students and schools of different characteristics and compares the results when participants are randomly presented with different assignment mechanisms. Qualitatively, the experimental results are indeed consistent with theoretical predictions. The percentage of participants who declare their true preferences under Boston is very low, whereas under Gale-Shapley and TTC, it is the majority. Gale-Shapley is the most stable, followed by Boston and TTC. TTC is the most efficient, followed by Gale-Shapley and Boston. However, the efficiency costs of Gale-Shapley are quantitatively small. This has led to a trend in recent years to replace Boston with Gale-Shapley (for example, in New York, Boston, and England), as reflected in several case studies we will examine below.

One limitation of experiments is that they rely on small groups of students and simulate preferences that may not be representative of real-world ones. Therefore, it has been crucial to complement experimental evidence with data from real education markets, specifically administrative data. As a result, a significant number of studies use administrative data, leveraging system changes to explore and refine the connection between theory and practice.

The most widely used mechanisms around the world are Boston and Gale-Shapley.

In the case of Boston, a key issue is quantifying the relevance of strategic behavior and its heterogeneity across different types of families. This is important because if some families are less capable of being strategic, Boston may lead to less favorable assignments for them. Calsamiglia and Güell (2018) study this question using administrative data from the city of Barcelona. Since the mid-1990s, school assignment in the city has operated under the Boston mechanism. Parents submit a list of preferences (up to 10 schools). As explained in the previous section, in the first stage, the first-preference school is considered. If there is no excess demand, all students are assigned to that school. If there is excess demand, spots are allocated based on students' priority points.

Table 1 shows the importance of neighborhood and other criteria for assignments. A student living in the school's neighborhood receives 30 points. If they do not live in the neighborhood but their parents or guardians work there, they receive 20 points. If neither of these applies but they live in the district (outside the neighborhood), they receive 15 points. If they simply live in the same city, they receive 10 points. Having a sibling in the preferred school adds 40 points. Additionally, extra points are awarded to families with disadvantaged socioeconomic characteristics, which are granted regardless of the school and received by only 10% of applicants. In summary, all else being equal, it is much more likely to be accepted into a school within one's neighborhood. Schools outside the neighborhood where a student can be accepted are likely to be those with lower demand.

To what extent does this influence families' demands? It is possible that families want to attend their neighborhood school regardless of the points.

How many families are giving up their truly preferred option out of fear of losing their best option in their neighborhood? To answer this question, Calsamiglia and Güell (2018) leverage a change in the definition of neighborhoods. Before 2007, the city was divided into neighborhoods based on administrative divisions. A problem with this division was that it did not accurately capture the distance to schools. For example, families living near the border of a district did not have priority points for schools just across the border, even if they were very close. Additionally, depending

Table 1 Priority points in case of excess demand for a school, Barcelona

Category	Points
Basic Points	
Siblings	
The applicant has a sibling in the preferred school	40
Neighborhood	
Residence in the neighborhood of the preferred school	30
One of the parents/guardians works in the neighborhood of the preferred school	20
Residence in the administrative district (not neighborhood) of the preferred school	15
Residence in the city of the preferred school	10
Socioeconomic Characteristics	
Low-income family	10
Applicant, parent/guardian, or sibling with a disability	10
Extra Points	
Socioeconomic Characteristics	
Large family (three or more siblings) or single parents	15
Applicant with a chronic digestive disease	10

Note Neighborhood criteria are mutually exclusive. *Source* Calsamiglia and Güell (2018)

on the district's density, the number of schools for which a family had priority points varied. The 2007 reform changed this definition. The neighborhood was redefined based on the distance from the family's housing block, ensuring it included the six closest schools: three public and three semi-private (privately managed but with subsidized tuition). As a result of the reform, for each family, we can distinguish four types of schools: (1) schools for which they had priority points and retained them; (2) schools for which they had priority points but lost them; (3) schools for which they previously had no priority points but gained them; and (4) schools for which they never have priority points.

The data show that the probability of applying to a school where priority points were lost drops by 50%. Conversely, the probability of applying to a school where priority points were gained doubles. This suggests that strategic behavior plays a significant role in school choice under the Boston mechanism, in line with theory. Families tend to apply to schools where admission is almost guaranteed in most cases (58%), take risks in 40% of cases (where their enrollment depends on a lottery), and only in 2% of cases do they apply to schools where admission is practically impossible. Additionally, the authors identify 20% of families exhibiting a naive demand pattern: they take risks in the first round, but their second preference is always full in the first round (making it inaccessible).

Not all families who apply for a school end up enrolling. The data from Calsamiglia and Güell (2018) allow the identification of families with an external fallback option (i.e., a private school). Since families who take risks secure their spot through a lottery, those who succeed and those who do not are nearly identical. The results show that about 13% of those who do not secure a spot end up enrolling in a private school, compared to those who secure a spot through the lottery. This result is important because it shows that having a fallback option allows families to take greater risks and also explains some behavior that initially appears naive or excessively risky.

The data also show that those with an external fallback option (and who take risks) have a higher socioeconomic status than those who choose the safe option. However, those who take risks without a fallback option have a socioeconomic status similar to those who choose the safe option. These results are particularly interesting because they show that, given the same fallback option, strategic behavior is not linked to socioeconomic status—an important concern in manipulable mechanisms like Boston. In other words, the difference in strategic behavior by socioeconomic level in this case is explained by the ability to avoid a poor assignment, not by differences in sophistication.

Would the results have been different under Gale-Shapley or Top Trading Cycles? Calsamiglia et al. (2020) use Barcelona's data to estimate the joint distribution of preferences and strategic sophistication, conducting a counterfactual analysis of outcomes and welfare under each system. They find that switching to Gale-Shapley would yield worse results, but Top Trading Cycles would improve the situation. However, there would always be winners and losers.

Finally, new technologies present opportunities to provide real-time information during the application process to improve school choice outcomes. For example, a recent experiment by Arteaga et al. (2022) provides real-time warnings in the school choice systems of Chile and New Haven, leading 22% of applicants at high risk of being unassigned to add schools to their lists, reducing the risk of non-assignment by 58% and increasing the added value of enrolled schools by 0.10 standard deviations.

4.2 School Choice and Segregation

School choice systems often prioritize schools close to the family's place of residence or work. This follows an obvious logic, aiming to minimize travel distance and maximize parental involvement in the school. However, the flip side is that residential segregation—i.e., socioeconomic differences between neighborhoods—also becomes school segregation.

Residential and school segregation pose a significant limit to equal opportunities. For example, Chetty et al. (2016) study the results of the "Moving to Opportunity" (MTO) experiment in the United States, which offered housing vouchers to randomly selected families to move from high-poverty housing projects to lower-poverty neighborhoods. Moving to a lower-poverty neighborhood when children are young (before age 13) increased college attendance and earnings, and reduced single-parenthood rates. On the other hand, Goux and Maurin (2007) find, with data from France, that a teenager's performance at the end of secondary school is strongly influenced by the performance of other teenagers in the neighborhood—in line with what we explain in Chapter 3c about the peer effect. Arenas and Hindriks (2021) estimate that desegregation policies have significant impacts on intergenerational mobility at a very low efficiency cost. A natural question, therefore, is whether it is possible to design school choice mechanisms in a way that minimizes segregation. As we will see, the existence of neighborhood points and reserve options in the form of private schools play a central role in answering this question.

Calsamiglia et al. (2021) study the possibility of cardinal segregation. This arises when households with identical ordinal preferences react to the choice mechanism with diverse strategies and end up with different school assignments. It turns out that under Boston, school choice can be characterized as a choice between a lottery of schools and a safe school. The variation in the degree of risk aversion toward schools can, therefore, result in differences in the optimal applications to send. Intuitively, this condition requires privileged families to be willing to take greater risks. The existence of private schools exaggerates these effects and further hinders equal educational opportunities by reducing the quality of peers in the worst public schools. Those who can pay or value private schools end up with greater chances of getting their child into the best public schools. The notable and worrying implication is that the assignment to free public schools is affected by differences in households' willingness to pay for a private school.

On the other hand, Calsamiglia and Miralles (2023) study a case characterized by the existence of a school that everyone wants to avoid, and a Gale-Shapley assignment. Their results show that if priority is applied for neighborhood schools, and the market is large enough, all families end up being assigned to their local neighborhood school, regardless of their preferences. The intuition is as follows: all families outside the area of the *undesirable* school request the neighborhood school first and get it. In contrast, all families in the area of the *undesirable* school, even if they request it last, end up being rejected by the others, already filled by neighborhood families, and end up in the *undesirable* school. This intuitive mechanism illustrates the importance of a public policy that seeks to avoid the existence of such a school at all costs.

Exercise 6: Explain, using a simple example, how the existence of an undesirable school for everyone combined with neighborhood points and a Gale-Shapley assignment makes all families end up being assigned to their neighborhood school. Compare it with a case where preferences are heterogeneous and there is no undesirable school.

In Spain, Gortázar et al. (2023) analyze the case of Madrid, where the assignment mechanism is Boston, with a points criterion similar to that of Barcelona. The authors take advantage of the fact that in 2013, priority points for proximity within the city were eliminated to analyze the issue empirically. The results show that eliminating residence-based priorities increases assignment to schools outside the district and to schools located further from the family home. Initially, the response comes from families with children born in Spain, although gradually other families converge. Most families access slightly higher-quality schools, especially the children of parents with lower educational levels. Therefore, eliminating residence-based priorities seems to help families from lower educational backgrounds access better-performing schools, potentially leading to better long-term outcomes. Although a complete welfare evaluation is difficult to make when we cannot interpret preferences as true, given the Boston mechanism, the authors also show that families exercise more choice and participate more in the school choice process.

Kutscher et al. (2023) study the implementation of a Gale-Shapley mechanism in 2016 by the Chilean government, as a central component of a major educational reform aimed at promoting social inclusion and reducing school segregation. The authors take advantage of the fact that the reform came into effect in different areas of the country in different years, to compare changes in segregation that took place before and after the reform.

The results show that the reform barely changed average school segregation. However, this result hides considerable heterogeneity between school districts, depending on their prior residential segregation and school supply. On the one hand, the centralized system expands school choice, and it is likely that some low socioeconomic status families use the new system to send their children to better-quality public or voucher schools that are further from their homes. However, this will not necessarily reduce school segregation if high socioeconomic status students anticipate it and respond by moving to private schools. The results of Kutscher et al. (2023) show that municipalities with a higher representation of public or voucher schools experienced a decrease in school segregation, while municipalities with more private schools experienced an increase in school segregation. This pattern of school change is especially intense for high-income families. These results are very consistent with the proposed theoretical mechanism, and again, the role of reserve options appears fundamental in understanding the outcomes of school choice mechanisms.

Finally, it is important to highlight that although centralized school choice systems formally transfer the power of choice to families (according to established priorities), schools still have some influence, subtly. Research by de Lafuente (2021) illustrates this channel very well. In a randomized experiment, emails were sent to more than 2500 schools in the Community of Madrid, in the period prior to the 2018 student enrollment process. In these messages, three types of fictitious couples, one Spanish and two Romanian, requested to visit the school. The respective Romanian couples indicated different levels of cultural assimilation with the origin of their child's name. To improve comparability between family profiles, a series of socioeconomic characteristics that influence selection toward assimilation and affect discrimination were controlled.

The results show that immigrants who choose a foreign (Romanian) name for their children have a response rate of 9 percentage points lower, compared to a base response rate of 77% for natives. On the other hand, the decision of immigrant parents to give their child a native name significantly reduces discrimination by 50%. Qualitatively, these results hold regardless of school characteristics, although the statistical power of the sample to detect such differences is lower. Given these results, it is easy to imagine that these differences in response rates explain differences in information, and potentially, in demand for those schools. In this way, schools can incentivize demand from demographic groups they are more or less interested in, by putting up more or fewer barriers to obtaining information about the school, and generating segregation.

5 College Choice

The problem of college choice has many similarities with that of school choice: it involves assigning a finite number of students to a finite number of college places. In many countries around the world, college assignment is done centrally, using the same mechanisms—mainly Gale-Shapley—with some modifications and different concerns.

In college choice, admission priority is centered on academic merits. Proximity usually plays a formally nonexistent role (although obviously travel costs come into play as an important factor in demand). In some countries, quotas are established for demographic or socioeconomic groups whose participation in the system has traditionally been lower.

The main decision when designing the college choice system is the definition of priorities. In practically the entire world, priority is defined by performance in standardized entrance exams, often in conjunction with academic performance in high school. In the case of Spain, the high school average grade accounts for 6 points, and the evaluation of the high school for college access (EBAU) up to 8 more points, reaching a maximum of 14 points. Previously, the EBAU had less relative weight (until 2010, the high school average grade accounted for 6 points and the EBAU 4). The use of standardized tests to determine enrollment priority has advantages and disadvantages. The main advantage, obviously, is that skills are measured with a common metric (within each Autonomous Community, with some autonomy in the high school curriculum). The main limitation is that skills are measured on a single day and in a specific exam format. For example, performance in such tests can be quite uneven among demographic groups, without necessarily reflecting different potential college performance. Arenas and Calsamiglia (2022) show, with data from Catalonia, how the 2010 reform negatively affected women's admission scores (whose performance is much higher than men's in high school, and similar in the EBAU), without that difference being related to differences in expected college performance (in Chapter 5c, we will see many more gender differences in education).

Another important decision regarding priorities concerns the relative weight given to different subjects. For example, in case of a tie, students who have taken more relevant subjects for the requested degree can be prioritized. In practice, in Spain, this materializes through the weights that each degree assigns to the grades of the modality subjects.

Students' priority is usually summarized in an admission score. This has the advantage of facilitating the quantification of cut-off scores in each college degree (i.e., the admission score of the last student who managed to obtain a place), and therefore, the evaluation of the student's access probabilities in each degree. Cut-off scores are usually strongly correlated over time, but even if they are not, the information is public and easy to take into account. In Spain, college admission is managed by the Autonomous Communities. The assignment process is the same everywhere, but applicants must fill out an application for each autonomous community where they consider enrolling. The number of preferences that students can declare is usually, unfortunately, limited, which can incentivize certain strategic behavior and inefficiencies. However, public information about cut-off scores very likely minimizes the probability of strategy errors or differences in sophistication in practice.

Exercise 7: Imagine that only 3 options could be requested for college admission, with a Gale-Shapley assignment. How do you think it would affect the demand for the most desired degrees? Why?

6 Conclusions

This chapter has examined the impact that school choice can have on the effectiveness and equity of the educational system. It has been highlighted that allowing families to choose the school can be an interesting strategy to motivate the improvement of educational institutions. However, for this to work, it is crucial that demand is guided by families' preferences regarding aspects that the school can influence, which in turn would motivate them to keep improving. Nevertheless, we have found that, on the one hand, families do not always have the necessary information about the various dimensions that determine the suitability of the school for their child and that, even so, their ability to choose a school is greatly affected by the imposed priority system. On the other hand, schools do not always have the capacity to adapt to the needs of demand, as the level of autonomy of the center is usually limited. Likewise, aspects such as the composition of peers in the school, which depend on the families that the center attracts, are strongly influenced by the prioritization systems of demand. Finally, we have also observed that school choice has externalities that can affect the equity of the system, influencing the levels of observed segregation. Moreover, we have seen how the existence of schools that are not desired by the majority of families can deactivate the transformative potential of school choice, while perpetuating the presence of schools with difficulties.

References

Abdulkadiroğlu, A., P. A. Pathak, J. Schellenberg, and C. R. Walters. 2020. Do parents value school effectiveness? *American Economic Review* 110 (5): 1502–1539.

Arenas, A. and C. Calsamiglia. 2022. *Gender Differences in High-Stakes Performance and College Admission Policies*. Tech. rep., Institute of Labor Economics (IZA).

Arenas, A., C. Calsamiglia, and J. Hindriks. 2021. Intergenerational mobility and unequal school opportunity. *The Economic Journal* 131 (635): 1027–1050.

Arteaga, F., A. J. Kapor, C. A. Neilson, and S. D. Zimmerman. 2022. Smart matching platforms and heterogeneous beliefs in centralized school choice. *The Quarterly Journal of Economics* 137 (3): 1791–1848.

Beuermann, D. W., C. K. Jackson, L. Navarro-Sola, and F. Pardo. 2023. What is a good school, and can parents tell? Evidence on the multidimensionality of school output. *The Review of Economic Studies* 90 (1): 65–101.

Bisin, A., and T. Verdier. 2001. The economics of cultural transmission and the dynamics of preferences. *Journal of Economic Theory* 97 (2): 298–319.

Calsamiglia, C., C. Fu, and M. Güell. 2020. Structural estimation of a model of school choices: The boston mechanism versus its alternatives. *Journal of Political Economy* 128 (2): 642–680.

Calsamiglia, C., C. Fu, M. Güell, and M. Güell. 2018. Priorities in school choice: The case of the boston mechanism in barcelona. *Journal of Public Economics* 163: 20–36.

Calsamiglia, C., C. Fu, M. Güell, M. Güell, F. Martínez-Mora, and A. Miralles. 2021. School choice design, risk aversion and cardinal segregation. *The Economic Journal* 131 (635): 1081–1104.

———and A. Miralles. 2023. Catchment areas, stratification and access to better schools. *International Economic Review*.

Cantillon, E. 2017. Broadening the market design approach to school choice. *Oxford Review of Economic Policy* 33 (4): 613–634.

Chen, Y., and T. Sönmez. 2006. School choice: An experimental study. *Journal of Economic Theory* 127 (1): 202–231.

Chetty, R., N. Hendren, and L. F. Katz. 2016. The effects of exposure to better neighborhoods on children: New evidence from the moving to opportunity experiment. *American Economic Review* 106 (4): 855–902.

de Lafuente, D. M. 2021. Cultural assimilation and ethnic discrimination: An audit study with schools. *Labour Economics* 72: 102058.

Fack, G., and J. Grenet. 2010. When do better schools raise housing prices? evidence from paris public and private schools. *Journal of Public Economics* 94 (1–2): 59–77.

Gibbons, S., S. Machin, and O. Silva. 2013. Valuing school quality using boundary discontinuities. *Journal of Urban Economics* 75: 15–28.

Gortázar, L., D. Mayor, and J. Montalbán. 2023. Residence-based priorities and school choice. *Economics of Education Review* 95: 102384.

Goux, D., and E. Maurin. 2007. Close neighbours matter: Neighbourhood effects on early performance at school. *The Economic Journal* 117 (523): 1193–1215.

Hastings, J. S., and J. M. Weinstein. 2008. Information, school choice, and academic achievement: Evidence from two experiments. *The Quarterly Journal of Economics* 123 (4): 1373–1414.

Kutscher, M., S. Nath, and S. Urzúa. 2023. Centralized admission systems and school segregation: Evidence from a national reform. *Journal of Public Economics* 221: 104863.

Loviglio, A. 2023. *School quality beyond test scores: The role of schools in shaping educational outcomes*. Tech. rep., Dipartimento Scienze Economiche, Universita'di Bologna.

MacLeod, W. B., and M. Urquiola. 2019. Is education consumption or investment? Implications for school competition. *Annual Review of Economics* 11: 563–589.

Mizala, A., and M. Urquiola. 2013. School markets: The impact of information approximating schools' effectiveness. *Journal of Development Economics* 103: 313–335.

Vega-Bayo, A., and P. Mariel. 2018. School choice across different regions of spain. *Hacienda Pública Española* (227): 11–36.

Educational Inequality

Marisa Hidalgo-Hidalgo and Iñigo Iturbe-Ormaetxe

1 Introduction

The educational levels of the population have increased in recent years in most countries. In OECD countries, the average proportion of people aged 25–34 with tertiary education (university and higher vocational training) has increased from 26% in 2000 to 47.4% in 2022.[1] In the same age group, the proportion who did not complete upper secondary education (Baccalaureate or Intermediate Vocational Training) has fallen from 25.8% in 2000 to 13.9% in 2022. There are still large differences between countries, from 1.6% in Korea to 32.9% in Turkey and 43% in Mexico. Among European countries, the highest dropout rate is in Spain (26.5%). In this chapter, we see that school dropout is closely associated to the socioeconomic characteristics of the individual. In particular, individuals with parents with low educational attainment are more likely to drop out of school.

Educational inequality is a very relevant issue from the point of view of public policies, among other reasons because of the future consequences of education, both in terms of employment outcomes (greater probability of employment, higher wages) and also in health or social participation. There is also broad consensus that part of this association reflects a causal relationship (Lochner 2011). Given these positive effects of education, a society in which some groups are systematically left behind condemns these groups to a disadvantaged position in the future.

[1] https://data-explorer.oecd.org/.

M. Hidalgo-Hidalgo (✉)
Department of Economics, Universidad Pablo de Olavide, Seville, Spain
e-mail: mhidalgo@upo.es

I. Iturbe-Ormaetxe
Departamento de Fundamentos del Análisis Económico (FAE), Universidad de Alicante, San Vicente del Raspeig, Spain

A. Cabrales and I. Sanz (eds.), *Economics of Education*,
https://doi.org/10.1007/978-3-031-90911-5_13

Equity in education is, in fact, a central issue in most countries. The Sustainable Development Goals adopted by the United Nations in 2015 with the ultimate goal of "ending poverty, protecting the planet and ensuring that by 2030 all people enjoy peace and prosperity" advocate "ensuring inclusive and equitable quality education and promoting lifelong learning opportunities for all."

Of course, educational inequality can be a reflection of income or wealth inequality in the society. What is the situation in the European countries in terms of income and wealth inequality? The most comprehensive database on inequality is the World Inequality Database coordinated by Facundo Alvaredo, Lucas Chancel, Thomas Piketty, Emmanuel Saez, and Gabriel Zucman (see wid.world). In Figure 1, we represent the Gini index of the distribution of income (before taxes) and wealth in Europe in the last forty years.

The Gini index is a classic measure of inequality that takes values between 0 and 1, where 0 means maximum equality (all individuals have the same income) and 1 means maximum inequality (a single individual owns all the income). Therefore, higher values of the index indicate greater inequality. According to the World Inequality Database, among EU countries, the Gini index for pre-tax income was 0.48 in 2022, and it ranges from 0.37 (Slovakia) to 0.62 (Lithuania). Also, in the chart below, we see that the Gini index has not experienced large fluctuations in the last 30 years. As for wealth, it tends to be more concentrated than income. The latest Gini coefficient for the EU countries is 0.76 in 2022. As for income, it fluctuates from a minimum of 0.61 (The Netherlands) to a maximum of 0.88 (Ireland). In the figure, we observe that the Gini index for wealth has also remained quite stable over the period for which we have data.

In conclusion, it does not seem that in the last forty years there have been great fluctuations in income or wealth inequality, at least if we consider the Gini index. According to this, in principle, we should not expect to find great inequalities with respect to educational levels. However, as we see later, this is not what we find in the data, which may be paradoxical. This is what we try to illustrate throughout the chapter, but to do so we have to start by discussing how we measure education and what measure of inequality we use. This is what we do in Sect. 2. In Sect. 3, we present evidence on educational inequality in Europe with respect to school dropout rates, university population and scores in standardized international tests. In Sect. 4, we talk about the possible consequences of current educational inequality. In Sect. 5, we discuss the causes of educational inequality as well as possible solutions. Finally, in Sect. 6, we briefly discuss other inequalities in the educational context and conclude.

Exercise 1: In addition to the Gini index that we have used to construct Fig. 1, there are other measures of inequality in the literature. For example, the percentage of income (or wealth) owned by the richest 10% of individuals, or the percentage of income (or wealth) owned by the richest 1% of individuals. In the wid.world database, you have data on these two measures for several countries, they present them as the "top" 10% and as the "top" 1%, respectively. Download the data for a country of your choice for

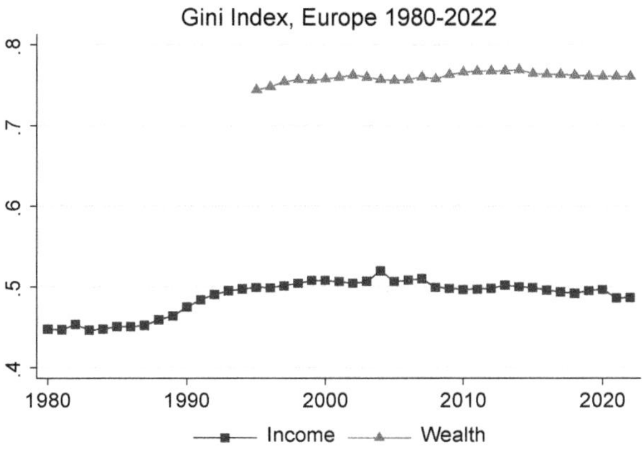

Fig. 1 Inequality in income and wealth in Europe (*Source* World Inequality Database)

> the period 1980–2021 and build a figure similar to Fig. 1. How have these indicators evolved over the period? Is this evolution similar to that of the Gini index?

2 Measures of Educational Inequality

The first problem when measuring educational inequality is deciding how to measure an individual's educational level. Some authors use the number of years of education of the person. In this case, a measure of inequality could be the standard deviation of the years of study of the adult population. As it is a measure of the degree of dispersion of the data with respect to the mean, a higher standard deviation means greater inequality (see Ram 1984, 1990, among the first works to use it). Another option is to use the educational Gini index as Checchi (2001), or Castelló and Doménech (2002) using data on educational levels from Barro and Lee (2001). In addition to the Gini index, it is possible to calculate a broader set of dispersion indices, including the Theil index (see Meschi and Cervini 2014, for an analysis of educational inequality using these two indices). However, the use of years of education is problematic for several reasons. First, it is a measure that may overestimate individual education (this would be the case, for example, among those who repeat a year). To avoid this first criticism, measures of the educational performance of the individual are often used, i.e. measures of the highest educational level attained. Two widely used measures are whether or not students have completed upper secondary education (school dropout) and whether they have completed university or higher vocational studies. Second, a common criticism of using the number of years of study is that it makes comparisons across countries difficult, as an additional year of study may be very different in a developed country than in a developing country or even within the same country over time. The increasing availability of comparable data on student performance on international tests has facilitated the use of other measures, confirming that quantity and quality of education do not always go hand in hand (Hanushek and Woessmann 2010).

We propose different measures of individuals' education and as a measure of inequality we use the gap in terms of different educational measures between individuals from different groups. Specifically, we consider two forms of educational inequality:

(a) Inequalities between individuals from different social groups. We analyze the gap in different educational variables: scores (or grades) and academic achievements (educational levels achieved). We also consider different types of social groups depending on, for example, family education or socioeconomic level.
(b) Inequalities in outcomes across the lifespan, e.g., employment status and poverty, among individuals with different levels of education. Here, we study the gap in different work outcomes between these groups.

We focus on the case of the European countries. To do this, we are going to use two large databases, EU-SILC and PISA:

(1) EU-SILC is the acronym for *European Union Statistics on Income and Living Conditions.*[2] EU-SILC is the main instrument for the study of poverty and social exclusion in the EU. We are going to use the 2011 and 2019 editions as both incorporate a special module in which participants provide information about their families when they were fourteen years old.[3] The objective is to obtain data on the family environment at a crucial moment for the development of the individual. Among other things, individuals indicate what level of education and occupation their parents had, what the economic situation of the household was, etc. For the analysis of this chapter, we focus on individuals between 30 and 60 years of age at the time of the survey. In this way, we ensure that they have completed their fundamental training period.[4]
(2) PISA is the acronym for *Programme for International Student Assessment* that the OECD has been conducting every three years since 2000. It measures the aptitudes of fifteen-year-old students in three areas: mathematics, reading, and science. In this chapter, we use the editions from 2000 to 2022. The PISA database provides, in addition to data on student performance on achievement tests in the three disciplines mentioned above, individual-level information on demographics (gender, immigration status, month of birth), socioeconomic background (parents' education and occupation), and school-level variables

[2] EU-SILC is conducted by Eurostat, the statistical office of the European Union.

[3] The one of 2011 is called "Module on Intergenerational transmission of disadvantages," while the one of 2019 is called "Intergenerational transmission of disadvantages, household composition and income evolution."

[4] The 2011 and the 2019 editions have data from the 27 countries in the European Union plus Iceland (only 2011), Norway, Serbia (only 2019), Switzerland, and United Kingdom (only 2011). We include all these 32 countries in our analysis.

(ownership, location, size). For consistency with the analysis using EU-SILC, we select the same set of European countries in PISA.[5]

Bonus Material Box: World Inequality Database on Education In addition to the databases discussed in this chapter, there are several others available for conducting similar analyses. One notable example is the World Inequality Database on Education (WIDE), developed by UNESCO (https://www.education-inequalities.org). This comprehensive database compiles data from national surveys in over 170 countries and offers an interactive platform for generating maps, graphs, infographics, and tables. Users can easily download, print, or share the visualizations online. WIDE allows for comparisons of educational outcomes across countries and within different groups in the same country, focusing on inequality factors such as wealth, gender, ethnicity, and location.

As previously discussed in Chapters 3 and 4 on the educational production function, educational achievement results from the combination of various inputs. Some are innate to the student, such as biological sex, genetic inheritance from parents, their education, occupation, and income. Others depend on the student's own efforts, such as the dedication they put into their studies, along with factors related to the characteristics of schools (e.g., public spending, classmates, etc.). In this chapter, we present evidence of inequality in educational outcomes based on various socioeconomic factors. However, the educational disparities we highlight may also stem from other unobserved variables. It is important to distinguish this from inequality in educational opportunity, which specifically measures the extent to which these outcome disparities are driven by inherited circumstances beyond an individual's control. While some may argue that a certain level of inequality in outcomes is acceptable, as it could reflect differences in effort or innate ability, there is much less consensus regarding the acceptability of inequality in opportunities among students (see the classic references of Roemer 1998, or Fleurbaey 2008). Apart from this argument of social justice, the existence of inequality of educational opportunities is also criticized based on arguments of efficiency to the extent that it can lead to an inefficient allocation of resources. The work of Ferreira and Gignoux (2014) analyzes inequality of educational outcomes and educational opportunities using PISA 2006 data for OECD countries and finds that inequality of opportunity explains up to 35% of all disparities in educational achievement. More recently, Marrero et al. (2023) also study inequality of educational opportunities using PISA 2018 for a set of European countries and use more precise measures of personal circumstances. Thus, they find that inequality of educational opportunities represents, on average, 32% of total educational inequality in Western Europe, with substantial variation between countries.

[5] The following link provides a list of countries that have participated in each of the PISA assessments since 2000. https://www.oecd.org/en/about/programmes/pisa/pisa-participants.html.

3 Evidence in Europe

In this section we describe educational inequality in Europe between individuals from different social groups with respect to three educational outcomes: school dropout, obtaining a university degree and PISA test results.

3.1 School Dropout and Family Characteristics

According to Eurostat, the early dropout rate from education and training is the percentage of people aged 18 to 24 who do not complete upper secondary education and do not follow any type of study-training in the four weeks prior to the interview conducted for the Labour Force Survey (see also Chapter 1 of the descriptive introduction to this book). In 2022, the dropout rates for the EU-27 were 11.1% and 8.0% for men and women, respectively.

In this section, we use EU-SILC data and propose as a definition of school dropout the percentage of individuals who report having an educational level below upper secondary and that differs from the traditional definition of dropout which does include those who have completed secondary school but have not continued studying. This approach allows us to track their evolution over time, as the individuals in the sample were born between 1951 and 1989. It is important to note that this definition differs from the one used by Eurostat, which focuses exclusively on individuals aged 18 to 24. For the sample as a whole, school dropout is 21%. In the figure below we see the evolution of this rate separately for men and women born between 1951 and 1989, grouping individuals into five-year intervals. Note that since the surveys are conducted in 2011 and 2019, the youngest in the sample are 30 years old, while the oldest are 60 (Fig. 2).

The trend in dropout rates is positive, as they clearly decrease over the period. We also see that the pattern is different between women and men, as can be seen from the difference in slopes. The dropout rate for women born in the 1950s was higher than that of men, but from the second half of the 1960s their dropout rates became lower. For the youngest cohort in the sample, there is a difference of four percentage points in favor of women (11% versus 15%).

Exercise 2: We have seen two measures of school dropout, on the one hand, Eurostat and on the other hand the one we use with EU-SILC data. Discuss the differences between the two measures. In particular, do you think that the measure used in the chapter can over- or underestimate the dropout rate compared to Eurostat's?

We now analyze the inequality in dropout rates according to family characteristics. Our main criterion is the educational level of the parents. Many authors have

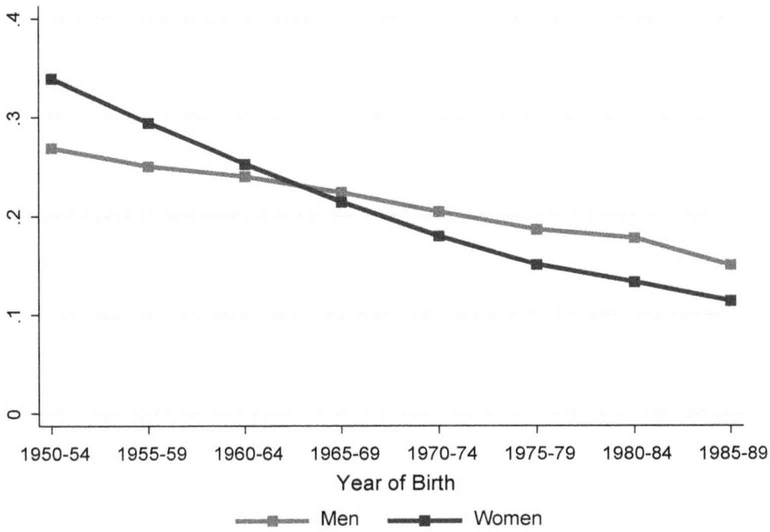

Fig. 2 Proportion of individuals in each cohort who do not complete secondary education (*Source* EU-SILC)

documented the existence of a positive and strong association between the educational levels of parents and children (see Holmlund et al. 2011). In our case, we divide individuals into two groups according to the education of their parents. We classify an individual as belonging to an "educated" family when either his or her mother or father (or both) completed upper secondary education. We classify the rest of the individuals within "uneducated" families. In other words, neither the father nor the mother have more than compulsory secondary school. The proportion of individuals in educated families in our sample is 46%, with a clear positive trend over time. Among those born in 1950–54, just 28.5% grew up in educated families, but this proportion exceeds 68% for those born in 1985–1989. Taking the sample as a whole, the dropout rates for women and men from educated families are 6.1% and 6.8%, respectively. In contrast, for individuals from families with a low educational level, these rates rise to 33.4% and 33.9%, respectively. Figure 3 shows the time trend of these rates.

Figure 3 is very interesting and shows two very different worlds. For women the trend is clearly positive, with dropout rates falling in both types of families. The differences also narrow up to the cohort born in 1975–1979, although they increase again thereafter. For men the picture is completely different, with dropout rates remaining practically stable throughout the period. Essentially, dropout is concentrated among people whose parents have a low level of education, which has very important implications for intergenerational mobility, as it indicates that the educational disadvantages of parents are transmitted to their children.

To complete the analysis, we estimate a linear regression model where the dependent variable is binary, taking the value one if the individual did not complete upper

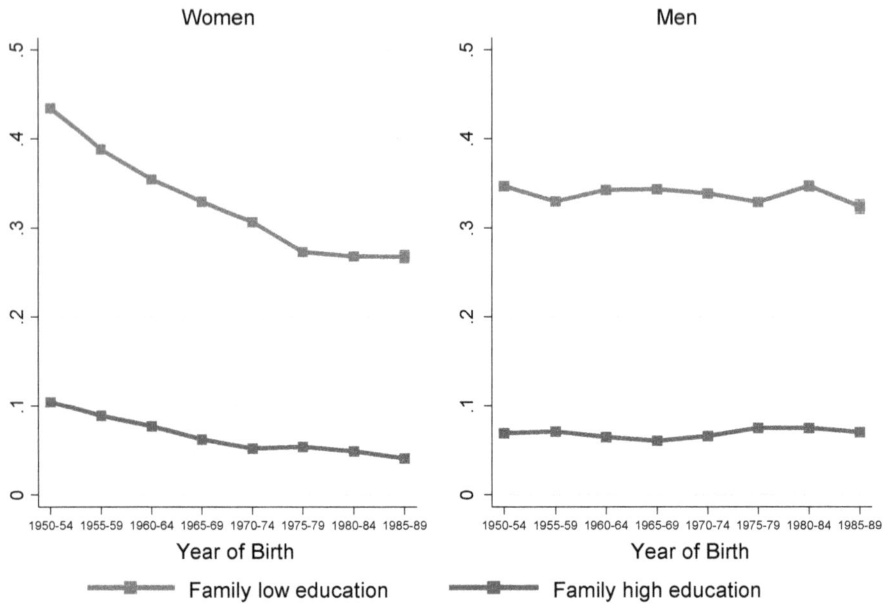

Fig. 3 Proportion of individuals in each cohort who do not complete secondary education by family type (*Source* EU-SILC)

secondary education. The key explanatory variable is also binary and takes value one if the subject comes from an uneducated family. In addition, we include other four explanatory dummy variables (gender, migrant status, poverty indicator when teenager, raised in a rural environment) together with regional fixed effects. The estimated coefficient of the main explanatory variable is 0.17 (standard deviation 0.001).[6] This indicates that the probability of not completing secondary education is 17 percentage points higher for individuals from low-education families compared to those from highly educated families. This effect is substantial, given that the average probability of not completing secondary education is 21.1%.

Exercise 3: In the linear regression we just looked at, we also include a variable that takes value one for women (and zero for men). The estimated coefficient of this variable is -0.0048 (standard deviation 0.0012). How do you interpret this coefficient? We also include another variable that takes value one if the individual was raised in a rural area (zero in another case). The estimated coefficient of this variable is 0.054 (standard deviation 0.0013). How do you interpret this coefficient? Do you think it is reasonable for it to take a positive value? Why?

[6] The number of observations in the regression is 361,990.

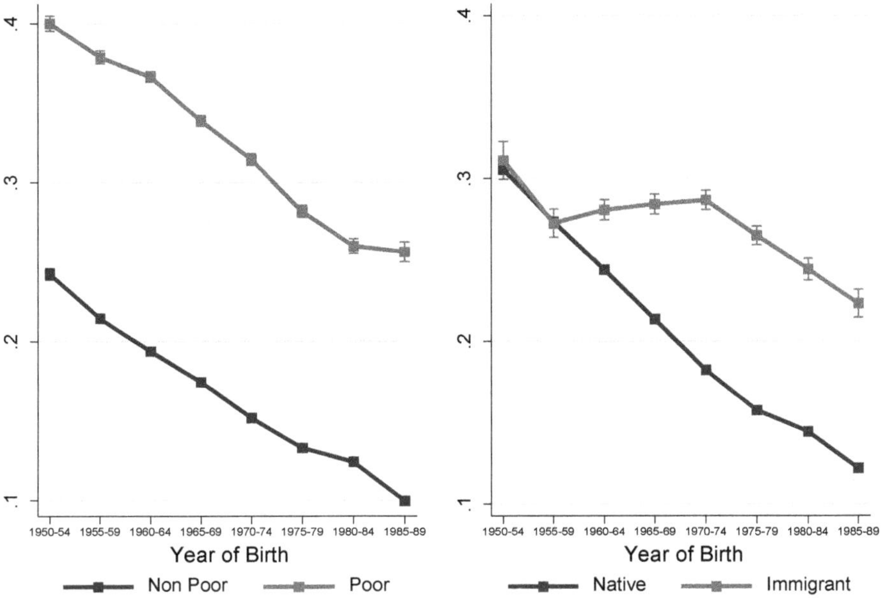

Fig. 4 Proportion of individuals in each cohort who do not complete secondary education. By family type (*Source* EU-SILC)

The EU-SILC database also has other interesting features about the family environment. For instance, it includes data on an individual's family financial situation when they were fourteen, as well as the nationality of their parents, among other factors. A key question is whether the individual had their basic school needs, such as books and equipment, covered at age fourteen.[7] Below we use some of these variables to dig deeper into the above results.

In Fig. 4, we represent in the left panel the dropout rates by dividing individuals according to whether they grew up in a poor family (the family's economic situation when they were fourteen was very bad, bad, or moderately bad) or not. In the right panel, we distinguish between natives and immigrants. We define as natives those individuals born in the country in which they take the survey.[8]

In the left-hand panel, the result is similar to Fig. 3. For individuals from poor families, the dropout rate is very high, although over the period it has dropped from 40 to 25.6%. For individuals from more advantaged families, the rate has dropped from 24 to 10%. In the figure, we also observe that educational inequality associated with family poverty status remained stable for generations born between 1950 and 1984 but increased for the latest cohorts, those born in the years 1985–1989.

[7] This question is only in the 2019 round.

[8] We also consider as natives those who have either one father or one mother (or both) who were born in the country.

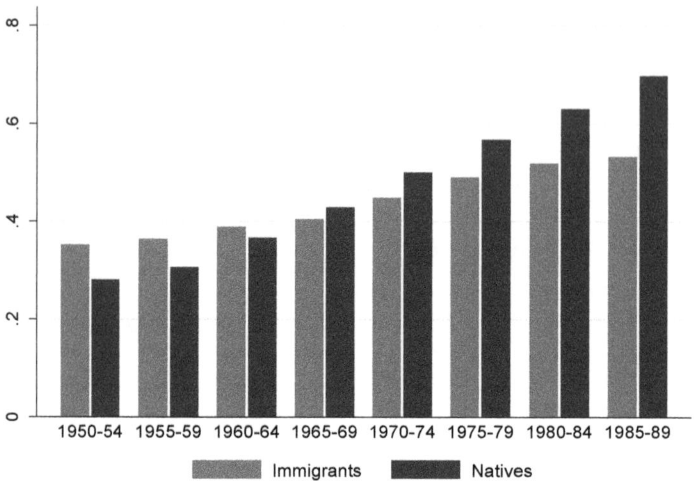

Fig. 5 Fraction of individuals from educated families (*Source* EU-SILC)

In the right panel, we see that for cohorts born in the 1950s, school dropout rates are similar for natives and immigrants. However, in the 1960s and the first half of the 1970s, the situation for immigrants worsens. This negative trend is corrected for the second half of the 1970s and for the 1980s, although the differences between the two groups remain. For the latest cohorts (1985–1989), the dropout rate for natives is 12.2%, while for immigrants it is 22.3%, almost double. One reason for this may be that the composition of the immigrant population has changed over the period. To see this in more detail, in the following graph, we represent what percentage of each group (immigrants vs. natives) comes from a family with education beyond compulsory secondary education. We see that the educational level of the parents of immigrants was better than that of natives for the cohorts born in the 60s and first half of the 70s, while the situation reverses from the second half of the 70s onwards. This result is consistent with that of Fig. 5.

Finally, a brief comment on the question of basic school needs when the individual was 14 years old. Of the total respondents, only 5.6% stated that these basic needs were not met, usually due to financial problems. This can be seen as an indicator of particularly negative personal circumstances. In fact, the school dropout rate for this group is 49.5%, more than double that for the rest of the individuals (20.3%).

3.2 Country Analysis

The aggregate analysis in the previous section may mask the existence of major differences between countries. For example, the trajectory of countries in the South may be very different from that of countries in the North or from that of former

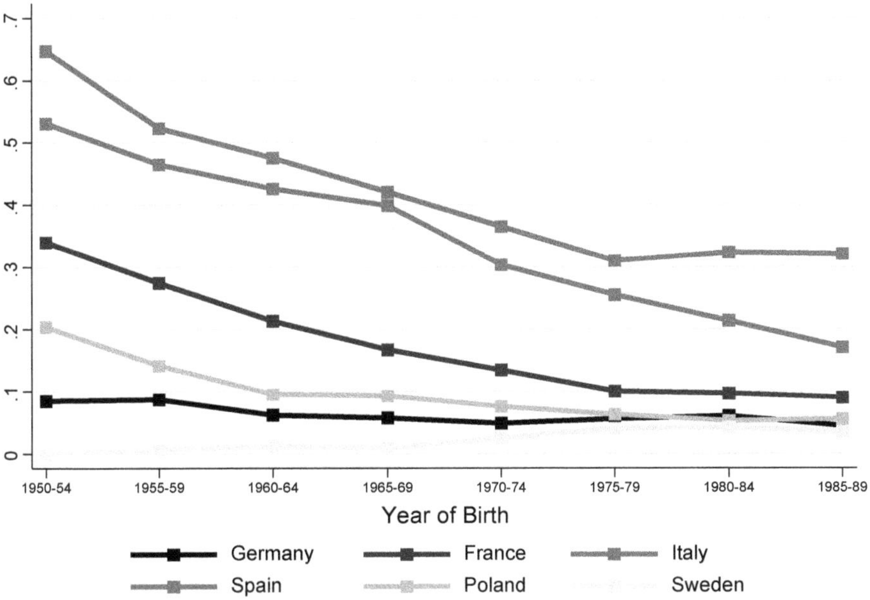

Fig. 6 Proportion of individuals in each cohort who do not complete secondary education. Six European countries (*Source* EU-SILC)

communist countries. In principle, we could reproduce the above analysis for each of the 32 countries in the sample, but this may be too cumbersome for the reader. We will therefore focus on the five countries in the European Union with more than 20 million inhabitants (Germany, France, Italy, Spain and Poland) and we also include Sweden as a representative of the Nordic countries. In the following figure, we see the evolution of the dropout rate in these six countries (Fig. 6).

We see very important differences between countries. While in Sweden, there is practically no dropout (although the situation has deteriorated in the last cohorts), in the two southern countries (Italy and Spain) the rates have been consistently higher. Furthermore, in Spain, the positive trend has stopped for the last cohorts, those born in the 1980s. The rest of the countries are in an intermediate situation. In the following figure, we break down the school dropout rate by family type for these same countries (Fig. 7).

This figure documents that educational inequality is greater in the two southern countries (Italy and Spain). We also see that in the latest cohorts in all countries the gap by family type has stopped narrowing and has even increased in the case of Sweden. In the following map, we represent the average difference in the entire sample in the school dropout rate between individuals from uneducated and educated families, by country. The gap in school dropout by family type is between a minimum of 0.4 percentage points in Sweden and a maximum of 52.7 in Portugal (Fig. 8).

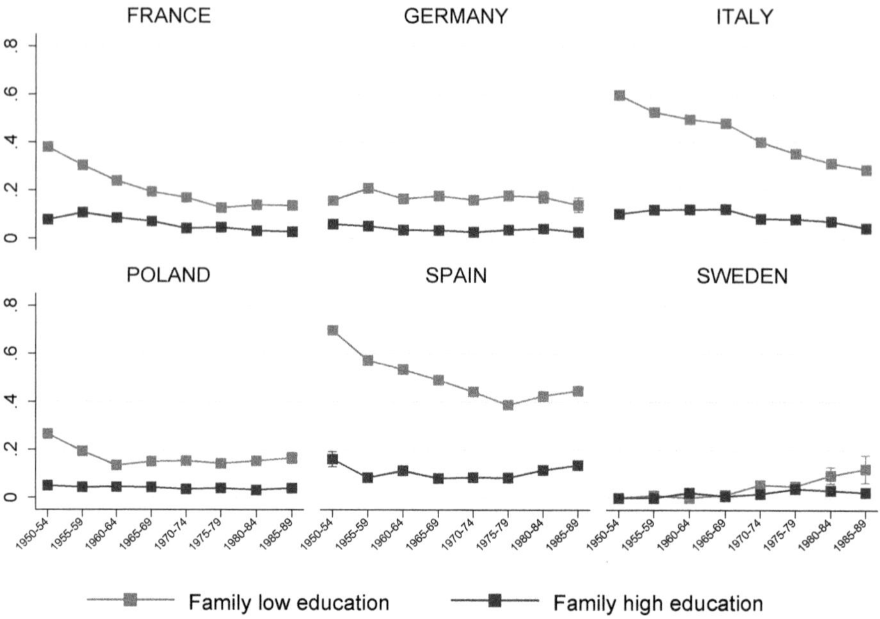

Fig. 7 Proportion of individuals in each cohort who do not complete secondary education by family type. Six European countries (*Source* EU-SILC)

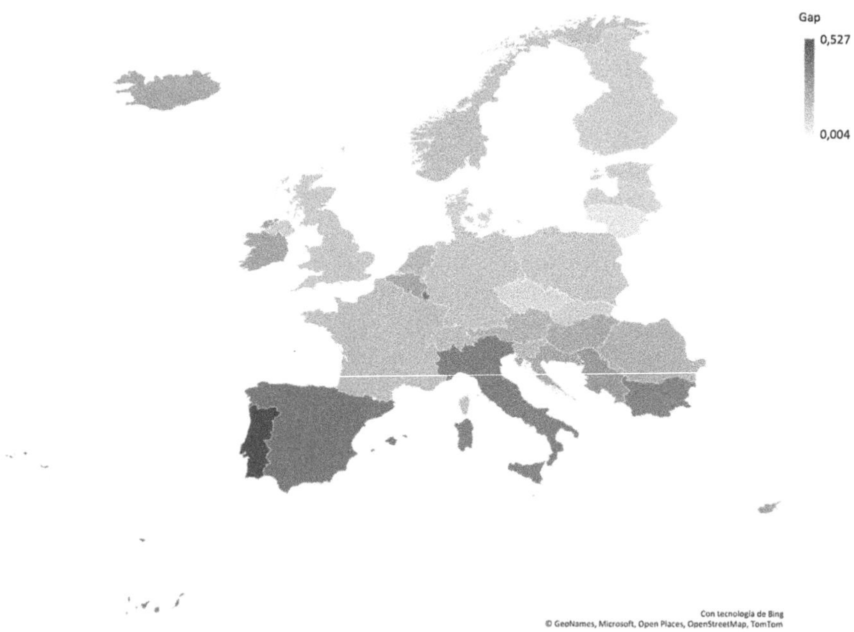

Fig. 8 Gap in school dropout by country and family type (*Source* EU-SILC 2011 and 2019)

3.3 Inequality in Access to University Education

In Sect. 3.1, we study inequality in terms of the completion of secondary education, a period in which parents' decisions, and therefore their characteristics, can have a greater influence on individual educational outcomes. However, in developed countries such as those in Europe and as indicated by Blanden et al. (2023), there is also inequality in higher education. At this stage, the influence of parents has a lesser impact although it is still present (for example, in terms of the field of study, the university to attend, the moment of entry into the labor market, etc.).

Here, we consider having completed university studies as an indicator of educational achievement. According to the most recent data from Eurostat, in 2023, 43% of the EU population aged 25–34 years had tertiary education. In the following figure, we represent what percentage of the population has higher education (university or Higher Vocational Training) in Europe, based on the educational level of their parents. The proportion of people with higher education in our sample (individuals born between 1950 and 1989) is 29.5%, although it increases with the age group to which the individual belongs. This proportion has increased from 20% among those born in 1950–1954 to 43% among those born in 1985–1989. In the following figure, we distinguish between men and women and analyze the inequality in this indicator between individuals from educated and uneducated families, as we did in the case of the school dropout indicator.

Figure 9 is very similar to Fig. 3. The proportion of women with university degrees has been equal to or greater than that of men since the 1960s, regardless of the educational level of the family. The percentage of the university-educated population has increased throughout the period for both sexes. The evolution of the university population in this period is very similar between individuals with educated and uneducated families, which implies that educational inequality remains stable in these generations. Specifically, for the most recent cohorts of men, the difference is around 28 percentage points (17.3% versus 45.1%), while for women, it is slightly higher, 31 points (28.2% versus 60%). The gap therefore remains very similar to that of school dropout (see Fig. 3) despite the fact that family influence seems to be lower.

3.4 Inequality in School Results

Differences in educational outcomes such as school dropout according to the socioeconomic background of the individual can arise at an early age (for a review of this evidence, see Attanasio 2015, or Currie and Almond 2011). In this section, we analyze the educational inequality between 15-year-old students from different social groups, specifically the educational level of the families, their migrant status, as well as their socioeconomic status. To do this, we use the results of mathematics and language in PISA. We also use repeating a grade as an educational measure,

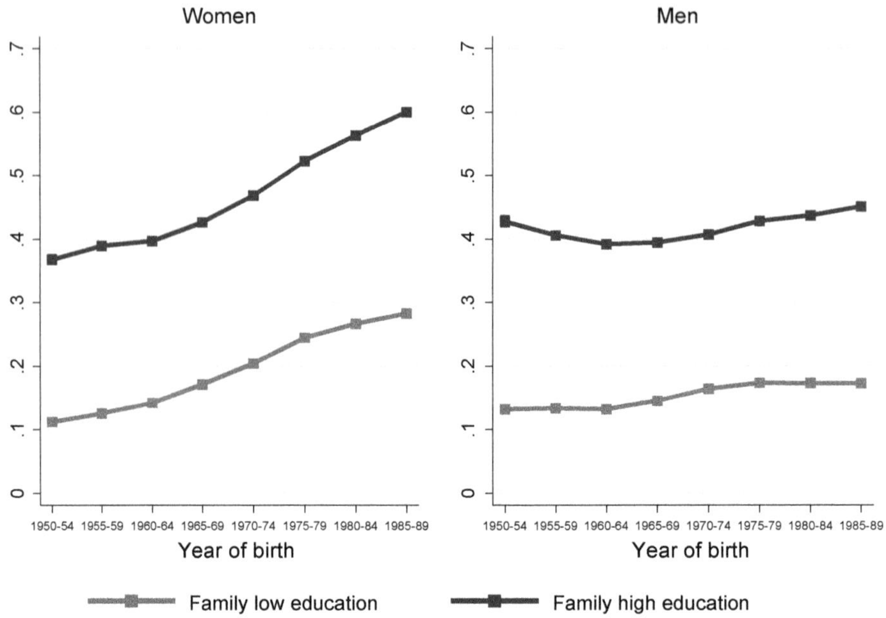

Fig. 9 Proportion of individuals in each cohort with university studies (*Source* EU-SILC)

as this is a circumstance that can be considered a good predictor of school dropout (see, among others, Cockx et al. 2019). School outcomes in mathematics are strong predictors of future outcomes, such as the likelihood of completing high school or attending university, or even individuals' wages and employment in the labor market (Joensen and Nielsen 2009; Rose and Betts 2004; Hanushek et al. 2015). On the other hand, learning to read and write is an essential skill. In fact, empirical evidence shows that basic literacy skills generate significant wage and employment gains in the labor market (Cherry and Vignoles 2016).

For this analysis, we use PISA data from several European countries, starting with the 2000 edition, covering individuals born in 1985. This allows us to connect the analysis to the most recent generations examined for school leaving using EU-SILC data. The following figures display inequality in PISA scores for mathematics and language based on family educational background. Here we define an educated family as one where either the mother or father holds a university degree. In the overall sample, 56% of students come from families with higher education.

We observe consistent disparities in both mathematics and language performance. In the most recent year for which data is available (2022), the gap in mathematics is 42.1 points, while in reading, it is 42.6 points. These differences account for 47.3% and 44.6% of the respective standard deviations. A striking feature of the data is the overall decline in scores in the latest edition. This drop is not due to significant changes in the sample of countries, as Luxembourg is the only nation that

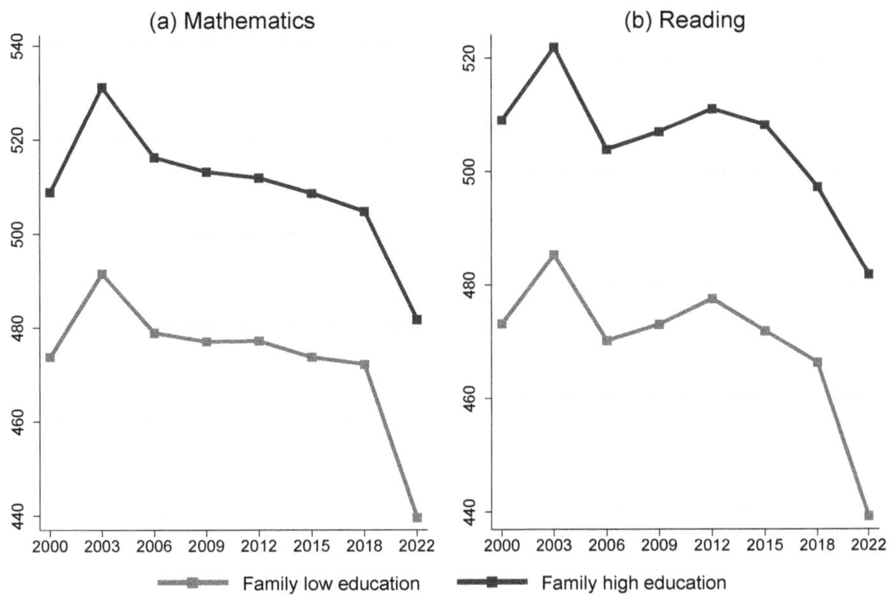

Fig. 10 Scores in mathematics and reading by type of family (*Source* PISA)

participated in 2018 but not in 2022. Experts suggest that COVID-19 exacerbated an already existing downward trend (Fig. 10).

Similar to our approach in studying school dropout inequality, we now categorize families based on their socioeconomic status and whether they are native or immigrant. To assess students' socioeconomic status, we use the ESCS index provided by PISA, which is constructed from three family-related factors: parents' highest educational attainment, the highest occupational status within the household, and household possessions, including books. In Fig. 11, we categorize PISA test participants from 2003 onward into quartiles based on their ESCS scores (the 2000 edition is excluded because a different measure of socioeconomic index was used). We calculate the mean scores for each quartile, ranking individuals according to their ESCS values. Those in quartile 1 represent the 25% with the lowest ESCS, quartile 2 includes the next 25%, and so on.

We observe a large gap between the scores of students in the bottom and top quartiles. In 2022, the difference in mathematics is approximately 86.1 points, equivalent to 97% of a standard deviation, with a similar gap in language. Moreover, the trends for all four quartiles have remained nearly parallel over the past 18 years.

Exercise 4: In the PISA database, you have data on the number of books, computers, and tablets of the student. Download the PISA data for a country of your choice from the 2022 edition and build a figure similar to Fig. 11 using these variables. What is the

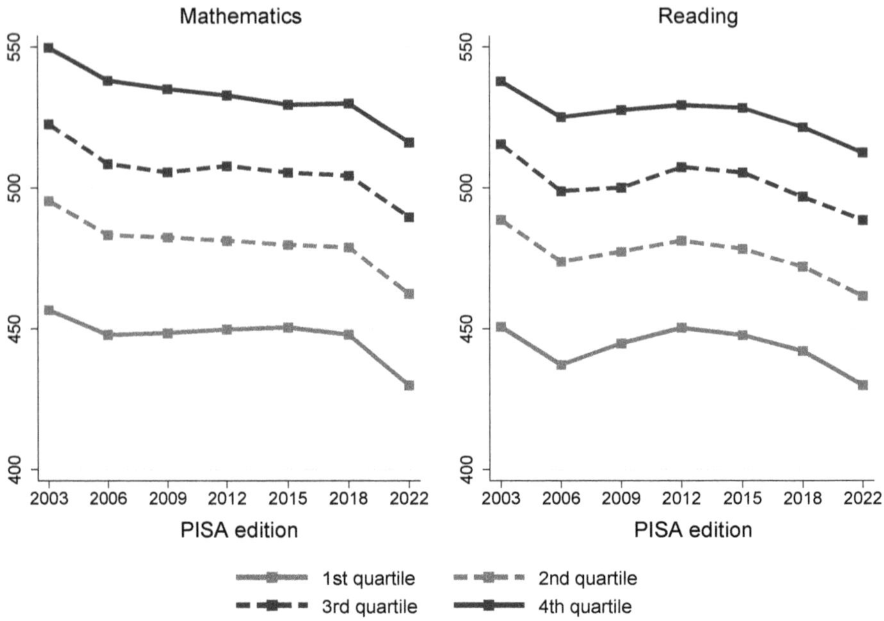

Fig. 11 Scores in mathematics (left) and reading (right) and ESCS (*Source* PISA)

> educational inequality in mathematics and language between students who have fewer than 25 books and those who have more than 100? And between those who have one or no computer (or tablet) and those who have more than one? Is it similar to what we observe using the socioeconomic index? Are there differences between inequality in mathematics and language depending on the type of materials they have?

Below, we present the inequality in PISA mathematics scores between students from immigrant and native families. The immigrant group includes both first- and second-generation students. We focus on mathematics scores, as language difficulties among some immigrant students may introduce measurement errors in reading scores (evidence suggests these difficulties can affect performance in language classes, see Resnjanskij et al. 2024).

As we can see in Fig. 12, there is a gap between the two groups that has slightly reduced since the 2015 edition.

3.5 *Inequality in Terms of Grade Repetition*

Repeating a year is a widespread practice in some European countries. Among PISA 2022 participants, more than 12% have repeated a grade at least once in primary or secondary school. There is also some evidence that students from disadvantaged

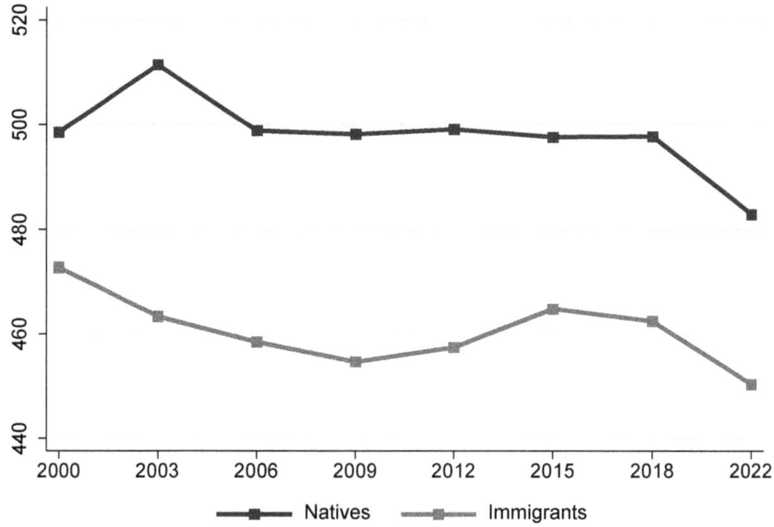

Fig. 12 Math scores and migrant status (*Source* PISA)

backgrounds are more likely to repeat a grade. According to PISA 2022 data for European countries, the proportion of repeaters per quartile of the ESCS index is 15.1% in the bottom quartile, 9.7% in the second, 5.9% in the third, and 3.5% in the top quartile. A student in the bottom quartile is 4.3 times more likely than one in the top quartile to have repeated a grade at least once. With this in mind, we examine educational inequality in terms of grade repetition and its recent trends. To do so, we analyze all PISA rounds that include data on whether a student has repeated a grade.[9] In Fig. 13, we explore the grade repetition rates based on family educational background. The gap between the two family types has widened in recent years, reaching a difference of 8.4 percentage points in 2022 (15.5% versus 7.1%).

Exercise 5: As some studies suggest, grade repetition is linked to school dropout. While the PISA database does not provide direct information on whether a student drops out, it does include data on their educational expectations. Specifically, there is a variable that captures the highest level of education a student expects to achieve. Download the PISA data for your country of choice in the last edition (2022). What are the dropout expectations for students who repeat versus those who do not? Is there a noticeable difference? How have these trends evolved?

[9] We have no information about repeated grades in the rounds of 2000 and 2006.

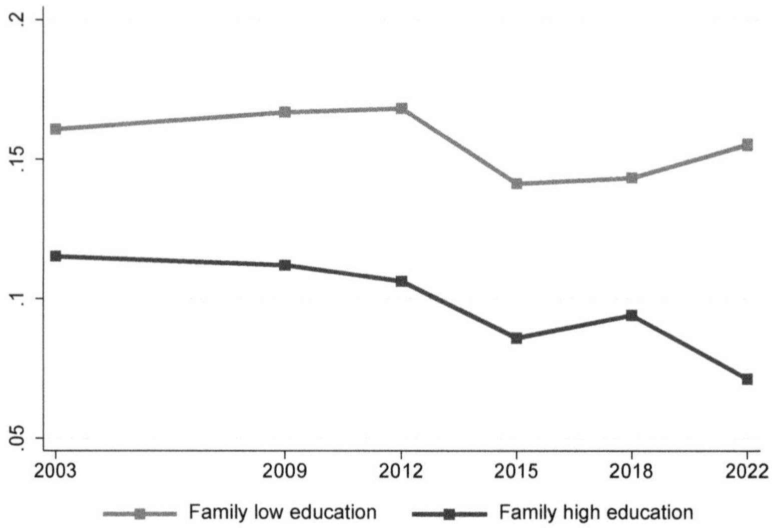

Fig. 13 Proportion of students repeating a year by type of family (*Source* PISA)

> **Bonus Material Box: Repeat a Course** The goal of repetition is to give students a "second chance" to master the knowledge and skills appropriate to their level. However, it continues to be a practice that is the subject of debate both within the educational and scientific community, as the identification of its effects is not obvious and the evidence is mixed (Allen et al., 2009). Among some of the most recent studies, Alet (2014) detects that short-term gains in test scores tend to disappear a few years after repetition. García-Pérez et al. (2014) find negative effects of repeating a year on academic performance in Spain. Finally, students who repeat grades are more likely to drop out of secondary school (Manacorda 2012; Jacob and Lefgren 2009; Cockx et al. 2019).

3.6 Country differences in scores

In this section, we briefly discuss country differences in PISA data. In Fig. 14, we compare the inequality in scores between countries using the criterion of socioeconomic status. The figure shows for each country the average score in the PISA 2022 score in mathematics (left panel) and in language (right panel), as well as the average scores of the bottom and top quartiles of the PISA socioeconomic status index (ESCS), as well as the gap between the two. Countries are ranked according to the average score.

From Fig. 14, we can make several observations. First, the gap in test scores between the top and bottom quartiles of socioeconomic status ranges from 61 to 123

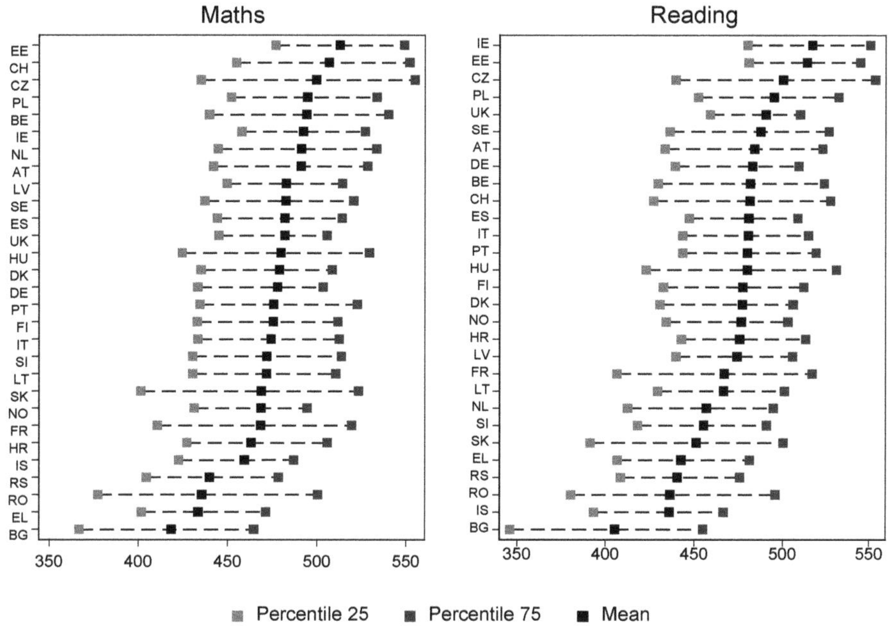

Fig. 14 Scores in mathematics and reading and ESCS by country (*Source* PISA 2022)

points in mathematics and from 51 to 115 in language. Notice that, in all countries, and in both mathematics and language, the performance of students from disadvantaged backgrounds is below the OECD average of 500 points. Finally, while the average gap between countries reaches 94 points in mathematics and 111 in language, the average gap by family environment is 85 points in mathematics and 82 points in reading.

In the next figure, we illustrate the potential trade-off between efficiency and equity, focusing on mathematics scores from 2022. Efficiency is measured by a country's average score and is represented on the horizontal axis. To assess inequality, we proceed as follows: first, we calculate the average mathematics score for students in both the bottom and top deciles of the ESCS index in each country. The ESCS index ranks students based on their socioeconomic status, and we divide them into ten equal-sized groups (deciles), with the bottom decile representing the most disadvantaged students and the top decile the most advantaged. Our proposed measure of inequality is the difference in average mathematics scores between these two deciles, which reflects the disparity in performance across socioeconomic groups within each country. We represent this measure of (in)equity in the vertical axis.

In the figure, we represent 29 countries, and the red dot represents the median of the efficiency and inequality measures. Countries located in the southeast quadrant are those that perform better than the median in both efficiency and equity, as they have a higher average score and a smaller gap between the top and bottom deciles. In the figure, five countries clearly fall in the southeast quadrant: Estonia, Ireland,

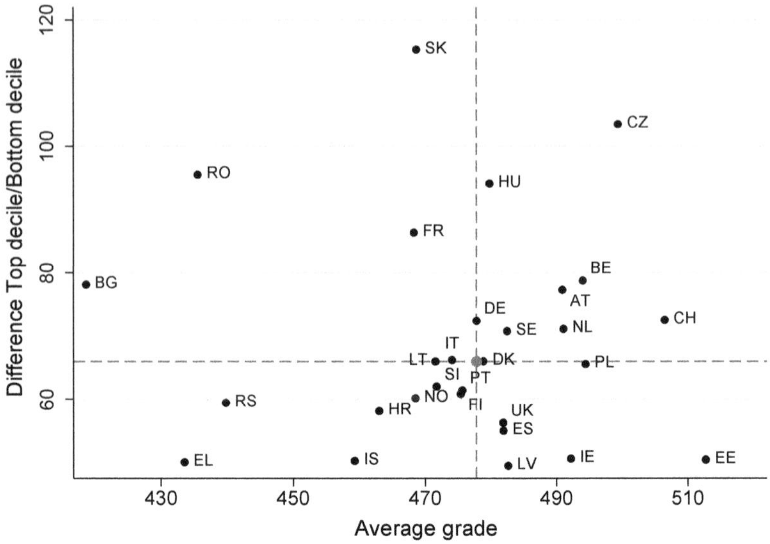

Fig. 15 Average score in mathematics and differences between the top and bottom decile (*Source* PISA 2022)

Latvia, Spain, and the United Kingdom, indicating both higher average scores and smaller disparities between deciles. In contrast, countries in the northwest quadrant—Bulgaria, Slovakia, France, and Romania—are in a worse position, with lower average scores and greater inequality. Lastly, the countries in the other quadrants perform better in one dimension but worse in the other, reflecting a trade-off between efficiency and equity (Fig. 15).

4 Future Consequences of Current Educational Inequality

The presence of individuals left behind in society leads to limited career opportunities, ultimately restricting social mobility. Social mobility refers to the capacity for individuals to overcome the disadvantages of being born into a low socioeconomic background throughout their lives. If a significant fraction of those from poor or under-educated families achieve only low levels of education, social mobility will be constrained. High mobility occurs when an individual's educational achievements are largely independent of their parents' educational background. Inequality and lack of mobility often go hand in hand. The "Great Gatsby Curve" highlights this connection, demonstrating a positive correlation between economic inequality and reduced intergenerational social mobility at the country level.

Educational inequality today not only has the potential to widen future economic disparities but also to intensify existing poverty problems. The European Union's standard measure of poverty is based on the "At Risk of Poverty or Social Exclusion" (AROPE) indicator, which identifies individuals living in households that meet at least one of the following three criteria:

(1) The family's disposable income is below the poverty line (60% of the country's median income).
(2) The family suffers significant material deprivation.
(3) There are adults in the home who worked less than 20% of their potential time during the previous year.

The AROPE rate is the proportion of the total population that is at risk of poverty or social exclusion. This is the main indicator for EU studies of poverty and social exclusion. According to the latest Eurostat data (2023), 94.6 million people in the European Union (21% of the population) are at risk of poverty or social exclusion. This rate varied from a highest value in Romania (32%), to the lowest value in Czechia (12%). In Fig. 16, we show the AROPE rate depending on whether the individual dropped out of school before the end of secondary school or not.

As we can see in Fig. 16, people who drop out of school have a much higher risk of being in poverty and exclusion. For the total sample, the AROPE rate reaches 18% for those who remained in school and 41% for those who dropped out. If we combine the information in this figure with what we saw in Figs. 3 and 4, we find ourselves in a poverty trap situation. People who grew up in poor or poorly educated families drop out of education earlier, condemning them to a higher risk of poverty and exclusion in their adult life.

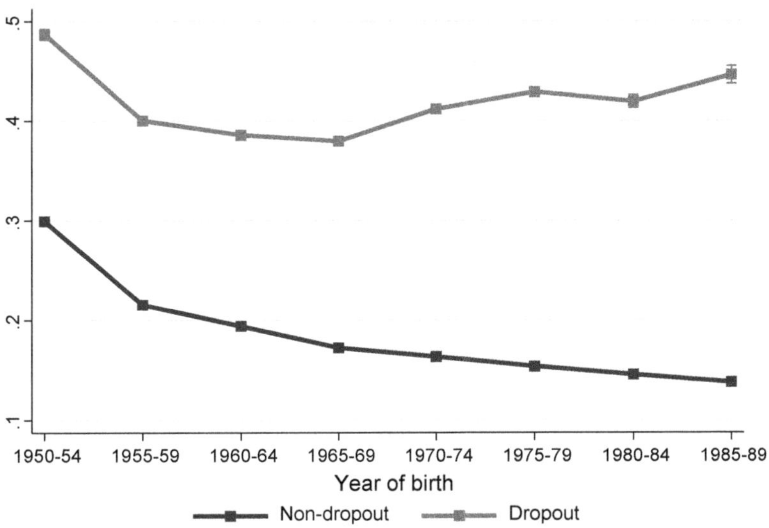

Fig. 16 School dropout and risk of poverty and exclusion (AROPE) (*Source* EU-SILC)

4.1 Educational Inequality and Social Mobility in a Context of Change in the Productive Structure

As Breen (2022) points out, between the 50s and 80s many European countries recorded high rates of social mobility. Among other possible factors, this could be explained by the fact that this was also a period of expansion of management and professional positions. This favored the promotion of people from less advantaged backgrounds without necessarily excluding children from advantaged backgrounds from such positions. However, in the last decades of the twentieth century, these structural changes were attenuated and the situation that now prevails in many other European countries is greater economic inequality (Blanden et al. 2023) and low social mobility (Breen and Müller 2020). The consequences that this can have on educational inequality, and how in turn education can contribute to reducing economic inequality in a context of change in the production model as a result of digital transformation, task automation, etc., is a question worth further exploring (OECD 2023).

5 Causes of Inequality and Possible Solutions

There are multiple causes of inequality between individuals who come from different family backgrounds (Piketty 2000). A first avenue is undoubtedly the genetic transmission of skills, the effect of which may be reinforced in the presence of selective matchings between individuals with similar abilities (see Clark 2021). On the other hand, despite widespread access to education, families with more education usually also have more economic resources, which allows them to spend more on complementary educational goods and services (e.g., language classes or extracurricular support classes). The higher educational level of parents can also translate, among others, into a greater interest and concern for their children's education since they have learned to value it more and also into a greater availability of time to help them with schoolwork. It is also obvious that, the higher the educational level of the parents, the more they are able to help their children in the most complicated subjects (mathematics). Parental employment status has also been observed to have effects on children's education (see Ruíz-Valenzuela 2020, for a review of the most recent literature). Finally, the social environment including the neighborhood and its impact on school choice, as well as on children's friendships, has been discussed previously in Chapter 3c. on the effects of classmates. This influence on the production of human capital is also a key factor in explaining educational inequality. Moreover, this inequality may intensify with increasing school segregation, as discussed in Chapter 5a on school choice.

The complex interdependence of these pathways contributing to educational inequality complicates the identification of the most influential factor or the one that most significantly perpetuates inequality throughout the entire process of human capital accumulation. In this chapter, we have carried out a descriptive analysis of educational inequality, without attempting to establish a causal relationship between the factors we have considered (education and family socioeconomic status) and the inequality we observe. Below we comment on some studies that have tried to identify causal effects between certain measures of socio-family characteristics and educational results.

Evidence on the relevance of socio-family characteristics in individual education is abundant. Björklund and Salvanes (2011) summarize this empirical literature, and analyze the main mechanisms behind this relationship, in order to isolate the weight of the characteristics of the parents. These authors find that correlations of educational outcomes between parents and children may in fact underestimate the role of socio-family characteristics. To do this, they use the correlations of years of schooling between siblings. This correlation can be considered a global measure of the importance of family and environment that reflects parental influences, but also other influences shared by siblings that are orthogonal to parental characteristics. After comparing sibling and intergenerational correlations, they conclude that siblings share educational advantages to a much greater extent than parent–child correlations reflect, implying that intergenerational correlations account for only a small portion of the effects of the family environment. On the other hand, they find that parental education only explains a small part of the factors shared by siblings.

Among the works that study possible causal relationships, it is worth highlighting the literature review by Holmlund et al. (2011), which focuses on quantifying the causal effect of parental education on children's educational and employment outcomes, isolating it from other factors previously mentioned, such as individual ability. Thus, based on an application with data from Sweden, they conclude that intergenerational correlations of education are largely due to selection and not to direct causal effects, even though parental education is the main driver. More recently, Bingley et al. (2021), using census data from individuals born between 1965 and 1985 in Denmark, delve into the relative influence of family and environment (neighbors and schoolmates) on both educational and work outcomes. Thus, they find that the family is the main explanatory factor of the correlation between income and educational level of siblings, and the prevalence of this effect is greater for women than for men.

To the extent that a large part of educational inequality arises at an early age (see Cunha and Heckman 2007, among others), educational interventions at these stages seem especially effective. Among the first programs aimed at improving educational opportunities for children from disadvantaged backgrounds are the Perry Preschool Program, Abecedarian and the CARE Programs, all developed in the 60s and 70s in the United States. The evidence on the impact of these programs is overwhelming. A recent summary of this can be found in Elango et al. (2015), who also compare the benefits of different types of interventions according to their universal or non-universal nature. The evidence on the effects of early childhood education programs, which has expanded markedly since the 1970s, is more ambiguous. However, while positive impacts are observed among children from less advantaged socioeconomic backgrounds (see, for example, Cornelissen et al. 2018), this expansion may not have fully precisely reached those groups that could benefit most from it (see Chapter 4a for a detailed analysis of the role of early childhood education).

Other interventions that can contribute to reducing educational inequalities are remedial education programs. These are designed to help the worst performing students achieve minimum academic levels, usually by attending classes after school hours and in small groups. Most of these interventions are conducted in adolescence when, as we have seen throughout the chapter, the differences in educational outcomes between students from different socioeconomic backgrounds are very evident. In fact, Guryan et al. (2023), focusing on adolescent beneficiaries of the Saga Education program in Chicago, show that the estimated cost–benefit ratio is comparable to that of many successful early childhood programs.

Such interventions are attracting increasing interest, especially in developed countries (see, for example, Carcillo et al. 2015, for an overview of these programs in OECD countries). Evidence on its impact on educational outcomes, however, is still scarce. Lavy et al. (2022) find positive effects on the long-term income of a program in secondary school students in Israel; García-Pérez and Hidalgo-Hidalgo (2017) and Battaglia and Hidalgo-Hidalgo (2024) found higher PISA scores and perseverance, respectively, among students in schools that followed a remedial program in Spain; Battaglia and Lebedinski (2015) focusing on an intervention aimed at Roma students in Serbia found no significant effects on their grades or school dropout. This type of intervention is not, however, exclusive to secondary educational stages. Alan et al. (2019) find positive effects on non-cognitive skills of an intervention on primary school children in Turkey; Battistin and Meroni (2016), who analyze a remedial education program in primary schools in Italy, find positive effects on mathematics grades. The debate on the most appropriate time to conduct this type of intervention is open (Battaglia and Hidalgo-Hidalgo 2023).

6 Other Inequalities and Final Comments

Throughout the chapter, we have illustrated the educational inequality between individuals from different social groups and we have focused on the level of education or family socioeconomic status to identify these groups. However, there are other dimensions that also generate educational inequality, among which belonging to ethnic minorities is very important. The Roma community is the largest minority in the EU: between 6 and 8 million people. The figure is much higher if we refer to the whole of Europe, reaching 10–12 million, that is, if we add the Balkans and other countries further east, such as Moldova, etc. (Communication from the European Commission 2011). The educational inequality between this minority, who live in precarious socioeconomic conditions, and the rest of the population is enormous. To cite an educational result that we have discussed in this chapter, the school dropout rate among the Roma population aged 18–24 in 2021 was about 70%, compared to less than 10% of the total European population (for more information on this and other indicators, see the report by the European School Education Platform 2023).

This inequality prompted the Council of Europe's recommendation to improve access to education for Roma students and combat all types of inequality in education.[10] Among the possible measures to achieve these objectives and for which there is empirical evidence, we highlight compensatory education programs again. Among this evidence, for example, Battaglia and Lebedinski (2022) and Battaglia and Lebedinski (2015) find positive effects in both the short and medium term of the Roma Teaching Assistant Program in Serbia.

Another source of educational inequality is the existence of special educational needs. According to the European Agency for Special Needs and Inclusive Education (2021), the number of students with special educational needs (SEN) in Europe varies across countries, but approximately 4–5% of the total student population falls under this category. In addition, the precise number of SEN students changes annually as member states improve their reporting mechanisms and policies around inclusive education. The European Commission and various agencies continue to monitor and provide data to enhance educational inclusivity throughout Europe (European Commission 2021). We do know that, in all countries of the world, people with disabilities have lower levels of education than people without disabilities: on average, people with disabilities are less likely to ever attend school, are more likely to be out of school, are less likely to complete primary or secondary education, have fewer years of schooling, and are less likely to have basic literacy skills (United Nations 2018). Thus, among the measures recommended by UNESCO (2021), we can highlight the need to evaluate the education these students receive, improve teacher training or investment in technology as a tool to reduce barriers.

In recent years, European countries have experienced a notable advance in their educational results, reducing existing disparities. However, significant inequalities persist, especially related to both family socioeconomic status and the dimensions mentioned in this section. It is crucial to accurately identify the causes of these disparities in order to design effective policies that can mitigate them. In addition, it is essential to carry out meticulous evaluations of the educational interventions implemented. Only by fully understanding these inequalities and their causes can we develop a truly equitable education system, offering equal opportunities for all students, regardless of their background or economic situation.

References

Alan, S., T. Boneva and S. Ertac. 2019. Ever failed, try again, succeed better: Results from a randomized educational intervention on grit. *The Quarterly Journal of Economics* 134 (3): 1121–1162. https://doi.org/10.1093/qje/qjz006.

Alet, E. 2014. Repetition: Medicine for a short-run remission. *Annales d'Économie et de Statistique* 111–112: 227–250. https://doi.org/10.2307/23646332.

[10] Council Recommendation of 12 March 2021 on equality, inclusion and participation of Roma (2021/C93/01).

Allen, C., Q. Chen, V. Willson, and J. Hughes. 2009. Quality of research design moderates effects of grade retention on achievement: A meta-analytic, multilevel analysis. *Educational Evaluation and Policy Analysis* 31 (4): 480–499. https://doi.org/10.3102/0162373709352239.

Attanasio, O. 2015. The determinants of human capital formation during the early years of life: Theory, measurement, and polices. *Journal of the European Economic Association* 13 (6): 949–997. https://doi.org/10.1111/jeea.12159.

Barro, R., and J. Lee. 2001. International data on educational attainment: Updates and implications. *Oxford Economic Papers* 53: 541–563. https://doi.org/10.1093/oep/53.3.541.

Battaglia, M., and L. Lebedinski. 2015. Equal access to education: An evaluation of the Roma Teaching Assistant Program in Serbia. *World Development* 76: 62–81. https://doi.org/10.1016/j.worlddev.2015.06.009.

Battaglia, M., and L. Lebedinski. 2022. With a little help from my friends: Medium-Term effects of a remedial education program targeting Roma minority. *Economics of Education Review* 86: 102196. https://doi.org/10.1016/j.econedurev.2021.102196.

Battaglia, M., and M. Hidalgo-Hidalgo. 2023. *Better early than late? Primary versus secondary school remedial interventions.* Mimeo Universidad Pablo de Olavide.

Battaglia, M., and M. Hidalgo-Hidalgo. 2024. Test endurance and remedial education interventions: Good news for girls. *The B.E. Journal of Economic Analysis and Policy.* https://doi.org/10.1515/bejeap-2023-0410.

Battistin, E., and E.C. Meroni. 2016. Should we increase instruction time in low achieving schools? Evidence from Southern Italy. *Economics of Education Review* 55: 39–56. https://doi.org/10.1016/j.econedurev.2016.08.003.

Bingley, P., L. Cappellari, and K. Tatsiramos. 2021. Family, community and long-term socio-economic inequality: Evidence from siblings and youth peers. *The Economic Journal* 131 (636): 1515–1554. https://doi.org/10.1093/ej/ueaa121.

Björklund, A., and K. Salvanes. 2011. Education and family background: Mechanisms and policies. In *Handbook of the Economics of Education*, Vol. 3, ed. E. Hanushek, S. Machin, and L. Woessmann, 201–247. Elsevier. https://doi.org/10.1016/B978-0-444-53429-3.00003-X.

Blanden, J., M. Doepke, and J. Stuhler. 2023. Educational inequality. In *Handbook of the Economics of Education*, Vol. 6, ed. E. Hanushek, S. Machin, and L. Woessmann, 405–497. Elsevier. https://doi.org/10.1016/bs.hesedu.2022.11.003.

Breen, R. 2022. The stubborn persistence of educational inequality, IFS Deaton Review of Inequalities, Institute for Fiscal Studies.

Breen, R., and E. Müller (eds.). 2020. *Education and Intergenerational Social Mobility in Europe and the United States.* Redwood City, CA: Stanford University Press.

Carcillo, S., R. Fernández, S. Königs, and A. Minea. 2015. NEET youth in the aftermath of the crisis: Challenges and policies. OECD Social, Employment and Migration Working Papers, No. 164, OECD Publishing, Paris. https://doi.org/10.1787/5js6363503f6-en.

Castelló, A., and R. Doménech. 2002. Human capital inequality and economic growth: Some new evidence. *Economic Journal* 112: C187–200. https://doi.org/10.1111/1468-0297.00024.

Checchi, D. 2001. Education, inequality and income inequality, LSE STICERD Research paper DARP 52, LSE, London.

Cherry, G., and A. Vignoles. 2016. What is the economic value of literacy and numeracy? Basic skills in literacy and numeracy are essential for success in the labor market. *IZA World of Labor*, 229. https://doi.org/10.15185/izawol.229.v2.

Clark, G. 2021. For whom the bell curve tolls: A lineage of 400,000 individuals 1750–2020 shows genetics determines most social outcomes. Unpublished Manuscript, UC Davis.

Cockx, B., M. Picchio, and S. Baert. 2019. Modeling the effects of grade retention in high school. *Journal of Applied Econometrics* 34 (3): 403–424. https://doi.org/10.1002/jae.2670.

Communication from the European Commission. 2011. A European framework of national Roma inclusion strategies until 2020. European Commission, Brussels.

Cornelissen, T., C. Dustmann, A. Raute, and U. Schönberg. 2018. Who benefits from universal child care? Estimating marginal returns to early child care attendance. *Journal of Political Economy* 126 (6): 2356–2409. https://doi.org/10.1086/699979.

Cunha, F., and J. Heckman. 2007. The technology of skill formation. *American Economic Review* 97 (2): 31–47. https://doi.org/10.1257/aer.97.2.31.

Currie, J., and D. Almond. 2011. Human capital development before age five. In Handbook of Labor Economics, Vol. 4, ed. D. Card, and O. Ashenfelter, 1315–1486. Elsevier.

Elango, S., J.L. García, J.J. Heckman, and A. Hojman. 2015. Early Childhood Education. NBER Working Paper 21766.

European Agency for Special Needs and Inclusive Education. (2021). *European Agency Statistics on Inclusive Education (EASIE).* https://www.european-agency.org/activities/data.

European School Education Platform. 2023. Addressing school segregation: Promoting inclusion of Roma communities. https://school-education.ec.europa.eu/en/discover/news/promoting-inclusion-roma-communities.

Eurostat, 2023. Living conditions in Europe - poverty and social exclusion. https://ec.europa.eu/eurostat/statistics-explained/index.php?title=Living_conditions_in_Europe_poverty_and_social_exclusion&oldid=584082#Poverty_and_social_exclusion.

Ferreira, F., and J. Gignoux. 2014. The measurement of educational inequality: Achievement and opportunity. *The World Bank Economic Review* 28: 210–246.

Fleurbaey, M. 2008. *Fairness, responsibility, and welfare.* Oxford University Press.

Fundación Secretariado Gitano. 2023. The educational situation of Roma students in Spain Executive Report. Madrid, Ministry of Social Rights and Agenda 2030.

García-Pérez, J., and M. Hidalgo-Hidalgo. 2017. No student left behind? Evidence from the Programme for School Guidance in Spain. *Economics of Education Review* 60: 97–111. https://doi.org/10.1016/j.econedurev.2017.08.006.

García-Pérez, I., M. Hidalgo-Hidalgo, and A. Robles-Zurita. 2014. Does grade retention affect students' achievement? Some evidence from Spain. *Applied Economics* 46 (12): 1373–1392. https://doi.org/10.1080/00036846.2013.872761.

Guryan, J., J. Ludwig, M.P. Bhatt, P.J. Cook, J.M.V. Davis, K. Dodge, G. Farkas, R.G. Fryer, S. Mayer, H. Pollack, L. Steinberg, and G. Stoddard. 2023. Not too late: Improving academic outcomes among adolescents. *American Economic Revie* 113 (3): 738–765. https://doi.org/10.1257/aer.20210434.

Hanushek, E., G. Schwerdt, S. Wiederhold, and L. Woessmann. 2015. Returns to skills around the world: Evidence from PIAAC. *European Economic Review* 73:103–130. https://doi.org/10.1016/j.euroecorev.2014.10.006.

Hanushek, E., and L. Woessmann. 2010. The economics of international differences in educational achievement, NBER Working Paper 15949.

Holmlund, H., M. Lindahl, and E. Plug. 2011. The causal effect of parents' schooling on children's schooling: A comparison of estimation methods. *Journal of Economic Literature* 49 (3): 615–651. https://doi.org/10.1257/jel.49.3.615.

Jacob, B., and L. Lefgren. 2009. The effect of grade retention on high school completion. *American Economic Journal: Applied Economics* 1: 33–58. https://doi.org/10.1257/app.1.3.33.

Joensen, J., and H. Nielsen. 2009. Is there a causal effect of high school math on labor market outcomes? *Journal of Human Resources* 44 (1): 171–198. https://www.jstor.org/stable/20648891.

Lavy, V., A. Kott, and G. Rachkovski. 2022. Does remedial education at late childhood pay off after all? Long-run consequences for University Schooling, Labor Market Outcomes and Intergenerational Mobility. *Journal of Labor Economics* 40 (1): 239–282. https://doi.org/10.1086/713742.

Lochner, L. 2011. Nonproduction benefits of education: Crime, health, and good citizenship. In *Handbook of the Economics of Education*, Vol. 4, ed. E. Hanushek, S. Machin, and L. Woessmann, 183–282. Elsevier. https://doi.org/10.1016/B978-0-444-53444-6.00002-X.

Manacorda, M. 2012. The cost of grade retention. *Review of Economics and Statistics* 94: 596–606. https://www.jstor.org/stable/23262090.

Marrero, G., J. Palomino, and G. Sicilia. 2023. Inequality of opportunity in educational achievement in Western Europe: Contributors and channels. *Journal of Economic Inequality* 22: 383–410.

Meschi, E., and F. Scervini. 2014. Expansion of schooling and educational inequality in Europe: The educational Kuznets curve revisited. *Oxford Economic Papers* 66: 660–680.

OECD. 2023. Education at a Glance 2023: Educational attainment and labor-force status. https://data.oecd.org/eduatt/adult-education-level.htm.

Piketty, T. 2000. Theories of persistent inequality and intergenerational mobility. In *Handbook of Income Distribution*, Vol. 1, ed. A. Atkinson, and F. Bourguignon, 429–476. Elsevier.

Policy Memo from the European Commission. 2021. Access to quality education for children with special educational needs. European Commission, Brussels. https://ec.europa.eu/social/BlobServlet?docId=20625&langId=en.

Ram, R., 1984. Population increase, economic growth, educational inequality, and income distribution: Some recent evidence. *Journal of Development Economics* 14: 419–428.

Ram, R. 1990. Educational expansion and schooling inequality: International evidence and some implications. *Review of Economics and Statistics* 72 (2): 266–274.

Resnjanskij, S., J. Ruhose, S. Wiederhold, L. Woessmann, and K. Wedel. 2024. Can mentoring alleviate family disadvantage in adolescence? A field experiment to improve labor-market prospects. *Journal of Political Economy* 132 (3): 1013–1062.

Roemer, J. 1998. *Equality of opportunity*. Cambridge, MA: Harvard University Press.

Rose, H., and J. Betts. 2004. The effect of high school courses on earnings. *The Review of Economics and Statistics* 86 (2): 497–513.

Ruíz-Valenzuela, J. 2020. Intergenerational effects of employment protection reforms. *Labour Economics* 62: 101774.

UNESCO. 2021. Inclusive Education and Learning for Persons with Disabilities, UNESCO International Institute for Educational Planning. http://www.iiep.unesco.org/.

United Nations. 2018. Education and disability: Analysis of data from 49 countries. Information Paper N. 49.

Gender Gaps in Education

Claudia Hupkau and Jenifer Ruiz-Valenzuela

1 Introduction

In most developed economies, women's educational performance has improved substantially in recent decades. Across OECD countries, women comprised 56% of first-time entrants into tertiary education in 2022 and constituted a majority of new entrants in every OECD country (OECD 2024). However, the percentage of women who choose to enrol in STEM disciplines (Science, Technology, Engineering, and Mathematics) remains low and has remained relatively stable over the past few years. These observations suggest two important gender gaps.

First, in most advanced economies, we observe a lower level of educational performance among boys compared to girls. One of the most commonly used indicators to capture this phenomenon is the percentage of early school leavers. As mentioned in Chapter 1, early school leaving is defined as the percentage of individuals aged 18–24 who meet the following criteria: (1) They have only completed lower secondary education or less and (2), they are not enrolled in any academic or training course.

In Fig. 1, we can see how, over the past two decades, the percentage of early school leavers among boys has always been higher than that of girls in the EU-27. Data for different countries show that the gender gap has decreased in countries like Portugal and Spain, but it is rising for countries that started the millennium with a lower gender gap (in the UK and Germany, for instance). Other indicators that

C. Hupkau (✉)
CUNEF Universidad, Madrid, Spain
e-mail: claudia.hupkau@cunef.edu

C. Hupkau · J. Ruiz-Valenzuela
Centre for Economic Performance (London School of Economics), London, UK

J. Ruiz-Valenzuela
Departament Economia, Facultat Economia i Empresa, Universitat de Barcelona (UB), Barcelona, Spain

Institut Economia de Barcelona (IEB), Barcelona, Spain

A. Cabrales and I. Sanz (eds.), *Economics of Education*,
https://doi.org/10.1007/978-3-031-90911-5_14

capture students' educational performance point in the same direction. Women tend to have higher test scores in standardised assessments and are significantly less likely to repeat a grade at primary and lower secondary levels (OECD 2024).

Second, according to Eurostat data on enrolments for the EU-27 countries shown in Fig. 2, we see that within STEM disciplines, the low percentage of women enrolled is mostly due to the low enrolment rates in the fields of Information and Communication Technologies and Engineering-related fields, with no discernible improvements over the last decade. Eurostat (2023) data on enrolments in tertiary education, shown in Table 1, reveal that during the 2021–2022 academic year, women were under-represented in Information and Communication Technologies (20.16% of enrollees), Engineering, and engineering trades (21.38% of enrollees).

Within sciences, women were also under-represented in Physical Sciences (43.46%) and Mathematics and Statistics (41.61%), while they were over-represented in Biological and related sciences (66.69%) as well as Medicine (62.45%).

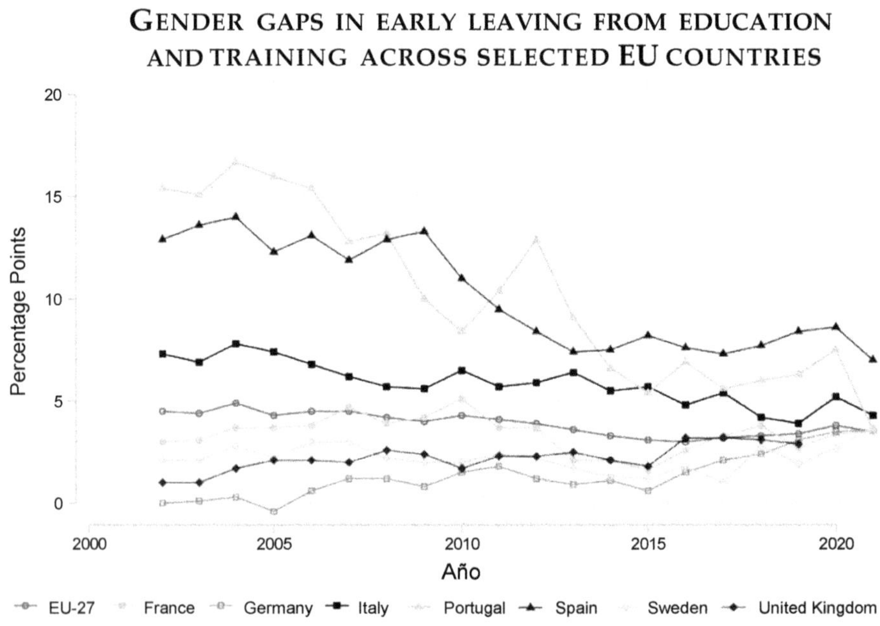

Fig. 1 Gender gaps in early leaving from education and training across selected EU countries (*Note* The graph represents the difference in the share of "early leavers from education and training" between males and females for selected EU countries. An early school leaver is defined as a person aged 18–24 who has completed at most lower secondary education and is not involved in further education or training; the indicator "early leavers from education and training" is expressed as a percentage of the people aged 18–24 with such criteria out of the total population aged 18–24. Based on information from the European Labour Force Survey. *Source* Ministerio de Educación y Formación Profesional [2023])

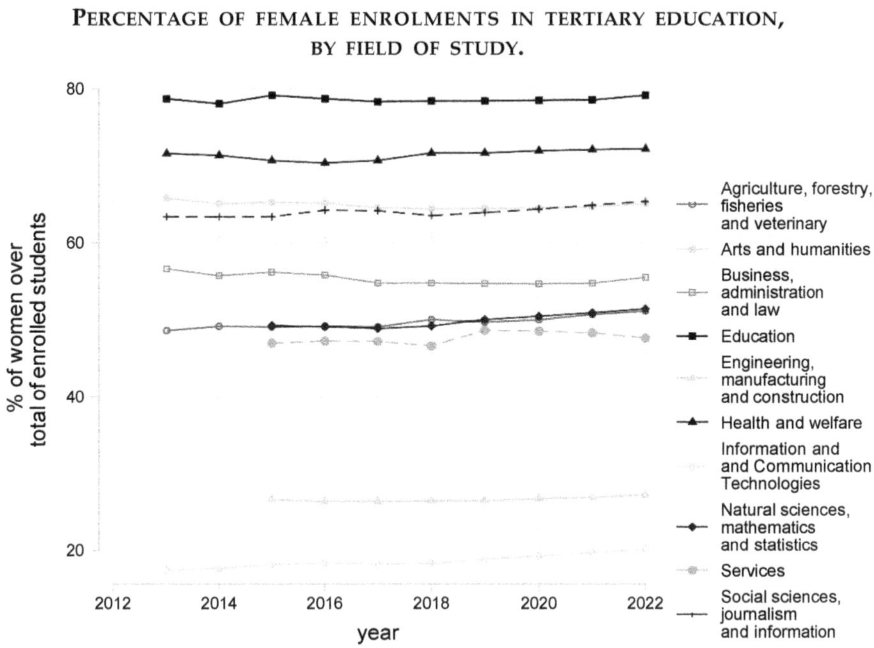

Fig. 2 Percentage of female enrolments in tertiary education, by field of study (*Note* Data for EU-27. The graph shows the per cent of women as a percentage of the total number of students enrolled in a specific field of study based on data from Eurostat [2023]. All students in tertiary education [levels 5–8], including short cycle tertiary education, Bachelor's or equivalent levels, and Master's and equivalent levels)

This gap is not limited to university course choices. Women are also under-represented in vocational training programs in STEM fields. This is a characteristic shared by most developed economies (Encinas-Martín and Cherian 2023).

In this chapter, we will try to understand the reasons behind these two main gender gaps in education. The reasons are closely linked to different inputs of the education production function, introduced in Chapters 4, 5, 6 and 7

1.1 *Why Should We Be Concerned About Gender Gaps in Education?*

In both cases, these gender gaps should concern us due to their negative implications for the individual as well as their effects on society as a whole.

Let us start with the first of the gaps described, that is, the lower level of educational performance among men. In *The Price We Pay: Economic and Social Consequences of Inadequate Education*, Belfield and Levin (2007) bring together a group of academic experts in the economics of education who, using data from the United

Table 1 Percentage of women enrolled in universities, by field of study. Academic year 2021–2022

Total of women enrolled: 54.63%			
Total Education	**79.16%**	**Total science**	**51.39%**
Training for pre-school teachers	87.60%	Biological and related sciences	66.69%
Teacher training without subject specialisation	78.73%	Physical sciences	43.46%
Teacher training with subject specialisation	62.78%	Mathematics and statistics	41.61%
Total Arts and Humanities	**65.06%**	**Engineering, manufacturing and construction**	**27.26%**
Arts	61.53%	Engineering and engineering trades	21.38%
Languages	75.71%	Architecture and construction	42.14%
Humanities (except languages)	51.43%	**Agriculture, forestry, fisheries and veterinary**	**51.09%**
Total Social sciences, journalism and information	**65.36%**	Agriculture	46.15%
Psychology	78.00%	Forestry	35.12%
Economics	44.89%	Veterinary	77.17%
Journalism and information	68.61%	**Health and welfare**	**72.16%**
Total Business, administration and law	**55.47%**	Medicine	62.45%
Business and administration	54.33%	Nursing and midwifery	84.96%
Law	62.69%	Social work and counselling	82.06%
Total Information and Communication Technologies	**20.16%**	**Services**	**47.62%**
Computer use	21.32%	Sports	30.07%
Software and applications development and analysis	18.67%	Travel, tourism and leisure	68.21%

Source Calculations based on Eurostat (2023), Table educ_uoe_enrt03. Students enrolled in undergraduate and postgraduate programs (tertiary education levels 5–8)

States, show how low levels of education are associated with a higher likelihood of unemployment and health problems, lower incomes, or criminal behaviour. For example, in one of the chapters, Enrico Moretti documents how high-school dropouts (those who do not complete the second stage of secondary education) are twice as likely to end up in prison as those who do complete post-compulsory secondary education. In addition to these individual costs, Belfield and Levin (2007) explain that there are well-documented costs for taxpayers and society in general:

- A lower level of individual income slows economic growth and tax revenues and puts pressure on budgetary allocations for welfare policies for low-income families.

- Poorer health levels increase the cost of public healthcare. In one of the chapters, Cecilia Rouse estimates that for each individual who completes post-compulsory secondary education in the United States, the government would save about $39,000 due to reduced use of public health programs.
- One of the negative externalities of low levels of education, which is more prevalent among men, is a higher likelihood of committing crimes. Enrico Moretti estimates that an additional year of schooling would reduce murders and assaults by nearly 30%, vehicle theft by 20%, and robberies and burglaries by 6%. Thus, he calculates that if an additional 1% of men aged 20–60 graduated from post-compulsory secondary education, the U.S. government would save over one billion dollars a year in justice system-related costs (judges, prosecutors, prisons, etc.).

These negative consequences of boys' lower educational performance are exacerbated by the growing polarisation of the labour market. Autor (2010) explains that job opportunities are increasingly concentrated at the tails of the job distribution. That is, we observe greater demand for highly skilled workers (who earn higher wages), less demand for jobs for workers with a medium level of qualification, and greater demand for low-skilled jobs (which typically pay very low wages). A lower level of educational performance among boys pushes them to be under-represented among highly skilled workers. In addition to the negative consequences in terms of employment or crime, David Autor provides evidence of the association between education and marital status: men who do not complete post-compulsory secondary education are less likely to marry.

Exercise 1

We have just described the negative consequences of having a low educational attainment for the individual, as well as the negative externalities for society in general. We invite you to discuss in class whether these negative externalities are worse when under-education is predominantly among men. A good article to support the discussion is the one written by David Autor in 2010 "*US Labor Market Challenges over the Longer Term.*"

The second of the gaps described, that is, the lower proportion of women in STEM disciplines, also has adverse effects on women in the labour market. At the individual level, graduates in these disciplines, whether university graduates or in vocational training programs, tend to work in industries (or economic sectors) and occupations with higher wages. The existing evidence suggests that both the economic sector and the occupation of workers are contributing to the persistent wage gap between men and women (i.e., women have, on average, lower wages than men) (Blau and Kahn 2017; Black et al. 2021). Moreover, due to the growing importance of artificial intelligence and data analytics for companies, demand for graduates in STEM disciplines is expected to continue to rise in the future. This would put upward pressure on wages in many STEM disciplines, contributing, if gender patterns in STEM enrolment do not change, to a widening gender wage gap.

We relegate the reader interested in understanding the relationship between field of study and its return in the labour market to Chapter 4b. Additionally, the chapter by Altonji et al. (2016) in the *Handbook of the Economics of Education* provides a good summary of the problems (and potential solutions) faced by researchers when estimating causal effects of returns to different fields of study.

In addition to these individual gains associated with STEM fields of study, there is evidence that STEM workers are essential for innovation, one of the main drivers of productivity growth. For example, with data from the United States, Peri et al. (2015) use instrumental variables (explained in Chapter 2) as follows. In the first stage, as an instrument to predict the growth of foreign STEM workers, they use variation over time in the proportion of visas granted to different nationality groups in different cities, including city fixed effects in their estimates. In the second stage, the authors obtain causal estimates of the effect of the growth of foreign STEM workers on the wages and employment of native workers. Their results show that a one percentage point increase in the growth of foreign STEM workers leads to a seven to eight percentage point increase in wages for native workers with a university degree. With these results, the authors simulate the effect of foreign STEM workers on aggregate total productivity, finding that inflows of foreign STEM workers explain around 30–50% of the aggregate productivity growth in the United States between 1990 and 2010. Therefore, in an international context, where there is a shortage of STEM workers, the under-representation of women in these disciplines may be significantly reducing aggregate innovation and productivity.

2 Drivers of Boys' Underachievement Relative to Girls

For most advanced economies, the data stubbornly show lower educational performance of boys compared to girls. In this section, we will describe some of the main factors that contribute to explaining this gender gap. Moreover, for each factor, we review and discuss in detail some of the most important research findings. The goal is not only to understand the factors but also to apply the knowledge on causal identification introduced in Chapter 2 and discuss how different authors have tried to address identification challenges.

We have grouped the potential reasons into four major groups. First, we briefly review differences in non-cognitive skills between boys and girls. Then, we address the role that families and, more generally, the socioeconomic environment play in explaining this gender gap (see also Chapter 5 on the impact of families on education). Thirdly, we review what the existing evidence tells us about the role of schools and potential teacher biases. Finally, we provide some insights into the relationship between labour market conditions, the opportunity cost of continuing education, and students' educational performance.

2.1 Non-cognitive Skills

Non-cognitive skills comprise character traits, personality, attributes, dispositions, social skills, attitudes, abilities, and personal resources that are independent of intellectual capacity. In Chapter 15, non-cognitive skills are defined in more detail, as well as how they are measured, what their determinants are, and their importance for the well-being of individuals throughout life. One aspect that highlights the importance of these non-cognitive skills is the role they play in determining students' academic outcomes. In this chapter, we address whether there are differences in non-cognitive skills between boys and girls that may be explaining gender differences in early school leaving.

The psychology literature has long studied the existence of gender differences in non-cognitive skills. A good example is the study by Else-Quest et al. (2006), which reports the results of a meta-analysis that examines gender differences in the temperament of boys and girls (i.e., character, disposition, or way of reacting to different situations). The authors of this meta-analysis use data from a total of 189 studies, meticulously selected (the selection process is exhaustively described in their article). The conclusion of this meta-analysis is that boys have lower levels of inhibitory control as well as perceptual sensitivity, and this is consistent with a higher incidence of externalising behaviour problems.[1]

In economics, several studies have linked lower levels of non-cognitive skills with worse academic performance. One of the first examples linking gender differences in non-cognitive skills with boys' poorer educational performance is an article by Nobel Prize-winning economist Gary S. Becker, and co-authors William H. J. Hubbard and Kevin M. Murphy. In that article, Becker et al. (2010) attempt to explain why women have surpassed men in terms of university enrolment by analysing the distribution of costs and benefits of attending university.

In general, the authors find that over the past four decades, the benefits of attending university, despite having increased more for women than for men, cannot explain the higher graduation rate of women in tertiary education. Among the costs, the authors separate what they call traditional (or monetary) costs from non-traditional costs, clarifying that the latter are determined in large part by differences in non-cognitive skills between individuals. Regarding the latter, the authors show two important gender differences. First, the average non-cognitive skills of women are higher than those of men. Second, women exhibit less variance in their distribution of non-cognitive skills. These two facts imply, according to their model, that women's supply elasticity is higher, for the same level of benefits of attending university. Thus, lower costs of attending university expressed in terms of higher (and less disparate) non-cognitive skills among women would in part be explaining why women have surpassed men in most developed countries in terms of tertiary education participation.

Harmonised descriptive data on non-cognitive skills for a wide array of countries is difficult to find—mainly due to the fact that researchers have reached no

[1] Externalising behaviour problems are outward-directed behaviours characterised by actions that are disruptive, impulsive, aggressive, or oppositional.

clear consensus as to what specific skills should be included under this umbrella term (Rammstedt et al. 2024). So let us exemplify this issue by using data on special educational needs for selected countries from the European Agency for Special Needs and Inclusive Education (European Agency for Special Needs and Inclusive Education 2024). Figure 3 illustrates the ratio of male to female students with special educational needs—those requiring targeted educational support due to disabilities or severe behavioural disorders. As the ratio exceeds one in all countries shown, boys consistently outnumber girls in the prevalence of special education needs. In England, Italy, France and Spain, the fraction of boys with special education needs more than doubles that of girls. Moreover, the gender gap is persistent and has barely changed, and if anything risen, in most of the countries shown. There is also evidence that boys spend fewer hours doing homework or school assignments outside of school hours. For example, with microdata from the Community of Madrid, Montalbán and Ruiz-Valenzuela (2022) show that boys spend fewer hours doing homework, and these differences increase as children grow older. In the fourth year of secondary compulsory education, girls do between 1.5 and 2.5 more hours of homework per week than boys. The gender gap is also higher the higher the level of parental education. These figures are consistent with what Gershenson and Holt (2015) find with time use data from the United States. The gross gap shows a difference of almost 1.7 hours per week in favour of girls. After accounting for gender differences in education in after-school time use, parental involvement, educational expectations, course selection and prior academic performance, the gender gap remains at one extra hour per week devoted to schoolwork by girls. These same authors explain how time spent doing homework is associated with an important non-cognitive skill: the willingness to learn.

In summary, differences in non-cognitive skills between boys and girls, such as a higher percentage of behavioural problems among boys or a lower willingness to learn, could be partly explaining boys' lower educational performance.

Exercise 2

In this chapter, we have seen that women have surpassed men in terms of the proportion who access and complete university education. We have also seen that boys are less likely to complete the second stage of compulsory secondary education. Discuss how potential differences in non-cognitive skills between men and women could explain this difference. You can help yourself with the reading of the references cited in this section.

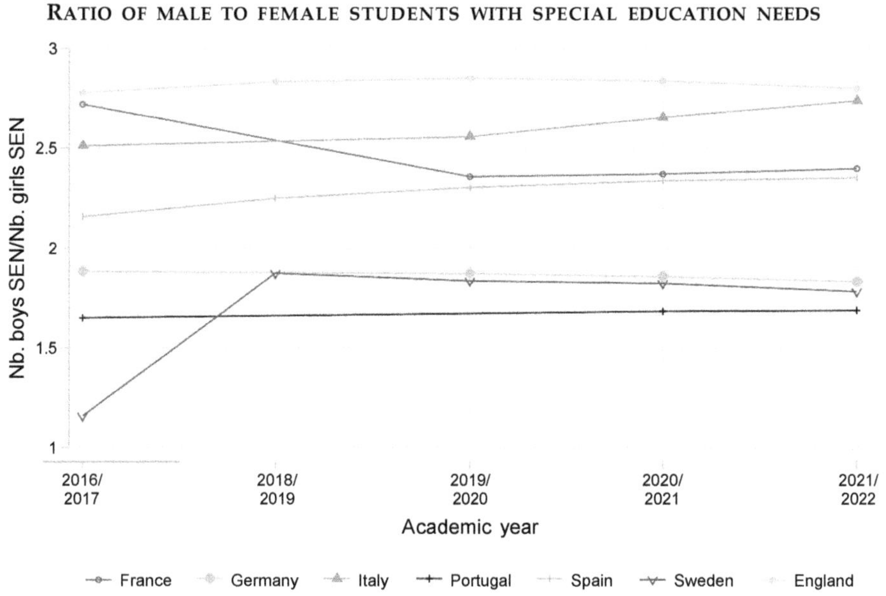

Fig. 3 Ratio of male to female students with special education needs (*Note* The data show the ratio of male to female students with special education needs, enrolled in any form of recognised education (6–18 years). Students with special educational needs are defined as those who have been assessed as such by educational guidance teams or services and who require, for a period of their schooling or throughout it, specific educational support and attention due to disability or severe behavioural disorders. *Source* European Agency for Special Needs and Inclusive Education [2024])

2.2 Families and Socioeconomic Factors

In Chapter 5, we have seen that families play an important role in their children's educational performance. Variables decided within the family, such as the economic resources invested in their children's education or other extracurricular activities, the time spent with the children, or different parenting styles, are considered inputs in the education production function. Could these different inputs have a differentiated effect on the educational performance of boys and girls? For example, does growing up in a poorer socioeconomic environment affect boys and girls differently? Do parents choose different education production function inputs based on the gender of their child?

Regarding the first of these questions, a hypothesis that has been tested with data from Florida by David Autor, David Figlio, Krzysztof Karbownik, Jeffrey Roth, and Melanie Wasserman, is that boys suffer worse academic consequences when they grow up in disadvantaged family environments (Autor et al. 2019). Estimating this differential effect is not easy. As the authors explain, there are two important challenges. The first is that the family environment is highly correlated with other inputs in the education production function, such as the parents' education level. For example, parents with higher education levels typically live in wealthier neighbourhoods with better schools. Thus, it is difficult to separate the impact of a disadvantaged economic environment from the impact of lower-quality schools or poorer neighbourhoods. The second challenge comes from the amount of data needed to implement and justify a credible causal identification strategy. Autor and his co-authors overcome these two challenges in a credible manner. They address the first challenge by comparing differences in academic outcomes between brothers and sisters. The assumption they make is that siblings who have been cared for by the same mother are exposed to the same family environment. The second assumption they need to make to claim that the effects found are causal is that there are no systematic differences between brothers and sisters by socioeconomic status at birth. They can verify this second assumption thanks to the fact that they have access to a database with very precise measures of maternal and child health at birth. With this data, they demonstrate that, at least in their sample, there are no significant differences between brothers and sisters at birth (or over time for the same mother). Despite having very good data and being able to directly compare the academic performance of brothers and sisters, the effect the authors find could be driven by a differential gender effect of the neighbourhood where students reside or the schools they attend (we will see later that these effects also exist). That is, lower-quality schools or living in poorer neighbourhoods could have an unequal impact on the academic performance of boys and girls. To control for this possibility, and only capture the effect of growing up in a disadvantaged family environment (and not of growing up in disadvantaged neighbourhoods or attending lower-quality schools), the authors include in their estimation variables measuring the quality of the schools that brothers and sisters attend, and they also include neighbourhood fixed effects. The final exercise indicates that, relative to their sisters, boys born into disadvantaged family environments have poorer academic performance, more disciplinary problems, and a higher level of early school leaving.

There are also differential gender effects of growing up in disadvantaged neighbourhoods. This is shown by Chetty and Hendren (2018), using a somewhat similar strategy, as they also rely on comparing different outcome variables between brothers and sisters. These authors use data from more than five million families in the United States who moved counties during the years observed in the sample. Thus, they can compare the outcomes of brothers and sisters who were different ages at the time of the move and were therefore exposed to different neighbourhoods (before and after the move) for a different number of years. The results show that for children who grew up in the 25th percentile of the income distribution, growing up (from birth) in a one-standard-deviation better county increases their income by approximately 10%. Children from low-income families are more likely to succeed in counties that have lower concentrations of poverty, lower income inequality, better schools, a higher proportion of two-parent families, and lower crime rates. And something important to explain gender gaps in school underachievement: the authors show that the outcomes of brothers vary more across areas (are more susceptible to the neighbourhood effect) than the outcomes of their sisters, and that boys have particularly poor outcomes in highly segregated areas.

A similar situation occurs with non-cognitive skills, which can influence students' academic outcomes and which literature suggests may be partly due to biological differences (see Chapter 15 for a more in-depth discussion). An article by Marianne Bertrand and Jessica Pan provides evidence that, in addition, growing up in disadvantaged environments, in their case measured by what they call *broken* families (single mothers or teenage mothers), has a more pernicious effect on boys than on girls (Bertrand and Pan 2013).

The conclusions of these three important articles help us answer the first question posed at the beginning of this subsection: Could different socioeconomic factors have a differentiated effect on the educational performance of boys and girls? The empirical evidence tells us that growing up in a disadvantaged family environment or neighbourhood has a more detrimental effect on boys than on girls, and therefore contributes to explaining the gender gap in school underachievement.

In addition to these socioeconomic environment effects, families choose the level of investment in education (e.g., monetary or time investments) for each of their sons and daughters. The literature analysing the impact of parental investments in education is extensive, and it is not our aim in this chapter to provide a comprehensive review of it. However, we would like to highlight some findings on gender differences in the time parents spend on educational activities with their children that emerge at very early ages. These differences could be explaining part of the existing gender gap in early school leaving. The availability of detailed survey data in Canada, the United Kingdom, and the United States has allowed Michael Baker and Kevin Milligan to test some of the findings in previous literature, which had concluded that parents tend to invest more time in childrearing activities when the offspring are boys. With data from very young children (i.e., from around nine months to five years), Baker and Milligan (2016) show that this greater parental engagement with boys does not occur at young ages but emerges later on. In fact, in all three countries, what the authors show is that both mothers and fathers spend more time on activities categorised as teaching (i.e., reading, singing, learning to use numbers and letters) with their daughters, and these differences are observed as early as nine months of age. Using data from the United States Time Use Survey, Bertrand and Pan (2013) find that this is especially true in single-mother families.

To conclude, is the time invested in educational activities chosen differently depending on the gender of the child? There is some evidence that the answer to this question is affirmative, at least in developed countries, and that this could be explaining poorer educational performance of boys compared to girls.

Exercise 3
Use the evidence in Bertrand and Pan (2013) and Baker and Milligan (2016) to discuss the role that parental preferences (e.g., whether mothers or fathers prefer to have daughters over sons) may play in determining the investment of resources (i.e., time and/ or money) they make in their sons' and daughters' education. What other reasons do these authors mention to explain the different educational investments parents make depending on the gender of their children?

2.3 School and Teachers

Earlier in the book, we have seen that it is not only families who, with their decisions, affect the educational performance of their children. Several inputs in the education production function, which vary at the school level, can explain important differences in student performance (see, for example, differences in class size in Chapter 4; or differences related to teacher quality in Chapter 7). In this chapter, we will focus on a couple of aspects related to schools and teachers that could explain boys' poorer educational performance: potential teacher gender biases and the under-representation of male teachers in different stages of compulsory education.

Let's start with the role of potential biases that teachers may have regarding boys. In Sect. 3, we will see the existence of implicit (and explicit) biases among teachers that may be negatively conditioning girls' performance in science and mathematics-related subjects. However, there is also evidence that teachers have biases that negatively affect boys. For example, economist Camille Terrier (2020) uses data on students in France that contain an essential feature: they have information on both the grades given in French and maths by teachers (non-blind scores) and the grades obtained by students in the same subjects scored by an external evaluator who does not know the student (blind scores). One important clarification that Terrier makes is that both tests (external and nonexternal) are designed to measure the same set of skills. With this data, Terrier constructs a measure of the degree of gender bias that teachers have, defined as the average gap between girls' non-blind and blind scores, minus this same gap for boys. That is, if the difference between the score given by a teacher and the score given by the external evaluator is greater for girls than for boys, that teacher would be giving higher grades to girls and would appear classified in the data as exhibiting a gender bias in favour of girls. Another crucial element for her empirical strategy is that teachers are assigned quasi-randomly to classes. Aggregating the data at the class level, the variation that Terrier exploits comes from comparing the progress of girls (relative to boys) in classes with more biased teachers, and the progress girls make (always compared to boys) in classes with less biased teachers. Terrier's findings highlight that teacher biases have a negative impact on boys' progress during secondary school in both mathematics and French.

Other recent studies, with data from different regions of Spain, confirm these findings. For example, with data from the Basque Country, Gortazar et al. (2022) find that teachers evaluate worse those groups of students who are, on average, lagging behind in school. This is the case of boys.

Let's now analyse the potential role that the under-representation of male teachers in different stages of compulsory education may play in boys' poorer educational performance. For example, in 2021, across OECD countries, only 4% of teachers in pre-primary education were male. In primary schools this share goes up, but only to 18%. Even in lower secondary education, the fraction of male teachers stands only at 33% (OECD 2023). Thus, as it occurs for girls with the lack of role models in STEM (as we will see in Sect. 3), there is an almost total absence of male teachers in early childhood and, to a great extent, also in primary education. Several studies in the academic literature have provided evidence that having a teacher of the same identity can positively affect students' academic performance. Thus, a lower proportion of male teachers in the early stages of education could be negatively affecting boys' educational performance. This is what a study published by Thomas Dee in the *Journal of Human Resources* (Dee 2007) finds. Their study uses data from a survey in the United States that allows them to observe the same student, and their performance, in different subjects and with teachers of different gender. That is, Dee can study what happens to a student's performance when the student is assigned to a male teacher and when he is assigned to a female teacher (*within-student comparisons*). His results indicate that the assignment of a same-gender teacher significantly improves both girls' and boys' performance, as well as the teacher's perception of the student's performance and the student's engagement with the teacher's subject. This result is relevant to explain potential performance differences—especially in reading—between boys and girls, given that, as we have seen, most teachers, from early childhood to secondary education, are women.

Another very recent example is the one studied by Ursina Schaede and Ville Mankki (Schaede and Mankki 2022). To analyse this issue, Schaede and Mankki use a Finnish reform that eliminated the mandatory 40% quota of reserved university places for male primary school teacher candidates. This reform allows them to study the question in a differences-in-differences (DiD) context using data from before and after the reform. But these authors go a bit further and combine their DiD context with the instrumental variables method (DiD-IV). That is, these authors find an instrumental variable (an exogenous source of variation) for the dependent variable of interest, which in their case measures the municipal-level gender composition of primary school teachers. The instrument they use is the interaction between the before and after the reform, with information on mandatory teacher retirements that occur each year at the municipal level when teachers reach the age of 60. As the authors put it "If municipalities have open positions during the time when quota cohorts enter the teacher market, they will be more likely to hire candidates from a pool with relatively more male rookie teachers compared to municipalities that have to fill open positions once new teacher cohorts selected without the quota are entering the teacher market."

The first thing these authors find is that the elimination of the mandatory 40% quota of male teachers effectively reduces the proportion of men admitted to primary school teacher training from 40 to 20%. In the second stage, they examine effects on variables that measure students' educational performance and, in their case, find that students exposed to a higher proportion of male teachers achieve higher educational levels and also do better in the labour market. These results hold for both boys and girls, leading the authors to conclude that the existence of the male quota improved the teacher selection process.

There are many more studies in this area, and we will see some in Sect. 3, but what these two studies suggest is that increasing the number of male teachers in the early stages of education could increase boys' educational performance without harming the educational performance of girls.

2.4 Labour Market Conditions and Opportunity Cost of Continuing Education

In the introduction to this chapter, we saw in Fig. 1 the evolution of the gender gap in early school leaving. One characteristic to highlight from the graph is the sharp decrease in the gap since the Great Recession of 2008 in Spain. Spain, with a high fraction of the male population working in the construction sector at the time, was one of the countries hardest hit by the economic crisis, at least when it came to the share of people who became unemployed. These associations in the data suggest that the labour market, and in particular the availability of low-skilled jobs, may play an important role in the decision to leave school early.

To see the connection between labour market conditions and educational decisions, let's think of a simple human capital accumulation model (Becker 1962) (the reader can also review what was discussed in Chapter 10). When compulsory education ends, a student has to decide whether to continue studying or enter the labour market. It is possible that the student (or their family) compares the expected future income stream if they continue studying for another year with the expected income stream if they immediately enter the labour market. If a high unemployment rate is a general indicator of labour market conditions, it may indicate both lower initial wages for school leavers and a lower probability of finding a job upon leaving school. In both cases, this would translate into a reduction in the expected value of income streams if the student decides to enter the labour market immediately, thereby reducing the percentage of students who leave school early. On the other hand, an economic crisis environment in which a family member loses their job could force other family members to enter the labour market. Rees and Naci Mocan (1997) show a negative correlation between the level of unemployment and early school leaving, indicating that the first channel seems to be more relevant.

In the context of the 2008 economic crisis in Spain, the sector where most jobs were destroyed was construction, a sector that employed mainly men, with a wide availability of low-skilled jobs. This likely reduced the opportunity cost of continuing education disproportionately for boys, as their job opportunities were more affected than those of girls. This is precisely what Ainoa Aparicio-Fenoll studies in her article published in the *Journal of Human Capital* in 2016. In that article, Aparicio-Fenoll (2016) explains that the housing boom generated substantial variation in returns to education over time and across regions, primarily for boys. She also argues that the housing boom was exogenous to pre-existing differences in educational outcomes between men and women. This is why she can use an instrumental variable estimation strategy (see Chapter 2). More precisely, in the first stage, the author instruments differences in educational returns between men and women with the level of construction activity at the provincial level. In the second stage, she estimates the effect that these variations in returns to education have on educational variables. Specifically, for young people aged 16 to 18, she shows that a 10% decrease in the wage ratio of educated individuals to uneducated individuals (i.e., relative wage increase in low-skilled occupations) leads to a 2% decrease in the probability of being enrolled in school.

3 What Factors Explain Lower Participation of Women in STEM?

As we saw in the introduction to this chapter, women are less likely to enrol in subjects related to STEM disciplines, such as computer science or engineering (see Table 1), and remain under-represented in occupations related to these areas. The current consensus coming from research in the field of the economics of education is that differences in the maths abilities of boys and girls cannot explain the gender differences in educational and professional choices (Breda et al. 2018). If girls' cognitive abilities are very similar to boys', what then explains this phenomenon? In this section, we will analyse some of the factors behind the existing gender gap in choosing mathematics-intensive degrees in tertiary education as well as STEM occupations.

3.1 Comparative Advantage

Historically, it has been argued that the lack of women in STEM fields, and more specifically in maths-intensive sciences, is due to girls' lower performance in this subject. However, in most developed countries, this difference is now almost non-existent. Figure 4 shows the evolution of the average score difference between boys and girls in the reading and maths sections of the Program for International Student Assessment (PISA) across a selection of OECD countries. The data show that at age 15, boys and girls have, on average, very similar performance in mathematics. The latest available data for 2022 shows a gender gap in favour of boys of just under 10 points for the OECD average. However, girls have a significant advantage over boys in reading, about 25 points on average for the group of OECD countries participating in this test. Moreover, when girls outperform in mathematics as well, as is the case in England (Cavaglia et al. 2021), the gender gap in favour of women tends to be larger in Language.

In a study in the journal *Proceedings of the National Academy of Sciences (PNAS)*, economists Thomas Breda and Clotilde Napp show that a potential explanation for the gender difference in STEM specialisation choices may lie in women's comparative advantage in reading and men's comparative advantage in mathematics. The concept of comparative advantage is one of the oldest in economics, developed by British economist David Ricardo in the early nineteenth century.

This concept states that even if a person is more efficient than all others in one task—for example, doing laundry— it may be preferable to pay someone to do it for them. Why? Because each hour spent on these tasks has an opportunity cost, and they might be better off using that time on a task where they are more productive, such as cooking. If this is the case, that person has a comparative advantage in this other task (cooking). Translated into our context, this concept suggests that even if a girl is very good at mathematics, if her language skills are superior, she should pursue a discipline related to reading, literature, or the humanities rather than a discipline related to mathematics.

In the aforementioned study, Breda et al. (2018) use PISA data for 64 countries and 300,000 15-year-old students and calculate, for each student, the difference between their maths and reading performance on the PISA tests. The first thing they show is that the difference between a student's performance in reading and maths is 80% of a standard deviation (SD) higher for girls than for boys, a magnitude considered very large. In other words, the scores in maths and reading are much more similar for boys than for girls, suggesting that girls have a much stronger comparative advantage in language than boys do in mathematics. Second, these authors construct an index that measures the student's intention to study maths-related subjects in post-compulsory secondary education, at university, as well as intentions to choose a maths or science-related occupation. The gender gap for this STEM Specialization Intentions Index amounts to 22% of a standard deviation in favour of boys worldwide.

In the next step, the economists attempt to explain where the differences in the STEM Specialisation Intentions Index between girls and boys come from. It could be argued, for example, that it is due to boys' better skills in this subject. However, the authors show that when they control for maths ability in a linear regression of the "STEM Specialisation Intentions Index" on a variable indicating gender, the estimated gender gap in the STEM Specialisation Intentions Index is reduced by less than 10% worldwide and in most of the countries under analysis. In contrast, the difference between boys and girls in their intention to pursue maths-related careers disappears almost entirely when controlling for individual differences in maths and reading skills. In other words, these authors can explain the gender gap in the STEM Specialisation Intentions Index when they control in their regressions for students' comparative advantage in mathematics or reading. Overall, the study shows that

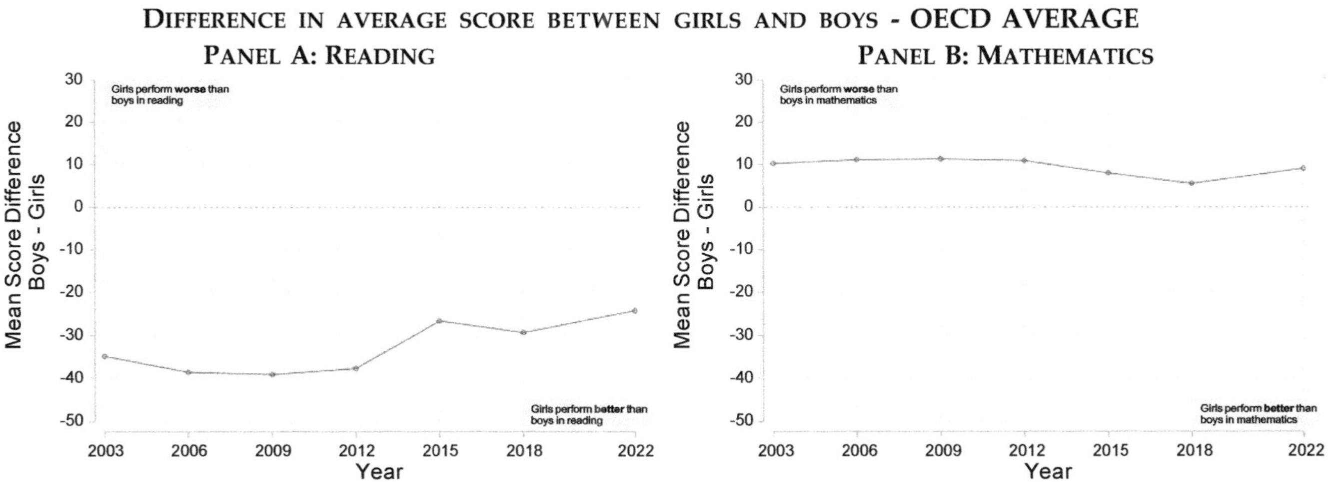

Fig. 4 Difference in average score between girls and boys—OECD average (*Note* The data show the gender difference in PISA exams between average score for male and female students in reading [Panel A] and mathematics [Panel B]. Original data from PISA Database, OECD. We plot data from OWiD [2024])

the difference between a student's performance in reading and maths can explain up to 80% of the gender gap in the intention to choose maths-related courses in post-compulsory education (Breda et al. 2018).

3.2 The Role of Culture and Social Norms

We just saw that girls tend to perform better in language than in mathematics, and boys perform better in mathematics than in language. Moreover, the difference in performance between these two subjects tends to be larger for girls than for boys. This raises the question of why we observe such disparate skills between these two subjects for girls.

One possible explanation is related to culture and social norms. There is considerable evidence suggesting that in countries where gender stereotypes are stronger, the gender difference in maths performance is higher. One such study is by Luigi Guiso et al. (2008), published in 2008 in the journal *Science*. The authors use data from PISA 2003 for 40 countries, where 15-year-old students were assessed on the same maths test, and show that the average score for girls in maths was 10.5 points lower than that of boys (equivalent to 2% less than boys' average score). To explore the role of culture and social norms in explaining these differences, they rank the participating countries according to various measures of gender equity. For example, they use the *World Economic Forum Gender Gap Index* (GGI), which reflects women's economic and political opportunities, education, and well-being. By regressing the gender gap in maths performance at the country level on the gender inequality index of that country, they find that more egalitarian societies have a much smaller gender gap in maths performance. In fact, they find that if a country like Turkey—with a low level of gender equality—had the same level of gender equality as Sweden, the gender gap in maths skills in Turkey would disappear.

It could be argued that the authors are simply detecting an incidental correlation between gender equality indices and the gender gap in maths. For example, it could be that the factor that reduces the gender gap in maths is actually economic development. Since economic development is also positively related to gender equality in society, we run the risk that if we do not include an economic development variable in the regression, the coefficient of the gender equality variable will capture both the effect of the gender equality index and the effect of the economic development variable. That is, if we leave the economic development variable out of the equation, we could obtain biased estimates due to an omitted variable problem (the reader can refer to Chapter 2 to refresh this concept). The authors attempt to address this problem by including an interaction between gender and the logarithm of GDP per capita (which would be measuring the level of economic development of each country). Their results show that the relationship between the gender equality index and the difference in maths exam scores holds. Therefore, differences in economic development between countries, which could be explaining, in turn, differences in the culture or social norms of a given country, are not what would be explaining the results of Luigi Guiso and co-authors.

The study cited above suggests that culture and social norms may play an important role in explaining the gender gap in performance in STEM subjects and, consequently, in the choice of STEM fields in tertiary education or STEM occupations. However, there could be an alternative interpretation of the results presented. For example, in those countries where girls perform relatively better in maths and where the gender gap in maths is zero or even in favour of girls, it is possible that women are better prepared, access better jobs, earn higher wages, and have more political power (Nollenberger et al. 2016). This would result in greater gender equality in these countries, and the indices used in the previous study would capture this. Therefore, the estimates presented earlier could suffer from a reverse causality problem (see Chapter 2).

To address this problem, in a study published in 2016, economists Natalia Nollenberger et al. (2016) employ a strategy used in the field of epidemiology, based on two key aspects (Fernández 2011). First, they focus on second-generation immigrants in the same host country to study the effect of gender values. This allows them to study the effect of a single aspect of culture—values passed down from generation to generation—because the institutions and social norms to which individuals are exposed in the host country are the same for everyone. The second aspect is that although second-generation immigrants were born and raised in the host country, it is likely that their families passed on different cultural values to them depending on their country of origin.

Like Guiso et al. (2008), these economists also use PISA data, but for the years 2003, 2006, 2009, and 2012, with a sample of 11,527 second-generation immigrants whose families immigrated from 35 different countries and who lived, at the time of the PISA test, in nine different host countries. The empirical strategy consists of regressing the individual score on the PISA maths test on a variable indicating whether the individual is female and the interaction between the variable indicating whether the gender is female and the GGI index of the country of ancestry. The most important aspect of the identification strategy is that their regressions include fixed effects of country of ancestry, host country, and cohort, as well as individual control variables. They also include an interaction between the host country indicator and the variable indicating whether the student's gender is female to account for variation in gender education gaps that may arise from cultural or institutional differences between host countries. The coefficient of interest is that of the interaction between female gender and the GGI index. This coefficient indicates the gender differences in maths outcomes between second-generation immigrants that would be explained by differences in the cultural values passed down by their parents.

The results indicate that a one-standard-deviation increase in the GGI of the parents' country of origin is associated with a reduction of 7.47 points in the PISA gender gap in maths. This represents 29% of a standard deviation in the gender gap, measured among the countries of ancestry included in the sample.

It could be argued that other sources of heterogeneity among individuals, aside from their cultural beliefs about gender, could be affecting their academic outcomes. One problem could be that girls from more egalitarian countries may be in schools that favour girls, for example, because they have more female teachers or because they have more teachers of their own ethnicity (Dee 2005). If we ignore these factors, the estimates of the effect of culture could be biased by the effect of omitted variables (see Chapter 2). The authors include a series of additional controls to address potential biases and find that their estimates are robust to these inclusions. They conclude that policies aimed at changing cultural beliefs about women's roles in society can be crucial in reducing the gender gap in maths.

Exercise 4

Discuss how the reverse causality problem makes it difficult to study the impact of culture or social norms on the gender gap in maths. How did Nollenberger et al. (2016) try to overcome this problem in their study on second-generation immigrants?

Exercise 5

This exercise requires downloading data that is freely available online. First, download the latest available data on the Gender Inequality Index for several countries, provided by the United Nations on their website. Second, download the latest aggregated PISA performance data by gender and country and calculate the gender gap in maths performance. This aggregated data is available on the OECD website. Using statistical software such as Stata or R, merge the two datasets. What is the correlation between the gender gap in maths performance in PISA and the ranking in gender inequality? You can obtain this correlation by running a regression where the gender gap in maths performance is the dependent variable and the gender inequality ranking is the independent variable. Discuss the results and compare them with those of Guiso et al. (2008).

3.3 Gender Stereotypes

Cultural beliefs or social norms about women's roles in society are important in explaining the gender gap in maths. The literature in the economics of education has studied more specifically the role of gender stereotypes in explaining gender gaps in

STEM discipline or occupation choices. According to the definition of the United Nations High Commissioner for Human Rights, a gender stereotype is a generalised view or preconceived idea about the attributes, characteristics, or roles that women and men have or should have. Given what we have seen earlier in this section, we might ask the following: Are there negative stereotypes about women in the field of mathematics, or more generally, in STEM fields?

Italian economist Michela Carlana answers this question in a study published in 2019 in *The Quarterly Journal of Economics*. Specifically, Carlana (2019) studies how teachers' stereotypes and gender biases can affect their assessment of girls' performance in mathematics. Stereotypes conveyed by teachers can be especially harmful to students, as it has been shown that they affect the development of academic self-concept. If a girl perceives from her teacher that she does not have high mathematical abilities, this can lead to low confidence in her maths skills, which in turn can negatively affect her maths performance. To assess the effect of gender stereotypes on the gender gap in maths, Carlana (2019) measures the gender biases of 1,400 teachers in northern Italy using the Gender-Science Implicit Association Test (IAT). This test was developed by social psychologists in 1998 (Greenwald et al. 1998) and has been widely used in studies of racial and gender biases. The test consists of two tasks. First, subjects are asked to sort male names and scientific concepts to one side of a screen and, on the opposite side, to sort female names and concepts related to the humanities. In the second task, participants are asked to sort female names and scientific concepts on one side of the screen and male names and humanities-related concepts on the opposite side. The underlying idea of this test is that if individuals have implicit associations between male gender and scientific concepts, they will perform the first task (which asks them to categorise male names on the same side of the screen as scientific concepts) more quickly. Additionally, teachers were asked about explicit biases or associations, such as their beliefs about gender differences in innate mathematical ability, as well as an explicit question aimed at measuring more traditional gender values. In the next step, Carlana employs two strategies to identify the causal effect of gender stereotypes. The first strategy consists of a regression that measures the gender gap *within* the same class. That is, with observations of students grouped in classes, Carlana can include fixed effects of the class in her regressions. This allows her to make a comparison while keeping constant all the characteristics of classmates, the school, and the teachers (see Chapter 2). Specifically, she runs a regression of the score obtained on a maths exam or the academic choice made by an individual in a given classroom on the interaction of a variable indicating the student's gender with the standardised IAT score. The coefficient of this interaction measures how the assignment of a maths teacher with a higher level of gender stereotypes affects the gender gap in the class. In the second strategy, she compares students of the same gender within the same cohort in the same school. This allows her to separately analyse the effect of stereotypes on girls and boys.

The first result Carlana shows is that the gender gap in maths performance increases by one-third (from 0.15 to 0.20 standard deviations) in classes assigned to a maths teacher who implicitly associates boys with maths, compared to classes assigned to a teacher who associates girls with maths. The second result, using her second strategy, shows that having a teacher with a "masculine maths" attitude has a negative effect on female students, while a "feminine maths" attitude has a positive effect on female students. In contrast, teachers' gender stereotypes do not affect boys' results. Moreover, she shows that stereotypes are particularly harmful for girls with low maths performance at the beginning of secondary school. These results are consistent with the *stereotype threat* theory developed by social psychologists Claude Steele and Joshua Aronson (Steele and Aronson 1995). According to this theory, the mere fear of confirming a negative stereotype (e.g., "girls are bad at maths") causes cognitive stress and reduces performance, leading to the confirmation of the negative stereotype and a vicious circle.

This study shows how gender stereotypes can contribute to the gender gap in maths during secondary school. It is important to note that, as discussed in Section 2, other studies have shown that there are also teachers with negative biases against boys, and this may explain boys' poorer overall school performance. It is also important to remember that on average, the gender gap in mathematics as measured by PISA is very small. There are many girls with high mathematics performance, and yet we still see that girls remain significantly under-represented in both STEM specialisations in post-compulsory education and STEM occupations.

Teacher gender biases are just one of the possible channels through which gender stereotypes can negatively affect women's maths performance. Another recent study published by the *Centre for Economic Performance* at the London School of Economics analyses the role of gender stereotypes within the family. Nicoletti et al. (2022) use survey data on Australian parents' self-reported beliefs about their children's maths and reading skills and match this data with administrative records on children's performance on national standardised tests in maths and reading at ages 8–9. The authors show three interesting results that would confirm the existence of negative stereotypes about girls' maths abilities, also within the family. First, these authors find that parents are more likely to overestimate boys' maths skills than to overestimate girls' maths skills. Second, they find that parents' bias towards overestimating boys' maths skills disappears after receiving information about their children's academic performance (i.e., once they receive information about their children's performance as measured by standardised tests). Finally, they show that parents' gender bias against girls helps explain the widening gender gap in maths skills during childhood. This suggests that exposure to gender stereotypes within the family negatively influences girls' ability to reach their full potential in STEM disciplines.

3.4 Lack of Role Models in STEM

One possible explanation for why many girls, even those who achieve very good results in maths, do not choose STEM university degrees, vocational training, or occupations, is the lack of female role models in these areas. Since women are so under-represented in some STEM fields, the likelihood of girls finding a female role model in those fields is low. On the one hand, it could be the lack of *female teachers* in STEM disciplines that negatively affects girls' motivation to continue studying these disciplines. On the other hand, it could be the lack of *role models in the professional and academic world* that causes girls to underestimate their possibilities in this field.

The first channel, i.e., the lack of female teachers in STEM subjects, has been widely studied. One of the first articles is that by Scott Carrell, Marianne Page, and James West in *The Quarterly Journal of Economics* (Carrell et al. 2010). The main challenge faced by these authors is that the teacher's gender may not be random. Thus, female students with higher maths skills might choose a female maths teacher because they feel that a female teacher would treat them in a less biased way, and therefore, they might perform better than with a male teacher. If this were the case, it would introduce selection bias into the estimates. A regression that relates teacher gender to academic outcomes and/or course choices in college would be biased by the fact that high-skilled female students choose to enrol with female teachers instead of male teachers, but these students would have performed well even if they had chosen to enrol with male teachers. The reader may recall the concept of selection bias in Chapter 2.

To address this challenge and obtain causal estimates, the authors use a specific feature of a U.S. university, i.e., the random assignment of students to maths and science teachers and the fact that all students have to take certain mandatory introductory and follow-up courses in maths, physics, chemistry, engineering, history, and English. This randomisation and the requirement to take certain courses prevent biased selection of students into (1) teachers who may systematically vary in their gender biases and (2) maths-related subjects.

The authors show that exposure to a female teacher has a significant effect on female students' performance in maths and science classes, as well as on the likelihood that top-performing female students will continue to take maths and science courses in the future and graduate with a STEM degree. In contrast, teacher gender has no impact on the outcomes or choices of male students. However, the effects of teachers are not easy to interpret. They could be due to gender differences in teaching practices and classroom behaviour, rather than the fact that female teachers act as role models for girls.

Another study directly analyses the effect of being exposed to a female role model. Breda et al. (2023) evaluate a real-world program called "For Girls and Science" (*Pour les Filles et la Science*) launched in 2014 by the L'Oréal Foundation to encourage girls to explore STEM careers. The program consists of one-hour interventions during school hours led by young female scientists or young professionals employed in the Research and Innovation division of the L'Oréal group. They use data from 19,451 students in 416 10th-grade classes and 185 12th-grade classes (science track) in public and private high schools in the Paris region. Half of the classes were randomly assigned to receive a visit from one of the 56 participants. The other half received no intervention. The impact of this program can be measured causally due to its design as a randomised controlled trial (see Chapter 2). A crucial aspect of the program is that in the French system, students make irreversible educational decisions at the end of 10th and 12th grade. After the first year of high school

(10th grade), approximately 80% of students continue in the general high school in the last two years (11th and 12th grade), and 20% move towards technological high school. At the end of the last year of high school (12th grade), students choose the programs they want to study at university. This allows them to study the effect of the program on enrolment in science, technology, engineering, and mathematics at university.

In 10th grade, classroom visits had no detectable impact on the likelihood of boys and girls enrolling in the science track in 11th grade. In contrast, the program induced a significant increase of 2.4% points in university enrolment in STEM disciplines among 12th-grade girls, equivalent to an 8% increase over the baseline rate of 29%. The effect on boys was insignificant. In terms of the mechanisms that might explain this change in girls' choices, the authors show that the intervention positively affected the *perception of science-related jobs*. In contrast, the intervention did not affect girls' self-reported affinity for science subjects, did not improve academic performance in these subjects, and only slightly improved their self-concept of maths. This indicates that the problem of women's under-representation in science-related jobs may stem from a misconception of these jobs, rather than from a lack of confidence or skills in these areas. The authors cite as an example the possible perception that jobs in scientific fields (such as engineering) have a greater difficulty in balancing work with family life.

3.5 The Role of Competitive Contexts

As described in Sect. 3, the average gender gap in maths has decreased in recent years and is now almost non-existent in most developed countries. However, the data still show a lack of girls among the highest-performing students. This is illustrated in Fig. 5, which shows histograms of score distributions in reading and maths on the 2018 PISA test. Girls outperform boys on average and are over-represented at the top of the distribution in reading. For maths, the score distributions almost overlap, but in the right tail of the distribution (where the top-performing students are), there are more boys than girls. Why are there fewer girls than boys among the best in maths?

Increasing evidence points to an explanation that may be uncomfortable: the differences may be partly attributed to the differential way men and women respond to competitive exam environments. In this section, we will analyse evidence suggesting that this is the case. As Muriel Niederle and Lise Vesterlund point out in a seminal article published in the *Journal of Economic Perspectives* (Niederle and Vesterlund 2010), the competitive pressures associated with taking exams can lead to outcomes that do not reflect the results that would be obtained in less competitive environments. In other words: the fact that boys perform better on certain tests and under high competitive pressure does not necessarily imply that their maths skills are better than girls'. Due to the way exams are administered and the fact that many academic opportunities depend on exam results, women are likely to be at a disadvantage by not reaching their full potential in highly competitive exams.

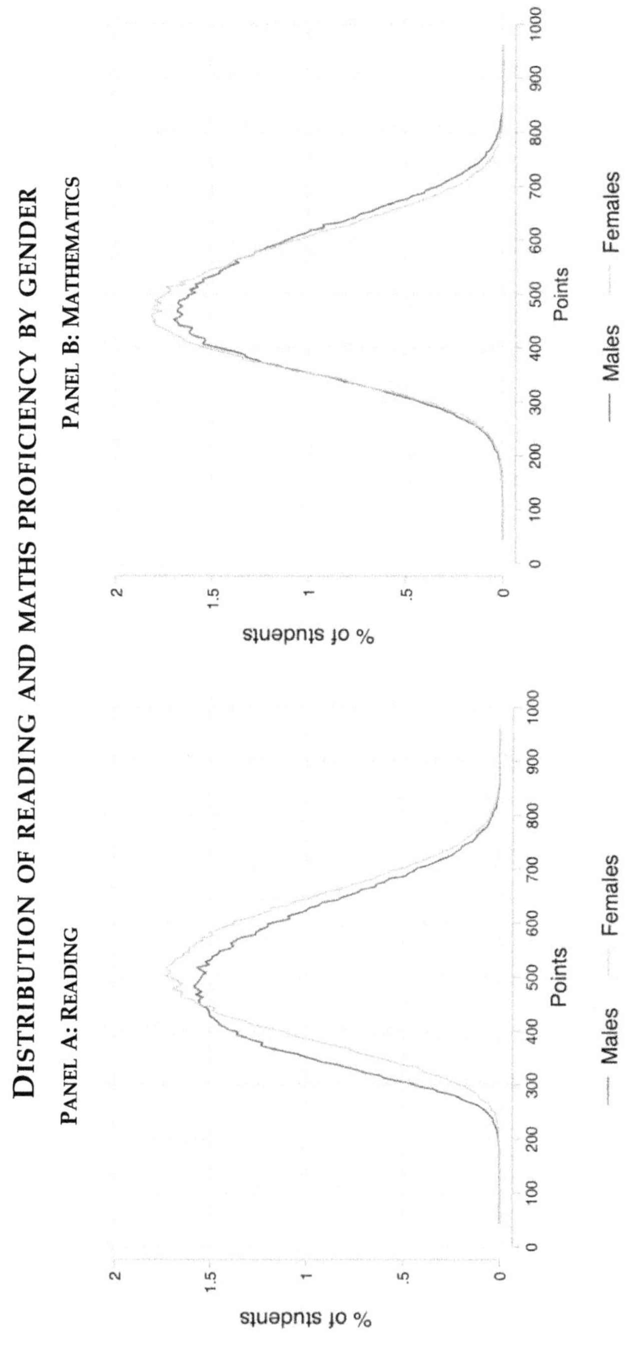

Fig. 5 Distribution of reading and maths proficiency by gender (*Note* This figure is a histogram of the PISA scores in language and mathematics from the 2018 PISA study using a five-point score interval. *Source* Figure II.7.4 from OECD [2019])

A recent study that analyses the effects of competitive environments on the gender gap in maths is by economists Nagore Iriberri and Pedro Rey-Biel (2019). Using data from the *Concurso de Primavera de Matemáticas* (Spring Mathematics Competition) in Spain, they show that although girls have similar or even higher maths grades than boys, boys perform better than girls in the competition, and as they progress from one round to the next, this gap increases. In the first round, which takes place in the participant's school, the gender gap is 34% of a standard deviation. In the second and final round of the competition, which takes place at a public university in Madrid, the gap increases by 9% of a standard deviation. The authors show that the increase in the gender gap between the two rounds is due to an increase in the competitive pressure as participants move to the second and final round, and not to alternative explanations, such as differential selection of boys and girls for the competition, discrimination, or different reactions between boys and girls to the increased difficulty of the questions between the first and second rounds. One interesting aspect of the competition is that unanswered questions are rewarded compared to incorrectly answered questions (participants receive zero points if the answer is incorrect, one point if they do not answer, and five points when the answer is correct). The authors show that girls leave more questions unanswered than boys, and this difference increases in the second round. This suggests a greater risk aversion and a lower willingness to guess among girls, as a possible explanation for why a gender gap emerges in the context of a competition, compared to the context of normal maths classes. Therefore, the way in which unanswered questions are rewarded or penalised can have a significant effect on the gender gap in this type of competition.

In another study, the same authors conduct a large-scale natural field experiment to test and understand the mechanisms underlying gender differences in the willingness to guess (Iriberri and Rey-Biel 2021). The context of this experiment is again the *Concurso de Primavera de Matemáticas*. For the experiment, they vary the way unanswered questions are scored. For the first 13 of the 25 questions on the exam, students receive zero points for both unanswered and incorrectly answered questions, and for the last 12 questions on the exam, incorrect answers score 0 and unanswered questions score one point. The latter implies a reward for not answering. Correct answers always score five points. By having multiple observations for each student (one per question) and two ways of scoring unanswered questions for each individual, Iriberri and Biel can compare each participant's willingness to guess in each context, as well as overall performance on both parts of the exam. That is, they can use a research strategy that includes student-level fixed effects. The results show that in the first part of the exam, which has no reward for not answering, women omit more questions than men (0.17 standard deviations more relative to the mean), even though the dominant strategy would be to answer all the questions when there is no reward at all. And most importantly, this difference increases (by an additional 0.14 standard deviations relative to the mean) in the second part of the test, where unanswered questions are rewarded with one point. The conclusion of this study is that a scoring rule that rewards, even slightly, the omission of questions can work to the detriment of girls and contribute to a greater gender gap in competitive maths exams.

Exercise 6
Discuss other areas of high-stakes exams where the design of the exam could negatively affect women's performance. What policy recommendations would you give to change their design to be more equitable?

4 Conclusions

International data stubbornly show that boys perform worse in education and that women remain under-represented in university courses and careers related to STEM disciplines (Science, Technology, Engineering, and Mathematics). In this chapter, we have summarised some reasons why we should be concerned about these two major gender gaps and have discussed some of the possible explanations for these phenomena.

In the case of boys' poorer educational performance, we analysed the role of non-cognitive skills, the role of families and socioeconomic factors, the impact of schools and teachers, and finally, we gave some insights into the relationship between labour market conditions, the opportunity cost of continuing education, and student performance.

Regarding the under-representation of women in STEM, we examined the role of culture, social norms, and gender stereotypes, the lack of female role models among maths and science teachers, as well as in many science-related professions, and finally, the role of competitive contexts.

Although all the factors analysed are relevant, and knowledge in this field has advanced considerably in the last decade, we are far from understanding all the underlying causes of the gender differences observed in our education systems, and it is likely that many factors interact with each other.

References

Altonji, Joseph G., Peter Arcidiacono, and Arnaud Maurel. 2016. The analysis of field choice in college and graduate school: Determinants and wage effects. In *Handbook of the economics of education*, vol. 5, 305–396. Elsevier.

Aparicio-Fenoll, Ainhoa. 2016. Returns to education and educational outcomes: The case of the Spanish housing boom. *Journal of Human Capital* 10 (2): 235–265.

Autor, David. 2010. US labor market challenges over the longer term. Federal Reserve Board of Governors.

Autor, David, David Figlio, Krzysztof Karbownik, Jeffrey Roth, and Melanie Wasserman. 2019. Family disadvantage and the gender gap in behavioral and educational outcomes. *American Economic Journal: Applied Economics* 11 (3): 338–381.

Baker, Michael, and Kevin Milligan. 2016. Boy-girl differences in parental time investments: Evidence from three countries. *Journal of Human Capital* 10 (4): 399–441.

Becker, Gary S. 1962. Investment in human capital: A theoretical analysis. *Journal of Political Economy* 70 (5): 9–49.

Becker, Gary S., William H. J. Hubbard, and Kevin M. Murphy. 2010. Explaining the worldwide boom in higher education of women. *Journal of Human Capital* 4 (3): 203–241

Belfield, Clive R., and Henry M. Levin. 2007. *The price we pay: Economic and social consequences of inadequate education*, Brookings Institution Press.

Bertrand, Marianne, and Jessica Pan. 2013. The trouble with boys: Social influences and the gender gap in disruptive behavior. *American Economic Journal: Applied Economics* 5 (1): 32–64.

Black, Sandra E., Chandra Muller, Alexandra Spitz-Oener, Ziwei He, Koit Hung, and John Robert Warren. 2021. The importance of STEM: High school knowledge, skills and occupations in an era of growing inequality. *Research Policy* 50 (7): 104249.

Blau, Francine D., and Lawrence M. Kahn. 2017. The gender wage gap: Extent, trends, and explanations. *Journal of Economic Literature* 55 (3): 789–865.

Breda, Thomas, Elyès Jouini, and Clotilde Napp. 2018. Societal inequalities amplify gender gaps in math. *Science* 359 (6381): 1219–1220.

Breda, Thomas. 2023. Julien Grenet, Marion Monnet, and Clémentine Van Effenterre, "How effective are female role models in steering girls towards stem? Evidence from French High Schools." *The Economic Journal* 133 (653): 1773–1809.

Carlana, Michela. 2019. Implicit stereotypes: Evidence from teachers' gender bias. *The Quarterly Journal of Economics* 134 (3): 1163–1224.

Carrell, Scott E., Marianne E. Page, and James E. West. 2010. Sex and science: How professor gender perpetuates the gender gap. *The Quarterly Journal of Economics* 125 (3): 1101–1144.

Cavaglia, Chiara, Stephen Machin, Sandra McNally, and Jenifer Ruiz-Valenzuela. 2021. Gender, achievement, and subject choice in English education. *Oxford Review of Economic Policy* 36 (4): 816–835.

Chetty, Raj, and Nathaniel Hendren. 2018. The impacts of neighborhoods on intergenerational mobility II: County-level estimates. *The Quarterly Journal of Economics* 133 (3): 1163–1228.

Dee, Thomas S. 2005. A Teacher like me: Does race, ethnicity, or gender matter? *The American Economic Review* 95 (2): 158–165.

Dee, Thomas S. 2007. Teachers and the gender gaps in student achievement. *Journal of Human Resources* 42(3):528–554.

Else-Quest, Nicole M., Janet Shibley Hyde, H. Hill Goldsmith, and Carol A Van Hulle. 2006. Gender differences in temperament: A meta-analysis. *Psychological Bulletin* 132 (1): 33.

Encinas-Martín, Marta, and Michelle Cherian. 2023. *Gender, education and skills*. OECD Skills Studies. Paris: OECD Publishing.

European Agency for Special Needs and Inclusive Education. 2024. European Agency for Special Needs and Inclusive Education—EASIE data tables by country. Available at: https://www.european-agency.org. Accessed 21 October 2024.

Eurostat. 2023. Students enrolled in tertiary education by education level, programme orientation, sex, and field of education. Available at: https://ec.europa.eu/eurostat/databrowser/view/educ_uoe_enrt03custom_12997606/default/table. Accessed 24 September 2024.

Fernández, Raquel. 2011. Chapter 11—Does culture matter? In *Handbook of social economics*, ed. Jess Benhabib, Alberto Bisin, and Matthew O. Jackson, vol. 1, 481–510. North-Holland.

Gershenson, S., and Stephen B. Holt. 2015. Gender gaps in high school students' homework time. *Educational Researcher* 44 (8): 432–441.

Gortazar, Lucas, David Martinez de Lafuente, and Ainhoa Vega-Bayo. 2022. Comparing teacher and external assessments: Are boys, immigrants, and poorer students undergraded? *ISEAK Working Paper*, July, 115: 103725.

Greenwald, A. G., D. E. McGhee, and J. L. K. Schwartz. 1998. Measuring individual differences in implicit cognition: The implicit association test. *Journal of Personality and Social Psychology* 6: 1464–1480.

Guiso, Luigi, Ferdinando Monte, Paola Sapienza, and Luigi Zingales. 2008. Culture, gender, and math. *Science-New York Then Washington* 320 (5880): 1164.

Iriberri, Nagore, and Pedro Rey-Biel. 2019. Competitive pressure widens the gender gap in performance: Evidence from a two-stage competition in mathematics. *The Economic Journal* 129 (620): 1863–1893.

Iriberri, Nagore and Pedro Rey-Biel. 2021. Brave boys and play-it-safe girls: Gender differences in willingness to guess in a large-scale natural field experiment. *European Economic Review* 131: 103603.

Ministerio de Educación y Formación Profesional. 2023. Estadísticas Laborales - En- cuesta de Población Activa (EPA), Tabla aban_1_02. Available at: https://estadisticas.educacion.gob.es/EducaJaxiPx/Tabla.htm?path=/laborales/epa/aban/l0/&file=aban_1_02.px&L=0. Accessed 7 March 2023.

Montalbán, José and Jenifer Ruiz-Valenzuela. 2022 ¿Cómo aumentar el acceso de las mujeres a disciplinas científicas y técnicas en la educación superior? Esade EcPol Policy Brief, 29.

Nicoletti, Cheti, Almudena Sevilla, and Valentina Tonei. 2022. Gender stereotypes in the family. IZA Discussion Paper, 15773.

Niederle, Muriel, and Lise Vesterlund. 2010. Explaining the gender gap in math test scores: The role of competition. *Journal of Economic Perspectives* 24 (2): 129–144.

Nollenberger, Natalia, Núria. Rodríguez-Planas, and Almudena Sevilla. 2016. The math gender gap: The role of culture. *American Economic Review* 106 (5): 257–261.

OECD. 2019. PISA 2018 Results (Volume II).

OECD. 2023. Education at a Glance 2023.

OECD. 2024. Education at a Glance 2024.

OWiD, "Average Performance of 15-Year-Olds in Mathematics, Reading, and Science," Available at: https://ourworldindata.org/grapher/average-performance-of-15-year-olds-in-mathematics-reading-and-science, 2024. Our World in Data. Accessed: 24.9.2024.

Peri, Giovanni, Kevin Shih, and Chad Sparber. 2015. STEM workers, H-1B visas, and productivity in US cities. *Journal of Labor Economics* 33 (S1): S225–S255.

Rammstedt, Beatrice, Clemens M Lechner, and Daniel Danner. 2024. Beyond literacy: The incremental value of non-cognitive skills.

Rees, Daniel I., and H. Naci Mocan. 1997. Labor market conditions and the high school dropout rate: Evidence from New York State. *Economics of Education Review* 16 (2): 103–109.

Schaede, Ursina, and Ville Mankki. 2022. Quota vs quality? Long-term gains from an unusual gender quota.

Steele, Claude M., and Joshua Aronson. 1995. Stereotype threat and the intellectual test performance of African Americans. *Journal of Personality and Social Psychology* 69 (5): 797–811.

Terrier, Camille. 2020. Boys lag behind: How teachers' gender biases affect student achievement. *Economics of Education Review* 77: 101981.

Non-cognitive Skills

Ildefonso Méndez and Gema Zamarro

1 What Are Non-cognitive Skills?

Economics research has demonstrated that there is a set of skills, independent of intelligence quotient, which are particularly malleable at early ages and have a significant impact on well-being throughout childhood, adolescence, and adulthood. This finding has opened the door to the design of interventions and programs that stimulate the development of these skills. These programs have proven to be particularly effective, especially when they are effectively targeted at the child and youth population, to reduce the intergenerational transmission of poverty, improve social-emotional skills, improve, for example, coexistence, early school dropout, etc.

This chapter reviews the current state of scientific knowledge about non-cognitive skills, their relevance in educational, labor, personal, and health outcomes, their determinants, and the characteristics of effective programs and interventions for stimulating these skills from an early age.

The U.S. Department of Education defined non-cognitive skills in 2013 as the set of character traits, personality, attributes, dispositions, social skills, attitudes, capabilities, and personal resources, independent of intellectual ability. They are presented in contrast to what is considered intellectual ability, but together with it, they help predict fundamental elements for well-being in life, such as academic and labor performance, health, and social well-being.

Non-cognitive skills is the term used by economists for this set of individual qualities and is a broad concept that encompasses a multitude of interrelated attributes, defined and studied mainly by experts in psychology. Given their interdisciplinary origin, these skills have been referred to by multiple names in the fields of economics,

I. Méndez (✉)
Universidad de Murcia, Murcia, Spain
e-mail: ildefonso.mendez@um.es

G. Zamarro
University of Arkansas, Fayetteville, AR, USA

A. Cabrales and I. Sanz (eds.), *Economics of Education*,
https://doi.org/10.1007/978-3-031-90911-5_15

psychology, education, and philosophical literature, including personality traits, character or temperament, executive functions, virtues, social-emotional skills, and non-cognitive skills, among others. These different terms emphasize different characteristics of non-cognitive skills. Concepts such as personality, character, or temperament emphasize the permanence and hereditary nature of non-cognitive skills, while concepts like social-emotional skills or non-cognitive skills emphasize the fact that these skills can be learned.

Executive functions, on the other hand, are a series of mental processes that enable planning, maintaining attention, remembering, and managing multiple tasks simultaneously, and they form the basis for some non-cognitive skills. Executive functions rely on three types of mental processes: working memory, cognitive flexibility, and inhibitory control. Inhibitory control is the component most directly related to the economic concept of non-cognitive skills. Working memory allows us to hold and manipulate different pieces of information within a short time. Cognitive flexibility enables us to maintain and shift our focus based on different demands in our environment. Finally, self-control helps us set priorities, and resist distractions and impulsive reactions. These executive functions are highly correlated with one another and work together with each other.

Executive functions and non-cognitive skills contribute to academic performance, labor outcomes, and social well-being. However, this relationship does not necessarily work in the opposite direction. While there is a significant hereditary component to non-cognitive skills, estimated to be between 30 and 60% (Bouchard & Loehlin, 2001), as explained later in this chapter, these skills develop throughout life, with critical periods during childhood and adolescence. Their development is influenced by cultural factors as well as the family and educational environment.

Figure 1 illustrates a diagram showing how the various non-cognitive skills defined in this section relate to each other, the factors that influence them, and the impact these skills have.

2 How to Measure Non-cognitive Skills?

Obtaining measures of non-cognitive skills is not an easy task. Most researchers and evaluators use survey-based measures, where respondents' non-cognitive skills are assessed by studying their responses to a series of multiple-choice questions. However, survey-based measures can be biased if respondents answer in socially acceptable ways that do not necessarily reflect reality. This phenomenon is known in the literature as "social desirability bias." Another source of potential bias in survey-based measures of non-cognitive skills is the possibility that respondents may differ in their use of the questions' response scales. This phenomenon, known as "reference group bias," can be a significant issue when comparing levels of non-cognitive skills between groups or geographic areas from different cultures (or cultural traditions).

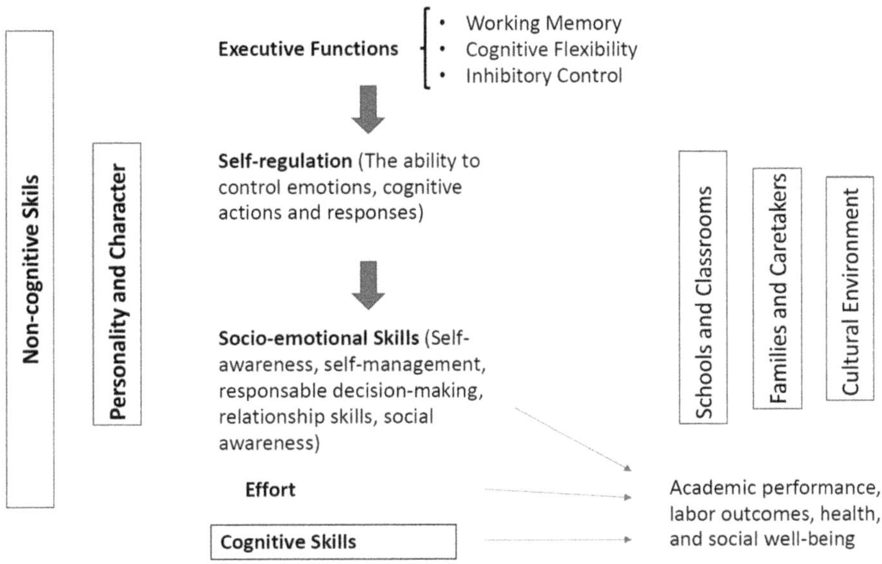

Fig. 1 Executive functions, socio-emotional skills, and academic, labor, and well-being outcomes

An alternative way that researchers have measured non-cognitive skills without relying on surveys is through the direct measurement of certain behaviors associated with various non-cognitive skills. For example, researchers have used academic behaviors such as course grades, attendance records, or school expulsions as measures of low student motivation.

Another alternative is to measure specific non-cognitive skills through experiments, using direct tasks where the level of competence related to a particular non-cognitive skill can be observed while a participant is performing a specific task. A classic example is the marshmallow test designed by Mischel et al. (1972) to measure levels of self-control in children. Lastly, recent literature proposes the use of paradata or metadata—"data about data"—from exams and surveys to obtain measures of non-cognitive skills.

2.1 *Measurement Through Surveys*

The primary way researchers have attempted to measure various non-cognitive skills is through questionnaires in which respondents answer a series of questions, often using what is known as a "Likert scale" to indicate their level of agreement or disagreement with a series of statements. Two widely used examples in the literature include questionnaires to measure the five personality traits (the Big Five) and the perseverance and passion for long-term goals Grit scale.

2.1.1 Personality Measures: The Big Five

Multiple studies in psychology and economics have used the Big Five taxonomy to measure the following personality traits: Openness, Conscientiousness, Extraversion, Agreeableness, and Neuroticism. Openness captures individuals' tendency to experience and learn new things. It is related to imagination and creativity. Conscientiousness reflects levels of perseverance, focus, impulse control, and the ability to achieve goals. Extraversion measures the ability to relate to others, emotional expressiveness, and social interaction skills. Agreeableness assesses empathy toward others, altruism, and levels of affection. Finally, neuroticism measures an individual's physical and emotional capacity to cope with daily stress. Those with high levels of neuroticism often experience frequent anxiety and irritability in response to everyday stressors from work or personal life.

Following the pioneering work by Fiske (1949), researchers in psychology have studied and developed various questionnaires to capture personality traits, finding that these questionnaires consistently measure five dimensions of personality. For example, John et al. (1991) and John et al. (2008) developed a series of questions known as the Big Five Inventory, which consists of a questionnaire with 44 statements where respondents indicate their level of agreement on a five-point Likert scale, ranging from 1 (Strongly Disagree) to 5 (Strongly Agree). Overall, the Big Five personality model and its questionnaires are among the most widely used in psychological research and, more recently, in economics as well.

2.1.2 Long-Term Perseverance Measures or "Grit"

Duckworth et al. (2007) define "Grit" as the tendency to maintain interest and effort over time to achieve long-term goals. Along with her co-authors, psychologist Angela Duckworth developed two possible questionnaires to measure the concept of "Grit." These questionnaires can be accessed online here: https://angeladuckworth.com/grit-scale/.

Similarly to the Big Five inventory, the questionnaires for measuring "Grit" consist of a series of statements where respondents report their level of agreement on a 5-point Likert scale. These statements include, among others, phrases such as "I am a hard worker," "I am diligent," or "New ideas and projects sometimes distract me from previous ideas and projects." For the Spanish version of the long-term perseverance or "Grit" questionnaire, see the work of Arco-Tirado et al. (2018).

2.1.3 Limitations of Survey-Based Measures

Despite the evidence supporting the validity of questionnaires like the Big Five inventory or "Grit" scale, this method of measuring non-cognitive skills has significant limitations. In particular, as previously mentioned, survey-based measures can be affected by two important biases: "social desirability bias" and "reference group bias." These biases occur when respondents tend to provide answers that are more socially acceptable ("social desirability bias") or when they differ in their use of response categories based on their culture or social group ("reference group bias"). For example, when students are asked about their level of school motivation and are instructed to respond on an ordinal scale, like those presented in the Big Five inventory or the grit-scale questionnaire, their individual standards of what it means to be a motivated student may influence their responses. Specifically, the concept of what it means to be a motivated student is likely influenced by cultural factors and the context of their schools. This means that two students with the same objective level of motivation, but who live in different regions, come from different cultures, are of different genders, or attend different schools, may respond differently. For instance, studies have shown that students in the United States, who identify with an Asian background, tend to score lower on the "Grit" scale compared to those who do not identify as Asian, despite the higher average academic performance of Asian students.

The anchoring vignettes method is proposed as a potential solution to measurement issues caused by differences in reference values or "reference group bias." This method involves asking respondents to evaluate not only a specific concept, such as their levels of motivation, but also the same levels represented in a series of hypothetical scenarios called vignettes. These vignettes are short stories describing a hypothetical person with a certain objective level in the concept being measured. Since all respondents evaluate the same vignettes, assuming they interpret them in the same way, the observed differences in their assessments of these hypothetical stories can be interpreted as differences in their individual standards and reference points used in their responses. Under the assumption that respondents apply these same individual standards when evaluating the hypothetical vignettes and when assessing themselves, the evaluations of these vignettes can be used to adjust their responses and correct for biases. For more details about this method and its applications in the PISA study in Spain, see Zamarro (2021).

2.2 Direct Measures of Behavior

Given the limitations of survey-based measures, researchers have sought alternative methods to directly assess behaviors related to different non-cognitive skills. In some cases, researchers utilize existing administrative data related to student behavior within the educational system. Another alternative involves behavioral measures through experiments, where participants are asked to perform a direct task in a laboratory setting, and their performance during this task is quantified as a measure of a specific non-cognitive skill.

2.2.1 Using Administrative Data

In some cases, educators and researchers have used administrative data to measure behaviors related to students' non-cognitive skills. Various academic behaviors, such as absenteeism, course grades, incidents of behavioral problems, and school expulsions, are linked to students' motivation and academic effort. These behaviors can help build early warning indicator systems for potential school dropouts. Typically, these behaviors manifest low levels of self-control, conscientiousness, or "grit," which are associated with a higher likelihood of dropping out of school. For further discussion on the issue of school dropouts, see Chapters 1 and 13.

An important issue with measures of non-cognitive skills based on administrative data is that these behaviors are only partially determined by non-cognitive skills. There are other factors that may be associated with these school behaviors, independent of non-cognitive skill levels. For instance, while course grades may reflect low levels of self-control, conscientiousness, or perseverance, they can also indicate other family factors and limited resources in the household. Moreover, these family and personal factors may, in turn, be related to non-cognitive skills, as described in Fig. 1, which can affect students' self-esteem and performance. This can lead to significant endogeneity problems if one is interested in studying the causal effect of non-cognitive skills on other variables. For further discussion of such empirical issues, see Chapter 2 of this book.

2.2.2 Behavioral Measures Through Experiments with Direct Tasks

Given the limitations of measures based on administrative data and surveys, researchers have developed direct measures of non-cognitive skills through experiments and direct tasks in laboratory settings. These laboratory measures aim to control conditions as much as possible to limit the influence of external factors on non-cognitive skill assessments. Participants are asked to perform specific tasks related to particular non-cognitive skills, and researchers then quantify their performance on these tasks.

A classic example in this category is the famous marshmallow test developed by Mischel et al. (1972). This test was designed to study the ability of children aged four to six to delay gratification. The researchers worked with preschool children at a school that was part of Stanford University. In a series of tests, the researchers asked the children to wait before eating a marshmallow, altering the conditions of the wait. If the children managed to wait, they were given two marshmallows. The researchers measured the number of minutes and seconds the children were able to wait as a measure of their ability to delay gratification, a skill related to self-control. Mischel and his colleagues concluded that children could increase their wait time using distraction strategies. Those who were able to wait longer distracted themselves by looking away, covering their eyes, or talking to themselves to avoid focusing on the marshmallow. In the third section, we discuss the marshmallow test in more detail and the implications of these experiments.

This type of direct task measurement has several important limitations. First, they tend to be costly, which limits the ability to collect large data samples, although this limitation is improving with the advent of new technologies. Second, it is unclear how representative the results obtained from these laboratory tests are for more general everyday contexts (external validity). Finally, it is challenging to administer these tests multiple times to study the evolution of non-cognitive skills, as participants become familiar with the test after their first attempt. This familiarity can lead to biased results in subsequent assessments, often skewing them upward.

Given the challenges of rigorously measuring various non-cognitive skills, researchers have continued to explore alternative measures. Recently, the use of paradata or metadata—essentially "data about the data"—from exams and surveys has been proposed to obtain measures of non-cognitive skills.

2.3 Using Metadata or Paradata to Infer Measures of Non-cognitive Skills

Successfully taking an exam or survey requires not only the necessary subject knowledge but also self-efficacy, conscientiousness, and self-management to stay focused on the task. Therefore, measures based on the metadata or paradata from exams and surveys—such as the time spent answering difficult questions, whether questions are answered quickly without a minimal response time, if questions are left blank, or if answers are provided randomly—can help assess non-cognitive skills related to self-efficacy, conscientiousness, self-management, or perseverance.

These paradata or metadata-based measures are akin to a natural experiment in economics. While the metadata/paradata is not designed to be a direct measure of non-cognitive skills (just as a natural experiment isn't designed as a laboratory experiment), the information they naturally capture can indicate different levels of relevant non-cognitive skills. The use of exam or survey metadata or paradata can be seen as an intermediate method between using administrative data and conducting behavioral measures through direct task experiments. Although the metadata typically comes from assessments taken by students in an educational context, the conditions under which these tests are usually conducted are more standardized than the behaviors captured in administrative data during a typical school day.

Regarding exam paradata, emerging research has shown that the time students spend answering questions, particularly the rate of rapid guessing, serves as an indicator of their academic motivation. This motivation is related to other measures of non-cognitive skills, such as self-efficacy, self-management, diligence, and perseverance. In this respect, studies have also demonstrated that students who do not dedicate enough time to answering exam questions and attempt to guess rapidly on 10% or more of the questions tend to have lower course grades, higher absenteeism rates, and more behavioral problems in school.

In addition to response time, researchers have studied other behaviors when students take an exam. For example, Borghans and Schils (2012) propose examining the rate of decline in performance as the test progresses, across standardized tests such as the PISA test developed by the OECD. Specifically, they investigate how the likelihood of answering exam questions correctly decreases depending on the order of the questions, from the beginning to the end of the exam. Using PISA data, where the order of questions varies across different versions of the test and each version is randomly assigned to students, which allows them to control for question difficulty, they find that the rate of decline in the test is not strongly related to the final score, indicating that this decline in performance does not largely capture students' cognitive abilities. On the other hand, using data from exams with characteristics similar to the PISA test but conducted in England, Borghans and Schils (2012) show that 16-year-old students who exhibited a greater decline in performance throughout the exam had lower levels of conscientiousness, ambition, and school motivation, as well as lower employment rates and wages in adulthood, 20 years later, even after accounting for the total test scores. Based on these results, the authors conclude that the rate of decline can serve as a measure of non-cognitive skills related to intrinsic motivation and perseverance.

2.3.1 The Predictive Power of Student Effort in Surveys

In addition to exams, students increasingly complete surveys in school to gather their opinions on various topics, such as their perceptions of their school and teachers, or to collect data about their economic and social situations. These surveys, much like standardized exams, also require students to pay attention and exert effort in answering the questions. Researchers have proposed measuring the effort students put into these surveys as a possible measure of non-cognitive skills related to conscientiousness, motivation, and diligence. In particular, researchers suggest studying two types of behavior that demonstrate little effort from the student: the percentage of survey questions left blank and the extent to which students respond unpredictably or randomly. These two behaviors have been found to be related to measures of non-cognitive skills based on surveys, such as conscientiousness and "grit." Additionally, it has also been found that a lack of effort in surveys by students is correlated with the levels of education attained, employment, and wages later in life, even when accounting for cognitive ability levels and family socioeconomic status.

For example, Hitt et al. (2016) use data from six longitudinal studies representative of the adolescent population in the United States. All participants in these studies took a cognitive skills test in their first year of participation and completed surveys collecting demographic data and their opinions on various topics. The authors argue that, for students, these surveys conducted in school are perceived as school assignments and can therefore be used to measure students' academic motivation through the effort they put into these surveys. They then measure the percentage of survey questions that students left blank or responded "I don't know" in each study's surveys. Using a linear regression model, the authors examine the relationship between survey effort in adolescence and the level of education attained in adulthood (for more discussion on linear regression models, see Chapter 2 of this book). The authors controlled for family and personal characteristics related to the costs and benefits of obtaining a higher level of education. Importantly, they also controlled for the cognitive skill level of the respondents. They find that in models with both the non-response rate in the survey and the level of cognitive skills included, the non-response rate was still a statistically significant predictor in four of the six studies. The effects, when significant, ranged from 0.10 to 0.30 years less education for each one standard deviation increase in the non-response rate. This effect compares favorably with the effect of increasing cognitive skill by one standard deviation, which corresponded to an increase of between 0.10 and 1.44 more years of education, depending on the study. The authors also examined the relationship between non-response rates and income and employment levels in adulthood, finding that while there is an initial significant relationship, it is largely due to the higher levels of education attained.

2.3.2 International Differences, by Regions, and by Gender

Research in economics of education has increasingly recognized that student performance on standardized tests, such as the PISA test, reflects not only students' knowledge in the subject but also their effort and academic motivation. This is supported by findings from studies like Gneezy et al. (2019), which demonstrate how performance on these tests can be influenced by offering students monetary incentives. As a result, researchers have used metadata and paradata from these tests to examine the extent to which differences between countries, regions within country, or student groups (e.g., by gender) can be explained by varying levels of motivation and effort among students. Interested readers may also refer to Chapter 5c for more details on how differences in non-cognitive skills by gender impact certain educational outcomes.

In their analysis of the performance decline rate using PISA test data, Borghans and Schils (2012) document significant differences across countries in this measure of effort and estimate that around 19% of the observed variation in PISA results between countries could be explained by different rates of decline in performance throughout the test. Zamarro et al. (2019) corroborate these findings by using both the rate of decline in performance and other effort measures based on metadata from the survey following the PISA test, such as the percentage of questions that students leave blank and the rate of responses that can be considered unpredictable or careless. They estimate that all these measures of effort could explain between 32 and 38% of the variation observed across countries in PISA scores. As shown in Fig. 2, both studies find that, along with Greece, Spain is one of the countries that exhibits the greatest decline in performance throughout the test, as the line depicting performance decline from the beginning to the end of the test has a steeper slope in these countries, suggesting a deficit in non-cognitive skills related to diligence and persistence.

Balart and Cabrales (2014) show significant differences in the rate of decline on the PISA test also across regions in Spain, but they conclude that these differences can largely be explained by regional variations in the socioeconomic characteristics of the

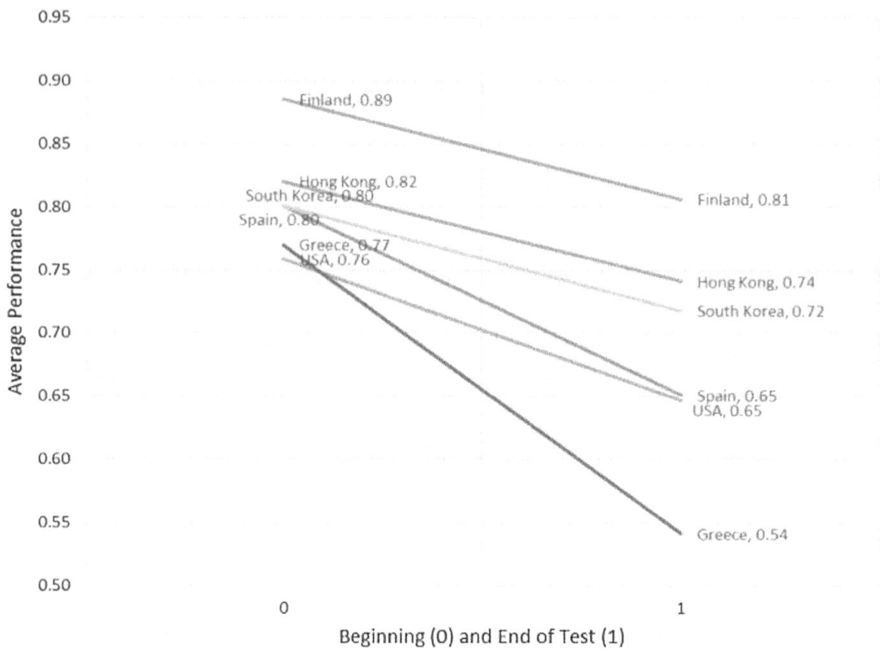

Fig. 2 Performance at the beginning and at the end of the PISA test, by country (*Source* Zamarro et al. [2019])

students. Zamarro (2021) further notes that there may also be a cultural component that explains the differences between Spanish regions, given the correlations found between the non-response rate in the PISA questionnaire, the rate of rapid guessing on the test, and the historical literacy rates in Spain (see Fig. 3).

The literature has also consistently shown that girls exhibit higher levels of effort on these types of tests than boys. Balart and Cabrales (2014) and Balart and Oosterveen (2019) demonstrate that being a girl and having a higher proportion of girls in the classroom are associated with less decline in performance during the PISA test. Similarly, Zamarro (2021) also shows greater effort from girls in Spain in measures of academic motivation, the percentage of questions left blank in the PISA survey, and the rapid guessing rate in the test. This greater effort from girls implies that they compensate some of the gender gap in performance on the test with increased effort. As a result, once gender differences in effort are accounted for using statistical methods, it is found that gender gaps in performance in subjects like mathematics and science could be larger than initially believed. For more details on gender differences in education, see Chapter 5c.

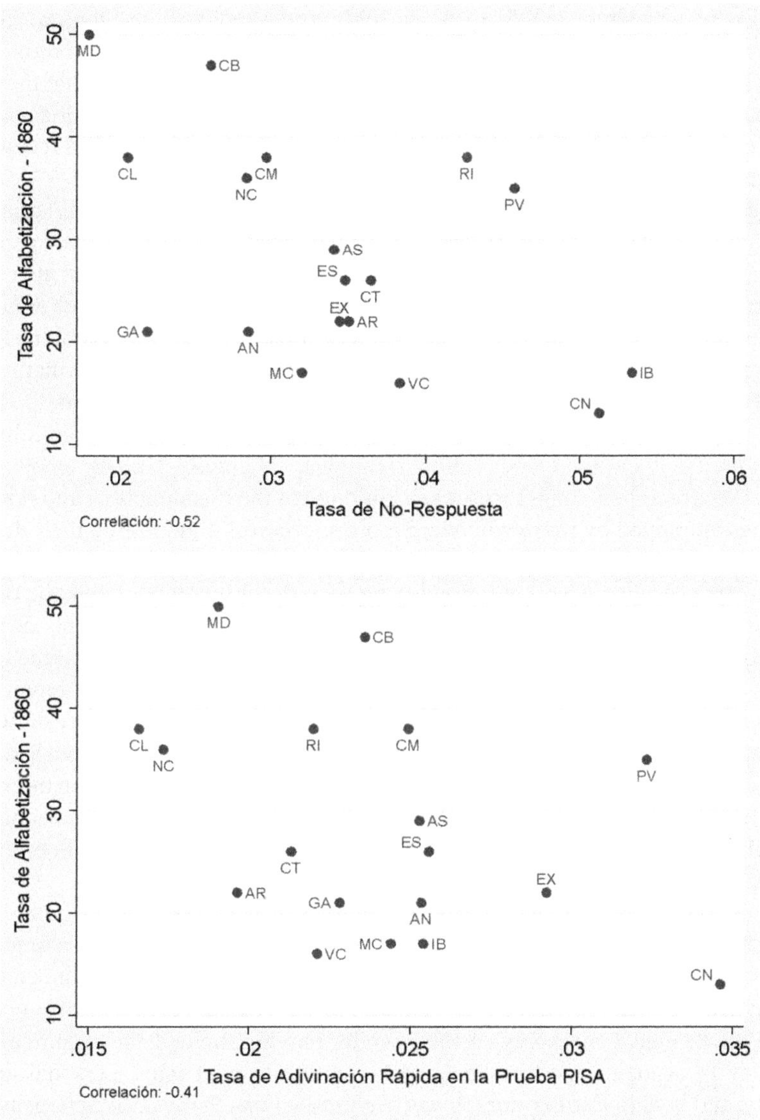

Fig. 3 Non-response in the PISA survey, rapid guessing in the test and historical literacy measures by different regions in Spain (*Source* Zamarro [2021])

3 Don't Eat the Marshmallow!

In the 1960s, one of the most well-known and replicated experiments in the history of psychology was conducted. Walter Mischel, an Austrian psychologist at Stanford University, devised an original test of delayed gratification aimed at children.

The concept was simple. A 5- to 6-year-old child attending the Stanford University daycare is taken to a room without stimuli or distractions and asked to sit at a table with a plate containing a marshmallow. They are then informed that they have two options: they can eat the marshmallow at any time, or they can wait a specified number of minutes, which they can track using an analog clock, and then receive two marshmallows.

Given that for a child of that age, a treat like a marshmallow is a powerful reinforcer and an object of desire, the marshmallow test represents a struggle between emotion and reason. What's interesting about this battle is the disparity of forces: at ages 5 to 6, the brain areas that manage emotions, such as the limbic system and the amygdala, are mature, while the prefrontal cortex—the latest part to fully develop in the human brain, responsible for executive functions and thus rationality—does not mature until around ages 20–25. In this battle, Goliath represents the present moment, the "carpe diem," and emotion, while David symbolizes rationality, delay, and the inhibition of the impulse to eat the marshmallow right away. Naturally, Goliath tends to win. Mischel recorded how long it took each child to eat the marshmallow and noted the strategies employed by those who were more successful in inhibiting their desire to eat it immediately.

The surprise came when, in following up with the children who took the original test, Mischel and his co-authors found that, all else being equal in terms of family background, those children who had better resisted the temptation to eat the marshmallow at ages 5–6 generally performed better academically, had higher-paying jobs, greater life satisfaction, lower body mass index, and managed stress more effectively than those who had succumbed to temptation earlier. This finding, published in the last decade of the previous century, sparked a profound debate about the role of character education—what some refer to as the malleable aspects of personality—and self-regulation or socio-emotional skills, as emphasized by others, in promoting lifelong well-being.

In this context, studies emerge from economics, psychology, and the combination of both disciplines, analyzing the explanatory power of these malleable dimensions of personality or socio-emotional skills and their role in determining inequality in society. The application of economic modeling and strategies for identifying causal effects on available measures of these skills has highlighted the significant role they play in academic performance, early school dropout rates, personal and job stability, and health. Furthermore, it has been shown that these skills, independent of IQ, are transmitted from parents to children both genetically and through example. Investments in early improvement programs for non-cognitive skills among socially disadvantaged groups are one of the most promising approaches for reducing social inequalities, due to their effects on the participants' development as well as the development of their children. In the following section, we will review the available evidence.

In 2018, Watts, Duncan, and Quan set out to replicate the results of Mischel and his colleagues' original studies using a larger and more representative sample from the United States. Watts et al. (2018) confirmed positive correlations between the waiting time of children in their sample and academic performance. However, the association was considerably weaker than the one Mischel and his co-authors originally documented and disappeared when comparing children from the same socioeconomic and cognitive development levels. Additionally, Watts et al. (2018) found no relationship in their study between the waiting time of children at age 5 and their socio-emotional behavior measures at age 15. These new findings from a more representative sample highlighted the importance of socioeconomic and cultural factors in the levels of non-cognitive skills, even though the marshmallow test was designed to limit their influence.

4 Determinants of Non-cognitive skills

4.1 Genetics

The research conducted in recent decades has shown that the attributes, dispositions, attitudes, and resources that give substance to non-cognitive skills are shaped from early childhood, and even before birth, as a result of the interaction between genetic and environmental factors. Buser et al. (2023), for example, demonstrate that genes play a significant role in determining our endowment of cognitive and non-cognitive skills and, therefore, partially explain the inequalities in educational and labor achievement that, in turn, determine the inequality in the distribution of income, wealth, and well-being in a society.

The role of genes in determining non-cognitive skills is particularly documented in clinical populations, that is, individuals with learning difficulties, such as attention deficit hyperactivity disorder (ADHD), and/or individuals with special educational needs, such as autism. Thus, the most significant risk factor for having a child with autism is having one or more relatives with autism. In this scenario, the probability of having a child with autism is around 20%, which is 10–20 times higher than in the general population. In the case of ADHD, this probability is 80%.

Bouchard and Loehlin (2001) conclude that, in the general population, indicators of non-cognitive skills obtained from information about the behavior or conduct of generation n are transmitted to members of generation n + 1 at a rate ranging from 30 to 60%. It can thus be concluded that, while genes play a significant role in determining non-cognitive skills, environmental factors have an even more relevant role for most social groups or communities, especially those at risk of social exclusion, in the determination and evolution of these skills.

4.2 Environmental Determinants

Among the environmental factors highlighted by the research are stress, the parenting style of parents or regular caregivers (which is also discussed in Chapter 3b of this book), family size, and a factor that we could define, in a general sense, as companionship, which reflects the quality time that the child enjoys individually with their parents, regular caregivers, or teachers.

Family income has been used in economics as a proxy for various factors whose presence depresses the development of non-cognitive skills: stress, emotional instability of parents, their lower likelihood of accompanying the child in their development and spending quality time with them, or exposure to unsafe or violent environments. Fletcher and Wolfe (2016) find, using a sample of schoolchildren residing in the United States aged between 5 and 11 years, that family income has a significant and increasing explanatory power regarding children's socio-emotional adjustment. Specifically, these authors find that the likelihood of a student displaying appropriate social skills, such as cooperating with peers or avoiding problems caused by impulsivity, such as aggression toward a peer, is causally conditioned by family income.

In this regard, the evidence reviewed by Diamond (2013) confirms that factors such as growing up in a household at risk of social exclusion, being a member of a socially discriminated minority, or exposure to violence or lack of safety have a very harmful effect on the development of the brain's executive functions. Specifically, children living in households at risk of social exclusion show average executive functioning at the age of 4 years, which is 30% lower than that of children not exposed to poverty at the beginning of their school life. This adverse differential translates into a lower likelihood of maintaining attention in class, transitioning flexibly between activities, or engaging in socially valid interactions with peers.

The evidence in Farah et al. (2006) suggests that these differences based on family income increase with age. Specifically, adolescents aged 10–13 years living in households at risk of social exclusion show, on average, working memory that is 50% lower than that of students living in middle-class households. The unfavorable differential at these ages reaches 60% in terms of behavioral inhibition, the component of executive function most closely related to the economic concept of non-cognitive skills.

Diamond (2013) identifies the stress characteristic of households at risk of social exclusion as the determining factor in the causal relationship between family income and the development of non-cognitive skills. Abundant evidence in the fields of psychology and medicine highlights the pernicious effect of prolonged exposure to stress on the development of the prefrontal cortex and, consequently, on executive functioning. Furthermore, it is evident that less advantaged households in terms of income are those where there is greater stress, where urgent matters permanently take precedence over important ones, providing a less favorable context for stimulating reflection in children, which is a true determinant of adequate executive functioning (Zelazo, 2003).

4.3 Parenting Styles

In relation to parenting style, Diamond (2013) points out that children whose parents are very protective or controlling, and those who base their children's education on punishment, consistently show lower levels of executive functioning than those with parents who promote their children's autonomy. Generally, the level of self-regulation in children is higher in households where more enriched language is used, where parents ask open-ended questions that encourage their children's reflection, and where they verbalize their problem-solving strategies. These factors are also closely related to family income as a synthetic indicator of context.

Another relevant factor for the development of a child's non-cognitive skills is who their primary caregiver is. This factor is closely related to the previous one, the parenting style of the children. Ao et al. (2021) find that children residing in China who are primarily cared for by their grandparents show systematically higher levels of external locus of control than those cared for by their parents. That is, children who are regularly cared for by their grandparents are, all else being equal regarding other characteristics such as family income, more likely to believe that success or improvement is due to factors outside themselves, such as luck, fate, or initial family conditions. This result can be explained by the different parenting styles of parents and grandparents. The latter tend to adopt a style more focused on enjoying time with grandchildren and shared leisure activities, with fewer limits, less discipline, less involvement in academic tasks, and generally less stimulation of the grandchildren's autonomy.

The latter result suggests that being regularly cared for by grandparents may lead, all else being equal regarding other characteristics such as family income, to a lower growth mindset in children. This concept, originally developed by psychologist Carol Dweck, has been shown to be one of the non-cognitive dimensions with significant implications for academic performance and children's self-esteem (Alan et al., 2016).

Specifically, we can say that a child has a growth mindset when they understand that it is sustained effort and perseverance that allow them to improve their results. A growth mindset enables children to recognize that mistakes are an intrinsic part of the learning process and therefore valuable. Above all, an adequate dose of growth mindset preserves their self-concept by making them aware that results improve with practice and effort and are not explained by static endowments of supposedly unchangeable factors like intelligence or physical abilities for sports.

The antithesis of a growth mindset is a conceptualization of intelligence and other personal factors as static and insensitive to effort and practice. Thus, children with a fixed mindset often fear making mistakes; they do not want to test themselves in new contexts for fear of not performing equally well and frequently use phrases like "I am not good at this" shortly after starting something new.

The findings from Ao et al. (2021) suggest that countries like Spain, where balancing professional and family life depends on informal support provided within the family environment—particularly from grandparents—achieve suboptimal endowments of non-cognitive skills in young people as a result of this form of social organization.

4.4 Family Size

The number of members in the family unit is another factor highlighted in the literature as a determinant of a person's non-cognitive skill endowment. Juhn et al. (2015) demonstrate, using a representative sample of the U.S. population, that the substitution effect between the number of children (quantity) and investment per child (quality) also affects non-cognitive skills. Specifically, these authors find that an increase in family size due to the birth of a new member leads to lower parental investment per child, reducing both cognitive and non-cognitive skills, approximated by behavioral difficulties, in children.

The concept of parental investment refers not only to monetary investment in educational institutions, tutoring centers, etc., but also to the quality time spent with each child. This latter aspect directly leads us to another key determinant highlighted in the literature, which we can define as accompaniment. Accompaniment refers to the time that an adult (parent, grandparent, or teacher) dedicates individually to a child. The importance of feeling part of a group, whether it be family or classroom, has been emphasized in numerous publications as a determinant of the motivation and effort that a child puts into what they do. Additionally, having individualized time with reference adults in each context is essential for feeling that one belongs to that context.

4.5 School Environment

The relevance of accompaniment in determining non-cognitive skills is evident, for example, in research indicating that smaller school groups achieve better results in non-cognitive skills (Dee & West, 2011; see the chapter on class size, 3a, in this book), or in studies showing that grandparent care yields better outcomes in non-cognitive skills than formal alternatives like daycare due to the individualized attention grandchildren receive (Morando & Platt, 2002). Evidence regarding family size also points in this direction.

Teachers also play a significant role in determining their students' non-cognitive skills. This is supported by the findings from Cheng and Zamarro (2018) and Jackson (2018). The latter study demonstrates that teachers affect not only their students' academic performance but also a wide range of behaviors such as absenteeism, expulsions, retention, etc. Specifically, Jackson (2018) finds that when considering the effect of teachers on both the performance and behavior of their students, the impact teachers have on the long-term overall development of their students nearly doubles. Meanwhile, Cheng and Zamarro (2018) develop measures of teachers' non-cognitive skills that provide information not captured by commonly considered indicators while demonstrating their impact on student performance. For more information on the role of teachers in developing their students' cognitive and non-cognitive skills, see Chapter 3d.

4.6 Culture

Culture is undoubtedly another determining factor in the endowment of non-cognitive skills among the young cohorts of a country. Fernández and Fogli (2009) define culture as the set of beliefs and preferences that shape individual decisions, which vary systematically among groups defined by their geographical location and/or social position, and which are transmitted from parents to children. The prolific literature on the impact of culture, as defined above, has shown its relevance in decisions regarding fertility, labor supply, geographic mobility, formation of new households, regulation of the labor market, etc. In this regard, Mendez (2015) demonstrates that a significant fraction, between 10 and 30%, of the differences in performance among developed countries for their 15-year-old students in the standardized PISA test is due to the effect of culture on determining the dominant non-cognitive skills in each country. Specifically, Mendez (2015) analyzes to what extent the PISA performance of second-generation immigrant students with different backgrounds but residing in the same country is influenced by the qualities deemed important to foster in a child in their father's country of origin when he was young. Thus, those young people whose parents lived in countries that considered it essential to promote effort, perseverance, autonomy, and delayed gratification achieve better results in mathematics, science, and language when controlling for other personal characteristics, school characteristics, institutional factors, and grade level. Furthermore, Mendez and Zamarro (2018) find that this cultural factor also has a significant effect on the educational level ultimately attained.

It is worth noting that available evidence also shows that environmental factors impact the development of a child's non-cognitive skills from conception. In this sense, Li et al. (2024) find that the frequency and intensity of torrential rain episodes during pregnancy affect both cognitive and non-cognitive development in children in India. Specifically, episodes occurring during the first trimester of pregnancy have a greater negative impact on child development.

5 Interventions That Improve Non-cognitive Skills

There are numerous interventions designed to improve the non-cognitive skills of specific population groups, typically defined by the presence of a deficit in these skills, or of the general population.

Heckman and Kautz (2013) conduct a thorough review of the literature on the evaluation of interventions aimed at improving the well-being of certain social groups, usually disadvantaged populations. These authors review more than 20 programs whose evaluations meet the requirements of identifying the effect of interest in a methodologically appropriate manner, testing for the presence of that effect several years after the intervention, and identifying its impact on measures of non-cognitive skills and different dimensions of development such as: IQ, academic performance, educational attainment, health, criminality, substance abuse, employment status, labor income, etc. All analyzed programs have a minimum duration of one year, with two years being the most common duration for programs aimed at households with children under 4 years old.

The analysis conducted by Heckman and Kautz (2013) confirms that the most effective interventions—those that improve the well-being of the target population to the greatest extent and whose effects appear to be more persistent over time—are those directed at disadvantaged households with preschool-aged children. Specifically, the most cost-effective interventions are those aimed at households with children under 5 years old. Thanks to the evaluated programs, these children were able to improve both their academic performance and their educational attainment in adulthood, their health, their labor income, and reduce the likelihood of encountering legal issues compared to what would have happened had the program not been implemented in their homes. Therefore, it can be stated that an effective program will be even more so the younger the children in the household it targets.

Heckman and Kautz (2013) find that the only effective programs for sustained improvement in IQ over time are those aimed at households with children under 3 years old. This result suggests that the critical period for improving this measure of intelligence extends from conception to approximately 3 years of age. After that age, the determining factors for cognitive development are largely predetermined. In contrast, a person's non-cognitive skills can be improved through well-defined interventions both in early childhood, by working with their parents or usual caregivers, and throughout compulsory schooling, adolescence, and adulthood. However, the effectiveness of this intervention will be greater the younger the individual is.

Cunha et al. (2010) explain this latter result by finding that skills, whether cognitive or non-cognitive, show marked dynamic complementarity. In other words, the levels of a skill at one age determine the productivity of future investments in skills. These authors find that, unlike non-cognitive skills, cognitive skills are only malleable during the early years of a person's life. Although dynamic complementarity explains the greater productivity of investments in non-cognitive skills at younger ages, investments in these skills at later ages still show significant returns. Finally, these authors find that non-cognitive skills contribute to the improvement of cognitive skills, while causality in the opposite direction is less relevant.

These results suggest that the most effective interventions for improving the quality of life of children in socially disadvantaged households will be those that achieve sustained improvements in these children's non-cognitive skills over time. The results analyzed by Heckman and Kautz (2013) confirm this intuition.

Another common characteristic of the most effective programs is that they involve parents, either mandatorily or by motivating them to participate. This result makes sense considering that the most effective programs work with families who have preschool-aged children and therefore focus on training parents who become more suitable models for their children to assimilate these new habits or non-cognitive skills through imitation. Specifically, some of the most effective programs, such as the Perry Preschool Program or Head Start, include sessions conducted in the homes targeted by the intervention to directly shape parents' behaviors. The lower estimated effectiveness for programs aimed at adolescents coincides with the fact that none of these programs involve adolescents' parents or conduct home sessions.

One of the most evaluated and effective programs, the Perry Preschool Program, was aimed at 3- or 4-year-old children from low-income families, predominantly Black children with an IQ below 85 at age 3. The program offered two-and-a-half hours of intervention from Monday to Friday at a center for children and home visits to shape parents' behaviors and strengthen bonds with their children. The Perry Program lasted two years. After this time, both families randomly selected for the program and those excluded were enrolled in the same center.

The results from randomized evaluations show that the Perry Program improved academic performance and reduced the likelihood that these children would encounter legal issues years later, with positive effects—though less robust—on educational attainment and labor income. The key to this effectiveness lies in improving these children's non-cognitive skills since the program only had transient effects on IQ.

Children participating in the Perry Program engaged daily in thinking routines such as "plan-execute-reflect," where they were taught to create a plan, execute it, and reflect on deviations from both their original plan and its execution as well as on outcomes achieved. Reflection was done with teachers at the center and with their classmates. They were also accustomed to working with peers to find solutions to problems encountered while pursuing their goals.

Finally, another aspect to highlight about interventions or programs that effectively stimulate the development of non-cognitive skills is that, in some cases, such as the Perry Program, the benefits of the program are transmitted to the next generation. Thus, Heckman and Karapakula (2019) find that the children of participants in the Perry program significantly benefited from their parents' participation in the program. Specifically, these children had fewer behavioral problems at school, higher levels of education and employment, and lower rates of involvement in criminal activities compared to the children of non-participants. Similar results are obtained by García et al. (2023) for the children of African American participants living in disadvantaged households. Furthermore, Heckman and Karapakula (2019) find that the siblings of participants in the program also benefited significantly.

The Perry Program could well be defined as a program aimed at stimulating children's executive functioning. Specifically, the goal of the Perry Program could be defined as helping children develop the habit of thinking before acting, that is, stimulating inhibition. To achieve this, likely with visual supports, they were reminded of the need to generate a plan, execute it, and finally reflect on any deviations between what was planned and what was achieved.

Additionally, as suggested by Vygotsky in his seminal contributions, reflection was carried out among peers, which contributes to more meaningful learning and improved executive functioning. Thus, the Perry Program fostered the habit of thinking before acting, stimulating executive functioning or non-cognitive skills among participating students—something inferred from evaluation results indicating that it improved children's behavior.

Using criteria similar to those of Heckman and Kautz (2013) regarding the selection of evaluations for analysis, Diamond and Ling (2016) provide a comprehensive review of the effectiveness of programs designed to improve executive functioning.

Diamond and Ling (2016) review over 80 interventions ranging from computer programs aimed at stimulating specific dimensions of executive functioning, such as working memory, to interventions that constitute genuine curricula designed to enhance executive functioning in the general school population—similar to those evaluated by Heckman and Kautz (2013), with some programs like Tools of the Mind included in both reviews.

In general, the interventions reviewed by Diamond and Ling (2016) have smaller sample sizes than those analyzed by Heckman and Kautz (2013), while also conducting less long-term follow-up on intervention effects. Nevertheless, their results are qualitatively consistent with those obtained by Heckman and Kautz (2013) and are particularly complementary by providing details on program design and implementation as well as its uneven effectiveness among students with different neurodevelopmental profiles—an aspect often overlooked in evaluations conducted from an economic perspective.

The findings from Diamond and Ling (2016) confirm that stimulating executive functions requires a period for assimilating new habits; that is, consistent exposure to a stimulus-response sequence within a specific context. In this regard, it is noteworthy that the programs reviewed by Heckman and Kautz (2013) had a minimum duration of one year, extending up to two years for the most effective programs.

Additionally, Diamond and Ling (2016) conclude that interventions focusing on a specific dimension of executive functioning—such as inhibition or working memory—do not usually transfer their benefits, if any exist, to other dimensions of executive functioning; thus they yield lesser benefits than could be obtained with a more holistic approach. This result suggests that considering all dimensions of executive functioning in program design may be particularly relevant for its effectiveness.

The concept of executive functions has a significant advantage over non-cognitive skills because it is already integrated into the educational world. Thus, while both teachers (in early childhood and primary education) and professors (in secondary education and beyond) are often unfamiliar with a concept constructed by exclusion from IQ—such as non-cognitive skills—almost all are familiar with brain executive functions and their relevance in cognitive, emotional, and social development among children and adolescents.

Executive functions have been highlighted as determinants for learning and the acquisition of socio-emotional skills among students with learning difficulties and/or special educational needs. Thus, students with diagnoses of dyslexia, dyscalculia, attention deficit with or without hyperactivity, autism, giftedness, etc., typically require professionals with precise knowledge of how to stimulate the development of executive functions to facilitate their learning and social inclusion.

In recent decades, the benefits of stimulating the brain's executive functions for the entire population have been confirmed, not just for individuals with clinical diagnoses, especially when such stimulation occurs at an early age. This issue is particularly relevant given that current cohorts of 5-year-old children are lagging in executive functioning compared to 5-year-olds from previous generations (Smirnova, 1998). Despite the relevance of executive functioning for balanced development (cognitive, emotional, social, and physical) in children, recent studies indicate that according to early childhood educators themselves, more than half of their students do not possess effective executive functioning skills while pointing to poor executive function as the main challenge for the teaching-learning process (Rimm-Kaufman et al., 2009).

Despite scientific evidence supporting the importance of self-regulation capacity and the need for its stimulation—especially from an early age—the current school model in Spain and in almost all developed countries remains focused on cognitive aspects and the progressive and sequential accumulation of regulated knowledge. This way of conceiving education is more suited to a country undergoing initial industrialization than to one aspiring to a productive model change centered on innovation and creativity. It leaves crucial aspects such as student motivation, development of self-confidence, stimulation of inhibitory control, other dimensions of non-cognitive skills like growth mindset, and generally executive functions in the hands of each teacher's good practices, criteria, voluntarism, and individual personality.

The evidence reviewed here suggests that notable benefits could arise in terms of reducing poverty and inequality in Spain from interventions aimed at disadvantaged or less advantaged households with very young children—even before their birth. Specifically, since schooling in Spain is virtually universal from three years old onward, our suggestion has two components: (i) develop and evaluate programs aimed at future parents and regular caregivers (the parents themselves, grandparents, nurseries, etc.) of children under three years old; (ii) develop best practice guides illustrating how to achieve the socio-emotional developmental goals that autonomous communities typically set for children aged 3–6 years.

The effectiveness of these interventions will be optimized if they are defined based on best practices for stimulating non-cognitive skills and executive functions; last at least one year; and actively involve parents and teachers by creating a culture or project linking educational centers and homes that can be generalized to other contexts.

By training teachers at an educational center in best practices conducive to stimulating non-cognitive skills and executive functions, we will contribute not only to the cognitive, emotional, and social development of all students but also to creating schools where the inclusion of students from disadvantaged backgrounds who have learning difficulties or special educational needs is more likely. This is precisely the goal of the Educar para Ser project developed by some authors of this chapter; it is present in over 40 schools in the Community of Madrid and is currently undergoing experimental evaluation in China. It is also worth highlighting the Pentabilities program by the Bofill Foundation which uses digital tools to stimulate students' socio-emotional skill development.

6 Conclusions

- Non-cognitive skills are a broad concept that includes personality traits, attributes, dispositions, social skills, attitudes, capabilities, and personal resources, independent of intellectual ability.
- Given their interdisciplinary origins, these skills have received multiple names in the economic, psychological, pedagogical, or philosophical literature, including personality traits, character or temperament, values, executive functions, socio-emotional skills, and non-cognitive skills, among others.
- Measuring non-cognitive skills is a complex task. Survey-based measures suffer from significant biases, which has led researchers to seek alternative measures based on administrative data and metadata from exams and surveys that students take in school.
- Although there is a significant hereditary component to non-cognitive skills, these skills develop over a lifetime with critical periods during childhood, and their development is influenced by cultural factors and the family and educational environment.
- Stimulating non-cognitive skills from an early age has notable positive effects on performance and school coexistence, early school dropout, delinquency, health status, specifically substance abuse, occupational category, wage income, and overall well-being throughout life.
- Furthermore, the benefits of effective interventions in stimulating non-cognitive skills tend to be greater for socially vulnerable groups and are transmitted from parents to their children.

Exercises

Exercise 1. Imagine you are interested in studying the relationship between motivation and academic performance. You have data from a student survey at the beginning of the academic year and measure their performance at the end. In a regression analysis between these measures, you find a negative correlation. It seems that higher motivation is associated with lower performance. Define the concepts of "social desirability bias" and "reference group bias." Explain how these could account for the negative relationship found between motivation and educational performance.

Exercise 2. In your own words, explain the possible mechanisms by which, in your opinion, the most cost-effective interventions are those aimed at younger children.

Exercise 3. The Power of Reflection.

The day-and-night task was designed to analyze the self-regulation skills of 4- and 5-year-old children. It is a simple game where they are asked to say "day" if they see an image of the moon and "night" if they see an image of the sun. In the first round of the game, it was estimated that 56% of the children answered correctly. Next, a comparable sample in terms of socioeconomic and educational characteristics was asked to play the game, but they were allowed to listen to a children's song for three seconds before responding and after seeing the image. In this case, the percentage of correct answers rose to 89%.

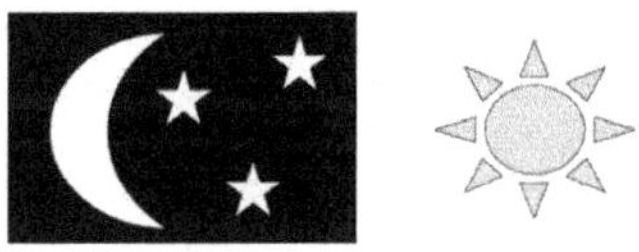

Day Night

What do these results suggest to you? How do you think the habit of reflection can be encouraged in a secondary classroom? Do you think that asking to raise your hands for answers to questions in class promote reflection?

Exercise 4. The power of an M&M.

A study measured the IQ levels of a large group of primary school students and classified them into three groups: high, medium, and low. A few months later, the researchers remeasured the IQ of these students with different questions. Half of the students in each group, randomly selected, were offered an M&M for each correct answer.

The IQ scores did not vary between the first and second tests, regardless of whether they were offered the M&M or not, among high and medium IQ students. However, low IQ students who had the incentive of the M&Ms increased their average IQ by 45%, while the average IQ of low IQ students without the incentive remained unchanged.

How do you explain these results?

Do you think eating M&Ms can make you smarter?

What do you think traditional measures of intelligence assess?

Exercise 5. Choosing extracurricular activities.

Parents are deciding, along with their 8-year-old child, on the extracurricular activities for this school year. The parents, who have read about non-cognitive skills, want to choose an activity that contributes to their child's overall development (cognitive, emotional, and social). They are considering the following options: soccer, Tae-Kwon-Do, singing in a choir, playing a musical instrument, and the Kumon method for math.

Which of these activities would you recommend, and why?

After consulting with their child, he makes it clear that he is only considering soccer and Tae-Kwon-Do. Which of these two would you recommend, and why?

References

Ao, X., X. Chen, and Z. Zhao. 2022. Is care by grandparents or parents better for children's non-cognitive skills? Evidence on locus of control from China. *China Economic Review* 71: 101734. https://doi.org/10.1016/j.chieco.2021.101734.

Alan, S., & T. Boneva, and S. Ertac. 2016. Ever failed, try again, succeed better: Results from a randomized educational intervention on grit. *The Quarterly Journal of Economics* 134.

Arco-Tirado, J. L., F. D. Fernández-Martín, and R. H. Hoyle. 2018. Development and validation of a Spanish version of the Grit-S Scale. *Frontiers Psychology* 9:96. https://doi.org/10.3389/fpsyg.2018.00096. PMID: 29467705.

Balart, P., and A. Cabrales. 2014. La Maratón de PISA: La Perseverancia como Factor del Éxito en una Prueba de Competencias. Monografías Sobre Educación. Fundación Ramon Areces y Fundación Europea Sociedad y Educación.

Balart, P., and M. Oosterveen. 2019. Females show more sustained performance during test-taking than males. *Nature Communications* 10: 3798. https://doi.org/10.1038/s41467-019-11691-y.

Borghans, L., and T. Schils. 2012. The leaning tower of Pisa: Decomposing achievement test scores into cognitive and noncognitive components. Retrieved from http://www.sole-jole.org/13260.pdf.

Bouchard, T. J., Jr., and J. C. Loehlin. 2001. Genes, evolution, and personality. *Behavior Genetics* 31 (3): 243–273. https://doi.org/10.1023/A:1012294324713.

Buser, T., R. Ahlskog, M. Johanneson, P. Koellinger, and S. Oskarsson. 2023. Using genes to explore the effects of cognitive and non-cognitive skills on education and labor market outcomes. *Tinbergen Institute Discussion Paper* TI 2021-088/I.

Cheng, A., and G. Zamarro. 2018. Measuring teacher non-cognitive skills and its impact on students: Insight from the measures of effective teaching longitudinal database. *Economics of Education Review* 64: 251–260. https://doi.org/10.1016/j.econedurev.2018.03.001.

Cunha, F., J. J. Heckman, and S. M. Schennach. 2010. Estimating the technology of cognitive and noncognitive skill formation. *Econometrica* 78 (3): 883–931. https://doi.org/10.3982/ECTA6551.

Dee, T. S., M. R. West. 2011. The non-cognitive returns to class size. *Educational Evaluation and Policy Analysis* 33 (1): 23–46. https://doi.org/10.3102/0162373710392370.

Diamond, A. 2013. Executive functions. *Annual Review of Psychology* 64 (1): 135–168. https://doi.org/10.1146/psych.2013.64.issue-110.1146/annurev-psych-113011-143750.

Diamond, A., and D. S. Ling. 2016. Conclusions about interventions programs and approaches for improving executive functions that appear justified and those that despite much hype do not. *Developmental Cognitive Neuroscience* 18: 34–48. https://doi.org/10.1016/j.dcn.2015.11.005.

Duckworth, A. L., C. Peterson, M. D. Matthews, and D. R. Kelly. 2007. Grit: Perseverance and passion for long-term goals. *Journal of Personality and Social Psychology* 92 (6): 1087–1101. https://doi.org/10.1037/0022-3514.92.6.1087.

Farah, M. J., D. M. Shera, H. Jessica, L. Savage, M. Betancourt, Joan, L. Giannetta Nancy, K. Brodsky Elsa, Malmud, and H. Hallam. 2006. Childhood poverty: Specific associations with neurocognitive development. *Brain Research* 1110 (1): 166–174. https://doi.org/10.1016/j.brainres.2006.06.072.

Fernández, R., and A. Fogli. 2009. Culture: An empirical investigation of beliefs work and fertility. *American Economic Journal: Macroeconomics* 1 (1): 146–177. https://doi.org/10.1257/mac.1.1.146.

Fiske, D. W. 1949. Consistency of the factorial structures of personality ratings from different sources. *The Journal of Abnormal and Social Psychology* 44 (3): 329–344. https://doi.org/10.1037/h0057198.

Fletcher, J. M., and B. Wolfe. 2016. The importance of family income in the formation and evolution of non-cognitive skills in childhood. *Economics of Education Review* 54: 143–154.

García, J. L., J. J. Heckman, and V. Ronda. 2023. The lasting effects of early-childhood education on promoting the skills and social mobility of disadvantaged African Americans and their children. *Journal of Political Economy* 131 (6): 1477–1506. https://doi.org/10.1086/722936.

Gneezy, U., J. A. List, J. A. Livingston, X. Qin, S. Sadoff, and Y. Xu. 2019. Measuring success in education: The role of effort on the test itself. *American Economic Review: Insights* 1 (3): 291–308. https://doi.org/10.1257/aeri.20180633.

Heckman J. J., and G. Karapakula. 2019. *Intergenerational and Intragenerational Externalities of the Perry Preschool Project*. Working Papers 2019-033, Human Capital and Economic Opportunity Working Group.

Heckman, J. J., and T. Kautz. 2013. Fostering and measuring skills: Interventions that improve character and cognition. NBER Working Papers 19656, National Bureau of Economic Research, Inc.

Hitt, C., J. Trivitt, and A. Cheng. 2016. When you say nothing at all: The predictive power of student effort on surveys. *Economics of Education Review* 52: 105–119. https://doi.org/10.1016/j.econedurev.2016.02.001.

Jackson, C. K. 2018. What do test scores miss? The importance of teacher effects on non–test score outcomes. *Journal of Political Economy* 126 (5): 2072–2107. https://doi.org/10.1086/699018.

John, O. P., L. P. Naumann, and C. J. Soto. 2008. Paradigm shift to the integrative big-five trait taxonomy: History, measurement, and conceptual issues. In *Handbook of personality: Theory and research*, ed. O. P. John, R. W. Robins, and L. A. Pervin, 114–158. New York, NY: Guilford Press.

John, O. P., E. M. Donahue, and R. L. Kentle. 1991. *The big five inventory-versions 4a and 54*. Berkeley, CA: University of California, Berkeley, Institute of Personality and Social Research.

Juhn, C., Y. Rubinstein, and C. A. Zuppann. 2015, December. *The quantity-quality trade-off and the formation of cognitive and non-cognitive skills* (No. 21824). NBER Working Paper.

Li, S., Y. Chen W. Wei, G. Fang, and W. Duan. 2024. The increase in extreme precipitation and its proportion over global land. *Journal of Hydrology* 628: 130456. https://doi.org/10.1016/j.jhydrol.2023.130456.

Mendez, I. 2015. The effect of the intergenerational transmission of noncognitive skills on student performance. *Economics of Education Review* 46: 78–97. https://doi.org/10.1016/j.econedurev.2015.03.001.

Mendez, I., and G. Zamarro. 2018. The intergenerational transmission of noncognitive skills and their effect on education and employment outcomes. *Journal of Population Economics* 31 (2): 521–560. https://doi.org/10.1007/s00148-017-0661-0.

Mischel, W., E. B. Ebbesen, and A. R. Zeiss. 1972. Cognitive and attentional mechanisms in delay of gratification. *Journal of Personality and Social Psychology* 21 (2): 204–218. https://doi.org/10.1037/h0032198.

Morando, G., and L. Platt. 2002. The impact of centre-based childcare on non-cognitive skills of young children.

Rimm-Kaufman, S. E., T. W. Curby, K. J. Grimm L. Nathanson, and L. L. Brock. 2009. The contribution of children's self-regulation and classroom quality to children's adaptive behaviors in the kindergarten classroom. *Developmental Psychology* 45 (4): 958–972. https://doi.org/10.1037/a0015861.

Smirnova, E. O. 1998. Development of will and intentionality in toddlers and preschool-aged children. *Moscow: Modek*. Razvitie voli i proizvol'nosti v rannem i doshkol'nom vozraste.

Watts, T. W., G. J. Duncan, and H. Quan. 2018. Revisiting the marshmallow test: A conceptual replication investigating links between early delay of gratification and later outcomes. *Psychological Science* 29 (7): 1159–1177. https://doi.org/10.1177/0956797618761661.

Zamarro, G. 2021. Motivación académica, habilidades no cognitivas y brecha de género en matemáticas y ciencias. El caso de España. Monografías Sobre Educación. Fundación Ramon Areces y Fundación Europea Sociedad y Educación.

Zamarro, G., C. Hitt, and I. Mendez. 2019. When students don't care: Reexamining international differences in achievement and student effort. *Journal of Human Capital* 13 (4): 519–552. https://doi.org/10.1086/705799.

Zelazo, P. D., U. Muller, D. Frye, and S. Marcovitch. 2003. Abstract monographs of the society for research in child development. 68 (3): vii–viii. https://doi.org/10.1111/mono.2003.68.issue-310.1111/j.0037-976X.2003.00260.x.

Index

A. Cabrales and I. Sanz (eds.), *Economics of Education*, https://doi.org/10.1007/978-3-031-90911-5

www.ingramcontent.com/pod-product-compliance
Ingram Content Group UK Ltd.
Pitfield, Milton Keynes, MK11 3LW, UK
UKHW021700040126
466613UK00006B/43
9783031909108